A STAR BOOK

Life and Times of REMBRANDT

R. v. R.

ORIGINALLY PUBLISHED AS
"R. v. R. THE LIFE AND TIMES OF REMBRANDT VAN RIJN"

BY
Hendrik Van Loon

GARDEN CITY PUBLISHING COMPANY, INC.
GARDEN CITY, NEW YORK

COPYRIGHT, 1930, BY HORACE LIVERIGHT

PRINTED IN U. S. A.

REMBRANDT

To

Dr. Alice R. Bernheim

List of Chapters

FOREWORD	Explaining how I came to write this book	xiii
CHAPTER 1	How I happen to remember that it rained on a certain day in November of the year 1641	3
CHAPTER 2	I meet Saskia for the first time and find her a very sick woman	22
CHAPTER 3	Concerning the people who were my friends during the days of my youth	33
CHAPTER 4	How we amused ourselves when the world was simpler than it is to-day	52
CHAPTER 5	Under what circumstances I first had met Rembrandt	57
CHAPTER 6	A disagreeable woman is as a rule a very disagreeable woman	63
CHAPTER 7	Saskia's illness	68
CHAPTER 8	I begin to learn something new about art when Rembrandt invites me into his studio	71
CHAPTER 9	Rembrandt paints a very large picture which he expects to make him famous	79
CHAPTER 10	And as a result of this picture Rembrandt becomes the joke of Amsterdam	99
CHAPTER 11	We take a walk and talk art with an honest miller	102
CHAPTER 12	Rembrandt meets my friends and Saskia grows weaker	105
CHAPTER 13	Saskia quietly goes to sleep for all time	114
CHAPTER 14	Saskia is buried and Rembrandt goes back to work	117
CHAPTER 15	Rembrandt unexpectedly calls and borrows fifty guilders	123
CHAPTER 16	I learn a few things about Saskia's family	127
CHAPTER 17	I relate a few interesting stories about my grandfather	135
CHAPTER 18	Under what peculiar circumstances my grandmother happened to marry my grandfather	144
CHAPTER 19	A honeymoon in the year 1572	149

List of Chapters

CHAPTER 20	Even as a very young child I had strange doubts about the fifth commandment	155
CHAPTER 21	Of the brother whom I had and lost	162
CHAPTER 22	I ask my brother to return to me	176
CHAPTER 23	My brother comes home	179
CHAPTER 24	Rembrandt asks me to call	182
CHAPTER 25	I have the honor to dine with one of the Burgomasters	185
CHAPTER 26	We take another trip into the country and discuss diverse methods of navigation	206
CHAPTER 27	I decide to become a voluntary exile from my own country	210
CHAPTER 28	Of the difficulties of being a "surgeon" and not a "doctor medicinae" in the year I sailed for America	216
CHAPTER 29	I depart for a new world	230
CHAPTER 30	The town of Nieuw Amsterdam proves somewhat of a disappointment, but what a marvelous country!	243
CHAPTER 31	His Excellency the Governor grants me an audience	247
CHAPTER 32	Religious bigotry and political shortsightedness prove not to be confined to the eastern shores of the Atlantic Ocean	252
CHAPTER 33	We try to save a woman who has been cast into the wilderness by her neighbors from the North and fail	260
CHAPTER 34	Bernardo and I set forth to find the Lost Tribes and some territory fit for agriculture, and neither of us is very successful	263
CHAPTER 35	A fairy tale in the wilderness and what became of it	282
CHAPTER 36	News from home	291
CHAPTER 37	The ten Lost Tribes are joined by one more	301
CHAPTER 38	I have certain doubts about the superior virtues of the so-called "white men" as compared to their copper-colored brethren of the New World	304
CHAPTER 39	I talk politics with My Lord Stuyvesant, who takes a gloomy view of things	309
CHAPTER 40	I receive bad news from Amsterdam and decide to return home	319
CHAPTER 41	I reach Holland safely but find the old home town surrounded by the troops of the Prince of Orange	327

List of Chapters

CHAPTER 42	The Prince is forced to give up his nefarious designs and for the first time in many years I am able to fry eggs on my own kitchen table	343
CHAPTER 43	I write my official report and what became of my recommendations about affairs in America	349
CHAPTER 44	There was one woman I loved and I lost her	352
CHAPTER 45	Our neighbor, Menasseh ben Israel, decides to leave Amsterdam for London	356
CHAPTER 46	We once more fight the English	364
CHAPTER 47	I meet my colleague, Dr. Ephraim Bueno, who had taken care of Rembrandt's family while I was in America	366
CHAPTER 48	Concerning the position of artists in a commercial country	371
CHAPTER 49	Two of my old friends are gone and in my loneliness I begin to see a little more of Rembrandt	375
CHAPTER 50	Rembrandt becomes talkative and favors me with a few of his views upon Art	379
CHAPTER 51	I begin to understand that all is not well in the big house on the Jodenbreestraat	391
CHAPTER 52	Jean-Louys gets a new servant, and I hear for the last time from Bernardo	400
CHAPTER 53	I visit my banker and learn something about the deplorable state of Rembrandt's finances	415
CHAPTER 54	I once more take up my search for some drug that should kill the pain of those about to undergo a surgical operation	421
CHAPTER 55	I found a new sort of hospital	428
CHAPTER 56	The ministers take a hand in Rembrandt's affairs	431
CHAPTER 57	Hendrickje has a child and the clergy of Amsterdam express their opinion upon my researches in the domain of painless surgery	439
CHAPTER 58	I notice that by losing my credit I have also lost the respect of a good many of my fellow-townsmen	443
CHAPTER 59	I lose a faithful banker and an even more faithful friend	457
CHAPTER 60	Our Jewish neighbors, who have come to us to escape from the intolerance of their Spanish masters, show	

List of Chapters

	that religious bigotry is not restricted to one sect or religion	462
CHAPTER 61	My son begins the education of his father	474
CHAPTER 62	We build a new town hall and Rembrandt almost paints a picture for it	479
CHAPTER 63	Rembrandt receives a caller. He proves to be an official from the Bankruptcy Court	494
CHAPTER 64	The house on the Jodenbreestraat stands still and empty	499
CHAPTER 65	Our fugitives from the Spanish Inquisition show that they were intelligent and eager pupils and young Baruch d'Espinoza is forced to leave Amsterdam	503
CHAPTER 66	Rembrandt shows signs of beginning old age	510
CHAPTER 67	Hendrickje goes into business	515
CHAPTER 68	Hendrickje and Titus form a partnership but are not very successful	520
CHAPTER 69	The van Rijn family finds a new house	522
CHAPTER 70	I pay a visit to a strange colony of people who actually think for themselves	527
CHAPTER 71	I get Rembrandt an order for a final picture	534
CHAPTER 72	A chapter mostly personal and not devoid of encouragement	539
CHAPTER 73	Poor Hendrickje goes to her final rest	540
CHAPTER 74	Jean-Louys sails forth into space	543
CHAPTER 75	A forgotten man in a lonely house goes on painting pictures	550
CHAPTER 76	Rembrandt has one more pupil	553
CHAPTER 77	For the first time in my life I meet a real statesman	555
CHAPTER 78	And still Rembrandt continues to paint	562
CHAPTER 79	Titus marries	565
CHAPTER 80	I read a final chapter in Genesis	567
EPILOGUE	By a distant descendant	569

THE LIFE
AND TIMES OF REMBRANDT

R. v. R.

IS AN ACCOUNT OF THE LAST YEARS AND THE DEATH
OF ONE

Rembrandt Harmenszoon Van Rijn

A PAINTER AND ETCHER OF SOME RENOWN
WHO LIVED AND WORKED (WHICH IN HIS CASE WAS THE SAME)
IN THE TOWN OF AMSTERDAM
(WHICH IS IN HOLLAND)
AND DIED OF GENERAL NEGLECT AND DIVERSE OTHER UNFORTUNATE
CIRCUMSTANCES
ON THE FOURTH OF OCTOBER OF THE YEAR OF GRACE 1669
(*God have mercy upon his soul*)
AND WHO WAS ATTENDED IN HIS AFFLICTIONS

BY ONE

Joannis Van Loon

DOCTOR MEDICINAE AND CHIRURGEON IN EXTRAORDINARY
TO A VAST NUMBER OF HUMBLE CITIZENS
WHOSE ENDURING GRATITUDE HAS ERECTED HIM
A MONUMENT
LESS PERISHABLE THAN GRANITE AND MORE ENDURING THAN PORPHYRY
AND WHO
DURING A MOST BUSY LIFE
YET FOUND TIME TO WRITE DOWN THESE PERSONAL RECOLLECTIONS
OF THE GREATEST OF HIS FELLOW-CITIZENS
AND WHICH ARE NOW
FOR THE FIRST TIME PRESENTED
(PROVIDED WITH AS FEW NOTES, EMENDATIONS
AND CRITICAL OBSERVATIONS AS POSSIBLE)
BY HIS GREAT-GREAT-GRANDSON, NINE TIMES REMOVED

Hendrik Willem Van Loon

IN THE YEAR OF GRACE 1930
AND IN THE TOWN OF VEERE
WHICH IS IN ZEELAND

Foreword

EXPLAINING HOW I CAME TO WRITE THIS BOOK

Amsterdam, October 9th, 1669
In the house called De Houttuyn

We buried him yesterday and I shall never forget that terrible morning. The rain, which had been pouring down ever since the beginning of the month, had ceased. A cold and gloomy fog had thrown a dark and chilling pall over the whole city. The empty streets seemed filled with a vague sense of futile uselessness. The small group of mourners stood silently by the side of the church-door, waiting for the coffin to arrive.

Last Friday, a few hours before he died and during a moment of semi-consciousness, he had whispered to me that he wanted to rest next to Saskia. He must have forgotten that he had sold her grave long ago, when Hendrickje passed away and when he was caught without a penny and had been forced to sell the family lot in the Old Church to buy a grave for his second wife. I promised him that I would do my best, but of course the thing was out of the question. I am glad I told him this lie, for he went to his last sleep fully convinced that soon all would be well and that his dust would mingle with that of the woman he had loved in the days of his youth.

And then three days ago Magdalena van Loo called. I had never cared for her. I had found her mean and jealous and apt to whine, but I had tried to like her on account of her father-in-law and of the poor boy she had married.

She told me a long rambling story about some gold pieces which apparently had belonged to Cornelia and to her. Over and over again she repeated the same sentences: "I am sure father took some of that money before he died. And now what shall we do? We can't even buy milk for the baby. I am sure father took it," and so on and so forth.

Then followed a long and circumstantial account of her being sick and being unable to nurse the baby herself. I tried to reassure her. The money undoubtedly would be found. Had she looked for it carefully? No, she had not, but she felt convinced that the old man had appropriated some of it. For weeks and weeks he had sold nothing. He had just sat and stared or he had scratched meaningless lines on the back of some old copper plates. He had been without a cent when Titus died, for uncle Uylenburgh had paid for the funeral. That she knew for a fact. All the same, the old man had been able to buy himself food and drink, especially drink. He must have stolen some of Cornelia's gold, and "half of it was to come to me!" It was impossible to get her mind off the subject and so I asked her whether the sexton had been around to see her about the funeral.

Then she broke into tears once more. She felt so ashamed that she could not possibly hope to survive this last humiliation. The sexton had not come himself. He had merely sent one of the grave-diggers. The man had been drunk and quite rude. He has asked her how much she could pay and she had answered that she wanted things done very simply and could not afford more than five guilders. He had laughed out loud. People from the poor-house were given a better burial than that, but then, of course, what could one expect of those fine gentlemen who never did a stroke of work, who merely sat before an easel all day long and gave themselves airs! Finally he had got her into such a state of vapors that she had cried out for the shoe-maker who lived on the ground floor to come and help her. He had taken the unruly ruffian by the scruff of the neck and had thrown him out into the street and that, at least, had made her happy.

I then asked her whether that was where matters stood and she answered yes and at once went off on another tirade, telling me that no woman had ever been treated as she had been treated ever since she had married into that irresponsible family of painter people, and much more to the same effect, until in sheer despair I had ordered a hackney-coach and had driven her to the Roozengracht to see the sexton of the West Church (a man I cordially detested, but what will you? The corpse could not remain above ground for ever) and had asked him what he meant by such conduct. At once the miserable creature became most obsequious. He apologized for the behavior of his grave-digger, and then annoyed me with his confidences. "If only you knew, Doctor," he said, "how hard it is to get good workmen these days! The job does no longer pay so very well and what is found in the old graves nowadays is not worth the digging. Ever since it has become the custom to bury people merely in their shrouds, the money has gone out of the grave-digging business."

I bade him hold his tongue and after some preliminaries we settled on a "full funeral"—that is to say, sixteen men to carry the coffin and the usual length of broadcloth to cover the remains. I paid him fifteen guilders and gave him some extra stivers for beer-money for the men, and he promised in advance that everything would be done in a first-class manner, very quietly and with great dignity.

But when I got to the church yesterday morning, the men were there, but they gave every evidence of having visited the alehouse before they went to work and I felt so strongly upon the subject that I mentioned it to Abraham Francen, one of the master's old friends, who was leaning against a tree in the yard.

Foreword

"This is an outrage," I said.

But one drunken scoundrel heard me and scowled at me and gave me an evil look and—

"And why not?" he leered. "Our friend here didn't mind a drop himself at the right time, did he?"

When I called the sexton to task, he merely repeated what he had told me the day before—that it was terribly difficult to get respectable men for his sort of work. For now that the war with England had come to an end, everybody had plenty of money and nobody wanted to be a gravedigger any more.

Finally we came to the spot that had been chosen and without any further ceremony the coffin was lowered into the grave. I had meant to say a few words to bid my old friend a last farewell, but I was not given the chance, for as soon as the ropes had been pulled out from underneath the coffin the sexton said quite loudly: "Come now, my men, don't stand there doing nothing and just looking sheepish. Get busy! We have four other customers this morning." Whereupon we all turned around (there were, as I said, only a handful of us) and I walked to the part of the church reserved for divine service and I knelt down (something I had not done a single time these last five and thirty years) and I prayed whatever God might hear my supplication that he might deal mercifully with the soul of this poor, suffering mortal, who had given so much to this world and had received so little in return.

Then I slowly walked home, but while crossing the Dam, I ran across old Vondel, the poet. He had changed so greatly since I last saw him that I hardly recognized him. He seemed sick and he was shivering beneath his shabby, threadbare coat. It hurt me to see such a person in such a condition. The town these last few months has been full of a strange new affliction of the lungs, and those who were weakest were of course the first to be attacked. I asked him whether he had breakfasted and he said "No," but then he rarely took anything before noon. I suggested that we have a cup of coffee in one of those new taverns that make a specialty of this beverage, and he accepted my offer with pathetic eagerness. He even mentioned that there was a new coffee shop a few doors away where the coffee was very good and the prices were not exorbitant. I must have looked surprised, for he added, "You see, these places are often patronized by sailors and there is always a chance that one of them may bring me news of my son."

The human heart is a strange thing. Small loss when young Vondel was packed off to the Indies, these many years ago. The boy was an utter misfit. He drank. He gambled. He ran after women, and what sort of women! He was directly responsible for his father's financial failure. And here the old man was wasting his few hard-earned pennies, drinking coffee in mean taverns because some day one of the sailors might perhaps bring him some news of "his darling child."

We sat down and I pretended to be hungry and ordered some bread and cheese. "You might keep me company," I suggested to Vondel, and he consented. But a moment later he jumped to his feet. "Pardon me," he said, "but there is Captain Jan Floriszoon of the *Dolphin*. He got in yesterday from Malacca. He may have news for me from my boy."

"Bring him over here," I called out, and a moment later the captain appeared. He was a sailor of the old school, hard as nails and thrifty as the Bank, but not unkind. Yes, he would take something. He would take something with much pleasure. It was a cold and wet day. A gin and bitters would not be amiss. He had had a most prosperous voyage, only a year and a half for the round trip and less than forty percent of his crew had died. Ever hear of a certain Jan van den Vondel? No, never! Could not remember that he had ever run across him. But that of course meant nothing. There were so many ships and India was a big country, hundreds and thousands of islands. Some day the boy would undoubtedly show up and come back.

The captain was more considerate than I had expected a man of his caliber to be and I asked the poet how he himself was getting along. Vondel, with an eager face, hastened to inform me that things could not be better. Poor devil! He reminded me of a patient I had visited the day before in the poor-house and who had asked me not to let him die because he had been allowed to raise a crocus in his little room and he was afraid that the poor little plant would not be able to survive if he were not there to take care of it.

Here I was, sitting face to face with the greatest genius that ever handled our language—a shabby, broken-down clerk—and he was explaining that he really had every reason to feel deeply grateful for the way in which fate had treated him.

"Their Lordships have been most kind to me," he explained. "Of course, the pawn-shop can't afford to pay me very much, but my needs are small and besides, I have a lot of time for myself. With the exception of Saturdays, when we stay open till midnight, I rarely work more than ten hours a day and quite often they allow me to come a little later in the morning, that I may make the rounds of the harbor and ask for news of my son. Within another year I hope to get my pension. I want to finish my last play, 'Noah,' and I must get at it before I am too old to handle a pen."

And so on and so forth. Until the honest captain interrupted him and turned to me and remarked with a polite bow that he was pleased to have made my acquaintance, for he had often heard of me from his sister, Anneke Floriszoon, the wife of Antony Blauw, whom I remembered as one of my patients a number of years ago, and then he ordered another gin at my expense and drank to my health and said that he was glad to see that the Amsterdam chirurgeons took their work seriously and were going about at such an early hour of the morning. But I told him that I rarely visited this part of Amsterdam at that hour, but that I had happened to cross the Dam on my way home from the funeral of a friend.

"And who might that be?" the old poet asked, "for I am not aware that any one of importance has died."

"No," I answered, "I suppose not. He died quite suddenly. Yet you knew the man. It was Rembrandt van Rijn."

He looked at me with slight embarrassment.

"Of course I knew him," he said. "A very great artist. Of course, I could not always follow him and he thought very differently from me upon many subjects. For one thing, I don't believe that he was ever truly a Christian. But a great painter, nevertheless. Only tell me, Doctor, are you sure it was not an impostor? For Rembrandt, if I recollect rightly, died five years ago, yes, more than five years ago. He died in Hull in England. He had gone there to escape from his creditors. That is, if I remember correctly."

"Hull?" interrupted the captain. "Hull nothing! I know all about that fellow. He did a piece once of Joris de Caullery with whom I served as second mate in the battle of Dover in '52 when we licked Blake. Yes, I know all about him. It was he who had that quarrel with the dominies about his servant girl. But he went to Sweden some six or seven years ago. I have a friend who sails to Danzig, and he took him to Gothenburg in '61 or '62. He told me so himself and so I know it to be true."

"Nevertheless, my good friends," I answered, "Rembrandt died last Friday and we buried him this morning."

"Strange, very strange!" Vondel murmured. "Died right here in this town, and I did not even know he was still alive!"

"Well," said the good-natured captain, willing to make all the world feel as merry as he did himself and signaling to the waiter to bring him a third gin and bitters, "well, that is too bad. But we all have to die sooner or later and I am sure there are plenty of painters left. So here is to you, gentlemen! Happy years and many of them!"

  .   .   .   .

Hofwyck, Voorburg, October 23, 1669.

Two weeks have gone by and a great many things have happened.

The evening of the funeral I dropped in at the house on the Roozengracht to prescribe a sedative for poor Magdalena who was still worrying about that little bag of gold that had belonged to Cornelia and her and that had disappeared. A few days later, Cornelia was to find it behind a pile of clean sheets, but just then Rembrandt was still suspected of having stolen his daughter's money and so Magdalena wept and whined until at last she dropped off to sleep and I went back to the hospital and composed a letter to My Lord Constantin Huygens who had had some dealings with the dead painter in the days of the late Prince Henry and who had been ever full of admiration for his genius, and late that same night I carried it to the skipper of the boat to The Hague, who promised me as a personal favor that he would deliver it to His Lordship the next morning together with some official-looking documents which had been entrusted to him by the Burgomasters and had to do with a vacancy in the Board of Aldermen.

Three days later I received an answer from the famous old diplomat, who by this time must have been well past seventy.

> "I have to thank you, my dear Doctor," so he wrote in his precise Latin (for he never got over the feeling that a letter in the vernacular was a breach of good form, almost as inexcusable as paying an official call without a ruff or finishing a dinner without wiping off one's mouth), "I have to thank you for your favor of October the ninth and I was deeply shocked to hear your most unfortunate news. I knew him well, this extraordinary miller's son, upon whom the gods had bestowed such exceeding gifts. What a sad—a most sad ending! But such seems to be the fate of those among us who dare to storm the tops of high Olympus. In any other country he would have been deemed worthy of a national funeral; kings would have felt honored to march behind his bier. But did not the Athenians banish Pheidias? And what reward but a sentence of death did Florence ever bestow upon the greatest of her many gifted sons?
>
> "I am an old man now, my learned friend, and I live far away from the vapid noise of the turbulent world. I have had another (and serious) attack of the gout and writing does not come easily to me these days. You must be in need of a change of scene after these most distressing events. Why not visit me here in my quiet retreat for a few days? I have little to offer you but a most cordial welcome and some of that noble vintage from the ancient city of Avignon, which almost persuades an old heretic like myself that there must have been some good in the institution of a Supreme Pontiff. For truly, the men who grew that wine must have been past-masters in the art of living.
>
> "Farewell for the nonce and send me your reply by messenger. Tell me the hour of your arrival and a carriage will await you at Veur and it is only a short ride to the humble roof of your most faithful and obedient servant,
>
> "C. H."

I had no reason to refuse. Young Willem was away at his studies in Leyden. The excellent Jantje could look after the household and my cousin Fijbo (one of the Frisian van Loons, come to settle in Amsterdam three years ago) could take care of my practice. I answered that I would accept with pleasure and three days later I took the boat for the south.

An uneventful trip, except for an acrimonious debate between a short,

Foreword

fat man who looked like a clergyman (and proved to be a shoe-maker) and a tall, lean fellow who looked like a shoe-maker (and proved to be a clergyman) who for some obscure reason revived the ancient quarrel about "homoousian" and "homoiousian" and got so excited about the "unbegotten begotten son" as opposed to the "ever begotten son" that they would surely have come to blows if the skipper had not threatened to throw them both overboard unless they moderate their language.

Except for this unfortunate incident, unavoidable in a country like ours where everybody is certain that he alone possesses a key to the right kind of Truth, the voyage was pleasant and dull (as a pleasant voyage should be) and at Veur I found Pieter, the old coachman, waiting for me and an hour later I was sitting in front of a bright open fire in that corner room that I knew so well and that looked across the fields all the way to the leaning tower of Delft.

I can't say that I ever enjoyed a holiday quite so much. For a holiday it has been so far, in the best and truest sense of the word. A holiday enlivened by good talk, good fare and the constant consideration of a courteous host. Indeed, if this strange new land of ours had done naught but produce this one man, I would not consider the experiment to have been a failure. He has been everywhere. He has known every one. Yet he has remained as simple as the gardener who delighted him yesterday with a few fresh radishes. He writes Latin like his native tongue, but handles our obstinate language as if it were the pliable vernacular of Ariosto. He is well versed in music and has fair skill in the art of drawing and painting. His mathematical ability has come to glorious fruition in his son Christiaan, who is now in Paris making further experiments with his pendulum clock. He seems to have suffered some financial reverses during the recent war with England, but the simplicity of the household is so perfect in all its details that life at the court of the Grand Monarch himself could be no more agreeable than existence here at Hofwyck.

I spend the morning in my own room which overlooks the old marshes of Schieland, now turned into fertile pastures. There is an excellent library on the ground floor and I am urged to take as many books to my own quarters as suits my fancy.

Old Pieter, who has been with his master for almost forty years, brings me my breakfast and informs me about the state of the weather which has been fairly good since I arrived last Thursday.

At one o'clock I take a short walk in the garden which has been laid out according to the French taste (and which the French for some unaccountable reason call a "Dutch garden"). At two o'clock we take a short drive and the afternoon and evening we spend together. And of course the conversation almost invariably turns to the loss of our friend of the Roozengracht.

I am a physician and familiar with death. I am not much of a churchman and cannot for the life of me understand the gruesome delight with which Christians, ever since the days of the Catacombs, have been pleased to enlarge upon the horrors of the charnel-house. The people of ancient times were much more rational in their attitude toward that sublime sleep that is bestowed upon us as a pleasant sample of eternity. They knew that the world only exists through contrasts. That there is no light, unless there be darkness, no joy unless there be sorrow, no life unless there be death. I accept their wisdom and it is not so much the fact that Rembrandt has ceased to exist that worries me (God knows, life held little of pleasure for him) as the realization of the utter futility of all effort.

I sometimes am afraid of the conclusions to which this sort of reasoning may lead us and yesterday My Lord Huygens read me a serious lecture upon the dangers of this sort of speculation.

"Have a care," he said, "or I shall have to send your doubts to my neighbor, the learned Jew, and he will wash them in a mixture of Cartesian and Baconian philosophies and then he will bleach them in the light of his own merciless logic and when they are returned to you, they will have shrunk to the three letters Q.E.D. neatly embroidered on the remnants of something that only a short while before was still a fairly useful garment that might have kept people from freezing in the realm of doubt."

"No," I answered, "that would not solve the difficulty. I have little love for that strange celestial potentate whom our Calvinists call their righteous Jehovah, but neither do I want the Almighty to be reduced to a mathematical formula. And my worries are not of the theological variety.

"I knew Spinoza in the old days, before his own people so kindly tried to murder him. A charming man. A learned man. An honest man. But I am a little wary of those philosophers who try to weave their spiritual garments out of their own inner consciousness. I am not enough of a mystic and prefer the 'Praise of Folly' to all the metaphysical cogitations in the world. No, what worries me is not the fate of poor old Rembrandt. He is either entirely out of it or he is trying so hard to solve the problem of reducing the Light Everlasting to a few smears of chrome-yellow and flake-white that he will forget everything else. No, it is something else that is on my mind."

"The living, rather than the dead?"

"Exactly. Here we are. Since we got our freedom, our land has been blessed beyond anything that has ever been seen before. Our dominies, with their usual sense of modesty, take all the credit upon themselves and see in these riches an expression of approval of the Lord Almighty and an endorsement of the policies of the House of Orange. They may be right, but it seems to me that our fortunate geographic location may have as much to do with our favorable rate of exchange as the approbation of an ancient Jewish deity who had tantrums and liked the smell of burning entrails. I hope I am not offending you?"

My Lord Constantin shook his head. "These are hardly the expressions I would have used when I dined with King James (of blessed memory) and dozed my way through the endless sessions of the Great Synod. But here we are alone and old Pieter is deaf and, to tell you the truth, I too prefer one page of Erasmus to all the homilies of the sour-faced doctor from Geneva. So go ahead and tell me your troubles."

"Well, as I was saying, here we are part of a strange new experiment in state-craft. We have turned a swamp into another Rome. We rule black people and yellow people and red people—millions of them in every part of the world. Until a short time ago we kept a larger standing army than any one had ever dreamed possible and we paid for it and it did not ruin us. We probably have a larger navy than any other country and, somehow or other, we seem to have enough funds to keep the ships going without an unusual number of riots.

"We juggle with slices of territory larger than the Holy Roman Empire as if we were children playing with marbles, and one day we take a few hundred thousand square miles of forests in North America and say that they belong to us and half a century later, we trade them off for a couple of hundred thousand square miles of sugar lands in South America and nobody knows and nobody cares and it really makes no difference either one way or another.

"We supply the whole world with grain and with fish and whalebone and linen and hides and our store-houses fairly burst with the bales of nutmeg and pepper that are dumped into them twice or three times a year and in between we fight a couple of wars and the people at home go to church and pray for victory and then go back to business and make a little more money and speculate in Indian shares and in tulips and in Spitzbergen sperm-oil and in Amsterdam real estate and lose fortunes and gain fortunes as if they never had been doing anything else all their lives and as if we had not known their fathers and grandfathers when they were perfectly respectable bakers and butchers and candle-stick makers who had to work devilishly hard for every stiver they made and were contented if once every fifteen years they could afford a new suit of Sunday clothes.

"But that is not so much what fills me with such anxiety for the future. We have all of us got to begin sometime. When the Emperor of Austria tried to raise funds on the Amsterdam exchange to develop his mercury mines, he had a prospectus printed to prove that he was descended in a straight line from Julius Caesar, but in the days of my grandfather, whenever old Charles of Habsburg got full on Louvain beer and French cognac, and was told by my grandpapa that no human stomach on earth could stand such atrocious mixtures, he used to weep and ask him what one could expect of a fellow who was half Spanish peasant and half Flemish bastard and whose earliest ancestor had driven a Swiss ox-cart as a sutler in the army of Charlemagne.

"Perhaps he exaggerated a bit, but when the great French Queen visited Amsterdam and the Burgomasters forced her to listen to endless speeches about 'Your Majesty's illustrious forebears, the enlightened rulers of Tuscany,' or wherever it was, I remember that when it was my turn to be presented and she was told that I was the consultant physician of the Hospital of St. Catherine, and silly old Witsen, who knew my aversion to drugs, said, 'Yes, Your Majesty, and he has prescribed more pills in his day than any other man now alive,' the old Queen smiled rather sourly and said, 'Monseigneur, I know all about pills. I have got three of them in my coat-of-arms.'

"No, it isn't that we are rich that worries me. It is rather pleasant to see every one well fed and decently clothed and it never did any harm to a man's self-respect to have an extra change of linen. But what are we going to do with all our wealth? The envoy of His late Majesty James of England (the tactful one who is said to have given a party the day they killed old John of Barneveldt) in his usual charming way wrote to his royal master and asked what one could expect of a country that was merely 'a counting-house defended by a navy?'

"But that Puritan boor was right. At least in part. As long as our merchants are able to make one hundred percent on their money, by buying something for a guilder and selling it for two, and as long as the common people are fairly obedient to Their Lordships, and go to church three times on Sunday, we ask no questions and we are contented to be rich and smug and not any too finicky in our pastimes, but when it comes to something not of this earth earthy, we let our greatest poet handle a goose-quill in a dirty pawn-shop ten hours a day to keep himself from starving; we drag the greatest painter of our time through every court in the whole bailiwick and a couple of rice-peddlers who have just spent thousands of guilders for an escutcheon with sixteen quarterings swindle him out of his last pennies and even your fine old Prince has to be dunned eight or nine times before he will pay him.

"And what happens to Rembrandt and Vondel has happened to all the others. The King of Spain and the King of Denmark and the Emperor and the King of England and even that wild potentate of Muscovy (wherever that is) keep agents in Amsterdam to supply them with the work of our great men. And we quietly let them die in the poor-house as if they were so many tramps."

I talked along that vein most of the afternoon and My Lord Constantin listened with great patience, but I do not think that he answered me very fully. Perhaps he did, but I am a bit hazy about it.

I am tired and have a pain at the back of my head. I shall go to bed and finish this to-morrow.

Hofwyck, December 20, 1669.

For a while, it looked as if there were to be no "to-morrow" at all.

I must have caught a cold on the day of Rembrandt's funeral, for I remember that I had one or two chills on board the canal-boat when I traveled to Voorburg, and that my teeth were chattering when I reached Hofwyck. I hear that my kind old host consulted with no less than three doctors from The Hague and when they were unable to break the fever, he had sent to Leyden for a young professor who was experimenting with the cinchona bark and who gave me of his tincture with apparent success, for from that day on I am told that I began to improve.

And whether my affliction was "march poison," as the ague fits and the dry heat seemed to indicate, or an attack of the "English sweat" which had been so common during the last century, or some entirely new disease come to us from America or Asia, upon that point my learned professional brethren do not seem to have been able to make a decision. But the cinchona bark was apparently quite effective (I shall try it on my own patients as soon as I return to practice) or perhaps it was the excellent care which I received at the hands of my good host which kept me from joining the Great Majority.

Most important of all, I do not appear to be suffering from anemia or any of the other after effects which are so common and so disastrous in cases of this sort. But as soon as I was allowed to sit up and as soon as I once more began to take an interest in my surroundings, I noticed (what had so often worried me with my own patients) that I seemed mentally exhausted and could not rid myself of a few simple thoughts which kept repeating themselves in my mind and kept repeating and repeating themselves until I was ready to shriek and had to be restrained from doing myself bodily harm.

After a few days there was a slight improvement, but then it began to look as if something in my mind had congealed at the moment I was taken ill and that it refused, no matter how hard I tried, to let itself be thawed out. The death of Rembrandt, I am willing to confess it, had made more of an impression upon me than almost anything else that had ever happened to me. I had come to Hofwyck full of his sad fate and until I was taken ill, I had thought and talked of practically nothing else.

All during the fever, whenever I wandered in my delirium (so My Lord Constantin told me last week) I had been fighting Rembrandt's battles. No doubt he had deserved a better fate and no doubt most of our people are hopelessly indifferent about the really great men who bring honor to our nation. But I used to be possessed of a certain philosophic calm and I used to accept the iniquities of this world with great and satisfying equanimity of soul.

Whenever as children we got greatly excited about some particularly stupid piece of business on the part of our neighbors, our grandfather used to warn us to remember the safe advice of our famous cousin Erasmus that "Since the world loved to be swindled, we might just as well let it be swindled." He admonished us to keep strictly to honest practices in our own dealings with mankind, but not let ourselves be upset every time we came in contact with some particular phase of human folly.

"For once you begin to take the human race too seriously," he warned us, "you will either lose your sense of humor or turn pious, and in either case, you had much better be dead."

In a general way I had always been able to stick to this wise and tolerant rule of conduct. I had never wasted much time pitying my fellowmen nor had I indulged in too great expressions of merriment when for the millionth time in history I watched how they hoisted themselves with the petard of their own willful ignorance. I had simply accepted them as I found them and had not tried to improve too much upon God's unfortunate handiwork.

But now something had happened. Try however I might, I could not rid myself of the obsession that in one way or another I was responsible for the death of my friend and no matter how hard my host and my doctor friend from Leyden tried (he knew something beyond mere powders and pills, which I can't say for most of my colleagues) I could not purge my poor, tired brain of the vision of that last terrible morning in the West Church, with the grinning pall-bearers and the drinking, cursing grave-diggers who handled that sacred coffin as if it had held the carcase of some indifferent lout, killed in a drunken street-brawl.

And yet, if life, if my life at least, had to go on, I must first of all purge my mind of these all-too-persistent depressions and I knew it and at the same time I could not do it and then the consciousness that I knew it and could not do it added itself to my other tribulations, and thereupon Hell itself held no such terrors as I experienced during those weeks I was trying to regain my physical health and to establish some sort of mental equilibrium.

And I know not what the end would have been, had not My Lord Constantin, trying to divert me and so get me away from my own depressing thoughts, one day called on me in the company of the learned Jew of whom we had been talking a short time before I was taken ill.

I had met Spinoza several times before in the olden days in Amsterdam and I had once visited him in Rijnsburg, but so many things had happened since then, that I had almost forgotten what a charming and simple-minded fellow he was. Of his ideas, as I have said before, I have never understood a great deal and anyway, theological and philosophical speculations have never been very much to my taste. But Spinoza proved a veritable godsend to a man recovering from a long illness and I bade him (with my host's gracious permission) to come again and to come as often as he could.

He was living in very modest quarters in the village of Voorburg, which was only a few minutes away, and quite frequently, after he got through with his day's work, he used to drop in for a short talk. I admired the liberality of mind of my host, for soon the people of The Hague must have heard that Hofwyck was being patronized by the most dangerous heretic then alive and five days after his first visit (which took place on a Tuesday) not fewer than three clergymen in that gossipy village (God forbid that it should ever acquire the dignity of a town) made veiled allusions in their sermons to "the influence which certain people of libertine principles were said to be gaining once more upon those in close connection with the House of Orange."

But as My Lord Constantin merely shrugged his shoulders when he heard of it, I did not let it worry me and continued to enjoy the visits of this keen-eyed young Jew with the soft Portuguese accent, who actually seemed to believe that all the eternal verities could be reduced to mathematical equations.

Now whether my host had mentioned my strange mental affliction to this amiable and kindly prophet (great Heavens! what an improvement that boy was upon the average ranting and maundering rabbi of his quarrelsome tribe!) but in the most tactful way he one day brought the conversation upon the subject of Rembrandt and how shocked he had been to hear of his untimely death and how much he had admired his work—especially his etchings which were more in keeping with his own mathematical turn of mind, and then he asked me to tell him about the last days of the great master and about his funeral and of course, I was only too delighted and he repeated this performance three days in succession, and then quite suddenly one day he said:

"You know, Doctor, you are bound for the lunatic asylum, and they tell me it is not pleasant in there."

To which, with unusual calm and clearness of vision, I answered: "Yes, my friend, I know that, but what can I do about it?"

To which he gave me the totally unexpected answer: "Write it all down and get rid of it that way, before you go insane. That is what I am doing myself."

Amsterdam, April 3, 1670.

The cure has worked.

And I, in my old age, discover that I have most unexpectedly become the father of a book.

I did not mean to write one, for I am a physician and not an author, but what of it? These pages will be carefully packed away among my other belongings. They have no literary value. My son is not interested in such things and they will never be published, no matter what happens.

And Rembrandt, if he knows, will understand.

My task is finished. And now I must go back to the business of living, for I have loafed long enough and there is work to be done, a great deal of work.

Two weeks from next Monday I shall be seventy years old. That is not as old as my good host of Hofwyck, who is well in the seventies, but neither is it an age to take lightly. Ten more good years at the very most. After that—whatever follows.

And so I bid farewell to this labor of love which has well served me during my days of reconvalescence.

From now on, my hand shall only touch the scalpel. May it be as true and honest in all things as the brush that lies on my desk, the only tangible memory of the dearest of my friends and the greatest of my race.

JAN VAN LOON.

List of Illustrations

Rembrandt — *Frontispiece*

	FACING PAGE
The Church	36
Portrait of Saskia (1633—lead pencil)	37
Facsimile of Letter to Huygens	68
The Windmill	69
Johannes Lutma	132
The Death of the Virgin	133
Self Portrait (About 1666)	164
The Three Crosses	165
Elizabeth Van Leeuwen (Wife of Rembrandt's brother)	228
Rembrandt's Brother Adriaen	229
Rembrandt's Mother	260
Rembrandt's Father	261
Three Heads of Women	324
Hendrickje Stoffels (About 1652)	325
Rembrandt Painting Hendrickje	356
Cornelis Claesz Anslo	357
The Jewish Synagogue	420
Bankruptcy Notice	421
The Old Man Seated in an Armchair	452
Self Portrait (About 1659)	453

R.v.R.

The Life & Times of Rembrandt van Rijn

Chapter 1

HOW I HAPPEN TO REMEMBER THAT IT RAINED ON A CERTAIN DAY IN NOVEMBER OF THE YEAR 1641

It was late in the evening of one of the last days of November of the year '41 and it was raining very hard.

Let me tell how I happen to be so sure about this. I have a very bad memory for dates and for names, but a curiously strong gift of recollection for all sorts of completely irrelevant details which most people find it only too easy to forget.

Now in the spring of '41, my uncle Gerard, from whom I have inherited my present house on the Houtmarkt in Amsterdam, died. It took all summer to settle his estate, but early in October (I have forgotten the exact date) I received word from Veere that everything was ready and would I please come and sign the necessary papers. I was very busy at the time and asked whether these legal affairs could not be attended to by correspondence. But notaries are notaries, all the world over. It was money in their pocket to make the affair drag as long as possible and they informed me that I had to come myself.

And so I bade farewell to my patients and after four fairly uncomfortable days in draughty boats and damp beds (our village inns are as bad now as they were a hundred years ago) I reached the little town where I had spent the only happy days of my entire childhood. I had not been in the place for almost ten years and at once noticed a difference. The harbor seemed less full of ships. There were fewer people in the streets and one rarely heard a word of English, whereas in former days, English and Scotch had been as common as Dutch and every child had been able to swear almost as readily in one language as in the other.

I stayed at the inn and it was very dull. In former days there always had been at least a dozen guests. Now there were only a decrepit-looking Scotchman and a German. The Scotchman had come to wind up his affairs, and the German (a dull citizen from Danzig with a pockmarked face and such extraordinary ideas of cleanliness that at first I thought him to be a Pole) was apparently trying to get hold of a good piece of business for very little money. Neither of these worthies was very pleasant company, and please remember that it rained steadily, day and night, all the time I was in Veere and that I was forced to share the tap-room with these fossils for two solid weeks, before the lawyers and the notaries were ready to submit the last of their dockets, affidavits, quitclaims, transfers and licenses.

Rather than listen to the shorter English catechism (as composed privately by the Scotchman's grandfather and as recited by the grandson with touching regularity after the sixth or seventh hot toddy), or playing chess with the spurious Teuton (who had to be watched like a hawk lest he make queens and knights do certain things which nature and the rules of the game had never intended them to do), I used to withdraw to my room and rather than spend my evenings perusing those bales of official documents (without which no decent citizen of our republic can either hope to enter or leave this world) I would read such trash as had been left behind by former visitors and which the proprietor of the establishment kept behind lock and key and to which he invariably referred as his Temple of Solomon. It was pretty terrible stuff but the endless rain storms had so thoroughly spoiled the road to Middelburg that it was impossible to send to that city for fresh literary supplies and in consequence I was bored beyond words.

Then I made a great discovery which filled my heart with sudden and unexpected visions of a happy fortnight. My good uncle in his younger days had been one of the suitors of a young lady whose fame since then has spread far and wide and who will be remembered as one of the most resourceful women our country has ever produced. But she was after bigger game than a mere ship-builder and she had given herself in marriage to a youthful lawyer of French descent but Dutch parentage, who had started his career as a sort of literary infant prodigy; who ere he was ten years of age had recited his own-made Greek hexameters before half of the crowned heads of Europe; and who at the tender age of twelve had commenced to edit and revise a dozen of the most ponderous and erudite among the minor prophets of Latin literature. A most facile juggler of easy-flowing verse, who one day would compose him a drama on Adam in exile, the next week would turn out a history of the rebellion of the Netherlands and in between these manifold activities, would find time to devote himself in a most thorough-going fashion to the pursuit of the law and the costly pastime of practical politics.

When this incredible young man presented himself as a candidate for the hand and the favor of my uncle's inamorata, when this wandering encyclopedia of classical and legal information began to bombard the simple Veere girl with endless love letters, couched in terms of truly Ciceronian eloquence, her other swains (of whom there were many, for in those days she had not yet fallen a victim to those fits of temper which afterwards were to turn the Grotius household into such a merry hell) had felt that their cause was lost and had tactfully withdrawn. But of course they had been very curious to see what manner of man had so ignominiously defeated them and when the happy pair descended from the boat that had brought them from Holland to spend their honeymoon with Maria's parents, they had all been present at the dock and in a spirit of good feeling had presented the new Mrs. Grotius with an enormous bouquet of roses, an unexpected attention which the delighted young bride had rewarded with kisses for the entire assembled multitude.

A few of the boys had been curious to see what effect this outburst of osculatory generosity might have upon the happy groom, but he apparently had taken no notice of the incident, being too much occupied with the unloading of two vast trunks, filled with books, and upon which he bestowed so much attention that he had neither eyes nor ears for his beautiful wife.

This strange honeymoon had given rise to many rather ribald jokes, for the lovely Reigersberg child was an entirely normal product of that fertile Zeeland clay which raises the most powerful horses, the richest grain and the bluest of all blue grapes, and it was generally conceded that in matters of the heart, the young lady had no need of a printed edition of Ovid's "Amatory Art."

In her despair Maria had turned to my uncle (who was a little older than her other childhood friends) and had favored him with her confidence.

"Hugh is a fine fellow," she had told him, "and I am very fond of him. He is very devoted to me and I like being the wife of so important a man, but I hate to go to bed with Martianus Capella, and Cicero, although no doubt a most talented orator, is a dull companion in the morning when the sun is shining and the wind is blowing and the birds are singing and all those ancient worthies seem a hundred million years dead and buried."

In consequence of this interview my uncle, who was the incarnation of commercial honesty, had committed the only crime of his life. While the Reigersberg family was away on a state visit to their relatives in Middelburg, he had broken into their house and had removed the contents of the two fatal trunks to his own attic where he had carefully hidden them behind a worm-eaten chest that had stood there ever since the days of his great-grandmother.

Of course the affair had leaked out (small cities are proverbially leaky when it comes to the domestic affairs of their inhabitants) and my uncle had acquired a reputation for unselfish loyalty which stuck to him (as a mild and amiable joke) until the end of his days.

Now in my despair I remembered the existence of this long lost treasure. I sent the old housekeeper to investigate the attic. She reported that it contained nothing but two moldy chests of drawers, a trunk filled with discarded clothes, and a pile of books in various stages of neglect and decomposition and all of them fit for the rubbish pile.

I, however, knowing the contempt mixed with fear and suspicion which the illiterate feel toward the printed word, told the old lady to take a bucket of water and a sponge and set to work to remove the ravages of almost fifty years of neglect as best she could. She murmured a few vague words about "No good ever coming of all this book-learning," but I encouraged her by telling her that she might keep whatever books of sermons might be found among my uncle's hidden relics, and two days later, neatly packed into three large clothes-baskets, this extraordinary collection was delivered at my door.

I approached those books with a feeling of shyness and respect. I seemed to be committing a sacrilege. There, on the fly-leaf of each book, stood a name that had carried the fame of our country into every corner of the civilized world. But because the erstwhile owner of these imposing-looking quartos had steadfastly defended the principles of mutual forbearance upon which our commonwealth was based, he had been driven into ignominious exile by those selfsame bigots and Pharisees who had been responsible for the violent death of my dear Lord John of Barneveldt.

It is said that when the great King Gustavus Adolphus was killed at the battle of Lutzen, a copy of Grotius' work on international relations was the only volume found in his tent except his Bible and that His Majesty never went to sleep without reading one or two chapters from the New Testament and from this treatise on the laws that should regulate the behavior of nations, whether at war or in peace.

And yet even while I was sitting there, aimlessly handling these parchment bindings, that marvelous man who had ever been received by emperors and kings as their equal could not return to the land of his birth because an ill-tempered French theologian with a bad liver and the hallucinations of a village Messiah had decreed that tolerance was an invention of the Devil, that there was only one way of salvation to which he and only he and his disciples held the key and which was therefore closed to all those whose charity and kindliness of spirit forbade them from sharing the arrogant conceits of the two-penny dictator of a mean Swiss town.

And these reflections, together with the apparent hopelessness of our age-old struggle against human stupidity and ignorance, filled my heart with such despair that soon I sent the books back to the attic whence they had come, and braving the endless dampness, set forth to find a somewhat more energetic form of diversion of the spirit than the patient perusal of Aratus, Arienus, and the commentaries of the late and unlamented Scaliger.

Of course all this is only indirectly connected with the fact that it rained very hard and very continually during the fall of the year 1641. And if this manuscript should ever fall into the hands of some one else (which God forbid!) he might well remark, "The poor old fellow is wandering all over the place."

But I would answer him: "Dear friend, isn't all of life a matter of jibing and tacking and sailing all over the place? Has any one ever undertaken to navigate the high seas of experience without continually being driven hither and yon by the storms of adversity and the currents of ill-fate?" And I shall peacefully continue my literary peregrinations as the spirit moves me, for that is the way I have lived and that is the way I hope to die. I shall be immobile and stationary for many years to come, but that will happen when my craft is safely anchored near the consoling shores of some convenient cemetery.

And now let me return to that dreary and rain-soaked fortnight in the fall of the year 1641 when I sat shivering in a village inn, signed legal documents all day long and passed through one of the weirdest adventures of a career that has been rather full of extraordinary incidents.

Because I was restless and bored, I used to take long solitary walks. One evening I was struck by a most extraordinary noise that issued forth from two rather poor-looking houses, not far from the ancient church of Our Lady in a part of the town occupied by fishermen, many of whom hailed from the near-by village of Arnemuiden, where the people were experiencing difficulties with their harbor.

After a little study, I vaguely recognized a few of the better known tunes of Petrus Dathenus and I thought: "Oh, well, here are some of the children of Zion come together for a little private worship," and I forgot all about it until one night (it must have been between six and seven o'clock of the evening, for I had just finished my supper, but it was already quite dark) just when I passed the bigger of the two houses, the door opened and four men appeared carrying an enormous wooden box from which there issued such a cackling, gobbling and guggling as I had never heard before in all my livelong days.

And the next evening at precisely the same hour I beheld (this time, however, coming from the other house) a small procession of women and children, heavily loaded with cages and crates which seemed to contain a miniature menagerie of all the better known household pets and which (though in a different manner) produced almost as many cacophonic sounds as the wooden contraption which had attracted my attention the night before.

My curiosity was now thoroughly aroused. It did not seem a matter of very great importance, but I was bored and when one is thoroughly bored in a small town, even the clandestine transportation of a humble hencoop means a most welcome diversion. I made it a point to walk past these two houses every evening after dinner. It used to get dark shortly after four o'clock, and what with the rain and the absolute lack of any sort of street illumination, there was little chance of detection.

I was familiar with the religious tendencies of the simple fisherfolk who inhabit these southern islands and the singing and shouting alone would hardly have attracted my attention. I would have thought that some new Elijah had arisen or that some obscure John the Baptist was busy trying to impress his neighbors with that consciousness of sin which ever since the beginning of history has allowed the prophets of Heaven to lead a comfortable and dignified existence at the expense of their neighbors—and the next moment I would have forgotten all about it.

But the large bundles and boxes did not quite seem to fit into the general order of things and in a casual way I mentioned these to my notary friend during one of our interminable sessions at his office. This office, by the way, was situated in the same house in which the excellent Valerius, his predecessor in office, had made his interesting collection of contemporary war songs. All music, however, had long since departed from the premises and life had become dreadfully serious.

The good man was terribly upset by what I told him. He was so startled that he dropped his pen into the lime-pot instead of the ink-stand and then in trying to salvage the pen (for he was a careful book-keeper), dribbled lime all over the papers which meant that each and every one of them had to be copied again and that business—for that day at least—had come to a standstill. And when I tried to quiet him down, with such simple speeches as: "Why get excited about so small an occurrence?" and: "Just a few pious brethren holding a little private meeting—no use bothering about them," or words to that effect, he flew into a veritable rage.

"Simple indeed!" he bellowed. "Simple indeed! and singing psalms while they are betraying their country!" and he burst forth out of the office and to my horror I saw him pass by, a few minutes later, followed by the sheriff and two deputies, all of them armed with swords and halberds.

Now in order to understand this remark, you ought to know that during the early forties, the people were in a terrible state of both suspicion and suspense. Don't ask me why, for I could not possibly tell you. Such attacks of unrest are very much like the epidemics of a mysterious disease. One day everybody is well and happy, and the men sit in the taverns and drink their ale and tobacco and talk business and the women swap stories across the doorsteps and little boys and girls play in the gutter and every one is sure that all is well with the world, or at least as well as ever it can be. And the next day, those same men are dead, and terror-stricken women are desperately clutching at their whimpering children, lest the green-eyed monster get hold of them and drag them to an untimely grave.

Yet nothing has happened. The evil winds that carry disease have not blown from east or west, or south or north. None of the dreaded comets that influence our lives have appeared upon the horizon. No vapors (as far as any one could notice) have arisen from either river or sea to cause this blight. The affliction is there and those who believe that everything has been predicted since the beginning of time say: "This pestilence comes to us as the vengeance of a just God to punish us because we loved Satan too much" and those who hold that Evil is all-powerful in this world stammer: "It is Satan who wants to chastise us because we loved God too much," and those who are convinced (upon very slender evidence, I must confess) that our universe is based upon reason and understanding, confess: "We don't know. We may know in the fullness of time, but at present, we are still too deeply steeped in ignorance and prejudice either to know or to find out."

And all this holds good with equal truth of those strange spiritual maladies that have afflicted the nations of our globe as long ago as the days of Genesis and Deuteronomy. The sun is shining and the harvests stand ready and peace reigneth on earth. The swords have been hammered into plow-shares and kings and potentates call each other "Brother." Ships sail across the seven seas and merchants trade far and wide without the slightest fear of molestation. It looks as if the dream of the great King Henry of France was about to come true and that henceforth a Parliament of Nations shall settle the difficulties that arise between the different countries without the usual idiotic appeal to violence and bloodshed.

And then, almost overnight, something happens and Paradise is turned into Hell, that same English merchant who has been dealing with his Dutch rival in peace and harmony for twenty or thirty years, has become an untrustworthy scoundrel and must be watched from the moment he sets foot on our soil, until he leaves it again. Otherwise he might poison the wells or set fire to hospitals and orphan asylums and in a hundred other ways show what a fiend he really is and has been all the time he was being received as a welcome guest.

Substitute, if you wish, Frenchmen for Englishmen or Russians or Turks and substitute Danish for Dutch or German or Spanish, but the result will be the same. The moment this "dementia maxima" descends upon earth, human reason ceases to function and no matter what those, who are able to think a little clearer than the majority of their fellow-citizens, will say or suggest or do or write, the illness must take its natural course, until having slain its thousands or tens of thousands, it departs once more as mysteriously and as suddenly as the plague or the black death or that strange sweating sickness of which nearly one tenth of the people of Amsterdam died only three years ago.

Well, during the early forties we were once again threatened by an outbreak of this unpleasant international delirium. Nominally we were still in rebellion against our lawful sovereign, the King of Spain. But I doubt whether more than a dozen people among all my vast acquaintance knew the name of the King whom they were supposed to be defying. To the younger generation, even such names as Leyden or Haarlem, that had filled my heart with horror when I was a child, meant practically nothing. They probably remembered that those cities had suffered a succession of sieges and that their people had eaten rats and mice and the bodies of dead men and women rather than open their gates to Alva's hirelings. But I doubt whether they took those yarns about starvation and heroism very seriously.

They would listen to grandpa with polite patience, but when it came to his stories of Spanish tyranny and cruelty, they were apt to shrug their shoulders. It was almost forty years since the last of the Spanish garrisons had been driven from the northern parts of the Republic and the cap ture of Breda had shown that the enemy could no longer hold his own even in the South, where the populace had remained staunchly faithful to the old religion and where the names of Calvin and Luther were identified with the Beast of the Book of Revelation.

In the Far East, the capture of Ceylon and Malacca had filled the last gap in the road to the Indies and ships bound for Java could now travel as safely and comfortably as the daily canal-boat between Amsterdam and Haarlem. The opening up of Japan had proved a most lucrative business and the merchant who sent a ship to Hirado or Deshima and did not make a full five hundred percent on his investment thought himself cheated out of his legitimate profits and was apt to petition the government to get himself reimbursed for his trouble.

The whales of Spitzbergen continued as plentiful as in the days of Barendszoon and Hudson and the town of Smeerenberg had three saloons for every try-house.

In Brazil, Count John Maurice of Nassau was busy laying the foundations for a new empire that was to offer greater opportunities for speculation and investment than anything we had ever undertaken before. The West India Company was growing rich on the slave trade to Spanish America. The Baltic grain trade was still entirely in the hands of our own people and by smuggling flour to the starving people of Spain (what did a war mean to these poor hungry wretches?) and by making them pay through the nose for every sack of wheat, our merchants were gathering in enough money to pay almost half the costs of our admiralties.

As for the industries at home, the mills were working overtime, for all this rich plunder from all over the world had to be prepared for the market—the wood had to be sawed, the rice had to be husked, the wheat had to be ground, the tobacco had to be cut, the spices had to be cleaned, the fish had to be dried and in order to keep the vast fleets of merchantmen continuously on the high seas, ships had to be built and ships had to be repaired and sails had to be made and the rope-yards had to be kept busy and everywhere there was such terrific activity that those who went hungry did so solely because they were either too incompetent or too lazy to grab their share of the golden manna which poured down upon us from a kindly disposed Heaven.

I know that I am talking like that famous master of rhetoric who at the opening of the University of Utrecht tried to prove that the inhabitants of the Low Countries were no other than the two lost tribes of Israel, at last come into their own. But I want to give an adequate picture of the background against which those regrettable events took place, which I am now about to relate.

I am not sufficiently familiar with the people of the South to know whether they perhaps are incapable of enjoying themselves without a consciousness of imminent danger. But those of us who descend from the race of the Batavians seem to have an infinite capacity for needless suffering, both of the body and the soul. I remember how once as a boy I was invited to go sailing on the Zuyder Zee and a very persistent wind from the south-west carried us to the shores of Friesland. It was the first (and last) time I visited this distant province and I was struck by the immense richness of its meadows and fields. "Surely," I said to myself, "these peasants ought to be happy and contented." But wherever we went we saw none but dejected faces and heard naught but talk of great despondency and discouragement, until an honest yeoman from the neighborhood of Franeker, liberally supplied with vast quantities of that excellent gin which is a specialty of the city of Leeuwarden, could at last be induced to tell us the cause for so profound a feeling of dejection among the Frisian husbandmen. "It is the potatoes," he explained, "the damn potatoes! The crop is marvelous this year—never had a crop like it before—not a bad one among them—and we are up against it—what shall we now give to our hogs?"

Well, in the year '41 the whole of the Republic was enjoying such prosperity that every one was more or less worrying about "feeding the hogs." And since no fault could be found with the government, the conduct of the war, the management of the various trading companies or even with the wages that were being paid to the artisans, the people eagerly began to look for some other cause for discontent.

In no other way can I explain the strange feeling of hostility and suspicion that then arose against the kingdom of England with which so far we had lived on a footing of a most complete and cordial unity. Wherever I went I heard stories about British perfidy and British malice and British knavery and people who had never seen a Britisher in all their lives, who would not have known one had they seen one, would tell me hair-raising stories about the personal characteristics and habits of a race with which they were as familiar as they were with Eskimos or Tartars.

What struck me as even more amazing was the sudden personal hatred against the person of His Majesty the King. This poor sovereign was now held to blame for all the sins of his fathers and even more for those of his cousin, the late Elizabeth of Tudor. That red-haired fury had undoubtedly used us badly and it is true that the English episode in the Low Countries had ended most unfortunately for all concerned. But I never could see that it made very much difference under such circumstances whether the Queen had actually slept with the man who afterwards was to become the leader of the expedition to Holland (as many pious people stoutly maintained, though God knows they had never been able to peep into Her Majesty's bedroom) or whether she had led a chaste life and had died a virgin (as all of her subjects so firmly believe). That particular "Sweet Robin" had not been the sort of man that ought to have been sent upon that sort of an errand and the Queen, like many another woman in a humbler position, had merely mistaken a neatly turned leg for a neatly turned brain, and that was all.

But no, the old virago must now be dug out of her grave and be held responsible for everything from the unpaid bills of her dear friend Leicester to the treason of Stanley and York, though there was hardly a man alive to tell what sort of treason these two Englishmen had committed. As for poor King James, he was called a true son of his mother, for genealogical details rarely interest the multitude, and when once upon a time, in the cabin of the *Rotterdam*, I tried to prove that he was not the son of Elizabeth of England but of Mary of Scotland, whose head had been cut off by her British cousin, I was immediately pounced upon from all sides and a very excited apothecary, who knew for certain that I was an agent in the pay of the English minister, was all for throwing me overboard and he might have succeeded in making things very uncomfortable for me, hadn't the skipper (an old friend of my grandfather's) descended into the cockpit and offered to brain the first person who laid hands on his beloved doctor.

Indeed, I could never see what reason we had to hate this unfortunate monarch, who had allowed himself to be cheated out of the greater part of the indemnity which we still owed him for the English expedition of 1596. I love my pipe, and I shall always think that a man who is capable of writing a treatise against tobacco shows a regrettable lack of the common decencies of civilized existence. But all this outcry against the shuffling old Scotchman seemed very silly to me and what can I say about the deluge of abuse that was now being heaped upon his son, who, if we were to believe the news-sheets, had more than enough troubles of his own.

Of course as so often happens in similar outbreaks of national fury, the person who was suspected and accused of any number of crimes had really nothing to do with the case. He was merely a convenient dummy, and as England was one of our closest neighbors, the British rulers usually had to play the rôle of scape-goat when the real offending parties lived behind the Pyrenees or on the other side of the Danube and were therefore out of reach of the public wrath. And it was clear to any one who had paid any attention to the political development of that day that fear of the Church rather than fear of the English was at the bottom of the panic that was sweeping across the country.

The fact that the Queen of England had recently appointed a diplomatic representative of her own in Rome had somehow or other become public property. Brussels in those days was the center of all European intrigues and our spies, well supplied with money, had first choice of all the scandals and gossip of at least half a hundred foreign courts. The comings and goings of Father Carr, who acted as Her Majesty's intermediary between the English court and the Bishop of Rome, were closely watched by Their Lordships at the Hague and when Her Majesty used the uprising among the so-called Puritans (a sect of very strict Calvinists who were in very close relations with our own people) to collect vast sums of money from those of her subjects who had secretly remained faithful to the Papist cause, the fat was in the fire and from a hundred pulpits one heard the dreaded word "Jesuit" followed by the even more terrible threat of a "return of the Inquisition."

In how far there was any truth in the widely spread story of a Jesuit plot to murder the Estates General and overthrow the Republic, I do not know. But of course ever since the murder of good Prince William by a poor, bigoted Frenchman who had been encouraged to commit this crime by an enthusiastic Jesuit from Treves, and ever since the murder of Henry III by a Dominican friar and the attempt upon the life of his successor by a pupil of the Jesuits and the final murder of this good king by a poor maniac who was known to have tried to become a member of that terrible society, the people of our country had been convinced that Rome was preparing for a counter-offensive and meant to reconquer the lost provinces as soon as an opportunity should offer itself.

The plot to blow up the members of the House of Parliament, who had voted for the expulsion of all Catholic priests from England, had caused a tremendous sensation in our country and ever since (and it must have happened more than thirty-five years ago) it had been rumored that the Scarlet Woman would stop short at no act, however vile or repugnant, to reëstablish her dominion over the people of our own country.

Of course, all these stories were greatly embellished during their rounds of the taverns and ale-houses. Acquaviva, the General of the Jesuit Company, was closely identified with Antichrist and hundreds of thousands of otherwise intelligent burghers fondly believed that he breakfasted every morning on a couple of stolen Protestant babies. Every ship arriving from a Mediterranean port was carefully searched, lest a cargo of figs and dates might prove to be really a cargo of Jesuit friars, and even in far distant Brazil and Java, everything that went awry was the fault of one of the disciples of Loyola.

Let the King of Jacatra object to the price he received for his coffee, and at once it was known: "A Spanish Jesuit from Manila has had access to the princely ear and is trying to start trouble between the company and the natives." Let a cacique of the Recife refuse to supply a sufficient number of Indians to work on the fortifications of Macao and of course he has taken a bribe offered him by a Portuguese Jesuit from Rio.

Meanwhile at home, even in the most remote parts of the country provinces, the mysterious influence of the Jesuits was ever a subject of daily discussion. It was enough for a boy who had played hookey to explain his absence from school by a "dark-faced, dark-haired man who spoke with a foreign accent and promised me some candy if I would follow him, and who frightened me so terribly that I ran away and did not dare come home until after dark," to set an entire village in motion and make peasants, heavily armed with blunderbusses and scythes, search the highways and byways for the traitor who had threatened their child.

Upon some rare occasions such bands of crazy yokels actually caught a Papist, but invariably he proved to be some perfectly harmless priest who had ventured back into the country, notwithstanding the drastic laws against the Papish idolatry, or some kind-hearted soul bent upon an errand of mercy at some isolated farm-house where people of his faith were dying and had asked for his assistance. For though I am quite convinced that men like Acquaviva or Vitelleschi would have sacrificed hundreds of their enemies without the slightest pang of conscience, if by so doing they could have brought a single erring soul back into the fold, and would have burned thousands of my neighbors with utter equanimity of soul if they had thought that it would further the cause of their beloved Church, neither the Neapolitan nor his Roman successor were fools and they knew that the time had not yet come for a concentrated action in our particular part of the northern world. But they rather approved of the mental terrorism which the mere mentioning of their name was able to call forth and they encouraged the myth of their omnipresence and omniscience in every possible way. That the terror-stricken people, looking for somebody to hate and unable to lay their hands upon any bona fide Jesuits, had then fastened their anger upon the King of England, who was at war with his Calvinistic subjects, and whose wife was known to be a friend of the Pope, why, that was just a bit of great good luck which they meant to turn to their own advantage as soon as the opportunity should offer itself.

This is rather a long-winded explanation of a very simple situation, but I had to tell all this if I were to make quite clear how an innocent evening perambulation (the result of a man's boredom in a rain-soaked little town) could lead to such absolutely unforeseen complications and could become the cause of great misery to a large group of perfectly harmless religious fanatics.

I have already written down that I had last seen my notary friend when accompanied by the arm of the law he was hurrying in the general direction of the church near which the houses were located about which I had spoken to him. I am by nature averse to all forms of public disorder and excitement and whenever I see a crowd in the distance, I usually take the nearest side street, rather than be brought face to face with some drunken brawl or a quarrel between husband and wife. From the agitated behavior of the old legal dignitary and the presence of the sheriff, I understood that my perfectly harmless remark must have created some sort of excitement. I felt sincerely sorry that I should have been the cause of this upheaval. I had mentioned the matter from sheer lack of suitable topics for conversation and not to start an inquiry which might end God only knew where and how.

And so, rather than await further developments, I returned to my room and ordered my dinner which consisted of a fresh shrimp salad, but when I asked for the meat, the girl who waited on me came rushing back from the kitchen, all pale and trembling, and explained to me that the cook was gone.

"Why so?" I asked her. "Is there a fire or a flood?"

"Oh, no, Sir," the poor creature replied. "Much worse! They have discovered a plot to murder all of us in our beds to-night!"

Really, this was getting to be too silly for words. A chance remark to a decrepit old scribe and a whole town thrown into the madness of a panic. I took my hat and rushed to the house of the notary. He had just returned from the Town Hall. He welcomed me with outstretched arms. His hands were shaking as if he had just lifted a weight too great for his strength.

"Magnificent!" he shouted. "Magnificent! We shall never forget what you have done for us."

At this I grew angry.

"Listen," I objected, "please listen to me for one moment. I am sorry I ever opened my mouth about those poor devils. I thought it would make for conversation and you know I have a hard time keeping my mind on your damned legal paraphernalia. But these poor fellows probably belonged to some new sect of religious lunatics, and now what have you done to them?"

"Done to them?" the old fellow interrupted me. "We have done to them what they deserved. They are locked up, all of them, eight men and eight women and seventeen children, locked up in the cellars of the Town Hall. To-morrow they will send troops from Middelburg and take them to the Abbey where they will be safer. We are too near the coast here."

"But for Heaven's sake," and I tried to stop his flow of words, "for Heaven's sake, man, be reasonable! The whole town has been turned topsy-turvy because I was bored and went walking in the rain and heard a few fishermen singing their hideous songs and because I made a casual remark about . . ." But I got no further, for Mr. Notary arose from his seat with great dignity and with a voice quivering with emotion he proclaimed:

"There is nothing ever 'casual' in the sight of God. I know your indifference in religious matters. But let me tell you that you were the instrument in God's hand, through which we may yet save our dear country."

"Save it from what?"

"From Antichrist!"

For such was the state of apprehension and uncertainty which dominated the minds of vast numbers of people of that day that a single careless remark of an inconsequential visitor could in less than ten seconds change an amiable and easy-going old conveyancer into an eager young Torquemada and could turn a well-balanced little town of peaceful citizens into a seething mass of open-mouthed lunatics for no better reason than that some one somewhere had whispered the word "Jesuits" and "British spies."

Of course, what happened afterwards has become common knowledge. The news-sheets and year-books have seen to that.

The day after I had indulged in this disastrous conversation (thank God, it taught me a lesson never to be facetious with those who take themselves seriously) a detachment of soldiers appeared from Middelburg and amidst the cat-calls of the assembled populace of Veere and amidst threats of the gallows and the block marched the poor victims to the capital of the Province. It was pouring, for the rain never seemed to cease during the latter half of that year. The sight of the small children wading through the mud of the ill-paved road, shivering and dazed and anxiously clutching the skirts of their mothers, was quite painful. And the burghers of Veere, being by nature rather kindly, had already begun to repent of their fury of the day before. And so suddenly a few peasant carts appeared from nowhere in particular and first the bedraggled infants were loaded on board and then the women and finally even the men were permitted to ride, so that they did not reach Middelburg in too exhausted a condition.

As I, entirely against my will, had been the cause of all this commotion, I took a horse and rode to Middelburg very early the next morning and I went to see the law officers and explained just exactly how all this had come about and tried to convince them that in all likelihood the prisoners were neither British spies nor Jesuit agents, but belonged to some obscure religious sect which had invented a new religion of its own and was practicing a strange ritual, like the Baptists who believe in total immersion or the Collegiates who have no ministers to address them and who consider every human being a potential prophet to whom the others should listen whenever the Spirit moves him.

In the end even these suspicious magistrates understood that I had been right and in less than a week's time the prisoners were discharged and were sent home with a small gift of money to compensate them for their suffering. And then it all came out, and an absurd story it was!

In a near-by village on one of the other islands a certain Reverend Jodocus Poot had started a new sect. The Reverend Jodocus was not a regularly ordained minister of the gospel. He had begun life as a tailor. Then he had married a girl from his native town of Ierseke with some money. He had taken a few lessons in Latin from the local minister, had bought himself a few inspiring-looking books, and quite by chance had got hold of Reuchlin's "De Arte Cabbalistica" which had so impressed him that thereafter he had completely discarded the New Testament, which he declared to be a Pauline heresy (don't ask me how he came to this conclusion, for I would not be able to tell you!) and had set up shop as a sort of Protestant rabbi, ready to explain and interpret the more obscure passages of the books of the Pentateuch.

During his studies he had come to some very queer conclusions and as a result his disciples would wear no clothes beyond those absolutely necessary for the sake of Christian decency, for any protection (in the form of an overcoat or gloves) against the blasts of winter would have been open defiance of the will of God who had divided the year into a cold season and a warm one and whose will must be obeyed at all costs. Neither, if they were farmers, would they fertilize their fields, for if God had intended them (the fields) to be covered with manure, He would undoubtedly have attended to that matter at the day of creation. Nor, if they were sailors, would they learn to swim, for if God meant them to be drowned, it was not within their humble human province to frustrate His designs by keeping afloat until they were saved.

This noble orator (he could out-distance and out-shout every dominie within the whole province of Zeeland) had made a good thing out of his peculiar form of theology. Like a second John the Baptist he refused to accept any remuneration for his exhortations, but once a year his followers were allowed to bring an offering to Jehovah through his most unworthy servant, the Reverend Jodocus Pedesius, for although the good man was a sworn enemy of all book-learning, he had Latinized his name as soon as he had given up the tailor's bench for the pulpit.

He therefore was able to live a happy and carefree existence, but in order to maintain his hold upon his disciples, he was continuously obliged to increase the strength of the spiritual potions which he offered his audiences three times on Sundays and once on Wednesday evening.

Indeed, he reminded me (through what I heard of him, for I never saw him in the flesh) of those musicians who are so addicted to playing fortissimo that in the end, when they really wish to accentuate a passage, they cease to produce music and merely make a noise. The terrible rainstorms of the last four months had given him a new and bright idea. One day he publicly announced that a careful study of Genesis VI-IX had convinced him that the end of the world was near at hand, not through fire, as had so often been predicted, but through another deluge. The Lord was in despair about the wickedness of his recalcitrant children (like all the half educated, the Reverend Jodocus loved big words) and the fastnesses of the great ocean were about to be broken up and the windows of Heaven were about to be opened.

"Prepare, all ye sinners, for the Day of Judgment is at hand, when those who have worshiped the Beast and the Image shall drink of the wine of the wrath of God and shall be tormented with fire and brimstone in the presence of the holy angels and in the presence of the Lamb!"

By this time a number of lay-preachers had fallen under the spell of Pedesius' eloquence and throughout the Island of Walcheren quite a number of shoe-makers and tailors (cobblers and habit-makers lead a sedentary life and have much time for solitary meditation) were busily engaged spreading the Pedesian doctrines. The most violent among these was a cordwainer in the near-by town of Arnemuiden which ever since the Reformation had been a stronghold of the "precise" doctrine, as the stricter sort of Calvinists used to call their own brand of theology. This honest man, who was slightly lame and besides suffered from the "morbus demoniacus" (he was never so inspired as when he had a "fit," his parishioners used to say with pride), welcomed the idea of a second deluge with such vehemence that he soon out-rivaled all other Pedesians by the vividness and lucidity of his descriptions of the rapidly approaching aquatic catastrophe.

He even could give the exact date. It was to take place on Friday, the fourth of November, of the year 1641, at thirteen minutes past eight in the morning.

It appeared during the trial that two families of Veere fishermen had belonged to the congregation of this strange prophet, that for more than five years they had regularly walked from Veere to Arnemuiden (a distance of some three hours) to hear the messages of this limping herald of doom, and that in the end they themselves had begun to have hallucinations.

One small girl of seven especially had been pursued by strange dreams and during one of these an angel by the name of Ameshaspentas had appeared at the foot of her bed (the angel, according to description, had been a very beautiful woman dressed all in gold and with silver wings) and had commanded her to tell her parents and her uncle that they and their families alone among all the creatures of this earth had found favor in the eyes of the Lord; that they, and they alone, would be spared during the coming flood; and that they must hasten and build themselves an Ark in which to save themselves and a couple of all the birds, the insects and the mammals which then inhabited the surface of the planet. Nothing was said about the fishes. It was supposed that they would take care of themselves.

Now it happened that the fishermen unto whom this message came were dreadfully poor. Their vessels were old and leaky and there was not a soul in the whole town who would offer to give them a stiver's worth of credit. Furthermore, they had seen pictures of elephants and dromedaries and all sorts of strange animals which lived in far-off countries and how were they to get hold of these and how were they to capture the birds? And in trying to catch a couple of wasps, the youngest child had been badly stung and both his hands had been so swollen that they had to send him to the leech.

There indeed was a problem. But it was settled by the little girl, who most conveniently had another dream, during which the angels Abdiel and Zadriel had told her not to worry about this detail. Not only was the Lord incensed about the behavior of the human race, but the majority of the animals, too, had been guilty of grave wickedness and it would suffice therefore if the future Noahs took only such beasties as lived on the Island of Walcheren.

The big boxes, therefore, which originally had attracted my attention, contained nothing more ferocious than a few rabbits and a few chickens and a couple of hares and pheasants and two small pigs. These poor dumb creatures had been completely forgotten while the trial lasted. Neither had any one dared to approach the fatal ships, for during the first few days there issued from their respective holds such a weird agglomeration of doleful sounds that every one supposed the crafts to be haunted and when the rightful owners finally returned to their vessels to release their live-stock, they found that all of the poor prisoners had died of starvation, except one small weasel, who had broken out of his cage and had grown fat upon the remains of his neighbors.

Thus ended this strange episode which was entirely due to my own lack of discretion in trying to pass small-talk with people who recognized no coin but the Eternal Verities and which would never have occurred had not the fall of the year '41 been such a period of such incessant and relentless rainstorms.

Incidentally just before I left Veere to return to Amsterdam, the notary handed me a small package which my uncle had entrusted to him, with instructions not to give it to me until I should have obeyed the different stipulations of his somewhat complicated and rather elaborate testament. As I had now signed all the necessary papers, had paid over (without a murmur, I am happy to say) the various sums that he had willed to a number of local charities and in a general way had tried to behave like a decent heir (as I had every reason to be, since I had held the old gentleman in a very sincere and grateful affection) I was allowed to open this mysterious message which came to me from the other side of the grave.

It contained a letter, dated Veere, May 1st, of the year of Grace 1623, which read:

"MY BELOVED NEPHEW:

"You have chosen the one profession which I myself would have followed, had I not been forced by outward circumstances to enter a business career.

"Now there are several sorts of doctors, in this world—those who regard themselves as messengers of our dear Lord, sent to this earth to minister to the needs of the poor and the miserable and those who exercise their trade as if they were selling draperies or cheese, instead of dispensing the mercy of God. I have watched you very carefully these last twenty years and believe that I know your character as well as my dear sister would have known it had she been spared to see you grow up. I have often wished that you had been more thoroughly imbued with the seriousness of life or had understood a little more clearly that the whole of our existence on this earth is merely the prelude to the vastly greater joys of Heaven. But perhaps our dear Lord in His wisdom does not yet think that the time has come to incline your heart towards Him to whom the highest of our mountains are but a grain of sand and who holds the oceans in the hollow of His hands as if they were drops of water.

"Meanwhile, although you confess yourself a disciple of the old Pagan philosophers, I have never discovered in you that pride of wisdom and that contempt for the humble in spirit which so often mars the usefulness of those who call themselves the true followers of Plato and Aristotle.

"I think that you will go far in your chosen field of work and I remember that you have quite frequently told me of the efforts that are being made by some of the most eminent of our chirurgeons to alleviate the pains of those who must undergo surgical treatment. I do not in any way wish to influence you in your career, but if you would devote yourself to the study of such artificial catalepsy (you will have to forgive an old wood-merchant if he is not entirely up to the nomenclature of medicine) I for one shall most certainly not be displeased and I can think of no other pursuit of human happiness that would have been more in accordance with the wishes of your sainted mother.

"Therefore, and in order that you shall not be obliged to spend all your time upon an ordinary practice, but shall have full liberty to experiment with different narcotics, I have this day invested the sum derived from the sale of my branch office in Flushing in ten securities of the recently re-chartered United East-Indian Companies. They are Common Stock, entirely safe and not apt to be greatly influenced by the fluctuations of the stock-market and they represented a capital of about 30,000 guilders. If they should bear an average interest of eight percent (as it seems not unreasonable to expect) they will assure you an income of 2,400 guilders a year. This is not a great deal of money, but we are simple folk and it ought to be sufficient for your needs if you will remain faithful to the mode of living to which you have been accustomed since the days of your childhood.

"You will of course understand that this is not an outright gift to you as my nephew, but a sacred trust which I bestow upon you as an instrument which in God's hand and through the mercy of our Saviour, Jesus Christ, and through the industry and application of your own unworthy brain may lead to the mitigation of some of that misery and pain which have been our share ever since that terrible day when Adam in his willful disobedience defied the wrath of a righteous Jehovah.

"Farewell, and think in kindness of
"Your devoted Uncle,
"Gerard van Loon."

I walked home that night through the pouring rain with the envelope carefully tucked away in the inside pocket of my coat. I was so moved by this letter that I did not examine the further contents of the small package until I was back in Amsterdam. I was totally ignorant of financial affairs, having thus far lived entirely by my practice, except during the years of preparation when my uncle allowed me a small stipend and I therefore took these shares to my good friend, Lodewijk Schraiber, who was a merchant with connections both in Paris and London and whose knowledge of such things was only surpassed by the respect he enjoyed in commercial circles.

He slowly loosened the thin red ribbon with which the small bundle of securities had been fastened together, spread them out upon his table. Then he put his hand across his bald head, as he was wont to do whenever pleased, and said:

"Your uncle has done pretty well by you, eh?"

I agreed that the old gentleman had always been most kind and lenient to me.

"And now he made a loafer of you!"

This puzzled me and I answered that Amsterdam being one of the most expensive cities of the whole world (as was well known to all those who came there from other towns to transact business), I could hardly expect to go and live on my income, since it would average me only 2,400 guilders a year.

"Then you don't know," and he looked at me in a puzzled way, "what these shares are worth?"

"Yes," I said, "ten times three thousand guilders, or thirty thousand guilders in all."

"And you never heard that they have increased just a little in value?"

"No," I replied, "have they?"

"A mere trifle. Only six hundred percent!"

"Great Heavens! Then now they are worth more than 30,000 guilders?"

"Haven't you ever learned to do simple sums in arithmetic?"

"I have, but that was long ago."

"Well, to-day they are worth exactly 180,000 guilders."

. . . . .

And that was another reason why I remembered that the fall of the year '41 was very rainy, for not only did it pour in the streets, but through the thoughtfulness of this kindly old gentleman, I was quite unexpectedly placed in a position where all my future cares of a material nature were washed away as if by magic, and where I could now give all my time and strength to the work of my choice—the study of those drugs which eventually (so I hoped) would elevate the chirurgeon from a mere butcher (which he now only too often was) to a merciful prophet of new health and a new hope of life.

Chapter 2

I MEET SASKIA FOR THE FIRST TIME AND FIND HER A VERY SICK WOMAN

The fall of the year '41, therefore (as I hope to have proved beyond a shadow of doubt), was a period of endless rainstorms and the month of November was by far the worst. There were floods, and a great many head of cattle were drowned and the cities lay drenched by the endless dampness and the walls were covered with mildew, for as it had begun to rain before the peat had been shipped to town, the available fuel was all water-logged and either refused to burn at all, or filled the room with such vast clouds of smoke that most people preferred to shiver rather than choke.

There was a great deal of sickness and when Jantje, the second-maid (for I could afford two servants by now and have ever held that the highest form of thinking goes best with the most comfortable mode of living, and I firmly believe that Thomas à Kempis would have been a more enjoyable and more useful philosopher if he had spent his days in the pleasant tower of the Sieur de Montaigne rather than among the sandy hills of Overijsel)—when Jantje entered and told me that there was a girl who had come to ask me to visit a sick woman, I thought: "Oh, well, another case of a bad cold! I wish that they would leave me in peace."

For by this time I had practically discontinued my general practice. I still went to the hospital every day because I wanted to learn as much of surgery as I possibly could, but I took no further private patients and spent all my days in a small workshop or laboratory which I had fixed up in the basement of my house where I had a large fire-place (which I heated with coal) and could experiment without the danger of setting the house on fire.

I went into the hall and found not a girl but a middle-aged woman, whose face did not in the least appeal to me, and I was about to send her away and bid her go and find some one else, when she interrupted me in a scolding tone of voice and said: "If it were not a matter of great urgency, my master would have sent for some well-known physician, but my mistress seems to be dying and they told me to get the nearest leech I could find—any one would do."

Somehow or other, the utter lack of graciousness, the painful directness of this person who had come to ask a favor and found the opportunity to offer an insult, appealed to my sense of humor. The good Doctor François Rabelais, who cured more people by his laughter than by his pills and poultices, would have been delighted with this sharp-tongued shrew. He probably would have given her in marriage to Pantagruel and his life thereafter would have been about as merry as that of Socrates during his more domestic periods. And so I did not answer her as I should have done, but took my cloak and followed her.

We did not have far to go. We went down the Houtkoopers Gracht and turned to the left past the Anthonie Sluys and into the Anthonie Breestraat, where we stopped before a two-story brick house which looked as if it were the house of some well-to-do merchant.

The door was opened almost before we had knocked and an anxious voice asked, "Is that the doctor?" To which my unpleasant companion sharply answered, "Well, it is some sort of a leech. He was the nearest one I could find. I hope he will do." To which the voice replied, "Keep a civil tongue in your head, my good woman, and ask the Master to step in while I get a candle."

For indeed the hall was very dark and it was filled with the sharp odor of some acid which made me think for a moment that I had come to the house of a person who occupied himself in his spare time with experiments in alchemy. But when the candle was lit, I saw at once that this was not a laboratory, for the small table in the center and the chairs were all of them covered with drawings and sketches, and against the walls (though I could only see them dimly) there stood a number of canvases, but they were painted in such somber colors that I could not make out the subjects they represented.

Nor could I place the man who had apparently made them. He was a stockily built fellow with the shoulders and arms of a mason or carpenter. Indeed, the first impression I got when he opened the door was that of some better-class working-man, some one accustomed to heavy physical exercise but at the same time trained to read charts and architectural plans —perhaps the foreman of a building company. Such a fellow, however, would hardly have lived in a house of his own on one of the best streets in town, but in that strange city of ours, with new blocks of houses going up like mushrooms and new fortunes being made overnight (especially by those who were in some way connected with the board of aldermen) all things were possible and some of the best houses on the Heerengracht belonged to people who only a few years before had never seen a fork or known the use of a napkin. And so I quietly accepted the situation and asked: "Where is the patient?"

"In the Big Room," he answered, and his voice struck me, for it was very gentle and not in the least in keeping with his somewhat rough and plebeian exterior. Wherefore, while I removed my coat (which was wet, for of course outside the rain was pouring) and now suspecting that I had to deal with a member of my own class, I introduced myself and said:

"I am Doctor van Loon."

And he extended his hand (he had put the candle down on a chair to help me with my cloak) and gave me a slight bow and said: "I am glad you came, Doctor. My name is van Rijn and it is my wife who needs your services," and he picked up the candle once more and led me across the hall into the room situated in the rear part of the house. Here a small oil lamp was burning and there was a fire and as a result it was not quite dark and I got a general impression of the apartment, and it increased the feeling of discomfort which had come over me when I first entered the house.

It is always very difficult to define such emotions and a doctor is at a disadvantage, for he lives so closely with his patients that he often loses track of the sequence of events, and because this particular patient eventually died, it would be easy to argue that those presentiments of doom which had struck me so forcibly when I first entered that house had been invented by me long after the final disaster; indeed, that my unconscious self had invented them as a consolation for the complete failure of my ministrations.

But in this instance at least that was not true. As I have already taken the opportunity to explain, I am not a religious man in the usual, conventional sense of the word. I am, alas, a true descendant of my gloriously blasphemous grandfather, who having had his ears cut off by one brand of religion and his livelihood destroyed by another variety, decided that he would compose himself a new faith of his own which he did by rejecting everything except that famous law of Christ which bids us be pleasantly spoken and amiable to our neighbors—that rule of Kung-fu-Tze, the great Chinese philosopher, which states that the truly wise man minds his own business, and one single line borrowed from a famous Latin poet, who fifteen hundred years before had discovered that there really was no reason in the world why we should not speak the truth with a smile.

To this mixture compositum I had added a liberal supply of the writings of a Frenchman by the name of Michel de Montaigne, who was just then beginning to be known in our country and who (in my opinion) gave us the most honest book that has ever been written by the pen of mortal man.

In this home-made system of theology (which my grandfather bestowed upon me much as my grandmother revealed unto me with profound injunctions of secrecy the family recipe for the making of a perfect omelette, an art almost as simple yet as complicated as that of saving souls)—in this concise but exceedingly handy "Guide to Every Day Happiness" there was no room for spooks, miracles and ectoplastic manifestations of a premonitory nature. It was then the habit in our city (a habit not restricted by any means to the more ignorant classes) never to undertake a single action without first consulting a sooth-sayer. Some patronized crystal-gazers and others went to the descendants of the ancient Haruspices who explained the future from the bowels of some unfortunate cat who was slaughtered for the occasion. Many took great stock in the stars and not a few tried to read the divine mysteries by a study of names or numbers or a handful of grass, plucked at random from some near-by churchyard.

I never fell a victim to any of these absurd superstitions. Sometimes I wished that I had been able to become a confirmed pyromancist or rhabdomancist or psephomancist (or whatever these strange cults call themselves), for if once I could have convinced myself that red-hot irons or fountains or pebbles were able to reveal the intentions of the Almighty, I might have been able to believe (as the vast majority of my neighbors did) that all the wisdom of the ages lay buried between the covers of a single book, writ two or three thousand years before by a tribe of wandering shepherds and peddlers whose ignorance was only surpassed by their love for bloodthirsty detail and their conviction that they and they alone held the true key to salvation.

And so, with the possible exception of a slight leaning towards predicting the weather by means of a game of lansquenet (a harmless enough trick which I had learned from the captain of a Swiss regiment of foot, and which failed as often as it came true), I never took any interest in the supernatural and let myself be guided exclusively by the dictates of my conscience as revealed unto me by the wisdom of Socrates, and by the sum total of those scientific conclusions which had been left unto us by the great sages of the ancient world.

Therefore when I speak of certain chill premonitions which gripped me when I entered this house, I do not refer to anything supernatural. But I hold with Pythagoras of Samos that there is neither life nor death— that all creation is but the tangible expression of one Primeval Force, just as all clouds and rivers and glaciers and snowstorms, yea, even wells and subterranean sources, are manifestations in somewhat different forms and shapes of one vast body of water which encircles and covers the greater part of our globe.

I further believe with him that nothing can ever be added to this original mass of what the Greeks called Energy nor that anything can ever be taken away from it. As a result of this profound conviction, I am able to anticipate Death (that hideous bugaboo of all my Christian friends) without the slightest qualm of fear. For I know that there is neither beginning nor end, but that all life is merely the visible manifestation of that Eternal Continuity which is the one and only mystery we shall never be able to fathom or understand.

But when the time has come to surrender that spark of Energy which one has been allowed (for a shorter or a longer period) to borrow from the great store-house of the Eternal Force, there are certain unmistakable evidences of the impending change, such as occur in nature just before a thunderstorm or just before the eruption of a volcano. What these consist of, I could not possibly tell. I have never been able to classify them as I am able to classify the flowers in my garden or to describe them as I can describe the symptoms of an affliction of the throat. But I have met people in the street or in some merry company and suddenly I have known that "that man" or "that woman" would not live much longer and very shortly afterwards I have heard that he or she had died before the end of a month or a week. And I have had the same experience with animals and even with plants. Once I remember a young couple who had but one child (and could never have another) and who concentrated every thought upon their small offspring. The boy was guarded day and night by two maids who had been carefully trained never to let him out of their sight. He was not allowed to go to school lest he breathe the air contaminated by the breath of the other pupils, but he was taught by private tutors. He never even was taken for a walk, but was made to play in the garden, a very large garden, by the way, so that he had plenty of room for exercise. I knew the father slightly (he had studied law at the University of Leyden while I was taking my course in anatomy there) and he had shown me the boy and had proudly boasted that this son of his some day was going to be one of the greatest people our country had ever produced and that he was going to take no chances with his safety or his health. I knew that he was going to be disappointed and that the poor infant would not live very much longer, but of course I said nothing. A few weeks later the boy, while playing in his garden, was stung by a wasp. It hurt him and of course he scratched, as any one will do under the circumstances. And three days afterwards, he was dead from blood poisoning.

Millions of little children are stung every year by millions of wasps and nothing happens. But this particular boy was doomed and if it had not been a wasp it would have been a bee or a stroke of lightning or a falling beam, but something somewhere would have arisen across his path to bring about this unexpected result. I have never seen it to fail and the moment I entered this house on the Anthonie Breestraat, I knew: "Here the eternal process of change is about to take place and there will be crape on the door before the passing of another year."

And then I ceased to think any further upon the subject (this whole meditation which fills so many pages of script had flashed through my mind in less than two seconds) and I assumed that air of grave concern which sick people expect in their physicians and which often proves itself much more beneficial than barrels of powders and hogsheads of pills.

The patient was lying in a big bed that had been built within the wall, for only the very rich have thus far taken to the French custom of sleeping in those four-postered affairs that stand in the middle of the room and are exposed to all the draughts of the night. By her side there was a cradle and I had to move it before I could come near enough to examine her. I asked the husband to let me have his candle and whispered to him to ask if his wife were asleep. But ere he could answer, the woman had opened her eyes and in a very low and listless tone of voice, she said, "No. I am not asleep. But I am so tired—so dreadfully tired."

And then I sat down by the side of the bed and went through the examination which is customary upon such occasions and asked a number of questions, but these seemed to exhaust the patient so terribly that I made the ordeal as short as possible, felt her pulse, which was very weak and very irregular but much too high, put my hand on her forehead and found it to be cold and moist and then covered her up with her blue counterpane (I had noticed that everything in the room was blue, the walls were covered with a bluish tapestry and all the chairs had blue seats) and told her to try and sleep and that I would soon send her a potion which would make her rest. Then I turned to her husband (and where had I seen that man before? While I was sitting by the side of the bed, it had suddenly come over me that I had seen him somewhere before—but where?) and beckoned to him that I wanted to speak to him alone and he once more picked up his candle, went to the door and said to the nurse (the woman who had called for me and who had waited all this time in the hall and who now acted in a somewhat guilty way, as if she had been listening at the keyhole):

"Geertje, you watch over your mistress and take care of the child, while I go upstairs a moment with the doctor."

And together we climbed the stairs and went into a big room in the front of the house which was so full of vases and plates and pewter tankards and old globes and bits of statuary and strange, outlandish-looking swords and helmets and pictures . . . pictures everywhere . . . pictures on the walls and pictures leaning against the chairs and leaning against the table and leaning against each other, that for an instant the thought struck me, "This man is a dealer in antiquities, and not an artist at all."

But a moment later he bade me be seated (on a chair from which he had first removed a heavy book bound in parchment, a dozen or so etchings or sketches, and on top of it all a small Roman bust of some ancient emperor or general), and he did this with so much grace and ease of manners that I came back to my first impression of a painter or an engraver, only I could not quite remember ever having heard his name before, and yet all the while I felt that I ought to know who he was and furthermore, I knew positively that this was not our first meeting.

He then carefully picked up a large lacquered box and a small cup and saucer which together with two small porcelain figures had been balancing perilously on the seat of another chair, placed them on a table crowned with the grinning head of a blackamoor, and sat down, folded his hands, threw back his head with a curious gesture (which is so common among short-sighted people) and said in an even tone of voice:

"You need not lie to me. Her illness is very dangerous, isn't it?"

To which at first I made no reply, and then in order to gain time, I said, "It may be dangerous or not. But before I draw any definite conclusions, you had better answer me a few questions," and I asked him about his wife's previous history with considerable detail and what I heard, confirmed the worst of my fears and suspicions. They had been married seven years. No, his wife was not an Amsterdam girl. She came from Friesland, across the Zuyder Zee. He himself was born in Leyden. His father had been a miller and had died eleven years before at the age of sixty-two and his mother had died only a year ago at the age of fifty-one and there had been six children, two girls and three other boys besides himself. They had all of them been well enough as far as he knew. "Of course," he said, "that had really nothing at all to do with the case of poor Saskia, but I am thinking of my Titus, for the baby does not look very strong to me and I want you to know that from my side at least he comes of fairly healthy stock."

But from his wife's side the report was not quite so favorable. "You see," he explained to me, "she is really of much better family than I and I have noticed that somehow or other, such children don't seem to get along as well in the world as we who slept three in a bed when we were very young and who were left to shift for ourselves."

I might have heard her father's name. He was that Rombertus van Uylenburgh who had been lunching with the Prince of Orange when Gerard murdered him. He had been Burgomaster of Leeuwarden and had been sent to the Prince to talk about the political situation in the North. He, van Rijn, had never known his father-in-law, for the old man had died in '24 when Saskia was just twelve. There had been eight other children in the family but after the death of the parents (the mother had died a year or so before the husband) the home had been broken up and Saskia had come to Amsterdam with her cousin Hendrick who had a curiosity shop and occasionally dealt in pictures and there he had met her and then she had sat for him for her portrait a couple of times. "In the beginning, the Uylenburghs had been a little aloof," the painter told me, "but Hendrick, who was not much of a business man, borrowed some money from me and he probably felt that I would not dun him quite so easily if his young relative posed for me and, besides, the poor girl knew very few people in Amsterdam and was rather bored and liked a little excitement and coming to my studio with her sister was quite an adventure, for you know what the respectable world thinks about us painters." The end had been that they had become engaged and then they had been married. "And now," he continued, "I am afraid that I shall lose her, for ten months ago, a short time before our boy was born, she had a hemorrhage and she hardly lived through the confinement and this evening, just before we sent for you, she had another one, not quite as bad as the first, but it showed that there still is something the matter with her and the surgeon who usually tends her has himself fallen sick of some malady of the lungs and until he recovers, I wish that you would look after her, for you live near by and she often has such terrible attacks of suffocation that I think she will die and I would like to have a doctor who is not too far away."

This did not seem the most fortunate of grounds for the choice of a physician, but the man interested me (where had I seen that face before?) and he was such a strange mixture of a rather arrogant grand seigneur and a helpless child and the whole house with its jumbled masses of pictures and furniture and china and Roman senators struck me as so utterly incongruous in our respectable city of Amsterdam, that I agreed to accept the case and told him so.

And he said, "Thank you," though without any great show of gratitude, and apparently wanted to go back downstairs, but I bade him to be seated again, for what he had told me was all very interesting, but there were a few other questions I wanted to ask him before I could express any opinion upon the chances of recovery.

"Have there been any other children besides the boy downstairs?"

"Yes, several. A boy who was born a year after our marriage and who died while quite small, and two girls who also died soon after they were born."

"What did they die of?"

"Nothing in particular. They just did not seem to have strength enough to live. Their mother was too weak to nurse them and that may have made some difference, but even after we had found an excellent wet-nurse, they did not gain. They never cried. They just lay very still and then they died."

"And the present child was strong when it was born?"

"No! Not very. For several hours after he was born, the boy looked as if he too were going to die right away." Then the midwife had given him a cold bath and he began to cry and that apparently had saved him. But his mother had never been able to nurse him. They had a nurse now, the woman who had been sent to fetch me, and who was now taking care of the sick woman downstairs. But the child did not gain and it cried a good deal and it looked terribly pale.

Then I asked him a question: "Have you another room in the house, except the big one downstairs, where you could put the child up for the time being?"

"Yes, several. There is one downstairs and there is this room and my studio and the room with the etching-press."

"Which one has most sun and air?"

"The one in which my wife is."

"Is there no other?"

"A small one where my press stands."

"Let the child sleep there."

"But then it will be impossible to work there. I have four boys who do my printing for me. They have just started on a new plate of Dominie Anslo. Yesterday I pulled the first three proofs and changed the plate a little. But to-morrow they are going to begin work on it. I have had orders for twenty-five copies. It will be a great nuisance if I have to turn that room into a nursery."

"Nevertheless, the child had better not be in the same room with the mother for some time."

"Then you know what she has?"

"No, I don't. I am not certain. I may know within a day or two. Meanwhile, the nurse had better take the little boy to your printing room. She can probably fix herself some sort of a bed in there."

"We have an extra cot."

"Very well."

"And you will come again to-morrow?"

"I certainly will."

"And there is nothing you can do now?"

"Nothing. She will probably be very tired. She ought to sleep as much as possible. I will pass by the apothecary on my way home and will order him to make her a sleeping potion. If she is restless you can give her two small spoonfuls in some water every other hour. But don't give it to her more than three times. I don't want to tax her heart too much. And now I had better be going."

The painter got up from his chair and opened the door for me. Once more I noticed the powerful shoulders underneath the blue linen smock and the broad forehead and the sad, troubled eyes, together with the common nose and the broad chin that was almost a challenge to the world to come and be damned. A strange mixture of the gentleman and the hod-carrier and where had I seen it before?

On my way out I passed through the sick room but the poor woman seemed to be asleep. I put my hand upon her forehead, which was cold and clammy. She had apparently no longer any fever, but her color had grown worse. When I had first seen her, she had been very pale with a brilliant red spot on both cheeks. Now the red spots were gone and the color of her skin was an unhealthy gray. Her pulse had grown so weak that I could hardly notice it. I put my hand upon her heart. It was beating, but very faintly. She was a very sick woman indeed and seemed to have reached that point of exhaustion when the slightest shock might be fatal. If she could sleep through the night, we had a fine chance to bring her back to life in the morning, but I was not very hopeful.

Just then I heard the angry voice of the woman who had come to fetch me and who was now talking to the painter in the hall.

"I won't do it! I just won't do it!"

And when he answered, "Sh-sh! Not so loud. My wife will wake up," she continued even more sharply, "Sh-sh yourself! I just won't do it."

"But the doctor says you must."

"Bah! Doctors don't know anything. The idea! I have taken care of children all my life. I never heard such nonsense. It is just a little cold your wife has caught. All this fuss about a little cold! But of course, doctors must give you their fool advice so that they can ask you for more money."

At that moment, the sick woman woke up and softly whimpered. I tiptoed to the door and spoke sharply to the nurse. "You will do what I say," I told her, "or to-morrow I shall report you to the medical guild. You may not care for my opinion, but you will care if you never get another case."

She looked at me with great arrogance.

"All right, Doctor," she said sweetly. "I shall do what you tell me," and she went into the room to get the child.

Van Rijn saw me out to the front step.

"I am sorry," he apologized, "but it is so terribly hard to get a good nurse just now."

"Yes," I answered, "but if I were you, I would get rid of this woman as soon as I could. I don't like her eyes. She looks as if she might go crazy any moment."

"I will try and find another one to-morrow," he promised me, and then I bade him farewell and turned to the left to go to the Oude Singel where I knew that there was an apothecary who kept late hours, as he was an amateur musician and had once sold me a viola da gamba of his own making.

I found him still at work in a little room at the back of the house. He had a theory that the tone of fiddles depended upon the sort of varnish that was used and had for years been experimenting with different sorts of oil and resin. He had just obtained a new sort of resin called "copalene" or some such thing—a funny-looking yellow mess which he had ordered from England. He wanted to tell me all about it and how now his fiddles would sound like those of the great Nicolo Amati of Cremona. But it was late and I was tired and I bade him wash his hands and go to his dispensary and mix me the dose which I meant to prescribe for my new patient. While he was busy with his bottles, I asked him whether he had a boy who could run an errand and deliver the bottle.

"Is it far?" he asked.

"About ten minutes. That big house in the Breestraat. The second one from the Saint Anthonie Lock."

"You mean the new house of Rembrandt?"

"I thought his name was van Rijn?"

"So it is. I think he comes from Leyden and his father owns a maltmill on the old Rhine. But he is usually known by his first name."

"Then he is well known?"

The apothecary looked at me in wonder. "They say he is painting quite a number of pictures for the Prince of Orange. He must be pretty good."

"Yes," I answered. And then I went home and when I passed by the Breestraat, I noticed that there still was a light in the upstairs room.

"A strange man," I said to myself. "And soon he will be a very unhappy man. But where did I ever see that face before?"

Chapter 3

CONCERNING THE PEOPLE WHO WERE MY FRIENDS DURING THE DAYS OF MY YOUTH

I was soaking wet when I came home and so I took my clothes off and put them to dry in front of the fire in my bedroom. The only luxury that came into my life when I inherited that small fortune was an open fire in my bedroom and though it was regarded as a sacrilege by my friends who called me a "weakling" and a "Sybarite" and predicted every sort of disease as a result of this self-coddling process, I was never so happy as when I woke up and saw those cheerful flames enacting all the plays of the famous Mr. William Shakespeare upon the beams of the ceiling, and as for my friends—well, they may have disapproved of this "voluptuous incandescence" as one of them addicted to the "Metamorphoses" of Ovid called it, but I noticed that they were apt to gather together in my bedroom upon every possible occasion and that they lingered there long after the time had come to return to their own frozen closets. This evening while a blast of hail (for now that winter was approaching, we were getting a mixed diet of rain, snow and hail), was threatening to smash my costly window panes, the little bits of smoldering peat looked more inviting than ever. I took the kettle that hung over the fire, made myself a hot rum-punch, opened the doors of the bedstead and crept between the sheets.

I slept soundly for a couple of hours.

Then my cat Cocaine (I had called the animal after a new American plant which seemed to bear pain-killing qualities and which had recently been brought to Europe by a Spanish friar) wanted to get in (I had closed all the windows on account of the rain) and I had to get up to let the leisurely creature get into the house and then she insisted upon having some milk, and she took her time about drinking it (or eating it or whatever cats do with milk, for they seem to eat and even chew it) and by the time she got through, and of course wanted to get out again, I was so thoroughly awake that I could not go back to sleep, but lay rolling over in bed and thinking of a million things—as one will do under such circumstances and then suddenly and for no apparent reason it struck me where I had seen that man's face before and I remembered the whole episode which for a few days had threatened to throw our entire city into a state of turmoil and revolution and which had completely passed out of my mind, what with my recent adventures at Veere and the rain and everything.

It must have been in the year 1628. I am not absolutely certain, but I think that it was a few months before the capture of the Spanish treasure fleet by Admiral Piet Hein, an event which also ended in a riot, as the sailors wanted a bonus of seventeen months' wages and only got sixteen and in their fury pulled down several of the buildings of the West India Company, where the golden millions were said to lie hidden.

Yes, it must have been the year '28 and I had been in Amsterdam a little over a year and I had just opened my first office on the Bloemgracht, which was not as famous then as a couple of years later when Jan Blaeu moved there from the Damrak and began to print his tremendous atlas there on those nine presses which were called after the nine muses and which gained almost as great a reputation as their Greek sisters.

The Bloemgracht then was in a comparatively new part of the town and for a young physician it seemed to offer better opportunities than one of the older neighborhoods, where the rents were so much higher.

I passed by the house the other day after the funeral of Rembrandt, for the Bloemgracht ran parallel to the Roozengracht, and it was a melancholy trip, for the days I spent in that little house were the happiest days of my life. It is true that I was very poor, but my God! what glorious friends I had!

And where are they now? Two of them are dead, and the third one has gone back to his native country. At first he used to write to me. Then came a letter saying: "The sun is setting over the waters of the Golden Horn. The cypresses of my garden are throwing long shadows upon the walls of Shah Zadeh. Soon the time will come when I shall receive an answer to those questions which used to puzzle us so many, many years ago. Farewell, dear friend. Life has been good." And after that, silence.

I asked an acquaintance, whose ships ply between here and the Levant, to try and get me some news about old Selim. After eight months, one of the captains who knew a little Turkish, sent me a report. Selim was still alive, but no one had seen him for almost six years. He had inherited his father's wealth and was considered one of the richest men of Constantinople. As soon as he had come into his fortune, he had closed his harem, had liberally endowed all of his wives, and had sent them back to their villages, thanking them for their charming company of the last twenty years and wishing them that peace and quiet which he himself now expected to enjoy. He had then ordered a small house to be built in the middle of his vast gardens and had surrounded it with a high wall. His old palace, which had been completely rebuilt a decade before, he had given to the city as a home for orphans on condition that any dog or cat who strayed into the premises must be fed and lodged for as long as he or she cared to stay. He had then sent for his children (there were fifteen sons and eleven girls) and against all precedent he had offered to divide his fortune among them equally and give it to them right away instead of letting them wait until he died, on condition that they would accept a settlement and sign some sort of quit-claim which relieved him and his executors of all further worry about family jealousies and family quarrels.

When that had been done, he and one old and trusted servant had retired to the little house in the garden—the single door that gave access to this small paradise (for it was filled with the choicest of flowers and shrubs) had been barricaded—and once a day a cart came with provisions which the old servant pulled up in a basket which he had previously let down from the top of the wall. The grocer and the baker and the butcher were paid by a French banking house in Stamboul to which Selim had entrusted a small fund for that purpose on condition that he would never be bothered with an accounting. He received no visitors. He refused to receive letters and sent none except once, when to the astonishment of his neighbors (who never grew tired of watching these strange proceedings) he had asked that a letter of his be transmitted to an address in Amsterdam and had given the baker-boy who took charge of the transaction an order for ten Turkish pounds on his French banker. No one knew whether he was dead or alive, but the basket of food was delivered regularly every day and so it was presumed that he and his servant were still alive. That was all the honest skipper had been able to find out, but it was enough.

Selim had done exactly what he had always threatened to do and rather than live in a world he despised, and too much of a gentleman to leave it until his appointed hour, he had retired to the contemplation of beautiful flowers and little humming-birds and bumble-bees. A strange ending for a man who could have ruled an empire! But how very sensible!

Jean-Louys de la Tremouille, the famous skeptic, the man who professed to be subject to no ordinary human emotion, got so homesick for his own people after he had finished his last great work on mathematics that together with his man-of-all-work, a poor devil of a former galley-slave who had been condemned to the bagno for having been kind to a Huguenot minister, he set sail for France in a tiny boat and was probably lost at sea, for we never heard of him again after that day.

And as for Bernardo Mendoza Soeyro, that strangely romantic creature with his tender body and his brave soul, one of the few people who had ever been in a prison of the Inquisition and had lived to tell the tale, died full of years and glory (but far away from his friends) as an Indian chieftain in a small village of the Mohegans.

I have every reason to be grateful that I was born in a time so active, so full of color, so rich as the present. But most of all do I give thanks that I was able to start my career in a city which in more than one sense of the word happened to be the center of the whole civilized world. For where else on this planet would it have been possible to bring together such a strange group of human beings as right here in this incredible town of ours? The son of a French duke, a young man who through ancient precedent was allowed to remain covered and seated in the presence of his sovereign and now a quiet student of mathematics and philosophy, living unobtrusively in a couple of rooms of an old tower; a Sephardic Jew, descendant of kings of Israel, a wanderer, no parents, no relatives, no wife, no children, no home, poor as a church-mouse and proud as a peacock, at one time one of the richest students of the University of Salamanca, now contented to make a bare living as the bookkeeper for old Isaac Ashalem, who lived in the Lazarus Street and dealt in dried Norwegian fish and Greek currants; and then Selim, whose real name we never were able to discover (it was too complicated, he told us, and anyway it could not be spelled out in Dutch), whose father had been grand-vizier to Murad IV, the conquerer of Bagdad, who at the age of ten had had forty servants of his own and who had quarreled with his father, a most devout Moslem and passionately devoted to his brilliant son, because he had once dared to serve him with a new sauce containing a few drops of Malaga, who had then been obliged to leave the country and was living in Amsterdam in amiable splendor and explained his presence in these northern climes by his desire to translate Homer into Arabic, "In order," as he used to say, "that my compatriots may learn of the glorious deeds of their ancestors, for what after all were the Trojans but the earliest keepers of the holy road to Stamboul and what were the Greeks but the predecessors of those predatory Christians who have ever since the beginning of history tried to deprive the people of Asia of their legitimate possessions?

Remains the question—how did four such utterly different characters ever happen to meet each other and in so simple a house as mine?

Well, that I could not tell you.

It was one of those mysteries which one accepts but does not question. I think that I first met Selim, who dressed in European clothes but looked for all the world like the pictures of Solomon which were to be found in the Bibles of my childhood. I ran across him, if I am not mistaken, in the "Cave of Despair"—an inn which for a time was a close rival of the "King of Bohemia" and where a few of us used to gather on Friday evenings to play draughts and chess. He was a brilliant but most inconsequential chess player, who would overpower his opponents with his openings and then, when the game seemed to be his for the taking, would lose interest and of course would lose the game.

As for Bernardo (who was so very particular about that "o" at the end of his name) I happened to see him one cold winter morning on the Ververs Gracht. He was going to his place of business (the fish shop of old Ashalem) and a mob of little boys had chosen him as the target for their snow-balls. That in itself was harmless enough, but as the victim refused to pay any attention, neither grew angry nor accelerated his pace, the urchins decided to mix their snow with certain other ingredients

THE CHURCH

PORTRAIT OF SASKIA
(1633)
lead pencil

which are forever present in a busy commercial city where all the hauling is done by horses. When this failed to bring forth the desired results, they started to abuse him.

"Ah, the dirty Yiddisher! Kill the Yiddisher!" and other expressions even less flattering but equally obnoxious. Then one of the boys fished a piece of ice out of the canal and was about to heave that at the poor Jewman when I lost my temper (something I am very apt to do upon such occasions) and gave him a sound whack across the ears.

For some strange reason, there seems to be a superstition in our community that children must not be interfered with during their more playful moments on the highways and byways of our good town. At school for seven or eight hours of every day they are cuffed and spanked and are forced to suffer all sorts of indignities to both their courage and self-respect. They are made to recite endless verses from the less intelligible chapters of the Old Testament and are forced to learn a vast number of things which can never be of the slightest possible practical value to any human being. In short, while they are in the class-room, they must behave like little angels. But the moment they are back in the fresh air, they are cheerfully permitted to behave like little demons and no good Dutchman of my time would have dreamed of interfering with the sweet darlings while they were destroying flowers or cutting down shrubs or making life miserable for the stray cats and dogs of our alley-ways.

When that young man therefore discovered that a grown-up person had dared to deprive him of the pleasure of throwing a miniature ice-floe at a perfectly harmless stranger, he was so surprised that he dropped his missile and abruptly turned around to see who it was that had undertaken to play the rôle of God. But in so doing, he slipped and fell and hit his head against a tree and although he had got no more than a scratch, he set up such a terrific yell that soon from all the houses there appeared irate fathers and even more irate mothers asking in no uncertain tone of voice who it was that had dared to chastise their little darling. Of course, the wounded brat made the best of his opportunities, hastily smeared the few drops of blood all over his face until it looked as if he had just escaped from the massacre of Saint Bartholomew's night and then shrieked, "He tried to kill me. He is a dirty Papist. He tried to kill me!"

Well, to make a long and not very interesting story as short as it can possibly be, ere five minutes had gone by I was the center of a mob of wild Indians who were all for pitching me into the canal. And they might have succeeded, for a short time before I had sprained my left arm and I was therefore fairly helpless. But suddenly (how it was done, I do not know, although it happened right before my eyes) half a dozen of the loudest-shouting ruffians were sprawling on the snow and the rest were running for dear life and I heard a voice with a strange guttural accent say: "You had better come with me right away before they discover that I am alone," and here was that mild-looking Jew, who only a few minutes before had seemed to be too meek to fight back the children that were tormenting him, wiping five very bloody knuckles on the edge of his very shabby coat as if he had just taken part in a duello and was ready to accept the apologies of his former opponent.

So much for our first meeting with Bernardo.

Jean-Louys joined us a little later and he too entered our circle completely by accident. He had come to Amsterdam in the early thirties (for he was a little older than the rest of us) and for years he had not spoken to a soul (finding his neighbors little to his liking) until he felt obliged to buy himself a dog—"from fear," as he explained to me once in a rare moment of confidence, "that I would lose the use of my vocal cords."

He belonged to that class of apparently open-hearted people who are really much more secretive about their own affairs than the close-lipped brethren who pride themselves on the fact that no one will ever be able to read their emotions. He talked easily, yea, fluently, about his past, but in the end one knew exactly as much as one had known in the beginning, which was nothing at all.

Now by nature, I am not a gossiping sort of person. Most of my life I have gone my own way and I have done a large number of things which were perfectly clear to me but not in the least clear to my fellow-countrymen. It may be different in big countries like France or England, but in the small cities of a small republic like ours, everybody considers himself his brother's keeper and as a result, I have for years been an interesting topic of conversation for most of my neighbors, and the more they were puzzled by my behavior, the less flattering they were in their comment. I knew of course that a really high-minded man should be completely indifferent to the remarks his friends make about him behind his back, but it so happens that I am not sufficiently aloof not to care. It took me years before I could accustom myself to the sneering looks and the whispered remarks of the honest bakers and butchers among whom I spent my days and, what was infinitely worse, among whom I was obliged to make a living. The tortures I suffered during that period taught me to be exceedingly lenient and careful in my judgment about the acts of others and not to condemn my fellow-men even when all the appearances were against them.

And when I now confess that I made a careful study of the antecedents of our delightful French friend, I do not want to appear in the light of the usual small-town busy-body. I happen to be a scientist and scientists are people who prefer a world of law and order to a universe of chance and guess. When they run across a brilliantly intelligent human being who quietly defies all the laws and regulations of the community in which he lives—who plays the profligate grand seigneur in a commonwealth of penny-saving shopkeepers—who openly proclaims his disbelief in

Heaven or Hell in a community where ninety-nine percent of his neighbors are upset by the fear of doing or saying something that in some way might be contrary to the will of God—and yet succeeds in gaining great happiness out of existence and in achieving a most perfect equanimity of soul, they of course want to know how this could possibly have come about and they will study the strange phenomenon until they have come to understand it as closely as one human being can ever hope to understand another.

In the case of Jean-Louys it took me several years and this is the story of his life, as I finally came to know it.

His real name I saw but once. He had asked me to witness a deed of gift of certain farms and houses to his wife, and I went with him to my notary whose mother was a Huguenot and who therefore spoke French as fluently as he spoke Dutch and I listened while the endless document was being read. There were seven or eight Christian names, Jean-Louys, François, Antoine, Henri and a few others which I have forgotten. Then followed an enumeration of titles, a page and a half long: Baron de la Tremouille, Baron de Seignerolle and Peletier-Desorts, Knight of the order of Saint Lazarus of Jerusalem, Knight of the order of Malta, Knight of the order of Our Lady of Mount Carmel, Hereditary Keeper of the Falcons of His Majesty the King, and a vast variety of dignities which meant as much to me as the enumeration of the ninety-nine holy attributes of the Moslem God with which Selim loved to delight us after he had partaken of his third glass of forbidden gin and water.

But these honors which (if I am rightly informed) meant more to the average Frenchman than his wife and children and his property, sat lightly upon the shoulders of this tall, slow-moving young man with the high forehead and the aquiline nose, who at first called himself Vicomte de Legre, after a small river near Bordeaux, upon which most of his property was situated. When he grew tired of the mute admiration with which the plain citizens of our republic stared at a live vicomte, he threw the "de" overboard, let go of the "Legre," and henceforth was known simply as Monsieur Jean-Louys.

For the first forty years of his life he had been an only son. And as his mother had died at his birth, it looked as if he would be the sole heir to his father's estates and his father was deemed one of the richest men in the whole of Gascony. But at the age of sixty-five the old gentleman (who was of a vigorous nature) married a girl of eighteen from Bilbao, just across the Spanish frontier, and exactly nine months later, Jean-Louys had a little brother. He had never seen the child, having left his native country before the child was born, but when his father died, he had treated him most generously and to the best of his knowledge the young man had used the greater part of his inheritance to buy himself a captaincy in a regiment of Royal Musketeers of which some day he hoped to be the commander-in-chief.

There had been no sisters and poor Jean-Louys, left alone with his father in the enormous castle on the banks of the Legre, had spent a lonely but most extraordinary youth. For the old Baron de la Tremouille like so many people of his age (he was born in 1570) was a fanatic upon the subject of education.

Of course, a nobleman of his rank could not attend a university like any ordinary commoner. Therefore Monsieur de la Tremouille, père, as soon as he had succeeded his father (the boon companion and minister of King Henry IV, who could be of an exceedingly liberal nature towards those who served him well) had surrounded himself with a veritable court of learned and eloquent humanists. A refugee Byzantine, by the name of Simon Hagiadopoulos (there still were a few Byzantine refugees peddling their learning, although it was more than a century since the fall of their city), and the learned Theofrastus Molestus, the famous editor of the speech of Appius Claudius Caecus (a ten-page pamphlet upon the study of which Molestus had spent the greater part of thirty years), taught him the rudiments of Latin and Greek syntax until the restless baron, bored by so much erudition, got the old scholars appointed as professors of rhetoric and ancient history to the University of Grenoble and imported a young Italian by the name of Paolo Parentese who paid less attention to grammar, but who with the help of an unexpurgated copy of "The Golden Ass" of Apuleius taught his pupil a fair amount of Latin in less than a year and then remained for an extra twelve months to explain the mysteries of the "Decameron" in the original tongue of Giovanni Boccaccio.

In the meantime, a fourth teacher had appeared in the person of Rabbi Sholem ben Yehiel, who was to give instruction in Hebrew. For although this tongue was pre-classical rather than classical, the Gascon country-gentleman, in abject awe before everything even remotely connected with the Rebirth of Civilization, decided to follow the full program as laid down by the immortal John Reuchlin. All the great humanists had taken lessons in Hebrew, therefore the Baron de la Tremouille, who meant to be considered their humble disciple, meant to take lessons in Hebrew as well. But the experiment was not a success. Forty years spent in reading and explaining the less intelligible parts of the Talmud to the over-eager and under-nourished children of the Viennese Ghetto had not exactly fitted poor Sholem ben Yehiel for the task of teaching the delicate mysteries of his holy hieroglyphics to an old French country squire who rode ten miles every morning before breakfast and ate five hearty meals a day except on fast-days, when he made it six, because he held that fish was less nourishing than meat or venison. Nothing could come of such an arrangement.

Before they had even reached the fifth letter of the alphabet, the student and his professor had engaged in such a terrific battle of words that that same afternoon, the Rabbi together with his books and many scripts had been packed off to Arcachon with the injunction never to set foot again on the premises. The departure of the pious Talmudist in a dense cloud of dust, followed by the jeers of all the villagers (who had greatly, though secretly, objected to his presence and had even gone to their priest to ask him to lay the matter before the authorities at Bordeaux) and the outbreak of fury on the part of M. le Baron which extended over a period of several months, had attracted a great deal of attention and this attention had changed into admiration when the Bishop of La Rochelle preached a sermon upon the subject in which he commended the Gascon nobleman for his loyalty to the faith, for although the world was most sadly afflicted by the tendencies of an age which boldly dared to proclaim the wisdom of the pagan philosophers superior to that of the Fathers of the Church, this noble knight took his stand with the saints when he defended his Saviour against the ill-conditioned attacks of an unbelieving Jew.

This story was ever the delight of Jean-Louys, who had heard it a thousand times from his different nurses, his gardeners, his stablemen and all the other retainers of Château Tremouille, who had promoted the hapless Rabbi to the rank of Satan and who loved to depict their master fighting with his bare hands against the claws and hoofs of the Evil One.

When he reached the years of discretion, Jean-Louys had one day asked his father about the truth of the matter. The old man had burst out laughing. "Devil be damned!" he said, pounding the table with his fist, so that at least one decanter of wine fell upon the floor, "Devil be damned! That fool Jew wanted to tell me that trout tastes best when fried in butter and would not agree with me that it ought to be done in olive-oil, and so I chased him away."

But after this unfortunate occurrence, the Baron had decided that perhaps he had been a little too old to devote himself to classical studies with that patience and devotion which such studies demanded. He did not intend, however, to let this experience go entirely to waste. What he now needed was a brand new son who should be taken in hand while a suckling babe and should be turned into a combination of Lorenzo de' Medici, William the Conqueror and Dante, by a new educational method which had just been explained to him by a friend who lived in the neighboring province of Guyenne.

To find the prospective mother for this infant prodigy was the work of a few days. Her rank and riches did not matter, the husband had enough of those for two people. She must have health and beauty. A candidate richly provided with both was detected in a near-by village. Her father was a day-laborer and the girl could neither read nor write. But she had the finest set of teeth in ten counties and she could carry a small calf as easily as if it had been a kitten. Incidentally she had been engaged for three years to a poor sheep-farmer of the Lake of Caran, but that of course was a negligible detail.

She was duly washed and garbed by the old women of her hamlet and the marriage took place with as much solemnity as if she had been a princess of the blood. Exactly nine months after her nuptials, she had given birth to a sickly child, had lived long enough to whisper, "I hate it!" had turned over on her side and had died.

The infant, however, with the help of a devoted aunt, had managed to live until the age of four when his father took him in hand and exposed him to that famous system which was to change a puny Gascony baby into a superman. What had ever put these strange pedagogical notions into the old Baron's head, Jean-Louys did not know. He had once asked his father whether it was not the same system as that which had been followed by M. Pierre de Montaigne in educating his son Michel. Whereupon the father had soundly boxed his ears and had asked him: "Since when have the la Tremouilles been obliged to get their inspiration from a family of fish-dealers and Jews?" and had sent his son to bed without supper.

The details of this extraordinary pedagogic experiment were related unto me in great detail, for Jean-Louys never tired of enumerating the glorious absurdities of the scheme.

"You know," he used to say, "every town is filled with inventors who spend half of their lives devising elaborate methods by which they can drive smoke down the wrong side of the chimney and by which they can make their ships sail the wrong way. My father belonged to that class of enthusiasts. At the end of twelve years of training, I knew exactly as much as the average child that has been to an ordinary school for half the time. I had learned enough Latin to be able to translate the inscriptions in the village cemetery. I could spell my way through a Greek sentence, but I did not know what it meant. I could hum a song, but could not carry a tune. And whenever I mounted a horse on one side, I fell off on the other. Clearly my father knew that he had made a mistake. But he was an obstinate old fellow. The son had failed him. Very well, he would try a grandson. And so they set forth to find a wife for me.

"They could not find one in all Paris, but reports came from Pampeluna on the other side of the Spanish frontier that there was a virgin in that town of such exceeding pulchritude that even a king might wish her for his consort, though I have never noticed that sovereigns were very particular about the looks of their females. Anyway, Papa crossed the mountains, severely criticized the strategic methods displayed by Roland at Roncesvalles, and a week later he returned with my fiancée.

"She did not speak a word of French, but my God! how lovely she was, and I considered myself a lucky devil. A day after our marriage, I knew the truth. She was dumb, and she used a perfume that smelled like sandal-wood and reminded me of my dead ancestors in the family crypt. Also she was very pious, but she became pregnant almost at once and the eager grandfather was contented.

"The child was born in January and at the age of one, my father took it in hand. He had come to the conclusion that he had begun too late in life with me to accomplish anything. This time he meant there to be no mistake. And little Jean-Louys II moved from the nursery to the school-room before he was twelve months old. I sat alone with my wife.

"The poor woman! She was terrible. It had been the pride of her family that they lived in the same house in which Inigo de Loyola (you remember the converted rake who turned saint?) had been nursed after part of his leg had been blown away by a French cannon-ball. That had been in the days of her great-grandmother, but it seemed that the family had never talked of anything else ever since. They had been presented with part of the bone that had been cut out of the leg of the holy man and she had brought it with her when she came to Tremouille, 'to insure her happiness in marriage.'

"Well, that was the beginning of her affliction. She got what our doctors called 'the malady of the reliquaries.' She began to collect souvenirs of sanctity. I was a good Catholic in those days and still may be, for all I know, but too much is too much, even in the matter of saints.

"In the beginning, while I was quite crazy about her (she was so incredibly lovely, though she was rapidly growing stout and was developing a slight mustache) I did not mind how much she spent, but when she used the entire revenue of our estates for a period of three years to build a shrine for the splintered fibula of a defunct Spanish warrior, who had fallen fighting the blackamoors, I became slightly agitated. I tried to talk to her, but she told me I was wicked and devoid of all piety, that her confessor had told her before she left her native land that all Frenchmen were mockers of God and that now she knew it to be true, but that she meant to save the soul of the father of her child, no matter how much it might cost me and that she had sent to Meaux for a tooth of Saint Fiacre, from whose intervention she expected great results for our vineyards and an added revenue which she hoped to spend upon further objects of sanctity.

"Of course, the good Lord, who dearly loves his little joke, provided southern France with such a marvelous summer that that year we derived about twice as much money from the sale of our wines as ever before. And of course the tooth of Saint Fiacre was responsible.

"The extra revenue was invested in a piece of the elbow of Saint Faro. That may have been accident, or good salesmanship on the part of the dealer in Meaux who had sold her her first purchase.

"After that in quick succession she acquired a lock of hair of Sainte Dorothea to improve the quality of our apple cider (but Dorothea's hair proved less successful than Fiacre's bicuspid, for myriads of caterpillars descended upon our apple orchard and we did not have a decent apple to sell for four whole years) and a piece of the thumb of Saint Fridolin, to give us good weather for our harvest (but we had a plague of locusts which ate all our grain), and next a pearl of the crown of Sainte Gertrude, which failed, however, to kill the mice (as it should have done, according to the written guarantee by the Prior of the Cloister of Nivelles who arranged the transaction), and then (without further reference to our agricultural needs) a bit of the skull of Saint Athanasius; the original sword of Saint Pancratius; the original ax of Saint Boniface; a piece of hail which had lain in the hand of Saint Barnabas and had become so miraculously petrified that it looked for all the world like a common pebble; a feather from the wing of the dove of Saint Basilius; a link from the chain of Saint Paulinus of Nola, the original goose-quill with which Saint Jerome had written the Vulgate; a bottle containing some ashes from the pyre of Saint Polycarp, the martyr; the other half of the coat of Saint Martin of Tours, a shoe of Saint Hedwig of Silesia, and a leaf of the castor-oil plant of Jonah, although I never quite understood by what right this unsuccessful prophet of woe, who had lived and died eight hundred years before the birth of our Saviour, happened to be included among the Christian martyrs.

"All this represented a considerable outlay of money, but the upkeep was even worse. For each and every one of those relics had to be encased in a golden receptacle, richly adorned with the pearls and emeralds which were one of the proudest heirlooms of our family. And then she began to build little chapels all over the place, each one dedicated to his own little saint, until our estate began to look like a vast cemetery. Next, each one of these chapels was entrusted to the care of one or two guardians, who of course had to be paid for their services and of course I was supposed to do the paying. From far and wide, people began to flock to our estates to visit the shrines and as was quite inevitable, the relics began to perform miracles. Saint Pancratius specialized in toothache while Saint Cyprian made the lame walk and Saint Faro cured the seven-day itch. It was a lucrative business, not for me but for the holy men who administered these clinics. And soon there was bitter rivalry between the different shoulder-blades and finger-joints and molars, and pitched battles were in almost daily occurrence.

"As for me, I had not only become entirely superfluous, but even a little ludicrous. Of course, I tried to bring my wife to reason. But it was no use. She went about dressed up as a nun and declared that she had had a vision of Saint Clara who had told her that in time our place would become a second St. Damascus in which she (my wife) would play the rôle of Saint Francis' former lady-friend.

"I had stood for a good deal, but this began to look a little too much like spiritual adultery to me and I decided to leave. My father, who notwithstanding his extraordinary educational notions was an excellent man of business, had greatly increased the revenue of our estates. I asked him for a yearly allowance. He asked me what I wanted to do and I answered that I wanted to go abroad.

" 'To do what?'

" 'To study.'

" 'To study what?'

" 'Everything. Nothing in particular.'

" 'That will exactly suit your taste.'

"And he bade me farewell as cheerfully and happily as if I had informed him that I was going to Bordeaux for a few days to order some new clothes.

"A week later I left. I really don't know whether I was happy or unhappy. My wife had long since left me for her weird collection of celestial remains. My child had been estranged from me and a Greek grammar and a Latin dictionary formed an unpassable barrier between father and son. I suppose that I ought to have asserted myself long before then, but for one reason or another I had allowed things to drift and of course I had lost out and so I wandered and having always had an interest in military tactics and being somewhat of an amateur mathematician, I finally drifted towards the Low Countries, because there at that moment past masters of that game were playing each other for the highest stakes and I thought that there I would be able to learn more than anywhere else. I went first of all to Brussels and then to Cologne, for I could not very well tell the Spanish authorities that I was on my way to join their enemies and from Cologne I went by boat to Rotterdam and there I took the shilling and enlisted in a regiment of infantry with the promise that I would be allowed to enter a company of artillery as soon as an obliging bullet should have caused a convenient vacancy.

"But in those days the art of siege and counter-siege had been carried to such a pitch of perfection that there were very few casualties and so I did my turn of duty in a regiment of the line and it was dull work, though the hours were easy and I was able to read a great deal.

"And now a strange thing happened. Those same classics that had driven me to desperation when I was able to read them sitting comfortably in an armchair at home, became a positive source of delight when I read them by the flickering light of a candle in a leaky tent surrounded by a dozen snoring ruffians and sick unto death from the terrible food which a stealing commissary-sergeant had thought good enough for the shivering cannon-fodder entrusted to his care. And of course that strangely indifferent luck that had without any apparent reason turned me, the heir to vast estates, into a homeless wanderer (a solvent wanderer with money in his pocket, but a wanderer, nevertheless) followed me even here.

"The Dutch and Spanish concluded a truce that was to last twelve years and contrary to the general expectations, they remained faithful to the terms of the agreement. Military life became garrison life, a dull succession of totally useless duties, marching to no place in particular—standing guard over nothing in particular—polishing guns and swords that were never to be put to any practical use. It was pretty terrible, but in a first moment of enthusiasm, I had enlisted for five years, and there I was.

"Then one night we were garrisoned in some God-forsaken little village in Brabant amidst a sullen population which hated us because we had taken away their churches, had removed all the pictures and statuary, had covered the walls with three inches of white-wash and had turned them into hideous Calvinistic meeting-houses. And there was nothing to do, absolutely nothing but drink and gamble and read and then do some more drinking and gambling and reading with an occasional turn of duty! Well, one night I was standing guard and it was raining cats and dogs and the roads were lakes and I heard a soldier from another regiment come wallowing through the mud. When he was quite near me, he slipped and almost fell, but instead of the string of oaths which I was expecting, I heard the well-known lines of Horace: 'Desiderantem quod satis est, neque tumultuosum . . .' Whereupon I continued: '. . . Sollicitat mare . . .' and so on and so forth and then of course, we spoke to each other and I discovered him to be a fellow-Frenchman, a fellow by the name of Descartes, a commoner, but an exceedingly intelligent person who seemed to have made almost as much of a failure of his education as I.

"Well, we came to be good friends and in the year '19, when our enlistments ran out, we decided that life in the Low Countries was too dull for a couple of honest philosophers and as there was chance of trouble in Germany (I have forgotten now what it was all about. I think it had something to do with the election of a new king of Bohemia) we went east and took service with the Habsburgs and we fought or rather we stood and waited and finally we ran at the battle of Weisserberg and then the war petered out and we were once more out of a job.

"I soon became convinced that the Descartes man had a much better brain than I and being trained by the Jesuits and not by a father with a theory, he knew how to study. But through my association with him I found that I was not quite as much of a blockhead as my dear father had always tried to make me believe. I discovered that I had a brain and that brain was beginning to demand that it be satisfied, just as my stomach would demand that it be satisfied after a long and tiring march.

"But unlike my stomach (which would digest anything except pork, cucumbers and radishes) my brain was very particular in the choice of its food. Philology did not interest it very much and theology it would utterly reject. I tried a mixed diet of philosophy and history, but it remained indifferent. I talked it over with Descartes. He, lucky dog, had no such troubles. For this quiet-spoken Tourainian was somewhat of a mystic and although one of the most brilliant scientists I have ever met, he also believed in dreams.

"Yes, he was a regular Saint Paul and one night he had a vision. We were in Neuburg in Bavaria and we had been rolling dice (for Descartes was a great gambler and would risk his last penny on a pair of sixes) and we had drunk a quantity of a very sour wine which they grew along the banks of the Danube and whether it was the wine or the fact that he had lost about forty thalers to me, I don't of course know, but that night he dreamed that he was to be the prophet and founder of a new science and that idea got hold of him so firmly that soon afterwards he resigned from the army and began to prepare for what he called his 'mission.'

"He was a restless person, forever on the move. I heard that for a while he drifted back into the army and that he was present at the siege of La Rochelle, when the Protestants and the English were driven out. And of course he has spent a great deal of his time right here in Amsterdam, as you probably know.

"Well, anyway, there I was all alone, bored to death by life among the dull and bigoted peasants of Bavaria and try as I might, I could not dream dreams, and whenever I had visions, I knew that it was the sour Suabian wine and not a message from High Heaven. And then one day, while looking aimlessly through some volumes at a bookstore in Munich (where we had gone into winter quarters) the bookseller came up to me and asked me whether I had not been a friend of Herr René Descartes, and that this Herr Descartes was a swindler and a scoundrel for he had ordered a work of mathematics to be sent to him all the way from Edinburgh in Scotland and the book had arrived and it cost three thalers, but Herr Descartes had never appeared to claim it and as no one else wanted it and it could not be returned (Scotch publishers never allowed you to return books) it was a total loss and therefore Herr Descartes was a swindler and a scoundrel and a great deal more to the same effect.

"To stop the garrulous Teuton from any further abuse of my friend, I paid him his three thalers, put the little volume (it was no more than a paper-bound pamphlet of about 150 pages) into my knapsack and departed. But three thalers were three thalers. I could easily do without them, but like all good Frenchmen, I was careful of my money and driven by the instinct that I must always get my money's worth, I one day picked it up and read it. God knows, the title was forbidding enough. 'Mirifici Logarithorum Canonis descriptio, ejusque usus, in utraque trigonometria' and a lot more which I cannot quote from memory.

"But that little book proved my Damascus. Suddenly my eyes were opened to my true mission in life. The author, a young Scotchman and some sort of a mathematical infant prodigy, had like myself started out with an interest in the problems of modern artillery and was the inventor of a gun that could fire ten times as fast as any of the cannon we had used heretofore. But as his fellow-countrymen used their pieces of ordnance merely to kill each other on account of their eternal theological squabbles, he had turned his mind to more peaceful pursuits and had invented a new method of computation by which one could substitute addition and subtraction for multiplication. I shall not try and explain his idea to you, for your practical medical mind would not be able to grasp something so beautifully abstract. But this was the fodder for which my mind had been waiting all those many years. I got out of the service as quickly as I could and went down the Rhine once more to find a ship to take me to Edinburgh and visit this young genius. But in Rotterdam I heard that he had died from the gout or something. He was still quite young when he returned to the ultimate zero, and how he had had time to do all the work he did and think all the thoughts he thought, I don't know and neither does it matter very much. As far as I personally was concerned, he had served his purpose. I was quite ready to devote the rest of my days to those calculations which he, in his own words, was willing to leave 'to others less afflicted by the ailments of the body.'

"I moved to Amsterdam, took those rooms in the old mill of the Rijzenhoofd which you know and have never again left the town nor do I ever mean to leave it until I shall be quite through with my tables of logarithms, and that, according to the best of my knowledge, will take me between two and three hundred years."

. . . .

So much for the story which Jean-Louys told me about his past and the reasons which had brought him to our city. There remains the story of how we first met.

Jean-Louys was the perfect type of the French gentleman, ever courteous, ever willing to be agreeable, ever ready to laugh at himself or at Fate, a brilliant mind and inexhaustible curiosity about everything and everybody and totally incapable of learning a single word of a foreign language. He had spent almost six years of his life in the service of the Habsburgs, and did not know a word of German. He lived in Holland for more than forty years and never got beyond "ja" and "neen" and even those two words he managed with such a strange intonation that half of the time people understood him to say "yes" when he meant "no" and "no" when he meant "yes." Furthermore, like the vast majority of his fellow-countrymen, he could never accustom himself to any food except French food. The way our roasts were done reminded him of a cannibal feast "where savages swallow large slabs of raw meat." Our marvelous vegetables were spoiled for him because "we drown them in water." He tried a succession of cooks, Dutch, French, Polish, even a

Tartar who claimed that he had been chef at the court of the Grand Duke of Muscovy, but all to no avail. He was slowly dying of starvation until he decided to do his own housekeeping. He led a most regular existence, got up at six, lit his candle and worked at his logarithms, took a cup of bouillon and a slice of bread at nine, worked at his tables until twelve, ate his dinner, read for an hour in Xenophon (of whom for some strange reason he was inordinately fond), worked at his mathematical tables until six, ate his supper, puttered around his rooms and went to bed at eight with the exception of Saturdays, when he called on me after supper and when we played chess, and of the Sunday afternoon, which we usually spent with the Turk and the Jew.

But after a few years of this sedentary life, he began to suffer certain internal discomforts and a leech to whom he went (for like all Frenchmen he had implicit faith in the curative power of a good bleeding) told him that there was nothing the matter with him but a lack of exercise. Unfortunately, like most brain workers, he detested exercise and so he compromised by going forth every day to buy his own provisions and in order that the walk should do him some good, he selected a vegetable store and a meat shop near the Kloveniersdoelen on the Amstel River, fully twenty minutes away from his own place of residence. He could not speak Dutch but he could pay and he always paid cash and so he was a welcome customer, and furthermore he smiled so pleasantly that the fat old vegetable woman took quite a liking to him and let him roam through her fruit stalls at will and often when she was in the rear of the house, taking care of her brood of chickens, the Frenchman would simply take whatever he needed and would deposit as much money as he thought was necessary on the window-sill and would depart.

Now it happened during this period that the whole country had gone crazy about tulips. We had been raising tulips for quite a number of years, but no one had thought much of them. Indeed, a number of florists regarded them as a rather objectionable foreign weed which never ought to have been imported into a respectable Christian country. And then quite suddenly, and for no reason known to either God or man, all the world began to buy tulips and raise tulips and sell tulips and speculate in tulips and hyacinths, and even the humble crocus was worth its weight in gold. Overnight, a single bulb which in the olden days had sold for a couple of stivers might bring a thousand or two thousand or even three thousand guilders and in one instance, in the town of Alkmaar, a new variety called the "Admiral of Enkhuizen" sold for not less than 5200 guilders.

Now when a whole nation goes mad, no matter for what cause, it is useless to try and reason about it. In God's own good time, order will be reëstablished, a few people will have made a lot of money, many more will have lost all they had and everything will be as it was before until the next outbreak of wholesale lunacy.

And I would not have paid any attention to this unfortunate business if it had not been for a most absurd incident which occurred during the spring of the year 1637.

I was returning from my morning's duty at the hospital and I was just about to cross the bridge which led to the city's quarry-works, when I heard a terrific noise issuing from a small vegetable store on the corner of the old Singel. A woman was letting loose such a flow of profanity in such a marvelous mixture of different low-class dialects that I could not help but listen with that rapture which one feels before a perfect work of art. Whenever she gasped for breath (which occurred every two or three minutes) a man's voice would try to answer her in the most polished of French phrases. A delighted crowd of loafers stood in front of the store, eagerly awaiting the moment when hostilities should begin that they might take the side of their poor abused fellow-citizen and pitch into the dirty little Frenchman who undoubtedly had been up to one of the usual tricks of his untrustworthy race. I had not the slightest desire to get mixed up in this business, but the Frenchman, seeing some one who looked as if he might speak a few words of his tongue, suddenly rushed out of the store, grabbed me by the arm and said, "Monsieur, for God's sake, play the good Samaritan and tell me what this is all about!"

The fury of the vegetable female having meanwhile spent itself somewhat, she also accepted my offer that I should act as interpreter and the story which then slowly unraveled itself would have delighted the heart of Boccaccio or one of those other famous tellers of tales.

As I have said before, Jean-Louys for quite a long time had been in the habit of coming into the store and helping himself to whatever he wanted if the greengrocer happened to be occupied with her domestic duties. One day he would take spinach and the next day it would be a cabbage or a cauliflower or whatever happened to be in season. Of course, Jean-Louys, like all people from southern climes, was very fond of onions.

Well, the previous day, while rummaging through the shop, he had come upon something that for all the world looked to him like some new and slightly larger variety of onions. He had put them into his basket, had left two stivers, the usual price for a couple of onions, had taken them home, had mixed them into his salad and had found them to be absolutely without taste. This morning he had gone forth upon his customary errands a little earlier than before, intending to complain about those savorless onions ("for what is the use of an onion unless it be really an onion?" he asked me with true Gallic logic) but no sooner had he made his appearance than Madame had heaved a cabbage at him, followed by a couple of rich, ripe cucumbers and a very unripe and hard-skinned melon. He had tried to argue, had pointed to the onion basket and had shaken his head in token of disgust, but then the fat had really been in the fire and the ensuing quarrel might have ended in a general massacre when I happened to make my appearance and was so unceremoniously invited to act as intermediary.

What had happened was really absurd beyond words. The good vegetable woman, like everybody else, had been speculating in tulips. She had taken her life's savings out of the stocking in which they lay hidden among her extra woolen towels and had invested every penny she owned in two bulbs, a "semper Argentus" and a "Paragon of Delft." At eleven o'clock in the morning of the day before they had been delivered by the skipper of the Haarlem boat, just when the third youngest child had stung itself on a wasp and set up such howls that the mother had been obliged to go to its assistance.

Well, with one thing and another, she had forgotten all about her precious treasures and not until she had come back to the store in the afternoon had she realized what had happened. The two stivers lying patiently by the side of the regular onion basket had told the tale.

Jean-Louys never winked an eye. He had eaten the tulips and he meant to pay for them. The greengrocer's wife vowed that the French Baron was a perfect gentleman and he, from his side, proclaimed that now he was a greater personage than the King of France. "For His Majesty," so he reasoned, "spends a thousand florins a day on all his meals. While I, all alone, consumed a salad worth two thousand."

And then he accepted my invitation to a less elaborate and costly meal and that is how our friendship started.

Chapter 4

HOW WE AMUSED OURSELVES WHEN THE WORLD WAS SIMPLER THAN IT IS TO-DAY

During the winter we only saw each other on Saturday evening, but when spring came, the four of us often used to meet on Sundays for a walk into the country and afterwards we had dinner either at a tavern in town or in the rooms of Jean-Louys' tower or on the Rijzenhoofd.

For of course we had rather placed ourselves outside the pale of polite society. A Jew was pretty bad. A Turk was a little worse. But a Papist was beyond the limit. A combination of the three, plus a Dutchman who was suspected of being a Libertine (the word in my youth did not mean a "rake" as it does to-day but merely a "liberal" in questions of theology) was something which the good town of Amsterdam had never seen before and hoped never to see again.

The reverend clergy, of course, was greatly upset by this conspicuous friendship among four people who by every rule of the game as played in their church (this metaphor would make them shudder, could they read it) ought to be each other's mortal enemies and ought to hate each other with venomous fury. But when a young man, recently graduated from the University of Utrecht and full of zeal for the True Doctrine as taught exclusively in his own academy of learning (which had been founded only a short time ago to counteract the dangerous influence of Leyden, where science was now being taught and which therefore had acquired a terrible reputation for "radicalism")—when this misguided young orator delivered himself of a learned allocution in which he suggested that those four mysterious friends whose comings and goings so much interested the good people of Amsterdam would have made ideal citizens for the late and unlamented city of Sodom and that the authorities ought to take a hand in the matter, the Burgomaster did take a hand in the matter and warned this brilliant exponent of Christian charity that a repetition of this oratorical masterpiece would lead to a sentence of expulsion and confiscation of his household goods, whereupon he hastily changed his attitude and by way of apology preached a sermon extolling the virtues of Hagar, as the mother of the Moslem religion, and giving great praise to Mahomet, whom he placed among the major prophets, right between Elijah and John the Baptist.

This put him once more into the good graces of Their Lordships of the Town Hall, who were contemplating a little private treaty of commerce and friendship between themselves and the Sultan of Turkey and who did not want to see their plans come to grief because a half-literate peasant from a village in some muddy polder did not approve of the private conduct of a young foreigner of distinction, who was the son of a famous padisha and who recently had been appointed Ottoman consul to the city of Amsterdam.

Exactly what this consulship amounted to, we were never able to find out, for all commerce between the Levantine harbors and Holland was carried on by Dutch vessels and although there were quite a number of Armenians in our country, they would hardly appeal to a Turk in case of help or need. But Selim liked the distinction which his new title bestowed upon him and he made use of his official position to send his distinguished father a large number of complicated mechanical devices, clocks from Switzerland that said "cookoo" when the hour struck and watches from Nuremberg with little ships painted on their dials, and a bronze hen that walked and a cock that crowed and flapped its wings, and other similar toys which seem to delight the hearts of children and foreign potentates.

To gain the good will of the skippers to whom he entrusted these treasures, Selim always gave them imposing-looking letters of introduction. The first captain to deliver such a message afterwards confessed that he had done so in great fear and trepidation. He had run all over Amsterdam, trying to find some one who could translate it for him, but his search had been in vain. And when he finally presented himself and his letter at the palace gate of Selim Senior, he did not know whether he was carrying his death-warrant or a note on the imperial treasury. When five minutes after his arrival he suddenly saw himself surrounded by a hundred long-bearded savages with red breeches, yellow coats and green turbans, he felt that his last hour had come and that he was about to be taken to the drowning-pool. When these ferocious-looking creatures took all his clothes from his back and garbed him in a long silken dressing gown (at least so it looked) and removed his shoes, he began to hope that he might be decapitated rather than suffocated between silken pillows. But as soon as this ceremony had been performed, the hundred dancing dervishes, with one accord, fell upon their knees, threw their hands up to high Heaven, and shouted "Ka-wa-wah! Ka-wa-wah!" which the skipper afterwards learned meant "welcome." And from that moment, until a week later, when he was allowed to return to his vessel, the poor sailor had lived a life of such luxury as he had never been able to imagine, even in the most licentious of his dreams. For the old Padisha dearly loved his son, and though he would never be able to forgive him the indiscretion of that alcoholized gravy, he wished him well and would stop at no trouble or expense if in that way he could further his boy's career. Such stories, greatly embellished during the course of many repetitions, had elevated Selim to the rank of a Prince of the Realm and the city fathers of Amsterdam expected great things of him during the forthcoming negotiations.

From that side, therefore, he had nothing to fear. As for Bernardo, the fact that he had spent three years in solitary confinement in a dungeon of the Inquisition gave him a peculiar position in a community which still sent its children to bed with the threat that the Spaniards would get them if they were not good. Indeed, he enjoyed that distinction which a fishing-village bestows upon the sole survivor of a famous shipwreck. He was a man to be pointed at with awe and to be treated with consideration, no matter what he did.

Finally as for Jean-Louys, he was one of those fortunate people who carried their passport upon their face and who had a "laissez passer" for all countries and for all classes of society in the charm of their manners.

Such types as he are very rare in our Republic. Once upon a time we had had an aristocracy but it had been killed off during the bloody years of the Reformation and during the first decade of the rebellion. But we never had a court, in the French or English sense of the word. William of Orange, had he lived a few years longer, might have made himself the center of such a court, in the truest and noblest sense of the word. But his sons missed all talent for the higher graces of life. I have, in my humble professional quality, attended them both, upon one or two occasions when they needed the services of a surgeon. They were Germans and remained Germans all their lives long. Marvelous fighters, great masters of strategy, equipped with excellent, mathematical brains. But they always smelled slightly of horses and frequently of that bad perfumery which is so beloved of ladies of certain professional qualities. Frederick Henry was better than his older brother Maurice, but even he would have made a sad figure at the palace of St. James or in gardens of the Tuileries. And as for Their Lordships, who are our actual rulers, with their coats of arms and their liveries and their armorial carvings upon their solemn church-pews and their stout wives in satins and pearls, why, they are merely tradespeople disguised as dukes. They know it and we know it and they know that we know that they know that we know it and as a result, they are never at their ease, but always must endeavor to play a rôle for which they are fitted neither by nature nor inclination.

One of the few exceptions to this rule was my dear friend and protector, Constantin Huygens. I remember once, shortly after my recovery from that illness which overtook me in his house in Voorburg that he decided to give me a few days relaxation by a boating-party. We were bound for the city of Gouda but when only a few hours out, near the village of Bleiswijk a sudden gust of wind broke our mainmast and the little yacht had to come to a standstill until the damage should have been repaired.

It was Saturday afternoon. On Sunday, of course, no one would do a stroke of work, there were no masts to be had there anyway, and we found ourselves doomed to spend three days in as God-forsaken a little hamlet as I had ever visited. There were six of us and if we had been left to ourselves, we would have hated each other after the first day and would have cut each other's throats the second. What we would have done on the third, I do not know, but it would have been pretty terrible. Then My Lord Constantin came to the fore and made so wonderful a display of that tact and good sense which he had learned during his youth in France and England and Italy that those three days of exile from the civilized world will ever remain in my memory as one of the most agreeable incidents in my life.

Before we had been in that dreary village an hour, he had discovered that the grouchy landlord was a great fisherman and he talked to him of trouts and sturgeons (which the poor fellow had never seen) and of salmon and for good measure he threw in a couple of whales, until that mean sutler went into his cellar and produced the only good bottle of wine that had ever been served in his place. Next he got leave to visit the kitchen and he got that slovenly maid interested in a story about a visit he had paid as a young man to the Doge of Venice and how the Italians could make the most wonderful dishes with the help of a little brazier of charcoal and she worked her head off before her stove, until we had a meal fit for Master Dandolo himself. Then after the meal, when he heard that there was an old peasant living near by who could play the old-fashioned theorbo, but who had been snubbed once by a singing teacher from the city and now refused to perform before the gentry, he walked all the way to the man's house, told him how as a boy he had played the lute before James I, until that happy rustic carted his home-made theorbo all the way to our inn and amused us all night long with his songs and would not take a penny for his trouble, but thanked us humbly when he took his leave for the great honor we had bestowed upon him.

For three whole days this sort of thing continued. From somewhere or other an old copy of Horace was produced and we spent many amusing hours trying to translate some of his less difficult odes into a semblance of Dutch. And there was fishing and there were walks and there were a couple of stray pups we had picked up on our walks and a kitten which was a terrible drunkard and used to lick the wine out of our glasses until it was so tipsy it could not keep its eyes open, and the last evenings we gave a performance of the Frogs of Aristophanes as serious-minded Vondel would have written it and Spinoza in an enormous wig made out of rope played Dionysus and put so much pathos into the rôle, filling in long spaces with the Hebrew prayers he had learned as a child (and which we pretended was the original Greek) that the peasants whom we had invited to attend this noble production roared with laughter and stamped their feet so violently that he had to give an encore.

Well, this same rare quality of mind which was so characteristic of My Lord Constantin, and which invariably made him say the right thing at the right moment in the right tone of voice and which allowed him to project himself into the tastes and preferences and prejudices and superstitions of others, the gods in their wisdom had also bestowed upon the heir of the house of Tremouille. He had been taught to go through life with a minimum of social friction and as a result, no matter in what situation he suddenly found himself, he could remain superior to it and dominate it. For without the slightest sacrifice to his own principles, or dignity, he was able to placate those who at first felt inclined to oppose him until he had gained their good will and respect. And after that of course the rest was easy.

During the first year of his voluntary exile, he had plenty of chances to exercise this wonderful faculty. He was a mysterious person and mysterious people are not welcome in small communities that are on all sides beset by enemies. But this opposition soon passed away and when his knowledge of mathematics enabled him to suggest several changes in the handling of heavy siege-guns (for like Napier, his teacher, he was keenly interested in the science of ballistics) and his recommendations were accepted by the Prince, who not only favored him with a personal letter but sent for him to visit him in his camp, his place in the community was so firmly established that never thereafter and until the day of his departure was he subjected to the slightest annoyance. Even the clergy left him alone, though he made no secret of his opinion that the change from a man-made religion to a book-made religion had caused more harm than good and that nature was a matter of organized common-sense, rather than the haphazard product of some deity who had wanted a week's entertainment.

Chapter 5

UNDER WHAT CIRCUMSTANCES I FIRST HAD MET REMBRANDT

Thank God, I am not trying to write a book, for here I have wasted a dozen goose-quills writing about my dear friends, while I ought to have been busy with my patient. But poor Saskia was such a colorless person that she could not make herself interesting even on her death-bed while her husband came to play such a rôle in my life that every detail connected with our first meeting had become important to me. When I left his house that rainy evening, I was worried by a vague recollection of having seen the man before. I will now tell under what circumstances this happened and then it will be seen that my strangely assorted companions had something to do with it. Besides, they were such wonderful people, it does me good to write about them. And in a private diary that is not meant for publication, such little excursions ought to be allowed.

And so I continue my story once more by going a few years back (which is the way most stories in life are told) and it is April of the year 1626 and this time it does not rain, but the sun is shining and it is Easter morning and the good people of Amsterdam have all gone to church, but the bad people, Selim and Jean-Louys and Bernardo and myself, have decided to start forth upon a new venture this day and hire ourselves a small yacht and sail to the island of Marken. This was quite an undertaking, for the people of that isolated sandbank were of a savage nature and enjoyed a reputation as amateur pirates and highway robbers which made most travelers keep far away from their shores unless they were itinerant ministers of the Gospel, when they could count upon a most cordial welcome.

But Selim declared that he had had great experience along that line from a trip which he had once taken as captain of a Turkish man-of-war to the northern shores of the Black Sea, a desolate and swampy region inhabitated by wandering tribes of a strange race, called the Slavs. How Selim had ever got himself appointed commander of a war vessel, when he managed to be seasick while crossing the harbor on a ferry-boat had always been a puzzle to me. But by that time I had learned not to wonder at anything pertaining to the morals, the habits or the customs of the wily follower of the Prophet. Furthermore we were accompanied by Jean-Louys and his ability to win the good will of almost any creature on either two or four legs was such that I thought him capable of taming even those wild men of the Zuyder Zee.

Anyway, we had arranged that we should meet at ten o'clock near the Montelbaans Tower, the old tower near the harbor which twice a month was the scene of great gayety and great misery, when the soldiers and sailors who had signed up for service in the Indies embarked from there for Batavia amidst the beating of many drums, the singing and shouting of a thousand tipsy women and the general jubilation of the crimps who felt that they had done their duty as soon as they had delivered this latest batch of human cattle into the hands of their new master and were now entitled to a few days of drunken relaxation. The rest of the time, however, the tower stood in dignified silence and it seemed an ideal meeting place for four respectable citizens bound upon a peaceful picnic.

I was a little earlier than the others, not having to come quite so far, but as soon as I had reached the Oude Schans, I had felt that there was something unusual in the air. Excited men and women were standing in small groups along the side of the canal, and all of them had their eyes fixed on a single house (a perfectly commonplace, respectable house such as you might find in any street in Amsterdam) and occasionally some one would shout, "I saw one of them!" or "The whole place is full of them!" or again, "There is one now! He is trying to get across the roof!" followed by a cry of "Look out! They are going to shoot!" Whereupon every one would run as fast as possible to find safety behind a tree or the bales of merchandise that were lying beneath tarpaulin covers awaiting the return of the stevedores on Tuesday morning.

The whole thing seemed too absurd for words. Our town was famous for its orderliness. The militia was a heavy-fisted organization and Their Lordships, who could under certain circumstances be persuaded to overlook ordinary misdemeanors of a private nature, knew no mercy when it came to rioting. If one rioted and one was caught, one was hung from one of the windows of the Town Hall and that was all there was to it. "Go as far as you like," the Burgomaster seemed to say. "Rob each other occasionally and even kill each other occasionally, but keep the peace of the community and do not upset the system of law and order as laid down by our wise decrees."

The idea therefore of a riot and of all things, on Easter morning, seemed little short of preposterous and I turned to a tight-lipped individual with mean yellow eyes, who was standing by my side and who was apparently drawing great personal satisfaction from this unusual proceeding.

"Pray tell me," I asked him, "what is this all about?"

He at once grew suspicious.

"Oh, don't you know? Why, that is curious, that you shouldn't know!"

I assured him that since I had only come a few minutes before, I had hardly had time to know.

"Well," he said, "the house is full of Arminians. They are holding a service there and they just tried to kill a child and use its blood for their ceremonies."

Of course, if I had been sensible, I would not have continued this conversation. But in those days, I suffered from a dreadful spiritual complaint. I simply could not get over the notion that since all men had been created after God's image, they also must be endowed with certain primitive faculties for logical reasoning. Of course I knew that some people were not quite as bright as others, but I always told myself that that was merely the result of different backgrounds and different opportunities for development. "Give them a chance," I would tell my friends when they informed me that I was a silly-minded old fool. "Give them a chance. They have never had one. No one has ever appealed to their higher instincts. Talk to them! Reason it out with them and sooner or later you will find their vulnerable point and they will be forever grateful to you for having shown the right way towards the Truth."

I was so thoroughly convinced of the correctness of this point of view that almost every week I would waste endless valuable hours in utterly futile discussions with people to whom even the proposition of $2 \times 2 = 4$ was an unfathomable mystery and something to be regarded with profound suspicion, as it did not occur within the pages of Holy Writ. And no one short of a perfect lunatic would have undertaken to start an argument with that type of religious zealot and under such circumstances. But I was not very bright in those days and still believed in the efficacy of orderly argumentation and I answered:

"But surely, my dear sir, the people have not revived that silly old lie about the Jews for the benefit of the Arminians?"

Good Lord! how the fellow bristled! But he was the typical coward. He turned to a group of men and boys who had stationed themselves carefully behind a dozen big wooden boxes.

"Hey, boys!" he shouted. "I have caught one of them. This fellow here is a black Arminian. Come and get him."

Wherefore the crowd left its shelter and swooped down upon me and no doubt would have attacked me, when suddenly the door of the house opened and a dozen men and women, like frightened rabbits, made a dash for life and liberty towards the left of the street, which did not seem to be so well guarded. With a howl of joy, the mob rushed after its victims and I was left standing alone, looking as sheepish as one does when one is conscious of having done something very foolish.

But a pleasant voice behind me said: "Trying to solve the problems of this world by the usual appeal to reason, or just merely a friendly little argument?" And there were Jean-Louys and Bernardo and they said: "Selim was here a moment ago but he left, as he said it always hurt his tender Moslem heart to see Christians murder each other and he is waiting for us in the Ridder Straat and you had better leave before these brutes come back."

But ere we could turn into the next side street, we heard the beating of drums and from the north a company of militia was coming marching along, and so we found ourselves caught between the rioters and the soldiers and not contemplating our position with any pleasure (for the mob looked as if it wanted to fight) we stood aimlessly still for a moment and then when Bernardo said, "There! Look, there is a tavern!" we made for the door of the inn just as some one from the other side was trying to lock it.

Indeed, our attempt to force our way in almost led to another violent encounter, when suddenly and by a stroke of great good luck, I recognized the inn-keeper as an old patient of the city hospital and he recognized me too, for he said: "Come in as fast as you can, for there is going to be trouble and I don't want them to plunder my house."

For the moment at least we were safe and having nothing better to do we sat down and ordered three glasses of gin and asked our host what had caused all the trouble and he said that he was not quite sure either but apparently one of the houses further down the street belonged to a member of the Arminian community. Since the followers of Jacobus Arminius had been read out of the Church by act of the General Synod half a dozen years before, they had been in the habit of meeting at this house on the Oude Schans to listen to one of their ministers and fortify each other in their misfortunes by common prayer and an avowal of faith. These clandestine meetings were of course against the law and the clergy of Amsterdam had protested violently, but the Arminians or Remonstrants or by whatever name they were called, were industrious and respectable citizens and Their Lordships of the Town Hall refused to proceed against them, even if those black-souled sinners publicly confessed that they had serious doubts upon the subject of predestination and infant damnation. As long as they paid their taxes and were discreet about their weekly gatherings, they could sing and pray and preach as they liked and Their Lordships would most certainly not interfere.

Well, this morning some boys who had stayed away from Sunday-school had used the stoop of this house for a game of knuckle-bones and they had been very noisy about it and some one had come out of the house and had told them to go and play somewhere else. But of course, no other stoop would do and half a dozen times they had been told to go away and half a dozen times they had used vile language until the poor Arminian, forgetting all the precepts of his creed, had lost his temper and had boxed the ears of a young lout who had called him a name which I shall not here repeat. The youthful mucker, instead of taking his medicine, had shrieked that he had been murdered. A few passers-by had taken his side as is the habit of our common people who, regardless of the merits of the case, will always support one of their own class. Some one else then had raised the cry of "The Arminians and the Papists are in that house!" and the fat had been in the fire. For by this time the angry horde had been augmented by those who were returning from early service and they were in no mood to obey the orders of the officer of the guard who marched up to them all alone and bade them disperse.

I was looking through a little peephole in one of the blinds which had been hastily pulled across the windows, for the rattle of breaking glass told us what was happening a few doors away. I saw the officer parley and then hesitate. Evidently he did not want to use force, but that one short moment of trepidation was enough to decide the fate of the besieged worshipers. The crowd set up a terrific yell and a fresh volley of stones and sticks and mud was directed against the offending house. But one of the stones, either intentionally or accidentally, hit one of the soldiers who were waiting at some distance. He was perfectly willing to see the dirty Arminians get their just rewards, but he would be damned if he would stand there and have his nose broken by a brick and just stand there and do nothing about it. I saw him level his musket. At the same moment, one of the leaders of the rabble, an evil-looking ruffian with a cobble stone in each hand and a long knife held between his lips, in a sudden outburst of fury turned on his heels and made for the officer who still alone, and with his sword undrawn, was absolutely unable to defend himself, and undoubtedly he would have killed him, had not the soldier fired his gun and caught the assailant right between the eyes. The man dropped his knife, threw up his arms, stones and all, jumped about four feet in the air and fell down dead.

This was the sign for a general mêlée and during the next half hour there was a great deal of desultory fighting and several of the crowd were taken prisoner and since the danger of a bombardment was now considerably less, we persuaded our host to let us open the blind, for such outbreaks of popular fury are very interesting to people with a philosophical turn of mind and we did not want to let the opportunity go by of studying our neighbors in the act of breaking skulls and windows for the greater glory of their mysterious God.

And then suddenly I saw something that struck me as most extraordinary. Leaning against a tree and standing there as unconcernedly as if he were all alone in the park drawing a bird or a squirrel, a young man was making a sketch of one of the inevitable beggars who had hastened to be present when the plundering should begin (our beggars have a very sensitive nose for that sort of thing) and who now with some of his colleagues was debating whether they had better go on or whether they should retreat as the game had been spoiled anyway by the arrival of the guards. A few evidently were in favor of seeing the thing out, but others of a more cautious nature seemed to be in favor of flight.

While they were still debating this point, the battle between the rioters and the soldiers suddenly took a fresh impetus from the arrival of a number of sailors from some near-by East Indiamen, who armed with cutlasses were all for showing the damned heretics that they could not preach their stinking doctrines in their city and hope to get away with it. It was a bitter fight and many heads were broken and many fingers were split and stones flew to and fro, but through it all that strange young man kept working away at his sketches and appeared totally unconscious of the fact that at any moment he too might be killed. All three of us were fascinated by the sight of him. He was very simply dressed, like a student or a better class artisan and he wore his hair long as was then the fashion. But he had eyes, and all three of us remarked on those eyes.

"We must speak to him," Jean-Louys cried out, delighted with so much sang-froid, "and we must invite him to accompany us on our trip. He will be very useful in our negotiations with the natives."

But finally, when the soldiers had swept away the rabble and we could open the door and go out on the street, the young man was gone. We looked for him everywhere, but could not find him. And so we gave up the search and thanked our host and gave him a handsome tip (for maybe he had saved our lives) and went to the Ridder Straat and at the appointed tavern found Selim busily engaged in explaining the mysteries of a ring he wore to the serving girl, who was so fascinated that she had let him put an arm around her—"So that she should be closer to the subject"—as he explained to us when we entered.

Of course, our picnic and our sailing party had been spoiled for that whole part of the town remained smoldering with anger for several days and it was not safe to get too close to a pleasure yacht. The people felt full of righteous indignation. They had tried to protect their homes, their families, their children, against the pollution of a terrible heresy and as a reward for their devotion to the cause of True Religion they had been shot down like dogs. The idea that any one under such circumstances could be so utterly indifferent to the interests of the community as to go sailing for pleasure might have caused a new outbreak and at the suggestion of Jean-Louys we went to his tower and he made us an omelette in the true French style (they don't use flour in France for their omelettes as we do and get something much lighter and much more digestible than our own domestic pancakes) and Selim made us a strange dish of little bits of meat and rather pasty-looking flour which he called Ish-kebab, which he informed us was the favorite dish of His Majesty Murad IV and Bernardo mixed us a salad after the true Portuguese style which was not unpleasant although a little too oily and garlicky and I sat wondering who this strange young man might have been who could lose himself so completely in his task that he kept on drawing pictures while all around him, people were killing each other.

For a long time his face continued to haunt me. But I never saw him again. Until that rainy evening in the month of November of the year 1641 when suddenly it dawned upon me, as I lay tossing in my bed. The strange young man of the riot of fifteen years before was none other than the husband of my new patient. It was Rembrandt van Rijn.

Chapter 6

A DISAGREEABLE WOMAN IS AS A RULE A VERY DISAGREEABLE WOMAN

When I called again at the house in the Breestraat, I mentioned the riot of fifteen years before as we sat in the studio after I had visited my patient. I had been right. Rembrandt had been there. Just by chance. For at that time he was not living in Amsterdam. He had been there for a short time in '23, studying with Lastman, but in '26 he had been back in Leyden, and he had only been in Amsterdam for a fortnight to try and sell some of his pictures. The trip had not been very successful. The pictures were bad, but not quite bad enough to find a customer and he had returned to Leyden, as he explained, "because the meals at home cost nothing and because I could send my laundry to the family wash."

As for the incident of the riot, yes, he remembered vaguely that there had been a lot of shouting while he was drawing, "but I really have forgotten," he added. "All I remember is that I found myself face to face with one of the most picturesque hoodlums I had ever seen. I have always had a secret liking for those wandering vagabonds, who obey neither God nor man. They neither spin nor weave or whatever it is that they are supposed to do. They lie and steal and cheat and loaf and gamble and get hung or die miserably by the side of the road, but they make no pretense to be anything else and when they are dirty, they are dirty, and when they are drunk, they are drunk, and one knows what one is painting. I will show you the one I saw that day. I have done him in an etching. Some other time—when I have not got this worry—then I will look it up for you—some other time—when Saskia is better."

"Better!" I thought. "You poor devil, I ought to tell you right now. But why should I? She won't live a day longer for my telling you. No! You might as well have hope until the final end." And so we talked of this and that and the other thing, but mostly of this and that, as the "other thing" (taking it to mean the events of the big world) did not interest my new friend in the least.

I sometimes tried to bring up the sort of subjects that were of importance to the average run of my patients, the trouble the King of England seemed to have with his people and how it would affect our own trade if there should be war between the King and his Parliament, and the difficulties that never seemed to come to an end between Sweden and Denmark about the tolls in the Sund, and how it would mean a great loss to our own grain-trade if there were an open outbreak of hostilities and how it might force us to take sides just when our navy was needed for a final attack upon Spain, and what a lot all that would cost and how some one had written a book to prove that somewhere between Asia and America, in the southern part of the Pacific there must be a large piece of land and how certain merchants in our town were interested in the idea and wanted to send out an expedition to discover this mysterious land and take possession of it and exploit it, which would mean a wonderful new source of revenue, but to all these problems he nodded a polite "yes" without ever offering a suggestion of his own.

And then I talked of art, of which (with the exception of music) I am entirely ignorant, and I told him of two pictures by an Italian, whose name I had forgotten but they represented the Colosseum by moonlight and the ruins of the Forum early in the morning and I said what an inspiration it must be to any young man to be able to go to that wonderful country for a short while and study the ancient masters, and he said, yes, perhaps it was a good thing for a few of them. If they were born to be bad painters, they had better be bad painters on the other side of the Alps than on this side, and of course, the old masters had been wonderful, the greatest painters that had ever lived, but the story they had to tell was best told by their pictures and these one could see in Holland just as well as anywhere else.

For it really did not matter much where one painted, but it all depended upon how one painted and all these hundreds of young men, ruining their families because they had to learn their art abroad, had better stay home and join the bakers-guild or become tailors or longshoremen, for if they had talent, it would show itself even if they never left their own little alleyway or their own room and if they had not, all the Italian sunsets and French sunrises and Spanish saints and German devils would not turn them into real artists.

And when he was still quite young and had only painted a few pictures—it must have been in 1630 or '31—My Lord Constantin Huygens, who had seen his work and that of his friend Jan Lievens had told them that what they were doing was very nice and really very promising, but they were an arrogant couple of brats who thought that they were so smart that no one could teach them anything, and if only they would go to Italy for a while and study Raphael and Michelangelo, they might really amount to something. But they had answered that they could not afford to waste their time on such a long voyage and they had stayed right where they were and after all they had learned their trade just as well as the others and they had never lost the habit of working, which was one of the worst sides of the life 'neath the pleasant Italian skies, with all the women in the world at one's disposal and even more wine.

So that was that, and invariably after a couple of minutes our minds went back to the sick woman in the Big Room downstairs and the baby in the Small Room upstairs and what the chances were for the mother's speedy recovery and whether the child had inherited her weak constitution or whether he would pull through. As for the child, I really knew nothing about it. It looked strong enough but it was restless and wept a great deal and this annoyed the mother and tired her. For of course, as soon as I was out of the house, the nurse would find a pretext to move the child from the etching room upstairs back to the living room downstairs.

If I happened to come in upon such an occasion, there always was a vague excuse. The Master had to use his press that morning, or the room smelled so badly of ink that it had to be aired and they were afraid that the child would catch cold or she had to tend to the baby's laundry and could not leave the child alone while she was in the garden. And so on and so forth.

The reason for this opposition was not hard to find. The old-fashioned dry-nurse holds a curious position in our community. She is usually a woman of very simple origin, but because she spends her days in the houses of the rich, she has acquired a certain dignity of manner which deceives a great many people. There are undoubtedly a number of members of that profession who are faithful and efficient and competent and who render exceedingly useful services. But there are all too many who are lazy and indifferent and who do more harm than good with their superstitions and their methods which go back straight to those Middle Ages when men knew sometimes how to die but rarely how to live.

These women are really a menace to the community. They come into people's houses when everything is topsy-turvy and when the husband is half crazy with fright. They quickly succeed in surrounding themselves with a nimbus of indispensability. "If it were not for them, of course everything would have gone wrong, but they saved the mother and they also saved the child," and more of the same sort, until the poor male parent believes that a fat, complacent woman with the mind of a cow is the savior of his domestic happiness, and bows to the creature as if she were a goddess. And the relatives too fall a victim to this nonsense and the dry-nurse shows them the beautiful new infant and pockets her tips and allows everybody to wait on her as if it were she and not the mother who had gone through the ordeal of child-bearing.

Whenever she sees that she is in danger of losing her exalted position, she draws upon her large stock of so-called "nurse's tales" and frightens the poor parents with stories about children who suddenly grew an extra couple of hands or who died of mysterious diseases or who were eaten up by werewolves because the dry-nurse was not there to drive away the devils and spooks and the bogeymen which cause those afflictions with one of those mysterious but efficacious abracadabras of which they alone possess the secret.

Yes, I have known of cases when the dry-nurse, who felt that she was being neglected, deliberately doped the child with a weak solution of gin and milk so as to "save it from a horrible death" and thereby gain the everlasting gratitude of the entire household, which did not know that the "cure" consisted in substituting milk for gin and allowing the child to sleep off the effects of its youthful debauch.

The nurse in the painter's family belonged to this latter category. She was an unpleasant-looking person with large, coarse features and an arrogant voice with a whine in it. Such a combination may seem impossible but she really was possessed of it and reminded me of certain curs which are able to yelp and bark at the same time. She was (as I afterwards discovered) the widow of an army-trumpeter and often talked of the days when she had had her own place and had not been obliged to eat other people's bread. Her game was so simple that any other man would have looked through it right away. She knew enough about sick people to understand that the man for whom she worked would soon be a widower. She meant to fill the empty place. She probably felt that I, as an outsider, might not be so easily deceived and would try to warn the husband, for the whole thing was so transparent that it could not well remain hidden from the patient to whom any sort of excitement might prove fatal. Hence she had a double reason to hate me. In the first place, because as a doctor I was bound to disapprove of a great many things which to her were part of an ancient ritual and an easy way of getting some extra money, and in the second place because I might upset her plan of becoming the second Mrs. van Rijn.

It may seem that I pay more attention to this woman than she deserves, for the world is full of hysterical and scheming females and they are rarely very interesting. But soon after the death of Saskia it appeared that I had been right in my diagnosis of Geertje's hidden intentions and for years, the poor painter's life was made miserable by this former servant and her lamentations and complaints.

From all this Rembrandt might have saved himself if he had done what I bade him do and had sent her packing. But this man, who was without mercy for himself when it came to his work, who would actually live and sleep and sit and paint and walk in his clothes for weeks at a time if he got interested in a problem of light and dark, who would content himself with a slice of bread and a couple of herrings as his only meal for months at a time because he was too busy with an etching to think of anything else, this slave-driver who kept his mind and body going full tilt until he pitched himself headlong into an early grave, was weak as butter when it came to women.

He did not understand them and in his heart of hearts, I think he rather disliked them. He was a vigorous fellow with the strength of a bull and other qualifications which are usually associated with that useful animal. And therefore he was sometimes in dire need of a woman, just a woman, any woman would do. He was by nature exceedingly kind-hearted and, of course, the other sex was quick to recognize this defect in his armor and to use his vulnerability to its own advantage. As a result Rembrandt was forever in some sort of trouble about his domestic relations.

The truth of course was that a man like him should never have been married at all. For no matter what sort of union he contracted, the moment he promised that he would love and cherish a certain female for the rest of his days, he was uttering a lie. He had already given his word to some one else, years and years ago, and she was a most jealous mistress and would never let go of him.

Once shortly after Saskia's death I tried to explain this to one of her relatives, a respectable Frisian dominie. He was horrified.

"Then you mean to say," he stammered, "that my poor niece was married to an adulterer?"

"Yes," I answered, "just as much as any other woman who undertakes to become the life-companion of a man who is more in love with his work than with anything else."

For that, alas, was the truth. And it caused a vast amount of misery to a few human beings and brought inconceivable beauty into the lives of millions of others.

This balance sheet will please a few and others will throw it away in disgust.

But nature ofttimes chooses strange ways her miracles to perform.

And who shall say that she is wrong?

Chapter 7

SASKIA'S ILLNESS

Yes, Saskia was a very sick woman but like so many sufferers from phthisis, she was totally unaware of the seriousness of her condition. She felt weak, of course, desperately weak at times, and the fever slowly burned up her strength. She was losing weight at a terrible rate of speed, but she felt no pain, no discomfort, and except for an occasional fit of coughing, she would hardly have known that there was anything the matter with her at all.

Perhaps the Gods, who are not renowned for their mercy in dealing with the ailments of the human race, recognized that this affliction was just a little more than most people would be able to bear unless mitigated by some spiritual anesthetic, consisting in this instance of an irrepressible form of gayety and a steadfast optimism which makes it impossible for them to believe that there is no hope and that death is merely a question of weeks or months, or at the best, a few years.

Every time I visited the house on the Breestraat, Saskia was doing "just a little better than the last time you saw me, dear Doctor." She was so lovely and so pathetic and so patient and so totally ineffectual that my heart was full of pity for her and sometimes I bought a few flowers for her from the flower-woman just around the corner of the Anthonie Sluys, a strange old creature who was said to be the widow of a ship's captain, who had been eaten up by the savages of some mysterious Indian island, but who as I found out one day was the relict of a plain sailor hung for insubordination and who had invented the story of her romantically consumed spouse in order to attract more customers.

Upon such occasions, Saskia was as happy as a child and one day I remember I had brought her a bunch of country violets and she made a little wreath and put it on the head of the baby, for of course, no matter what I might say the child continued to live in the big downstairs room where the mother lay dying. She even tried to make little Titus dance on her knees while she was sitting propped up in her chair in front of the fire. But the effort was too much for her and she had a coughing spell and when I tried to make her lie down, she refused and said she would be all right as soon as she had taken some of her medicine.

This puzzled me, for I had given her no medicine except a sleeping potion, knowing only too well that in the whole of the pharmacopoeia no drug was to be found that could prevail against the onslaughts of this dreadful disease. And then I discovered to my horror that that unspeakable nurse had prevailed upon her to try the mixture of a well-

FACSIMILE OF A LETTER TO HUYGENS

THE WINDMILL

known mountebank who had come to Amsterdam a few years before and pretended that he was a Babylonian prince who had discovered the secret formula of King Solomon's elixir of life, hidden among the ruins of the temple of Jerusalem. He was an absolute fraud. But he wore a long bright red cloak and a green turban and he was a very clever scoundrel who had had an enormous amount of experience in almost every city of Europe and had worked his way out of at least a dozen jails and he played upon the emotions of his patients with as much agility and virtuosity as if he had been the late Jan Sweelinck trying out the organ of some humble village church, and his waiting room was always filled with eager crowds of suffering mortals who listened to him with great awe and declared themselves cured before they had even left his house.

He advertised that since he had been sent by God he was not allowed to charge for his services and indeed, the consultation itself was entirely free of charge. But in order to prevent a relapse, he persuaded most of his customers to buy a couple of bottles of his famous "Elixir Vitae" which he sold at a florin apiece. I now had a chance to examine this mixture for as soon as we had put Saskia back to bed and she was resting quietly, I took my departure, but was careful to remove the bottle. At home I examined the contents as well as I could and found that it consisted of licorice, camomile and water with a dash of sugar to make it a little more palatable. No wonder this quack could afford a handsomer carriage than any of the regular members of our Surgeons' Guild.

I spoke to the husband the next day about this incident and told him what I had discovered, that this licorice water might not be directly harmful to his wife, but neither would it do her any good, as she needed plenty of milk and eggs, but that she must avoid all things that would tend to upset her stomach or spoil her appetite. He was very angry and promised to dismiss the nurse at once. When I returned the next day, I found her gone. I expressed my joy and asked where the child was.

"Oh," the painter answered with a somewhat sheepish look, "the nurse is taking the child out for a little walk. She said that she thought it needed some air and it was such a lovely day!"

A lovely day indeed! A sharp eastern wind was making the blinds rattle. The streets were full of dust. When I came into the sick room I found it filled with smoke. And the mother lay gasping in her bed.

"The nurse said it would be all right," she whispered to me hoarsely, "but there is such a storm and it is blowing down the chimney and I could not get up and I called, but no one heard me." And she wept bitterly for this was one of the rare days when her customary cheerfulness had left her and she felt very sorry for herself.

I was thoroughly angry with van Rijn and I made no attempt to disguise or hide my feelings. He had remained upstairs in his studio as I knew he would, for he felt so utterly helpless in the midst of these domestic upheavals that most of the time he tried to persuade himself that they did not exist by locking himself up in his studio and keeping his mind engaged upon his work. I now told him in no uncertain tones that something had to be done or I would no longer be responsible.

Then I suddenly realized that he had never yet understood the seriousness of his wife's illness. His thoughts had been so completely concentrated upon his paintings that nothing short of a brutal and point-blank announcement of imminent disaster could break through the man's "unawareness" of his physical surroundings. Now he went to the other extreme. He accused himself bitterly of his neglect, called himself his wife's murderer, carefully washed his brushes in a jar of turpentine, carefully wiped them upon a rag, took off his painter's blouse, turned his easel away from the light, went out of the door, locked the door behind him, went downstairs, sat himself down by the side of his wife's bed, took her hand and said: "Saskia sweet, now I shall be thy nurse." And as far as I know, he never left her room again until she died.

For he loved this woman very deeply and very tenderly. Indeed, he loved her as much as he was ever able to love anything made of flesh and blood, and not of canvas and paint or the gold-gleaming copper of the etcher's plate.

Chapter 8

I BEGIN TO LEARN SOMETHING NEW ABOUT ART WHEN REMBRANDT INVITES ME INTO HIS STUDIO

After this there was some sort of order in the big house on the Breestraat. Van Rijn had put a cot up in a corner of the Big Room. A cleaning woman had been called in and the bottles of acid and the pans with rosin had been removed to a small cabinet to the left of the front door. One or two paintings which smelled too strongly of fresh varnish had been temporarily relegated to the studio upstairs and the peat-fire had been changed for one of wood. It cost a good deal more, but as the man seemed to be making plenty of money, there was no reason why he should worry over a little extra expense. The nurse Geertje was still on the premises, but she carefully kept out of my sight. Three times a day she was permitted to bring the child to see its mother and on those occasions, if mere looks could have killed, I would have died as miserably as Saint Sebastian, for her eyes were as powerful as a whole regiment of Roman archers. But as long as she obeyed my instructions I did not care how little she loved me or how much she hated me. It was my duty to try and prolong the life of my patient for as long as it could be done. She needed rest and regular hours and she now had both, for van Rijn guarded her day and night with a patience and care which were as touching as ineffectual.

For once in his life he had escaped from the dreadful mistress who heretofore had never given him a moment's respite. He did not touch a brush and although I had heard that he had been ordered to do a large piece for the new clubhouse of the Town Guards, I never saw him busy with any sketches. I asked him whether it had been finished and he said no, it had been begun, but it could wait and that people would like it anyway and that he did not care a tinker's dam whether it was ever finished or not if only he could keep his wife alive and get her better. And he used to sit by her side for hours and speak to her softly, which seemed to be the best way to make her go to sleep, for after ten or fifteen minutes she would close her eyes and lie very still with a smile upon her lovely face and she looked so young, not a day older than twenty, that it seemed incredible that she was going to die very soon; but our art has never yet found a way to combat this affliction and so the winter passed and the new year came and I knew that it would be Saskia's last one and I was quite miserable about it when something happened in my own life that made me completely forget the difficulties of the van Rijn household. For we human beings are so complicated that the miseries of our neighbors mean nothing to us the moment we ourselves get into trouble. And it was during this winter that an event occurred which for a time threatened to upset the whole of my existence and which made me an exile from my country for almost a dozen years.

Now it was customary in those days for each of the members of the Surgeons' Guild in town to give a course in anatomy for the benefit of the students of medicine and those leeches and barbers who wanted to prepare themselves a little more thoroughly for their daily tasks. The last time I had given this course of lectures and demonstrations had been in the summer of the year 1636, and now I was told by the Dean of our Guild to prepare myself to teach elementary anatomy once more during the months of March, April and May of the coming year. As I had devoted myself almost entirely to the study of drugs during the last decade, I was a bit rusty and felt the need of refreshing my memory and so I went to Anatomical Hall of the Surgeons' Guild, situated these last eight years on the second floor of the Saint Anthonie Gate, right above the local meat-market, a somewhat unfortunate location as it gave the ribald minded a chance to make rather pointed remarks about this close proximity between butchers and doctors.

I must confess that I had not been near the place since my last lectureship and I was surprised to find one side of the wall entirely filled with a large picture, showing Doctor Nicolaes Pieterszoon in the midst of his students. Pieterszoon had gone far since the day he posed for this portrait, for he had been High Sheriff of our town and had been elected Burgomaster two or three times. Also he had taken the name of Tulp after a large tulip that stood carved in the façade of his house on the Keizersgracht.

The picture struck me very forcibly for in it I found something which I had rarely discovered in any other painting—though I must confess at once that this form of art had never been my strong point. As a child I had always wanted to draw, but my father, with his narrow religious ideas, felt convinced that young people should be trained to do that which was most distasteful to them, rather than be allowed to follow their natural bent. Therefore when it became apparent (from my eternal scribbling on slates and walls and rarer pieces of paper) that I had not only some gift for drawing but an absolute urge to express myself in lines and curves, representing a large variety of subjects from our old maid Jacoba to Jonah being spewed out by the whale, my father then and there decided that I must become a musician.

He did not ask whether I had a good ear, whether I had the sort of fingers one needs to become an experienced player of the violin. He "decided," and in my youth when a father "decided" a child obeyed and that was all there was to it. And so from the age of six until I was fourteen I went twice a week to the room of Signor Tomasso Staccato, player-in-extraordinary and virtuoso of the Chamber to his Grace, the late Marquis Ercole II of Este.

The little Italian, if he spoke the truth, must have been about a hundred years old, for Ercole, as I happened to discover one day in a history of architecture, lived during the first half of the sixteenth century. But such small lies, due to the vanity of simple-minded and otherwise loveable people, are easily pardoned and Signor Staccato was one of the most charming men I have ever met. He played the violin, the viola da gamba and viola da basso with equal dexterity and was besides no mean performer on the clavecin, an instrument of great charm and much more dependable than the viols which in our wet and damp climate are apt to be as moody as the spoiled wives of indulgent husbands.

There was a tradition, when I was a child, that all music teachers were fair game for naughty little boys and that it was the holy duty of the pupils to make the lives of these poor creatures as miserable as they possibly could. And of course music-teachers were supposed to be artists and artists could not handle the birch like ordinary school-masters, for it would have been beneath their dignity to spank any one. Signor Staccato carefully stuck to this rule, that there must be no physical violence mixed with his teaching. But at one time in his career he had acquired a bow made out of steel. Good God! I still shiver when I think of that long, thin steel bow which used to descend upon my fingers with unexpected violence whenever I did not pay sufficient attention. "B flat," he would say in his falsetto voice, "and you played B sharp," and both B sharp and B flat were accompanied by a short, sharp whack across the knuckles with that fatal bow. If that seemed too mild a form of punishment he would discover that the left hand was not in the right position and then it would be hammered into the correct place with a quick succession of rapid blows. "There!—a little further back if you please, my child—a little further back—still a leetle more!" Bang! Bang! Bang!

It was a strange system to make one learn to play the violin. But somehow or other, it worked, and although I had very little talent, I learned to render some of the simpler pieces of Orlando di Lasso and Arcadelt with a certain degree of accuracy. But my playing was something I had learned out of a book. It was not something that came out of the heart, and whereas if I had been allowed to follow my natural inclination, I might have developed into a fair draughtsman, I had now reached the age of forty, an indifferent performer on the viol and hopelessly ignorant of that form of graphic self-expression towards which I had always felt so strongly inclined.

I had in the meantime seen a great many paintings. Our city was full of them. It sometimes seemed to me that our town would burst from sheer riches, like a sack too heavily loaded with grain. Our harbors were more crowded than ever. The streets near the Exchange gave one the impression of a continual county-fair. During the morning hours, when the musicians played on the Dam, one saw as many Turks and Germans and Blackamoors and Frenchmen and Britishers and Swedes, and even people from far-away India, as one did Dutchmen. All roads appeared to be leading to Amsterdam and the great rivers of the world flowed no longer towards the North Pole, but carried their ships right to our port—ships bulging with spices and with silks and with grain and with whale-oil and every product from the shores of the Seven Great Seas.

There were those who believed that these wonderful blessings were being poured into our laps because as a nation we had found special favor in the eyes of God. How or by what means, I failed to understand, for it never struck me that we were much kinder or more generous or more humble than many of our neighbors and those surely were the virtues which ought to have appealed most directly to the Almighty Ruler of Heaven. And as far as I could reason things out (though I was careful to keep this opinion to myself) we owed this prosperity to the fortunate circumstance that we had been obliged to fight so long and so bitterly for our mere existence. The weaker ones among our people had died long ago. They had not been able to survive the endless sieges, the hunger, the anxiety for parents or children who at any moment might be hanged or burned or broken on the wheel. The strong ones had survived. And when the enemy was driven off our territory, those strong ones were so full of energy and enthusiasm, that they had to find some new outlet for their surplus of high spirits. The sight of a map would drive them crazy with excitement. Our small country could no longer hold them. They had forced the King of Spain to his knees. Old Charles of England had his hands full with that psalm-singing rebel called Cromwell. Louis of France was just nobody at all, and his mother and her dear friend the Cardinal, who ruled France between their quarrels and their bickerings, did not count except as agreeable topics for scandal and rather ribald tavern songs. The Swedes and Danes might be bothersome with their silly quarrels, but somehow or other, the straits that led to the Baltic grain fields would be kept open and a curse upon both of them if they tried to interfere with our honest trade. Finally there were the minor potentates of Germany and the Mediterranean, but they were just funny without being bothersome.

And so, for no other reason than that they must ever and again prove to themselves what fine fellows they were, my neighbors must go forth and pull the pigtail of the Emperor of China and singe the beard of the Sultan of Turkey and pull the tails of the polar bears in Spitzbergen and make love to the daughters of the Cacique of Virginia and drink beer in the pagodas of India and light their pipes with the eternal lamp of some holy shrine in Calicut and do any number of scandalous, dangerous and altogether outrageous things which ought to have cost them their lives, but which on the contrary filled their pockets with ducats and made them twice as foolhardy and brave and devil-may-care as they had ever been before. But of course after ten or twenty years of this sort of life, they would grow a little too old for this sort of pastime and then they would retire from the business of storming the gates of Heaven and Hell and would turn respectable and they would buy themselves large and uncomfortable houses in one of the newly laid out parts of the town (and how they were robbed by our good burgomasters who speculated in this sort of real estate as if the whole city were their private property and they were responsible to no one no matter how much they stole from the community) and of course they must show their neighbors how rich they were (what is the fun of having bags and bags and bags of money if no one knows it?) and so they filled their houses with elegant French chairs that weighed a ton and with Spanish chests that only a mule could move and with pictures—rows and rows and still more rows of pictures.

I don't suppose that most of them knew what those pictures were about or cared a straw for them either one way or the other. But they knew that in the older days the abbots of the churches and the princes of Italy and Spain and the barons of England and the nobles of France had adorned their houses with paintings and so of course they must have paintings too. As a result, wherever I went, whether my patient happened to be a simple butcher from the Voldersstraat or a rich Indian merchant living on the fashionable side of the Heerengracht, I found myself surrounded by miles and miles of colored canvases. Some of them were probably very good and a few of them were undoubtedly very bad, but most of them were of a very decent quality, as the Guild of St. Luke maintained the highest possible standards and no one could hope to qualify as a master until he had spent years and years in a very exacting and very difficult apprenticeship.

But for one reason or another, I had never known much about this form of art until I met Rembrandt.

Of course there always had been certain pictures I liked and others I did not like quite so well. I had taken them more or less for granted. A portrait of a man or a woman was that same man or woman made of linseed-oil and diverse pigments instead of flesh and blood. A landscape in a golden frame was not in any way different from that same landscape as I could see it from my own front windows. A lamb-chop or a dead fish in color was still a lamb-chop or a dead fish. It was all very fine and very clever, but it was dead.

And now I suddenly made the discovery that such things could have a soul.

I don't like that word "soul." It smacks too much of those theological discussions I have heard going on around me ever since I was a child, but just now I can't think of any other expression that describes equally well what I mean and so I shall let it go at that and repeat that I suddenly came face to face with the animate quality of supposedly inanimate substances (for what else is a picture but a bit of hemp covered with a messy layer of vegetable matter?) and I was forced to realize that the terms "dead" and "alive" were a little less definite than I had always presumed them to be.

This dawned upon me not slowly and gradually through my conversations with Rembrandt (who however could rarely be induced to talk about his work) or through the contemplation of those paintings by different famous masters with which the walls of his house were covered. The first revelation came to me quite suddenly that morning I went to the rooms of the Surgeons' Guild and stood in front of the portrait of Nicolaes Tulp and half a dozen of my colleagues, busy with some anatomical demonstration. I had known Claes Tulp ever since I had come to Amsterdam and was on pleasant speaking-terms with most of the other men whose faces appeared on the picture. During my student days I had attended hundreds of dissections. I understood that it had become fashionable among the better-known among my colleagues to have themselves painted carving up some unfortunate victim of the gallows or the poor ward. Together with the whole town I had laughed when one rather vain old physician, who had engaged in a bitter professional quarrel with one of the young men, had ordered a portrait of this sort and had bribed the artist to make one of the "students" look like his hated rival, thereby drawing attention to his own superior position in life. And together with the whole country I had roared when the younger man, not to be outdone in civilities of this sort, had favored the Surgeons' Guild with a large canvas (not particularly well done, I am sorry to say) in which he himself was shown "demonstrating" the entrails of a very unappetizing corpse, which bore a striking if somewhat greenish resemblance to the learned Professor who had humiliated him in picture No. 1.

But all of those popular "anatomical lessons" were mere records of past events. They told the spectator that "on such and such a day, in such and such a room, Doctor A., surrounded by Doctors B., C., D. and E., had dissected the mortal remains of the late F. and had found that the praecentral gyrus was still situated between the postcentral gyrus and the superior frontal gyrus (as it ought to be) or had opened up the abdomen and had decided that the patient had died of a distemper of the liver, brought about by years and years of assiduous toping."

Well, I don't know how to explain it, but Rembrandt's picture of Nicolaes Tulp was different, quite different. It did not merely tell a story. It gave tangible expression of an abstract idea—an idea so all-preponderant that the story connected with it dwindled down to insignificant proportions, like the piece of inconsequential parchment upon which the original of the Sermon on the Mount was first written by those who heard the great prophet lay down the law of human forbearance.

Nicolaes Tulp ceased to be a distinguished and fashionable practitioner in the most opulent town of that period—the brilliant son of a rich father—a clever politician who four times in succession got himself appointed to the highest office in his community—a distinguished anatomist and an executive of no mean talent who had reorganized the entire pharmaceutical system of his own time. Instead, he became the living symbol of that divine curiosity which prying into the secrets of nature may some day set the human race free from most of its manifold ills and miseries.

And the faces of the men around him were no longer those of humdrum hard-working leeches, come hither to learn a few things and perhaps improve their standing in the medical world and charge a little higher fees than before and buy their wives new silken dresses for going-to-meeting. Those eyes looked beyond the corpse stretched out before them. Those eyes saw more than the tendons of a single arm. They were gazing into the mystery that underlies all existence—the one hopeless and eternal mystery: "What was it that made those muscles move?"

I am trying to make my own impression clear to myself and I am afraid that I am not succeeding very well. Nor did I derive much support in my speculations from Rembrandt when we were sitting together one night in the etching room. (Saskia had had a bad attack of coughing but at last she had fallen asleep.) I told him what had happened to me and I grew rather rhetorical and used big words and spoke of art and the mission of art, the way I had heard certain painters and sculptors speak when they spent an evening together at a tavern and some one paid for their drinks.

He was interested, but not particularly interested or surprised.

"You always impressed me as an intelligent person, Doctor," he said, "and those little sketches which you have shown me are quite nice. You may not have learned as much as some of the boys who went to art-school, but the Lord was good to you at birth and you started out with a whole lot more than any of those poor devils will ever get, no matter how hard they work. And yet, here you are, forty years old, or even more, and you have never yet discovered what all truly intelligent people have known since the beginning of time."

"And that is?" I asked him.

"That nothing counts in this world except the inner spirit of things."

"Meaning the immortal soul of man?"

"Meaning the immortal soul of everything that was ever created."

"The immortal soul of tables and chairs and cats and dogs and houses and ships?"

"Just so."

"And the immortal soul of books and scissors and flowers and clouds?"

"Exactly."

I was silent for a while. Then I looked at this strange man with the tired eyes and the tired droop of the strong unwieldy shoulders.

"How many people in all the world will be able to understand that?"

He smiled and lifted up both hands in a gesture of resignation. Then he answered me slowly: "Well, perhaps three or four in every hundred. At the most, four. In very exceptional cases, five."

"And the others?"

"They will never know what we are talking about, but they will have their revenge."

"In what way?"

"They will let us starve to death."

The conversation was rapidly getting beyond my depth.

"Good night," I said, and held out my hand. He took it.

"Good night, Doctor, and thank you and if you have a few moments after dinner to-morrow, say at three or two-thirty, I wish you would come here. There is something I want to show you." And with that he showed me through the hall and bade me good night.

It was a dark night and it was raining. In the house of the Rabbi, a few doors further down, a light was still burning. Menasseh ben Israel was busy with his presses. He was always busy with those presses and people said he printed his books from golden letters. He was a clever man of great learning, a simple and loveable character. For a moment I thought that I would drop in and see what he was doing. But just then the tower of the South Church struck twelve. Bang—bang—bang—bang—

One could write a book about that, I thought. The spirit of the hour-glass, the spirit of the clock. Bang—bang—bang—bang—birth, life and death—happiness, sickness and health—hope and despair—bang—bang—bang—bang.

It was a good mood in which to go to sleep. I pulled my cloak around me a little closer and I turned the corner.

The door of a tavern opened and closed. Drunken voices filled the street.

"Lemme tell you," a man was drooling into the ear of another. "Now, what I am talking about, when a thing is so, it is so, and not otherwise, see? and when a man is so, he is so and that is all there is to him, see?"

"Sure, Jan, I see," the other answered.

"That's good," the tipsy philosopher volunteered, "for if you didn't agree with me that what is so, is so, I'd have knocked your damn head between your shoulders, see?"

The other one said that he did.

I left them to their discussion and I went home.

It was still raining when I lifted the latch.

Chapter 9

REMBRANDT PAINTS A VERY LARGE PICTURE WHICH HE EXPECTS TO MAKE HIM FAMOUS

The next morning I spent at the hospital. Then I went home for dinner and a little after three I called at the Breestraat. The patient was having one of her bad days. Nevertheless she had insisted upon leaving her bed and was sitting in a chair, propped up with many pillows. The child was on her lap. The nurse was busy hanging some clothes to dry near the fire. I had told her not to do the washing in the same room with the sick woman, but of course she had not obeyed my instructions. She grumbled something when I entered, picked up the baby's things, threw them into a wicker basket, slammed the door behind her and left.

"She has one of her terrible days, when I can do nothing with her," Saskia complained. "Sometimes I almost think she is mad."

"I am sorry," I replied, "your husband ought to have discharged her long ago."

"I know it. But he hates to be bothered with such things. He is a good man and he tries to interest himself in the household. But his heart is in his work. And she is very devoted to the baby and you know how little I can do. But soon I shall be better. I feel ever so much stronger than I did a few weeks ago. I looked at myself in the mirror to-day. My cheeks were as red as before I had this attack of a bad cold. Don't you think I look well?"

I assured her that I had never seen her look so beautiful. Nor was it necessary for me to lie. The poor woman had a raging fever and her cheeks were flushed a deep, dark crimson. What she had taken for a sign of new health was merely the harbinger of death. Four months from that day, or at least five or six, she would be resting beneath a slab of granite in the Old Church. It was our duty to make her last few days on earth as happy as possible. I said something nice about the child, who was a very fine boy, but like all children, had an instinctive dislike of sick people and was trying hard to get away.

"Isn't he lovely?" she asked, trying to lift him up but finding him too much for her slender arms. "Oh, he is such a darling! And we are going to make a sailor of him."

"Not a great painter, like his father?"

She slowly shook her head. "No," she said, "I want him to be happy and carefree, and I don't believe artists ever are."

"But surely you cannot doubt that Rembrandt is happy! He has his work. He has you"—I noticed my mistake and hastily tried to correct myself.—"He has you and the baby and . . ." But here she interrupted me. "You were right the first time," she said. "He has his work and in his spare time, he has me and then he dresses me up to look like a princess (which I am not) or like a fairy-queen (which I am even less) and I become part of his work!"

"The most beautiful part," I suggested with a smile.

"Oh, well, it is very kind of you to say that but all the same, I am only part of his work, and never part of his life."

"You became part of his life when you gave him this lovely child."

She looked at me with a puzzled expression. All her cheerfulness left her and her high spirits made way for a sudden fit of melancholia. "Do you really believe that?" she asked me with a puzzled look. "For if I didn't think so myself, I would want to die to-morrow. Now I am contented to wait until the day comes, and I am afraid it will come soon enough."

I tried to contradict her with the usual foolish stories which are the stock-in-trade of our profession, but just then Rembrandt entered the room. He was in great anger and was swearing most heartily.

"The idiot!" he shouted. "The perfectly hopeless, clumsy idiot! I thought that I had at last shown him how to use that press. The last time he soaked the paper until it turned to pulp as soon as one touched it. And now he has put the plate underneath the roller without using any felt. The copper is bent like a hoop. I shall have to do the whole thing over again. I might easily have sold a hundred copies. Old Dominie Anslo is always good for a hundred copies, and the Mennonites don't mind what they spend when it comes to pictures of their preachers."

Saskia held out her hand, a very white and very thin hand, but lovely of shape. "Come and sit down here for a moment, my dear," she asked him. "Why don't you tell the boy to go home? If he is just a common nuisance, you surely don't want him around in your place."

At once her husband's anger vanished. "I had thought of it," he answered, "but the next one would probably be just as bad or even worse. And this one pays me a hundred florins a year for the privilege of being one of my pupils. But I will tell you what I will do. Don't we need some kindling for the fire?"

"We always do."

"Very well. I shall turn him out into the yard to cut wood. I shall tell him that the exercise is good for his biceps and that a painter needs strong muscles. A brilliant idea. And I owe it to you. If I had been left to my own devices for another two minutes, I would have fired him, and now, my good doctor, you and I will take a little walk and I will show you something and perhaps I will tell you something—that is to say, if my wife will let you go for a few minutes?"

Poor Saskia made a faint effort to smile, but it was not a very successful one. The color had once more left her cheeks. She looked wasted and coughed terribly while we carried her back to bed.

"She ought not to be doing so much," I warned when we were out on the street.

Rembrandt shook his head. "I know it," he said, "but how can I keep her in bed when she insists upon getting up? Besides, if I didn't help her, she would call for the nurse."

"I thought you would get rid of the woman?"

"I wanted to. And I tried to. Really, I tried very hard. But it was rather difficult. You see, I am very busy and it would have taken a great deal of time . . ."

I understood. This man knew only one thing in the world and that was his work. He had acquired a household. Sooner or later, we all do, and most of us manage to muddle through. But this poor devil, who was a giant when it came to his own particular form of art, was a miserable little dwarf as soon as he found himself face to face with the silly troubles of daily life. He was willing to try and solve problems of light and dark which no one before him had ever dared to tackle. But when he was called upon to read the riot act to a shrew of a nurse who was a menace to the health of his wife and child, he got frightened and ran away.

Well, we all are as we are and what we are and there is no use trying to change the human race from one thing to another, for it just can't be done. And with this wise reflection I followed my host into the street when he stopped and asked me:

"Do you mind, if before we go to the Amstel we take a short walk through the Jewish quarter? You will see some rare sights." And I answered, "Of course not," and so instead of turning to the left we turned to the right and soon we found ourselves in a world that was as different from the rest of the city as the moon from the sun.

The reason for this strange development in our city was a very simple one. Forty years ago this suburb had been a swamp. Later on it had been drained after a fashion but the houses were still very damp and so they could be rented to no one but the poorest among the poor. Of these there were vast quantities, for ever since we had declared ourselves independent from Spain, our town had been a haven of refuge to tens of thousands of people from every part of the world. Some of them had come because they had heard that we were rich beyond the wildest dreams of avarice and that therefore it was much easier to make a living in Holland than anywhere else. Others belonged to one of the innumerable sects that had sprung up immediately after the Reformation. These had hastened to the great and free Republic because they either hoped to escape persecution at the hands of their enemies or (as happened quite as frequently) because they thought that in a country where the magistrates were reported to be very lenient, they might be able to do a little persecuting of their own.

Then during the eighties of the last century, Portugal had been annexed by Spain and of course the first thing King Philip had done was to pass an edict by which he had deprived his newly acquired territory of the only people who ever thought it worth their while to do a little work.

My grandmother used to tell me how in the nineties, when the first of the Portuguese immigrants began to arrive, people used to flock to the shores of the Y whenever it was reported that a ship with fugitives was about to enter the harbor. And she described the terrible conditions on board those vessels, men and women and children all huddled together with their few belongings (they never were given more than twenty-four hours' warning before they were expelled and were obliged to sell their houses and real estate and their merchandise during those hours besides doing their packing) and how quite often when the hatches were opened it was found that half of them had died or were on the point of passing away from lack of food and drink and fresh air and how the survivors would be taken on shore and given milk and bread and were taken to the houses of private citizens to recuperate, among great manifestations of horror and pity.

And my grandfather, with a noble oath, was apt to interrupt her recital at this point to fulminate against the Reverend Clergy who denounced that sort of public charity because the Jews, some fifteen hundred years before, had killed one of their own prophets. "As if," so the old man tried to defend the Sanhedrin, "there has ever been a people that has not murdered its great men!" And then the old lady would bid him remember that he was a Christian and must not say such things and he would roar with laughter and would say, "A Christian? Me? I am a rebel, a good, honest rebel, and I have fought all my life and I have cursed all my life, and I never let a chance go by to get hold of an honest drink or a dishonest woman, and I have killed my enemies and I have loved my friends and I have hated the Pope of Rome and that bastard Pope of Geneva. Long live the Prince! and when I die, I shall go straight up to God and I shall tell him just what I think of him, and everything he has done to all those I loved and then undoubtedly I shall go to hell and I shall be a rebel there as I have been on earth, but thank the Lord, it won't be as cold there as among the harp-strumming little angels with their freshly laundered petticoats!"

And then these two charming old people would look at each other with great and sincere affection and being very ancient and rather feeble, they would smile a pleasant smile and before you could count three, they would be fast asleep, holding each other's hand as if they had been married only day before yesterday.

They have been dead now for a good many years and the former immigrants have grown rich and have moved to a more fashionable neighborhood. But every year some new recruits arrive from foreign lands and in the part of the town through which Rembrandt took me, one still hears more Spanish and Portuguese and Yiddish and German than Dutch; the shops still look like bazaars and the food continues to smell like the devil. And as for the women who live there, for reasons unknown to the astonished Gentiles, they still persist in shaving their heads and bedecking themselves with wigs that are as silly as they are unbecoming.

I had rarely visited this Little Jerusalem, for these people have their own doctors (very good ones, too, though they favor some extraordinary remedies) and whenever I had time for a little fresh air, I preferred to go to the harbor and watch the ships come in. But Rembrandt seemed to know this part of the town by heart and was apparently on speaking terms with half the population, for wherever we went, he was greeted with great obsequiousness and caps were taken off to "der Meister" as if he had been a burgomaster or some great official instead of being merely a painter.

But he explained it to me at once. "Don't think for a moment that they are so civil because they have the slightest understanding for my work. I am a good customer. I pay cash whenever I can and I don't bargain more than is necessary. That is all." And then he told me that this ghetto was a veritable treasure-house and contained more color than all the rest of Amsterdam put together.

"You know how it is," he said, stepping aside to avoid the contents of an unmentionable piece of domestic furniture which was being emptied from a second-story window, "our civilization is drab and gray. We seem to regard color as an expression of the sinful flesh. Our men are dressed in black, our women are dressed in black, our children are dressed in black, our churches look like white-washed sepulchers. When we give a party, we all sit around with sour faces until we get very drunk, and then we behave as Jan Steen shows us in his pictures, and a clever boy he is, too, even if he came from Leyden, the same as I do. I wish that I knew something more about my own family. I don't mean my brothers and sisters. They are good people, but they don't interest me, and to tell you the truth, they are pretty common-place. My grandparents, too, were dull, small trades-people from a village near Leyden. They had never been anywhere. They had never seen anything. But how about my great-grandparents or still further back? Was there ever an Italian in our family or even a Fleming? For they tell me that the Flemings are much more lively than we are. I bought a picture of Rubens once and it was wonderful! Then again, our religion may have something to do with it. It is hard to tell. I have known a few old people who could remember back to the days before Amsterdam and Leyden had gone reformed. They say that life was much gayer then than now. It was not very pleasant to have quite so many priests and deacons and monks wandering aimlessly through the streets, but if you left them alone, they left you alone and provided you went to mass once in a long while, no questions were asked. To-day, every time you smile, some one comes around to read you a couple of chapters from Job, just as a warning. Of course, in the end, the Church had to go. We are a slow-moving people and we don't think very fast but at least we think. All that had to disappear, but I sometimes wonder whether I would not have been happier if I had been born in Italy."

"Did you ever think of going there?"

"Of course I did. Every youngster who paints thinks of going to Italy at some time in his career."

"But you never went?"

"No. I thought of it seriously in '31. I even talked it over with Jan Lievens when we were studying together in Leyden. We could have got the money too. That malt-mill of my father was not doing badly at all and there were some rich people who were taking an interest in us. But it seemed a waste of time. I was very unhappy in those days and did not think that I would live long. I wanted to use every hour of daylight and could not afford to waste a couple of months trying to get to a place where the daylight probably was not so very different from what it is here. Of course there have been some great masters in Italy. But I can see their work just as well in Amsterdam as in Rome. They bring it to us by the ship loads. I have copied quite a number of them. They are being sold as genuine, but, then, our art dealers would sell pictures by St. Luke himself if they saw a chance to make a profit. Funny that the only apostle who was not a Jew should have done so much to make the Jews rich, with all due respect to my dear cousin Uylenburgh, for he is in the art business too. And so am I, in a way, for a few days ago I let him have another thousand guilders. What he has done with it, I don't know, but I will sell you my claim for half of what I paid!"

While this conversation was going on, we had almost reached the outskirts of the Jewish quarter and I asked Rembrandt whether he hadn't forgotten that he was bound upon some errand.

"I know," he answered, "but that is in still another part of the town. I just instinctively turn to this warren whenever I go out. But I am after something better to-day than I can find here. I think that I have got hold of a genuine bit by Michelangelo. I have only seen it once. Then they asked too much for it. It is a small thing, the head of a child. If they will let me have it for fifteen hundred guilders, I shall take it."

He mentioned the sum as casually as if it had been a couple of shillings. I had heard that he got a great deal more for his portraits than any one else and of course everybody knew that he had married a rich wife, but I was not quite prepared for such nonchalance. The habits of my very simple childhood stuck to me pretty closely and I asked whether that was not a great deal of money for one picture. He seemed a bit surprised at the question but answered that he did not think so.

"I suppose, when you look at it from one point of view, it is a good deal of money. But Michelanglo was a very wonderful painter. No, I don't think fifteen hundred guilders is too much. I am getting more than that myself."

"For a single picture?"

"Yes, and if you will have patience with me for a few minutes longer, I will show it to you. But first I must go down the cellar for a little light."

The "cellar" to which he referred when we came to it proved to be the basement of the old archery-house on the Singel. The archers had long since been blown out of existence by the musketeers and their club-house was now merely a sort of better class tavern, where one was allowed to look at the pictures of famous old warriors in exchange for a bottle of wine or a few glasses of beer. The top floor of the building was rented to a glove merchant who used the attics to dry his skins and in the basement (as I now saw for the first time) there was an antique shop, run by a Jew whose name was mentioned on a sign outside the door, but it was so covered with dirt which obliging children had smeared upon it that I could not read it. This worthy man was garbed in a long cloak that reached to the floor and beyond, so that he was continually tripping over his own garment. It looked like a relic from the flood and had seen very little water since that day Mount Ararat once more raised its summit from among the waves. As the rooms were very dark and the owner of the premises hid his face behind very black and very bushy whiskers, one was continually bumping up against him and he was forever begging one's pardon in a jargon compounded of two thirds Portuguese, one sixth German and one sixth Dutch with a liberal sprinkling of what I took to be the original language of King David's psalms.

I discovered to my great amazement that Rembrandt not only understood this home-made dialect, but actually spoke it with great fluency for once the product of Michelangelo's brush had been produced from a corner where the darkness was not only visible but also tangible, he addressed himself to the hirsute dealer in such an eloquent mixture of all the less current vituperations of the different tongues just enumerated, that I was quite sure the two men must come to blows at any moment, in which case I decided that I would not take sides, but would make for the exit with all possible speed. But nothing happened. On the contrary, after half an hour's animated conversation, during which (as far as I was able to comprehend) frequent references were made to the immediate ancestors of the contending parties, they separated in the best of spirits. Rembrandt had succeeded in forcing the price down by one hundred florins. But the art-dealer from his side had persuaded him to buy the frame, which he swore was worth two hundred guilders, but which he would let him have for half the amount. The whole transaction therefore, as far as I could see, remained in the statu quo ante. Each party to the deal, however, seemed profoundly convinced that he had got the better of his opponent. Wherefore everybody was happy and we parted with mutual expressions of esteem and a promise to return as soon as there was another bargain to be had.

The fresh air was pleasant after this entrance to purgatory. I awaited some explanation of the mysterious proceedings that had taken place in the catacombs of art, and I got one.

"I wanted that picture," Rembrandt confessed, "and I wanted it badly. The old Jew asked too much. I got it for a hundred guilders less."

"But the frame! How about that frame? He charged you a hundred guilders for it."

The poor painter looked puzzled, like a child that has been caught in some foolish expenditure of a hard-earned stiver. But he quickly recovered. "After all," he asked in a somewhat querulous tone, as if I had unjustly accused him of wasting his son's patrimony, "what is the money for in this world of ours except to spend it? Fifteen hundred guilders is rather a large sum. But next week, next month, at the very least, I shall have eighteen hundred florins coming in for some work I have just finished. And I did want that painting and I wanted it badly!"

With which irrefutable piece of logic we retraced our steps whence we had come, crossed the Rokin and then turned to the right until we reached the Amstel. In the olden days, before the great expansion that followed in the wake of our declaration of independence, this had been the outer limit of the city's territory. There had been only a few scattered houses along the banks of the stream (it really was a canal, but our poets loved to compare it to the Tiber or the Seine or the Thames) and the gardens and open spaces had been much in demand by the archers of the old militia companies who used to come together here on Sunday afternoons for target practice.

During the latter half of the fifteenth century, when all the little cities of our country fought each other (just as the nations nowadays are forever making war upon their neighbors) a heavy bulwark had been erected at this point. The name of one enormous stone tower which still stood intact and was called "Swijght-Utrecht" or "Keep-Quiet-Utrecht," showed only too clearly from what side danger had threatened our forefathers. The Bishop of Utrecht was no longer a menace for he had ceased to exist shortly after the construction of this dungeon and the walls now extended far beyond the other side of the Amstel. But the brick monster continued to stand where it had been built in the year 1482. But it was now a perfectly peaceful part of the famous Kloveniersdoelen, the meeting-place and club-house of the culverin-carrying town companies which had succeeded the archers of medieval fame as soon as gunpowder had been invented.

During the great war of independence, those town companies had rendered the most signal services. Without them we never would have been able to gain our freedom, for the German and the Swiss and English mercenaries whom we hired to fight for us from time to time were professionals who had nothing much to gain and everything to lose and in nine cases out of ten they disappeared when the fighting began and did not return until the signal had been given to begin looting.

Of course twenty years ago, when all those things I am here writing down happened, there was no longer a single enemy within a hundred miles of Amsterdam, except an occasional prisoner-of-war, brought in by the fleet. But every self-respecting young man thought it his duty to join one of the town companies and devote some of his spare time to the practice of arms. That many of those militia regiments were rapidly degenerating into mere social organizations, without the slightest military ambition or strategic value, was becoming more evident almost every day. But such a development seems inevitable (if the history I have read means anything at all, which I sometimes doubt) and in order to be perfectly fair, I ought to state that several crack companies took their duties just as seriously as their fathers and grandfathers had done before them and certainly in the year 1650 when William II made his dastardly attack upon our beloved city, they proved that they were fully able to handle the situation and forced the foolish princeling to return whence he had come with no other glory than a pair of wet feet. And during the early forties (and please remember that I am telling you about certain events that happened in the year 1642 and therefore a very long time ago) there was a sudden return of interest in the noble profession of arms.

The different companies were trying hard to attract desirable recruits and all the social and economic advantages of associating one's self with this or that or the other captain were carefully enumerated and made a subject of conversation in all of the better-class taverns. (The more notorious dram-shops were equally interested, but from a somewhat different angle, as the town-militia was also the town-police and the sworn enemy of all lawbreakers and rioters.)

Now since the beginning of time, it has been the proud privilege of the children of Mars to be more resplendent in their outer raiment than ordinary citizens, who follow a peaceful if more lucrative and useful profession. Nature, when she began her interesting task, bestowed her gifts of beauty and attractiveness almost exclusively upon the male members of the different sorts of animals. I do not claim that I have an inner knowledge of her secret intentions, but she probably thought that it would be better for the future development of her menagerie if the males should be more attractive than the females and if the competition for favors should not come too exclusively from one side. But when she finally came to the human race, she had either grown tired or had become discouraged, for she changed her policy completely and arranged things in such a way that among us mortals the woman should be the attractive member of society, while the man might look like anything or nothing at all. The women of course have made the best of their advantage while we poor men are still trying (though mostly in vain) to find some compromise by which we would be able to make ourselves a little less painfully plain than we were apparently meant to be. Scholars and other learned doctors put on beautiful silken garments whenever they can find an excuse for doing so. Judges affect scarlet and ermine. I have never seen a priest of the old church in his official garments, for they are not allowed in our city, but from the stories of my grandmother, I judge that the multi-colored coat of Joseph was as nothing compared to an archbishop or a cardinal in full canonicals. That old church, by the way, was very wise in more ways than one and it recognized the need of the average human being to revel in color once in a while by providing a special season when every clodhopper and lout was allowed to dress up like a royal duke and strut about like a lovesick peacock.

But the soldiers have understood the value of a gaudy appearance better than any one else. With them, it probably was a matter of necessity. Their profession, except in times of peace, offered few advantages. Endless marches along hot and dusty roads, bad sleeping-quarters, poor food and the danger every moment of losing an arm or a leg or getting a ball through one's brain. There had to be some compensation to attract the unwary and beguile the simple minded into taking the king's shilling.

Of course this could have been accomplished by raising the men's wages, but then the officers no longer would have been able to regard their regiments as profitable sources of revenue and they would have asked for better pay for themselves and all the royal treasuries of Europe would have gone bankrupt. Also as an inducement to enlistening discipline might have been slightly relaxed and there might have been a little less flogging and hanging, but this would have been impossible in view of the sort of people who took most readily to the business of organized murder. The easiest way out was to allow these honorable jail-birds and paupers (and when I call them that I surely offer no insult to the average members of a regiment of mercenaries) to garb themselves as if they were really fine fellows, instead of being mere deplorable cannon-fodder. This gave them a feeling of superiority and the average man will go through almost any hardships and will suffer every form of indignity and degradation if in the end he is allowed to feel himself (if only for a moment) superior to his fellow-beings.

This incidentally accounts for the noble behavior of so many criminals on the scaffold. By assuming an attitude of noble resignation, they place themselves hand and foot above the mob of jeering hoodlums who surround the gallows and they jump off the ladder, saying to themselves, "Ah, what a fine fellow I am, compared to this rabble!" It also accounts for the readiness of hundreds of thousands of poor yokels who leave their plows and the simple pleasures of an humble rustic life to prance about dressed in plumes and gold braid for one hour each day, though they are forced to obey the whims of a drunken and bullying drill-sergeant for the other twenty-three.

I hope that all my medical diagnoses may be as correct as this estimate of the motives that inspired the brave heroes who used to strut down our streets whenever we were obliged to hire extra troops for our operations against the Spaniards. It will be understood that I am not now talking of the ordinary citizen who, exasperated by the endless hangings and quarterings of our dear Liege Lord finally rose in open rebellion.

They fought because they had to, just as they would go and work on the dikes whenever their city was threatened by floods. It was a matter of live or die and quite naturally they preferred to take a chance at living, even if they had to expose themselves to a little occasional dying in order to accomplish this very sensible purpose. But there was very little outer glory connected with their martial careers. I am too young to have known many of these men myself, but I have seen their pictures, honest, simple citizens, butchers and bakers and shipowners with honest, plain faces and great big hands that could cleave an ox or pull a sail as well as the best of them. Their officers would perhaps wear an orange scarf to set them apart from the rest of their men, but that would be the only bit of color in the whole picture.

But to-day, whenever a company sallies forth to guard a gate that really needs no guarding, or patrol a wall that is as safe as my own back yard, both the common soldiers and the lieutenants and captains resemble warships on parade. They have plumes on their hats and gold braid on their coats and they wrap themselves up in yards and yards of colored scarfs and every sixth man waves a flag that is as big as a house and the servant girls and the scullery maids leave their kitchens to stare at these gallant heroes and to admire them and to giggle at them and the poor fools feel flattered by these basement attentions and spend a night shivering in a guard-house (instead of snoring comfortably by the side of their spouses) and they will repeat the performance next week and week after and week after merely for this short period of popular glory. And when they get themselves painted, they pose around a table that looks as if great King Louis of France were entertaining the Ambassador from the Republic of Venice, and they are all of them dressed up as if they were the keepers of the harem of the Grand Padisha of Turkey and they dine on dishes that our grandfathers would have regarded as the last word in useless luxury and altogether they disport themselves as if they were the sort of young British lords who once in a while honor our city with their visit and they tell me that the artists have to send to Paris to get some of the gilt that has to be laid on the swords and arquebuses.

All of which many and varied meditations passed rapidly through my brain as we were walking in the general direction of the Kloveniersdoelen, for I knew that it was used as a meeting place by some of the smartest regiments and that the captains' rooms were filled with pictures by van der Helst and Govaert Slinck and Claes Elias and I feared that Rembrandt, having started the day bright and early by buying himself a genuine Michelangelo, might wind up the afternoon by dragging me through one of those things I dread most of all—a picture gallery.

And when he stood in front of the entrance-gate and he said: "Let us go in here a moment," the worst of my fears was about to be realized. These buildings had been added to so often and they were by now composed of so many remnants of walls and towers, bits of old walls and decapitated pieces of even older private houses, that one almost needed a guide to find one's way. But Rembrandt opened the door of the taproom (no military club-house has ever been perfect without a well-provided bar) and said: "It has been quite a walk. You will like a glass of beer. I am not a member of this honorable guild, but I have worked here on and off for quite a long time and they let me use their common-room. Come in."

We sat down and Rembrandt ordered two mugs of beer. Then he said: "You must be hungry! You are not? Do you mind if I eat something? The meals at home have become a little sketchy since Saskia was taken sick and I have had nothing all day and so if you will pardon me . . ." and he asked that they bring him a plate of fried eggs and one of fresh herring and some bread and he went after the food with a most excellent appetite and between the beer and the fish he told me why he had brought me there.

"I don't want to talk about myself," he said, "but these last four years have been rather lonely and I have had a pretty hard struggle, what with an ailing wife, a pretty difficult family-in-law, a new house which is really much too big and expensive for me, and a few other little items with which I shan't bother you, as you probably have troubles enough of your own. But I shall tell you something and then you will know what is going to happen. It is always pleasant to be on the inside of things. It makes one feel that one really is somebody. And something very interesting is going to happen here soon. Are you sure you don't want any of this herring? It is exceedingly good. But never mind, and here is my story.

"You know that I come from very simple folk. And you know how they look upon such things in our Republic. In Flanders, they think so much of Rubens that they make him an ambassador. They tell me *there* is a man in Spain by the name of Velasquez who is said to be the greatest painter that ever lived. I have never seen anything he did, but I have heard that he can make an empty room look really like an empty room and that is the hardest thing of all. I may learn to do that too, but it will take me another twenty years of practice. But I hear that this Don Diego Velasquez is held in such great esteem that he is allowed to sit in the presence of the King, when all other courtiers, even the highest nobles in the land, must stand and do homage. And when he is in Rome, the Pope is happy to receive him and invite him to live in the private villa of the Medici family.

"Well, we can't all be the same in this world and every country handles such matters according to its own notions of what is right and suitable and what is not. Here people look upon an artist as a better-class laboring man. Some of us make money. None of us are rich, but some of us get fairly good wages, not any better than those which a dike-worker or a book-keeper or a baker's assistant makes with much less trouble. And so our parents don't mind and are rather proud of their little boy who is sometimes allowed to associate with gentlemen, that is, when he is allowed to paint their portraits, though of course they always fear that in the end he will share the fate of Roghman or old Hercules Seghers and die in the alms-house or break his neck in a grog-shop.

"That these poor fellows came to such an end because their neighbors were too dull to appreciate them, that never seems to dawn upon them. They think it a good joke that Hercules finally had to paint his pictures on his old shirts and the back of his old breeches and had to sell his etchings to the butchers of the Rokin for wrapping-paper. 'My steak came this morning, packed in Tobias and the Angel,' says one, and his friend roared with laughter and answers: 'I bought a landscape the other day, paid five guilders for it—it was on a piece of the old man's pants. Ha! ha! ha!' And they go and put a thousand or ten thousand guilders in a 'sure' investment that some one sells them on the say-so of his grandfather who knew a man who had met a Spaniard or a Pole who had told him that he had heard from some one, whose name he could not remember, that it was a good thing.

"You know this to be so and I know it to be so and all of us know it to be so, but I for one had seen enough of poverty not to want any more of it than I had to have. Some people can stand misery better than others. I loved old Seghers. He was a great man. Hercules has forgotten more about painting and etching than most of us will ever know. I was a youngster and he was quite an old man when I first came to Amsterdam and I did not see him often. But one night I went to his place with a few friends. A bare room with a horrible-looking woman in one corner doing something to a large stone jar filled with vegetables. She seemed to be his wife. Half a dozen dirty children on the floor and the old man with a pleasant bun on, completely oblivious of the mess around him, working at a storm, as fine a piece of painting as I have ever seen. He had fastened it against the wall with two nails and he stood in front of it. The wife wanted to know what we had come for and asked me whether we were sheriffs?

"That afternoon, the Jew with whom he did business had brought him back his last etching, the finest piece of work he had ever done. Sorry, but he could not sell it. And Hercules had taken a copper file and had cut the plate into four pieces because he could not afford a new one and must work. He was crazy with work. He worked morning, noon and night. They say he was a drunkard. Well, drunken people don't paint the sort of pictures he did. But sometimes it got to be too much for him and then he would take a glass or two, just enough not to hear the bawling wife and the howling infants.

"That afternoon, it seemed, while she had gone out to pawn his easel, he had stolen the last sheet out of the children's bed and had cut it up to be used as canvas. I shall spare you the rest. I was not very rich then and, anyway, he had nothing for sale as everything had been either pawned or had been bartered away for butter and eggs and milk for the children. Afterwards, with a great deal of trouble, I got hold of six of his pictures. You may have seen them in my house. One of them is hanging in the front hall and one in the side room and a few others in the little alcove behind the side room. I keep them all over the house, in the first place because I like them immensely and in the second place because they are a constant reminder. They take me back to the day when I stood in Seghers' stable (it really wasn't a house he was living in) and said to myself: 'Rembrandt, my boy, you are a good deal of a dreamer and you are apt to do foolish things. Well, do all the foolish things you want, but see that you get paid well in the meantime. A plumber and a coppersmith get paid for what they do. See to it that you get paid too.'

"Besides, I need a lot of money. I like color around me. I need it. I would have died in a place like that of Hercules in less than a week. I want to buy things. I hate haggling. I hate to beat old Jacob down for a couple of guilders. And when I go to an auction and see something I would like for my collection, I go ahead and let them push up the price and I know that in the end I will probably pay more than the thing is worth, but I have to have it, and that is all, for when I want something, I want it then and there and not next week or a year later. I must be able to make experiments if I am to do good work. Saskia is a lovely woman. You ought to have seen her a couple of years ago when she was still a girl and before she got so sick. But I must try her out, test her, so to speak, see what is in her, dress her up in silks and satins and hang pearls on her and rubies, paint her a hundred different ways. Poor child, I don't think she always enjoyed it. But she was very good-natured about it. I needed that sort of foolishness to find out what I could do and she said yes. She is really very sweet. She always says yes and I suppose at times, I am very unreasonable. All that is, however, beside the point and I will tell you what I am going to do. Want to smoke?"

The herring was gone and the fried eggs were gone and the beer was gone and I said: "Yes, I would enjoy a pipe." And so Rembrandt ordered two fresh mugs and two pipes of tobacco and then he leaned his elbows on the table and leaned over to me and went on:

"You know that I have been doing a great deal of portrait work. I could give you names, but they are neither here nor there. People came to me to sit for their portraits. I painted them and they paid me four or five and sometimes even six hundred guilders. I don't know why. Even van der Helst never got more than that amount for a picture as big as a house with a dozen or twenty figures and that meant a lot more work than I had to do, for each one of those twenty fools would think that he was the handsomest of the crowd and would insist upon being done in great detail. So you see I was about the only one who had no kick coming. I was even asked to do some pictures for the Prince. I don't think he liked them any too well for I believe that His Highness is more interested in the pretty ladies of Jake Jordaens than in religious subjects and I hear that he is going to build himself a new palace in the woods and that he is going to use no one but Flemish painters. But that may be just studio gossip. You know how much there is of that nowadays and I finally got paid, though I had the devil's own time collecting and I would never have got a penny if it had not been that My Lord Huygens, who thinks all the world of my work, had got the bills approved.

"But what I mean is this: everybody had heard of me and it became the fashion for rich people to have themselves painted by me.

"'Very well,' I used to say to myself, 'I shall paint you and sometimes I shall even paint you as you want to be painted.'

"For I needed the money. Our first child was coming. There was the new house into which I wanted to move (I had to mortgage it rather heavily) and there were all the other things I wanted. People used to say that I was a lucky devil because I had married a rich wife. But Saskia was not rich. There were nine children and old Uylenburgh had been too busy with politics to pay much attention to his estate. I have never seen him, for he died some eight years before I met my wife.

"The old fellow was quite a famous character. You must have heard of him. He was dining with Prince William the day he was called away from the table and was shot by what's-his-name, that friend of the Jesuits whom King Philip hired to murder him. Then he was burgomaster of Leeuwarden and sheriff but he was so busy with public affairs he had very little time to look after his own interests.

"When he died, each of the children was supposed to get about forty thousand guilders. Quite a sum, I grant you, and my neighbors of course added an extra couple of zero's and made it four hundred thousand. They might have made it forty million florins, for all the actual cash we ever saw. For everything was invested in farms and houses and as soon as we wanted to divide the estate, the farms could not be rented and the houses could not be sold. And of course I am living here in Amsterdam and the other heirs are living in Friesland, a couple of days away.

"Did you ever have anything to do with Frisians? A strange race. The most obstinate and pig-headed people there are in the world. And stingy! My God! Only a couple of years ago I had to go to law to get a few thousand guilders that an aunt had left her in '34. Six whole years of waiting. When we finally got it, the other heirs tried to cheat us out of the interest—out of six years' accumulated interest—and I had to hire a lawyer and spend two hundred guilders on fees before my wife could pry a penny loose from those dear relatives of hers.

"They are a nice tribe! They kiss every stiver a dozen times before they spend it and when I made a lot of money painting portraits and bought a few pictures and statues and things (just because I liked them, and after all, it was my money I spent and not theirs, so why should they worry?) they must jabber to all the neighbors about the 'scandalous way in which I was squandering Saskia's patrimony' and I had to go to law once more and sue them for libel and then they perjured themselves all over the place and the judge said that he could not do anything and threw the case out of court.

"Did that stop them? Of course not. They went right on and I had to bring suit once more in Friesland before I heard the last of this famous 'squandering of my wife's patrimony.' Squandering, indeed! When I need thirteen thousand guilders cash to buy the house in the Breestraat, I have to give notes that will keep me busy for the rest of my days. Do you think I would have done that if I could have laid my hands on a little cash? No, that story of the poor painter and the rich wife is so much moonshine. We are not poor, and I have enough to keep living the way I want to live, but I intend to be careful.

"Only you know how it is! I get interested in a subject. I see or rather I feel a lot of things others don't see or don't feel. I put them into my picture and the man who sat for his portrait and considered himself a fine fellow gets angry, says the likeness is not there or I have given him a look in his eyes that will prove to his neighbors that he is a miser or mean to his wife, and in the end he either refuses the picture or he will offer to pay me half of what he promised.

"This won't do, for just now I am not only painting for the sake of my 'art'—whatever that may mean—though you will hear a lot about it if to-night you will go to the Dirty Towel or the Dark Cellar and will listen to the brethren of the brush who come together there every evening to drink their beer and talk of their plans. No, just now I want to make all the money I can. I have got to pay for that house and Saskia will probably be sick for quite a long time and the boy will have to go to a good school and to the University afterwards.

"Besides you know how it is; there exists a fashion in portrait-painters as well as a fashion in women's clothes. I have been the fashion now for several years and I know what many people are hoping to say soon: 'Oh, yes, that man van Rijn! He was quite good a little while ago, but he has lost something of his old—well, what shall we call it?—of his old pep and stamina.' And what they mean of course is that I am beginning to paint them as they are and no longer as they want to think that they are and now I will show you— Hey there, Hendrick, bring me the bill for what we have had. Thank you!—I shall now take you upstairs, and I shall show you."

Hendrick dutifully brought the bill, observed that it was remarkably good weather for the time of year (since it had not rained for almost three entire days) pocketed the change without Rembrandt paying the slightest attention to him, and bowed us out of the door. We then turned towards the left, walked up two flights of broad and comfortable stairs and came into a large room which was used as an assembly hall whenever some important matter made it necessary to call the entire company together. It was quite dark when we entered. The high windows were covered with green baize curtains. On the walls I vaguely noticed one or two pictures—large pictures—the usual company-portraits that one would expect to find in such places. Then, when my eyes got accustomed to the dim light I saw that at the other end of the hall there was a vast wooden structure, supporting an enormous canvas, the most gigantic picture I had ever seen, but what it was meant to represent I could not make out.

Suddenly Rembrandt pulled the curtains aside and the room was flooded with brilliant sunlight and I suffered a physical shock, as if I had been struck in the face by a palette full of the richest colors ever devised by the hand of man. Homer, who undoubtedly was the greatest master of the word that ever lived, might have been able to revaluate an impression like that into terms of words. Dante would have mumbled something divine but obscure. Montaigne would have smiled and kept silent, but I, being only a humble leech, and a simple Hollander could only say one word: "Damnation!"

Whereupon Rembrandt, who was not given much to outward manifestations of affection, threw both his arms around me and shouted: "Splendid! For now at least I know that one person has understood what I meant to do."

And then he pulled a heavy bench in front of the picture, once more closed the curtains that were furthest away from the picture (thereby fairly forcing the figure in white in the center of the painting to march right out of the frame), made me sit down, himself sat down with his elbows on his knees, rested his chin in the palms of his hands (a favorite position of his whenever he was thinking very hard) and said:

"Now you know why I dragged you up here. This is my chance! My great chance! It came to me by accident. The company of Captain Banning Cocq was going to have its portrait done. First they talked of van der Helst doing it and then some one wanted Flinck and some others wanted some one else again but one day My Lord of Purmerend came to me and said he had seen the portrait I had done of the mother of Jan Six and the one of Dominie Anslo and his wife and he liked the way in which I had arranged the good dominie and his wife, with the books on the table and the man talking to the woman—not two people just sitting, but a husband and wife really talking to each other and being interested too in what was being said—and he had had an idea. His company wanted to have its picture painted. Most of the men wanted the usual thing—soldiers and officers all grouped around a table with a couple of pewter plates filled with dead oysters and a lot of wine bottles—everybody looking very proud and very brave and slightly the worse for having eaten so much. What he wanted to know—hadn't this sort of thing been done a little too often? Wasn't there some other way in which such a picture could be painted?

"Well, at first I was a little frightened by the idea. For I had never tried my hand at large groups of people. But then I said that I would try if he gave me a few days to think it over. He answered that he would be delighted and would I come and see him when I was ready.

"So I set to work, but most of the sketches I did not like at all and I threw them away. And then suddenly it came to me, as I told you coming up here, that those regiments of volunteers don't mean so very much in our day. As a rule they are just an excuse for pleasant social gatherings. But that is because we are living in times of peace. Probably if there were another war (of course I know we are still at war with Spain, but who cares? The Spaniards are broke and we are rich and we can hire all the men in the whole wide world and let them do our fighting for us.) If there were another war they would once more amount to something. And there is a very definite ideal hidden somewhere in the idea of an 'armed citizenry.'

"It is easy to poke fun at those pompous house-painters and gin-distillers and fish-mongers marching forth in plumes and feathers, toting heavy swords and lances and carrying gigantic arquebuses and powder-horns as if they were going to drive the Turks out of Europe when all of us know that they are going to spend the greater part of the night throwing dice in the guard-house and drinking small beer for no more serious purpose than to prevent the peasant women from Buiksloot and the Beemster from smuggling their butter and eggs and chickens past the revenue officer at the city gate.

"But that is only part of the story and by no means the most interesting part. Those men are the sons and the grandchildren of just such house-painters and gin-distillers and fish-dealers who got hanged and burned and broken on the wheel, fighting for something that was on their conscience, something that had nothing at all to do with selling gin or codfish or printing-houses, for God knows, they could have done that just as well while they were being ruled by a king as while they were being ruled by Their Lordships of the Town Hall. There was something in them somewhere, that made them rather fine and noble. Well, if it was there, I was going to find it and paint it.

"And so I went to see My Lord of Purmerend one evening in his house on the Singel (you know the big one with the dolphin which de Keyser built originally for his father-in-law, the old burgomaster) and he was most kind to me and even introduced me to his family and then we sat in his office and I took some paper (I can't talk without drawing at the same time) and I explained to him what I wanted to do—paint him and his men just as they were leaving the arsenal for a turn of duty—everything still in great disorder, one old fellow beating the alarm and some of the soldiers taking down their pikes and others getting their guns ready and little boys and little girls getting out from underneath the feet of the men (there are always a couple of kids running around on such occasions) and the inevitable dog that is present at every parade and always in the midst of it and one Man who is The Leader—one man who has himself in hand and who knows what he is doing, who is quietly going ahead because he realizes that the others will follow no matter what he does.

"I am not quite sure that I am making myself clear. But you told me that you had liked my picture of Nicolaes Tulp. Well, in that case I did not paint a learned doctor giving a lesson in anatomy. I tried to make it mean something a little more general—a little more abstract, if you allow me to use one of the big words of your French friend, the Count. I tried to paint science, rather than a group of scientists. Just as here I have done my best to give one an impression of 'civic duty' rather than merely show them a number of inconsequential citizens doing their own little particular duties. Do you follow me?"

I did follow him. I followed him so well that for a moment I could say nothing in reply. It is strange that anything that is really "perfect" affects me that way. Most people when they see a perfect sunset or hear a perfect song or see a perfectly beautiful woman, grow eloquent—shout —wave their arms—climb on chairs—feel that they must do something, anything at all, to let the world know how deeply they have been impressed.

With me, it works the other way.

I grow absolutely dumb and can't say a word.

If anybody interrupts my gloomy meditation, I will curse him as if I were the stevedore of some Indiaman who had slipped on the gang-plank and had dropped a bale of rice on his own feet. Then I fall back into that utter silence of desperation which overtakes me whenever I happen to find myself face to face with something really beautiful and only after hours of silent wandering along the back streets or sitting alone in a darkened room, am I able to regain my normal composure.

But Rembrandt, who was not always the most tactful of men and apt to be rather brusque and short-tempered, seemed to understand what had happened to me, for he found an excuse to bid me farewell.

"It is getting late," he said. "I just heard the chimes play and I think the clock struck six. I shall run back home and see how poor Saskia is faring. I am sorry that I have taken so much of your time, but now you will understand why I brought you here. I had to do something really big, something tremendous, to make the people see what I can accomplish when they give me free rein. And this picture will do it. The world will hear about the trick. I shall have more customers than ever. I shall be able to make experiments. I shall have greater freedom than ever before and all through this picture, for, mark my words, it will make people talk."

Chapter 10

AND AS A RESULT OF THIS PICTURE REMBRANDT BECOMES THE JOKE OF AMSTERDAM

Rembrandt was right.
People talked about his picture.
As a matter of fact, they have not stopped talking yet.
The first result of this "new departure in artistic arrangement," of this attempt "to put an idea into colors" and "translate an emotion into lights and shades" was a gigantic roar of laughter. The members of Captain Cocq's company started it. Their wives and children laughed next. Then their sweethearts laughed. Soon the whole town laughed and then quite suddenly the victims of this "unseemly hoax" ceased to be quite as hilarious as they had been in the beginning. For a joke could be carried too far and they were the ones who would have to pay, weren't they? And pay for what? That is what they asked each other and asked all those willing to listen.
Pay a hundred or two hundred guilders apiece for the privilege of having the back of their heads shown or their feet or one hand or one shoulder?
Pay a hundred or two hundred guilders for the honor of being a dim, unrecognizable figure, amidst a number of dim, unrecognizable figures in the dark recesses of an enormous gate, "a piece of animated shade," as one funny observer remarked, while others who had not paid a penny more had been placed right in the center of the stage and in the full light of day?
What had that poor fool tried to do, anyhow?
What had he been thinking of while he was painting this picture?
Surely one man's money was as good as the next!
And when one had paid one's share, one was entitled to as good treatment as one's neighbor. This business of showing favors would never do. Not if they, the soldiers, knew anything about it. They were not such simpletons as this stranger seemed to think. There had been pictures of boards of regents and military companies in Amsterdam long before this smart young man had left his native mill in the distant town of Leyden to come and tell the benighted people of the metropolis how (in his opinion) the thing ought to be done. All he had to do, if he really cared to find out (but he probably thought that he knew better than any one else) was to pay a visit to the Town Hall or to the orphan asylums or to any of the guild houses. He would then see what the customers who paid him their hard-earned guilders had a right to expect from the

artist they employed, and so on and so forth, with a great deal of talk of "going to law about it" and downright refusals to pay money for value not received.

But it was not only the rabble in the street who talked that way. Men and women who surely ought to have known better joined in the chorus of abuse. Vondel, our great poet, driven to despair by those bright peasant lads who disguised as ministers of the Gospel and shepherds of the human soul were every whit as narrow-minded and intolerant as the worst of the ancient Inquisitors, had bade farewell to the Calvinist community a year or so before and had boldly proclaimed his return to the church of his fathers. I can't exactly say that his friends were pleased. My Lord Hooft of Muiden bade him never darken his door again. That seemed rather superfluous and I made bold to tell him so one day when he had asked Jean-Louys and myself to visit him at his charming old castle where he kept open house over the week-end and with a rare gift for the social amenities of life entertained poets and painters and musicians without ever letting them fly at each other's throats.

"How happens it," I asked him, "that you, My Lord, a true liberal in mind and thought and act, now take the side of those who think a man's conduct should be judged by the religious company he keeps?"

"Stuff and nonsense!" he replied. "I got irritated because that foolish old poet made such a great to-do about his so-called conversion. Calvinism is a curse. I agree with him fully. It is a curse which eventually will destroy us. But the Roman creed that went before was just as bad. Neither of them ever seemed to have heard of a certain Jesus of Nazareth who bade us love each other and be of good will to our neighbors. Now I can understand a man who comes to me and says: 'Sir, I have the measles. I don't like them. And so I want to go ahead and be cured.' But I can't follow him when he whines: 'I have got the measles, I don't like them and therefore I think that I will exchange them for the small-pox.'"

That being more or less the attitude of most of his former friends, the poor fellow, who besides had just lost his wife and had found himself all alone in the world with a good-for-nothing scoundrel of a son, began to growl and snarl at everybody and everything, as an outlet for his own misery and self-reproach. Besides, like so many of his kind, the poor poet was of a very jealous disposition, and being some twenty years older than Rembrandt, he had never forgiven him that he, the upstart, had gained fame and riches, lived in a noble mansion and had married a beautiful woman, while he, the modern rejuvenated Homer, the divinely inspired bard, acclaimed by all the world as the greatest word-painter of modern times, was obliged to sell stockings for a living. He now saw his chance and composed a ditty in which Rembrandt's work was compared with that of his rival, Govaert Flinck (a perfectly competent manufacturer of "official" pictures, but without the slightest touch of originality) and was of course found wanting on account of its "artificial gloom and its pedantic use of shadows and half lights" and he wound up by dubbing the former "the Prince of Darkness," a witticism that stuck to Rembrandt for all the rest of his days.

The other painters, also dearly loving a colleague who had done pretty well in a worldly sense, were not slow to catch up with the general chorus of disapproval. They talked of their poor, misguided friend, who seemed to have shot his bolt in this latest picture and let it be known that they had of course always thought him a great man, but that it was a pity he had reached the limits of his art at such a comparatively tender age. Still others, especially the art-dealers with whom Rembrandt had refused to do business, were even more to the point.

"The temporary infatuation of the public, which had made this eccentric young man the fashionable painter of the hour, has now probably reached its end," was one of their more good-natured comments. While in their less guarded moments, they simply shouted: "Another bubble that has burst!" and rubbed their hands in anticipatory glee.

Why go on with this sad recital of human stupidity?

My wise doctor-friend, who three thousand years or so ago wrote that very wise book which we call "Ecclesiastes" summed it all up in the words: "Vanity of vanities, and all is vanity."

Here was a man who had dared to think a new thought and tell a new truth. Proudly he had turned to his fellow-men saying these noble words: "Behold! a little yellow and a little black and a little green and ocher and red and presto! I change them into an Idea." And the Philistines had loudly guffawed, had poked each other in the ribs and had shouted: "The clown! The mountebank! He wants to show us! Teach us! Tell us! As if we were not bright enough to know what we want for ourselves!"

And from that moment on, Rembrandt was doomed.

He might have returned to fame at some royal court, and indeed, it would have been better if right then and there he had moved to England or France. But in a Republic, such a thing was impossible. He had set himself up to be better than his neighbors. There was only one answer—death and oblivion.

The only question was: How long would it take the pack to get and devour him?

Chapter 11

WE TAKE A WALK AND TALK ART WITH AN HONEST MILLER

Of course there were exceptions to the general chorus of disapproval. There were a few people who "suspected" that something very fine and extraordinary had been added to the sum total of the world's beauty. There were others who went beyond "suspecting" and who felt convinced that this was one of the most beautiful things ever wrought by the hand of man.

I frequently discussed the matter with my friends during our Sunday walks which continued as in the older days. It was interesting to get the reactions of those three men, so utterly different, yet bound to each other by the ties of a common understanding.

Selim was the least interested of them. "Why," he used to ask, "all this fuss about something quite as useless and immaterial as a bit of canvas, covered with white lead and zinc and old extracts from dead vegetables and dead animals? No, the Prophet was right. The human race ought not to care for such trifles. There are more important things in this world than men and women made of linseed-oil and madder."

"Such as?" he was asked.

"Men and women of flesh and blood, especially the latter," he replied, and refused to devote any more of his energy and strength to a discussion that seemed so far removed from his charming and simple little universe.

Bernardo took it all very calmly. A man who has stood tied up against the wooden pole that was to be his own funeral pyre and who has lived to tell the tale can look upon the affairs of everyday life from such a high and such an immeasurably detached point-of-vantage that little items like frustrated careers and ruined reputations mean nothing to him, or less than nothing.

We had walked out to a mill not far from the plague house (about half an hour beyond that part of the city's bulwarks called "de Passeerder") and the miller, glad to have some one to amuse him on a rather dreary Sabbath, had invited us to come in and drink a glass of beer. Even here in this remote spot the story had become known, for it seemed that Rembrandt had often sketched the mill and had even promised the people that he would some day make an etching of it and they all liked him, for he always had a pleasant word for the children and often brought them a bit of candy and once even a toy house which he had carried all the way from town. The miller therefore was a heavy partisan of the painter and cursed the soldiers, who, he said, were no good anyway and much more proficient at the business of drinking than that of fighting.

"And what is more," he said, and his eyes shone with honest indignation, "if they make it impossible for this man with all their foolish talk to gain his livelihood in the city, all he needs to do is to come out here, for we like him and we will see to it that he does not starve. If he can paint animals too I have got a job for him right away. We have a pet hog. We are so fond of it, we have never been able to kill it. If he will paint it for us, I will gladly give him five brand new guilders."

We reassured him and told him that Rembrandt still had a few friends and was in no immediate danger of starvation, whereupon the excellent fellow said, "That is good," breathed deeply three or four times, and dozed off, to spend the Sabbath afternoon in his usual fashion by taking a nap and getting rested up from the excitement and the worry of the previous week.

This left us to ourselves and it was then that Bernardo delivered the only commentary I ever heard him make upon the case. "I may seem to be lacking in enthusiasm," he remarked slowly, "but you must not forget that I am reasonably well versed in the history of my own country. I suppose the histories of other countries would be very much the same, but perhaps we started writing our adventures down a few years earlier than our neighbors and so we know a little better what happened than some other countries.

"Well, what did happen? We produced great spiritual leaders who were able to reason things out for themselves and show us the way out of the wilderness of ignorance through which we had been wandering for a much longer period than the proverbial forty years. Did the people appreciate them and joyfully acclaim them as their kings? I never heard of it. Upon a few rare occasions, they cried Hosanna because it flattered their national pride to think that the Jewish race had been bright enough to give birth to such wonderful prophets. But they soon grew tired of giving praise to one whom they must (whether they liked to or not) consider superior to themselves and then they stoned him or threw him before the wild animals. Why should you expect your own people to be different?"

Jean-Louys, too, assumed an attitude of aloofness, though he knew a good picture from a bad one and had expressed the greatest admiration for one or two small sketches which Rembrandt had given me and which I had had framed and which were hanging on the walls of my dining-room. But he liked to play at being a sort of philosophic St. Simeon Stylites.

"My dear children," he announced solemnly, "why get all het up about some new folly of the human race? There is only one friend in this world upon whom you can always depend, who will never betray you, no matter under what circumstances, who will always be true, who will not humiliate you before your circle of intimate acquaintances by some signal act of public idiocy."

"And who might that be?" Bernardo interrupted him. "Perhaps the tables of stone of my great-uncle Moses?"

"By no means," the Frenchman answered quietly, "but the tables of logarithms of my great teacher, Napier. But if this ancient medico here will do something for the good of our souls, I suggest that he invite us all to his house some time and let us meet this painting prodigy from the town of Leyden. Imagine a great man coming from a town full of professors! But bring him in some fine day and we will tell you what we think of him."

Whereupon we made our adieux to the good miller, who had returned to consciousness and was now standing in front of his window to inform us that if it did not rain it would probably stay good weather, and we walked back to town and went to Jean-Louys' tower, and he cooked us a chicken in the French style (that is to say, in a large earthen pot together with all sorts of vegetables and a noble brown sauce) and we remained until all hours of the night and we were genuinely happy and we spoke of a thousand and one different things, but what we said I no longer know, for whenever friends talk among themselves, they add so much of mutual respect and good will to the mere spoken word that no human being, be he ever so well-versed in the art of writing, could ever hope to do justice to such a conversation.

"Faithful friends are the medicine of life," said Ecclesiasticus.

God be praised, that old Israelite knew whereof he was talking.

Chapter 12

REMBRANDT MEETS MY FRIENDS AND SASKIA GROWS WEAKER

The meeting between Rembrandt and my friends took place much sooner than I had expected and this is the way it came about.

A couple of times a week I would go to the painter's house and we would spend the evening playing back-gammon. I don't know whether anybody still takes an interest in this game, but thirty years ago it was quite popular.

Saskia had now reached the stage where she could no longer leave her bed and Rembrandt used to sit by her side and read to her from the Bible. For she no longer expected to get better. The optimism of the first four months had been replaced by a profound and very pathetic form of melancholia. She did not complain. She did not rage against her fate, as so many of her fellow-sufferers do. She had resigned herself to the idea that she must die young and must leave her child to the care of strangers. She was almost too weak to care very much, but she sometimes complained that it lasted so long. She was tired. She was most dreadfully tired and she wanted to go to sleep, but she was too tired to come to rest and she used to beg me to give her something that would make her forget, at least for a short while, and I sometimes let her have a little theriaca, but that compound seemed to have little effect upon her and the poor girl would lie tossing in her bed all day and all night long, her cheeks flushed and her lovely eyes wide open—a picture of abject misery and yet there was nothing that we could do for her except sometimes read to her from those chapters in the New Testament which she remembered from her childhood and which brought back the days of her youth when she had been as strong and well as the best of them.

After an hour or so, however, even listening to the quiet voice of her husband would exhaust her and she would whisper to him and ask him to cease. But at the same time she would beg not to be left alone.

"I shall be alone so long," she once said to me with a little smile. "I shall be alone so long before either Rembrandt or the boy joins me. I want their company every minute of both day and night as long as I can still have it."

And so every evening the baby's cradle was carried to one corner of the room (I insisted that the child be placed as far away from the mother as possible on account of the danger of contagion) and Rembrandt would light the candles on the table that had been pushed against the wall, so that the light would not disturb the patient and he would read to her for an hour or so, until she showed signs of exhaustion and then he would occupy himself quietly with his own business. He would sharpen a steel needle for his dry-points or he would examine a plate and correct some corner that had not come out as he wished or he would sign the pictures his pupils had printed that day in the little alcove upstairs. But his eyes were not very strong, he had suffered slightly from near-sightedness since early childhood and drawing or etching by candle-light would give him a stinging pain right behind his eye-balls, and so whenever I could join him for a game of back-gammon, he would be most grateful to me and he would go down into his cellar and return with a bottle of a very wonderful Rhenish wine which was called "The Milk of Our Lady" and which most certainly was worthy of that name.

But after a short time, the clicking of the dice as we threw them upon the boards got to be too exhausting for Saskia. We then threw them upon a heavy wad of fine muslin, the muslin he used to wipe his plates with, but even then sometimes one dice would slightly touch another and the patient invariably complained that the noise sent shivers all through her and as we could not talk either, and neither of us had the slightest liking for cards, we were hard put to it to find some way of passing the evening without just sitting and staring at each other.

Then one day I happened to mention to Rembrandt that I had just learned a new game from Jean-Louys which was very interesting and took a considerable amount of thought and foresight and which was called "chess" and which was so old that some people said it had been played by the heroes outside of Troy and which originally had been a war game, devised for the amusement of the Shahs of Persia, who used to be great potentates and who had ruled Asia until great Alexander had come and had deprived them of their power and had taken away their land to give it to his own generals.

The very name, calling forth visions of Oriental tyrants with beautiful diamond-studded turbans, lying in tapestried tents in the heart of some wind-swept desert, surrounded by dashing knights and armor-covered elephants bearing turreted castles on their ponderous backs, appealed to his imagination and he at once asked me to introduce him to my friend and let him learn the game too.

I waited until Saskia was feeling a little better and then one evening I invited both men to my house for supper. They took to each other at once and became fast friends. And this was rather curious, as they represented two entirely different classes of society and as Jean-Louys treated even the most distinguished among the Dutch patricians with that mixture of civil aloofness and amused condescension which the rich Amsterdam merchant would bestow upon a former butler who had gone to the Indies, had done rather well by himself and had now returned to the city of his former activities with a couple of million rupees and who had become a personage whom one must treat with a certain amount of economic respect, while at the same time keeping him at a respectable social distance, never for a moment allowing him to forget that the gap between inherited and recently acquired wealth was a divinely ordained institution across which no earthly wealth could ever hope to build a means of escape.

The Count de la Tremouille was the incarnation of what is commonly called "good breeding." Never during all the many years we spent together have I heard him give offense unintentionally, which surely is the highest tribute one can pay to a man's standard of courtesy. Like all wise people, he moved through life vertically rather than horizontally, but no matter in what company he found himself, I have never known the occasion upon which this unpretentious exile was not sitting "at the head of the table" or when anybody felt inclined to offer the man with the funny accent the slightest familiarity.

How and in what way he had acquired this gift of dominating his surroundings without in any way trying to dominate his audience, I do not know. But he had it and as a result, while he himself never seemed to remember that he had been born the Baron de la Tremouille, his surroundings were never quite able to forget it and even his fishdealer would insist upon selling him six pence worth of shrimps as if he had been a foreign potentate, come to negotiate a great international loan. Upon very rare occasions, however, the invisible courtiers who seemed to watch every one of his thoughts and actions were given a day off and silently departed for a quiet evening in town. Then his brain resembled a munificent, royal palace, from which all the guards had fled. The doors and windows stood wide open and one could enter at will, to wander through the vast halls and admire the accumulated treasures of recollection and observation, or to find a quiet nook in the formal gardens at the back of the edifice and there meditate upon the strange vicissitudes of the great adventure commonly known as life.

But in order to enjoy this privilege, one had to be recognized as a blood brother of the mind. Mere physical relationship counted for nothing, affinity of feeling for everything. I have seen a first cousin of M. le Baron come all the way from Gascony in connection with some question of an inheritance, sit for hours in the little kitchen that lay just off the study, cooling his heels and swearing impatiently because Jean-Louys was talking to the first-mate of a whaler who could neither read nor write but who had observed curious irregularities of behavior on the part of his compass while passing those extreme northern shores of Lapland where it is said that there are a number of vast iron deposits.

And it is a well-known fact that the Baron de la Tremouille forgot to attend the dinner which the Burgomasters of Amsterdam were giving in honor of a cousin of the King of Denmark (in the vain hope of obtaining a slight reduction of the Sund tolls by getting His Royal Highness disgracefully drunk on Dutch gin) because he had promised to sit up with his sick shoe-maker, an amateur philosopher of a singularly amusing trend of thought, who had made a careful study of the anagrams by means of which the Reverend Jacobus Bruinesteek had proved that the Psalms of David had really been written by King Solomon, who had applied these to the Revelations of St. John, and the Gospel of St. Luke, and had come to the somewhat startling conclusions that Judas Iscariot had written the former, while the latter was the work of Pontius Pilate.

One never knew therefore what reaction to expect from a meeting between one's ordinary friends and this strange product of French feudal practices and neo-mathematical theories except that his outward manner would always be in inverse ratio to the respect he inwardly felt for his new acquaintance. When he was sublimely polite, the case was hopeless. When he was just every-day polite, there was hope and one might give the candidate another chance. When he dropped all reserve, the victory had been won. During the first five minutes after I had introduced Rembrandt to him, I was in great fear that the encounter would be a failure. For the painter, conscious of his own low birth (his Uylenburgh in-laws had seen to that) was awkward and surly and ready to take offense at the slightest provocation, or even provide a little of the provocation himself.

The dinner was to be at my house, but Jean-Louys had promised to do the cooking. He held that cooking, after mathematics, was the greatest contribution towards human progress. "After all," he often asked, when his sleeves rolled up to his elbows, he walked between his study and the kitchen beating his eggs and his oil and quoting profusely from Ennius and from Simonides of Ceos, "after all, in what consists the difference between man and beast except in the possibilities of the former to learn the art of dining, while the latter is forever doomed to feed? I grant you that most men still are in the state of savagery when they take food for the mere pleasure of filling their bellies. I grant you that the vast majority of our fellow-citizens still handle their forks and spoons as if they were a farmer loading a wagon of hay. But a few have at last seen the light. A few of them 'dine.' Whereas my dog Nouille, the noblest beast that ever pulled a fox out of a hole, a creature of such intellect and refinement that if he could only have worn a wig and cassock they would have made him Cardinal-Archbishop of Paris, had the table manners of a hog and unless he were very closely watched, would regale himself with delicacies which were more fit for a starving hyena than for an over-fed turn-spit."

And unless he were interfered with at this spot, he would proceed to explain that a man's table manners were the safest index to his general character, that one could measure the degree of a friend's greed or honesty by watching the way in which he moved his fork or knife to his mouth. If the progress of the food from the plate to lips were even and uninterrupted, one could trust that guest for any amount up to a hundred thousand francs. If, on the other hand, the moment the food approached the mouth, there was a snatching movement on the part of the teeth and a hurrying on the part of the fingers, then that person had still a few hundred thousand years to go before he was fit to associate with civilized people.

All of which was very amusing, but a little dangerous in view of the "catch as catch can" method of eating which was still being practiced by the majority of our neighbors. And alas! Rembrandt was no exception. When he was hard at work upon some new picture or when he was struggling with a new idea for an etching, he could be terribly absent-minded. Upon such occasions he seemed to be completely oblivious of his surroundings. As I have already written down in a former part of my diary I have known him to go without either food or drink for as long as two days and two nights at a time. Then when he finally broke his fast, his table manners were rather painfully reminiscent of the days in the Weddesteeg, when the six van Rijn infants were all of them standing around the paternal table, dipping their spoons into the common bowl of pap and fishing out the few chunks of meat left behind by their father and mother. Now he not only had his work to worry him (I knew that he was finishing a portrait of the Widow Swartenhout and the old lady, who had a will of her own, despite her seventy-five years, was not the easiest of sitters) but also had a very sick wife on his hands and a rather sickly child (not to mention a hellishly ill-tempered nurse), I had good reason to fear that he might be in one of his vague and irritable moods and then one never could foretell just exactly what he would do or say or how he would react to the simplest remark, if by some miraculous stretch of the imagination it could be construed as a reflection upon his personal behavior.

And when Jean-Louys appeared from the kitchen in his shirt-sleeves, wearing an apron over his silk ruffles (for though he affected no colors in his outer garments, he remained scrupulously faithful to the reigning fashions until the day of his death), carrying a large blue Delft bowl full of batter and loudly quoting Seneca's "Convivae certe tui dicant, Bibamus!" suddenly I had the feeling: this party is going to be the wreck of an old friendship. For Rembrandt, who knew a very little Latin but no French whatsoever, looked as if he were going to say: "Well, my fine young man, and what about it, and have you lived here all this time without learning enough of our language to wish me at least a civil good morning in my own tongue?" But Jean-Louys, without paying the slightest attention, greeted him with a very deep and ceremonial bow and said in the nearest approach to Dutch I ever heard issue from the mouth of a Frenchman, "Mijn Heer, I welcome the successor of Pheidias, who did not think an old woman making pancakes a subject beneath his august dignity. Wherefore with your kind permission, I shall now make you an alemette the recipe of which I got straight from the chief cook of the Abbot of Thelème."

Whether Rembrandt got the allusion to the greatest of all the past masters of ancient France, I had reason to doubt, for as he often told me, he lived for the day and not for day before yesterday. And I am afraid that not half a dozen people in the whole town of Amsterdam knew (or cared) what sort of friars had inhabited the delectable abbaye of old Doctor Rabelais' invention. But the reference to the pancake woman, a rather mediocre etching of his early days which hardly any one knew, greatly flattered his pride. And he at once dropped the bristling attitude with which he had watched the advent of our amateur cook, bowed low and answered with a courtly wave of the hand:

"And if the product of your art, Monsieur, comes up to what certain reports of your culinary powers make me anticipate, then even great Jupiter would consider himself fortunate to be invited to this feast."

Which so surprised and delighted de la Tremouille that he almost dropped his bowl of batter on my instrument case, bowed even lower than before, pronounced himself Monsieur van Rijn's most humble servitor and ever after treated him with such marks of esteem and good will that the French commercial agent (who was supposed to collect business information for his royal master, but filled most of his letters with social gossip of what he supposed to be the better sort of Amsterdam society) filled three entire letters with the details of this famous meeting and hinted in no uncertain terms that M. de la Tremouille was rapidly approaching that stage of democratic debasement where a hint to the judicial authorities of Amsterdam and a Lettre de Cachet held ready at the nearest frontier town might not be out of place—a fine piece of diplomatic reasoning which in the course of its peregrinations towards Paris was duly copied by the post-master of The Hague, was forwarded by him to My Lord Huygens, and so reached my humble home in Amsterdam with a request for the recipe of that famous alemette, which he spelled wrong and called an "omelette."

But to return to our dinner-party, we really had a very pleasant evening. Selim at first held himself slightly aloof. "The graphic arts," he offered as an excuse, "are not quite in my line. The Koran does not allow me to take an interest in them."

"And in which chapter, my friend, does the Koran mention the graphic arts?" came the voice of Bernardo, who knew that this excellent follower of the Prophet (not unlike a good many Christians) never gave a thought to these holy works except upon those frequent occasions when he needed their authority to talk himself out of doing something which he really did not want to do. For example, whenever he went to the house of friends and was offered beer, which he detested, Selim would solemly lift his eyes toward Heaven and in a sepulchral voice he would declaim: "Alas and alack! does not the Angel Gabriel in the fifth verse of the second Sura declare unto the faithful: 'In the name of Allah, the compassionate compassioner, abstain, ye lovers of righteousness, from all those things that benumb the spirit.'"

But should his host take the hint and dive into his cellar for a bottle of Burgundy (which the young Moslem dearly loved) then Selim would proceed: "But what does the Prophet himself in the twenty-third verse of the eighteenth Sura have to say upon the duties of those who wander abroad in foreign lands? 'Listen, all ye faithful, and act ye so in all ways that he who offereth ye food and drink shall never feel himself slighted, for true hospitality is the founding-stone of friendship, the bulwark of goodwill.'" And he would continue to misquote these highfalutin passages until either the supply of wine had been completely consumed or the rest of the guests had passed underneath the table.

He would, however, be a little more careful with his texts whenever Bernardo was present, for the Jew, having spent several years of his life in a Portuguese prison in the company of a holy man from Fez had used the endless hours of this interminable bondage to learn the greater part of the Koran by heart, in return for which he had taught the poor blackamoor the Psalms of David, the book of Judges and the Canticle of Solomon. He had long since thrown this useless intellectual ballast overboard, but enough remained to allow him to control the more phantastic statements of our amateur Moollah and the quarrels of these two Semites about the relative merits of their ancestral creeds (for neither of which either one of them felt the slightest respect) added a great deal to the gayety of our small society.

It caused considerable scandal among our Christian neighbors (who were never invited to our parties, yet knew everything we had said and done as accurately as if they had been present in person) but they were as a rule too busy fighting among themselves to pay very much attention to our hilarious heresies. And this evening, Selim, true to his custom, had no sooner relieved himself of his noble sentiment about the Koran and the art of painting, than he asked for a pencil and paper and spent the rest of the evening entertaining my small son with accounts of the glorious deeds of Harun al-Raschid, illuminating his talk with very amusing little pictures in which that great warrior was depicted in the act of decapitating rows and rows of Crusaders with such bloodthirsty realism that the poor infant could not sleep for five nights in succession.

As for the rest of us, immediately after dinner we went to my workroom and spent the evening playing chess. Jean-Louys, who claimed that this game was the best remedy for gout and nagging wives (the two evils he most dreaded) had recently taken a very serious interest in it and had made it a subject of careful study.

"What will you?" he used to ask. "I can work at my tables for only eight or nine hours a day. After that the figures put their hats and coats on and begin to dance minuets all over the page. I have got to do something to keep myself from going woozy and I can't live without mathematics, just as others can't live without gin or rum or theology or women

There is music. But that is no longer what it used to be. Too much sentiment in it nowadays. And so let us have the board."

We got the board (a home-made affair, for in the whole of Amsterdam I had not been able to get one and in most shops I had been told that such a thing did not exist) and Jean-Louys got out his copy of Ruy Lopez (a little book which he had ordered all the way from Sevilla in Spain) and he turned to page nineteen and carefully followed all the instructions from opening to attack and in eighteen moves, he had been checkmated by Bernardo, who had learned the game only the week before and who had no more idea about "gambits" and "end plays" than I had of raising pheasants, but who beat us all with a regularity that was as much of a surprise to us as it was to himself.

But what interested me most of all was Rembrandt's reaction to this game. I had already taught him the moves, king—one square at a time, forward, backward, sideways—castles up and down the whole line as may be desirable—knights one square forwards, two squares sideways—etc., etc., and much to my surprise he had learned it in an astoundingly short time. One or two evenings had been enough to give him a general idea of the game. But he played chess as he painted.

I have said before that he would rarely talk about the theory of his art and used to say that one hour of practice was better than a week of discussion and I do not believe that he ever put a single thought upon the subject on paper, although he had quite a gift for expressing himself in writing. But a few nights after our dinner party he approached the subject himself and what he said was quite interesting.

"I like your Frenchman," he said in connection with some remark of mine upon the excellence of Jean-Louys' virtuosity as a cook. "I grant you that he makes a most excellent pancake, but these fancy dishes are not very much to my taste. I am accustomed to simpler fare. But I like him for the line he follows in playing that strange new game and it is upon 'line' that everything in this world depends.

"You know that I have a number of pupils. Some of them have been rather successful. Flinck has already made his mark and you will hear of Bol and Douw, for they are sound craftsmen and know their trade. Of course I did not really teach them very much. In their own way they are just as good as I am. It just happens that I am a little older and have had time to learn a few tricks which I can hand down to them.

"But of course, people see that Flinck has got a new commission from the Prince or they hear that Bol is painting a dozen portraits a year and they say to themselves: Here is our little Willem or our little Jantje and he is making wonderful pictures with that box of colors grandpa gave him for Saint Nicholas. We must send him to this man van Rijn and let him grow up to be as great an artist as Eeckhout or perhaps as the master himself and make a lot of money and go about all dressed up in silks and plumes, for you know what foolish ideas there are abroad about a profession which counts so many of its most honored members among the inmates of the poor-house.

"But what can I do? I can't make a living merely painting portraits. I need pupils. None of those boys are very easy to handle. They are young and models are willing. I have not got the slightest inclination to play the school-master, but I can at least be careful that I don't waste my time upon material that is too absolutely hopeless. And so I have made it a rule that they must bring me their drawings.

"Their drawings, mind you, not their paintings. For almost anybody, if he is not absolutely color-blind and has had a good teacher, can learn to paint some sort of a picture. But a line never lies. Give me a scrap of a man's drawings, anything at all, and in five seconds I will tell you whether he has any talent or whether he had better become a brewer.

"Besides, painting is not merely a question of technique. There has got to be temperament, character, personality. Without those, there is no life and the world is dull enough as it is. No need to clutter it up with miles of dead canvas. Yes, a painter should learn his trade and be able to finish a picture, attend to all the details just as a tailor should be able to finish a suit of clothes or a carpenter to finish a cupboard.

"Perhaps I don't make myself quite clear. There are others who could tell you much better what is in my mind than I can tell you myself. But mark my words, a man has a 'line' or he has not. And that Frenchman has a line. He has got it in his manner. He has got it in his manners. He has got it in his pancakes. He has got it in his chess. He has got it in everything. While I . . ."

I looked at him in surprise, for this was a new note I had never heard before.

"While you?"

"While I have got too much of it in my drawing and too little in my life. But I am still young. Give me a few more years of experience, and I too may learn."

Chapter 13

SASKIA QUIETLY GOES TO SLEEP FOR ALL TIME

Rembrandt did learn certain things about life and he learned them much sooner than he had expected. It was a fortnight after our dinner-party and the painter and I were spending an evening as usual, watching over Saskia.

I had long since given up all hope of ever being able to do something for her. I had brought in two of my colleagues who had studied her disease in Grenoble and in London. As with patients of this sort a great deal depends upon their own state of mind and they must be encouraged in their strange belief that they will soon be cured (their occasional attacks of melancholia are the worst thing that can happen to them) my learned rivals had been introduced to her as art-dealers from Antwerp who wanted to inspect Rembrandt's etchings and she felt quite flattered that two such distinguished-looking gentlemen should have come all the way from Flanders to pay homage to her husband's genius and had asked a good many questions about Rubens, whether he really had been paid a hundred guilders a day while he was painting a picture for some one and whether his wife had really been as handsome and well-dressed as she had heard and whether she had ever posed for him in the nude, because that was something she herself never could have done, however much she might love her husband.

To which they had answered to the best of their ability and being experienced physicians and therefore accustomed to the telling of many innocent lies, they had so well acquitted themselves of the task that Saskia was quite satisfied and had dozed off, firmly convinced that she was a much better-looking woman than Helen Fourment and also, to a certain extent, a much more respectable one, since she had sometimes appeared in her man's pictures as Flora but never as Venus.

Then we had bade Rembrandt leave us and the three of us had examined the sleeping woman, for the short interview had already exhausted her waning strength, and I had shown them my record of the case and they both had looked solemn and they both had shaken their heads and the first one had whispered, "mors," and the second one had whispered, "mors," and then we had waited a few minutes to make the husband believe that we were discussing the matter in detail and that there still might be some hope and the elder of the two doctors had said: "One month more, at the very most." And the younger had answered, after the fashion of young physicians who try to show their superior experience before an elder confrère: "It seems to me that she might live another six weeks."

But I had said nothing, for I had seen her lose weight steadily for the last two months and I knew that it was a question of days rather than weeks and I took them upstairs and we all uttered some platitudes to Rembrandt, who had used that half hour to pull two proofs of a little etching of the three Magi, on which he had been working for quite a long time and which he now offered with a few complimentary words to my two doctor friends who were rather touched, for there was something very pathetic and almost naïve about this man who kept on laboring as unconcernedly as if his little household were not, at that very moment, on the brink of collapse and extinction.

Then they bade him farewell, declining his offer that he show them some further hospitality in token of his gratitude for their services and we went downstairs to the big hall and made ready for our evening's game.

Saskia was still asleep. Her right hand, very white and dreadfully thin, was resting on the counterpane. She had always been very fond of flowers and now that summer had come at last, Rembrandt brought her some fresh roses every morning. One of these she had stuck in her hair to give herself a more festive appearance, before the arrival of the "Antwerp art-dealers." It lay on her pillow. It was a very red rose and her cheeks by contrast looked even more pallid than usual. But she was breathing easily and regularly and there was a smile on her lips. I softly pulled the curtains of the bed together and tiptoed back to the table.

"She seems to be doing very well," I said. "What will you play, backgammon or chess?"

"Chess," Rembrandt answered. "I think that I can beat you to-night. The last time we played, I lost my queen almost at the very beginning. I will do better to-night."

I took two pawns and let him choose.

He pointed to my left hand and got red.

We began in the usual way, king's pawn, queen's pawn, king's bishop, queen's rook and whatever followed. I have forgotten how the game ran, but I remember that after only five or six moves, he had brought his queen out and was using her to force me into a defensive position. I warned him. What he was doing had a certain quality of brilliancy. It might make him win the game in about ten or fifteen moves, but only on condition that I overlooked a counter-attack which I could make with my knights, in which case his lack of reserves would put him into a fatal position. I watched him closely. He was so engrossed in his own calculations that he seemed completely unaware of the danger that threatened him from the side of my knights. I warned him once more. "This is all very fine," I told him, "but you are playing this to win."

"But this is so amusing," he answered. "I know that I am running a few risks but I have the position well in hand. I shall beat you the next move if I can extricate my queen."

"But can you?" I asked him, taking his bishop's pawn and thereby opening an avenue of attack for my bishop.

"I think I can— Why, it would be absurd if I couldn't! I had the game in hand only a moment ago and now—"

"And now," I answered, "I have your queen and you are mate in three moves."

He pushed back his chair.

"Too bad," he consoled himself. "Too bad. I thought that I had you this time. Let me try again. Just a moment till I make sure that Saskia is all right."

He picked up one of the two candles, went to the bed and pushed aside the curtains. Then he turned to me and whispered: "Look how quiet she is to-night! I never saw her sleep so soundly. She must be really getting better."

I stood by his side and put my hand upon her heart.

Saskia was dead.

Chapter 14

SASKIA IS BURIED AND REMBRANDT GOES BACK TO WORK

I am writing this in the year 1669 and Saskia died in '42. That is twenty-seven years ago and twenty-seven years are a long time in a man's life. I can't complain about my memory. It is causing me very little trouble, and as I shall be seventy next year, I have no right to expect too much. The greater part of my contemporaries are either dead or rapidly becoming senile and the former are better off than the latter.

What Fate holds in store for me, I do not know. But when the end comes, I hope that it will be sudden and swift and that I shall never have to pass through those periods of slow mental decay which seem to be the inevitable concomitant of old age.

But I have noticed something curious whenever I try to reconstruct the events of my own past. I can recollect the most unimportant details of my early childhood. I still know with absolute assurance what presents I received on Saint Nicholas day when I was seven and eight and nine and ten. I could tell you what we had to eat on the few occasions when we entertained guests. Could I handle a pencil, I would be able to draw you the absolute likeness of all my school-teachers and most of my friends.

The same holds good for the two years I spent studying anatomy and surgery at the University of Leyden. Every detail of every day, almost every detail of every hour of every day, is firmly fixed in my mind. But suddenly after my twentieth birthday, the picture becomes hazy. I still know in a general way what occurred during the years that I practiced medicine in Amsterdam, but I often lose track of the sequence of events. For example, I will remember with perfect clarity that such and such a person fell ill of such and such a disease and I could give you a fairly accurate account of the development of his case. But should you ask me to name the year, I would be hopelessly at a loss. I would be obliged to answer that I did not know. It might have been '46 or '56 and then again, it might have been '49 or '59. I just simply would not know. I could tell you whether the patient had a temperature on the third or on the fourth day of his affliction, but I might be off on the date all the way from five to ten years.

I have often speculated upon the true nature of this curious mental trick and I think that it is due to the increase in speed of both the months and the years as we grow older. When I was ten years of age, a single day resembled eternity, only on a somewhat smaller scale. It was composed of twenty-four hours, each one of which bore a distinct character of its own and offered countless possibilities for new adventures and fresh experiences.

Gradually human existence became more commonplace. One got up, did one's work, ate a few meals, talked to a few friends, worried a bit, laughed a bit, read a few chapters in a book and went to bed again.

The humdrum became the normal. One commenced to accept whatever Fate had in store without murmuring, for what was the use of trying to fight God? At first, of course, there still were the seasons. The spring, when the trees and the plants were in flower, the summer when it was hot, the fall when the grain was harvested, the winter when it was cold and one was obliged to wear heavy woolen coats and mufflers.

But after one's fiftieth birthday, even those natural divisions of the year seemed to lose their importance. One no longer grumbled about the frost or the heat or the rain or the snow. They were there! Impossible to do anything about them, anyway. That was the last great surrender. From that moment on, time ceased to have a personal entity. It became a smudge. Some gigantic joker had wiped his dirty thumb across the vault of Heaven and that was called life. Then the last final sleep and grateful oblivion for the rest of eternity.

Those thoughts have been continually in my mind during the last twenty years. Hence dates and hours mean very little to me and as I have never been in the habit of keeping a diary until now, as I never saved a single letter or a single scrap of paper that was in any way connected with my own existence (it seemed such a silly thing to do, as if my own funny little adventures were really of the slightest general importance), as, in short, I am writing this entirely from memory, I find it rather difficult to state when exactly Saskia departed this life or even when she was buried.

She died (I am quite sure about that) some time during the summer of 1642, for I remember that it was during the same year in which Tasman discovered that mysterious island in the Pacific Ocean which was called Nieuw Zeeland, after my beloved Zeeland, and sailed around the great south land about which we had had so many strange reports during the last forty years.

As always I was interested in any reports he might bring home about the narcotics in use among the natives. Everywhere in the world the inhabitants seem to have some favorite way of bringing about temporary forgetfulness. In most instances they were only interested in their miserable hasheesh as a momentary means of escape from lives that were none too happy. But I am convinced that some day we shall find a plant which will enable us to do something infinitely more important to perform surgical operations without that dreadful agony which now turns the operating-room into a torture chamber and makes people avoid the hospital as if it were the lepers' house. And there always is a chance that one of those explorers, coming back from distant parts of Asia or Africa or

America, shall bring us the answer to this age-old question. I had therefore made it a rule to keep track of all new voyages and when I heard that this new big island, called van Diemen's Land (after My Lord Anthony van Diemen, the governor-general of the Indies, who also conquered Formosa and who had equipped this most recent expedition)—when I heard that it was inhabited by woolly-haired aborigines who could make battle-axes return to their hands after they had thrown them at their enemies, I decided that people clever enough to invent such a curious device (the true nature of which I never heard explained) might also have discovered some new methods of bringing about a state of artificial oblivion. But the reports that were printed about these new explorations remained exceedingly brief and far from satisfactory. Finally I addressed a letter to the directors of the India Company and was informed that Their Lordships were conducting a business enterprise and were not managing a museum of natural curiosities and had no information to give me upon the subject in which I seemed interested.

Well, that famous voyage happened in 1642 (though I only heard about it two years later) but the date stuck in my memory, for the very silly reason that I had had a dispute with one of Rembrandt's brothers-in-law whether Lutjegast in which Tasman was born was situated in Friesland or in Groningen and finally I had bet him a rijksdaalder that it was in Groningen and not in Friesland and he had taken me up and I had been right and he had never paid me that rijksdaalder, claiming that by rights the hamlet ought to have been a part of his native province. (A pretty feeble excuse, it seemed to me.) And ever since, when some one said, "Sixteen-hundred and forty-two," I instinctively added, "Tasman from Lutjegast and Saskia, too." It was a foolish little jingle and not a very dignified one, but as long as the particular compartment of our brain occupied by our memory resembles a pawnshop the morning after a fire, with everything helter-skelter and in hopeless disorder, I suppose that such absurd combinations are inevitable.

Anyway that terrible rime allows me to remember that the poor girl died in the year 1642 and that is enough for the present purpose. She died in the summer of '42 and if I am not mistaken, it was during the middle of June, for the push-cart vendors were selling their first cherries and there were flowers everywhere, and the trees along the Burchtwal looked fresh and green as we slowly carried Saskia to her last resting place.

When we came to the Old Church, we found that the officials had not expected us so early and that the building was still locked. The coffin was put down while some one went to get the sexton and we all stood around in a small group and we wanted to say something and we did not know quite what to say and the noise of the traffic in the near-by Warmoesstraat served as a background for our silence and then all of a sudden, there was the grating sound of heavy bolts that were being pushed aside and the doors opened slowly as if pushed aside by invisible hands, and inside everything was very quiet, but in the distance some one was hammering at a bench that needed repair and I looked at Rembrandt and I saw that he had turned pale, as if they were hammering nails into his wife's coffin.

We buried her right underneath the small organ, not far away from the monument erected to Admiral van Heemskerk who had died off Gibraltar and who had been the first man to try and reach the Indies by way of the North Pole.

The ceremony took only a few minutes. The heavy black cloth which had completely covered the casket was carefully folded up by two of the professional pall-bearers who performed this office with such absurd dignity that they reminded me of my grandmother and her maid Rika, doing the sheets when the half-yearly laundry came home. Then the coffin was placed upon two heavy ropes. Eight men, four on each side, took hold of the ropes. The minister stepped forward with an enormous Bible which he opened and placed on a small wooden stand which had been placed there for the occasion and while he read the one hundred and third psalm, Saskia was slowly and silently lowered into the cavernous darkness of her open grave.

I have gone to many funerals in my day and every time I have been struck by the inability of the creed of Calvin and Luther to express its emotions in anything beyond mere words. The music in our churches is hideous. The singing is atrocious. We cover the walls with a dozen coats of whitewash, we paint the ceiling gray, and we varnish the benches until they are stained a dark brown and then we ask the congregation to come and sit still on incredibly uncomfortable seats while some one talks to them.

In our churches, some one is forever telling somebody else what he ought to think or do. Instead of agreement there is argument. Instead of being urged to lose our souls in quiet contemplation, we are exhorted to follow the intricate subtleties of violent controversies and to take sides in never-ending disputes. Heaven knows, I do not wish a return of those good old days of which our Catholic neighbors are secretly talking. Deprived of their ancient shrines and obliged to worship their own Lord in the attic of some innocent-looking warehouse, they must of course look back to the period before our town went Protestant as a sort of Paradise Lost. But their church had to go. It was too foreign to the nature of our people and we shall have to continue our present way until we shall be rid of it for all time.

No, it is not that I want. But I can't for the life of me see why we had to go so far in the other direction and why everything we do must be ugly and devoid of symbolic meaning. Most people are starving for a little color in their lives. They hunger for some variety of mysterious emotion that shall (for the moment at least) allow them to forget the all too brutal facts of human existence.

We fortunate ones who are not forever beset by the necessities of finding enough to eat and to drink and maintaining a roof over our children's heads, don't know what the poorer classes suffer. We go in for music or for painting or we write sonnets or study mathematics or lose ourselves in the works of the ancient philosophers. But all those roads of escape are closed to them. The Church alone can give them relief. And I never enter one of these sepulchral places of worship without wondering why our churches are so hopelessly one-sided and always appeal to the brain but never to the emotions.

Take that funeral of Saskia. Surely if there was a tragedy it was the death of this lovely creature. She was young and until a few months before her death, very lovely. She was married to one of the most remarkable men of her day and age, who was devoted to her and could have given her a life full of beauty and interest. She had a child. She had many friends. She was not very bright, perhaps, but no one asked of her that she be able to translate Auveer into Latin hexameters.

And then she died. Died before she was fully thirty years old. Died and left everything she loved behind, to become a mere number in a row of hideous graves and molder away in a threadbare shroud until her poor bones should be evicted to make room for some new candidate.

A ghastly tragedy, the negation of everything that men and women are supposed to live for. But a marvelous opportunity for the Church to stand forth as the prophet of hope, to maintain boldly and in the face of all this incriminating evidence, that life is good and that death is but another form of living, to surround these assertions with beautiful gestures and honest music, with symbols that should speak uncontrovertibly of the Eternal Verities.

Instead of which a young farmhand, speaking an accent that betrayed no breeding whatsoever, read some very fine verses, the meaning of which, however, he did not seem to understand in the least. Then sixteen men, who during the rest of the day were drivers of beer-wagons and eel-fishers, their working clothes badly hidden by long black cassocks and still smelling of the ale-house, took the large wooden box containing all this loveliness and with an ill-concealed "one, two, three!" they hurriedly lowered it into its stone cage. Then they turned away to carry the stretcher to the store-room in the back of the church where such paraphernalia were kept whenever there was no demand for their services, and hastened to the door to gather in the tips of the mourners.

I suppose there were those among us who wanted to linger a moment longer—to say something for the last time to the shadow that lay at our feet. But we were given no time. The minister left. The sexton was rattling his keys. There was nothing for us to do but to go.

And so we returned to the house in the Anthonie Breestraat and the nurse with the help of some of the neighbors had prepared a meal and the table was set in the same room from which they had carried the corpse away only an hour before (a dreadful and barbarous custom which we have undoubtedly inherited from our savage ancestors) and we were all of us bade to enter and regale ourselves.

I remained a few minutes, for not to have done so would have attracted too much attention. Then I looked for Rembrandt. He was not there. Driven by some sort of premonition, I softly tiptoed upstairs to the studio. Rembrandt, still in his mourning clothes, a long veil of black crape hanging down from his hat and black gloves on his hands, but completely oblivious of the world around him, was busy painting. I went up to him and put my hand on his shoulder, but he never turned his head and I don't think he noticed me.

For he was working once more at a portrait of Saskia, a portrait of Saskia as she had looked the day he had married her.

Chapter 15

REMBRANDT UNEXPECTEDLY CALLS AND BORROWS FIFTY GUILDERS

I left the studio without saying a word, talked to a few people downstairs, uttered the usual platitudes which belong to such an occasion, went home, changed my clothes and walked to the hospital where I spent the rest of the day. But to my great surprise, just after I had finished my supper, the maid told me that Mr. van Rijn had come to see me, and of course I bade him come in and asked why this formality of having himself announced, to which he replied vaguely that he did not know, and took a chair and sat down. Then I noticed that he was still in the same black clothes he had worn at the funeral and that there was something wild about the way in which he stared around the room.

In the case of any one else, I would have thought: "This man has been drinking." But he was dead sober and indeed it was not until much later, when anxiety about losing his eyesight was added to all his other worries, that he occasionally tried to find a few moments of oblivion by means of that false friend who dwelleth at the bottom of a brown jar of Schiedam gin.

There was but one other explanation for his disheveled looks; he was utterly exhausted.

I asked him whether he had had anything to eat that day, when he had last dined? He tried to remember, but could not. "Two or three days ago," he answered. And so I went into the kitchen and with my own hands prepared a meal of soft-boiled eggs and toasted bread and I sent the maid out for some milk, which I slightly heated, and he ate everything and then said: "I am dreadfully tired," and I took him upstairs and practically had to undress him (for he could hardly lift a finger) and I put him into my own bed and went downstairs again and made myself some sort of a couch out of chairs and cushions and the family Bible, which I used as a pillow, and blew out the candle and it seemed to me that I had hardly slept an hour when I was awakened by a loud banging on the front door, and of course I thought it was a patient and I went to the front door and to my great surprise, noticed that the sun was shining brightly and that it must be between eight or nine o'clock in the morning, and then I opened the door and there stood the nurse of little Titus, her hair hanging down her forehead and her bare feet in leather slippers.

"This is a fine thing to happen!" she began, but I shushed her and bade her come in and said sharply: "Keep a civil tongue in your head, woman. What is it you want?"

"Is he here?" she asked.

"He? What do you mean by 'he'?"

"Rembrandt."

"And since when do you call your master by his first name, or refer to him as 'he'?"

"Oh, well, he isn't so much, and for a widower to spend the night after his wife's funeral outside of the house! It is disgraceful! The neighbors will talk about it. They are already talking more than is good. It is disgraceful. And here I am, slaving myself to death to keep everything going nicely, and I cooked the finest meal ever served in our street after a funeral, and he does not even come down to say 'how do you do?' to a single one of the guests. And he forgets to give me money to buy beer and I have to pay for it out of my own pocket and then he does not come down to the meal and everybody will be talking about it!" and so on and so forth, an hysterical woman feeling very sorry for herself.

As there was no use arguing the case, I told her that she was a very badly used woman, that her master had been sadly negligent in his duties and that I would speak to him as soon as he had rested from the terrible exhaustion of the last few days, and having in this way quieted her somewhat, I prevailed upon her to go back home and take care of the baby and I would return with the master just as soon as I could.

The harpy actually left me and I returned to the dining-room to dress and to make up my mind what to say to Rembrandt, for although his household no longer needed my professional assistance, I felt that it was in even greater need of my services as a fairly sober-minded and not entirely unpractical human being. And when Rembrandt finally came downstairs, a little after eleven, and after he had eaten three ordinary breakfasts, I pushed my chair back (why can't one think with one's feet underneath the table?) and I said: "Listen, my good friend, but this will never do! If I have told you once I have told you ten dozen times, that woman ought to go. She is no good. She is irresponsible. I don't quite want to say that she is crazy but she isn't far away from it. Pay her her wages and let her go, but let her go right away, for unless I am much mistaken, she is rapidly losing her mind and she may end by murdering you or your child."

This startled him considerably and he asked: "Do you really think so, or do you say that because you do not like her?" To which I answered, not without some heat, that my personal likes or dislikes had nothing to do with the case, that in such matters I firmly believed in keeping professional and private opinions strictly separate, but that as a doctor who had done his best to save his wife and was now doing his best to save his son, I felt it my duty to warn him against so dangerous a companion, and I ended once more with the admonition: "Pay her and let her go."

But he answered that that was not as easy as it seemed and I asked him why? For the position between servants and master was clearly defined and regulated by the laws of Amsterdam. One might have to pay a servant or a nurse a few weeks extra wages, but that was all, and as long as the financial obligations were fulfilled, the magistrate took no notice when irate scullions stormed their council-chamber with their complaints and grievances. He might be obliged to give her a full month's wages, but then he would be able to ask her to leave his house at once, and good riddance.

All those arguments, however, seemed to make very little impression upon him. He kept repeating that it would not be so easy as I thought and finally took his leave, but just as I opened the door to show him out, he made a remark which puzzled me a great deal. "You are right," he said, "and I will do what you tell me. I will try to raise the money to-day."

"Raise the money to-day . . ."—a question of twenty or thirty guilders at the very most. "Raise the money"—when one lived in the biggest house on the Jodenbreestraat, bought pictures by Rubens and Raphael as if they had been ten-cent prints and was known to have married one of the richest girls of Friesland!

"I will try to raise the money to-day!" Thus far we had had tragedy. Now mystery had been added. And I decided to have a serious talk with him as soon as he should have recovered from the emotions of the last few days.

A man who any day could lay his hands on fifty thousand guilders in cash (every one knew that Saskia had not had a penny less) telling me that he would try and raise a servant's wages—no, something was wrong there.

But one can't very well ask questions of that sort and so I waited and went the usual rounds of my professional duties, for I knew that when people have something on their mind, they sooner or later must relieve themselves or go mad.

In the olden days, so I am told, one could go to a priest and tell him all about everything. Then came the new dispensation and people were admonished to address themselves directly to God.

And God lives so very far away and a doctor is conveniently near by, right around the corner. And so the doctor often gets the confidences that were really meant for the Almighty. I therefore made up my mind that I would not call at the Breestraat, and would wait, for the patient would appear soon enough.

Rembrandt, however, appeared to be struggling hard to keep his trouble to himself. The days grew into weeks and he never came near the Houtgracht.

And then suddenly one day when I returned from the hospital late in the afternoon I found him in my working-room. He must have been waiting quite a long time, for he had amused himself copying a bust of

Hippocrates that stood on my book-case, and the drawing was almost finished.

"I have come to speak to you about something," he said, without offering me the usual salutation. "I am in a rather difficult position. Can you let me have fifty guilders?" And then he told me his story, and it was a strange one, as you shall see for yourself.

Chapter 16

I LEARN A FEW THINGS ABOUT SASKIA'S FAMILY

"I am just back from the Old Church," he began. "I have bought the grave in which Saskia is buried. It is mine now and she will never have to lie there with strangers. I had to sell two of my pictures to raise the amount. I don't know what has happened. I had thought that they would bring me six hundred florins. I only got half. But the grave is mine. I went to the notary this morning. The papers have been signed and are in my pocket. Now could you let me have fifty guilders? I owe the nurse thirty for past wages and twenty for letting her go without the usual notice. Can I have the money?"

I told him that of course he could have the money, but why did he need it? It was a difficult subject. I decided not to try and be too delicate. Such mental operations are very much like physical ones, and the tender-hearted surgeons, who try to save the feelings of their patients, are the ones who do the most harm. And so I said: "Of course your affairs are none of my business and I would gladly give you a thousand guilders if you really needed them. But there is the house. You once told me that you had paid thirteen thousand guilders for it. You will grant me that I have never pried into your affairs, but one day when you were pulling a proof and I was talking to you in the little room upstairs, you remarked that you made between two thousand and three thousand florins a year from your etchings alone. Then there are your pupils. I don't know how much they pay you, but it ought to be a fairly decent sum. Then there are your portraits. There is the picture of Banning Cocq's company. The other day (it was at the funeral of Saskia, to be exact) young Uylenburgh, her cousin, told me that you had got five thousand florins for it. And then there is Saskia's inheritance. She must have had quite a good deal. Her father was a man of importance. I don't know what became of it, but I suppose you got some of it."

"I got everything."

"Well, you ought to be able to realize on it." (I hated to talk like a damn school-master, but in many ways the man to whom I was speaking was still a child.)

"I can," he answered. "It is merely a question of time. You see, Saskia had made a will about two weeks before she died. We did not tell you, because you had given orders that she must not be disturbed, and as a matter of fact, I did not know about it until it was all finished. But the thing had been on her mind for quite a long time and one afternoon, when I had gone out to talk about a new portrait, she sent the nurse to get her a notary. He came to see her and drew up everything in true legal form. She signed the documents nine days before she died and she left everything to me. It is understood that I will look after the boy and see that he gets a first-rate education and if I ever marry again, which I doubt, all the money goes to Titus. And some other details which are neither here nor there. But the most wonderful thing of all—and I never thought that the poor girl had cared quite so much for me—came at the end. She stipulated that I should never be asked to give any sort of an accounting. It is all mine to do with as I please. Of course, I shall merely regard it as a trust-fund for the benefit of little Titus. I may use some of it to pay for the house. Half of it has been paid already but I still owe some seven thousand florins on it and a few years' interest. In the end it will go to Titus anyway and so that means nothing.

"I am really much better fixed than ever before. But I have no head for business and I would rather paint three pictures than add one single sum of figures. And things have been sort of slow coming in these last six months. I know that people say that I got five thousand guilders for that big militia piece. Well, sixteen hundred is a little nearer to the truth, and even of that, I am not quite sure, for they now tell me that it is too large for the hall and they want to cut a piece off at both sides, and some of the soldiers who stood pretty near the edge of the picture threaten that they won't give me a cent unless they show up as well as the rest of the company. And then there are four or five of that crowd who claim that I have not done them justice. They don't want to be painted with their backs to the public. They say that they had agreed to pay an equal sum, all of them, and that therefore they have a right to as much canvas as their neighbors. One of them stopped me the other day on the Ververs Gracht and caused quite a scandal, and he was a sergeant, too. What did I mean by hiding his face behind the arm of another fellow, who was only a corporal and a man he did not care for to boot?

"Well, I did not lose my temper, though I was sorely tempted to do so. Instead I bought him a beer and took him to the Kloveniersdoelen and I spent an hour trying to show that beetlehead that I had tried to do something more than paint a nice, polite picture of himself and his companions, that I had not tried to paint one particular company of soldiers, but all the soldiers of all the ages, going forth to defend their homesteads. I made quite a speech. Did I convince him? Of course not! All my fine words did not make the slightest impression upon the creature's dumb brain. Whenever I thought that I had made my point clear, he would look at me and shake his head and say: 'I paid as much as the rest of them and I want to be shown as big as the rest of them, or I shan't give you a cent.' And in the end he got quite abusive and asked me whether the little girl in the center had paid her share and what she was doing there anyway, and then I gave up in despair, and I shall count myself lucky if I get half of what they promised me.

"You are right, I used to have quite a number of pupils, but you know how it is. Those who have talent are usually too poor to pay me anything and those who can pay have not got the talent and they are just a common nuisance. They might at least have given me some rest when Saskia died. Well, a few had the decency to go home. But half a dozen came from too far away to go home and they stayed. And one evening I heard a lot of noise in the attic (you know that is where they have their rooms) and I went upstairs to investigate and I heard two people snickering behind a door and then I heard the high giggle of one of the models, who had no business to be there at all, and then the boy said: 'And now we are in good company, for we are like Adam and Eve in Paradise.' So I told them that I would make that wish come true and would play the Angel with the Flaming Sword and would drive them out, and I threw them out of the house then and there, because I have got to have discipline in my own home, but of course people talked about it and as a result three of the other boys have left me.

"And so you see how it goes. I have several thousand guilders still coming to me for portraits I have done. But it seems that it is harder to collect nowadays than formerly. Some people claim that we may conclude peace with Spain almost any day now and that there will be quite a terrible crisis then, but why war should be more profitable than peace is something I don't quite understand. If I had ever kept books I would be able to tell you where all the money has gone, for I must have made quite a great deal these last ten years. And anyway, it does not matter. It is only a question of a few months—as soon as the formalities connected with the inheritance shall have been completed. You know how slow our courts are about such things. There must be a guardian for little Titus and the Chamber of Orphans must be consulted. I hate all such legal complications. I don't understand them. They worry me and keep me from working and so I just try to forget them. But everything will be all right in a couple of months.

"Meanwhile, it will be much better for everybody concerned if that damned nurse goes before the end of another day. I could sell something out of my collection, but then the whole town would say that those Frisian relations who said that I was a spendthrift and was wasting my wife's money had been right. I need fifty guilders and I need them right away and I need them very quietly. I can pay you back in September or October and I shall give you six percent, which seems fair. Can I have them?"

I said yes, he could have them, and went to the little safe in my bedroom in which I kept the East Indian shares I had inherited from my grand-uncle and I took out five golden riders and I gave them to Rembrandt and I bade him forget about the interest—it was just a small loan between friends, and that evening I wrote a long letter to a friend of mine in Leeuwarden, a young man with whom I had studied in Leyden, but who had given up medicine and had gone in for the law. He belonged to an excellent family which had remained faithful to the King of Spain after the outbreak of the revolution and had therefore been deprived of all its possessions. He often declared that while poverty might be no disgrace, it had very little else to recommend it to a sensible person, and he had made no secret of it then that he meant to marry money—a great deal of money—just as soon as he had the opportunity. He had been as good as his word. Almost immediately upon graduation he had married the daughter of a very rich cattle-owner from the neighborhood of Franeker. A former acquaintance who had gone to Franeker to finish his studies (finding Leyden a little too diverting for that constant application to his work which his father deemed necessary) had been present at the wedding. I ran across him one day when he was passing through Amsterdam and he told me all about it.

"The bride squinted and she was slightly lame," he informed me, "but she was an orphan and had two hundred thousand guilders in cash. The groom looked very meek and dignified and kept awake all during the service. He has bought out one of the best notary offices in the capital—specializes in farmers' cases, has become the financial adviser of every honest plowman in all of the sixteen counties—coins in the money almost as fast as the Mint can turn it out—is a very decent husband to the unsightly wife and is just as amusing and honest a companion as in the days before he got rich."

I wrote to this provincial Croesus and asked him to find out for me whether Saskia van Uylenburgh had really been as rich as people said and to give me all the particulars he could lay hands on—that I was not acting in an indiscreet fashion, but that I had a friend who was greatly interested, etc., etc., and would he please let me know by return mail.

Three weeks later I had his answer and his letter showed that he had not changed a bit from the days when we used to walk to Noordwijk on a fine Sunday afternoon to eat a supper of bread and cheese in the Golden Hyacinth and felt that this world was by far the best sort of a world anybody could wish to live in.

This is what he wrote:

"Ornatissime!

"Magno cum gaudio accepi letteras tuas atque maximo cum—now what in thunder was 'haste' in Latin? But anyway, I got your letter and the question you ask can refer to only one person, the great Maestro Rembrandtus van Rijn, painter-in-extraordinary to the Rabbis of Amsterdam and who not long ago, if I am to believe my correspondents, has given up the use of colors altogether and now distills himself a new sort of picture out of a mixture of soot, lamp-black and coal-ashes.

"For who else could be interested in the affairs of that poor Uylenburgh girl, who left here so long ago that few of her contemporaries remember her? Be reassured, however. I have done a little quiet investigating and here is my general impression of the case.

"I don't think that there is very much money in that particular quarter, or if there be any, that it will ever be of great use to him, as most of the renowned Uylenburgh millions exist only on paper, or wherever they exist 'in naturalia,' are so hopelessly mortgaged, hypothesized or hypothecated (take your choice) debentured and generally tied-up, that in case of a sudden sale, I doubt whether they would realize one twentieth of their normal value. I am on agreeable terms of professional cordiality with the notary who has handled the affairs of the family ever since the old man was elected sheriff for the first time and that must have been shortly after the flood. He threw up his hands in despair and said: 'Don't talk to me about that case! It will be my death yet. For now, so I understand, that the youngest daughter has died, the one who married that miller or painter or whatever he is in Holland, the widower will probably write us a letter and ask for a settlement but Solomon in all his wisdom could not unravel that estate.' And then he gave me many details, all in a perfectly professorial manner, and I shall not even try to explain his speech in plain Dutch, but I shall merely give you the gist of his observations.

"Old Rombertus van Uylenburgh, the father, had been quite a famous man in local Frisian politics. A big frog in a small puddle. During the critical years of the rebellion, he had several times been Burgomaster of Leeuwarden and he it was who conducted the negotiations between the Estates of Friesland and the Prince of Orange about choosing the latter to be sovereign ruler of the new commonwealth. But William was murdered before they had been able to reach an agreement. As you undoubtedly know old Rombertus was lunching with William the day the latter was shot and held him in his arms when he died. All this had brought a great deal of honor, but he had been away from home so much that he had little time to look after his own affairs.

"The mother had brought up the children, of whom there had been nine at the time of her death in '21 or '22. In '24 Rombertus himself had gone to join the angels. At that moment, two of the sons were engaged in the law and a third one had become an officer in a regiment of the line. Of the daughters, the eldest, Antje, is married to a certain Maccovius, a professor of theology in the University of Franeker, a rather unpleasant person of very violent convictions, but very popular among his neighbors whose views are about as broad as that of a birdseed. The second one, Hiskia, is married to Gerrit van Loo, who holds a political office in a little village north of Franeker. The third one, Titia, is married to a certain Frans Copal, who is engaged in business and who is said to spend much of his time in Holland. The fourth one is the wife of a Frisian gentleman of good family and some fortune, one Doede van Ockema, and the fifth one is the spouse of an artist by the name of Wybrand de Geest, a native of her own beloved town of Leeuwarden, who enjoys an excellent reputation as a portrait painter in this remote part of the world and who has done portraits of practically all of the members of the House of Orange who have ever visited Friesland.

"That, as our friends the French would say, is the 'tableau' of the immediate Uylenburgh family. There also are a vast number of uncles and aunts and cousins and second cousins and third cousins and some of them have remained at home, but others have boldly crossed the Zuyder Zee to try their luck in Amsterdam and of these you probably know more in Amsterdam than we do in Leeuwarden.

"Now as to the financial status of this Gens Uylenburghiensis. It is a most intricate matter, for as far as my informant knew, there never had been a division of the funds, and although the father had now been dead for almost twenty years, the estate had not yet been settled and it was doubtful whether a settlement would be possible at the present time, when the general fear that the war would come to an end has made money so tight that one is glad to pay twenty or even twenty-five percent for a loan of a few thousand guilders. In short, once upon a time there was a considerable fortune which belonged to the Uylenburgh children and of which they received so much per annum in the form of rents. But if any one of them should ever get into trouble and would ask for an immediate accounting, I am very doubtful whether the matter could be arranged without a dreadful sacrifice on the part of all concerned.

"Wherefore [so the letter ended], if your friend should be hard up for ready cash, I would advise him to go to the Jews and the money-lenders. They will give him better terms and they will prove to be more charitable than his beloved relations on this side of the Zuyder Zee. From all I have been able to gather, they are none too friendly towards this 'foreign' connection (any one not born within spitting distance of our beloved tower of Oldehove is considered a 'foreigner' in these parts) whose father ran a mill, whose brother is a shoemaker or some such terrible thing, who paints rabbis and associates openly with Turks and Frenchmen and other immoral races and who (something they will never forgive him) once paid 424 guilders for a picture by a certain Rubens who not only was an out-and-out Papist but who furthermore chose his subjects by preference from some heathenish story book, making it impossible for decent Christians to contemplate the same without a feeling of utter shame and mortification."

Then followed some very intimate and rather ribald remarks about the pleasant habits and manners of the populace among whom my old friend had cast his fortunes and the usual salutations in execrable Latin.

"Vale ornatissime atque eruditissime doctor medicinarum artium atque me miserum in hac urbe taediossissima visitare atque consolare festina.

"P.S.—You might send me some dried sprats as soon as the season opens. I confess to a liking for the lowly, petrified fish. In return for which I

JOHANNES LUTMA

THE DEATH OF THE VIRGIN

promise to keep you faithfully informed about anything that happens here in the matter of the U. family. But my general advice would be not to count on a penny. The money is there without a doubt. But how to get it away from the dear brethren and sistern—ah, my friend—there is the rub!

"P.P.S.—My wife wants to be remembered to you, ignota ignoto. She wonders whether you can find her a good cook in Amsterdam. Such a thing no longer exists in this part of the world. We have grown too prosperous. The wenches, all of them marry sailors, become ladies, and go about dressed up in silks and satins.

"P.P.P.S.—I meant bloaters, and not sprats. We can get sprats here by the ton, but the bloater is a delicacy. Ad nunc, vale definitissime atque favere mihi perge. . . ."

I put the document aside and did some fast thinking. Between the lines of his crazy letter, my old friend had told me everything I wanted to know and my heart was filled with sad forebodings. For by this time I had come to know Rembrandt quite well. He lived in a world of his own making and thus far life had been fairly easy to him. Now he had undoubtedly reached a crisis. His wife was dead. He had a small boy to bring up. It would cost a great deal to maintain the house in the Breestraat and public taste was rapidly changing and no longer looked with favor upon what people had begun to call his "phantastic experiments." The fact that he had asked me (still a comparative stranger) for a loan of fifty guilders, showed that he was very hard up for ready cash. Now if he had only been made to understand that he was poor and would have to begin all over again to provide for himself and his son, all might have been well, for he was a hard worker and never spent a penny upon his own comforts. But there was this strange streak of the grand seigneur in him. He must play fairy-godfather to his poor colleagues and whenever he went to an auction, he must outbid all the professional art dealers, just to show them that he was Rembrandt, the great Rembrandt, who need not bother about trifles.

If only he had been put face to face with the fact that he did not have a cent in the whole wide world! But he had fallen heir to Saskia's fortune! There was that pathetic will, leaving everything to her "beloved man" and leaving it without any restrictions or reservations whatsoever. If only she had insisted upon a guardian for her son, then there would have been a public appraisal and Rembrandt might have discovered what I now knew and what I could not very well tell him without running the risk of being called a busybody—a man who poked his nose into affairs that were none of his business.

My hands were tied and I was forced to stand by and see the poor fellow play the millionaire on the strength of a paper promise which was not worth its weight in lead.

Nevertheless, I might have done something, but just then an incident occurred that upset my own life so completely that it was years before I saw Rembrandt again.

And when I returned from my foreign travels, it was too late.

The bubble had burst, the house had been sold, and the painter was peddling his pictures from one pawnshop to the next, to buy bread for his children.

Chapter 17

I RELATE A FEW INTERESTING STORIES ABOUT MY GRANDFATHER

And now I come to that strange period in my life to which I have already alluded a few pages ago, when through circumstances over which I had no control whatsoever, I was an exile for almost eight years.

I have always been exceedingly sorry that this happened. I can never quite get over the feeling that things might have gone differently with Rembrandt if I had been there.

I am not thinking in the first place of the financial end of things. Since the death of my grand-uncle I really had more than I needed for my very simple needs and I might have been able to help him out of a few of his difficulties. But it would not have been an easy task. For Rembrandt (as I have said so often before) was absolutely blind on the subject of money. He was indeed blind upon most subjects related directly or indirectly with the business of living a quiet and respectable existence, as those terms were understood by the vast majority of his neighbors. He was a man possessed of a single idea. Within the realm of color and form, he felt himself like unto God. His ambition along that line sometimes assumed almost divine proportions. He wanted to capture the entire existing world around him and hold it his prisoner on canvas or paper. Life, alas, was so short and there was so much to be done. He had to work and work and work. He was sick. Never mind, he must work. His wife (one of the few persons who ever assumed the shape of a definite human being in his preoccupied mind) died. He must rush through the funeral and go back to work. He was acclaimed the fashionable painter of the hour and made twenty or thirty thousand guilders a year. Put them away in that cupboard over there or go to the Jew around the corner and buy out his whole stock of curiosities or give them to some poor devil of a fellow-painter who lies starving in a garret. Do anything you want with the money, as long as you don't bother him by talking about it. For he must work and life was short and there was a great deal to be done. A letter has just arrived from the sheriff saying that a number of outstanding notes are long overdue and should be paid right then and there or there would be difficulties. Visits from the Honorable Masters in Bankruptcy. Forced sales—fines—imprisonment, even. Fiddlesticks! it is winter and at three o'clock in the afternoon it is too dark to paint. One has to be economical and save every minute in times like these. The sheriff is a fool. Tell him so. Bid him come or stay away, for it is all the same as long as one can only work and work and work. No, a man like that could not be helped with an occasional check—with the loan of a few thousand guilders. They would have meant just as much to him as to a beaver busily engaged upon building a dam, or a bird constructing its nest.

All one could do for an unfortunate fellow like this, mad with the beauty of the outer world, crazy with joy at the myriad manifestations of the mysterious inner spirit, was to give him some understanding and then some more understanding and still more understanding and ask for nothing in return. Amen.

For the lonely pioneers who do the work that the rest of us shirk ask for very little. They are willing to go hungry and to slave for mean wages and to be humiliated by those who in God's own good time, in a thousand different ways, won't be allowed to hold the stirrup of their horses.

But they die unless at least once in a long while some one comes their way who stops in his tracks and bids them a cheery good-morning and casually remarks: "That is a pretty fine piece of work you are doing there."

For such is their nature.

And it is part of the penalty they pay for the greatest of their manifold blessings—the weregild they must contribute for never having grown up.

Here I must call a halt.

I had intended to write about a very dear friend, now dead and gone, and from the very beginning I had meant to keep myself and my own affairs as much as possible out of these recollections.

But when two lives are as absolutely entwined and interwoven as those of Rembrandt and my own, it is very difficult to accomplish this as completely as I meant to do it.

The next few pages therefore will be mainly about myself. But I shall be very short and above all things, I shall try to be honest.

My grandfather was an almost mythological figure to me. I knew him well, for he did not die until I was almost thirty. But when I was young, the men who had taken part in the great struggle for liberty were fast dying out and the few survivors were regarded with that awed respect which the Greeks would have bestowed upon the Titans, had one of them managed to escape from Tartarus to find his way to Athens.

As a young man, while serving as first-mate on a ship that plied between Rotterdam and Antwerp, he had once been caught with a copy of a Dutch New Testament which in the kindness of his heart he had promised to bring to a Lutheran minister awaiting a sentence of death in one of the Flemish prisons. He himself (as far as I was ever able to find out) took very little interest in theological questions. Whenever a dispute of that sort arose (and in our Republic, next to the making of money, people seem to have very few other interests) he would leave the room and whistle for his dog and go out for a walk, if it were daytime, or if it were night, go to bed and read the colloquies of Erasmus, which were an everlasting source of entertainment to him and which he could enjoy in the original, as shortly after the siege of Haarlem he had spent a year in a Spanish prison and had shared his cell with an Anabaptist preacher who happened to be quite a scholar and had whiled away the tedious hours of their common confinement by teaching his room-mate the rudiments of the Latin grammar.

No, he belonged to that vast group of men and women who had happened to be born just about the time Luther and Calvin had started their reformatory activities and who had been so thoroughly exasperated by the cruelty, the intolerance and the bigotry of both Catholics and Protestants that they had been obliged to seek a refuge among the philosophers of ancient days.

Nominally, my grandfather called himself a Christian.

In his heart, he was a contemporary of Socrates. Jesus, if he ever thought of him at all, he regarded as a well-meaning but rather futile and slightly bewildered young Jewish prophet, who in the aloofness of his primitive mountain village and totally ignorant of whatever lay beyond his own poverty-stricken hillsides (peasants always despise what they do not understand), had done more to arrest the normal development of the civilized world than any other agency, either human or divine.

He often talked to me of these matters during the last years of his life, but asked me not to mention it to any one else.

"What would be the use?" he would say. "Our wily old cousin was right. The average man is too weak to stand firmly upon his own feet. He needs some outward support, some pleasant fairy-story that shall make him forget the horrors, the boredom, the dull disappointment of his daily routine. Let him have his tales of giants and gods, his heroes and paladins.

"When you were a boy and believed in Santa Claus, Dominie Slatterius came to your father and said that this old saint was a relic of heathenism and you ought to be told and your father, being a fool, was ready to do so. I took the reverend gentleman by the scruff of the neck and threw him down the stoop and I told your father he would go the same way if he ever tried to substitute one of his dreadful Jewish fishermen or tentmakers for that amiable holy man who has made more children happy than all the church fathers and apostles together. That was not a very tolerant thing to do but look what has happened right here in our own country?

"Who started the great rebellion? A handful of men. What did they have to gain? Very little except the chance of being hung on the nearest tree. Of course, once the thing was under way, there were a lot of ardent patriots who knew that it was good fishing in troubled waters and who came over to our side. But who were the men who planned everything and took the risks and pawned their plate and their wives' diamonds and took extra mortgages on their houses to hire troops and buy guns and powder and ships and everything that was needed? A mere handful of honest fellows who hated to see poor devils of weavers and fishermen and carpenters being hacked to pieces and boiled alive and drowned like kittens merely because they happened to think differently from their neighbors upon subjects of which the neighbors couldn't possibly know more than they did themselves.

"I don't want to claim that we were saints. We were nothing of the sort. We drank and we cursed and we knew the difference between a handsome young wench and a homely old hag. And I don't swear that we would ever have moved a finger if it had not been for those endless processions of men and women, trudging patiently from the jail to the gallows, perfectly respectable citizens, hard-working little artisans with mumbling lips and staring eyes, going to be tied to a ladder and thrown into a slow-burning coal fire because they disagreed upon some utterly idiotic point of divine law with a fat old Italian who lived a thousand miles away, and who needed some money to give his daughter a suitable dowry.

"That is what started me. That and nothing else. And then, when it was all over, what did one see? The same men whom we had dragged away from the gallows by main force—those same men and women for whom we had ruined ourselves that they might think as they pleased—started murdering those who only a short while before had murdered them. The victim turned executioner, and the former executioners were now merrily dangling from a hundred trees. Could anything have been more absurd? We got rid of those hordes of mendicants and begging friars, because they were an obscene nuisance. And then, as soon as they were gone and we thought, 'Now we shall have peace,' our cities and our villages and our cross-roads and our homes were invaded by platoons of even more unpleasant brethren with long brown coats and long black faces, but every whit as stupid, as narrow minded, as objectionable, as their pestiferous predecessors.

"What is it all about, anyway?

"I am an old man. I have spent most of my life fighting for an absurd ideal of tolerance. And as soon as we had kicked the enemy out of the front door, he came in again by the back entrance.

"Bring me a pipe of tobacco and let me sit and smoke. It is the only sensible thing beside raising strawberries, and for that I am no longer young enough."

These conversations (and we had many of them, and they were all of them more or less alike) were typical of the old skipper and it will give you an idea of the sort of man he was. He must have been a terrific fighter in his day. He stood six feet three in his stockings and weighed well over two hundred pounds. He once figured out that he had passed through six formal sieges and taken part in eighteen naval engagements, not to mention skirmishes and three pitched battles upon those not infrequent occasions when the sailors waded ashore and joined the infantry. Several times he had been badly wounded, but he had the constitution of a young ox and even recovered from the blood-lettings with which in those early days my colleagues tried to cure everything from a broken leg to a case of anemia.

At one time or another of his career he must have accumulated considerable wealth. He once told me that during the expedition against Cadiz, when he commanded the second squadron, his share of the plunder alone amounted to fifty thousand ducats, and that was only one occasion among many when he had a plentiful chance to line his pockets with Spanish doubloons. What had become of all this money, I don't know. Nobody seemed to know. But he was the incarnation of generosity. He was so absolutely open-handed that in the middle of a battle he would have given his sword to his enemy, had the latter asked him for it, and would have continued to fight with his bare hands rather than say "no" to a courteous request.

Not that he was exactly poor when I came to know him a little better. He lived in a very decent house on the river front near Rotterdam and after the death of my grandmother he kept but one single servant, an old sailor whom he had once saved from being hung for an act of insubordination—a most excusable case of insubordination, as he explained to me, for the fellow had merely gone on shore to kill a landlubber who had stolen his girl from him. The old sailor was not only his devoted servant but also a perfect cook.

To return to my grandfather, he spent very little money upon his personal adornment, but a great deal upon books, and until the last years of his life he kept a small sailing-boat with which he used to putter around from morning till night and which at last was the cause of his death, for one day, leaving the harbor of Brielle, he saw how a small boy, who had been bombarding his craft with chunks of dried mud, lost his balance and fell into the water and was on the point of being carried away by the tide. He jumped overboard, saved the brat, gave him a most terrific walloping and continued his voyage without bothering to change his clothes. That night he had a chill and three days later he was dead from pneumonia, a fitting end for one who had spent his life doing the sort of things he had done.

When his last will and testament was opened, it was found that he had left every cent he possessed to an old sailors' home on condition that once a year a rousing feast be given to all the inmates upon which occasion they were to be allowed to get as drunk and hilarious as they pleased.

On the last day of his life he was visited by a minister. Rumor had gone about that the old skipper was on the point of dying and it seemed inconceivable that any one should go to his final rest without a word of commendation on the part of a duly ordained clergyman. The Reverend Doctor who made his appearance was a genial soul, the only one among the fourteen local shepherds who had sometimes been suspected of certain worldly inclinations. In the language of that day he was a "libertine," a man who took liberties with Holy Script and who was more interested in the spiritual message of Jesus than in the color of the cloak he had worn while delivering it. Upon this occasion his brethren had probably delegated him to call upon the dying sinner, as the one least likely to be shown the door. And the good dominie acquitted himself of his task with great dexterity, being neither too cordial nor too distant and aloof. He casually remarked that most people when they found themselves on the point of reporting for duty to the Great Commander of us all (a bit of joviality which was not appreciated by the patient) liked to have the opportunity to discuss their past record with some one who devoted all his time to matters of the soul.

"Dominie," the old man answered, "I know who you are and I have heard a good deal about you that I like. For one thing, most of your colleagues wish that you would slip on an apple skin and fall in a canal and drown. In this house, that is a recommendation. But what could you possibly hope to do for me?"

"Well," the reverend gentleman replied, "we might have a little talk about your chances of salvation. What for example has been your attitude towards the Lord's most holy covenants?"

"Yes," said my grandfather, "that is rather a leading question, but I like your courage and I will answer you. I think your Ten Commandments are a waste of time."

"But isn't that a dangerous remark for a man who is on the brink of the grave?"

"I don't see why. I am perfectly willing to have this out with the Lord himself. The best proof that he does not believe in them himself is the fact that he has never kept them."

"That is pure blasphemy!"

"Not in the least. But short of keeping the Sabbath, he has broken every one of them."

"I am afraid that I have nothing to say to you."

"Now there you go again, like a good Christian! Have a moment's patience with a dying man and I will explain. How about that idea of not killing your fellow-men? My dear friend, the whole Old Testament is full of killing. Your Jehovah is a mean and vindictive creature and suffers from tantrums like any badly brought up child. When he has one of his attacks (and almost anything may bring them on) he hits and strikes and thumps and prances like a drunken sailor in a bar-room brawl. Villages, towns, whole nations are wiped off the face of the earth—and what have they done? Often nothing for which an ordinary magistrate would dare to fine them.

"Take that business in Egypt. It has always struck me that the Egyptians were completely in the right. After all, it was their country. After all, the Jews had come to them to keep from starving to death and they had been pretty decently treated too. And according to what I have heard of them, they were a fine people—much nicer than their guests who were like the cuckoo and always put their eggs into another bird's nest. But they must be visited with all sorts of plagues and lose their children and suffer hunger and pestilence because your absurd Jehovah had another attack of anger and wanted to do a little smiting."

The minister looked perplexed. "I never heard it explained quite that way," he remarked.

"I am sure you never did and I am sorry if I should hurt your feelings. But that happens to be the way I look upon it."

"Anyway," in a feeble effort to spar for time, "that happened before he gave us his precious Law."

"Precious Law indeed! But afterwards it was just as bad. I know He kept the Sabbath, but that is about all. It was easy for him to tell us to honor our parents, as he did not have any himself to exasperate him with their everlasting complaints about being an 'undutiful child.' And as for the seventh commandment, have you ever thought of the way Joseph must have looked upon this divine command about respecting the integrity of another man's wife?"

The minister made ready to go, but the sick man held him back. "Don't go, Dominie," he said. "If this hurts your feelings, we will talk of something else."

"It does not hurt my feelings," the minister replied, "but it fills my heart with grief that any one who has spent his whole life among Christians should speak and think the way you do."

"That is just it! I have spent my whole life among Christians. When I was forty, I made a vow. I said to myself that if I met three Christians who really and truly lived up to the lessons of their master—three men or women who were truly humble and kind and tolerant and forgiving—yet professed themselves to belong to your creed, I would join the Church."

"And now you are how old?"

"Eighty-two, though I shall never see eighty-three."

"And you are still a pagan."

"No, Dominie, I am not that either."

"Then what do you call yourself?"

"Exactly what I am. Look here," and with great effort he pulled his night-gown from his left shoulder, for he was in terrible pain and very weak. "Look at this. Can you still see it after these sixty years? A big red letter H. The Inquisition burned it on my back so that if they ever caught me again, they would know me as a heretic and could treat me accordingly. When I come to the Gates of Heaven, I will show Saint Peter this and I am sure he will let me in, for what was he himself but a heretic when he turned his back upon the law of his fathers? And I will come to the throne of God and I will show him this and I will say: 'Holy Father, I fought sixty years for what I believed to be right and that red H is all I got to show for my labors. They gave it to me because I felt, like a very wonderful sage of olden times, that the still small voice from within was the best guide to follow in dealing with one's fellow-man.

" 'They burned it into my quivering flesh because they said I was a heretic—a person who did not hold with the established opinions. They meant it as a disgrace, but I have worn it as a badge of honor ever since. I don't know, God, what your intentions were with us poor mortals. Perhaps you ought to have devoted another week or fortnight to the business of getting our world started, for although I mean no offense, it is a pretty sad mess at the present moment and if all the history I have read means anything, it has been a muddle ever since you turned your back upon it and left us to the mercies of old Adam. Now I may be all wrong, but the only way in which I can see that anything will ever be accomplished is for some of us now and then to take an unpopular stand. The aye-sayers never get anywhere. But the no-sayers irritate the rest of their neighbors occasionally into doing the right thing. And I am a no-sayer, a heretic, a man who does not hold with the majority. As long as you turned me loose into this world with a mind of my own, I took it for granted that you meant me to do something with it.

" 'But that meant that I had to have doubts, to ask questions, to take every problem apart and see what I could make of it. Blame me and punish me, God, if I have done wrong, but I would have disgraced your Holy Name had I done differently and not used that brain you put into my skull to the best of my ability to show my fellow-men the way to a more reasonable world.' "

The old man exhausted himself by this supreme effort and lay panting for breath. The minister, who was really a very kindly person, tried to change the subject.

"Our Heavenly Father no doubt will know how to answer that question better than I can hope to do. But how about this world? You were a mariner. You depended upon a compass to set your course. And yet you lived without a single rule by which to guide your conduct."

The old man opened his eyes and smiled, though very feebly. "I am sorry, Dominie, but once more you are mistaken. I was quite young when I learned that my fellow-men had to be loved in spite of themselves, not to speak of trusting them. The only creature that I could depend upon, besides my wife (but she was an exception), was a dog. And I have never been without one since I was a boy of fifteen.

"I know you don't think very much of dogs. You won't even let them have a soul or go to Heaven. Think of golden streets with nothing but holy people and not a single dog! No, I have never spent either a day or a night without one of those four-footed companions. They cost me a lot of time, but they amply repaid me for my trouble. For dogs are very wise. Much wiser than men. People say they can't speak. Perhaps they know how but refuse to use their voice to save themselves an endless amount of bother and vague discussion. But they know all sorts of things we don't know, and they have a finer feeling for the difference between right and wrong than we do. And when I came home at night, or back to my ship, after the day's work (and pretty rough work it was at times) I would look my dog in the face and if he still wagged his tail at me, I knew that everything was all right, but if he didn't, I knew that something, somewhere, had gone wrong. It may sound a bit simple, but it is true, and best of all, it worked."

"And our system does not work?"

"Your system does not work. It merely talks and now if you will pardon me, I will go to sleep. I am not very strong any more and to-morrow, if you are right, I will have to engage in another conversation of this sort, and I still have to prepare my little speech."

"And if I am wrong?"

"If you are wrong, I shall be able to rest—rest for ever and ever."

"Then you are very tired?"

"Incredibly tired."

"Of living?"

"No, just of having been alive," and with this the sick man pulled the blankets around his shoulders and never spoke again.

The next morning the sailor-servant came to open the curtains and ask after his master's wishes.

But the skipper had received an answer to all his questions.

He was dead.

Chapter 18

UNDER WHAT PECULIAR CIRCUMSTANCES MY GRANDMOTHER HAPPENED TO MARRY MY GRANDFATHER

So much for my grandfather and now a few words about that even more extraordinary person who became my grandmother.

She died ten years before her husband, but I still knew her quite well and as she disliked her only son (my own father) as cordially as her husband detested him, she had concentrated all her love upon her two grandchildren. She was a tiny woman and she had never had the smallpox and her bright little eyes shone out from a face that had retained the complexion of a small girl, although it was well provided with wrinkles, for life as the wife of this extraordinary man had not been exactly easy.

"But it has always been interesting," she used to say when people tried to tell her how sorry they were for her that she, the daughter of an Antwerp burgomaster, had not been able to do better for herself and for the greater part of her life had been obliged to do her own housework and her own washing.

"It has never been dull for a moment, and what else counts except the few moments when we realize that we are something better than cabbages or cucumbers?"

But there was something else that set her apart from all other people in the minds of those who knew her. She had a smile. She rarely laughed and I have never known her to grin or to give a too exuberant manifestation of joy. But she was endowed with a most wondrous smile. I find it difficult to describe that smile. Rembrandt once showed me the reproduction (a very bad one) of a portrait painted by an Italian called Leonardo. It was the portrait of a woman, the wife, I believe of a Florentine merchant. That woman had the same smile, and it made her look as if she were the sole possessor of a terribly amusing secret which she could not impart to anybody in the whole wide world, but which kept her interested all the time and allowed her to rise sublimely superior to the common ills of mortal men.

I don't know anything about the private life of the Italian who was responsible for that painting. I think I have read somewhere that the lady in question was the third or fourth wife of a rich and old man and the anticipation of getting rid of him at an early date and becoming the mistress of a vast fortune may have kindled that inner glow of happiness which played around her eyes.

In the case of my grandmother the reason was more apparent and a great deal more creditable. Once upon a time and while she was still quite young, she had not only defied the power of Church and State, but had cheerfully thumbed her nose at all the established authorities and had so completely beaten them at their own game that for a moment at least she had been the most popular woman of western Europe.

She rarely talked about it and never mentioned it to us children, but I got the story from my uncle and this is what had happened.

My grandfather used to be mate on a vessel that plied between Rotterdam and Antwerp, while his brother attended to the family wood-yards in Veere. In those days no one was safe against the activities of thousands of spies—literally thousands of them. They were everywhere, and apparently never slept. A few of them were regular passengers on board my grandfather's boat, but he kept to his own business and was never much bothered by them. Besides, he needed all his time on the deck, for the King's Majesty being practically bankrupt, beacons and buoys and lighthouses had been deserted by their rightful keepers and navigation had become a matter of ability and of luck.

But that was not all. The inhabitants of the coastal regions, being deprived of the greater part of their revenue by the fact that no one any longer bothered about the old fast-days, but ate meat seven times a week, instead of fish (as they should have done), were turning more and more to piracy for a living. After all, they had wives and large broods of children to support and hunger has never been known to improve people's tempers nor increase their patience.

As the mariners of His Majesty's Navy (whose pay was three years overdue) took only a very luke-warm interest in protecting His Majesty's ports against freebooters, the honest fishermen sailed forth as buccaneers and soon were robbing friend and enemy with a sublime disregard for the rules of war or common decency. My grandfather's ship was twice attacked by them. Both times he got away without great damage but on the second occasion he was rather badly hurt by a bullet in his left arm. He had been warned to be extra cautious because among the passengers there was one of the Burgomasters of Antwerp and his daughter and they would have brought a handsome ransom had they been captured. He had not paid much attention to the old man. He had remarked to himself that the girl was a very handsome little creature, but though a cat may look at a king, the mate of a small trading-vessel had better not cast a too-longing eye upon the daughter of so great a magistrate as an Antwerp burgomaster. And he had forgotten all about her, except that when she went down the gangplank when he was standing waiting for the arrival of a doctor to bandage his arm and remove the bullet which was still imbedded in the muscles, the girl had suddenly turned to him, had whispered, "I think you are a wonderful man," and had thereupon departed.

Well, it was nice that she had noticed him, but life was full of a number of things that either had to be done or were agreeable in the doing, and he had promptly forgotten all about her.

Six weeks later on his third round trip he was arrested, denounced by a Dominican who had been on board and who had taken the trouble to go through the mate's luggage while the latter was attending to his business on deck. A copy of a Dutch translation of the New Testament, addressed to a citizen of Antwerp was found among his clothes. My grandfather was arrested and locked up in the Steen. He offered as his defense that he had carried that package with him in perfect good faith without bothering to open it or see what it contained. Yes, he believed that his friend had told him that it was a Bible, but he was a sailor, not a theologian. They showed him a passage (I think it was the gospel of St. John) where the apostle says: "And as we are saved through Christ Jesus" and where the translator had added the words: "And through him alone," as if it were possible to find salvation without the intermediary of a duly ordained priest and they asked him what he thought of that? He answered that he had really never thought of it at all, but that it seemed sensible.

They asked him whether he knew what had become of the man who had dared to print such violent heresies. He said no, and they told him that he had been burned at the stake. He answered that that seemed a bit severe for a mere four words and the chief Inquisitor, bidding him hold his tongue, told him that one word, yea, one single letter of one single word, was often enough in the sight of God to condemn a man to eternal punishment and he had answered that he supposed God was too busy with more important affairs to count the exact number of words in every book that was being printed, whereupon the president of the court lost all patience, called the young sailor a blasphemous fiend from Hell and a few other names which I have forgotten and after a moment's consultation with his colleagues, declared that the prisoner was hopeless, that it was not even necessary to torture him, as he had already confessed to everything the judges had suspected, and that they condemned him to be surrendered to the civil court which would know how to handle such a case and see that justice be done.

Up to that moment, it seems that my grandfather never even suspected the serious plight in which he so suddenly found himself. He expected that he would be fined or perhaps kept in jail for a couple of weeks. It was too absurd to punish a man more severely for a crime which he had really never committed. Besides, the book had not reached its destination and so he asked himself, in his simple way, "What harm has been done?" But the fact that he was removed from the common room in which all suspects were herded together and placed in solitary confinement in an evil-smelling dark hole, right underneath the watch-tower, gave him his first inkling that all was not right! He sat there in that smelly dungeon for three days without food or drink, was then heavily manacled and taken before the special court that dealt with cases of rebellion and within fifteen minutes he found himself condemned to be burned alive.

Of what thereafter happened, he only retained some very hazy recollections. All day and all night long he sat in his dark hole, sharing his loneliness with a small army of rats, as hungry as himself. Fortunately hunger and thirst tortured him so severely that he did not have much strength left to ponder upon his terrible fate. The whole affair continued to appear to him in the light of a very ill-timed joke. He just could not take it seriously. Tie a man to a stout iron post and pile fagots up all around him and set fire to those fagots and burn a living human being for no other possible reason than that he had been found in the possession of a book to which some poor fanatic had added four words of his own?. It was preposterous and it could not possibly be true.

Nevertheless, on the fifth day of his confinement, the executioner appeared in his dungeon, removed his irons and bade him change his clothes for a loose-fitting yellow cloak, richly ornamented with black devils chasing lost souls with long pitchforks (he remembered those little long-tailed devils dancing furiously up and down by the light of the flickering candle which the hangman had put on the floor). When the cloak had been neatly adjusted he told him that within another hour he would be visited by a priest who would hear his confession. The execution was to take place that same afternoon and there were seventeen other candidates for glory.

With these cheerful words, his evil-looking visitor had bade him godspeed and he had been left with his own thoughts until from sheer exhaustion he had fallen asleep, and had slept for what seemed to him at least a whole day and a whole night. Curiously enough, he had been right, but sailors often have a feeling for time which ordinary people lack. When he came back to life, he found quite a number of people in his cell and there were torches and the rumor of many voices and he knew that his hour had come.

He tried to get up, but he could not stand, and then to his surprise the chains were removed from his hands and his feet and he was asked whether he was strong enough to understand what was being said to him and he answered yes, that he thought he was and some one who looked like the clerk of some legal office read him a long paper, from which after an endless number of whereas's and wherefore's it appeared that ever since the memory of man, there had been a law in the land of Flanders according to which a man, condemned to death, would have his life spared if there were a virgin willing to marry him as he was being taken to the scaffold, ready to be executed; that there was a woman in Antwerp who had offered to take him as husband; that the counselors of the Inquisition had objected that this law did not hold in cases of "an offense against God," but that the highest authorities in the city had been consulted and had declared that the law held good, even in cases of "an offense against God"; that therefore the prisoner had to be approached and had to be given the choice between being burned alive or contracting matrimony with a totally unknown person, after which he would be exiled from the territory of Antwerp and the province of Flanders for all time.

My grandfather quite naturally chose the latter course. He imagined that some old hag had decided to use him as her means of escape from spinsterhood, but he was still young and life, even by the side of a homely female, with a hunchback and no teeth, was better than being slowly roasted to death in the public square of Antwerp. And he had answered yes, that he was ready to accept the lady's kind offer, though he must apologize for not appearing at his wedding in more fitting garments. Whereupon the clerk of the court (for that is who he was) said that the clothes did not matter, as there still was some other detail to be attended to, that the authorities could not run the risk of having so dangerous a person return to their province without means of recognizing him, and that as a perpetual souvenir of this memorable occasion, they had condemned him to be branded before they would surrender him to his lawful bride.

He was at once taken to the torture chamber, where everything was ready for his reception, and in less than five minutes the stench of burning human flesh told him that justice in the true Spanish fashion had been done and that one more person had been marked in indelible form with that letter H, which was reserved exclusively for heretics and prostitutes.

The pain and the anger at finding himself helpless and in the hands of a foul-smelling and slightly drunken butcher's boy, who was learning the executioner's trade in his leisure hours and who bungled the job and hurt him much more than was necessary, made my grandfather faint. When he came to he found himself in the Chapel of the Steen, and a monk was throwing water into his face.

"He is coming to," he said. "You can bring in the bride."

My grandfather prepared for the worst.

The door opened and in came the daughter of the Antwerp burgomaster who had been on board his ship that time they had been attacked by a band of hungry fishermen.

"I am sorry," she said, "that I am doing this to you. But you are too handsome a thing to die so young, and besides, I want you."

An hour later, the couple was on board a vessel bound for Flushing.

And that is the way my grandmother married my grandfather.

Chapter 19

A HONEYMOON IN THE YEAR 1572

This strange wedding led to a companionship so beautiful and so lasting that I have never seen the like of it. Those two people understood each other even when they were a thousand miles apart. And when they were together in a room they seemed to be one person. Yet neither of them seemed to be obliged to sacrifice his or her own personality in order to be the absolute counterpart of the other. For in all minor details, they stuck closely to their own individuality. My grandfather was a confirmed freethinker but one of the true sort who could be pleasant and tolerant to his neighbors even when he felt them to be hopelessly and completely in the wrong. My grandmother on the other hand remained faithful to the faith of her youth until the day of her death.

"There is not very much faith in it of the sort of faith you learn in your catechism," she used to explain to us when we were still very young children whenever we looked with fear and delight upon the Holy Family of beautifully colored earthenware that stood in the corner of her room, "and you precious darlings should not take it too seriously. But your grandmother is a simple soul and can't live without the fairy stories she used to believe as a child."

And she would tell us wonderful tales of saints who were boiled in oil and cut into little pieces or flayed alive, but who went on doing good to the poor just as unconcernedly as if nothing had happened to them, and she made the adventures of these holy men so natural and so real to us that my brother and I believed them all to be true and even began to write an illustrated history of the lives of the Saints—a literary enterprise which lasted exactly four weeks and carried us only from Adalbert of Prague to Afra of Augsburg.

For then our father, having been tipped off by the minister to whom we went for our religious training, discovered the manuscript, gave us both a sound thrashing and slowly burned our beloved pictures and our somewhat clumsy text over a small peat fire which had been lit especially for the occasion.

He then (as we afterwards heard) went to see his mother to complain of her action in telling us children a pack of lies, whereupon the old lady got so furious that she boxed his ears (boxed the ears of an Elder of the Dutch Reformed Church) and bade him be gone and leave the house forever. This does not sound like a happy family life, and as a matter of fact, the relations between my father and my grandmother were little short of grotesque.

How it was ever possible that such a man and such a woman, the incarnation of all that was good and true and brave and cheerful, should have given birth to the sad-eyed, morose and prejudiced creature who was the author of my being, is something I shall never be able to understand. I know that the old philosophers proclaimed that "nature makes no jumps." I am afraid that they were wrong, and that nature at times is the greatest "jumper" of them all. For, during my thirty-five years of practice I have seen her perform the strangest hops and bounds and capers. It may be that she acts according to certain definite though hidden laws of growth and development and that everything is for the best, which in her case means, "the inevitable." But I would have been a great deal happier if she had not chosen our particular family to demonstrate to what extents she could go when she was on one of her merry gambols.

According to those who hold that children born out of a great passion are the most gifted and the most brilliant, my father ought to have been one of the most remarkable men of his day and age. But circumstances interfered and whatever original impulses there may have been to give the child every possible advantage, they came to naught when the mother, just before the time of her confinement, was almost starved to death and for the greater part of three months had to subsist on a diet of boiled leaves and horse-meat.

That had happened in the year 1574. My grandparents had been married in the month of March, 1572. They had first gone to Flushing and when they found that they were no further molested by the Inquisition, they had gone to Veere to decide upon plans for the future. My grandfather had lost his job. Every respectable ship-owner was afraid to employ a man who had been branded like a common criminal. As for his wife, her noble act of self-sacrifice (for God knows, it took a great deal of courage on her part to take such a step) had completely estranged her from all her relatives. Her father had publicly cursed her. Her mother had died soon afterwards. My grandmother had written to her just before her death, but her letter had been returned to her unopened. In her pride, she had then completely broken with her own past, and to this very day I don't know her maiden name. I once asked her, for I was rather curious to know what blood might be flowing in my veins. She said: "Dear boy, I have never told any one and never shall tell any one. My life began the day I married your grandfather. Let that be enough."

She had been an only daughter and since according to Flemish law, a father could not disinherit his children, she ought to have come into a considerable inheritance. But this time the attorneys were prepared, and a clause was found in some ancient code (though to tell you the truth, it was no more superannuated than the law which had made it possible for her to marry my grandfather and save his life) by which all the money had been deviated to religious purposes before the death of her father and she had been unwilling to fight the case, as she wanted to be forgotten by all those among whom she had spent her childhood.

Anyway, the couple immediately after the great adventure were not only without funds but without the slightest prospect of making a living. Then one day early in April, when their last guilder was about to be spent, news reached Veere that a small squadron of freebooters, flying the flag of the Prince of Orange, had attacked the town of Brielle, a few miles to the north, and instead of plundering it (as had been their habit thus far) had decided to make it the center of operations against Spain.

The next morning, as captain of an eighteen-foot fishing-smack with eleven sailors and six arquebuses, my grandfather had left the harbor of Veere, bound for Brielle. He had been in luck. During the night a Spanish trading vessel carrying olive-oil from Cadiz to Amsterdam had run aground on the Onrust, a bank just off the mouth of the Scheldt. The dozen eager patriots, seeing the chance of a little extra profit, decided to attack the Spaniard, who measured at least three hundred tons. They waited till low tide and then five of them ran for the ship, which towered high above the yellow sand, leaning slightly over to one side, so that its guns either pointed to high heaven or were useless (on the leaning side) because the balls would not stay in them. The Spaniards tried to fire at their enemies with muskets, but they safely reached the vessel and crawling close to the bottom of the monster, they started making a fire out of some dried pieces of sail which they had carried with them.

The fire was not a success, but the rotten sail made a lot of smoke and the Spaniards, unaccustomed to this sort of warfare, surrendered for fear that they might be burned alive. Meanwhile a heavy breeze had sprung up from the west, the tide rose higher than usual, and grandfather not only succeeded in salvaging the vessel but brought it safely to Brielle where it was sold for 90,000 guilders, which after all the deductions for taxes and legal fees, gave each one of them the neat little sum of five thousand ducats.

It also drew the attention of the rebel commander to the young skipper of the Veere fishing-smack. He offered him a position on board his own vessel and in this way, grandfather drifted, entirely by chance, into the work for which he was most fit.

The next year he took part in the battle of the Zuyder Zee in which the Dutch for the first time captured a Spanish admiral and then he returned to Zeeland and took an active part in the operations which forced Middelburg, the capital of the province, to take the side of the rebellion.

Meanwhile in anticipation of difficulties in Zeeland (which, however, never occurred), my grandfather had sent his wife to Leyden where he had some distant relatives from his mother's side. As the Spaniards had tried to take the town but had retreated after a short while from fear of being drowned out of their trenches, this seemed as safe a place as any. But suddenly in the month of May they reappeared and cut the town so completely off from the rest of the country that during the first two months of the siege, only six people succeeded in breaking through the lines and reaching the headquarters of the Prince, who now lived in Delft, which was then considered the strongest fortress of the province of Holland.

The siege lasted six months and all that time my grandfather had only twice heard from his wife. Both times she wrote, "Doing well." But the last message, brought by carrier pigeon, carried the words: "Please hurry. I am getting terribly hungry." As indeed she was, together with the other inhabitants of the town, for the cows and pigs and sheep had all of them been eaten up—the horses were fast going, and the regular diet of the long-suffering people consisted of soup made from the leaves of trees and a hideous stew made out of grass and cabbages. Six thousand people had died of hunger or disease and the garrison was so weak from lack of food that there were hardly soldiers enough to man the guns. Nevertheless the town held out as the example of Haarlem, where the people had surrendered meekly to the mercy of the King's Majesty (and had been drowned wholesale by being bound back to back and then thrown into the lake), had taught them a lesson. And the local magistrates decided that everything should be done to save Leyden from a similar fate.

Early in August, the dikes near Rotterdam were cut and two weeks later a fleet of rafts and flat-bottomed ships stormed the first line of dams that was held by the Spaniards. Cursing and swearing and hacking and tearing, the exasperated crews swam and waded through the mud and through the hidden ditches and took these natural fortifications with their bare hands. What had once been a rebellion, had now developed into a war of extermination and all prisoners were drowned on the spot.

Even so, almost six seeks went by before the vessels came within the sight of Leyden. First, the wind was wrong, and next there was not enough water. Then the farmers of the region, in fear of losing their crops (they would have let their next door neighbor starve to death if in this way they could have saved their own crops), interfered and filled the holes in the dikes just as soon as they had been cut. Then the Rhine and the Maas turned traitor and carried less water to the sea than they had done for a hundred years and of course, this meant that the artificial lake to the north of Rotterdam ran practically dry. But late in September the wind changed. It grew into a storm. A spring tide on the night between the 29th and 30th of September did the rest. On the 3d of October the fleet appeared before the gates of Leyden and among the first to enter the town was my grandfather.

He did not find his wife at the home of her relatives. A neighbor, a pale shadow of a woman, told him that his relatives had all of them died but the strange lady who lived with them had been taken away to the house of My Lord Jan van der Does, one of the magistrates who seemed to have interested himself in her case. He actually found his wife at the given address, very cheerful, very brave, and very weak and on the point of giving birth to her first child. The midwife expected it within two or three days.

Conditions in the town were terrible. The plague had returned as a result of the terrible things the people had been forced to eat. The chances that the child would survive any such conditions were small. My grandfather consulted his host, the courteous and genial van der Does. He said: "This town will mean death for all women and children for a good long time to come. Get out of it."

"But where shall we go? Everything within miles has been plundered by the Spaniards."

But van der Does could help them. He owned some property in Noordwijk, that seemed to have escaped the attention of the invaders. If they could get a boat as far as Rijnsburg they could go the rest of the way on foot.

They got their boat and safely reached Rijnsburg, but when they came to Noordwijk, they found that the farm to which van der Does had sent them had been burned five months before. The tenants were living in the pig-sty out of which they had chased the usual inhabitants and were none too eager to take in any unexpected guests. But they knew that My Lord Jan owned a mill, a mill not far from Noordwijk. It had still been standing a few days before and probably would be intact as the Spaniards had already left a fortnight ago. It was another hour before they reached that mill. The door was locked. The miller had fled. By this time, the first pains of labor had commenced, and it was impossible to leave the poor woman any longer out there in the cold. My grandfather smashed a window and climbed inside and opened the door. From the near-by stable he brought in straw, a bed was made on the floor, a trough served as cradle. Empty grain bags were used as covers and a little after midnight on the seventh of October of the year 1574 my father was born.

Years afterwards I told this story to Rembrandt and he said, "Yes, I know that mill. I once visited it with my brother Willem. He was more interested in our family's history than I. He told me that that mill had been sold a year after the siege to my grandmother, whose second husband also had been a miller but why she had decided to sell it again, he did not know. Maybe because it was a grain-mill and it had become more profitable to go in for malt, now that the breweries were working overtime and everybody had money again and was drinking beer. And maybe because Noordwijk was too far away from Leyden. And maybe because, with a brood of children, they could not attend to two mills at once. Anyway, it no longer belonged to our people when I was born.

I saw it that once and a few months later, lightning struck it and it burned down to the ground. So that one monument to your father's glory is gone."

A monument to my father's glory!

Little did he know of what he was talking.

Chapter 20

EVEN AS A VERY YOUNG CHILD I HAD STRANGE DOUBTS ABOUT THE FIFTH COMMANDMENT

What then, exactly, was the matter with my father?

From the point of view of his children, everything.

He was quite a good-looking man, having inherited my grandfather's physical strength and a great deal of the personal charm of my grandmother. He was a man of many abilities. When he was young he used to play the lute with great dexterity, and during a visit to his uncle in Veere he copied most of the revolutionary tunes which the town notary, the famous Valerius, had collected during the early part of the rebellion, and he sung these with great success to his own accompaniment. At least, so I heard from some of his old friends, for when we were children, he never touched the instrument and declared all music to be an invention of the Devil. He also seemed to have had a great natural gift for drawing from nature. But nothing remained to show that he had ever taken an interest in such a worldly pastime.

When my brother and I were about fifteen years old, we called one day on a friend whose father possessed one of those famous "Libri Amicorums" which were so popular during the last century. It was a Sunday afternoon and as a great privilege we were allowed to see the pictures in this mysterious and delightful book instead of having to look at images of the deluge and the plagues of Egypt in the family Bible. And to our great delight, we found a picture drawn some twenty years before by our father and representing a young goddess and a young god telling each other something amidst a bower of vines. What they were telling each other was written underneath in a couple of verses, but neither of us was well enough skilled in the art of the penmanship of that day (a very flowery and curlycuey sort of writing) to be able to read them. But of course, as children will do, when we came home we proudly told of our discovery and how our father was a great painter and just as good, we felt convinced, as the wonderful men who had illustrated our Bible.

Our father said nothing to this, but quite contrary to his custom, which made him spend the Sabbath evening at home reading to us from the Old Testament (as far as I can remember, he never mentioned the New Testament to us), he left us immediately after supper and did not come home until at a very late hour. But when we called on the same friend a month or so later, and begged to see the wonder book, the young god and goddess were no longer there and we were too scared to ask what had become of them.

Of course, children never really "know" anything about their parents. They can merely "guess." But in our case, we were denied even that consoling luxury. All we could do was to suffer in silence, and suffer we did.

As soon as we were old enough to ask an occasional question, it was made clear to us that we had no will of our own. We were sinful, misbegotten creatures, hideous and loathsome in the sight of Jehovah (God was rarely mentioned to us), a stench in the nostrils of the Truly Righteous. These Truly Righteous, so we were gradually able to discover, were my father and those who agreed with him upon every comma and semi-colon of the Old Testament, but only in a very small and badly printed edition which had appeared in Amsterdam in the year 1569. All other translations were discarded as anathema, and the work of Satan, and if my father had had his way, they would have been gathered together and burned in the market square, right underneath the wooden nose of our great fellow-townsman, Erasmus, whom my father and his friends held in particular abhorrence on account of a little book which he had written in praise of that glorious Goddess of Folly, which ever since the beginning of time has ruled the world with much greater success than either Wisdom or Pity.

I find it difficult to reconstruct those years of mute suffering. My mother probably loved us, but the spirit inside of her had been killed by years and years of a most meticulous form of abuse of which my father seemed to hold the secret.

Were we ever really badly treated, in the ordinary sense of the word? No, I can't say that we were.

We had decent clothes. We ate decent food and never went hungry. We slept in comfortable rooms. We were sent to quite good schools and rarely were beaten more than any other children of that day and age, when it was considered necessary to spank the average boy at least once a day in order to remind him of his duty to love and honor his parents.

Then what made our existence such hell and cast such a blight upon all the rest of our lives and eventually brought such terrible disaster upon the heads of my brother and myself?

I hardly think that I can put the case into so many words. But here is a little incident I remember from the days when I received my first lessons in religious instruction. The dominie talked about our Father in Heaven and how God is so good to us that we must always call him Father and must approach him as if he were our real father, and I suddenly burst into tears and shrieked that I would then be obliged to hate God, that the word "father" was the most terrible word in the language, that I hated my father and would always hate him.

As I was taken sick the next day with the pox (of which on that occasion three of my other brothers and two of my sisters died) and probably was sick and feverish at the time of this occurrence, there probably was a special reason for this most unseemly outburst of honesty on the part of a child of nine. But all this is rather hazy in my mind. I recollect that the reverend doctor gave me a terrible beating and that I returned home more dead than alive, but too miserable to mind much what had happened.

That, however, was exactly the way I felt about that dreadful man whose very memory, after the lapse of fifty years or more, makes me shiver whenever I think of him.

The man was the walking incarnation of a spiritual spoil-sport. He loved righteousness (his own sort of righteousness, as I have already remarked) and hated everything else. He hated laughter and he hated tears. He hated the sun and he hated the moon. He hated the summer and he hated the winter. He radiated hate and gloom as other people radiate joy and contentment. His capacity for execration was unlimited and his ability to give concrete expression to his feeling of detestation surpassed even that of his deeply revered master, the tenebrous tyrant of the Sinaitic mountain tops.

If, as a child, we made ourselves a little boat out of a piece of cork and an old rag and a mast cut out of an old broom-stick (as every child brought up along the water-front was sure to do), he would wait until we had finished our craft and then he would smash it underneath the heel of his boot. If we painted a picture on an old China plate or a piece of parchment, he would slowly and deliberately hold it underneath the pump in our back yard until the colors were washed off. If we had a particularly favorite toy (and our grandparents were most lavish in providing us with houses and soldiers and little carts with real barrels and boxes on them) he would, as soon as he discovered that we had attached ourselves a little too seriously to one of those "worldly baubles," deprive us of our playthings and burn them on the peat fire that was supposed to keep our back room warm. If we showed a special liking for one of the boys with whom we went to school, he would allow us to invite him to our house, and then, when we all stood around the table, eating our dinner, he would find a way to humiliate the poor child until it could bear it no longer and broke out in tears or fled from this chamber of horrors, never to darken our door again.

He once urged us to invite all our little friends for a boat ride and hired a boat and made my mother spend days preparing food, and then, when we all, in our Sunday best, stood ready to embark, he told us that the party was off and that we had better go home to meditate upon "the benefits of disappointment."

In consequence of these occurrences, we gradually lost caste among all the other boys of our age and our will was so completely broken on the anvil of parental ill-will and bitterness that we became mere puppets in the hands of Fate, rudderless ships on the ocean of inexperience and doubt.

As a result, the terrible events took place which so completely changed the even tenor of my life and for almost eight years made me an exile from my own land and drove me away from Rembrandt at a time when he was perhaps most in need of such friendship as I was able to give him.

During my recent illness, when I was searching my mind for the causes of that strange melancholia which had so completely got hold of me, I discussed these matters with Spinoza, the man who more than any other has been able to dissect and understand the inner motives of the human heart. And while giving him an account of my father and of our childhood, I mentioned the episode of the Armada, that strange incident in my father's early years which quite by chance I had heard my grandfather tell one day.

It seems that during the early eighties of the last century, the King of Spain decided to eradicate all heresies from this world by destroying both England and Holland with one blow. For this purpose he ordered a fleet to be built of hundreds and hundreds of ships and an army to be equipped that was to embark on board those ships and conquer London and Amsterdam and then do whatever was to be done to bring all the people back into the folds of Mother Church. The men-of-war were to be built in Spain, but the soldiers were to be gathered in Dunkirk. For this special purpose His Majesty, who was practically bankrupt, had raised seven million ducats and the Pope had chipped in with an extra million. Naturally enough an expedition on such a large scale could not be kept a secret and as early as the fall of '86 the people in Holland knew what was going to happen.

Ambassadors were sent to London to discuss a general plan of defense with the English, but as usual, their Queen, who always insisted upon doing everything herself, could not quite make up her mind. One day she was all for fighting and the next she would send a letter to the King of Spain and remind him of the ancient friendship between their two respective countries and so on and so forth. And very likely nothing at all would have been accomplished if the Pope had not seen fit at that moment to issue a bull in which he called Her Majesty a bastard and a tyrant and graciously bestowed her realm upon her dear cousin of Spain, who was at the same time given the exalted title of "Defender of the Christian Faith." After that slur upon her birth, the old lady was all for fighting, and she began her operations with a raid upon peaceful Dutch merchantmen, and for a moment it looked as if the heretics (after the manner of heretics) were going to tear each other to pieces, but in the end the two nations came to terms and the Hollanders and Zeelanders undertook to watch and guard the harbor of Dunkirk, so that no troops should be able to reach the ships while the ships should be prevented from reaching the port and calling for the soldiers.

While Howard and Drake kept up a running fight with the great clumsy vessels which were at such a terrific disadvantage among the shallow waters of the Channel, a Zeeland squadron together with a number of ships from the admiralty of Holland, lay off the Flemish coast. My grandfather had been put in command of a fast sailing sloop of eighteen pieces, called in a spirit of fun *The Cardinal's Hat*. It was to act as a sort of guide for a squadron of fire-ships and was to try and pilot a few of these into the harbor of Dunkirk. As a rule, those fire-ships, well provided with grappling irons, had only a crew of about six men who started the pitch barrels burning as soon as their craft was safely headed for one of the enemy's galleons and then made for the little boat and rowed for safety while the rest of the cargo caught fire. Of course, my grandfather had taken his son along. A boy of fifteen in those days was supposed to take a man's share in the battles of his country and the son of an old freebooter was sure of a place of honor in an undertaking of this sort.

Furthermore, according to the story grandfather told me, my father in those days was a regular fire-eater. He was a good-looking devil, he was full of life and fun, he had been brought up on the stories of the glorious episodes of the early days of the rebellion. He knew all about sieges and pitched battles and hand-to-hand encounters on the slippery slopes of some muddy dike. He had seen the people whose ears had been cut off and whose noses had been slit by the Inquisition and his uncles and aunts had told him of the diet of mice and rats upon which they had subsisted when grain and meat had given out when the Spaniards had laid siege to their town. And as he was a bright and eager lad, full of imagination, he had vowed that some day he would do his best to avenge those hideous wrongs.

This was his first opportunity and he was going to show the stuff he was made of. He begged and implored everybody to give him a chance, until finally he was offered the command of the second of the fireships that were to be let loose against the Spanish vessels anchored peacefully in Dunkirk harbor that same evening.

A fire-boat, commanded by Hendrick van Cadzand, an old pilot who knew that part of the Belgian coast by heart, was to show the way, but everything depended upon quick work, for the instant these ships were detected, the expedition was at the mercy of the batteries on shore.

As soon as it was dark, the vessels made for Dunkirk and my father, holding the rudder, waved a cheerful good-by to his comrades and all went well until they were near the breakwater. At that moment, one of the Spanish sentinels on the pier fired his gun. It probably was an accidental shot and had nothing to do with the approaching vessels.

But then and there, something terrible happened to my father. He fainted. He fell into a dead faint. They threw pails of water over him and he came to, but every time a shot was fired, he would shriek and try as he might he could not keep from weeping or crouching behind the nearest bit of shelter. Through his clumsy maneuvering, the fire-vessels had got into disorder and the attack failed miserably. Of course, his behavior caused a terrible scandal. If he had not been the son of a father, known for his bravery, he would have been hanged immediately for cowardice. Under the circumstances, it was reported that he had suddenly been taken ill and had been sent home for treatment.

That was the story as I was told it and as I repeated it to Spinoza, and used it as an argument to prove that my father had always been an unreasonable and contemptible being. But he looked at me a long time out of his sad, black eyes, and then he said: "But don't you see?" And I answered "No," and he continued: "But it is all so very simple. Can't you really understand? You are supposed to take care of men's bodies and what have you learned about their minds, which so strongly affect those bodies? Nothing, I fear me. Now really, can't you understand what happened and how it all came about?"

I said no, that perhaps the recollection of the things I had suffered made me unfair, but that this seemed entirely in keeping with all I had ever known about my father. He ended life as a gloomy tyrant, who hated everybody and everything and whose chief aim during his waking hours seemed to be to make everybody miserable.

"And you don't know why?" Spinoza interrupted me.

"I can't say that I do. I suppose that he was born that way."

"But how about your grandfather's story which you just told me, of early years, of his courage, his fun, his good looks?"

"Nevertheless, he showed himself a coward."

"And that is just it. Some day we shall perhaps understand what cowardice is. Very likely we shall then be obliged to change our opinion about heroes too."

"You mean to say, in his case, that his fear of getting killed was stronger than his will to live and distinguish himself?"

"Of course it was. He probably had all the ambition and energy of your grandfather, who was then in the hey-day of his power. But he was born at the moment your grandmother had passed through a terrible experience. These two antecedents, these two personalities, clashed and were at war with each other right there within his soul. The stronger of the two won. He had a tremendous desire to distinguish himself. But something within himself defeated that impulse and defeated it quite ignominiously. As a result, he came to hate the world. . . ."

"Because he so thoroughly hated himself!"

"And he took his revenge upon his children."

"Because they were part of him—because in torturing them, he was really torturing himself."

Perhaps (as in so many other instances) Spinoza was right, though it was difficult for me to follow him quite so far.

He looked upon the problem from the pleasant and detached point of view of a professional philosopher. My father to him was merely an unknown quantity, an interesting x or y in the great mysterious equation of life.

Whereas to my brother and to myself, he was a fact, a fact that even at this late date makes me wake up sometimes in the middle of the night and shriek. For I hear silent foot-steps. Father is making his rounds, trying to discover something for which he can punish us to-morrow morning. Honor thy father and thy mother.

It is an ancient law. Perhaps it is a good law.

But methinks it is a little too one-sided.

Chapter 21

OF THE BROTHER WHOM I HAD AND LOST

My brother Willem was three years older than myself. He and I were the only children who had survived the pox when it attacked our family during the frightful epidemic of 1616.

Three years difference means a great deal when one is five or six, and even more when the age of ten has been reached. But from the very beginning we had been forced to make common cause. Otherwise our spirits would have been entirely crushed in that terrible and gloomy house which we were supposed to call our home. Of course, there was our mother who loved us very sincerely in her own way. But although she went through the gesture of being alive, got up in the morning, dressed herself, attended to the needs of the household, repaired our clothes, went to bed again at night, she had long since given up hope that anything would ever happen to set her free from the drudgery of waiting upon the will of a tyrant who found an excuse for every one of his selfish acts in the chapters of that dreadful Jewish history, the mere thought of which makes me shudder, now after a lapse of more than forty years.

Why had she married him? Well, he had been a "good party" in the usual sense of the word. He belonged to a respectable family, he had a good business, he would be able to provide for her and in those days, in our class of society, that was about all that mattered. His mania for fault-finding and his almost incredible capacity for making himself obnoxious had not yet assumed those outrageous proportions that were to make him a marked man in after life. He was moody and rather difficult. He also was reported to be rich and had fine prospects of growing richer as time went on. What more could one want?

And so my mother was married to him amidst the eager plaudits of her delighted family and never knew a happy day until that morning when she went forth to do her marketing, fell down in the street right in front of our door, and died then and there without so much as a sigh of relief that the end had come.

My brother and I were at school at the time this happened, but we were sent for immediately and when we came home, we were taken right into the room where mother lay dead. Her face was as white as wax, her hands were folded. She seemed to be asleep and in her sleep she smiled as if she understood why she had lived and why she had suffered and what it had been all about. But something gave me a terrible fright, a shock from which I never quite recovered—the firm expression of her lovely mouth told me that she had taken her secret with her and that I would never know it—that I was never going to find out the riddle of existence until I too should have passed beyond those portals from which there is no return.

I probably was too young to have reasoned it out in detail that way and these thoughts may have come to me much later. I am not sure, either one way or the other. I am growing to be an old man and my memory often plays me queer pranks. But ever since, when in the course of my professional duties, I have attended a death-bed, I have been struck by that same strange, other-worldly expression upon the faces of those who have just died.

They smile at us with infinite pity.

For they "know" and we poor mortals, who must go on bearing the burdens of existence, we can only "guess."

And the advantage is all with the still, white faces that now, after years of struggle and pain, have gained the greatest of all blessings, "peace and certainty."

My father, of course, took his loss in his usual selfish way. Somehow or other, he counted the sudden death of her who according to him was as yet "unprepared to meet her Creator" as a reflection upon his own piety. For a moment he ceased his studies of the Old Testament to search among the pages of the Book of Revelation for an answer to the question: "What have I done that I, poor sinner, should be afflicted in this manner?"

I doubt whether it ever dawned upon him that in dying my mother might have suffered certain inconveniences. She had been his wife, his hand-maiden, his cook, his seamstress, a convenient possession of which he had been proud on account of her beauty and her competent way of managing his household. Her loss meant an interruption of a pleasant routine and he sometimes seemed to feel that she had died merely to be disagreeable to him and put him to extra expense. And as the Apocalypse failed to give him an answer to his doubts, and he once more suffered a sense of utter defeat and futility, he grew even more morose than ever before and from that time on until we were old enough to leave the parental roof, our lives were one uninterrupted series of humiliations and sufferings.

It was then that my brother, with noble unselfishness, stepped forward to defend me against the tantrums and the unjust punishment of our mutual tormentor. And I from my side, hardly understanding what was happening, came to be bound to him by certain ties of gratitude and affection which were far stronger than the mere physical fact of sharing the same flesh and blood.

My dear brother was both father and mother to me in the truest sense of the word. He took care of me when I was sick (and I was never very strong as a child) and consoled me when I was punished for some imaginary infringement of the endless rules of conduct that were forced upon us to make us realize the seriousness of salvation. My father was dreadfully jealous of his son's influence upon me and more than once tried to break our intimacy by a threat of separating us and sending my brother to London under the pretext of having him serve his apprenticeship with an English goldsmith. But in the end he had to give in to the pressure that came from the side of our relatives who knew the miseries we suffered but were unable to interfere on our behalf, as the law was entirely on the side of the parents in those early days shortly after the Reformation and as children (in exchange for having been given the privilege of being born) were supposed to have many duties but not a single right.

Of course all the time we were growing older and bigger and finally the point was reached at which it was no longer possible to rule us with a cane. The day my father tried to whip me because I had smiled in church when the minister, reading the names of the ancestors of King David, had got his consonants mixed and had been forced to begin all over again, and had taken a heavy birch rod and then, after the first blow, had had it jerked out of his hand by my brother, who vowed that he would kill him if he ever touched me again, that day was probably the happiest day in his life, for now he had a grievance which made him akin to several of his favorite heroes of old Judean history—his own flesh and blood had turned against him.

He used that incident in a thousand different ways to make us feel his own spiritual superiority and we both thanked our stars when at last we were able to escape, my brother to take service with a well-known silver-smith in Leyden and I to visit the academy of that same town. But even then, although we were now free from daily, yes, almost hourly, interference with our own will, and the constant frustration of our most reasonable desires, we never quite succeeded in getting rid of that feeling of utter submission which came over us whenever my father spoke to us in his rôle as the Creator of our Being.

And when it was time for us to marry (and we were sufficiently well off through the death of our mother to marry quite young) we found ourselves supplied with wives with the choice of whom we had had nothing to do, but who had been selected for us by my father, because they were good Christian women and suitable mothers for such children as it might please Almighty Heaven to bestow upon us after our lawful union.

It happened that neither my brother nor I cared a whit for the women with whom we were thus unceremoniously thrown together. But we obeyed out of the sheer habit of obeying and we suffered the martyrdom of boredom because we did not know any better and because it never dawned upon us that love might mean something more than spending one's days and nights by the side of a female creature whom one detested at those rare moments when one did not merely bear their presence.

My wife (poor wretch, she was surely quite as unhappy as I, for she

SELF-PORTRAIT
(about 1666)

THE THREE CROSSES

had wanted to marry a draper's clerk and hated everything connected with poor people and their ailments)—well, my wife, fortunately for both of us, died shortly after she had given birth to a son. I buried her decently and lost myself in my studies, which soon meant infinitely more to me than all the women in the whole world. But my brother, who was a clever craftsman, but had no interest whatsoever beyond his profession and therefore had no means of escape, was thoroughly miserable and to make matters worse, the woman he had married proved to be both a shrew and absolutely averse to any sexual connection with the man whose name she bore but whose bed she steadfastly refused to share, except for the immediate purpose of having children, an arrangement which so thoroughly disgusted her husband that he never touched her again as long as he lived.

In the end, of course, such an unnatural way of living was to avenge itself in a most dreadful fashion. Early in the year 1650, my father died. He had tried to deprive us of our inheritance by giving all his money to an old men's home, but the courts quickly decided that such a thing was contrary to the law of the land and both my brother and I received several thousand florins besides a share in a number of houses on the Rotterdam water-front. I used my little capital to take a trip through the universities of northern Italy where medicine was then being taught much more successfully than at home. But my brother had been so terribly repressed for such a number of years that this stroke of good luck proved his undoing.

He had never known what it was to be a child or a boy. He meant to make up for lost time and at forty, he set out to recapture the joys of youth, of which he had heard a great deal but which he had never experienced at first hand. The thing was impossible and the poor fellow only succeeded in making himself slightly ridiculous without in any way getting repaid for his outlay in time and money and energy.

We had always been a very sober family and he therefore now felt it to be his duty to drink large quantities both of gin and beer. The gin made him sick and the beer made him sleepy. He greatly disliked the taste of both those beverages, but he had heard all his life of "Divine old Bacchus, to thee we lift, etc." and about the "good cheer of a group of jolly fellows with a pint of ale," and whatever other nonsense the poets have been pleased to compose upon this silly subject and now he was going to experience these joys or die in the attempt. Upon one occasion he almost had his wish and it took me weeks of hard work to bring him back to health. And during his period of reconvalescence, I used to remonstrate with him. An anomalous position. There I sat by the side of my hero and guardian-angel, trying to prevent him from making a fool of himself. It was all terribly humiliating and worst of all, the poor fellow could offer so many plausible excuses for his extraordinary conduct.

"I know that all this is absurd, especially at my age," he used to say, "but I will go crazy unless I have some sort of a fling now. I have never been allowed to do the things I wanted to do and all my life long I have been forced to do the things I did not want to do. I think that our father used to call that 'educating' us. I am forty-five now and there are whole pages in the record of my past existence that are a blank. I intend to write something upon them before I die. That is my good right and you should not try and interfere."

"But listen," I would argue, "there is a time and a place for everything. It is all right for you to drink milk out of a bottle when you are one. But it is a little silly when you are thirty. You can play with dolls until you are five. After that, the other boys will call you a sissy."

He shook his head sadly. "I know that you are right," he answered, "but I just can't help myself. I am angry with Fate. I am so damnably angry! I could go out and kill some one just because I am so angry. I have been cheated. We both have been cheated of everything that is most worth while.

"After all, what is our youth for? To gather such a rich stock of pleasant recollections that we can live upon them for the rest of our days. And what can you and I remember? Misery and tears and horribly dull hours and horribly dull days and even more horribly dull years. That terrible 'No' that stood at the beginning of every sentence our father ever uttered! Such a life isn't fit for human beings.

"You are lucky. You can escape among your pots and pans and all those books full of hieroglyphics. But look at me. I have got a job I hate. I wanted to be a sailor like grandfather, and I am forced to make ornamental salt-cellars for rich cattle-dealers who come in from the countryside and don't know how to use them once they have got them. I wanted to ride the sea in a great big ship and I sit all day long in a stuffy workshop. I wanted a woman of my own, children, I suppose. Look what I got! an animated edition of Holy Writ, not even nicely bound but in a dreadful linen cover."

Then I began all over again trying to convince him that while all he said was perfectly true, he did not make it any better by adding self-injury to the insults he had suffered at the hands of others, but all to no avail. He never went so far as to neglect his business. Somehow or other he managed to stick with great faithfulness to that bench and table he so thoroughly detested. But for the rest, he followed a course that could only lead to disaster. And then in an ill-fated moment, he joined a dramatic club.

These "rhetorical associations" or "master-singer societies" or "poets' unions" or whatever they were pleased to call themselves, had greatly flourished during the twelfth and thirteenth and fourteenth centuries, and every town and village had had a dramatic company of its own, enacting plays written by one of its members. Those plays, as a rule, had been pretty terrible, but they had served as an emotional outlet for a large number of people who otherwise would have spent their time singing bawdy songs in an ale-house. But during a period when everything was tinged with theology, even the theater could not escape.

First of all, the Lutherans captured the stage and used it to popularize their own doctrines. The Spanish authorities, not quite knowing what to do about that sort of propaganda, had quickly put an end to their performances. But not for long, as the Reformation was successful and the Catholics were sent about their business. But after a very short while, the Lutherans, who were too tame for our people, were replaced by the followers of Calvin and as soon as they noticed that people went to these performances not merely to be instructed but also to amuse themselves, they proclaimed theater-going a mortal sin and ordered all rhetorical clubs to be closed.

But the urge to rime and strut about on the stage and make a public exhibition of one's self was much too strong to be entirely suppressed and a way out was found when the amateur actors promised not to play for profit but to hand over all their revenues to the local hospitals and orphan asylums.

Those institutions had been in a state of painful bankruptcy ever since the days of the Reformation when the so-called "good works" had become highly suspicious as an invention of either the Devil or the Pope of Rome. As long as it was sufficient for a man's salvation if he "believed" the right thing, it did not matter so much what he "did." As a result of which the orphans went hungry and the sick remained untended, and a few extra guilders, even though they were derived from "play-acting," were more than welcome. It had seemed a very sensible arrangement, but in no time the Reverend Clergy was back on the job, bombarding Their Lordships of the Town Hall with complaints about this and that and the other piece of acting. One play was much too popish, the next was too full of liberal ideas, a third one showed a lack of respect for the cloth, a fourth one made sin too attractive, a fifth one failed to make vice unattractive enough, and so on and so forth, until the unfortunate day when old man Vondel, already seriously suspected of Papist leanings and an open and avowed enemy of the clerical zealots who had killed his political hero, John of Barneveldt, decided to write him a play in which it should be clearly proved and demonstrated that that unfortunate statesman had been the innocent victim of a great Calvinistic conspiracy.

Heaven knows he ought to have known better, after the authorities had almost clapped him in jail for making Mary Stuart, a sweet and innocent young thing, cruelly persecuted by an old and jealous hag called Elizabeth of England and showing all the virtues of this world to be on the side of Catholic Mary and none on the side of Protestant Bess.

No sooner had this storm in the theatrical tea-pot subsided when behold! there cometh the hurricane of a famous judicial assassination perpetrated well within the memory of the average man. There was a terrific outbreak of popular anger and of course my poor brother, all eager for what he called the "new emotions" and the "novel sensations," must take an active part in it. He had inherited his grandfather's liberal outlook upon life and being by nature a very humble man (most unhappy people are humble) he was the last person on earth to claim that one set of opinions was right and another was wrong. But when the clergy attacked poor old Vondel for his "secret Papist leanings" my brother must needs set up as one of the staunchest defenders of that unfortunate and misguided poet and make himself a mouthpiece of those who for one reason or another (mostly another) were known as the open and avowed enemies of the party then in power.

Their Lordships of the Town Hall were too clever to let themselves be dragged into a public debate, the outcome of which seemed very uncertain. They had other ways at their disposal to rid themselves of an uncomfortable opponent. They boycotted my brother's business and as he was dependent for his living upon the good will of the rich, he soon found himself without a single customer. Next the collectors of internal revenue paid an official visit to his premises and discovered that his merchandise had been assessed at much too low a value. An extra-assessment, and a fine for having sent in a false declaration, were the results of this investigation.

My brother, the soul of honesty, went to law about this and won his case, but the fees and the expense connected with all court pleadings in the Republic used up all his ready cash. At the same time his wife's relatives started proceedings before the magistrates, asking that their brother-in-law be forced to give an accounting of all his business relations during the last six years and hand over the greater part of his revenue to his "dutiful and pious wife, who had suffered grievously both in body and soul through the grave neglect on the part of her husband, who far from following his trade in a peaceful manner as behooved a good Christian and citizen, has wasted his time in the company of pamphleteers, play-actors, painters and other reprehensible characters, etc., etc." A whole catalogue of the most terrible grievances, mortifications, worries and annoyances, duly enumerated to show the eager populace just what sort of a person their highly respected neighbor really was.

Meanwhile rumor of this uproar had traveled abroad and the managers in England and France had not been slow to recognize its importance. Where there was smoke, there undoubtedly was fire and where there was so much discussion of theatrical affairs, there must be a vast number of people anxious to see a good play. The company from the "Théâtre du Pont Neuf" in Paris hastened to the Low Countries with Cyrano de Bergerac's "Le Pédant joué," dreaming of showers of well-rounded Dutch florins, and the Blackfriars Theater in London despatched a dozen of its worst performers directly to Amsterdam to entertain the natives of that distant city with the works of a certain William Shakespeare who seems to have been an actor in the days of Queen Elizabeth and who also on occasions wrote plays.

The interest, however, of the populace in the drama proved to be entirely theoretical, or rather theological. People delighted in discussing the problematical attitude of Jehovah towards the stage. But as for attending a single performance to see what the stage was really like, why, our good Calvinist neighbors would much rather have been broken on the wheel than consent to setting foot within the "Temple of Satan."

The French company therefore beat a hasty retreat, providing itself with sufficient money for the home voyage by selling all its costumes and stage-properties. The English troopers fared almost as badly. They opened their season with "Shylock, or the Merchant of Venice," a piece which proved to be highly distasteful to the Jews in our town. The day after the performance, the Dam in front of the Town Hall was one seething mass of excited Hebrews in long kaftans, wildly gesticulating and calling down violent curses upon the head of the poor scribe (dead, God knows how many years) who had so cruelly and unjustly called attention to one of their supposed racial weaknesses.

The magistrates, who just then were contemplating a rather important loan to finance the city's extension in the direction of the old Plague House, did not wish to start a financial panic and promised immediate redress. The Blackfriars people thereupon switched over to a play by a certain Ford, called "It's a Pity She's a Whore" which roused such a terrific storm of protest among the clergy that it had to be taken off after a single performance, when in their despair they chose a perfectly harmless piece by a certain John Fletcher called "The Faithful Shepherdess" which did not seem to have done very well in London at the time of its first performance, but which was quite a success in Amsterdam where people had not been spoiled in matters theatrical.

Now in the years of which I am writing, it was not customary for women to appear upon the scene. The female parts were taken by young boys who had been specially trained for this sort of work. But as a great innovation, the Blackfriars announced that the rôle of the Shepherdess would be played by a real woman.

Of the storm that thereupon broke loose, it would be difficult to give one who had not lived through these turbulent days an adequate idea.

Solemn processions proceeded to the Town Hall to offer petitions which ran all the way from humble and pious supplications for redress to open and avowed threats of rebellion. But the magistrates, being in an angry mood on account of a sermon preached a few weeks before in which a zealous young candidate for holy orders had publicly accused the Town Fathers of all sorts of improper speculations in connection with the city's extension (of which I wrote a moment ago), those magistrates were in no mood to listen to further remonstrances. They declared that they saw no reason to forbid the play in question and bade the petitioners be gone. When these honest citizens, undaunted by the failure of the day before, reappeared on the Dam the next morning, they saw that a number of gallows had been erected in front of the Town Hall and being able to take a hint, they dispersed and returned to their various professions.

But two nights later, the poor woman who played the rôle of the Shepherdess, at the beginning of the second act, was suddenly pelted with volley after volley of rotten eggs and bricks carefully packed in sheets of paper that afterwards proved to be parts of the petitions which the Burgomasters had refused to consider. She was hurt quite badly. The town guards were hastily summoned. A number of arrests were made and it was discovered that the gallery had been filled with people, none of whom had ever before graced a theater with his presence. But as every man, woman and child among them swore that they had not seen their neighbors lift a finger, let alone throw eggs or broken bottles in the direction of the stage, nothing could be done and the company, thoroughly defeated by the triumphant dominies, hastily left for London.

The unfortunate shepherdess, however, remained behind. Her arms and her face had been terribly cut and after trying to doctor herself for a few days, she was brought to the hospital where I cleaned her wounds and bandaged her and discovering that she was quite feverish, ordered her to be taken to a cot.

Even then she was not left in peace. On the day after she had been admitted to the God's House, a bottle of wine was received for her with a card which read: "From an admirer." This bottle was stolen by a boy in the porter's lodge. Immediately afterwards, he was taken ill with dreadful pains and convulsions. I happened to be on duty and was called for immediately, but before I could do anything, the poor fellow was dead. The bottle was discovered in his pocket, and suspecting foul play, I examined the contents. I found that the wine had been poisoned, though I never was able to determine the exact nature of the poison nor could I ever find out whence it had been sent. But when it is considered that this particular crime was still being punished by the rack and the wheel, and that the chances of detection in cases of that sort were very serious, then it will become plain how terribly excited some people had got about such a very simple affair as a woman playing the part of a woman in a theatrical play.

I mentioned this matter quite casually to my brother who happened to be staying with me for a few weeks in the hope that the silly agitation against him in his native town would meanwhile die down. I wish I had never broached the woman's name to him, for right off he flew into a terrible passion about those devils who would not even stop short at murder to further their own ends and who tried to make all people subject to their own prejudices, and as soon as the lacerated shepherdess had sufficiently recovered to leave the hospital, he hastened to pay her his respects and that was the beginning of the end, as far as he was concerned.

I don't want to be too hard on the poor female. I only saw her three times in all my life and as I had good reason to dislike her most cordially, my judgment about her would be hardly fair. This much I will say. She was exceedingly fair, but her beauty was like a bonfire on ice—it spread a wondrous light but gave absolutely no heat. And the same was true of her art.

She was, so I heard afterwards, the daughter of a man who had learned his trade with no one less than the famous William Shakespeare himself and who had been trained in the best traditions of what then was undoubtedly the best school of acting in the whole of Europe. And he in turn had taught her all he knew, which made it very difficult to find out exactly how much natural talent she actually had.

For "talent" and "training" are two very different things, as one comes to understand very soon when one has to deal with people in my profession. The possession of what we commonly call talent (the "well-balanced mind" of the ancient Greeks) allows the happy owner of this unusual quality to get along in this world without a great deal of training. While a great deal of sound training will make it possible for those, not endowed with too much talent, to find their way quite nicely and keep out of the poorhouse. Meanwhile there is a tremendous difference between the two, almost as much as there is between a rose grown by the good Lord and one painted by Melchior d'Hondecoeter, though the latter probably has no rival when it comes to rendering flowers on wood or canvas.

That same girl who was a most fascinating person when she went through her paces in the rôle of the Shepherdess, every line and every word carefully rehearsed by her father, became a dull and vain and highly irritating person the moment she was off the stage. My brother probably would have seen this for himself if she had not been made the object of such a bitter attack on the part of the dominies. The unreasonable hatred of the yellow-faced mob that had pelted her with stones on that fatal evening threw everything into a different light. She was Andromeda on the point of being sacrificed to the hydra-headed monster of religious bigotry while he was Perseus rushing forth to save her from her terrible fate. All this was pure nonsense. But it suited his starved power of imagination. All his life he had waited for a chance to play a noble and heroic rôle. In his heart of hearts he had wanted to be like our great-grandfather, but Fate had condemned him to spend his days by the side of a narrow-minded shrew sitting in a dingy room, hammering mythological figures on ornamental salt-cellars and chiseling phantastic coats-of-arms on those golden goblets with which our successful merchants celebrated the arrival of a son and heir to their recently acquired riches.

It really was not quite fair. The cards were stacked too heavily against this poor soul, starved so pitiably for a little color and a few emotions. Yes, my brother might have escaped if— But the word "if" has no place in the dictionary of human relationships and from the moment he first lay eyes on that woman, he was doomed though no one could have guessed how terrible his end would be.

I am an old man now and generally speaking I accept life as I find it. No use my trying to improve upon the handiwork of God. But if ever he contemplates a reorganization of his universe, I wish that he would rid us of one thing—the good woman who has the instincts of the courtesan. I have seen some of my younger (and older) friends do strange things when they fell into the clutches of the sort of females we are accustomed to call "bad." But their suffering and their humiliations could never bear comparison to the agonies that are suffered by the victims of the professionally "good" women. When it comes to despoiling a man of all those qualities which we associate with self-respect and common decency and pride of achievement, the "good" women can give aces and spades to their less fortunate sisters. For in everything they do, however mean and selfish and calculating their real motive, they will always fall back upon the one consolation, that they have still retained their virginity, though why our world should set so much store by something that is at best a mere biological detail, I, as a medicine man, am utterly unable to perceive.

The ancients, as far as I remember from reading a not inconsiderable number of classical authors, treated this subject much more intelligently than we do, as something beyond good and evil, a "brutum factum," an unavoidable and therefore "neutral" fact, that one had to accept together with life, like the necessity for eating or breathing or sleeping. But those unfortunate slaves who during the first four hundred years of our era crept to power by way of the altar and the confession-booth must hate this wonderous gift of Heaven as they must hate everything else that reminded them a little too closely of their former masters and of a system of civilization that had showered its benefits upon the Few at the expense and to the everlasting humiliation of the Many.

I sometimes wonder what would have happened to this continent of ours if we had received the message of Christ directly from Him without the discourteous intermediaryship of that loquacious tent-maker from Tarsus. For Paul, notwithstanding all his loud protestations to the contrary, was a Jew of the Jews and a Pharisee of the Pharisees. The nastiest and dirtiest and most degrading thing that has ever been said about love— that it is better to marry than to burn—could only have come up in the mind of some one who from father to son had been reared to regard women as a necessary evil, a piece of personal property, created solely for man's convenience and relief.

I know of course that to many honest Christians such a conception of things is most repellent. And the lovely edifices built all over our land to the glory of the Blessed Virgin bear witness to man's irrepressible desire to sanctify that greatest of all mysteries and make it an integral part of the divine law of our being.

But the Reformation (in our part of the world at least) was not a return to an older and nobler form of Christianity. It was the final triumph of Paul. It was a return to Judaism. And woman once more was pulled down from her pedestal to become a household drudge, a breeding-mare and part of her husband's less cherished possessions. Under those circumstances she had only one thing that was really her own until her lord and master claimed it for himself. And I suppose that was at the base of that strange belief that "purity" was something physical rather than something spiritual.

Needless to say I hated the woman who destroyed my brother and I repeat that I may be unfair when I try to make her the center of a religious and philosophic discussion, of which she would not have understood a single iota, and which at best, would have struck her as something that was merely nasty and altogether unworthy of the consideration of what she was pleased to call a lady. I therefore hasten to add that my sympathy at first was entirely on her side, when my brother, having fallen deeply in love with the object of his chivalrous devotion, decided that she must return his sentiments and run away with him to foreign lands, there to begin a new and glorious existence, etc., etc. I bluntly told him that he was crazy, that he was a married man and had no right to talk or think the way he did. And I called on the subject of his affection, then recovering in a small hostelry near the Damrak from her late inconveniences, to offer her my sympathy and suggest that she allow me to find accommodations for her safe return home.

But I was not accorded the reception I had expected. She gave me to understand in no uncertain terms that she was fully able to mind her own affairs and that she would depart when, how and in such manner as she might deem suitable and necessary. And so I took my hat and cane and departed fully expecting to hear that she had taken the next boat from Hellevoetsluis. But to my surprise she was still in Amsterdam a month later, still "recovering" and still protesting to my brother that she was a "good" woman and expected him to treat her as such, although at the same time allowing him to spend the greater part of his days in her company and depending upon him for everything from buying a new pair of stays to getting her the necessary papers to leave the territory of the Republic and providing her with funds for her current expenses, which my brother (having neglected his business beyond all hope of repair) was unable to meet and which he was forced to obtain from me, by giving me all sorts of feeble excuses for being "temporarily slightly embarrassed."

At last, thank God! I heard that she was leaving us. The wounds on her hands and face had fully recovered and there was no excuse for staying any longer in the inhospitable city on the Amstel River. She was to have gone early on a Friday in November and in the afternoon, I called at the house where my brother had taken lodgings when he first began to devote himself to the cause of the oppressed, or in plain language, ever since his imagination and his power of phantasy had got the better of his sense of reality and he had started out in quest of those problematic joys of early youth which had never been his share. His rooms were empty. There was a note on the table, addressed to me. It read: "Bless you, my dear boy. I have followed her. She needs me."

How she needed him I heard almost a year afterwards from a ship's captain who came to the hospital for the amputation of one of his thumbs, caught in a coil of rope. He noticed my name and asked me whether I had any relations in London. I told him yes, that I thought my brother had gone to live there.

"Strange," he said when he recovered slightly from the bottle of brandy which we had given him to bear the ordeal of cutting and sewing. "Strange that I should have met him in that rabbit-warren of humanity."

And he went on to tell me how one evening, walking down London Bridge to look at the shops, he had come across a man turning the leaves of a Dutch volume that was offered for sale among some old second-hand books, how he jokingly had remarked, "Well, Mr. Englishman, you won't be able to make much of that," and how the man had answered him, "But it is my own language."

How he had thereupon invited him to a near-by tavern and how his newly found friend had taken him to his rooms, very simple but very decent rooms, one of which was used for living quarters, while the other one served as a silver-smith's work-shop.

"That is how I make my living," the stranger had told him. "I have quite a trade. I make these so-called Dutch salt-cellars for the jewelers in the city. They pay me well. But then, I have to make quite a lot of money, for I have others to support besides myself."

"A wife and children?" the honest captain had asked with a sly nod. But the other, quite seriously, had answered, "No, I am not married, but I have obligations," and then they had talked of other things and soon afterwards the sailor had bade his adieux and had left to return to his vessel.

I asked my patient to take a letter for me the next time he went to London and four months later I had an answer. In a most affectionate way my brother thanked me for my eager interest in his well-being and happiness. "But don't worry about me," he begged. "Don't worry. I am perfectly contented with my fate. I have at last found something to worship. And angels themselves could ask nothing more or better of life than that."

The captain who brought me this message, however, was not quite so cheerful. He had taken some information about this strange, dignified man who seemed so absolutely out of place in a dingy house in a small alley just off Threadneedle Street and he had discovered that the former Shepherdess had bade farewell to the stage to become the lawful wife of a very doubtful young man who made a living as a juggler and sleight-of-hand artist, giving performances for the benefit of the nobility and having (according to a handbill which he presented to his rich patrons) been privileged upon several occasions to show his "art" to no one less than King Charles and Queen Henrietta Maria. In reality (as the captain discovered without very great difficulty) the young man was a card-sharp who operated in several of the less favorably known gambling houses that were maintained for the special benefit of the landed gentry on their annual pilgrimage to the national capital. But of late he had not been seen in his usual haunts and it seemed that he had retired completely from his somewhat dangerous profession. "I have married a rich wife," he was in the habit of boasting to his drinking companions, "so why should I work?"

"Rich wife?" I asked in surprise. "When the woman was here, she had nothing but the clothes on her back. What does he mean by rich wife?"

"It is your brother," the captain explained. "I am sorry to say it, but he supports not only the woman but also her husband."

"And in return?"

"In return he gets nothing. Absolutely and completely nothing. She is a most virtuous wife. She loves the young scoundrel she has married. He beats her and two or three times your brother had threatened to thrash him if he ever laid hands on her again. Meanwhile he sits in his little room and works, hammers and hammers and hammers all day long at his silver disks, making the most lovely figures and getting good pay (the highest paid craftsman in London he is, so I was told) and carrying it all to this miserable woman, who treats him as if he were her lackey and does not even say thank you."

"And he gets nothing in return for all his trouble?"

"Absolutely nothing, but a fair amount of abuse."

"Nor for his devotion?"

"Absolutely nothing."

And then I knew that the good captain was surely talking of my brother.

For no other man on this planet of ours would have been such a sublime fool.

Chapter 22

I ASK MY BROTHER TO RETURN TO ME

The last time I heard of my brother was in the fall of the year 1641, some eight or nine months before Saskia died.

One evening, when I was sitting by the fire (for it was raining hard and the room was cold and damp) a visitor was announced, and behold, it was my old friend the captain, whom I had not seen for almost two whole years.

"I have news for you," he said, "but you won't like it much. It is not very good news." And he told me how during his last visit to London he had been curious to see what had become of his friend the silversmith. He had found him in his old rooms, hammering away as usual. He had asked him for dinner on board his ship, but he said no, he could not come. He was too busy. He was busier than ever before. He had to make even more money than last year. And finally he had told the reason why. I asked my informant whether he could repeat it to me and he answered that he could.

"Fancy," he said, "that woman's husband now protests that he is of high and noble lineage. He lets it be whispered about that he is some vague connection of the House of Stuart and hints at certain indiscretions of the late Queen Mary. He is a dark-faced villain and talks a great deal about the southern blood of the Rizzios. But he is far from Italian in his love for that virulent usquebaugh, which his compatriots hail as their most important contribution to the happiness of nations. He is drunk every night and when he is in his cups, he becomes abusive of all the world and more especially of his wife, who waits upon him with dog-like devotion and publicly prides herself upon her steadfast loyalty, as one of the main duties of a good woman towards the man whom she has promised to love, honor and obey.

"But in the morning she goes to your brother to ask for the 'loan' of one or five or even ten guineas to tide herself and her husband over until he shall have received a remittance (ever overdue) from his estate in the Scottish highlands. And believe me or not, but the poor fellow accepts all this as the gospel truth. And he hurries to Threadneedle Street and borrows from the jewelers for whom he works until he can give her the sum for which she asks. And she takes the money without so much as saying 'by your leave' or 'thank you' and all day long he is beamingly happy, because he had been allowed—'privileged' he calls it—to be of some slight service to that incomparable creature.

"But that is not all. The husband, when he gets in his cups, is as rude as the captain of a Swiss regiment of lansquenets. He will abuse anybody and everybody in sight and I need not tell you that often leads to fights, for although the English are a peaceful people, they will only take so much insult and then they will hit back. Well, you will probably call me a liar when I tell you that your brother then takes his side, and steps forward to defend this miserable sot against the people who threaten to throw him out into the street. On one occasion he got hurt quite badly. An equally drunken Irishman, a descendant of the kings of Connemara (all Irishmen I ever bossed in my fo'c'sle are descendants of kings when they get a pint of our Geneva in them) began to brag about the glories of the court of Kilmacduagh or some such place as compared to those of the court of Scone or something to that effect and in a moment they had their rapiers out and your brother, in trying to separate them, got badly cut across the knuckles and could not do any work for almost two months.

"But the harpy and her husband did not leave him a moment's peace. What sort of a man was he anyway to leave them in the lurch at this important moment in their career when they might realize a fortune by selling one of their estates and investing the money in a new Muscovy company? And didn't he have very rich relatives in the Low Countries who could help him out until he could go back to work? How about the brother of his who was said to be one of the best-known surgeons in the richest town on the Continent? Surely he would do something for him if he explained the circumstances that had led to his unfortunate adventure. But your brother refused. He refused point-blank. His own humiliation was bad enough. No use letting his relatives at home know what had happened to him. I talked to him like a grandfather. I told him that now was the time to escape, now or never. He said yes, that he knew that I was right but how could he help himself?

"I said, 'Go back to Amsterdam. Your brother loves you. He will be only too delighted to see you again. He will give you his house. He will give you anything he has. I know, for he has told me so, time and again. He wants you back. Go home and be happy.'

"But he answered that he must have time to think. 'She would never let me go alone,' he finally said. 'She would follow me and she would bring her husband with her. That would lead to all sorts of scandals, for the fellow is utterly irrepressible when he gets a few drops of spirits in him. No, I must think this over very carefully. I want to see my brother, I want to see him most terribly. But I must not drag him down with me.'

"And so I left him, for the wind was blowing from the west and I had a cargo of some sort of funny striped English cows on board, and I was in a hurry."

"And that was the last you saw of him?" I asked.

"The very last. The next time I came to London, his rooms were closed. I asked his landlady but she did not know where he had gone."

"That was how long ago?"

"About six weeks."

And that was the last I heard from my brother.

I was to see him again once more, but not to speak to him.

Chapter 23

MY BROTHER COMES HOME

In the fall of the fatal year 1642, it was (as I have already written down) my turn to conduct the anatomical experiments which were held at the College of Surgeons for the benefit of the students who walked our hospitals.

Three years before we had moved into new quarters on the second floor of the St. Anthonie weigh-house and we were very proud of our institution. The clergy of course did not wholly approve of our efforts, but the fact that our laboratories were situated in rooms that had previously belonged to one of those amateur theatrical clubs which had caused so much scandal to the pious citizens of the town made them regard us, their successors, a little more leniently than they might have done otherwise. Furthermore, our institution enjoyed the cordial and avowed approval of Their Lordships of the Town Hall. As good merchants they appreciated the value of health in terms of guilders and quarters. A sick sailor or book-keeper was a dead loss, even if eventually he recovered. And not only did they protect us against those who thought it a sacrilege to pry too closely into the secrets of the human body, but they also gave us a liberal annual subsidy and they even passed a law that the remains of all those who died a violent death in the streets of the city should be surrendered to us for our investigations. We also drew for our daily supply upon the public wards of our hospitals but only when the patient had died without leaving behind any one who could lay claim to his body.

As Amsterdam, with its strict laws and its excellent system of town-guards, was a fairly peaceful town, the great majority of our customers came to us from the God's House, or hospital, but now and then some other unfortunate fellow would slip through after a drunken brawl in a tavern or as a result of one of those short-lived but violent popular upheavals which are very apt to occur in cities that are visited every day by thousands of sailors from every port of the inhabitable and from most parts of the uninhabitable globe.

We had two assistants who prepared the bodies for us. All we doctors had to do was to make an appearance at the appointed hour (usually late in the afternoon after we got through with our practice) and demonstrate some particular problem for the benefit of the students and the younger medical men, who flocked around the operating table. We followed a regular plan by which we tried to cover the whole field in a course of lectures and demonstrations covering the greater part of two years. But that fall I had been asked to deviate from the regular program and discuss certain problems of physiology which at that moment held the center of all our medical attention.

When I was quite a young student I remember how one day the lecturer who explained Galen to us had made a few sneering remarks about a certain Englishman called Harvey or some such name who had undertaken to prove that the blood in the human body was in a state of constant flux and not stationary as we had always held so far. The learned professor had grown very funny about the famous "circulator" who seemed to have discovered certain peculiarities of the human body which had remained a secret to all the famous medical investigators of ancient times. Young people are apt to be very conservative. They have been obliged to take such terrible pains to learn the few things they know, that they regard the man who tries to convince them of the opposite as their natural enemy. And all of us had loudly applauded our dear teacher when he continued to be witty at the expense of his British colleague.

But once mentioned, the idea would not die down. Some claimed that Aristotle had already drawn attention to this fact and others said that the eminent Doctor Servetus, burned at the stake by orders of John Calvin almost a century before (on account of some difference of opinion about the Holy Trinity), had also been of this opinion, though I was never able to get hold of the books in which he had tried to prove his point. But in the year 1628 this fellow Harvey had finally published his new theory in a book devoted exclusively to this subject and every medical man had read it or at least parts of it and for the last fifteen years our profession had been openly divided into "circulators" and "anti-circulators." Truth to tell, there were very few of the latter left at the time of which I am now speaking and the new theory had been so completely incorporated into the sum total of our observations and hypotheses which we sometimes erroneously call our "science of medicine" that it was decided to explain the subject in a special course of lectures and I was asked to give the first one of these.

I still remember the day. It was a Thursday and it was raining. It was so dark in the low-ceilinged rooms in which we met that it was necessary to light a number of candles. Furthermore, as word had gone about that we were going to discuss something comparatively new, a large number of idle people had flocked to our meeting place. For our so-called fashionable people are apt to be so exasperated by the emptiness of their existence that any novelty, however gruesome or extraordinary, is welcome provided it promises them a few minutes' respite from their own boredom. And for lack of a regular stage performance, they were more than willing to brave the horrors of the dissecting theater that they might boast to their friends, "Oh, you know . . . that new theory . . . I have forgotten which one . . . by that man . . . well, I just don't seem able to recollect his name . . . but you ought to have been there . . . it was just too fascinating for words. . . ."

All the same, since our institution was maintained by public funds, we were supposed to allow everybody who cared to come to make himself at home, though fortunately the greater part of that sort of an audience never stayed very long. After the first incision, they turned pale. After the second one, they turned green. After the third one they made for the nearest door.

That afternoon while going upstairs, I met one of our assistants. "Quite a crowd to-day," I remarked.

"Doctor," he said, "there is an awful mob up there. But they won't stay long."

Then I made some inquiries about the body upon which I was to demonstrate. "Is it a man or a woman?" I asked.

"A man," he answered. "They brought him here yesterday morning. They had found him just outside 'The Empty Wine-Barrel' on the Achterburgwal. A pretty low dive, that infamous 'Wine-Barrel.' The poor fellow must have been killed during a quarrel inside and they seem to have thrown him out for fear of the police. His face is in a terrible condition. I have covered it up. At least half a dozen slashes with a broken bottle or a very sharp knife. They don't know who he is, but then, this town is full of foreign scum, though this fellow's clothes looked quite respectable. Anything else I can do, Doctor?"

I said no and went upstairs and with a few words I explained the ideas of Doctor Harvey, that the blood circulates all through our body like the tides that at regular intervals sweep around the globe and how this theory had completely revolutionized the practice of medicine, especially in the field of surgery. And then I took up my scalpel and saw and opened up the chest and laid bare the heart and I took it into my hands to remove it and just then one of the students who stood on my right reached for his note-book which was in his left pocket and his hand brushed against the towel that had been placed across the head of the corpse and the small square of white linen fell on the floor and I recognized the face of my brother.

That is how he came home, and how I welcomed him, holding his dead heart in my hand.

Chapter 24

REMBRANDT ASKS ME TO CALL

A sinner in our town was a sinner. He had offended the majesty of God and must bear the punishment, no matter how undeservedly.

That same evening, after I had made my terrible discovery, I called on one of the Burgomasters who was under some slight obligation to me, as I had once taken care of his oldest boy and had pulled him through a very dangerous attack of croup. I explained to him what had happened and he sent his maid out (very few of our rich people dared to employ male servants, as this smacked too much of foreign manners) with a note for the High Sheriff, asking him to call for a few moments. The Sheriff came and promised that he would do his best to get some information upon the unfortunate incident. Meanwhile, the corpse of my brother remained in the dissecting room, for he was supposed to have come to his end as the result of "being the participant in an act of violence with one or more persons whose identity remained unknown." And according to the laws of Amsterdam, such a person could not be given proper burial but was either handed over to the medical profession or hanged from the gibbet outside the gate until his body rotted away or was devoured by the birds.

Fortunately the Sheriff was a very active man. In less than twenty-four hours, he came to my house with his news.

Two of his assistants had made a round of the different taverns and the first one reported as follows:

Three people, two men and a woman, apparently English, though one of them spoke fluent Dutch, had come to Amsterdam last Monday and had taken rooms in the inn run by an old woman known as Mother Joosten. They had stayed indoors most of the time, claiming that they still felt indisposed from the voyage which had been exceptionally rough and they had had their meals sent up to their rooms. One of the men drank a great deal and seemed to quarrel with the woman, who was apparently his wife. On Tuesday at about five they had gone out. Mother Joosten had asked them whether they needed anything for the night and they had said no, but the smaller of the two men had turned to her and had shown her a piece of paper on which he had written the word Houtgracht, indicating by gestures that he wanted to know where that street was. She had told him as best she could and they had departed.

Late that same evening the husband and wife had returned and had asked that their bill be prepared as they were obliged to leave early the next morning. Then they had told their landlady that they wanted to take another stroll and had gone out in the darkness.

In the morning when Mother Joosten knocked on their door, there had been no answer. The man and the woman were gone. They had left their baggage behind. It consisted of one very shabby leather trunk, containing a few odds and ends of personal apparel, without any value. The bill of nineteen florins and eighty cents (most of this had gone for gin) remained unpaid. (Bill annexed to the report.)

The second constable had followed their track after they had left the place of Mother Joosten. They apparently had started out to find me, for in the "King of Bohemia" where they had eaten and where one of the two men had drunk a great deal of French wine, they had once more asked the shortest road to the Houtgracht. When they left, the smaller of the two men was apparently very much under the influence of liquor and had stumbled across the door-step. He would have fallen if the woman had not caught him, but instead of being grateful to her for this assistance, he had cursed her and the other man had intervened and had suggested that they had better go home. But the smaller of the two men had said no, and had added something to the effect that that night would serve them as well as any other. Thereupon they had departed and it had been impossible to retrace their track.

They apparently had visited several other taverns but the inn-keepers, fearing that they might be implicated in a scandal and a scandal connected with murder and highway robbery (for my brother's pockets were absolutely empty when the body was found) had all of them lied like troopers. Yes, they had seen three people who answered the description given of them, but they had only entered their place of business for a moment and then had gone away, apparently in the best of spirits and that was all they knew, until the moment some highly respectable citizens, returning from a wedding, had stumbled across the dead body and had warned the police.

Under the circumstances and since it was becoming fairly evident that the victim had not been killed in a fight but had been deliberately murdered when he refused to show his companions the way to my house, Their Lordships felt that they might make an exception. They could not very well give me permission to bury my brother in one of the churches, but they had no objection if I could find room for him in one of the yards surrounding those places of worship where occasionally some of the poorer people were interred. I followed him to his grave one drab and rainy morning. But when I reached the cemetery, I found my three friends waiting for me. How they knew or how they had ever found out, I am unable to tell. But they were there and when the coffin had been silently lowered into the grave, Bernardo took a small book from his pocket and opened it.

"This poor man has suffered much," he said. "We will therefore bid him farewell with one short chapter of consolation." And he read the one hundred and thirtieth psalm. Then the sexton and his helpers quickly filled the grave and we went home.

At the bridge of the St. Anthonie locks, I bade them farewell, but Jean-Louys followed me.

"Friends," he said, "are the only dependable refuge in time of sorrow." And he came and stayed with me and said very little, but whenever I went out or whenever I returned home, he was there with a pleasant smile and a cheerful word of welcome. God knows how I would otherwise have pulled through those dreadful weeks.

And one evening, a few days later, a small flat package was brought to the house. Inside of it was a copy of an etching of "The Return of the Prodigal," and underneath it, in pencil, the words: "In Memoriam. Come and see me and let me share your sorrow. Rembrandt."

Chapter 25

I HAVE THE HONOR TO DINE WITH ONE OF THE BURGOMASTERS

When I was a small boy I was taught that all of life was tragedy, and when I grew a little older I sometimes tried to convince myself that all of life was comedy, but now, when I am fast approaching the traditional "three score and ten" I know that both those definitions were wrong.

Life is neither tragedy nor comedy, it is melodrama and melodrama of such a primitive sort that should any playwright dare to put it on the stage, his work would be hooted off the boards and he himself would be publicly derided as an impostor.

Here was my brother, the most peaceful and loveable of men—a hard-working and intelligent craftsman—just the sort of person to be the father of a cheerful family, spending the greater part of his days in quest of the unfindable and left for dead on the door-step of a mean ale-house. And there I was myself—a person with just one interest in life—to sit quietly in my study and try to find some way to alleviate the suffering of sick humanity—at best a very timid creature—rather afraid of life and perfectly willing to spend all my days in the same house on the same street in the same city with the same faithful friends—suddenly condemned to go to the other end of the earth and to spend eight long and lonely years in a wilderness which no white man had ever visited before.

It was all very strange and yet it seemed so hopelessly unavoidable. The hand of Fate was clearly discernible in everything that happened. I struggled as all of mankind has struggled since the beginning of time. I objected. I fought back. I cursed. I insisted upon an answer. And the gods whispered "Inevitable" and again withdrew behind the high clouds in indifferent aloofness.

Plainly it was impossible for me to continue much longer in a town where every stick and stone reminded me of the calamity that had overtaken me. My friends recognized this. They urged me to take a trip, to visit some of the universities of Italy where I would be able to see and hear much that would be of interest to my own investigations. But I lacked the courage and the energy.

I did my work and went to the hospital at the usual hours and made my rounds and saw my patients, but I resembled one of those automatic machines they make in Nuremberg—one that had been wound up long ago and the key of which had been mislaid by a careless servant.

Every day I felt myself grow a little weaker. Like most people of these northern climes, I had a very decided tendency towards melancholia. Thus far I had always rather despised the infamous "black humor" as a confession of moral weakness. And now, so help me God, I too was fast becoming one of its victims.

A few more weeks or months and I would begin to feel sorry for myself. That, as I well knew, was the beginning of the end. The next step would be a slow trip to the cemetery. Not from any wish to die so long before my time, but from a sheer lack of interest in keeping alive.

And then, just when I was beginning to tell everybody that the music had gone out of existence (I rather fancied that expression) and that the sky had lost its color and the flowers had lost their fragrance, in short, when I was beginning to be a terrible nuisance both to myself and to those who were patient enough to bear up with me, the "unexpected inevitable" or the "inevitable unexpected" that always stands hidden in the wings of the magnificent theater devoted to Human Folly, suddenly jumped to the center of the stage, whacked me gayly on the head with the jawbone of Balaam's ass, picked me up, threw me bodily across a couple of seas and oceans and left me stranded high and dry amidst such strange surroundings that I was soon forced to forget all about my own woes or suffer the indignity of being eaten up by a wolf or a bear. And the beginning of these strange adventures came to me in the form of a note which was delivered to me early one morning and in which My Lord Andries Bicker requested the pleasure of my company at his house on such and such a date for dinner and a private talk afterwards.

And this in itself was rather mysterious, for the Burgomasters of our good city did not as a rule extend their hospitality to private citizens like myself. It is true that I had visited his house once or twice in my professional capacity, but that was hardly a social introduction. And most of my neighbors still regarded me as a better-class barber. To-day the study of medicine is beginning to be elevated to the dignity of a science, and a few of us actually rank a little higher than mere leeches or pill-purveyors. But thirty years ago no mayor of the sovereign city of Amsterdam would break bread with a humble disciple of Aesculapius unless there was something he wanted to get from him and wanted very much indeed.

My Lord Andries Bicker was one of four brothers, who on the death of their father had inherited his vast fortune and then quietly divided the entire world among themselves as if it had been a parcel of real estate in one of the suburbs. There were those who said that the Republic ought not to be called the United Seven Netherlands but the United Four Bickerlands, and they were right. I have never been much interested in financial affairs. Perhaps that is not quite correct. I am interested in them, but in a vague sort of a way. Figures and statistics mean nothing to me at all. Tell me to-day that last year we imported eight hundred thousand lemons and four million pounds of rice and five hundred thousand pounds of almonds or that ten years ago the East India Company paid $22\frac{1}{2}$ percent dividend and last year only 18 percent and I shall answer you very politely, "Yes, indeed, and how very interesting!" But an hour later, I shall have forgotten all about it. But tell me that Jansen's father died of such and such a disease and his grandfather of such and such an affliction and if I am called in to see this same Jansen, fifty years hence, I shall have half my diagnosis ready before I have even entered the sick-room.

My grandfather, who was what you call a "practical man," more than once had held the Bicker family up for my youthful admiration. "The backbone of our country," he used to say. "Honest, hard-working people. There is no foolishness about them. In any other country they would be dukes and grandees and live in fine castles, and give themselves airs." (Grandfather could play the plain, simple democrat with great effect on such occasion.) "Just look at them! They must have two hundred ships between them and more shares in the big companies than any one else. Their income is a hundred times larger than that of many a German princeling who goes about boasting of his titles and his ancestors. And yet they continue to live right here in the midst of their wharves and breweries and store-houses and they tell me that they eat meat only once a week, like any ordinary citizen."

But these breweries and wharves and store-houses and those shares in East and West India companies and North Pole companies and South Pole companies meant nothing to me. But I had known both the father and the mother of these remarkable brothers and I was a good friend of the physician who had taken care of them for a number of years and I could have told any one of them offhand what he should eat and drink and what he should avoid and (had he been interested) I could have foretold him with a very fair degree of accuracy what illness would eventually take him to his grave. But as body and soul are not two different entities, as the church fathers of the Middle Ages told us, but are different expressions of one and the same mysterious occurrence, which we call life, I felt that I did not go too hopelessly unprepared to this strange meeting and that I would be able to hold my own in the conversation that was to follow, for I would understand the probable trend of thought of my host much better than he could possibly comprehend mine. Not that I expected anything very unusual. His Lordship probably contemplated some change in the conduct of the city's hospitals and wanted to consult a physician before he introduced the subject in the meeting of Their Lordships the Burgomasters.

But it came quite different, as I was soon to experience.

Our dinner too was more elaborate than I had anticipated. The whole family was present and I was introduced to the ladies of the household which was a signal honor to a member of my humble profession.

I was even taken aside to accept the solemn salutation of a very pretty little girl of six or seven, with a rich abundance of auburn curls. She made me a very pretty curtsey and said, "Good afternoon, Doctor," and I bowed low and kissed her hand with great formality. (For people are mistaken when they think that children don't observe our manners just as closely as we do theirs.) And I said, "Good afternoon, my dear, and what might your name be?" And she answered, "Wendela, sir, and I am staying with Uncle Andries because my sister has got the mumps," and then made me another curtsey and shyly ran back to her aunt who kissed her and said, "And now good night, little Mamselle, it is time you were in your coach with the white horses," whereupon she asked, "May I have just one pear?" and proudly marched off with her possession tightly clutched in her small right hand, the left one holding her long silken petticoats for fear that she might trip on the stairs.

I was not to see her again for a good many years and then under very different circumstances. For she afterwards married My Lord de Witt, whom many esteem the greatest statesman of our age, and she had a number of children, but after her last confinement in '65 she never quite recovered and I was called in on consultation and I had to tell her that as far as she was concerned, the Book of Life was closed and that another birth would mean the death both of herself and of her child, an announcement which seemed to fill her heart with great grief, "For," said she, "my husband is away so much of the time on business of state, and what shall I do to pass away the lonely hours, when the nursery is empty?"

But to return to our dinner. It was excellent and it was short, the highest praise one can give to that sort of function. It consisted of oysters and soup and a large roasted capon. "We ought to have sacrificed a cock to Aesculapius to-night," My Lord Andries explained while carving the fowl, "but seeing that it is not Aesculapius himself, but merely his trusted disciple, we thought that a capon would do just as well. Besides, these beasts are infinitely more tender than their less incomplete brethren." And he offered me the drum-stick, which was another token of honor for which I was not in the least prepared.

"These good people want something from me," I said to myself, and I soon found out that I was right. For immediately the feast had been served, the women bade us good day and my host and his brother Cornelis suggested that I follow them upstairs and they took me to a large room in the front of the house, the walls of which were entirely covered with book-cases and maps and bade me sit down in a low chair by the side of a large globe, and then the maid came in with a tray containing bottles of French wines and of Malaga and Madeira and glasses, and My Lord Andries filled me a glass and said, "Try this wine. It comes from Burgundy. It grew on the estate of a man who for fifty years faithfully served the King of France. Then he committed an act, most honorable in itself, but which went contrary to the personal interests of his Sovereign. He died in the Bastille and my brother and I, who had had business dealings with him, bought his vineyard to keep his wife from going to the poorhouse. Here is your good health."

And my Lord Cornelis took a large copper box, filled with tobacco, out of his pocket and handing me a fresh clay pipe he said, "Try this noble weed. It is of the same quality as that smoked by Sir Walter Raleigh on his way to the scaffold. He also had wasted fifty years of his life waiting upon a queen who called him an atheist for all his troubles and threw him over to please a silly boy who was her lover and serving a king who cut off his head as soon as he failed to find him that gold mine which everybody knew did not exist."

And then both brothers, lifting their glasses, said, "Here is to ourselves. God knows, we are coming on hard times."

And when my looks showed that I was slightly bewildered by this strange performance, they bade me light my pipe again (I always forget to keep those clay contraptions going and wish that some one would invent us a more agreeable way of inhaling the pleasant fumes of nicotine) and Cornelis said, "Fear not, dear Doctor, we have not lost our reason," and Andries added, "This is just our little joke, and now let us come to business," and he delivered quite a speech, which seemed so important to me that as soon as I returned home that evening, I wrote down everything I remembered of it and here are my notes of that evening.

"Doctor," he began, "we want your help. Perhaps you will think that we are slightly crazy but I can assure you that neither of us ever was in better health. Only one thing I must beg of you. All this must remain strictly between ourselves. Nothing is ever accomplished in an open meeting. God himself could not rule this world if he had to discuss everything he did with a dozen committees of arch-angels and was surrounded all the time by a mob of common little angels who more than half of the time would not know what he was talking about. What we are about to propose to you can only serve the weal of our own fatherland. But if our plans are to succeed, we must keep them a secret. At least for quite a number of years."

And when I had nodded my assent, he continued. "I don't want to give you a lecture on current politics, but you are no fool. Otherwise I need not assure you we would never have sent for you, which I mean as a compliment though perhaps I am a little too direct, but you have a good pair of eyes and an excellent pair of ears and you know just as well as I what is actually happening and more important still, what is going to happen in a couple of years.

"Of course you have heard what they say about us. That we run the Republic as if it were our own property. Well, what of it? We are business men. It is our duty to show profits. Is there any one who dares to claim that we don't make money? We make it for ourselves, but by making it for ourselves, we make it for every one else. Has this town ever been as rich as it has since the day our father joined the government? Has the Republic ever been as mighty as in these days when I and my brothers tell them how things ought to be done? There are a lot of lazy loafers who spend their waking hours in the taverns drinking mean gin and telling each other that we are tyrants, that we ought to be assassinated, that in ancient Greece and in ancient Rome the people ruled the state. Perhaps they are right, but this isn't ancient Rome nor ancient Greece. This is the Republic of the United Seven Netherlands and we now write the year of our Lord 1642.

"No, that 'vox populi' business and all that nonsense about democracy and Brutus and Caesar won't get us anywhere. Nor, to tell the truth, will it do us much harm. We are in power and we feel that we exercise this power for the common good. We therefore mean to keep it firmly in our own hands and we can do it, as the rabble will discover the moment it tries to start something. We are peaceful burghers. I and my brother would not harm a fly. But we must have law and order and prosperity! Let any one dare to interfere with us and he will swing outside the Town Hall windows and no mistake about it!

"But there is one little item that worries us a good deal. Some day, very soon, the war with Spain will come to an end. We are practically independent now, but when peace is signed, the whole world will have to recognize us as a sovereign commonwealth. What is going to happen then? And what will the House of Orange try to do? We have always been on good terms with those Germans. Old William was a great man. I have heard our grandfather speak about him. He knew him well. And so did our father. A very great man, wise and shrewd and very liberal. Not much of a soldier, but then, the world is full of soldiers and statesmen are as rare as roses in January. A terrible pity he was murdered just when we needed him so badly. A great many things would have come differently had he lived just a couple of years longer. But that is the way it goes in this world, and no use crying over spilt milk.

"His sons too have been very useful. But in a different way. Old William was a man of learning, a man of taste. He had vision and knew what was what. He would have made a good business executive. He knew how to row with the oars that were at his disposal. If he needed the support of the church party to further the interests of the land, he would go and associate with the ministers of the Gospel. If he thought that they were going too far and were trying to dominate the situation (and give that sort of people one finger and they will try to take the whole hand) he tactfully but sternly reminded them of their proper place and they went back into Clio's box until they were needed again. When there was fighting to be done, he not only found an army (and mind you, most of the time his treasury was completely empty, and did you ever hear of a professional soldier who fought for the love of the thing?) but he accomplished the impossible by enlisting the good will of all the different elements that under the leadership of a less clever man would have cut each other's throats long before they had seen a single enemy. But once the fighting was done, back they went again into their little wooden box, and that was that. He played on men and their emotions as old Sweelinck plays on his organ and as a result we had a decently balanced form of government. The Republic, as he saw it in his mind's eye, could have lived and might have lasted longer even than Venice or Genoa. But then he was murdered, and we got his sons.

"Excellent fighting men. Old Maurice never had a thought in his head except that it had to do with guns or horses or regiments of foot or ordnance. In the summer he laid siege to cities and in the winter he laid siege to women and I never heard of him to fail in getting whatever he wanted.

"But he was a German. His father had been a German too, but somehow or other, one never thought of him that way. He belonged to the world at large, but Maurice, for all his fine palaces and his courts and his gentlemen-in-waiting, always reminded me of an ordinary landjunker. He always smelled of horses and of stale beer, and when he dined at our house, we had to keep the windows open for a week afterwards.

"I am telling you now a few of our professional secrets. The crowd believe that the Stadholders of the Republic and the Burgomasters of Amsterdam are bosom friends, all coöperating most heartily for the ultimate benefit of our common country. Let them believe what they will. As long as we remain safely seated on those comfortable cushions of the Town Hall, we can afford a few amiable fairy-tales of that sort.

"But how long will we be able to hide the fact that we are really at cross-purposes? How soon before the man in the street discovers that all is not well? It has already happened once, upon one memorable occasion of which I need not remind you. Undoubtedly you are old enough to remember that terrible Monday the thirteenth. The greatest man our country had produced so far was murdered that day and murdered by the people for whom he had slaved for more than fifty years of his life. He had understood what few people before him suspected, that we were fast drifting towards a monarchy, and that the Republic would become another little German principality as soon as the Prince was allowed to forget that we, the people who make this commonwealth what it is, are his employers and pay him his salary as we pay that of any of our other servants.

"But of course Maurice would have been helpless without some political organization to back him up in his plans. I don't know who the bright man was who suggested that he make common-cause with the church party, but he did. And ever since, none of us have been quite safe. What happened to Oldenbarneveldt may happen to any of us almost any day. The present Stadholder is not a very strong man. He suffers from violent outbursts of temper and such people are always easily managed. Besides, he is too busy with his army. A marvelous fellow in his own field! Bois-le-Duc, Maastricht, Breda, Roermond, Wezel, he captured them all as neatly and as easily as a good chess player takes the pawns of his opponent. And not a single false move. But he is wasting himself physically. By the time he gets the last Spaniard out of our last city, he will be dead. He has a weak chest. Mark my words, we will sign our peace over his coffin.

"And then, what will become of all those German junkers who are now making a fine living as officers in our armies? We shall let our troops go the moment the war is over. Those captains and colonels and quartermaster-generals will all be out of a job and they won't like it. They have grown accustomed to three or four square meals a day, and plenty of wine. Do you think they will ever content themselves with the watery gruel of their beloved homeland, the beer-soup of Pomerania? I doubt it, and if all we hear of the way in which the Emperor's troops and the Swedes are chasing each other across the German lands is true, there won't be much even of that.

"Well, you can draw your own conclusions. They will want to remain right here where it is nice and comfortable and warm and where even the beggars won't touch their charity porridge unless it has about half a pound of sugar in it. And how will they accomplish this? By making themselves indispensable. And to whom? To the only man who has any need of their services, to the Prince.

"It is all very well to be the highest paid official in the Republic. But it would be a great deal more agreeable to step out of the salaried class and become an independent little potentate. I am not saying anything against the young prince. He is only a child. But at sixteen, a boy in his position is old enough to give us some inkling about his character and I don't trust that infant. I don't trust him for a moment! If he merely aspired to his father's place, why was he in such a hurry to marry the daughter of King Charles? Charles is hard up for money. He is having troubles with his people. I can't blame the people much, for their beloved sovereign seems a pretty slippery customer and he is costing them the devil of a lot of money. But of course he needs all the help he can get and so our young princeling was able to marry himself a princess of the blood at the moment the dear lady was going cheap.

"Well, what will he do next? He has the army, for as I have just pointed out to you, the officers know on what side their bread is buttered and a pleasant and solvent miniature court right here in Amsterdam or perhaps in The Hague would suit them remarkably well.

"But the army alone is not enough. We still have credit with the banks. We could send to Switzerland for a dozen regiments of infantry or we could buy half a dozen army corps from the Emperor, with cavalry and horses and all, enough to make an end to all this foolishness. And the navy is on our side and if the worst came to the worst, we could bring the men on shore and they are rough customers. But there are still a number of other people in this land of ours who have mighty little love for us and who would rally to anybody who promised them a chance to get even with their betters. That is the church party.

"I am a good Christian myself, as my father has been before me, and my mother too, and as I hope that my children will be after me. But those [and here His Lordship used a number of terms which I had never expected to hear from his lips and which I deem it wiser not to repeat] —but those stupid, narrow-minded, vain-glorious plow-boys, who have spent four years in some theological seminary and then come to town and frighten the rabble with their cock and bull stories about punishment and Hell and try to tell us—us!—how we should run the government of our own city and our own country! No, thank you, I'd rather flood the land again as they did when old Prince William was still alive and die in the last ditch than give in to these fellows one tenth of an inch.

"And that, I think, is the way all of us feel in the Town Hall. Well, of course the dominies know it and the Prince knows it and all his uncles and nephews and bastard little cousins know it. And there you have the lay of the land. As soon as the war with Spain is over, the war at home will begin. On the one hand, we the merchants who have made this country what it is, and on the other hand the Prince who wants to become a king and the rabble that believe everything he promises them and that see in him their savior who will lead them out of what they are pleased to call the wilderness of paganism into the promised land of that terrible man, Calvin."

Now when my Lord Andries got to this point, I thought it was time to rise respectfully to a few points of doubt. In the first place, had the House of Orange really ever had such ambitions as he had just implied? Surely, if they had wanted to make themselves the absolute rulers of the country, they could have done so repeatedly ere now. And in the second place, was he quite fair to the humble men and women who had fought and starved and died like flies during the first years of the great struggle for freedom and who had silently and contentedly borne such sufferings as would have broken the spirit of almost any other nation? But the Burgomaster was right there with his answer:

"I follow your objections," he said, "but don't you see that all this has changed completely since we practically gained our freedom? I will say this much for the doctrines of the learned Doctor Calvin, they absolutely suited the circumstances of the time. They were an excellent code of behavior for a town that was in a state of siege. They made men hard and women invincible. They put iron into the souls even of small children. It was a system that even the veterans of that old cut-throat Alva could not break. When he took Haarlem and drowned a couple of hundred of our people, they would grasp at the executioners with their dying fingers and would try to drag them down with them.

"But that sort of religion is of no earthly use to any one in times of peace. It is like the hammer of a smith that needs an anvil in order to function properly. Take the anvil away and it is just a useless tool that smashes people's toes when it is handed about and gets in everybody's way. Our ministers knew this and they still know it to-day. They must be forever standing on the ramparts of some beleaguered town. They must go snooping through the streets looking for hidden traitors. They must exhort and expostulate and urge and incite their poor disciples as if the enemy were still at the gate, ready to plunder and rape as did the soldiers of His Most Catholic Majesty. They must keep the people in a white hot rage against some threatening iniquity in their midst or go out of business altogether. And so for ever they are keeping the country in unrest and are forever setting the crowd off on a wild goose chase after a bugaboo that in reality does not exist.

"One day they clamor for the head of Oldenbarneveldt and keep the people happy with the lurid details of his execution. Then they must appoint a commission to examine the old man's affairs and show the world what a scoundrel he has been and behold! the commission reports that never in their lives have they come across so much honesty. That ends the search in that particular direction. But they are right away on the scent of a group of other miscreants and this time it is the members of some unfortunate sect that does not see fit to think of the Trinity as the old man in Geneva did.

"The Trinity is far removed from human affairs and it will be a long time before we shall really find out who is right in the matter. But that is a detail about which they don't bother. Those people don't think the way we do. Therefore they are in the pay of Satan. To the gallows with them! They made poor Hoogerbeets hang himself. De Groot is an exile somewhere in Sweden or France. And a couple of hundred of perfectly harmless preachers, some of the best and kindliest of men who ever trod this earth, are deprived of their livelihood, are making a living as bakers' assistants, have turned cobblers, have fled to one of those dreadful towns in northern Germany where they have to send their children begging in order to keep alive. All that is the work of the men of the great Synod.

"They are ideal shepherds for those who believe that they have seen the Devil sliding down our chimney on a long black broomstick and that we are making ready to massacre the children of Zion just as soon as the necessary formalities shall have been fulfilled with the King of Darkness.

"You think that I exaggerate? Well, think of what happened when you were young and the fights we had to fight right here in this city before we put an end to the tyranny of these clerical upstarts. What happened then taught us a lesson. This commonwealth was built upon the principle of live and let live, believe and let believe. That was the creed of Father William, and it is our creed to-day. We intend to maintain ourselves upon that basis. If we cannot do it, we shall fight. Meanwhile, like good merchants, we should provide for the future and that is why we asked you to come here. We are delighted to see you as our guest

But we also want to make you a business proposition. I shall light another couple of candles, to show you something. Meanwhile, have another glass of wine and fill yourself another pipe."

My Lord Andries went to a cupboard and took two candles which he fastened into a brass candle-stick and those he put in front of one of the large maps that hung on one side of the walls. He beckoned me to come nearer and I got up and I recognized one of Mercator's charts of the world, one of those new geographic maps that are said to have done so much to further the art of navigation.

"It is quite an old map," My Lord Andries remarked, "but it will do until the Blaeus give us a new one, which they have promised us very soon. Now look for a moment," and he showed me different parts of Asia and Africa and America, "all this belongs to us. Here all these islands," and he pointed to the Malayan Archipelago, "are possessions of the East India Company. Here, Ceylon has been ours for the last four years. Formosa old Carpentier has conquered. We have an open door that leads into Japan by way of Deshima. It is not very much of a door but a mighty profitable one. Here along the coast of Coromandel and Malabar we hold at least two dozen ports, we have a trading station at Mascate and control the trade in the Persian Gulf. Then down to Mauritius, and they say that Governor van Diemen is going to send Tasman to see what there is in this old story of several vast continents somewhere between Java and the South Pole.

"Sorry to bother you with these details. I sound like a schoolmaster, teaching a class of little boys their geography. In a moment you will see what I am driving at. Here on the west coast of Africa we possess a couple of harbors where our ships can get fresh provisions, then way up north here, Spitzbergen, where our whaling companies have built themselves a town where the money flows like sperm-oil, and down here in Brazil where we have a chance to build ourselves a vast empire of coffee and tea and tobacco, though unfortunately all this territory belongs to the West India Company and God knows how beautifully they mismanage it! And then here are all these islands in the West Indies. Old man Columbus surely was off the track when he mistook these bits of rock for part of the realm of the Great Mogul, but we are beginning to grow things on them and in due time they will pay their way. And then here in the north, the land we got from the discovery of Hudson. That is the spot to which we want to draw your attention for the moment, right here at the mouth of the Mauritius River, that one and this other bit of land at the tip of the African continent, right here where it says the Cape of Good Hope.

"I told you that we are afraid of what may happen to us as soon as we conclude peace with Spain and the soldiers join the great army of the unemployed, the people who are now working in our arsenals and navy-yards and powder-mills and who will have quite a hard time finding new jobs. Well we intend to be prepared. That is why we asked you to come here to-night. You can help us and I will tell you in what way, but first of all sit down again and have some more of this wine and another pipe of tobacco. The pipe will remind you of the fate that awaits those who put their faith in princes. But then, we are only burgomasters."

The glasses were filled and My Lord Andries took a sheet of paper and cut himself a new pen.

"I can think better when I have a piece of paper and a pen in my hands," he said. "You first had a lesson in practical politics and then one in geography. Allow me to add a little mathematics, the only science that should be of any real interest to the members of our merchants guild. Come over here near my desk and I will show you the conclusions we have drawn from many years of careful study."

With a few rough strokes he drew a picture that looked like a see-saw and two small soup-plates connected with pieces of string.

"What is this?" he asked.

"A pair of scales," I guessed, and I was right.

"That pair of scales represents the Republic," he continued. "That is the situation at the present time. The scales are well balanced," and he drew a small square in each of them and wrote in one of them "The Prince" and in the other, "The Merchants."

"In order that we may continue to be prosperous, this balance should be maintained. We merchants have no objection whatsoever to a strong central government. We are too busy with our own affairs to look after a lot of executive details, that can be much better attended to by the Stadholder, who is trained for that sort of work and whose family has made a specialty of it for God knows how many centuries. We need such a man in the Republic and we really don't care very much whether he wants to call himself a Stadholder or a King or anything else, as long as he does not interfere with our affairs and lets us free to make the money without which the commonwealth would be as helpless as a ship without sails. I am afraid that I am beginning to mix my different figures of speech. I am not a literary man, but I hope that I have made myself clear."

I told His Lordship that he had made himself entirely clear.

"Very well," he went on, and he drew another square in the soup-plate that had already been honored with the princely cargo. Then he wrote "The Church" inside the square and once more showed it to me.

"Suppose I add this extra load to one side of my scales, then what will happen?"

This mathematical catechism was beginning to amuse me.

"Then the balance would be disturbed," I answered.

"And in order to reëstablish that balance?"

"You would be obliged to find a counter-weight."

"Just so, Doctor! You ought to have been a mathematician instead of making pills. And what sort of a counter-weight would you suggest?"

I thought a moment and not wanting the conversation to become too serious, I said, "You might try moral persuasion."

The two Bicker brothers looked at each other and then lifted their glasses. "We must drink to that. 'Moral persuasion' to balance the dominies! A fine idea. But you know what became of the first man who tried to outweigh the power of a monarch by moral persuasion?"

I said yes, that I thought I remembered only too well.

"And of all the others?"

Again I nodded my assent.

"Very well, Doctor. Now be very bright for once and give us another guess."

"Money," I hinted.

"You are getting there. And how much money?"

"A great deal of it."

"An awful lot of it," My Lord observed.

"And even more," his brother added, and then he went on with his lecture.

"How is money made?" he asked me.

"By industry and perseverance."

"Yes, in the copy-books from which you learned your reading and writing when you were a little boy. But how is it really made?"

I told him that I had never thought of it. I was interested in only one problem, how sick people could be made well again. How was money made?

"Well," he observed in the tone of a school-master who is trying to be patient with a very dull pupil, "in a variety of ways. I don't want to go back all the way to the days of Moses and Julius Caesar or even those of those noble barons and knights who are now trying to marry our daughters if we are willing to give them enough of a dowry. I know the Greeks and the Phoenicians or whatever their names used to peddle their wares around the Mediterranean, and in the Middle Ages the Jews did a lot of buying and selling and had their teeth pulled out as often as some twopenny potentate was in need of a small loan. But generally speaking, before Venice and Genoa and Nuremberg and Antwerp and now our city taught them better, people made money by catching a few boatloads of their fellow-citizens by fastening dog-collars around their necks and forcing them to work for their own benefit as if they had been horses or dogs, which undoubtedly they were except that the man who killed a first-class stallion was punished a little more severely than the fellow who merely murdered a serf.

"But all that belongs to the past, at least in the civilized part of the world—which of course means our own part of the world. What the rest of our blessed continent does, hardly interests me. Perhaps from a business point of view, it is just as well that they remain a little backward. Meanwhile we will try and make 'profits.' Now what are profits? I have something that costs me ninety-nine cents and I sell it for a florin and I grow rich. I have something that costs me a florin and I sell it for ninety-nine cents, and I go to the poor-house. Business is really very simple. It merely consists in buying cheaply and selling dearly. All the rest is stuff and nonsense and belongs in one of those pamphlets about the 'rights of stockholders,' etc., that certain clever lawyers write in taverns when they have had a couple of drinks. Buying cheaply and selling dearly is the whole secret, and how can you do that best of all?"

Again I confessed my ignorance.

"You don't know? You really don't know? And yet it is so terribly simple. All you have to do is to get hold of some convenient little monopoly. Once you have got it, your troubles have come to an end. You can sit peacefully in your office and hire some one else to count your profits. Soon you will need a dozen people just to keep track of the figures."

I interrupted him with some irritation. "And that is where you need me? You want me to give up the practice of surgery and become a bookkeeper?"

His Lordship jumped to his feet. "God forbid," and he waved his hands in despair. "The world is full of good book-keepers, honest, intelligent, obliging fellows who will work all their lives for five florins a week and will never have a thought or a desire as long as they live. Book-keeper, fiddlesticks! Whenever we let it be known that the house of Bicker needs a new book-keeper, there is a line outside our door from here to Zaandam. No, we don't want you to turn book-keeper."

I looked at him in surprise. "Then, My Lord, how in Heaven's name do I come to figure in your plans and calculations?"

"Very simply. We want you to go and find that little monopoly for us," and once more His Lordship picked up his pen and began to do some figuring.

"In order to hold our own against the political combination we anticipate and fear," he said without looking up from his pothooks, "we need a great deal of added revenue. For this we need the exclusive hold upon one of the necessities of life. Most of these are already in other hands. The East India Company has got all the spices. They are out. The West India Company has got the slave trade. That is out. Besides, it is a nasty sort of business and I am not enough of a theologian to be able to drug my soul with those passages from Holy Script which elevate slave-raiding to the dignity of a semi-religious duty. Then in the North, there is whale oil and whale bone. But all this is in the hands of a single company and they won't allow any outsider to look in on their fishery preserves. Besides, I hear that they have gone after those poor dumb whales with such murderous violence that soon there won't be a whale left within a thousand miles of Spitzbergen. And suppose the French dressmakers decree that women shall not wear corsets any longer, what then would become of the whale-bone industry? It would lie flat on its back in less than a month.

"That does not seem to leave very much for us, does it? Of course, my brother and I are stockholders in all those companies and directors, and we get our share of the dividends. But the people on the other side of the fence, the partisans of the Prince are stockholders too and occasionally they are able to outvote us. And that is just what we don't want to happen. We want a monopoly of our own that shall be entirely in the hands of our own family and a few of our relatives, a water-tight and air-tight monopoly that is ours, to use as we shall see fit. And we think that we have found one.

"Let me give you a few more figures. Man has to eat in order to live. Granted! The staple article of daily consumption in most households is bread. Also granted! Bread is made out of a substance called grain. On that point there probably won't be any dispute. Where does that grain come from? Most assuredly not from the territory of the Republic. We have had two of our brightest book-keepers study this problem for three years. They have examined all the reports of the harbor-master and they have carefully gone through the tax returns of the commissioners of internal revenue. Here they are" (and he opened a drawer of his writing table and took out a blue cover which held a number of papers)—"here you are. Last year our city alone needed about forty-two thousand tons of grain, but one third of that went to the breweries and as you know, we make the beer for practically the whole of the country. The rest of the Republic used up another forty thousand tons. The total import was 160,000 tons so that almost eighty thousand tons were exported again and at an excellent profit I can assure you. For even under the present circumstances, our country has practically a monopoly of the carrying trade of all grain. Our agents in Copenhagen report that of the 793 ships that crossed the sound on their way from the Baltic to the North Sea, 702 flew the red, white and blue of the Republic. That is not a bad showing, is it? Of those 702, not less than 590 were bound for our city and more than half of those were loaded with grain. That grain is grown in Poland and Curland and Esthland, the old possessions of the German Order, and in Ukrania, which is part Polish and part Russian.

"In the olden days, this trade was easy enough. Of course the Danes with their infernal tolls made our lives miserable, but as long as we paid (although often enough we paid through the nose), we got our ships. But the political situation around the Baltic Sea is beginning to fill our hearts with fear. Poland is getting more disorderly every day. A republican monarchy, in which one foolish knight (be he drunk or sober, but as a rule he is drunk) has the power to upset any law that all the others want, such a country is bound to go to pieces sooner or later. The Swedes have conquered Esthland and Livland, but Gustavus Adolphus is dead, his daughter Christina (even if she had had sense enough to send for Grotius to act as one of her advisers) is—well, let us say rather 'unbalanced.' I hear that she has begun to see spooks and wants to travel to Rome to tell the Pope how to rule the world and then go into a monastery. That country, therefore, is out of our calculations for the present at least. All the Wasas have been a little bit crazy—very brilliant many of them—but always just a trifle unreliable.

"And then there is the famous Grand Duke of Muscovy, who now calls himself 'Caesar' and prattles sweetly of being heir to all the rights and prerogatives of the old Emperors of Byzantium. What all that will eventually lead to, God only knows. We have an agent in Moscow and he tells us that ever since Czar Ivan (you remember? The one who beat his son to death) the Russians have been talking of their 'ancestral rights' to the whole of the east coast of the Baltic. What those ancestral rights are I don't know. But I do know that there are a terrible lot of these wild people and once they are on the war-path, neither Swede nor Pole nor Prussian will be able to stop them.

"A nice little war in those parts that lasted let us say two or three years would make all of us starve. We need grain and Spain needs grain and Italy needs grain. We need it because there is more water than land in this country and no one so far has invented a method of growing grain in a swamp like rice. Spain and Italy need grain because they are so full of monasteries that there isn't room enough left to sow a few acres of wheat of their own. But think what it would mean to our carrying trade if we should be cut off from our base of supply in the Baltic! More than half of our ships would lie idle. And the greater part of the other half would be forced out of business because we would not have gold enough with which to buy the things we need from abroad. Now, Doctor, what is the answer?"

I confessed that I did not know.

"The answer is very simple. We must no longer content ourselves merely with transporting and selling other people's grain. We must grow it ourselves. And there are only two places where we can do that. One is on the Cape of Good Hope. But the East India Company would never allow us to settle there. Until now they have not taken possession of it themselves, but I hear that they may do so almost any moment and their charter gives them the right to claim the whole of southern Africa, as part of their dominions and then we would have done all our work in vain. I have no desire to be another LeMaire. That poor devil was no doubt well within his rights when he claimed that he had not infringed upon the charter of the company when he sailed to the Indies via Cape Horn. But old Coen took his ship away from him just the same and young LeMaire died from sheer disappointment and the father took the case to the supreme court and won it, but by the time the last judge had signed the last decree, the old fellow was a bankrupt and that is what would happen to us too if we were ever foolish enough to try it. No, there is but one way out. Come over here a moment," and His Lordship picked up a candle and went back to the map on the wall and pointed to the central part of the North American continent and he said:

"Right here and now we will tell you what you can do for us. All this of course belongs to the West India Company. It was given to them by the charter of 1621. But that company has never done well. I don't exactly know why. I suppose the East India Company has absorbed all our available surplus capital. In the Indies, almost everything will grow and the natives are patient little brown men who all work for you if you treat them badly enough. In America the natives will die rather than work for some one else. And the climate is annoying. No pepper, no cinnamon, no nutmeg. A few beaver-skins and a little dried fish and even for these you have to barter with a naked red man with feathers in his hair and a large battle-ax in his strong right hand.

"And they have been terribly unfortunate with the people they have sent out. They began wrong. That man Hudson may have been a fine navigator (I suppose he was) but he was about as loyal to his employers as those other Englishmen we hired to fight for us, and who sold Zutphen and Deventer to the Spaniards. I will say that he did a fine piece of work in sailing up the Mauritius River, but if Adriaan Block had not lost his ship off Manhattan Island (a strange accident that fire was too, but in this case a very fortunate one) and if Block had not been the man he was we would know no more about America to-day than we did when Hudson first invited the natives on board his *Half Moon,* and got them so beautifully drunk on Dutch gin. That was a pretty terrible performance and that bad beginning seems to have put a special hoodoo on everything we have ever tried to do in that part of the world. We have had a fine lot of men as governors of the Moluccas and Java, but there on the banks of the Mauritius, one terrible person has succeeded the other. Pieter Minuit was an honorable man. But the others, great Heavens, what a sad collection of incompetent scoundrels! May was a common clerk and not even an honest one. No one knows why he was ever appointed except that he happened to be on the spot when they needed some one in a hurry. Krol was a run-away dominie and absolutely untrustworthy. Van Twiller was a fool who thought that his good connections would keep him out of jail when he engaged in a little private speculation, as they afterwards did. Kieft, who is supposed to rule that colony to-day, is an undischarged bankrupt. You can still see his picture fastened to the gallows.

"He seems to belong to that unfortunate race of 'energetic' people who always must be 'doing' something, especially when they would serve their purpose much better by doing nothing at all. He got the company into a nice war with the natives. I have forgotten their names, Algonquins or something like that.

"The good ship *Fortune* came in port last week with a cargo of beaver-skins and I had a long talk with her captain. He used to work for us years ago when we had more breweries than we do now and needed more grain. He married a wife with some money and he put it into West India shares and then he went into the service of the company because, as he said, that was the only way to discover what they were doing with his funds. He has traded all over America from the Trask River to Cape Hinloopen. We are old friends and he knew that he could trust me. I learned more from him in five minutes' talk than from all the endless written reports of these half literate but long winded governors.

"The trouble with the Indians, so he told us, has been absolutely un-called for. Anybody with half a grain of common sense (uncommon sense is more to my liking but it is so terribly hard to find)—any one with half a grain of uncommon sense would have been able to avoid those difficulties. The savages in that part of the world seem to be harmless enough, a bit dirty and a bit lazy from our own point of view, but rather like children, good natured until they discover that you have tried to cheat them when they suddenly lose all control of themselves and slash and burn and kill until their anger is spent and they smile once more as if nothing had happened.

"Our friend had dealt with them for a dozen years or more. He had visited their villages and spent nights in their tents, absolutely unarmed and the only white man within a hundred miles. But nothing had ever happened to him. If it had not been for the slightly embarrassing and not entirely unodorous expressions of affection on the part of the wives and daughters of these poor heathen, he told me that he would rather settle down in almost any Indian village than in the place of his birth, which lies somewhere in the darkest interior of Friesland.

"You therefore need have no fear on that score. You won't be eaten up or burned at the stake or thrown to the dogs. I know that that has happened to a few of the Jesuit missionaries who operate in the neighborhood of Fort Orange. I am sorry for them, but why didn't they stay at home? Can you imagine a couple of priests and sorcerers of those Algonquins, or whatever the name, right here on the Dam near the fish-market, let us say, telling the dear public that is busy buying and selling shrimps and mussels, that they ought to stop buying and selling shrimps and ought to listen to the words of the Great White Spirit from the hills, who bids men and women paint their faces a bright red and stick a feather in their hair and say 'Walla, walla, walla' forty times in succession to escape the disfavor of the Great Black Spirit? Can you imagine such an episode and can you imagine what would happen to the poor heathen? Well, I can and I suppose you can too.

"No, the natives will be the least of your worries. You are a man of tact and we shall give you a shipload of these gimcracks and little mirrors and beads and bangles that seem to delight the hearts of those simple children of nature. And then, at your leisure, we want you to sail across the ocean and go to Nieuw Amsterdam. We have collected a great deal of information about you before we asked you to come here. We know that you are deeply interested in the problem of reducing the pain connected with those surgical operations that take place in our hospitals. Mind you, I don't say that they are not necessary, but I was a victim myself once. It was not much of an affair as such things go, but I still turn green and cold whenever I think of what they did to me. Very well, you let it be known that you are going to take a trip to America because you want to investigate those stories that are coming to us continuously about certain plants which the natives of the New World use to alleviate pain."

I interrupted His Lordship. "I am sorry," I said, "but why lie about it?"

But this rather downright question did not worry the speaker for a moment.

"In the first place," he continued, "it would not be quite a lie. My book-seller sends me every account of American exploration that appears. He has standing offers for such books in London and Sevilla and Lisbon. I can't read those printed in Portuguese, but I have those translated by a bright young Jew, a curious fellow who seems to be the only man who ever got away from the Inquisition and lived to tell the tale."

"I know him," I said. "He is one of my best friends."

"Really? Well, he is a bright fellow and ought to have a better job than he has now. We have offered to employ him ourselves, but he seems to be content to jog along. Well, as I was saying, I read every word that is being printed about those mysterious aborigines and what strikes me most is that they seem to know a great many things of which we, with all our learning, have not the faintest idea. They do seem to be able to deaden their bodies against pain. It may be just a funny story, like that one connected with the famous gold of Sir Walter Raleigh which proved to be some sort of copper or the Fountain of Youth of that old Spaniard whom they buried in the Mississippi (you see, I know my American geography) and so you won't be wasting your time if you consent to spend a few years collecting shrubs and weeds and interviewing medicine-men with rings through their noses."

I agreed that it would be a wonderful opportunity, but why not tell the truth?

"Because," my Lord Andries answered, "it would be one of those occasions where telling the truth would be fatal. What we really want to do, and now I am coming to the kernel of the business, is to get hold of vast tracts of land where grain can be grown at a very small cost. According to the best of our information, the coastal regions are too rocky and too densely covered with woods to be suitable for that purpose. But a few hundred miles inland, as I have found stated in any number of books, there are enormous plains where grain will grow almost over night.

All the land from the Atlantic to the next ocean (most likely it is the Pacific, but we are not sure yet. Hudson, so I hear, claimed to have found another sea much higher up in the north, a small ocean that may reach as far as Mexico) for all we know. All the land between the Fresh River and the South River belongs to the West India Company however. That organization is terribly hard up for money and the directors would listen with both ears if we offered to buy a few hundred thousand square miles and pay cash.

"That is what we want to do as soon as you come back and tell us that the soil is suitable for our purpose. We have the money and we mean to keep this a strictly family affair. No one outside of our own city will be allowed to invest a penny. No committees of Seventeen or Gentlemen Nineteen for us, if we can help it. This time the enterprise is going to be well managed. That is why we shall depend so greatly upon your report. If you tell us that the land will grow grain, we shall buy vast tracts. We are already at work upon a system of colonization. There are thousands of people in the Republic who would go abroad and settle in Java or Brazil or even in the New Netherlands if they were not obliged to go there in a state of semi-serfdom. If we find that we cannot work our farms without slave labor, we shall import a sufficient number of them from Africa. I don't approve of it much myself, but if that is the only way to make money, well then, we shall do as the others do.

"But what we have in mind will bear very little resemblance to those trading-posts which are the eternal stand-by of all our Indian companies. We want permanency. We want to turn our possessions over there (if ever we get them) really and truly into some sort of a New Netherlands. So that if things go wrong over here in the old Netherlands, we have another home in another world upon which we can fall back.

"Maybe I am a little too pessimistic. Maybe that young Orange prince is not bright enough or has not got courage enough to try and do all those things of which we suspect him. In that case, if we are successful, we shall have another source of income and a little extra pin-money is always acceptable even to the best of us. On the other hand, if things go badly we shall have a new fatherland. And new hope and courage for thousands of people."

He stopped abruptly and turned to his brother. "All this seems clear to you?" he asked.

"Perfectly," my Lord Cornelis answered.

"Then," turning to me, "have you any questions to ask?"

"Yes," I replied. "The one at which I hinted a moment ago. Why all this secrecy? Why not let everybody know what the purpose of my voyage is?"

"For a variety of reasons. In the first place, if the Prince and the Church people are conspiring to deprive us of our power and turn the Republic into a monarchy, they will of course take measures to prevent you from going, if they know what your mission is, and they will do their best to spoil our ideas, and as yet we are not powerful enough to hold our own against such a combination of forces. In the second place, if the direction was to hear of this, they would ask such extortionate prices for their land that the whole plan would come to nothing. In the third place . . ."

But I did not care to hear any further reasons. I already knew enough. My personal sympathies were entirely on the side of those two men who saw the ideals for which our fathers had fought so valiantly, go to ruin on the cliffs of selfishness, partisanship and religious bigotry. Of course they were business-men and figured things out in terms of florins and daalders, more than I would have done who lived vaguely in that realm of science where money is rarely discussed because it is so seldom seen in sufficient quantities to attract people's attention. But on the whole, I did not doubt the integrity of their motives. Only I would need a little time to think things over. I told them so and they agreed most readily.

"Take as long as you like, Doctor," they urged me most cordially. "We have expressed ourselves quite openly to you and have placed ourselves in your hands. Go home now, for you must be tired after listening to this lecture and let us know what you intend to do just as soon as you have made up your mind."

I bade my adieux and slowly walked home. When I crossed the bridge of the Saint Anthonie locks, I noticed that there was still light burning in the upstairs windows of Rembrandt's house. I had not seen anything of him since the funeral of my brother and thought that I would drop in for a minute. I needed some one with whom to talk things over before I went to bed, for I was much too excited to be able to go to sleep right off.

I knocked on the door but got no answer.

I knocked again and a little louder.

I heard people stumbling about in the back part of the house.

Finally the door was opened a few inches. The nurse of little Titus was standing there. She was holding a candle in her hand and looked at me as if she were ready to kill me.

"The master has gone to bed and can't be disturbed," she snapped. "Please go away." And she locked the door in my face.

I went home.

I didn't quite like what I had just seen.

Chapter 26

WE TAKE ANOTHER TRIP INTO THE COUNTRY AND DISCUSS DIVERSE METHODS OF NAVIGATION

The next Sunday was one of those incredibly fine days which we sometimes get in our part of the world as a compensation for all the rain and fog and slush and mud of the rest of the year. And so, although the regular season for our Sabbatical wanderings had already come to an end, we decided to take a walk and shortly after breakfast we left the Saint Anthonie Gate and walked to the Diemermeer.

I still remember the old "meer" as it was until a dozen years ago, a deep and malignant pool inhabited by wild ducks and wild geese and made unsafe by very ferocious poachers who liked to bring a little variety into their otherwise monotonous lives by robbing the occasional visitor and who were reported to have as little consideration for human life as some of my colleagues whose names, however, I prefer not to reveal to posterity.

But now that the lake has been converted into a polder and that some of our richest and even some of our most respectable citizens have chosen that spot for the erection of their country houses, the place is as safe as the inside of the bank and sitting peacefully in the tap-room of the Arms of Abcoude, one would hardly believe it possible that only a few years before, this selfsame spot lay covered underneath sixteen feet of water. After we had finished our meal, I told my friends of my future plans.

Perhaps this is not stating the case quite fairly. Way down deep in my mind I had decided already that I would accept the offer of the Bicker family. It was too fine a chance for me to escape for a while from a city where everything reminded me of the tragedy that had befallen our family, and furthermore I would be given the opportunity to make some very serious experiments in a field of science that seemed to me more worth while than anything else in the world.

Of course I would to a certain extent sail under false colors. My real mission would have to be kept a secret. But why not? When the late King Henry of France had to choose between his Protestant faith and the crown of France, he is said to have remarked that after all, the privilege of living in Paris as its sovereign master was worth an occasional visit to Holy Mass. I think that in due time I shall be able to pacify my conscience with that very shrewd observation of the man who gave us half a dozen witty words and one very fine sauce. But I have never been one of those strong and determined characters that could come to a decision one, two, three! and then close the door upon all further considerations because "they have made up their minds." In my case, the door of possible regrets almost always remains ajar, just a tiny little bit. And in order to be quite comfortable I need the reassurance of friends that I am really doing the right thing.

In this case they appeared to be unanimously agreed that this was the best thing I could possibly hope to do. They were sorry to lose me, for so long a time, but it was a rare chance. I absolutely must accept. They would write me about all that happened of any importance and would call on my small son to see that he fared well. (Good God! I had completely forgotten the child, but I supposed that I could safely leave him with the old nurse who took care of him anyway whether I was there or not.) And they would do anything for me they could, but I must say yes.

And so on and so forth, to the great secret joy of my "Demon," for though I am by no means another Socrates, the "still inner voice" that dwelleth within my breast can upon occasions shout louder than the most experienced of our town-criers, announcing the arrival of a fresh load of peat. And so we remained together until a very late hour, drinking a moderate amount and talking an immoderate amount and I, or rather the country of my future residence, became the center of an animated and learned geographical discussion during which Selim drew upon his vast knowledge of Moslem devils and monsters to populate the new world with a choice collection of satyrs and Calibans and ghouls, all of them anthropophagous and living by preference on the blood of surgeons and leeches, until he had completely exhausted the field of demonology when he switched from America to his own beloved Asia and depicted the charms of the gazelle-eyed houris and the black-haired peris in such colorful terms that a most respectable couple of Dutch people who sat at a neighboring table hastily bundled their daughters into their most respectable woolen shawls and dragged them to safety before this strange-looking "foreigner" should begin to put his seductive theories into practice.

In the meantime Jean-Louys (to the intense disgust of the landlord who, however, did not quite dare to remonstrate with a person of such palpable dignity) had poured some wine into a cup and by using his finger as his brush, had covered the freshly scoured wooden table with its beautiful white top with a variety of lines and curves which were supposed to represent a map of the countries bordering upon the Atlantic Ocean. And then calling for pen and paper, he set forth to figure out the distance between the roads of Texel and the mouth of the Mauritius River and he did this by means of a new method of nautical calculation which he had found the week before in a handbook on navigation written by a German professor of theology, who in his introduction had boasted that he would some day be recognized as one of the greatest of all marine experts as he had never seen either a sea nor a ship and therefore could not possibly be distracted from his "theoretical conclusions" by some of those so-called "practical observations" with which ship's captains were apt to disfigure their works.

In how far Jean-Louys had misunderstood or was now misinterpreting the "theory" of the learned man, I do not know, but when he came to the "theoretical conclusion" that the Atlantic Ocean was only half as wide as the Zuyder Zee, we decided that an occasional trip on board a fishing-smack might have done the erudite Teuton more good than the fifty years he seemed to have spent in his library in the genial company of those Babylonian and Ninevehian and Egyptian sources upon which he had based his contentions to the exclusion of everything and every one else.

"A fine system of navigation," Jean-Louys finally confessed, wiping the winish map of the Atlantic off the table with the help of his useless notes. "A splendid piece of work, as thorough a piece of investigation as half of the stuff that comes out of that mysterious land. A pity it was not published a couple of years before. It would have been of immense value to Jonah when he sailed his whale from Joppa to Tarsus. But I am afraid that you had better stick to Cunningham and Davis. That is to say, if you care to get there and if we, my friends, care to get back to Amsterdam before they close the gate on us, we had better be starting right now."

Thereupon he called for the landlord, still smarting under the damage done to his freshly cleaned table, made that sour-looking citizen the subject of an impromptu speech in which he not only praised the food and wine but also dwelled so impressively upon the charm of the man's tap-room, the beauty of his wife and daughters and the virtues of his cook (and all of this in broad Gascon French of which the innkeeper did not understand a word) that the poor fellow almost trembled with excitement and gratitude and would not let us go before we had all drunk his health in a special sort of French brandy which he had suddenly produced from a mysterious hiding-place and which, according to his story, had been brought him directly from the cellar of His Majesty, King Louis of France.

"No doubt a special gift which it has pleased His Majesty, my most august sovereign, to bestow upon you for just such a meal as the one with which you have just favored us?" Jean-Louys asked, using me as an interpreter.

"No, Your Worship, but I have a brother who is a cook . . ."

"On board a ship which plies between Amsterdam and Rouen."

The landlord stopped in surprise. "How did Your Worship know?"

"Because people who can afford to drink cognac like that, usually have brothers, who are . . ."

"Cooks on ships to Rouen!"

"Exactly."

And thereupon these two men who had suddenly discovered a common ground of philosophic interest by way of a brother who was a cook on a vessel from Amsterdam to Rouen, solemnly shook hands. Then all of us most solemnly shook hands and we walked back to Amsterdam through the light haze of the dying day and said little and thought much and were happy in each other's company.

But the gate was locked when we arrived.

And we had to pay two stivers each to get in and we had to listen to a short sermon on the part of the sergeant who was on guard and who in daily life exercised the profession of a shoemaker and who did not believe in "all this walking on the Sabbath just for the sake of pleasure."

"But, Sergeant," Jean-Louys stopped him, "we are not idle people. We are pilgrims returning from a long voyage."

"Long voyage!" the sergeant sneered. "I have been here all day long. I saw you go out this morning."

"But since then much has happened. We have made a great and profound discovery."

"I'd like to know what that was?"

"That even an humble cook on board a ship to Rouen may have his uses."

And then we bade the sergeant good night with great politeness and went to our respective homes.

But the next morning on my way to the Hospital I met My Lord Banning Cocq, who stopped me and asked me whether I and my friends had taken a walk to the Diemermeer the day before and I said yes, we had. And he answered, "I thought so," and I asked him, "Why, My Lord?" and he laughed and said, "Because my sergeant, poor devil, came to me in a state of great perturbation this morning and told me that he felt greatly worried, as he had let four lunatics into the town the night before, and then of course I knew it must have been you and your friends."

I thanked him sincerely for the compliment, for I knew that he was a genial man and would have dearly liked to join us on our walks if his position in society had permitted him to associate with a leech and a bookkeeper and a nondescript French nobleman, not to forget a Turk who made an open profession of his heathenish faith. But he shook his head rather sadly.

"My good Doctor," he remarked, "you are an older man than I. But I have been obliged to spend a whole morning keeping a half-witted trooper from running to the Burgomasters with a tale of four crazy men running wild in Amsterdam. Do you mind if I give you a bit of advice?"

I answered that of course I would be delighted.

"Then never try to be funny with common people. It does not make them happy and it will get you yourself into trouble. Good-by and by the way, I hear you are going to America on some sort of scientific expedition. . . ."

Chapter 27

I DECIDE TO BECOME A VOLUNTARY EXILE FROM MY OWN COUNTRY

"And by the way, I hear you are going to America?"

If I heard that once during the next six days, I heard it a thousand times. I had only told my friends and they were very discreet people. Besides they lived very solitary lives and hardly spoke to a soul from one week-end to the next.

The Bickers knew, too, but they would probably not think it to their advantage to let the fact be known before all their many preparations had been finished.

Then how had the news traveled abroad so fast?

To this day it has remained a mystery to me. But the experience strengthened me in my belief that there exists something closely akin to what I would like to call a "communal soul." And this communal soul is not restricted to densely populated countries. It functions just as effectively in the desert or in the wilderness or in the midst of a trackless forest as it does in the heart of Amsterdam or London. It travels with the rapidity of light which according to that learned friar, Roger Bacon, has a velocity that is even faster than that of a falling star. But whereas a stone cast from a height moves only in one direction, a bit of news that is of real importance to a vast number of people goes in all directions at once and recognizes neither east nor west nor south nor north nor up nor down, but seems to obey that same mysterious law which claims that nature abhors a vacuum, while it defies our mathematical maxim that no given body can be in two different places at one and the same time.

When I got up in the morning and had a cup of hot milk, my housekeeper said, "And so I hear, Master, that you are going to America, and what will become of me? and the child when I am gone?" And when I went to the Hospital, the old man who acts as a gate-keeper said, "Good morning, Doctor, and so I hear you are going to America." And when I left at noon and visited the barber, who is a member of the same guild as I and treats me with colleagual familiarity, he said, "Ah, my sly friend, I hear that you are going to leave us and are going to America." And so it went all day and in the evening after I returned home I found a note waiting for me from Rembrandt. It really was not a note, but an old sketch, underneath which he had scribbled a few words as follows:

"I hear that you are going to America and I want to ask you and your friends to drop in next Thursday evening, for I have finished a picture I want to show you."

This message I received with a certain amount of irritation. My reception at his house a few days before had hardly been of a sort to make me want to call again. Indeed, I was so annoyed by the recollection of what had happened on that occasion that I threw the letter into the fire, but it happened to land upside down and I saw that there was some writing on the back of the sheet and hastily fished it out of the flames (and burned my fingers in doing so) and I read:

"I am terribly sorry I missed you the other night. I was pulling a few proofs of a new landscape I had just started (most unsatisfactorily, so far) and the miserable woman never even let me know it was you who had called. I want to see you badly." And then three times underlined, "The woman is hopeless. I hope to God I shall be able to get rid of her positively before the end of next week."

I understood. The terrible nurse had had one of her attacks of ill-temper. "I hope to God I shall be able to get rid of her positively by the end of next week." A pious wish, to which I could say Amen with all my heart.

When the appointed evening came (the intervening days I had listened with such patience as was still at my command to one thousand three hundred and ninety-seven people telling me, "Oh, by the way, I hear that you are going to America!") I was detained at the Hospital by a boy who had been hit by the wings of one of the mills on the Blauwbrug bulwark and whose shoulder-blade had been horribly mutilated, and it was past nine o'clock before I reached the house on the Anthonie Breestraat. My friends were there and a middle-aged man of the Jewish race whom I recognized at once as a Rabbi of whom Rembrandt had made an etching a couple of years before and which had had a very favorable sale among the members of his congregation. I was now introduced to him and learned his name. He was the famous Samuel Menasseh ben Israel and Bernardo had often spoken to me about him for they were compatriots, they had both been born in Lisbon and had fled to the Republic when Portugal had been occupied by the Habsburgs and the Inquisition had been reëstablished in that unfortunate country.

His family, if I remembered rightly, had first gone to La Rochelle, but the eternal wrangling between the Protestants and the Catholics in that city had been very bad for business and the family had moved further away from home and had come to live in Amsterdam. The boy had been apprenticed to a painter, but he had wanted to study theology, until his father, old Joseph ben Israel, a well-known character about town and a practical man of great common sense, suggested that he practice both professions at the same time.

Of course as soon as there had been more than a dozen Jews in our town, there had been three dozen quarrels. What these quarrels were about, the rest of us were never able to discover, but a people that has spent two thousand years in endless and angry disputes about the relative value of inverted commas and semi-colons in a number of books which no sensible person takes the trouble to read, such maniacs of the written word can always find something to disagree about. And when in 1619 the government had granted them full religious liberty, they had celebrated the occasion by establishing three synagogues where there had only been one before. Menasseh fortunately did not belong to the extreme radicals and he was so broad-minded and so learned and so full of the true spirit of tolerant brotherhood that many Christians, exasperated by the sectorial hair-splitting of their own clergy, had fallen into the habit of going to his synagogue rather than attending divine service in one of their own churches. And even Catholic visitors of distinction had gone to Beth-Israel to hear this pleasant-voiced man hold forth upon the affairs of the day with such irrepressible good humor and in such fine temper of spirit that all the difficulties of this world seemed to solve themselves like the early fogs that are dispelled by the rays of the summer's sun.

All this I had heard long before I ever met him but I was to hear a great deal more that evening. For when I entered, the guests were sitting around the table examining a heavy volume bound beautifully in leather and Rembrandt, drawing me into the general conversation, said, "Look at this—I wish that I could draw the way our friend here paints." And he showed me a page of something which I could not read but which seemed to me to be a Hebrew edition of the Psalms, as it was printed in very short sentences and as the chapter was much briefer than those of the rest of the Old Testament.

I had guessed right, it was a Hebrew edition of the Psalms printed in the basement of the house diagonally across from that of Rembrandt where Menasseh lived and had also his workshop. Quite naturally the talk then drifted to the difficulty of getting foreign type in a city like Amsterdam and I learned to my surprise that there were not only two printing establishments that could handle Hebrew type, and that not only French and German and English and Spanish and Portuguese books were manufactured wholesale in our town, but that a great many Arabic and Persian and Armenian texts went forth into the world bearing the "cum privilegio" of the magistrates of Amsterdam, and when I expressed my surprise and asked the Rabbi how this had happened to come about, he answered, "Your rulers are very wise people. They are out after profit. Why shouldn't they be? They are business men and this is a business country. Did you ever hear of an innkeeper who could afford to ask too closely into the religious preferences of his guests and at the same time keep his trade? Well, I never did. And so they leave us alone as long as we don't say anything that is too disagreeable about themselves. And why should we? Imagine living in a country where there isn't any censorship!"

"But surely," I interrupted, "there is some sort of a censorship. You can't say just anything you want?"

"Almost anything you want. It is all in the saying. And as long as you don't print that Their Lordships of the Town Hall eat little children for breakfast or that they make a specialty of seducing little girls, you can go ahead and write whatever you want and the censors won't bother you any more than they do me," and then he continued (how nice to hear that once again!), "They tell me that you are going to America soon."

I said yes. I had heard something about it myself and I was beginning to feel that there might be some truth in the statement and I added in a spirit of fun, "Wouldn't your reverence care to come with me?"

But the good man suddenly became very serious and answered, "Yes. There is nothing I would like to do better than that. But the time has not yet come for God's people to come out of the wilderness," and when I showed, I am afraid, some surprise at this remark, he continued, "Most honored Doctor, you are a man of culture and breeding and do you mean to tell me that you don't know what has become of the Lost Tribes of the people of Israel? Why, they moved across the Pacific Ocean when it was still dry land and to-day they dwell in the land of America." And he made this extraordinary announcement so solemnly that all of us suddenly kept quiet and looked at each other in mute astonishment as if the door had opened and one of the ancient prophets had suddenly walked in upon us.

Upon such occasions it is almost inevitable that some one should make an utterly commonplace remark. I don't remember who was guilty, but of course some one said, "That is an interesting notion, but how about the Indians? Wouldn't they have killed them off long ago?"

But Menasseh, without showing the slightest sign of impatience, had his answer ready. "They undoubtedly would have done so if they could. But it would have meant suicide. For the Indians of America are the lost tribes of Zion." And he delivered us quite a lecture and told us how ten of the long-suffering tribes (I have forgotten their names and anyway, that is a detail), after the destruction of Jerusalem had wandered across Turkestan and China, how they had made converts on the way which still dwelled in Cathay, and had finally crossed over into that enormous tract of land that stretched its vast and uninhabited confines from the North Pole to the South Pole and that had been given unto them as their eternal heritage.

It was a very interesting story, but it did not sound very convincing to me. For one thing, remembering the trouble that small patch of land on the Mediterranean had caused to the world, the endless wars and quarrels with all the endless neighbors, I thought with horror of what would happen to us if we were to be faced by an entire continent filled with this peculiar race of men who had never been able to agree among themselves and who had never been able to agree with any one else either, and who seemed to have spent their entire time, ever since Abraham had set forth from the land of Ur, insisting that the whole world was out of step with the exception of themselves. But I held my tongue and did not say so, and as the nurse just then entered and in her usual surly way announced that supper was ready, the subject was allowed to drop and fortunately did not return to life amidst the excellent dishes of herring salad and boiled barley with sugar which awaited us in the front room.

And after supper Rembrandt took us up to his studio and showed us several sketches he had made of a landscape, an imaginary landscape with a couple of trees in the foreground, and told us that recently he had come into the possession of a number of sketches by a certain Altdorfer, a German architect who was apparently enamored of trees.

"That man seemed to regard trees as if they were human beings," he said. "Look at this and at this and at this. Those things aren't trees. They are wise old philosophers, who have spent a thousand years contemplating the follies of human existence. Look at this one with the blue background and the little man sitting all by himself at the foot of that grandfather among trees. That little man is so forlorn, so lonely, he would almost make you weep. And the tree stands in the foreground so fine and wise. Strange people, those Germans. I don't care to own any of their pictures, they don't seem to have a feeling for color. They think in lines, but they think more clearly and more distinctly than any of the rest of us. But when I asked Dirck Bleecker (the one who painted that terrible Venus for which the Prince paid him seventeen hundred florins cash, whereas I had to write seven or eight begging letters and wait God knows how many years to get a paltry six hundred for a Resurrection that was a hundred times better)—when I asked Bleecker, who had been in Regensburg on his way to Italy, whether there was any work of Altdorfer left in that town he answered me, 'Sure! a fine slaughter house and a couple of bulwarks outside the city gates.' Can you imagine it? Would it be possible in any other country? This blue tree and a fine slaughter-house! But I suppose he had to make a living. We all do."

Meanwhile in another corner of the room the good Rabbi was endeavoring to prove his point by a weird mixture of geographic and philologic and messianic information and was trying to make his hearers believe that the existence of such places as Dankhar and Dango and Dano showed the probable route taken by the tribe of Dan on its way from Palestine to the East. The argument sounded rather far-fetched to me. If Dankhar and Dango were to be accepted as evidence of the Israelites having been in Asia, how about Danzig and Danemark and the Danube as living testimony to their presence in Europe on their way from the old promised land to the new one?

For one short moment I thought of saying what was in my mind, but what was the use? Every one of us is entitled to at least one pet delusion. The most intelligent of men must be crazy on some one point to be really well-balanced and a useful member of society.

Menasseh was a delightful person, wise, witty and in everything he did inspired by a most good-natured tolerance towards all humanity. Why deprive him of the happy illusion that those tribes, so lamentably lost during one of the endless mishaps that were forever overtaking his people, had finally reached the shores of a better and happier land than that from which they had been forced to flee?

Why indeed?

I took another helping of herring salad.

Maybe at that very moment somewhere in the deepest abyss of the North Sea some ancient and learned herring patriarch was telling his great-great-great-great-grandchildren how some of their ancestors had swum away to parts unknown and had given birth to a race of gigantic whales that dominated the whole of the Pacific Ocean.

And meanwhile, mixed with potatoes and gherkins, I was eating them and thinking that they made really a very fine dish.

Chapter 28

OF THE DIFFICULTIES OF BEING A "SURGEON" AND NOT A "DOCTOR MEDICINAE" IN THE YEAR I SAILED FOR AMERICA

My Lord Andries proved a man of his word. No sooner had I let him know that I was willing to accept his offer than wheels within wheels began to move with that silence and efficiency one expects from a competent engine and within less than a week I was informed that the Amsterdam Chamber of the West India Company had appointed me one of its doctors with orders to proceed at once to the New Netherlands.

But then a strange difficulty presented itself, the sort of difficulty that could only arise in our Republic and that no one would have been able to anticipate.

My position in the medical world of Amsterdam had always been slightly anomalous. Everybody in the country belonged to one of the guilds as a matter of plain, everyday fact. When I was young and first went to Leyden to receive my training, I soon discovered that I had chosen a rather difficult career. The tremendous physical and intellectual energy which I had inherited from that glorious old man who had elevated our family from being "just people" to something just a little different had manifested itself in my case in the form of an insatiable curiosity about everybody and everything and an almost fanatical hatred of what I in my youthful arrogance used to deride as "human stupidity" and what, since then, I have learned to pity as merely another manifestation of that universal mental inertia which is born out of ignorance and fear. All around me I saw people suffering woefully and as a rule helplessly from a large variety of causes, most of which (please remember that I was only eighteen years old at that time) were entirely preventable.

I never was a very good Christian and I am quite sure I was not inspired by motives of a spiritual nature when I decided to devote my life to the study of medicine. I had never felt a particular urge to "love my neighbor" in the truly Biblical sense of the word. Loving some one at somebody else's command, even if that somebody else be God himself, has always been just a little too difficult for most people. But there was no earthly reason why we should not learn to "respect" our fellow-men. That meditation led me to a fresh difficulty. How could I respect a man when he was guilty of an error of judgment which had made him sick? There was only one way out of this puzzle. If I were to be true to myself, I must devote myself to the task of showing my neighbors just what sort of mistakes against the laws of nature and common sense they had committed to be as sadly afflicted as most of them were.

I am now more than sixty years old and during the last thirty years I have lived a very full life. I shudder when I think of the sublime self-assurance with which I approached the most perplexing puzzle of human life long before I had even begun to shave myself. But in a way I still hold that I was right though perhaps I might have expressed my opinions with a little less vehemence, and the other day, when I found an old anatomical note-book of mine on the title page of which I had written: "Mankind has only one enemy, its own ignorance. Let us destroy that ignorance," I felt a sudden happy pang of recognition and not entirely of regret.

The sentiment, after all these many years, sounded a bit hollow not to say platitudinous. But the boy who had composed it or had vaguely remembered it from one of Erasmus' colloquies and had transcribed it with many fine flourishes of the pen, had on the whole remained faithful to the promise of his youth. He hated "ignorance" when he was sixteen. He still hated it when he was sixty. The only difference was this, that now, having more or less reached the age of discretion and insight, he was beginning to realize that he was fighting against hopeless odds. The Good Book (this was the way my grandfather had reasoned) tells us that God created the world in six days and then took a vacation for the rest of eternity. If only He had spent one single extra day on His task and had devoted the Sabbath to giving men "reason," what a different world this would have been. But God did not and that is all there is to it and it is up to us to make the best of our bad bargain.

But if we try hard enough, we may be able to find a "compromise" and as that seems to be the only possible and definite answer to all the manifold problems of our existence, I feel that I have reason to consider myself a very lucky man. For all during my entire lifetime I have been able to do the things in which I was most vitally interested. Now I am approaching the end. Soon my time shall come to bid farewell to this curious planet. But if my heirs can put that on my grave as my one and only epitaph, I shall be contented, for I shall know that I have not wasted my time.

Meanwhile, when I was sixteen and still believed that there were such colors as "absolute white" and "absolute black" and "absolute red" and "absolute green" (Rembrandt has taught me differently since then), the question of my future career caused me considerable difficulties.

During the last fifty years there has been such enormous improvement in the field of medicine that it is almost impossible for the people of the present generation to understand the quandary in which those of us who aspired to be something more than mere barbers found themselves as soon as we had learned enough bad Latin and Greek to understand the hodge-podge of the so-called "learned" treatises of that day.

I think it was one of the great Arab physicians of ancient Spain who had drawn the maxim that "there are no sicknesses in this world, but that there are only sick people." By which of course he did not mean to deny the existence of certain definite afflictions, which almost any one with an ounce of intelligence can come to understand and diagnose (and sometimes even cure) but which was his way of saying that the individual is the basis of everything human and that we ought to judge each separate case upon its own merits.

But when I was young, the science of medicine was only slowly recovering from the complete intellectual apathy of the Middle Ages. The Church, with her eyes lifted upon an imaginary Heaven, was not sufficiently interested in the affairs of this world to pay much attention to the immediate physical needs of her children. As long as the immortal soul was saved, the perishable body was cheerfully surrendered to the million and one forces that work for decay and destruction. As soon as the tyranny of that unyielding institution was beginning to weaken, there had been a tremendous rebirth of that divine curiosity which is the cornerstone upon which we must base our sole hope for a better future.

But we, in our distant swamp along the banks of the North Sea, never felt the influence of such a movement until a century or more later. The universities of Palermo and Naples and Montpellier had been teaching anatomy hundreds of years before we ever suspected that such a thing was possible without invoking the immediate wrath of a vengeful God. In our cities there were a few people, often foreigners, who called themselves "doctors" and made a great to-do about their academic bulls (which not infrequently they had bought from a public scribe in a French or Italian market-place) but the great majority of the people, both in the towns and in the country districts, had been forced to content themselves with the simple services of the local barber. It sometimes happened that those barbers were intelligent men and could pull teeth and apply a poultice without killing their patients. But in most cases they were poor devils forced into their jobs because their father before them had belonged to the barbers' guild and because that was the only way in which they could make a living.

No wonder the general populace held them in light esteem. No wonder that both they and the so-called "doctors of medicine" were invariably mentioned in one breath with the quacks and mountebanks and other impostors who made our kermesses unsafe with their "infallible remedies" and their "unfailing cures" for everything from dandruff and corns to heart-failure and malignant tumors.

Then came the Reformation early during the last century, but that great spiritual upheaval affected the brain of the average man much less than people at this distance are apt to think. The spiritual world changed masters, that was all. Instead of taking our orders from a man whom no one ever saw because he lived behind the high walls of a Roman fortress, we were now supposed to obey a book that had been written so long ago that no one knew for sure who was responsible for its contents. In short, people fought valiantly to escape from one sort of tyranny to fall immediately into the clutches of a new despot who was almost as exacting as the old one and a great deal less human. What previously had been called green was now called yellow and what formerly had been called yellow was now called green, and that was about all the change there was.

And it was the same within my own field of work. The monks and nuns, of whom there were by far too many, were sent about their business. Hordes of holy mendicants now became plain, ordinary, everyday beggars. Formerly one had been obliged to receive them in one's house and feed them and lodge them and listen to their ill-mannered hiccoughing. Now one could surrender them to the police and have them flogged out of the city gate. That undoubtedly was a great step forward. But the decent and respectable men and women who had taken the words of Christ seriously (and of such there always were a few even during the worst days of the Church's downfall) they also were forced to give up their former profession and as most of these had devoted themselves to the care of the poor and the sick, our hospitals and almshouses suddenly found themselves deprived not only of their former revenue but also of the nurses and doctors who had thus far tended the lame, the halt and the blind.

The new creed loudly proclaimed its disbelief in the efficacy of good works as against the value of a correct spiritual attitude towards God. The old clergy with the wisdom acquired during centuries of a very close observation of human nature had never inquired too closely into the motives that made powerful princes and rich merchants suddenly disgorge a few hundred thousand guilders for the benefit of their hospitals or orphan asylums: "The orphans," so they reasoned, "have got to be fed and clothed and the poor have to be fed, and all that costs money. Let us gratefully accept the money and leave it to God to ask questions."

The new masters, inspired no doubt by the noblest of motives but without much practical experience along those lines, insisted that the gift in itself amounted to nothing. It was only the spirit behind it that mattered. And their parishioners were made to understand that all the good works in the world would not save them from one moment in Hell if their heart were not in the right place, and in many instances they were directly encouraged to stop giving their hard-earned pennies for public purposes.

Habit, however, was too strong or humanity was too decent, but this much I know, that the poor and the afflicted (in our cities at least) were never for a moment allowed to suffer through the hard-hearted righteousness of the new rulers. The saints were removed from their ancient niches and the chapels were turned into store-rooms and the fast days were no longer celebrated with an extra supply of wine or beer, but for the rest, everything remained pretty much as it had been during the last thousand years. The hospitals continued to be known as "God's Houses." Charitable old men and women continued to act as Boards of Regents and to administer the funds with scrupulous honesty. Pious girls continued to devote their lives to the care of their unfortunate fellow-citizens and continued to perform the most menial and disgusting tasks with that cheerful optimism that had been so characteristic of the old nuns.

And all of them were just as convinced as their fathers and grandfathers and great-grandfathers had been that existence on this planet was merely a preparatory experience, a gift of small account, and without any value except in so far as it led to the blessed happiness of Heaven or the dreadful punishments of Hell.

It was just as difficult to convince people of this sort of the necessity of taking proper care of the human body as it had been to persuade their predecessors that patients needed an occasional bath if they were not to die of infection, and hospitals remained, what they had always been before, almshouses and places of refuge for those too old or too sick to take care of themselves, quiet sanctuaries where they could be sure of a bed and a plate of porridge until merciful Death paid his final visit, but not (as many of us felt that they ought to be) temples of light and good cheer where the temporarily unfit were shown how to get themselves back to health and profitable employment.

Of course, whenever a sailor tumbled out of a mast and broke a leg or whenever a mason fell down from a scaffold and smashed his arms, some barber with a knack for surgery was called in to repair the damage. But those who suffered from an internal and not absolutely mechanical ailment were put on a diet of sermons and texts and for the rest were allowed to live or die as God and their own constitutions seemed to think best.

The "doctors," as differentiated from the mere "barbers" and "surgeons" who dwelled on a very much lower social plane, were supposed to occupy themselves with the problems affecting the behavior of all the invisible organs. And the doctors were few and far between, for there were practically no schools to train them and only a few of them could afford to visit one of those Mediterranean countries where the Moors held sway for a number of centuries. But here in the North, where we are centuries behind in the art of living, they could not learn very much of any importance to either themselves or to their future patients. I don't mean to imply that we lacked the necessary brains. The man who has done most during the last two thousand years to further our knowledge of the inner secrets of the human body was a Fleming. But he had to go to Italy to practice his art. As Professor Vesalius of Padua he could make a career. As plain Master Andries van Wesel he would have spent his days bleeding the good citizens of Brussels on week days and on Saturday he would have shaved their week's accumulation of whiskers and he would have counted himself happy if he had died as chairman of the barbers' guild.

Take the conditions in Leyden in the year 1617 when I made my appearance in that somewhat unsober seat of learning. The entire medical faculty consisted of only three professors, one who taught botany (for the benefit of future apothecaries), one who gave instruction in anatomy for the future chirurgeons and one who was supposed to hold clinical demonstrations to supplement the theoretical knowledge which the future doctors were supposed to gather from their text-books on medicine. Unfortunately at the time I registered, the plague had just visited Leyden and had killed more than one fifth of the total number of inhabitants, among them the professor of therapeutics and the professor of anatomy, the learned Petrus Pava, and the regents, for reasons of economy, had not yet decided upon their successors. But as it was felt that we should not be left in complete idleness, the dean of the theological faculty was asked to lecture to us upon the medicine of the ancient Hebrews. He was a ponderous and dull old patriarch with a long white beard and devoid of all eloquence. Besides we wanted to know how the art of healing had been taught in Athens, not in Jerusalem. But the plague had been followed by an even more serious epidemic of religious frenzy. The whole country was divided into sublapsarians and superlapsarians, people were thrown into jail and sometimes killed because they denied that children were already doomed to everlasting perdition while still in their mothers' wombs, and honorable clergymen with a record of fifty years of faithful service were deprived of their livelihood for no other reason than that they believed, or failed to believe, something which the majority of their neighbors held to be the gospel truth or an invention of Satan.

Leyden itself, where the quarrel had started, was of course seething with excitement. The University had always been suspected of "libertine" tendencies and the true believers had already founded a rival academy of their own in distant Groningen to keep the faith pure and free from the insiduous heresies of the learned and amiable Jacob Arminius. They were now contemplating a second university in Utrecht and perhaps from their point of view they were quite right. For our Alma Mater was the spiritual child of that small group of brilliant humanists who had been the intellectual body-guard and chief advisers of Prince William. The Great Silent One (more shrewd than silent, if we are to believe all the stories about him) had been that rare thing among mortals, a statesman with a concrete ideal. He had seen enough burning and hanging and quartering during the first twenty years of his life to satisfy him for the rest of his days, and he meant, should he ever acquire enough power, to establish a commonwealth in which all men should be allowed to seek salvation in their own way. The casual remark of one of the first rectors of the university he founded that "men could be led but never driven" had become the motto upon which our school had based its educational policy at least during the first half century of its existence.

In some ways this had been a dangerous experiment. The great majority of our students came from very humble homes. A few were very poor and a few were very rich. But all of them were far removed from the ordinary ties of parents and friends, and without any special preparation they found themselves flung into a community that was as little suited for a contemplative life as any place could possibly have been. The siege had left its stamp upon the manners of the town. The garrison that had occupied it for years afterwards had done likewise. The owners of the linen factories who paid their workmen miserable wages and filled the streets and alleys with a hungry and miserable set of men and women (not to speak of the children) had done likewise. And the climate had done the rest.

Left to their own devices, living in cheap quarters (for the town was dreadfully over populated and in bad need of a few thousand more houses), eating indifferent food in cheap inns, spending their evenings in cold and uncomfortable rooms without any other place to go, most of the students tried to find solace at the bottom of a bottle of wine or a jar of gin. And in most cases, five or six months of this sort of existence seemed sufficient to kill every vestige of intellectual curiosity and turn the eager young boy, who had left his native village prepared to do great things in the world outside, into a disappointed lad trying to get a degree with the least possible exertion and quite contented if the prestige of his official diploma helped him to get a safe and comfortable berth in the village or city of his birth, where such a document was still regarded as a guarantee of superior qualities and often proved a very handy key to place and preferment.

I am proud to say that there was a small minority which notwithstanding the many physical disadvantages of life and the disappointment of discovering that the royal road to learning led through the dismal swamps of boredom and pedantry, refused to surrender to the general atmosphere of the place and remained faithful to the enthusiasms of his undergraduate days. And curious to relate, they were the boys who most often got into conflict with the authorities. For whereas the faculty, during the period of clerical domination of which I am now speaking and which had begun shortly before I first matriculated in the year 1617, was willing to overlook a great many of the misdemeanors of the more rowdy elements among the students with a shrug of the shoulders and a jovial, "Oh, well, you know, boys will be boys," they were forever on their guard against what they called the "libertine tendencies" of the more independent-minded scholars.

It was a long cry from the days of the great teacher who laid down the maxim that it was better to try and lead men than drive them. It was the era during which Calvinism Triumphant was endeavoring to systemize and classify and standardize every manifestation of life and faith. To the average professor, independence of mind on the part of one of his pupils was anathema. And a tendency to inquire by personal investigation into the truth or error of the grandiloquent verities which the teacher had propounded from a hoary text-book, was a thing accursed in the sight of God.

The student body as a mass was ready to take the hint and asked no questions. And in return, when time came for examination, the professor from his side asked easy questions, and in this way everybody was happy.

But there were about a hundred of us who refused to submit to this new spiritual autocracy and we had to suffer in consequence. Most of us were the sons or grandsons of men who had taken an active part in the Rebellion. We seemed to have inherited something of the spirit of freedom that had inspired our fathers and grandfathers when they foreswore their legitimate sovereign on the ground that a monarch should be a father to his subjects and that they did not care for the sort of father King Philip happened to make.

Besides, the vast majority of the boys who came from such families had been brought up in an atmosphere of amiable skepticism. They had been taught to study the Scriptures from behind a pair of Erasmian spectacles, and from childhood on had been urged to take life with a pinch of that divine salt which is called "humor."

Such a point of view was, however, most abhorrent to the new sort of instructors. And although the "libertines" of my time were famous for their sobriety and their industry and without making a manifestation of their virtues, tried to lead reasonable and well-balanced lives, they were forever in trouble with the learned men who were supposed to rule this commonwealth of erudition. Let our friends, the "Regulars," stage a pitched battle with the denizens of the tenement districts, let them set fire to the house of a peaceful citizen on the ground that his daughter would make such a charming picture in her night-gown, let them engage in fights with harmless burghers returning from a picnic and make off with their wives and nothing would happen beyond a formal declaration of official investigation. But let one of the "libertines" so much as whisper a doubt about the erstwhile tendency of snakes to engage in conversation and he would find himself immediately ordered to appear before a board of inquiry and he would be obliged to eat humble pie of a very unpalatable sort lest he be prevented from taking his degree. Or let him merely "look" his doubts when the professor of exegesis expounded one of those eternal verities that are half as young as the Pyramids and are already showing much greater signs of wear and tear, and the faculty would be after him with the speed of the Amsterdam bucket-brigade, chasing a fire in the city's wood-yard.

We who were supposed to be studying the sciences secretly enjoyed this curious intellectual warfare and acquired great skill in lying in ambush while keeping clear from the traps that were placed in our own path. But the incident that brought about my expulsion was not of our making. It was the work of two cheerful roisterers, of two boys who were possessed both of brains and of money, but who long since had given up all hope of ever accomplishing anything at all in an academic way. They stayed on in Leyden because they were happy there and sometimes during their moments of semi-lucidity they could be very funny.

I have already noted that in the year 1617 in consequence of the plague the chairs of anatomy and therapeutics happened to be vacant and how the professor of theology had volunteered to fill the gap by lecturing to the future surgeons and doctors on the medicine of the ancient Hebrews. As a rule this good man gave his classes in his own home in a large room at the back of the house. But nobody ever came. This hurt his pride and he let it be known that on such and such a day he would demonstrate the seven deadly sins and the seven cardinal virtues in the anatomical theater of the University. This was an unusual thing to do. As a rule professors did not advertise their coming engagements as if they were quacks peddling nostrums. But that was not the end of the story. The day before this famous demonstration of the seven deadly sins and the seven cardinal virtues a little slip of paper on the bulletin board outside the rector's office let the people know that the lecture would be thrown open to the public and furthermore, "In order to make his points entirely clear, the distinguished speaker will avail himself of the corpse of a lying Arminian, hanged this morning for theft and false testimony."

Evidently he was going to have what in the parlance of the students was called a "circus."

On the morning of the day for this extraordinary occurrence, the anatomical lecture-hall was chock full of people. Half the student body was present. For it had been whispered about that our Light of Learning would improve the occasion by a scathing denunciation of all and sundry enemies of the true faith. In consequence whereof all the supralapsarians (or sublapsarians, I have forgotten which, but I mean the adherents of the late John Calvin) were present en masse, ready to give evidence of their principles by entering this much feared chamber of horrors which under ordinary circumstances they avoided as if it had been the lepers' hospital. But I also noticed a large number of young men who were famous for their devotion to the less studious sides of life and who were reputed to have sworn an oath that they would never attend a lecture until just seven weeks prior to their examinations. What they were doing there and why they had come at this unearthly hour, I didn't know. Probably for the same reason that had brought me, plain, ordinary curiosity.

Ten o'clock came. Five minutes past ten. The professor entered from the rear. There was terrific applause, also a very unusual thing. The professor sat down and beckoned to the assistants of the anatomical laboratory. They left the room but immediately returned bringing in a large wooden table on which there lay a corpse. But oh, my God! what a corpse! I have seen a great many dead people in my life. And some of them did not look so pretty. But this one was terrible, monstrous, incredible. The face was a bright green, the hair hanging down in long, disorderly streaks, was a nondescript yellow. A brilliant red piece of cloth had been thrown across the chest.

The professor began. But instead of sticking to his subject, he launched into a violent denunciation of all those who opposed his own views. Every point he made was loudly applauded by his adherents. The other party said nothing. Encouraged by his success, the foolish old man grew more and more bold. He jerked away the red cloth, exposing the corpse in all its gruesome nakedness.

"Ah, my beloved friends," he said in his best ministerial tone, "my poor, beloved brethren, to-day I shall speak unto you upon the subject of sin and virtue, the seven deadly sins and the seven cardinal virtues; the seven cardinal virtues as exemplified by the life of the blessed and spotless Lamb, the seven deadly sins all gathered together in the putrid breast of this miscreant, this devil in human form, who unwilling to listen to Heavenly council, followed false prophets, worshiped before false altars, thinking in his pride and folly, 'I, poor human mortal, can defy the laws of Heaven as laid down in God's own catechism as edited by his beloved disciples Zacharias Ursinus and Kaspar Olevianus in the year of our Lord, 1563, Amen.' Oh, my friends, what wickedness! what vicious greed! what dissolute contempt stand graven upon that brow, what salacious, misbegotten vileness!"

He stopped, his mouth wide open, for at that moment the dead man sat straight up on his table, gave a terrific sneeze, said, "Pardon me, Professor. But pray continue!" and laid himself down once more in the expectant position of a corpse momentarily awaiting the anatomist's scalpel.

For just the fraction of a second, every one stood still. No one dared to breathe.

Then pandemonium broke loose and the laughter that shook the windows came straight from the belly and went straight to the heart.

The whole thing was glorious. But not for very long, for a sallow-faced young theologian, dressed in sacrimonial brown and with an enormous white collar (all in the best orthodox fashion) walked up to the dead man and feebly hit him with a shaking fist, saying, "How dare you!" Whereupon the corpse gave him such a terrific whack on top of his wide-brimmed hat that that piece of wearing apparel would have come down upon his neck if it had not been stopped by his ears.

That was the sign for a free-for-all fight in which, I regret to say, the forces of Satan completely and quickly defeated the cohorts of righteousness, drove them out into the street and would have thrown them into the canal if the young divines had not shown a very definite aptitude for at least one pagan virtue by proving themselves quite as fleet-footed as Mercury and Achilles.

With the enemy gone, the others decided to make a day of it. From a near-by tavern they suddenly produced two bag-pipe artists and a drummer who opened the procession. Then followed eight bright young men carrying the table on which the corpse was reclining in a becoming but slightly indecent posture, throwing kisses to all the servant girls who at that hour in the morning (it being Friday, the traditional cleaning-day) were scrubbing the façades of their masters' houses. Then followed the men who had taken part in this strange resurrection, marching four abreast and chanting an inspired and a not very proper song to the tune of a bag-pipes. I followed them for a short distance as one will, caught against his will in such an affair, but not desirous of showing himself either aloof or superior to the pastime of rather amiable people who were making fools of themselves out of sheer good animal spirits. But as soon as I could conveniently do so, I slipped into a side street and went home.

Of course in less than half an hour the whole community had heard about it and thousands of town people joined the parade until the University authorities in their panic asked the magistrates to ring the riot bells. The garrison was called out and there was some fighting, but it suddenly began to pour, as it always does in Leyden whenever there is a celebration of some sort, and everybody rushed for home to get himself some dry clothes and a great deal of wet gin.

The next day it was announced that the lectures on anatomy and therapeutics were "discontinued for the season," and that, it seemed to me, was the end of the affair.

But a week later, I was unexpectedly invited to appear before the Rector and when I arrived at his office, I found about a dozen other students there, who without exception belonged to the group that was suspected of libertine tendencies. Without further ado we were ushered into the presence of the Rector, whom we found surrounded by his staff, including the unfortunate theologian who by his sheer eloquence had raised the dead.

Our names were read. We were asked whether we had een present that morning. I spoke up for the others, being somewhat older than the rest, and said yes, we had indeed been present as a matter of routine. We were supposed to follow certain lectures. The lecture had been given. We had been there.

Next question: Had we laughed at this unseemly incident?

Answer: Yes. How could we help ourselves?

Question: Had we taken part in the parade?

Answer: Only so far as the parade had followed the route we were obliged to follow in order to get home.

Question: Then we had been present at the parade?

Answer: In the same way that everybody who happened to be on the street at that moment had taken part in it.

Question: Please answer yes or no.

Answer: Yes and no.

Question: Do you think arrogance and defiance will help you?

Answer: I am merely telling the truth.
Question: That will do. Please step outside.

By what process of reasoning the learned doctors came to the conclusion that I had been the instigator of the whole absurd comedy, merely because I had laughed when it occurred, had afterwards stood around on the street with the others and had acted as spokesman for those cited before their august tribunal, I do not know. But I was expelled, together with half a dozen other students who had taken no more active part in arranging and executing this episode than I. The erstwhile corpse, whose father was one of the Burgomasters of Utrecht, was suspended for six months, and that was all.

But it had been a great victory for the orthodox party. All over the country, the dominies delivered fulminating speeches against those "rebellious spirits" who "in sheer defiance of Holy Writ had tried to bring ridicule upon the head of one of the humble servants of God." And naturally, whatever they said was accepted as gospel truth by their hearers and of course the hearers added a few embellishments to the story and of course my father was so shocked and angered by the occurrence that he threatened to send me to the Indies as a cabin-boy and of course my grandfather laughed so heartily that he almost had a stroke and then remarked, "Now you don't have to go back to this New Zion and you can learn your trade decently in some foreign city where they are all Papists anyway and don't worry about their convictions more than twice a year," and when I asked, "But where shall I go?" he answered, "Montpellier. Rabelais learned medicine there from the Jews and became a first-rate author and that is the place for a bad Dutch boy who won't take his dominie seriously."

Well, that is the way I happened to go to Montpellier, where I found that very much less difference was made between doctors and surgeons than at home. Even at that early age, I was most of all interested in experiments with narcotic drugs and the professor of clinical medicine happened to share my enthusiasm and urged me to qualify as a physician and not as a surgeon. Therefore when I returned to Holland, I was a full-fledged doctor who also had had considerable experience as a surgeon.

But then the difficulty arose that I had to make a living (all this happened many years before I came into my uncle's inheritance) and there were much better chances for surgeons than for doctors. I therefore joined the surgeons' guild, or rather, because there were not enough surgeons in our town to allow them to establish a guild of their own, I joined the wooden-shoe-makers' guild, of which they formed part. I never opened a barber-shop, which made the majority of my colleagues regard me as a silly upstart who believed himself too good for his trade. But I was not interested in scraping people's beards and stuck to surgery work. At times people also used to call me in as a doctor, but I never joined the guild of the physicians (they belonged officially to the peddlers' guild) and I was known as Master Jan, though many people, out of courtesy or in order to flatter my pride, called me Doctor van Loon.

But when My Lord Bicker applied to the Board of Direction of the West India Company for a berth for me as doctor in their colony of the New Netherlands, there was at once a tremendous outcry among the other medicine-men. I was a surgeon and not a doctor . . . I had never joined the physicians' guild . . . I had no right to call myself a doctor as I had only graduated in a foreign university . . . all the doctors in Amsterdam would in the future refuse to lend their professional services to the West India Company if I were allowed to sail as a doctor instead of as a plain surgeon . . . and so on and so forth . . . until I assured His Lordship that the matter was entirely immaterial to me, that I would just as soon go to America as a surgeon or even a leech (I drew the line at barbering) as in the quality of a full-fledged doctor. This satisfied my esteemed colleagues and on the seventh of February of the year 1643 I received my patent as ship's surgeon of the West India Company, with destination of New Amsterdam.

I was to sail in April.

A week before I left, Bernardo called on me. One could never tell whether he was sad or happy, but this time the animation of his voice told me that something extraordinary had occurred. I asked him what the good news was?

"I am going with you," he answered.

"Coming with me? Why—how—what are you going to do over there? Keep books for a fish-dealer? It is bad enough as it is here. What will the job be like over there?"

"I don't know," he replied, "and I don't care. I am through with fish and through with book-keeping. I am an explorer now. An explorer and an investigator."

"Investigator of what?"

"Of the lost tribes of Israel." And then he told me that Rabbi Menasseh ben Israel had been to see him, had told him that there were a number of Jews in Amsterdam who believed like himself that the copper-colored but black-haired natives of the New World were the direct descendants of the black-haired and yellow-skinned inhabitants of ancient Palestine. They were so convinced of the truth of this hypothesis that they had subscribed a certain sum of money to send some one across the ocean to investigate the matter.

"And you know," Bernardo remarked dryly, "ever since my little trouble with the Inquisition, I have been regarded by my fellow-countrymen as some strange physical phenomenon, a survivor from some great natural cataclysm of Sodom, a relic of the Flood. I am deemed the ideal messenger to send to the other end of the world and report upon the present status of my little nephews across the ocean. I hate my present job,

ELISABETH VAN LEEUWEN
The wife of Rembrandt's brother

REMBRANDT'S BROTHER ADRIAEN
(about 1650)

I know I was offered other work, but it would have merely meant that I moved from one set of ledgers to the next. I have done enough figuring in my life to last me for all eternity. I have sold enough fish to stock a dozen planets. And so I accepted almost humbly. You never guessed it, but I was born to be the hero of strange adventures. If you care to have me, I shall be your faithful traveling companion. But watch out for the adventures. Wherever I go, they follow me about. Probably because I look so little like the part!"

I answered him (and with absolute sincerity) that no one could have been more welcome to share my cabin and my loneliness.

And on the eighth of April of the year of Grace 1643 we left Amsterdam. Four days later we were on board the good ship *Dubbele Arend* bound from Texel to the mouth of the Mauritius River.

It was a brave little vessel of 320 tons and it was raining so hard when we lifted anchor that we could not see the buoys and ran on a bank. But the next high tide set us free. When I got up in the morning, the sun was shining brightly and the coast of Holland was no longer in sight.

Chapter 29

I DEPART FOR A NEW WORLD

I was to have spent two years in America. I stayed seven. And although I had many interesting adventures and many strange experiences, I feel that I am not entitled to enumerate them in a diary which after all might fall into the wrong hands.

For although I went across the ocean in the capacity of a surgeon of the West India Company, I was really in the service of My Lord Andries and his brother Cornelis. They suggested that I go and they paid for the trip. When I returned, I drew them up a detailed report containing all my observations and a few suggestions. They thanked me cordially and assured me that they were entirely satisfied, had no regret at the expense and hoped that from my side too the voyage had not been a disappointment. Then they asked me to keep the whole matter a secret until they had studied my records and had decided what to do. They would let me know within a few months.

But all sorts of things intervened. The Prince of Orange made his attack upon Amsterdam and the political party to which the Bickers belonged was forced to withdraw temporarily from the city's government. Soon afterwards, My Lord Andries and his brother Cornelis died and what became of my report I was never able to find out.

The younger generation of the Bickers, reëstablished in all their ancient dignities as soon as their brother-in-law and cousin, John de Witt, had deprived the House of Orange of its power (which he did shortly after my return to Holland), were very different people from their fathers and grandfathers. The new generation was beginning to lose contact with those business enterprises that had brought their ancestors fame and fortune. The Republic no longer had an established aristocracy. There were a few titled personages left, but they had lost all influence except in some of the more backward provinces of the east where those country squires had been able to maintain themselves in dreary glory in their lonely castles and where they continued to rule the peasants in a haphazard patriarchal way as they had done since the year one.

But by the middle of the seventeenth century the sons and grandsons of the men who had made the country what it was were beginning to regret that they must spend all their days as plain citizens with no other rank than the "My Lord" and "Your most Honorable, Well and Highborn Excellency," titles which they had bestowed upon themselves and which meant about as much as the high-sounding dignity of "Archbishop of Trebizond," held by an amiable little man who during the week professed to be a simple book-seller and who on Sundays in the attic of a house on the Oude-Zijds Voorburgwal read mass for the benefit of his Catholic parishioners.

In order to escape from this (to them) most humiliating position, these younger sons were trying to withdraw their money from business enterprises and were investing their inherited wealth in landed estates which had formerly belonged to the true nobility and which gave them a chance to write the names of a few villages behind the simple patronymic which they had received from their ancestors. During the next ten or twenty years, the old names would then be discreetly dropped and marriage with the daughters of impoverished domestic and foreign noblemen would do the rest. It was a bad day for the country when these young men, who ought to have spent their time on the Exchange, hastened every afternoon to the dancing schools of the Kalverstraat to let some former French waiter teach them the latest "elegances" of the court of King Louis. It is small consolation to remember that such a thing has happened in practically every other country that has grown rich through trade. For every one of those nations has either come to grief, or like Venice and Genoa is rapidly going to ruin to-day. Eventually we shall probably follow their example. I have only one consolation. I shall not be alive when that happens.

Of course, many things happen during eight years, and that is perhaps the reason I saw the change so clearly when I returned. The old Bickers had been so sure of their position in the community that they could associate with me, a simple surgeon, on terms of intimacy and friendship. The sons were polite but distant. They were afraid of what their friends would say. Suppose one of them had remarked, "Oh, I saw you with that leech to-day. Is that a new crony of yours?" My Lord Andries would have answered, "Yes, and what of it?" And the next day would have dealt that curious young man such a terrific blow on the Exchange that it would have taken him a couple of years to recover. The new generation was of a different mettle. They were much more polished and infinitely more suave than their fathers. They were not as ferocious in their hatreds. Neither were they as loyal in their affections. They were lukewarm and that, I fear, is a quality which one should only tolerate in certain kinds of vegetables.

About a dozen years after my return from America I heard that there were plans for a new and independent colony that was to be established in some part of the New Netherlands and was to be managed by the city of Amsterdam without the interference of the West India Company. It was an open secret that the latter was really in a state of bankruptcy and it would have been the right moment to acquire some of her property at a very low price. As soon as I had gathered a few of the details and had been told that the Bicker family was interested in the matter, I went to pay my respects and to offer my services if the directors of the new organization should desire some first-hand information upon a subject with which I was thoroughly familiar.

I was politely enough received but made to understand that I had better stick to my work in the hospital. I was somewhat taken aback by this attitude and guardedly referred to my report and to my willingness to elaborate it by word of mouth, should such a course be deemed advisable. There was a vaguely mumbled answer: "Report? Oh, yes, we know all about it. And now, if you will excuse us, there is a great deal of important business awaiting us. Yes, the man at the door will give you your cloak and hat."

The new company was actually founded, but in quite a different part of the New Netherlands from the spot I had suggested. It would be uncharitable on my part to say that I was actually pleased when it failed less than a dozen years later. But neither did I lose any sleep when I thought of the 600,000 florins the investors had wasted. After all, I had done my duty. And if the others refused to listen to my advice that was their affair and not mine. My own conscience was clear and as far as I was concerned, there the matter ended.

As for my observations in that distant land, since I had been sworn to secrecy before I left, I have never felt at liberty to speak of them to any one nor shall I mention them here. The results of my investigations about the so-called "narcotics" used by the natives of the New World in their practice of medicine have all been set down in my little book, "De Herbis Medicis Indorum," which was published in Leyden in the year 1652. And so there remain only a few personal details of the long voyage and since I am trying to put some order into the chaos of my personal recollections, it may serve a good purpose if I mention them.

First of all, the incredible six days while we were trying to make the English Channel in the face of a terrific southern gale. The *Dubbele Arend* was a staunch ship and the captain knew his business. Nevertheless we lost both our anchors, the fore-mast and half our sails and I suffered an amount of physical discomfort which I shall not forget as long as I live.

But it was not only the agony of aching bones and stomach that made those endless hours so miserable. None of the passengers were of course allowed out on deck, but even if I had been given permission to go out into the fresh air, I could not have done so as I was by far too weak to move my eye-lashes, let alone my hands and feet. I therefore lay flat on my back for almost seven solid days and nights, cooped up in a small, dark cupboard (we were not allowed to light even a candle, the ship rocked so terribly), and I had plenty of opportunity to think.

Now, even if my thoughts had been at all pleasant, this enforced residence in a tumbling, pitching, rolling tomb would have been bad enough. But just before I left, something else had occurred that had hurt me very badly and that was still causing me great distress.

I had bade farewell to all my other friends but I had kept Rembrandt for the last moment. I had grown very fond of this lonely soul and vaguely sensed a disaster in the household on the Breestraat. The Dircx woman was still staying with him. Under the pretext that little Titus had developed a cold and needed her care more than ever lest he die of the same disease as his mother, she was making herself more and more indispensable every day. She was undoubtedly very fond of the child, but in a strange and violent fashion, not pleasant to behold and decidedly dangerous for the object of her affection. One moment she would be kissing and petting the poor infant and the next she would scold it or cuff it for some trifling mistake which an ordinary, sensible person would have wisely overlooked.

As I had already told Rembrandt at least a dozen times, the woman was really not responsible for her actions. She suffered from "hysteria," a mysterious affliction of the womb already mentioned by Galen and not uncommon in females of her age. For days at a time she would be perfectly normal and then suddenly, without the slightest provocation, she would break into a fit of frenzied anger, would smash plates and dishes, would pull the clothes off her back and in other ways would make herself thoroughly detestable, while Rembrandt stood hopelessly by and tried to pacify her by the most extravagant of promises.

When these brought no relief he would appeal to her on behalf of "poor little Titus who needed her so badly," and she would burst forth into tears and that, for the moment at least, would be the last of the seizure. Twenty-four hours of sleep would completely restore her and she would be quite all right for another fortnight or so.

Once or twice, when the attacks were very severe, Rembrandt had sent for me, though there was nothing I could do. But every time I would warn him once again that he ought to get rid of the woman. She was too dangerous. People who suffer from the complaint of the "hysteria" are not only absolutely untrustworthy but they are very malicious and are very clever liars, and as they are absolutely unaccountable for their acts, they cannot be held responsible for what they either say or do.

In every possible way I tried to make the painter see the sort of trouble the woman might cause him. In a small religious community like ours, every artist was held to be a rake and a spendthrift. He might live the most strait-laced life possible, love, yea, even support his wife and children in decent comfort, and all the same his neighbors would say, "Oh, yes, a member of the guild of St. Luke. You know what *they* are! Better be careful and not see too much of him." When such a man was reported to be living all alone in one and the same house with the widow of a soldier, every one of these good Christians would be absolutely convinced that she was his mistress and they would shun this House of Sin as they would avoid doing a kind deed for some one who belonged to a different creed.

I told Rembrandt so, time and again, but it did absolutely no good. He would only get irritated. "Nonsense," he would reply. "Stuff and nonsense! The woman is a little difficult at times but no one could be more devoted to little Titus than she. She even thinks of making a will in the child's favor so that if she should suddenly die during one of her attacks— She has not done so yet, but she often speaks of it and that shows the way she feels about the boy—just as if he were her own son. Of course, I shall let her go eventually, but not just now. It would be unfair, after all she has done for the child."

But of course that was not the real reason why he was so slow in sending her packing. It was the old, old story. He knew of no life outside his work. He wanted to paint or etch, morning, noon and night. Nothing must interfere with the daily routine of the studio and the printing-room. A new housekeeper or a new nurse would mean a slight loss of time. He would be obliged to break her in, show her what was needed in that happy-go-lucky household of his. Out of devotion to his palette and his brushes, he neglected his own interests and those of Titus. Geertje Dircx, with all her failings, her tantrums, her everlasting whining and complaining, at least allowed him to work in peace, and that was all he asked of her or anybody else.

"But listen," I continued in a final attempt, "you are a portrait painter. A landscape painter does not come in personal contact with his public. He can be a drunkard and a scoundrel, but those who buy his pictures won't see him personally and so they won't care. But you draw portraits. People have to come to your studio. The general public is a terrible coward. The moment they hear some talk about Geertje and you, you are lost."

He could not see it. He just could not see it that way.

"If people care so little for my work that they won't come to my house because they think I sleep with the nurse, they had better stay away," was his only reply. And when I tried to reopen the subject, he impatiently interrupted me. "I know the woman is a fool," he said, "and I shall get rid of her just as soon as I can. But not just now. It would not be practical and it wouldn't be quite fair either. She will go soon enough, but give me time."

It was my last evening with him and there were a great many points I had wanted to discuss. But something had come between us. It was this miserable woman, and try as we might, we could not remove her from our consciousness. In the end, I made a fatal mistake. Rembrandt was a great painter, probably the greatest we ever had, but he was also of very simple origin and more than once some of his rich patrons had made him feel what they thought of the social status of an artist whose father had been a miller and whose brother was known to be a cobbler. Rembrandt was exceedingly sensitive about such slights (foolishly sensitive I thought), and because he was so sensitive and furthermore because at heart he was exceedingly shy, he could on occasions be one of the most abrupt and ill-mannered persons I have ever met.

On this particular evening he was at his worst. He was fond of me, as I was fond of him, and he hated to see me go. I too was unhappy and therefore terribly ill at ease. Otherwise I would never have been so foolish as to say what I did.

It was about eleven o'clock and I still had a great many things to do at home. I got up and lightly remarked, "Au revoir, and if ever you are in need of anything, write me and I will come right back."

He jumped from his chair. "I am not in need of anything," he almost snarled. "I am not in need of you or anybody else. It is very kind of you to offer your services, but I can take perfectly good care of myself, thank you."

I held out my hand. "Good-by then," I said.

"Good-by," he answered, but he did not take the hand I offered him, and he (on other occasions the most punctiliously polite of all my friends) let me find my way to the door alone.

All day long, the next twenty-four hours, I tried to find an excuse to call on him again. But my house was filled with people who wanted this or that and I had no opportunity to rush to the Jodenbreestraat and tell my poor friend that I was sorry, that everything was all right between us, and to show him in what friendship and affection I still held him. Then they came for the trunks and I had to go.

Such had been the manner of our farewell. The recollection of that terribly unhappy moment was almost worse than the sickness of which I suffered. And I thanked the good Lord when at last we reached Dover and I could once more place both feet firmly on dry land. I would have at least one whole week of decent sleep and decent food. And renewed vigor would give me strength to get rid of those recollections that had made me so unhappy the last nine days.

As I was soon to discover, our repairs would take much longer than any of us (the captain included) had thought, and we were in England for over a month. It was not a very pleasant month, either. The country seemed to be on the brink of a civil war and outsiders were as welcome as a falcon in a chicken-coop. Everybody suspected everybody else but all of them suspected a foreigner.

The first day I was on shore, I walked along the harbor and out of sheer boredom watched a gloomy-looking citizen who was fishing. Immediately he pulled up his net and barked at me, "You are a foreigner, eh? What are you doing here?"

I told him that I was a passenger on board a ship that had suffered from the recent storm and had been driven into port for repairs.

"Where from?" he asked.

"From Holland," I replied.

"Oh, Holland, eh?" he sneered. "Holland where the people call themselves Christians and then support the wicked enemies of God who would make this nation another Babylon."

I assured him that I had no idea of what he was talking—that as far as I knew, Babylon had been destroyed by Alexander the Great at least two thousand years before, and that the only reason for my standing there at that particular moment was my sincere desire to see him catch a fish.

But the man was in no mood for humor.

"You had better be gone," he threatened, "before I call the Sheriff. You are probably a spy. You are probably in the pay of your Queen."

"But listen, my friend," I interrupted him, "I have no queen. There is no Queen of Holland. There never has been one."

"Then what is the Stuart woman doing in your country?"

"Stuart woman? You mean the daughter of your own King Charles?"

"I do!"

"Well, she is the wife of one of our officials."

"So she is, and she is conspiring with her father to bring him back to London and kill all those who truly love God. Even now she may be sailing up the Thames with the navy of your dastardly country. Christians indeed! You are worse than Judas who betrayed our Lord for money."

I decided that I had to do with a madman and went my way, leaving the poor demented fellow to his illusory fish and his equally illusory "Queen of Holland."

I saw an inn and I went to the tap-room where I ordered a gin and water, as I had heard all my friends who had been in England tell that that was the national beverage of the British people. A few minutes later a fine-looking young cavalier with a noble lace collar and carrying a rapier at least eight feet long entered and sat at the table next to mine.

"Landlord," he called, "bring me a bottle of claret. I want to drink to the everlasting curse of that thrice-damned nation, the Dutch. Here goes!" and he emptied a bumper of what to me seemed an excellent vintage which should be sipped at leisure but never, under any circumstances, should be washed down one's throat as if it were beer.

The landlord, anticipating a profitable evening, bent over his patriotic customer. "And what, My Lord, might the Dutch have been doing now," he inquired, "that they should have incurred Your Lordship's displeasure?"

"What have they done now? *Now*, you say? What have they ever not ceased doing? Was there ever a more perfidious, contemptible and disreputable race on this planet of ours? What have they done now? Come here, all of you!" And here he addressed himself to a dozen pleasant-looking loafers who were standing in front of the bar and who, on the chance of a few free drinks, hastened to His Lordship's table.

"Sit down, all of you, and have a glass of this poison which our landlord calls claret. What have the Dutch done? Do you remember, my friends, how our gracious Sovereign most graciously allowed their Stadholder—some sort of high-sheriff, for all I know—to marry his royal daughter? A Dutch square-head marrying a Stuart! Very well. The deed was done. A royal princess," and here he lowered his voice, "dwelleth in The Hague—a genuine, honest-to-goodness royal princess dwelling in a Dutch hamlet. But what do you think? Were those fishmongers and cheese-merchants grateful? Not a thought of it! When Our Majesty got into trouble with those psalm-singing bastards of Hampden and What-do-you-call-him Cromwell, His Majesty sent his august consort to the Holland city to ask for their support in chastising his traitorous subjects. What I really mean, is to allow them to put their money for once into a cause that was wholly just and wholly righteous. What did they do?" Here he stopped for emphasis. "Nothing! absolutely nothing! Gave her a few thousand ducats and their good wishes! A few thousand, where they ought to have given millions. I know it for a fact. My brother is just back from Oxford. The Queen was there. A brave woman, a fine woman, one of God's noblest women! Had spent ten days at sea. Had braved death and seasickness without a flicker. And all that to be insulted by the damned Dutch with a present of a waiter's tip!"

I decided that it was apparently not a lucky day for the Dutch and I paid for my gin and water and went to my bed. But the next morning I thought I had better find out why we were quite so unpopular with everybody and I asked my landlady who the best surgeon in town was and I paid him a visit.

As a rule our colleagues in other cities are happy to see us for we often have heard of some new method of cutting the stone or applying the irons from those with which they are familiar and they are apt to learn something, just as we are ourselves. I found a crabbed old man, in a very cold room, with a woolen muffler around his neck, reading out of an enormous volume which proved to be the Book of Revelation, edited with myriads of notes by some English divine whose name I have forgotten.

No sooner had I told him that I was a member of the Amsterdam surgeons' guild, bound for the New Netherlands and driven into the harbor of Dover by inadvertent winds and that I wanted to pay my respects to one whose name was so generally and so honorably known ('flattery is the oil of all social machinery') than he closed the book before him with a loud bang, pushed back his chair and delivered himself of one of the bitterest denunciations to which I have ever been obliged to listen.

"Bound from the Old Netherlands to the New Netherlands, eh?" he asked. "The New Netherlands indeed! And who told you, you housebreaking robbers and pirates, that you could take a piece of land that belonged to the Children of Zion? The Children of Zion, I say and I mean it! When God meant to chastise us by giving us a Stuart to rule over us as our king, we who truly love Him and His service could only save His holy cause by carrying it to the other side of the ocean and founding a new and happier England amidst these savages, that were infinitely less cruel and blood-thirsty than our own Staffords and Lauds. God in His infinite wisdom had prepared this sanctuary for His own people when He sent Cabot across the ocean to take possession of all this part of America in our name, which is also His name. Then you came with your intrusions. You built yourselves castles within the realm of Israel. You raised armies to keep the Chosen People from their just reward. Now the hour of Judgment is at hand. The Evil One has arisen again. His name is Charles Stuart."

Here I interrupted him. "My very dear sir," I said, "I only came here out of colleagual politeness. The people in my country are greatly interested in the work of one of your physicians. I for one would like to talk of the ideas of Doctor Harvey."

I thought that the old man would attack me. "Harvey!" he shouted. "A vile and contemptible traitor. Harvey! a son of honest yeomen, who prefers to serve a popish king. Harvey, who this very moment is at Oxford to cure his royal master from the result of his youthful debaucheries!"

Once more I interrupted him, for the interview was getting to be very painful. I said that no doubt it was very sad that Doctor Harvey should have chosen to side with the wrong party (what did I know or care about his stupid parties? I had enough of them at home). And I argued that I had come to exchange some ideas upon science, not upon irrelevant religious quarrels. Those words, "irrelevant religious quarrels," brought about the explosion.

"Irrelevant!" the man hissed (if it be possible to hiss a word with so many r's) "irrelevant, sir! Just as 'irrelevant' as Pilate washing his hands of the ultimate fate of our Saviour. Here we have spent years building the New Zion, the New England, that at the great hour of our crisis we might have a weapon with which to strike at our enemy and save the old England. And here you, a member of the race that has steadily opposed us, that has almost ruined our plans, dares penetrate into my house and home and use the word 'irrelevant'! Out of my sight, sir! Out of my house!"

So that ended that third interview and I decided to go back to the ship and invite the captain for dinner and ask him what my pleasant-tempered British colleague had meant with his New Zion and how and why we poor Hollanders were accused of having interfered with the plans of Jehovah.

Captain Bontekoe, an honest sailor from Franeker and in contrast with most of his fellow Frisians a good Erasmian, had made nine previous trips to the West Indies and when I told him what had happened to me that afternoon, he was not in the least surprised.

"The same old story," he smiled pleasantly. "The same old story, or the same old fable, or the same old lie or whatever you want to call it. Look here, Doctor, I shall tell you the story in a nut-shell. The English take their souls seriously. They don't care much for the arts. They have to have some sort of an outlet for their emotions and so they quarrel about hymn-books and snakes that have talked or not talked, and infant damnation and other pleasant subjects like that and they burn each other and hang each other and draw and quarter each other with absolute good humor, but in the most murderous spirit imaginable. Until a couple of dozen years ago they were at least ruled by one of their own people. That made the hanging and burning a little less painful. It is much pleasanter to be sent to the scaffold by one of your own people than by an outsider. But red-haired old Bess, the wily old scoundrel, she died and they got the Stuarts to be their masters. They are no good, these Stuarts. They never have been. Besides, they are foreigners from a distant land; Scotchmen from Edinburgh, twice as far from London as Paris, four times as far as Amsterdam. The Stuarts have never understood their English subjects and the dear subjects have never understood their Scottish masters. And besides, personally they were no earthly good, very weak with women and even more so with their given word. A fine kettle of fish! And of course, sooner or later, it had to boil over. It seems to be boiling over right now. Parliament is in London, the King is in Oxford, and the armies of the two are somewhere between. We shall be lucky if we get away from here before they fight a pitched battle."

"Yes," I said, "that is undoubtedly interesting, but what in God's name has New Amsterdam got to do with that?"

"Nothing in the world of ordinary, normal people, but this afternoon, from what I can make up from what you tell me, you were not dealing with an ordinary, normal person. Don't forget that just now they are having the same kind of trouble in this country that we had thirty years ago. You know how that ended. We killed the only really great man we had ever had so far. In the end over here they will probably cut off the King's head. Mark my words! If Charles is not very careful, they will cut his head off. For these people (just as we were when you and I were still younger than we are to-day) have got themselves in a fine state of religious delirium tremens. They won't wake up and be cured until they have had the shock of their lives—some enormous sensation—a war—or a first-rate murder—or a trial, of the whole nation against one single statesman or even against the King. Can't you see it? All these sad-faced brethren sitting in some large hall behind an enormous Bible, turning the leaves and finding passages urging 'God's People' to commit tyrannicide or whatever the professors call it?"

"Yes," I interrupted him once more, "yes, Captain, I know and all this is tremendously interesting, but what does it have to do with New England and . . ."

"Pardon me," the skipper replied, "I am sorry, but I have been coming to this country on and off for the last thirty years. It used to be a damn amusing country, and now look at it! But you were asking a question.

You were asking me why this poor old leech was so angry with you to-day when you said you were a Hollander. Well, it is this way. He probably was one of the leading local lights in the camp of what they call here the 'noncomformists.' Thirty years ago you never heard of them. They may have existed, but they kept to themselves. Nowadays they are everywhere. Had one on board yesterday with some sort of city ordinance, that the crews of vessels, even foreign vessels, temporarily in the harbor of Dover, are expected to attend divine service on Sunday. Can you beat that? As if we came here for the fun of it!

"Well, where was I? Oh, yes, about New England. Yes, I have been there. Trip before last. Caught in a gale off Newfoundland, lost one of my masts, had to drop into Charleston harbor to get a new one. A convenient enough harbor, but, my God, what a people! I had to stay there four weeks. Never been so bored in all my life.

"There was another village nearby. It was called Boston. Same name as that place on the Bristol Channel. Everybody I met, when he or she heard I came from Holland, wanted to know all about the big synod of '18. The one the dominies held in Dordrecht when they held 180 meetings and spent 300,000 guilders to decide that a minister should dress in black and not in brown. That was not very important and it always seemed to me that they could have saved themselves a great deal of trouble and the taxpayers a lot of money by dressing them in black right at the beginning. But the first time I said so I got into serious difficulties. Afterwards, I just answered that I had been too young when this holy gathering was held to remember anything about it. And somehow or other, I got by with that reply, though many people suspected me of all sorts of terrible doctrines, in which, God knows, they were right.

"But, your question, why did they hate us down there where we are, near the South River or the Mauritius River or the Hudson (everybody calls it by a different name)?

"Well, don't you see, those poor deluded people are so thoroughly convinced that present-day England is going to perdition that they want to move to America, man, woman and child, bag and baggage and everything. That is what the grouchy old pill referred to this afternoon when he said that we were working against the forces of righteousness. They want a strong, independent state over there, run by the clergy (their clergy, of course, all the others are chased into the wilderness where the Injuns get them).

"But it is the devil of a place to start a new state. Rocky soil—a winter that lasts fourteen months of seven weeks each—no rivers—no ways of getting into the interior. Of course they never really wanted to go there.

"You studied in Leyden, didn't you? Ever walk through the Kloksteeg on a Sunday? Remember some terrific psalm-singing that went on there? Those were the people who first had the notion of that New Zion on the shores of America. They could, of course, have stayed right where they were. But they were peasants, cobblers, as simple a lot as I ever saw. I brought part of them from Delfshaven back to England in the summer of '20. As ungrateful a lot of people as I ever came across. Nothing had suited them in our country. Most of them had lived there a dozen years, but they didn't speak a word of our language. They complained about everything. They hadn't liked our food and it had always rained and our houses were too low and our boys had made love to their girls and that was wrong, for of course, they would never have dreamed of marrying their offspring to foreigners. Do you get that, Doctor? Foreigners! We were 'foreigners,' in our own country! Can you beat that? And then the war was beginning again, you know, after the Spanish truce, and they might have to serve in the army to defend a 'foreign' country—a 'foreign' country in which they had been given hospitality for a dozen years! And things at home were not going so well ('home' of course was Scrooby or whatever hole they came from) and they must go to Virginia and start a new country of their own.

"Of course the poor devils had no idea where Virginia was or how far away it was. For that matter, even to-day Virginia is just a name on the map. But they had heard about Virginia and that it was a good land and that one could grow tobacco there, thousands of pounds a year, and grow rich. They also told me that the colony was ruled by a godly man of their own persuasion who had passed a law that all people who did not believe every word in the Bible or did not go to church twice on the Sabbath day or who had doubts about the exact composition of the Trinity should be executed. Should be executed, if you please, for not going to church twice every Sunday! This fellow had been recalled a year or so before, but they did not know that, being the sort of fortunate people who can always just miss knowing what does not entirely fit in with their own plans or ideas.

"Very well! They got permission from the Virginia Company to settle within the jurisdiction of that august body, and they sailed from Plymouth or from Southampton, I forget which, but from somewhere in the south of England. Their captain did not know his business. If you compare his course with that of Hudson, fourteen years before, or even old man Smith who was what we call a 'fancy navigator,' it was pretty sad work. He landed his passengers, or whatever there was left of them—for they didn't seem to have known how to take care of themselves at all—he finally dumped the whole outfit on a piece of rock a couple of thousand miles north from the place for which they were bound, in the most miserable part of that God-forsaken wilderness of rocks and reefs that lies just south of the Saint Lawrence.

"He had the decency to offer to take them back on board his ship and try once more whether he could find the coast of Virginia. But they would not hear of it. They had had enough to last them for a dozen life-times. Better stay where they were and freeze than go back on that leaky scow and be seasick and drift about helplessly for another couple of months. Besides, now that they were on dry land they could eventually walk to Virginia. On the map it did not look very far. And then (and that is where we come in) they found a large chunk of that map covered with the startling legend, 'This belongs to the Dutch West India Company.'

"That made things different again. There were those same miserable 'foreigners' from whom they had just escaped after enjoying their hospitality for a dozen years. And they had got hold of the biggest river and they had built forts all along its borders and villages and cities. It was enough to make even a latter-day saint very mad. They wrote about it to London. The 'foreigners' by now had become 'intruders.' London looked through the archives. Old Cabot had first visited that part of the world (or rather had first seen it, for he never set foot on ground), in 1498. He had been sent out by Henry VII. Henry was King of England. Therefore everything Cabot had seen belonged to England. Could anything be simpler? On the basis that 'seeing is possessing,' the English government had most generously handed that whole part of the world over to a couple of English trading companies. Most of these had been failures and now that one of them at last was doing a little better we were found to be comfortably established right in the middle of all this 'exclusive' piece of English territory.

"No wonder they are annoyed. And no wonder the disappointed brethren who thought that they were going to erect the New Jerusalem on the spot where we have built our own town of New Amsterdam don't like it a bit. If you will follow my advice, don't enter into any further conversations with the people here. I shall hurry the repairs as much as I can for I don't like this country any better than you do. If possible I like it less. But sit quiet and don't talk with the natives. They aren't in a talky mood just now. Play checkers with that nice Jew friend of yours. Or back-gammon or whatever you like. But don't talk. Just pretend that you are dumb or that you can only speak Dutch. That is very much the same in the end and it will save us all a terrible lot of trouble."

And with these words the captain bade me a good night and I went to bed and read for a while in the "Praise of Folly" and thought how very little the world had changed during the last hundred years.

It was not a very brilliant thought, but it was late and I was sleepy.

Chapter 30

THE TOWN OF NIEUW AMSTERDAM PROVES SOMEWHAT OF A DISAPPOINTMENT, BUT WHAT A MARVELOUS COUNTRY!

The captain was as good as his word. In less than three weeks the repairs had been finished. Before the middle of May we had passed Land's End. The next day a heavy gale from the south almost blew us upon one of the rocks that surround the Scilly Islands. The wind changed. Then it died down. Then it veered around to the east and for the rest of the voyage we had splendid weather with a steady, stiff breeze which made us do the trip in less than a month.

To be perfectly sincere with myself, I did not in the least care for life on the ocean. I had heard the charms and the graces of this turbulent expanse of blue-green water chanted until I had come to believe that a sailor's life was the merriest of all. But those odes of praise must have been composed by Roman poets whose knowledge of nautical matters must have been derived from rowing across the Umbrian Lakes or wading across the Tiber. As for me, notwithstanding the discomfort of coaches, the stupidity of horses that are forever running you into a ditch or down a bridge, the terrible roads that are either mud-flats or dust-bins, and the wet blankets of most inns, as for me I shall travel on land every time I get a chance and let the sea be the sea for those who like to be uncomfortable on principle.

One day I picked up a little hand-book on navigation that was lying in the skipper's cabin. It informed me that seven-eighths of the planet was covered with water. Another one of God's little mistakes. At the end of this volume there was a short treatise on the rules of conduct of a captain towards his crew and vice versa. There were some charming items in it. But they struck me as a little too one-sided, for if I remember correctly, the captain could do about everything to the crew from flogging them several times in a single day to hanging them from the yard-arm or leaving them behind on an uninhabited island while the men from their side, if the treatment they had suffered had been sufficiently mild to allow them to recover from the after effects, had the right to complain to the ship's owners but only (and that was the interesting part) after they had first submitted to their punishment.

One day I saw how the system worked. As far as I could make out from talking to a large number of the sailors, Captain Bontekoe was conceded to be one of the kindest and most humane of commanders then in the service of the company. What some one a little less "good-natured" would have done under the circumstances, the Lord only knows. But this is what happened.

There was a nasty-looking young devil among the sailors who was said to be from Dublin. No one knew how he got on board, but at the last moment three men had been missing, the mate had sent to the gin-shops near the Montelbaans Tower for three extra men, "drunk or sober." He had found them, but in what state I need not tell. The crimp who had brought them on board had got his money and the ship was far out at sea before the poor devils discovered what had happened to them. Two of them took it good-naturedly. One ship after all was very much like another. The third one, however, seemed to have a girl in Amsterdam and he was wild with rage. His anger turned especially against one of his comrades in misery whom he held responsible for his fate. And one night he waited for him at the door of the fo'c'sle and mauled him terribly with his knife. I was called forward to bandage the victim. His face was in threads but he was a tough customer and recovered, although he had to go through life with only part of his nose left.

The next morning, with a glorious sun shining placidly upon a sea of shimmering silver, all the men were called aft by three short blasts of the bugler's trumpet. The young Irishman, his hands tightly fastened behind his back, was brought up from below. He had spent the night in the brig. The captain asked him whether he were guilty of having attacked one of his comrades. He nodded yes, he had done it, he was glad he had done it and would do it again if he had a chance. The captain disregarded the latter part of this speech.

"Fasten him to the mast," he said, "and be sure it is the same knife, for that is the rule of the sea."

The young fellow's arms were loosened and he was taken to the mast by the ship's carpenter. Then the knife with which the crime had been committed and which was now in the possession of the mate, was handed to the carpenter. With one quick blow and using the knife as a nail, he hammered the man's right hand to the mast, a little higher than his head, so that he would not lose too much blood. Then the bugler blew "dismissed" and everybody went about his business as if nothing had happened, leaving the poor devil standing there until he should have pulled the knife out of his lacerated hand by his own effort. But he remained obstinate. He had lost his girl and he no longer cared what happened. In the evening, the ship was pitching quite badly, but the knife held, and the prisoner still stood nailed to the mast. I went to the skipper and asked whether the time had not come to set the youngster free. Bontekoe shook his head. It just could not be done. The other men would take this as a sign of weakness and it was absolutely necessary for the safety of both the officers and the passengers (we carried two dozen emigrants between deck) that discipline be enforced in the old way, which as far as he, the captain, could tell, was the only possible way.

I went on deck late that evening. The man was still standing there. I felt such pity for him that contrary to all rules, I offered him a drink of gin. He refused. He refused it with an oath and kicked at me savagely with one of his heavy sea-boots. There was nothing to be done and I went to bed. In the morning, earlier than usual, I returned on deck. A little puddle of blood at the foot of the mast told of the tragedy.

I asked the mate who was on watch whether the boy had suffered any bad after effects from this long exposure and the loss of blood. He shook his head. "I don't know," he said. "He is gone. He was there at twelve. When we made the rounds at one, he was gone. The knife was lying on the deck."

"And the man?"

The mate made a gesture and I understood.

"Drowned himself?"

"Most likely. Those Irish people are very emotional."

And that, as far as I could discover, was the last time anybody gave the matter a thought. Whether it was due to this incident or whether we had an exceptionally well-mannered crew, I don't know, but we had no other adventures until we reached the mouth of the North River, the Mauritius River of Hudson's day.

During the last week I tried to pump the captain a little about the sort of people I would have to deal with. What was the Governor like and who was who and what in that strange land. But he was very chary with his information.

"You will soon enough find out for yourself," was all he would answer, "and I don't want to prejudice you."

"Yes," I replied, "but it would make it so much easier for me."

"Better find out for yourself though, Doctor. Better find out for yourself! As for me, I would rather spend a week with one of those painted savages the Governor is fighting just now than an hour with His Lordship himself."

"Then he is pretty bad?"

But the skipper remained firm. "I had a pretty dull life," he finally confessed, "and I can stand a bit of fun now and then. I am going to wait outside the fort when you return from your first interview with that noble potentate. I shall then conduct you to the second hero of the great comedy of Manhattan, the Reverend Doctor Everadus Bogardus. And I shall once more wait at the door until you return from that interview. Then we shall go to my good friend the leech (if he happens to be in town) and I shall treat you to the finest wild turkey on the island and you shall tell me all about it—the pleasant morning you spent with the officials. But don't ask me any further questions and spoil my fun."

And so I was in a state of complete and blissful ignorance when I put on my best broadcloth suit to pay my respects to His Excellency the Governor. Bernardo had wanted to accompany me, but at the last moment the skipper had interfered. "Don't take him," he had begged me. "He is a nice man and he probably is rather sensitive. Kieft does not like Jews and he might tell him so. Besides, it is better for you that you should go alone the first time. You may be a learned man, I have heard people say so and I have no reason to doubt it, but there are certain things you don't know yet. Go and get your little lesson."

Then I was rowed ashore. I was met by a group of dirty-looking children who stared at me with stupid faces and seemed indeed completely dumb until one of the sailors threw them some pennies, when they fell upon each other with such fury and amidst such terrific cursing as I had never heard before. I used this opportunity to escape from their embarrassing curiosity and hastily walked in the direction of the Fort. In my pocket I carried a draft on the Company's treasurer for 5000 florins and an order duly signed by three of the directors in Amsterdam requesting His Excellency, Governor Willem Kieft, to extend all possible aid and courtesy to Dr. Joannis van Loon, a surgeon and medical doctor of great repute who had come to the New Netherlands for scientific purposes and who should be given every facility at the disposal of the colonial government.

I felt myself a person of considerable importance. And I silently rehearsed the speech with which I would answer His Excellency's words of welcome.

Chapter 31

HIS EXCELLENCY THE GOVERNOR GRANTS ME AN AUDIENCE

The entrance to the Fort, which was also the official residence of the Governor, was away from the water-front and I therefore had to walk around two sides of the walls. There was no moat and the walls looked like the better sort of dikes one sees along the banks of the Zuyder Zee or between Veere and Vrouwenpolder. A number of sheep and a few cows peacefully nibbling the grass of this stronghold did not exactly give one the feeling that the colony was at the very moment engaged in a most dangerous war with its red-skinned neighbors.

The whole scene reminded me of the days of my youth, when I was perhaps seven or eight years old, when sometimes during the height of summer I was allowed to spend a few days with a distant cousin who had married a baker in the village of Ketel, about two hours distant from Rotterdam. A drowsy hamlet, drowsy chickens aimlessly picking at bits of grain, busy bees in enormous fur coats paying their matutinal calls upon all the flowers of the neighborhood and being quite noisy about it, and in the distance the slow but rhythmic blows of a steel hammer upon a steel anvil, everything incredibly peaceful, everything unbelievably far removed from a busy, work-a-day world. But Ketel lay buried and forgotten in the midst of the richest polder of Holland and this was the capital of a vast colonial empire. It was all very mysterious and a little bit upsetting. I was afraid that my speech would not quite fit the occasion. I hastened me to deliver it before I should have forgotten it entirely.

The gate was wide open. Indeed it looked as if it had not been closed for at least a dozen years. Two old men, apparently watchmen (for their halberds were leaning against the wall), were sitting on a bench. There was a checker-board between them and they were so engrossed in their game that they did not notice me. I waited patiently until they had both got at least one king and then I said, "Pardon me, but could you tell me where I can find His Excellency the Governor?"

The elder of the two who was sitting with his back toward the courtyard, pointed with his thumb across his shoulder and without looking up from his game said, "Over there, house on the left, you will find it all right," and quietly took three of his opponent's pieces.

The court-yard was clean enough but a large sow with a brood of very pink children was lying right across the foot-path. My dignity insisted that I remove this obstruction on my way to my first formal interview. But the beast weighed at least a thousand tons and refused to budge. I kicked it a couple of times, but it only grunted and waved one enormous hanging ear at me as if to say, "No use, mister, I am here and I stay here." So I gave the creature a wide berth and entered the first building on the right, a two-story structure which for all the world might have been a better class butcher-shop in one of the newer parts of Amsterdam.

Here too the doors stood wide open and I entered the hall without being challenged by any one. There was a door on the right and a door on the left. I chose the door on the right and knocked. A very unpleasant voice, with a decided German accent, bade me come in. At one side of the room a short, squat man with unkempt brown hair was cutting himself a new pen. He was so deeply engrossed in the business of cutting that pen that he never noticed me. I stood. He cut. The situation was embarrassing. But after all, I carried official messages from Their Lordships the Directors of the sovereign West India Company to His Excellency their Governor in the New Netherlands. I was a person of some importance. I was entitled to a little consideration. And when the pen-cutter, having botched his job, threw the offending goose-quill on the floor with a fine Teutonic oath and picked up another, to recommence the operation, I spoke up and said, "My good man, I am looking for the Governor. When can I see him?"

"You can't see him," he answered, without so much as giving me a look, "he is busy."

"Busy?" I answered. "May I ask how long it will be before I can see him?"

"When he ain't busy any more."

"When will that be?"

"When he gets this damn pen cut," and having decapitated his second goose-quill, he unconcernedly picked up a third one and once more let me wait in silence.

I was very angry by that time, but decided that I would teach him a lesson. I had my official letter of recommendation. In a moment he would know with whom he was dealing.

Finally he had got a pen that suited his fancy. He dipped it into the ink and scrawled something upon a piece of paper. Then he pushed his chair back and said gruffly, "Now what do you want?"

I pulled the letter of the Directors out of my pocket and laid it on his desk. He picked it up and looked at it. Then he called, "Van Tienhoven! Hey there, van Tienhoven, come here!"

A shabby-looking man of about forty came shuffling out of the adjoining room. "Tienhoven," the Governor said, "read this letter to me. I have forgotten my glasses this morning."

The shabby-looking man, apparently a secretary, took my credentials and reeled off the contents as if he were a notary, going over a sales-contract before a couple of witnesses. When he had finished he handed the document back to the Governor. "That is all," he said. "Do you need me any more? I am busy!"

His Excellency frowned a deep frown as if he were trying to puzzle out a question of momentous importance. He puzzled for at least five whole minutes. Then he said, "No, that will do. I will dictate an answer this afternoon. You can go now. I will talk to this fellow alone."

All that time he had kept me standing. I was tired after all those uncomfortable weeks at sea and involuntarily leaned with one hand upon the table. Suddenly he pushed his chair back and banged his desk with his fist.

"Stand up straight," he barked at me, "I am the Governor here. You are a leech in the pay of the Company. Stand up straight and listen to me. Those people over there in Amsterdam must be crazy. Here I am, having a war on my hands that has taken every single one of my men. If pressing business did not keep me here, I would be out at the front myself, this very moment. But I alas! must remain behind to organize the defense. I have sent to Holland for supplies—for soldiers—for money. And what do I get? A leech! a pill! a common barber, who brings me a letter saying, 'Please let this man pluck daisies and daffodils while you are busy fighting for your life.'

"Are they crazy? Do you think I am crazy? I won't submit to this. I know why they sent you. To spy on me. It is all the work of that damned Bogard, the Reverend Everadus Bogardus, the eminent divine. A fine Christian that most eminent and Reverend Doctor Everadus Bogardus! He got rid of my predecessor because poor drunken Twiller would not let him run the colony as he wanted to. Lied about him in Amsterdam, pulled wires. Sent letters to all his friends at home. Finally got his scalp. Now he wants mine. Preaches sly sermons about unfaithful servants wasting their talents. Calls on his parishioners and tells them how much better everything was in the days of old Piet Minnewit when the colonists were taught respect for their pastors and listened to the council of their holy men.

"Holy men indeed! Why, that fellow was so drunk last Sunday that he had to hold on to the table, giving us the sacrament. But what can I do about it? I am a man of action. If they would give me two regiments and fifty thousand guilders, there wouldn't be a native alive between here and Orange in less than six months' time. I tell them so, and what do they do? Send me a barber who wants to go about collecting pretty little flowers. No, my friend, you got into the wrong pew! I am a man of few words. You either go back where you came from and just as soon as you possibly can, or you take your orders from me and I will set you to shaving the garrison of this fort until I can ship you off to the front where you may be of some possible use if you can handle broken bones or know something about taking care of poisoned arrows."

I must confess that never in my life had I felt quite as sheepish as I did at that moment. There I stood like a recruit who was being scolded by his corporal for having omitted to clean the lock of his pistol. And the reception had been so absolutely different from what I had been led to anticipate, that I was completely at a loss what I should say or do next. Should I go away or should I remain where I was. I did not know and so I did nothing, as one is apt to do under such circumstances. But this did not in the least improve my position, for the Governor once more called out, "Van Tienhoven! Hey there, van Tienhoven, come here!" and when that poor slave appeared he ordered, "Show this fellow out. If he is still here within five minutes I shall have him flogged."

Outside the sun was still shining, the sow was still feeding her brood, the two old bewhiskered guards were still playing checkers. But in my heart there was such a turmoil of conflicting emotions, anger, bewilderment, revenge, hatred, and surprise, that I did the only thing I could do under the circumstances, I sat down on an old rusty cannon that was lying (for no apparent reason) in the middle of the road (like the sow) and then burst out into uncontrollable fits of laughter. Then I got up, brushed the dust off my clothes and turned the corner of the Fort. There the skipper stood with Bernardo and a strange man of pleasant appearance.

"Well," the captain asked, "did you have a nice time?"

"Good God!" was all I could answer.

Whereupon the skipper and the strange man clapped each other on the back right merrily and then broke forth into mighty guffaws, so loud and boisterous that a group of women who had been doing the family wash on the water-front put down their baskets filled with wet laundry and looked at us in great astonishment for such scenes of mirth were apparently not common in the good village of Nieuw Amsterdam. Gradually the peals of laughter ceased and I was duly introduced to the pleasant-faced stranger.

"This is Captain de Vries, Master Jan," the skipper said. "He is coming on board with us for a drink. Then we shall all go and dine with your good colleague, Doctor La Montagne. He has come to town with the captain. He has a house here and an old squaw who cooks for him. I have sent word that we would be there at two. The turkey has been ordered. I shall keep my promise and give it to you, even if you have not yet paid your respects to the eminent Everadus. I doubt whether he could receive you at such an early hour anyway."

"Busy with his sermon," Captain de Vries offered.

"Yes. Consulting the famous text of Genesis IX and re-living the whole episode to get sufficient local color. Save yourself that pleasure for some Sunday afternoon, Doctor. Perhaps you will then find him able to talk to you."

The allusion to Genesis was lost on me at the moment, but everything was so utterly different from what I had expected that I paid little attention to it at the time. When I had been in the colony for a little longer, I knew what the skipper had meant. But just then I merely smiled and followed the three men to the boat that was waiting for us at the landing.

The sailors were lying in the grass. In front of them stood an enormous Indian boy, looking a muddy brown and clad only in a garment that at home would have been known as a pair of swimming trunks. His legs were covered with mud. His eyes stared vacantly into space. A dirty broken feather had been stuck in his pitch-black hair, that had been braided like a woman's hair and that was also caked with mud. One of the sailors picked up a pebble and threw it at the giant. "Go along now, Jan Smeerpoets," he said. "Go home and tell the wives that there is nothing doing. Not a drop!"

The giant held out a very dirty hand. "Jenever," he moaned, "jenever."

"Nothing doing," the same sailor remarked, "not a drop."

The giant turned slowly on his heels and shuffled away.

The skipper looked at Bernardo. "Do you know who that is?"

Bernardo nodded "no."

"That is one of your long lost brethren. Nice fellow, ain't he?"

But Captain de Vries broke in. "Look here, Bontekoe, that is hardly fair. That is the way they are after we have taken them in hand and taught them a few things. Wait a few days and I will show you the original article. Then you will see something very different."

The boat pulled away from the shore.

When we rounded the outermost point of land, the dirty-looking savage was standing silently on a rock. His vacant eyes stared into space. His trembling hand was stretched in our direction. "Jenever," he was mumbling, "jenever—gin!"

And that is how I spent my first morning in the New World.

Chapter 32

RELIGIOUS BIGOTRY AND POLITICAL SHORTSIGHTEDNESS PROVE NOT TO BE CONFINED TO THE EASTERN SHORES OF THE ATLANTIC OCEAN

Those bad impressions, however, did not last long. I forgot them completely as soon as we reached the house of Doctor La Montagne. It was a low brick building standing in the heart of a lovely graden, just off the Breestraat, a wide cart-road that seemed to run due north. Doctor La Montagne apologized for not having been able to make more elaborate preparations for our reception.

"But this idiotic war keeps me very busy and I am rarely in town these days."

Then he led us into a small room with enormous oaken rafters and with a few fine prints on the walls. The table, made roughly out of a sort of wood which I did not recognize, had been set for six people. We sat on low benches and we were waited upon by an old Indian woman. The food was excellent but new to my taste. Especially the potatoes, of a yellowish color but much larger than those at home, attracted my attention. We had wine to drink but it was rather sour and a native product, as I afterwards learned. But the conversation was the best part of the meal. Here we were, three thousand miles away from home, and it might have been a Sunday in June and I might have been out in the Diemermeer or in Monnikendam with my friends, talking of all the latest news of the big world, listening to Jean-Louys telling us of a letter he had received that week from Descartes, who, so it seemed, was contemplating a visit to France—looking with ill-concealed suspicion at Selim, who was trying to convince us that Vienna was the natural capital of the Turkish Empire and that ere long (if he were to believe the letters he received from home) the Mohammedans would be once more marching upon the Austrian capital. Then, switching over to a discussion of the new tower of the South Church or of a dozen new etchings exhibited in the sales-rooms of Lucas Luce, paying our humble respects to Torstensson's latest victory over the armies of the Emperor and wondering what the Swedes would do next, and offering mild guesses as to what influence the death of Richelieu would have upon the new French loan, then being offered by the Wisselbank in the Vogelsteeg.

The same spirit of a well-mannered and tolerant interest in all affairs of heaven and earth, which took it for granted that the good Lord had created the whole universe for no other purpose than to offer human ingenuity and enthusiasm a happy and undisturbed hunting-ground, which I had learned to appreciate through the companionship of my friends in

Amsterdam, I now found here on a little island at the other side of the ocean. And I was once again struck by the fact how little outward circumstances have to do with that inner contentment that can come to us only from an exchange of ideas with congenial souls.

I have listened all my life to people arguing: "Englishmen are so and so," or "No Frenchman ever would have said such and such a thing . . .", or "No German would ever have done this and that," and at home they examine every man, woman and child upon the most intimate details of his or her pedigree before they will so much as say good morning to them. And I have heard all my life that "All merchants are money-grubbers," and "All doctors are quacks," or "All merchants are fine, up-standing fellows," and "All ministers of the Gospel are noble and devoted servants of mankind," but I have learned that it is quite impossible to lay down such laws about other races or other individuals.

The older I grow, the more I have become convinced that there are no "nations" and no "races" and no "classes of men"—that there are only individuals, that those individuals are good or bad—interesting or dull—wise or foolish—according to their natural inclinations, and that mysterious bent of character which we call "personality." And that first day I spent on the banks of the North River and all during those seven years during which I lived in the New Netherlands, I was continually running across further proof of the truth of this statement.

I came to know naked and painted savages whose manners were so exquisite that they could have been presented at the court of King Louis himself and would have been examples of good behavior and innate charm to the polished courtiers who surrounded that famous monarch. And not infrequently I ran across others that were just fat, cruel, lazy animals much too good for the bullets that were wasted on them.

I met simple farmers from some unknown village in the remotest corner of the colony who by thrift and industry and incredibly hard work had cleared wide acres of forest land and had built themselves fine homes where they lived in perfect peace and amity with all their neighbors and where they educated their children to be fine men and women, afraid of nobody and of such an independence of thought and action as was rarely found in the old country. And I have been obliged to spend the night underneath the roof of some worthless younger son of a good Amsterdam family whose parents had bought him a thousand acres of fertile grassland and who had been too lazy to raise a single crop or plant more than a dozen fruit trees in just as many years.

I am running ahead a little of my story. But that first afternoon in the New World convinced me that human nature is the same under every clime and this thought gave me courage to meet the many difficulties that beset my path as soon as I had let the Governor know that I was there on serious business and refused to let him intimidate me into going back home before my task was done.

As a matter of fact, and as I heard from Captain de Vries that same afternoon, Kieft was not a bad man nor as wholly incompetent as his enemies made him out to be. It is true that he was exceedingly vain, much given to banging the table and telling the world in general that he was a "man of action" and a "fellow who got results." But it is equally true that he was a tremendous improvement upon his predecessor, the unfortunate Wouter van Twiller, who had got the job because he was a nephew or a cousin or something of the van Rensselaers, the Amsterdam jewelers who had bought thousands of acres of land between New Amsterdam and Fort Orange.

It is true that Kieft was undoubtedly responsible for the outbreak of war with the natives. But it is equally true that there never had been a fixed Indian policy on the part of the government at home and that the different directors had never known whether they must treat the Red Man as their long-lost brother or must exterminate him as if he were merely some particularly obnoxious kind of vermin. And it would be unfair to accuse poor Kieft of never paying anybody anything he owed him when we remember that he himself was merely the hired man of a trading company that had been virtually in bankruptcy for more than ten years.

As far as I was concerned, I got along well enough with His Excellency, once his suspicions that I was a spy or a tool in the hands of his enemy, the Dominie, had been allayed. After that, he treated me with fair respect and in the end he even came to like me and gave me every opportunity to fulfill my mission.

Unfortunately he was recalled soon after my arrival. The terrible Bogardus (I met the man a number of times; he was the typical farmer's son from some hamlet in the hinterland who had come to might and power as a minister of the Gospel but who was constitutionally unable to live in a community without trying to set himself up as the village tyrant), this violent-mouthed and violent-tempered preacher of ill-will and sower of discontent was gradually making the position of the director absolutely impossible.

The whole town of Nieuw Amsterdam was divided into pro-Bogardians and anti-Bogardians. The affair was taking on the proportions of a public scandal. It would have been an excellent thing for the colony if at that moment the Board of Directors at Amsterdam had sent one of their members to investigate the matter on the spot. But these gentlemen refused to budge. The West India Company, to most of them, was only a side issue. Their true interests lay elsewhere and they continued to rule a country, a hundred times as large as the Netherlands, from some back room in Amsterdam, and clamored for reports, reports, reports, as if such matters could be decided by bales and bales of written reports.

I was accustomed to a certain amount of red tape from the charity organizations which handled the financial affairs of our hospitals in Amsterdam. But I never saw so many reams of paper go to waste as during the years I was nominally in the service of the West India Company. Everything had to be referred back to Amsterdam. If a man wanted to build himself a new chicken-coop he first had to ask permission of the Governor who in turn reported the matter to the Board of Directors at home, who in turn delegated this highly important problem to a special sub-committee. Then the special sub-committee would deliberate and report its findings to the Directors. They in turn would report the special sub-committee's findings back to the Governor in Nieuw Amsterdam, who would let the prospective coop-builder know what had been decided. Meanwhile at least a year had gone by. Very likely the owner of the chicken-farm had been killed by an Indian, trying to get hold of his pet-hen or the chickens themselves had been eaten up by a fox or the man had gone out of business to open a tavern and in that way, twelve valuable months and at least twenty-four guilders worth of paper, ink and red tape (not to mention the chickens) had been wasted upon a question that within any reasonably intelligently governed colony would have been settled in less than five minutes.

About two weeks after my arrival in the New World, I moved from Nieuw Amsterdam to Vriesendael, the country-place of Captain de Vries, who had bought this piece of land half a dozen years before.

After Governor Kieft had raged and stormed for a couple of days, complaining that he was forever being followed by a myriad of spies (everybody in Nieuw Amsterdam, in Kieft's eyes, was either a secret agent of the Directors or a hired assassin of his arch-enemy, the Dominie), after Kieft had raged and sworn that he would have me deported, that he would employ me shaving the garrison's whiskers, that (upon one occasion he went as far as that) he would have me hanged, he quieted down sufficiently to listen to the reports of Captain Bontekoe and the remonstrances of Captain de Vries. As a result, he sent for me and told me that he would allow me to stay, provided I kept out of his sight. I agreed to do this and mentioned that I had been invited by Captain de Vries to come and stay with him at Vriesendael until I should have got accustomed to the new country and should have learned something of the native language.

But his suspicious mind, influenced by years of alcoholic abuse, at once scented a plot. He knew that almost any day he might be recalled to account for the many difficulties that had arisen during his term of office. Meanwhile he seemed to fear that we might start a little private rebellion of our own, and talked of being murdered in his sleep, but finally (upon regaining a certain degree of sobriety) relented and graciously gave me permission to go to Vriesendael. As de Vries had acquired Patroon's rights when he bought his estate, this took me and Bernardo (to whom Kieft had taken a most unreasonable and terrible dislike) out of the immediate jurisdiction of the Governor and neither of us was sorry.

There remained the matter of getting enough ready money. The treasury was empty. But finally I was paid out 200 florins of the 5000 that were due me according to the draft given to be by My Lord Andries. I had brought another hundred florins in the coinage of the Province of Holland, and for the moment, at least, we were safe from immediate want.

It was that time of the year which the settlers called their Indian summer, and although it was late in October (at home it would be raining twenty-four hours every day) the weather was so mild that we could sleep out in the open without any danger to our health.

Bernardo and I, accustomed to living in small, close rooms, badly ventilated and usually filled with the smoke of wood and peat fires, experienced a rare delight in being able to spend so much of our time out-of-doors. Every morning brought us fresh surprises. One day it would be a deer that stood staring at us when we came to the brook to get water for our breakfast. One night it was a bear, who good-naturedly ambled away when we decided to pitch camp underneath the tree he had chosen as his prospective winter quarters.

In the beginning we were greatly frightened by the weird noises that arose on all sides as soon as the sun had disappeared behind the distant mountains. But we were taught that very few of the animals that prowled around at night were dangerous for human beings.

"They are merely going after their own affairs and they work in the dark, just as we work by the light of the sun," Captain de Vries explained, and soon I experienced a pleasant neighborly feeling toward all those nimble neighbors who loved and hated and destroyed and created while we lay rolled in our blankets and smoked a peaceful pipe of some of the excellent Virginia tobacco that was being smuggled into the territory of the Company by the boatload.

To me, still smarting under the terrible experience of that morning in the anatomical theater, the silence, and the beauty, of this lovely landscape came as a wonderful relief. All day long I was on my feet, carrying not only my blankets and possessions but also an extra ax and a heavy gun. For the first time in my life, I knew what it was to be so utterly exhausted by physical labor that it was impossible to think of one's private troubles. After four days of this sort of life, I could eat anything, could sleep at all hours, although my bed consisted of a couple of bowlders, and one morning I actually found myself singing a tune. I never did sing very well and the tune was some old ditty that had been popular in my student days. But the fact that I had forgotten myself and my own worries so absolutely and so completely that I was able to sing from sheer joy of being alive, showed me that I was on a fair way to recovery.

And when, full of this glorious new spirit, I chased a charming little beast in black and white fur and finally tried to capture it with my bare hands (it looked so nice and harmless) and discovered too late that this little wash-bear was in reality a full grown and very competent skunk and when in consequence of this encounter, I was banished from the rest of the party for a whole day, I did not loose courage. But I made my own fire and cooked for myself and did my own chores as if I had spent the whole of my life pioneering in some lonely wilderness.

By some miracle of nature, I, who since childhood had been beset by a million unaccountable fears, had suddenly set myself free from these alarms and nightmares. And from that moment on, America to me became Paradise regained, a land overflowing with all the good things of this world, the last refuge of hope for those who carry too heavy a burden of care or grief.

But how account for the miserable conditions in the little town we had just left? Why could not those people feel the way I did? Why could not they set to work instead of wasting their time in idle day-dreams talking to each other about the wonderful things they would have done if only they had been given a chance? They were being given every chance in the New World. What prevented them from getting out of the deep rut into which all of them seemed to have fallen?

De Vries, when I told him of the wonderful revelations that had come to me since I had turned my back upon civilization, did not share my views. "No," he said, "a few exceptional people, who bring something to this wilderness, who can fill the empty void of our forests with the product of their own imagination, are able to find contentment in leading just the sort of life we lead here. But these poor devils in Nieuw Amsterdam, what could you expect of them? When they are alone, they can hear their poor brains rattle. When it gets dark, they feel the touch of the werewolf's hairy snout, for that is all they learned as a child, that the night is filled with werewolves and ogres, and sly black devils who choke innocent wanderers. Of course, if they were made of sterner stuff, and eager to work themselves out of their own class, they would trek further into the wilderness, werewolf or no werewolf. But most of them are too lazy, too indolent or just too dull. Somehow or other they manage to get by and not quite starve to death. And if things go too badly with them, there is always the Company, which will rather spend a few guilders on charity than run the risk of a costly riot for bread."

"But why," I asked, "don't you get the better sort of immigrants?"

"Because we can't," de Vries replied, "because the Company won't let us. Those poor fossils in Amsterdam just simply can't get away from that word 'India' in their charter. India to them means riches—gold, silver, rubies, spices, plunder of all sorts. That is what India meant to Columbus almost two and a half centuries ago. That is what India means to most people to-day. But this is not the India where you can rob the peaceful little brown man of his belongings. This is America, where you have to work with your own hands or starve. But no, the Gentlemen Nineteen, who have never been here, and will never come here either, continue to prattle about their 'Indian domains.' To be sure, they add the word 'West' so as to differentiate their holdings from those of the 'East' India Company. But at heart, they continue to dream of easy riches. That is why they won't allow free immigration. That is why they stick to their absurd monopoly in beaver skins, when every child knows that the beaver is fast going the way of the dodo, that soon there won't be a beaver within a hundred miles from the sea-board.

"Don't think that we, who live over here, don't know all this. There are at least two dozen land-owners in the colony who feel exactly the way I do. And they write letters to the Directors, lots of letters and petitions and even printed pamphlets once in a while. But no, the Directors know best. Or they answer that there aren't enough people in the Republic willing to go so far away from home. All right, we tell them, if you can't find Hollanders, send us Germans. There are whole parts of Germany that are no longer fit for a wolf or a hyena to live in. First the troops of the Emperor came and stole everything. Then the Swedes came and stole the rest and carted it off to Stockholm. Then the Bohemians came, then the Haiduks came, God knows how all those people are called who now for well-nigh twenty-five years have been living at the expense of the poor Teutons. Those who have survived this system of progressive murder are men and women of exceptional character. They could do wonders over here. They would need a little assistance at first, but then they would begin to dig and cut and saw and in less than a single generation, half of all this territory would be converted into fertile farms. Given two generations and a fairly decent form of government and all these foreigners would be good Dutchmen. We would have a second Holland over here, to console and support the mother-country in her old age."

"And now?"

"Now? Why, the problem is so simple that any child can predict what is going to happen. The English are to the north of us and to the south of us. There is trouble brewing in England. Most likely there will be civil war. No matter who wins, the losing party will escape to the New World. If the King wins, as he appears to be doing at the present moment, thousands of people will go to Plymouth and to the region around the North Sea and Boston will outgrow Nieuw Amsterdam so fast that it will be almost funny. If the church people win (as they may do after a little while, seeing that they seem to be most dreadfully in earnest this time) then other thousands will come to Virginia to plant tobacco. In either case, we shall be the losers."

"We might be able to hold our own!"

"Hold our own with five thousand people who are in the pay of the

Company and have nothing much to lose by a change of government against fifty thousand who have come to this distant part of the world to start a new career? Doctor, use your reason! what chance would we have?"

And the good captain was right. We would not have a chance in the world!

Chapter 33

WE TRY TO SAVE A WOMAN WHO HAS BEEN CAST INTO THE WILDERNESS BY HER NEIGHBORS FROM THE NORTH AND FAIL

Soon after I had settled down in Vriesendael, Governor Kieft was recalled. His successor was already on the premises, a stern-faced old man with a wooden leg, a reputation for honesty and obstinacy and of such haughty bearing in his dealings with the colonists that one would have had to go to distant Moscow to find his counterpart.

I met His Excellency a month after his arrival. He was gracious enough and I suspect that before he left, My Lord Andries had sent for him and had dropped him a discreet hint about my mission. For although he never asked me any questions, he seemed to be fully informed about my plans and projects, but provided I did not interfere with the business of the Company, he let me feel that he would leave me strictly alone and that was really all I wanted.

The financial trouble too was successfully solved. His Excellency expressed his regrets that he was not able to pay me the entire sum at once. "But it would be dangerous anyway to carry such a vast sum around," he remarked, scratching the floor with his wooden leg, as he was in the habit of doing while talking to one of his subordinates. "Let us pay you a hundred florins a month. That surely will take care of your needs and see you through until you return."

Having made this arrangement, I began to prepare for a series of trips which should take me from one end of the colony to the other. Some of those voyages would be very difficult and very costly. I knew this after my first experience with winter travel. I was still at Vriesendael consulting maps and trying to persuade a dozen of the natives to accompany me, when word came to us of a disturbance among the Indians of the sound which separated the Lange Eiland from the main land. Captain de Vries was worried.

"That part of the country is very sparsely populated," he explained to me. "But about a half a dozen years ago, there was a violent religious quarrel in Massachusetts. There is a dominie over there by the name of Cotton who has been trying to turn Boston into a second Geneva. He and his followers mean to rule the city after their own sweet will and those who do not agree with them are urged to move away. Moving away very often means starving to death or being murdered by some of the natives. About four years ago, an English woman who had been foolish enough to start a fight with this man Cotton was expelled from the flock and came to live within our jurisdiction. Last night I heard in a

REMBRANDT'S MOTHER

REMBRANDT'S FATHER

roundabout sort of way that she was in trouble, that the natives meant to kill her. I shall go see whether I can be of any help to her. If you care to come, I shall be glad to have you, but you may never come back. It is a risky business as few white men have ever been where we shall be going."

I accepted the invitation with alacrity and early in December de Vries and I departed, accompanied by half a dozen natives who were friends of the captain. Bernardo stayed behind. His lungs had never been very strong and I thought it better that he should not expose himself needlessly to the cold winds that were beginning to blow out of the west and that cut through one's clothes like a knife and a very sharp knife at that.

Our voyage, by the way, proved a complete failure. We arrived on the spot about four months too late, as we found out when we reached the ruins of the houses where Mrs. Hutchinson and her disciples had been butchered by the Indians. Why they had been so brutally hacked to pieces we were never able to find out. The natives who lived in that neighborhood seemed harmless enough. We tried to get some explanation of their strang conduct but they were very vague when it came to details. No, they themselves had not taken part in the massacre. No, they did not know who had done so. Yes, they suspected that it was done by a tribe that had come from the north, but they could not tell, they did not know, they had been away fishing when it happened. When we returned, we were as wise as we had been before. De Vries firmly believed that it had been the work of a few renegade Indians from the north hired by the New Englanders for this special purpose.

"A man like Cotton is capable of anything when his ambition is hurt," he explained. "I hear that they rang the church bells when the good news of the massacre reached Boston. A creature like that has only one desire, to dominate his neighbors. Let anybody interfere with his plans and he will stop short at nothing, not even murder."

I was in no position to offer an opinion but I learned that the New World resembled the old one in only too many ways and I decided to proceed carefully. I spent the entire winter at Vriesendael and by the beginning of April, when it was possible to ford the countless little rivers of this part of the colony, I had everything ready for my voyage into the interior.

During all that time I had only received one letter from home. It was from Jean-Louys. He reported that my small boy was doing very well and apparently had forgotten my existence completely. He told me of certain rumors on the Exchange that the good ship *Princesse* carrying both the former Governor, Willem Kieft, and Dominie Bogardus to the mother-country (they must have made charming traveling companions!) had run on a bank or on a rock in the Bristol Channel which the captain had taken for the English Channel and that both Kieft and Bogardus had been drowned. Finally there was some news about the Rembrandt household.

"I called at the Jodenbreestraat a couple of weeks ago," Jean-Louys wrote. "Rembrandt was as cordial as always, but he seemed preoccupied. He was not exactly rude to me, but he was terribly ill at ease. He reminded me of those friends of my sinful childhood whom one sometimes met when they were dining or drinking in the company of a lady of lenient virtue. They were apt to be very awkward and rather rude for they were very young and had little experience of the big world and its devious ways.

"Of course our friend R. is an absolute child when it comes to the aforementioned ways of the world. He is paying close attention to business and has done some wonderful pictures since you left. He had finished a number of portraits, but I am afraid that very few new orders are coming in. He told me that he was doing well, but he had lost some of that open-heartedness that made him such a delightful companion in the olden days. Il y a quelque chose de louche dans cette maison-là. Don't ask me to explain, I couldn't. But I feel that all is not well with our friend. I wish to God he would get rid of that terrible nurse. I am afraid that she may be at the bottom of it all."

But this news no longer worried me. How infinitely remote all these problems seemed when looked at from that wide distance. I was glad to hear that my boy was well. Very glad indeed. I was sorry that my old friend seemed upset and was falling more and more into the clutches of that harpy. I feared for him, once the tongues of Amsterdam began wagging, once he had been cited publicly for "immorality" by some eager young preacher, anxious to make a name for himself by a bold and open attack upon the "immoralities of those proud and God-forsaking artists." It would mean his end, financially, socially and perhaps artistically. But I was helpless. And I was far away. And furthermore I stood on the point of losing myself into a part of the great American wilderness that to the best of our knowledge had never been visited by any other white man before.

It was not that I was no longer interested.

But I had found a new interest and the name thereof was The Great Unknown.

Chapter 34

BERNARDO AND I SET FORTH TO FIND THE LOST TRIBES AND SOME TERRITORY
FIT FOR AGRICULTURE, AND NEITHER OF US IS VERY SUCCESSFUL

Of my many voyages through the interior of the New Netherlands that kept me in America so much longer than I had planned, I am not at liberty to speak at the present moment. Those adventures have all been set down with great care in the diary I kept which together with my final report I surrendered to My Lord Andries upon my return to Holland. And since servants are sometimes curious and I don't know into whose hands these recollections will fall after my death, I do not think that I ought to repeat them here.

Nor shall I waste much time upon the interesting subject which had been my special hobby since I concluded my studies in Montpellier. The meager results of my investigations I laid down in my little book on the "Art of Medicine Among the American Indians." From that angle, the whole expedition was a mere waste of time and money. For the Indians, although possessing fair skill in the use of certain herbs, were just as ignorant about anesthetics as we ourselves are.

Quite frequently I heard of some wonderful medicine man who set broken bones or removed arrow heads without causing his patients any pain. But when at last I ran him down (often after a search which lasted two or three months) I invariably discovered that the reports of his performance had been greatly exaggerated and that either he used some sort of hypnotic influence (which worked well enough with these simple-minded natives) or that he followed the same methods we employ at home and filled the poor sufferer with such vast quantities of gin and rum that not infrequently they died of a stupor brought about by alcoholic poisoning, when they would have lived had they been kept perfectly sober.

No, from a purely practical point of view, this voyage was not a success. The only person who benefited from it was I myself. When finally I returned home, many of my friends used to pity me. "Eight years in a howling wilderness among painted savages. Good God! what a waste of time!" was a remark I not infrequently heard. But that was hardly true. I realize of course that I was not a second Marco Polo. I did not come home with a few million guilders' worth of diamonds and rubies, sewn in the seams of my clothes. Nor could I, even if I tried, astonish the world with stories about golden-roofed palaces and imperial crowns made out of one single piece of lapis lazuli. Outside of the few little brick houses in Nieuw Amsterdam, I never saw anything much more inspiring than a tent made out of cow-hide and made out of very dirty cow-hide at that. Nor can I truthfully say that lapis lazuli crowns were the fashion those years I spent in the New World. A few of the savages used to stick eagle feathers in their hair but as eagles were rare birds, even in those days, an ordinary barn-yard turkey was not infrequently pressed into service and a dejected-looking capon trying to hide his sadly damaged tail would often bear silent witness to the lack of discrimination with which young braves would often settle the problem of head-gear.

And during the whole of my seven or eight years (one lost all idea of time out there), I saw only one diamond and that belonged to the captain of a slave ship I once found at the mouth of the South River. It was a curious slave ship, or rather, it was a curious captain of a slave ship. The man was incredibly pious. Three times a day he would call together his crew and read to them from the Bible. Neither would he eat meat as long as he was at sea, for fear that such a diet would increase his carnal lusts and make him desire one of the poor black wenches that lay bound and gagged in the hold of the ship.

I tried to argue with him (for in those days I still believed that logic could move mountains or at least people) and prove to him that he could settle his problems overnight by choosing another trade, that no doubt it was a very fine thing on his part not to eat meat during the voyage for the aforementioned purpose, but suppose he give up his nefarious business? The world would be a great deal better for it, and he would like to be guaranteed a steak a day. But no, he could not do it. And why not? Because he had promised a woman in England the largest diamond in the world. Unless he brought her the largest diamond in the world, she would not marry him. And then he excused himself for it was six o'clock and he had to read a chapter from the Bible to his crew. I asked him which one he was reading to them that day and he answered, the first chapter of the Gospel of St. Luke.

Surely our good Lord harbors strange customers on his little planet. I had always known this. And I had always more or less rebelled against this arrangement. What the New World did for me was this: it made me accept humanity as God had made it, not as I thought that he ought to have made it or as I would have made it if I had been given the chance. This new attitude of mind was not the result of a sudden conviction. It came to me after two months spent on the flat of my back in a little wooden cabin somewhere in the heart of those endless forests which are to be found all along the western border of our American possessions.

Theoretically of course our colonies in America reach clear across from the Atlantic to the Pacific. But no one, so far as I know, has ever walked from Nieuw Amsterdam to the Spanish settlements in California. Most maps depict the northern half of the American continent as one vast mass of solid land, but this is merely guesswork. With my own eyes I have seen a lake that looked for all the world like part of a sea. The

Indians told me it was a lake and I had to take their word for it, but I would not be the least bit surprised if it were afterwards discovered that it was part of that branch of the Arctic Ocean which Hudson discovered on his last voyage and where he is said to have been murdered by his crew.

But of all the land that lies to the west of the mountains, we still know so little that everything I write down here is based upon speculation rather than upon knowledge. For one thing, I am no explorer. I never learned how to draw maps or how to handle a compass. Yes, I can see when the needle points toward the north and then say with a great deal of conviction, "We are now going due south or east or west." But that is about as far as my knowledge of that useful instrument goes.

My method of traveling was exceedingly simple. My Lord Andries having provided me generously with funds and the treasury of the colony having been sufficiently reorganized by industrious old Stuyvesant to honor my drafts, I was always well provided with cash. By this time, most of the Indians had learned that the funny-looking little round disks with the armored man on horseback were not just mere ornaments to be worn as ear-rings by their squaws, but were valuable talismans in exchange for which the merchants of Nieuw Amsterdam would give them almost anything their hearts desired.

It was rather a nuisance to travel with a big wooden box filled with Holland guilders, and there was a certain risk about it. But this risk I overcame by occasionally practicing my art as a healer. Indian medical methods, contrary to the glorious reports of many of the early discoverers, were primitive in the extreme. The patients were dosed with enormous potions of hideous-looking and -tasting liquids, brewed in great secrecy by professional sorcerers who as a rule were as ignorant as their patients were superstitious. The mortality among the tribes (especially among the children) was appalling. Quite often therefore I was able to pose as a miracle man by performing insignificant little operations which those people regarded as the work of a god. I encouraged this reputation as much as possible for it meant not only safety but a degree of comfort which few travelers had experienced before me. And when I heard that somewhere in the West there lived a number of tribes vastly superior in civilization and political organization to the natives who dwelled along the seaboard, I decided to pay a visit to these regions and see what opportunities they offered to those future wheat growers whom my Lord Andries and his brother hoped to settle in the New World.

As there was a certain degree of danger connected with a trip of this sort, I tried to persuade Bernardo not to accompany me, but he stubbornly refused. "After all," he reasoned, "I too am not entirely a free agent. I was given money for this voyage that I might find the Lost Tribes of Israel. I believe just as little in those Lost Tribes as you do. Ecbatana is the place to look for them, not America. and the girls of Babylon know more about them and why they refused to go back home to Jerusalem, than those in Nieuw Amsterdam.

"All the same, I am not here as a gentleman of leisure, amusing himself hunting rabbits and shooting squirrels. I am here as the emissary of a few pious Jews in Amsterdam who entrusted me with part of their hard-earned florins to perform a certain, well-defined task. The very name, 'The Five Tribes,' attracts me and intrigues me. I would never forgive myself if I did not use this opportunity to visit those long-lost brethren. There are only five of them, according to that French friend of Doctor La Montagne. That means that the other five are lost. Perhaps I will find those later. But for the moment these five will have to answer the purpose and I am going with you."

During the last month, the excellent Bernardo had changed a great deal. He was actually beginning to talk. And sometimes he even smiled. He explained this to me one day when we had walked some distance along the right bank of the North River and stood on the edge of a very high cliff overlooking the valley. He threw both hands up toward the high heavens and shouted: "Space! Endless, unlimited space! Thank God, that I learned the meaning of the word space before I died."

And when I said, "Yes, but you had space of this sort when we sat on the dikes of the Zuyder Zee," he shook his head. "I know," he answered, "but that was not quite the same. There I was like a bird, whom kind people allowed to play in the room. I could pretend that I was at liberty to amuse myself, but the cage was still on the table, waiting for me to return. Here it is different. Here, for the first time in my life, I feel that I am really free. There is no cage except such a cage as I wish to make for myself. I can wander a thousand miles toward the north and a thousand miles toward the south and a thousand miles toward the west and if I were not such a terribly poor sailor, I could sail thousands of miles toward the east and there would be nothing to keep me back.

"This suits some strange primitive instinct that lies buried in the heart of all of us Jews. We were a desert people. Our friends too often forget that. For thousands of years we never went near a city unless we had to. Hunger drove us to the high-walled towns of Egypt and Palestine. Then it was hunger for gold and for ease and for safety and comfort. The city corrupted us. We were not powerful enough to build ourselves another Babylon or Nineveh. We had to content ourselves with a mean little village of mean little tradesmen and narrow-minded priests, which our pride made us call the center of the universe. And there we grew into something that was absolutely contrary to our true inner nature.

"Our early prophets were men who dwelled in space—who worked in space—who thought in terms of space. Their successors looked out of their tiny, barred windows upon the dark court-yards of neighbors who were equally badly off and after a few hundred years of that sort of life, they came to the conclusion that all the world was a prison and in order to make existence bearable they chained the human soul to that philosophy of despair that lies buried within the pages of so many of their holy books. The Talmud, the Torah—I learned them by heart as a child—every line of them a leaden weight fastened to my soul to keep me from soaring too far away from the dungeons into which my people had crept out of their own volition, once they lost the touch of that freedom that had made them the salt of the earth.

"You think I exaggerate. But Moses proclaimed his Holy Law from the top of a mountain, not from a cellar in Jerusalem. Joshua spent his days on the battle-field. David sang his psalms while herding his father's sheep on the mountain-sides of Judea. Samuel took Saul from behind the plow to make him king of the Jews. Jesus was a country boy. He spent his childhood in a hamlet—a mere handful of houses on a hillside of Israel. He preached his sermons out in the open. Eleven of his disciples were fishermen and day-laborers. One came from the big city and his name was Judas.

"I want to join the immortal eleven—sunshine and rain and dirt and mud, honest sunshine and honest rain and honest dirt—working for my daily bread in the sweat of my brow—not counting somebody else's money or learning somebody else's wisdom by heart in a stuffy room where there has not been a ray of light for the last fifteen or fifteen hundred years."

And having delivered himself of this strange outburst, the longest single speech I had ever heard him make, the honest fellow went down to the Breestraat and bought himself a complete outfit, such as was worn by the professional beaver-hunters of the northern country and was as happy as a child that has been given its first grown-up suit of clothes and is going to take its first trip on the Haarlem canal-boat with papa and mamma and half a dozen of his little friends.

We left Nieuw Amsterdam late in August, when the sun was still blazing hot—spent a week at Vriesendael and then struck for the west along a trail that was hardly discernible from an ordinary squirrel's track.

The famous Five Tribes proved to be no myth, but a reality, and at first sight, a very formidable reality. Nor did they show any visible signs of joy at our approach. Instead they promptly surrounded our small party and conducted us politely but quite firmly to a small wooden stockade where they locked us up and left us to our own devices for three entire days and nights. Then some one who looked like a chief and spoke Mohawk came to ask us who we were—where we came from—what we meant to do in their country and finally how we happened to have Mohegan porters.

To this we answered through one of our Indians, who spoke a little Iroquois, that we were peaceful travelers, that one of us was a famous physician, that we came from a country far away across the big water, that we were merely visiting their country on account of the stories we had heard about the wisdom and learning of their medicine-men, and that the Mohegans had accompanied us to help us carry our luggage but would return to their own country as soon as we had had a chance to hire some of the local natives for that purpose.

He then asked who was the doctor. The interpreter pointed to me. The Mohawk looked at me, shook his head as if in some doubt, and went away again.

He returned that evening. Was I really a physician? Yes! Had I ever used a knife, as he had heard the white people could do? Yes! What was my specialty? Had I brought my instruments? Yes! Would I follow him? I would.

One of the Mohegans was permitted to carry my bag and the three of us started. We reached a village that was quite unlike any other Indian village I had ever seen. No one was visible, but from all the tents there came the noise of a low wailing. We went to the center of the village. Our guide withdrew. I took my interpreter with me and entered. The room was sparsely lit by a small fire. An old crone sat in front of it. The Mohegan translated. She was the mother of the head chief. Her son was ill. He was in great pain. He would soon die. Could I cure him? I answered that I would first have to see the patient before I could give her a definite answer. She said that she would take me to the place where he was hidden from fear that evil spirits might discover him and torture him still further. If I could cure him, I would be given freedom to roam through the territory of the Five Nations. If not, all of us would be killed.

This announcement did not tend to make me feel less nervous than I already was, but I followed the old squaw to a corner of the camp where I saw a small wooden house surrounded by a circle of smoldering fires. These fires had been lit to keep the evil spirits away. Inside the house lay a man of perhaps fifty years of age. His face was distorted with pain. His hands were clenched, his lips set tight. Six women, three on each side of him, were singing a low dirge.

I at once suspected an attack of the stone. I made a few inquiries and touched the abdomen. My first guess seemed right. I told the mother that I could cure her son—that he had fallen victim to a Devil who now lived in his entrails in the form of a large pebble—that I would capture this Devil and cut him out, provided they did as I bade them. The old squaw agreed. I kept the two wives, who looked huskiest, and sent the other four away. I told the mother to get me a torch. She went out and shortly afterwards came back with a box of candles which had probably been stolen from some murdered Dutch trader. I sent the mother away and told the interpreter to hold the candle while I made the incision. Meanwhile the two wives were to take hold of the hands of the patient and under no circumstances allow him to arise. I made the incision. I never knew such fortitude. The man hardly winced. I took the stone out with my forceps

(I don't believe in touching any wound with my hands, as my French colleagues do), and I bandaged the wound.

These natives have an incredible power of recuperation and I knew that in two or three days the man would probably be able to walk. I called the old mother back into the tent, told her to send all the wives away and spend the night with her son for fear the Devil might return. She asked me where that Devil was now and I said, "In my pocket. But he is still very lively. During the night, I shall tame him and in the morning I shall give him to you and you can drown him in the lake or burn him in a fire."

Then I went back to the stockade and slept a few hours. In the morning there was such shouting and such beating of drums that I feared for the worst. Undoubtedly the old woman had called in one of the native medicine-men (they always do) and the chief had died. I did not even take the trouble to eat my breakfast, firmly convinced that we all would be executed before noon. By and by the noise increased and a procession came heading our way. We were marched to the village but our baggage was kept behind, another sure sign to me that they meant to kill us.

Well, after an interminable walk, with at least a million wild savages excitedly dancing up and down beside us, we came to the village and there before his mother's tent stood my patient of last night, all dressed in his best leather coat and without a shred of my bandage of the previous evening. He was apparently feeling perfectly well and I now understood why the early explorers had given such glowing accounts of the medical achievements of the Indians. They committed, however, one small error of judgment due to faulty observation. The doctors of the wild men are atrocious, but their patients are perfect. For where else in the world would one find a man who less than twelve hours after being cut for the stone is able to walk home unassisted?

After this miraculous cure, our position of course became most agreeable. We were taken from the stockade and lodged in half a dozen tents in the heart of the village. Even the Mohegans, whom the Mohawks detest, were treated kindly. They were given an elaborate meal and were allowed to return to their country unmolested. And the next day, after I had presented the chief with his erstwhile tenant, had then taken the stone back from him, had placed it on a heavy bowlder and had smashed it with his battle-ax (fortunately it was a very brittle one and the trick worked to perfection), I was told that I could have as many guides and servants as I cared to, yea, that the whole tribe would follow me if necessary. I chose a dozen of the strongest and with them explored the country of the Oneidas and Onondagas in the north and towards the east without finding anything that suited my purpose, and then late in the fall I decided that I would make a dash for the west.

Bernardo was to remain behind and watch over our luggage while I and two guides started for a big river that was the frontier between the land of the Senecas and the Susquehannocks. The Senecas belonged to the Five Nations, but the Susquehannocks did not, and I was warned to keep out of their territory. I also was told that it would be better if I waited until next spring, but we were in the middle of an unusually fine Indian summer and I counted on being back in three or four weeks.

We entered the hunting fields of the Cayugas and one night about a week after we had left, we reached the top of a low hill from which one had a view of a large but melancholy-looking lake. On top of that hill the three of us spent the night. In the morning I decided to cross the lake if my guides could make me a canoe within a reasonable amount of time. They asked whether two days would be too long and I said no, that that would do very nicely.

They set to work and I decided to take a walk. A short distance from the shore there was a high cliff which interested me through its extraordinary shape. When I came nearer I noticed that it was part of the hillside where the soil had been washed away, and then I discovered a narrow gorge made by a river that had dug its way through the soft stone like a knife cutting through cheese. It was a geological formation entirely new to me, and the walk between the steep rugged walls fascinated me. After about ten minutes I came to a waterfall and had to return. But just before I came to where there was a curve in the riverbed, I stopped to give one more look at the scene behind me. For a better view I climbed upon a large bowlder, but no sooner was I on top than I heard a soft rustling sound and saw a tiny black snake hastily leaving a round pile of leaves which the wind had blown together into the hollow on top of the stone.

How it got there I never understood. Nor do I know to this day why it should have thrown me into such a panic, for I had been told over and over again that there were no dangerous snakes in this neighborhood. But such things will happen. From childhood on I had been taught to abhor every creeping thing and the little snake quite instinctively made me jump. I lost my balance, tried to catch myself by jumping for a much smaller stone that was lying near the riverbed, missed it and landed so unfortunately on the rocks below that I broke both my legs.

I knew by the pain that I had broken them. Then I knew nothing more, for I fainted.

How long I lay there, I don't know. When I came to it was quite dark. I saw too shining lights right above my nose. I reached out for a stone and the beast skuttled away. I heard its soft footsteps on the rocks. Then silence and the rush of the water and another fainting spell. But this time when I came to the moon was out. That was at least some consolation. I would not have to die in the dark. The pain continued to be almost unbearable, but there seems to be a limit to pain, just as there is a definite limit to heat or cold. And so I lay and suffered and had one of the most curious and interesting experiences of my whole life.

For now I experienced for the first time what it felt like to die. I had seen plenty of people pass into the other world. By far the greater part of them had been old men and women, broken by illness and too worn out by the hardships of existence to care very much either one way or the other. Death to them meant relief from monotony and hunger and the eternal grind of making both ends meet. There were a few who clung with almost superhuman obstinacy to the last spark of hope and fought death as bitterly as a pheasant mother fighting for its chicks. But most of them went peacefully to sleep like children who have spent the day on the sea-shore and are tired, very tired. And I had often wondered why they showed no greater spirit of rebellion, since life is the only gift of the gods of which we get only one helping, and when that is gone it is gone, and the plate is empty, and the dinner is definitely over. But now I knew.

If it had not been for the excruciating pain in my legs, I would have been really happy. All questions were being answered, all problems were being solved rapidly, quietly and smoothly. Doubt no longer existed in its manifold disturbing and perplexing fashions. At last I knew! For the first time since the day of my birth I was face to face with absolute and stark and inevitable Reality. And it was the most agreeable sensation of which I have any recollection. I was going to die. I was going to sleep. The little spark of intelligence and courage and hope and charity which I had borrowed from the Maker of All Things was about to be restored to the original owner. The few pounds of salt and water of which my mortal body was composed were about to be released and returned to the vast treasure-house of nature from which they had been withdrawn when I saw the light of day.

But these things did not seem to matter. I thought of them remotely and rather gratefully. I would never again see the face of my son. But he was a million miles removed from me at that moment. One way or the other, he would surely find his way in this world. I would never again hear the voice of Jean-Louys, of Bernardo, of Rembrandt, of any of my friends. But I felt that they would understand. They would remember little things I had said and done and to them I would be alive until their own hour had struck.

I had one regret. There were women in this world. I had read that some men had found perfect love. I had not. I had missed something. But my work had brought me many consolations, that had been denied other less fortunate creatures.

The pain was growing less. I was rapidly sliding down into a deep slumber, the sleep of all eternity, and I was content.

The pain was gone. The rock on which I was lying was soft and warm, a pleasant glow was touching my hands and cheeks. Yes, there was the wonderful old grandfather sitting in his chair and looking at me. "It won't hurt, my boy. We all must pass down that road some time. It won't hurt. Just let yourself go—a little more—let yourself go—" The moon would soon be hidden by the clouds, it was getting dark. The chimes of the town-hall were playing the hour—tinkelee tinkelee—tinkelee—bang—bang—bang—bang—bang—a flash of pain more hideous than any I had felt before shot through me—bang—bang—it must be seven o'clock—tinkelee—deedledee—dee—no! it was the half hour—bang—bang—nine o'clock—I was moving—I was lying in the arms of one of my Indian guides—bang—bang—it wasn't the clock that was striking—it was the noise of footsteps—the footsteps of the man that carried me—I was being taken somewhere—they had found me—I was not to die that night—I might not die at all—tinkelee—tinkelee—tinkelee—ting—a light was shining in my eyes—the pain was unbearable—I must die—then darkness and silence—I had fainted once more.

When I woke up the sun was shining. I was lying on a soft leather blanket. The hut smelled of fresh straw. The guide who had carried me was sitting by my side. "Sh," he said, and I closed my eyes and fell asleep once more.

Of what happened during the next few days I have only the haziest recollections, and I am never quite sure whether the things I am writing down are actually part of what I myself remember or whether they are bits of gossip I heard after I had recovered. It seems that my two guides had missed me when they stopped work. It was dark then but somehow or other they were able to follow my tracks and found me. They had carried me to a deserted village from which a small tribe of Cayugas had moved a year or so before. They had found a small wooden house and in this they had made me as comfortable as they could. They knew that I was badly hurt, that I had probably broken both legs, and they were afraid to touch me, for an Indian is always afraid of a sick man.

But they decided to help me in another way. On the evening of the second day I discovered what they had done. One of the two had stayed behind to take care of me if I should need anything. The other one was gone to get help.

On the evening of that second day, when I was fighting off the delirium of fever, I heard him return. He was not alone. A tall, thin man followed him and knelt down by my side. He was the strangest-looking individual I had ever seen. At first sight I took him for a native. A long leather coat, leather breeches and Indian shoes, long, unkempt and pitch-black hair hanging well down over his shoulders and an enormous knife stuck in his belt. But underneath these heavy outer garments he wore something that looked very much like a cassock, and his face was that of a white man.

I thought that he was a half-breed, and he looked so ferocious that my first impression was, "Why, here is one of the Cayugas who owns this village. He has come back to claim his home." And then I noticed that the fellow wore a heavy silver cross around his neck and I said, "Are you a priest?" and he answered, "Yes, my son, but to-night I am a bone-setter. First I shall pray for you and then I shall fix your legs. Don't mind the praying for you shall need it, once I get busy with those lower extremities." And he actually knelt by the side of my bed and reeled off a Latin prayer of which I did not understand one word, and then he got up and removed his coat and rolled up the sleeves of his cassock and beckoning to the two guides, he said, "Hold his arms," and once more he knelt by my side and got busy.

As those who have ever broken an arm or a leg well know, even the cleanest break makes an exceedingly painful operation. But two broken legs that have lain neglected for almost three days—no, I had better not speak about it. But all through my agony there ran a sort of professional pride in the dexterity with which this unknown man worked. Evidently he knew a good deal about surgery. He made no false movement. If I had to be in hell, he meant to keep me there as short a time as possible.

And I was lying flat on my back again, almost dead from exhaustion, and I was sleeping and I was slowly coming back to life, to find the cabin filled with smoke and one of the two Indians busy making a fire, and outside there was a terrific noise, a whistling, hissing noise, and the walls of the little wooden hut were leaning like the sides of a ship in a storm and I asked the Indian what had happened and he told me it was one of those blizzards which made this part of the country so exceptionally dangerous in winter and that it had come much earlier than they had expected and that it probably would last three or four days and that I must lie very still and not say a word and go back to sleep.

And when I woke up again the hissing, whistling sound was just as strong as ever, but the fire was burning brightly and suddenly I realized that I was going to recover. It might take me six weeks or two months, but I was going to recover and I had gone through the experience of dying for nothing and now I would have that experience twice, and truly, few people were ever so favored. And then my unknown doctor friend came in with his arms full of dry leaves (where he had found them, God only knows) and the Indians made me a new bed and then roasted a wild turkey which one of them had shot that morning, and soon that hut on the shores of that lake which did not even bear a name was as full of comfort and warmth and good cheer as the cabin of the Haarlem canal-boat on Saint Nicholas eve.

The guide, however, had been right. The blizzard continued for three whole days and nights and all that time I lay quietly in my corner while the others kept the fire going—went out for a couple of hours—returned with pheasants and woodcocks and occasionally with a few berries, and took care of me as if I had been their long lost brother. But on the morning of the fourth day, a Saturday, the white man did not appear for breakfast and when I asked whether he was not coming, the older one of the Mohawks said, "No, he is gone." And when I expressed some surprise that he should have left without giving me the opportunity to thank him for all he had done, he answered, "He will come back in two days." And true enough, on Monday towards the evening, the stranger returned and walked into our hut as unconcernedly as if he had gone just around the corner to get some fire wood. And when I said with a feeble attempt at a joke, "You could not keep away from home so long, I suppose," he replied, "That is right. I had to go back to my people and read mass and baptize two children, but now I shall stay with you for another five days."

Afterwards I discovered that "my people" lived some twenty miles away from where we were. In order to read mass to his people and at the same time take care of his white brother, this strange creature walked twenty miles, through three feet of snow, twice a week, and spent the rest of the time either helping the Indians with their traps, or bringing in fire wood or entertaining me with stories of his travels that made the wanderings of Marco Polo seem like an afternoon's promenade through the woods between Amsterdam and Naarden. He had been in the New World exactly twenty-five years. He had come to Quebec when he was twenty and had just been ordained. He had been trained in Louvain and according to all I know of that university (the worst stronghold of the worst form of reactionary feeling in Europe at the time of which I am speaking) he ought to have been a self-righteous doctrinary who would regard the death of a heretic as a welcome diversion in the monotony of his deadly missionary existence. But he explained this to me himself.

"It is the wilderness," he said, "that has done this to me. I suppose I am still a good Catholic. I try to be a faithful son of our holy church, but I am afraid that something has happened to me since I came here that has made me a very different man from the rigid-minded boy who left Quebec in 1622. Last year they sent some one from Canada to try and find me and tell me that I was entitled to a fourteen months' holiday and could go home for a rest. But I thought that I had better not return to civilization. My Bishop would lift his eyebrows and say, 'Cha! cha! a few years in a big city would do you no harm,' and very likely he would suggest that I be called to Bordeaux or Lyon or even Paris to give me a rest from my arduous labors, a sort of reward for faithful service, a reward that would last me the rest of my days, and some other man would be sent out here in place of myself and all the work I have done here would go to ruin in less than a fortnight and my dear Cayugas would be what they were when I came here and I would have lost my ears for nothing."

"Lost your ears?" I asked.

"Yes," he said, "that is why I wear my hair à l'Indienne. It happened the first year I was here. I had settled down in a village on the second one of the Big Lakes. Right among the Eries. The Eries were at war with the Senecas. You know how those Indian wars are. They begin about some trifle, a stolen halter or a nasty look from one chief to another. They flame up suddenly like a prairie fire and before you can say, 'My children, what is it all about?' a hundred villages have been wiped out. This time the Eries happened to win. The rumor spread among the Five Nations that the Eries were being helped by a great white sorcerer. They decided to get hold of that sorcerer to break the power of the lake-dwellers. I went about my business as if I did not know that there was a war. One night, going to visit a village at a little distance from the shore, I was waylaid by a bunch of Cayugas who had come to the assistance of the Senecas. They tied me to a stake in the regular Indian fashion and were going to carve me slowly to pieces. They began with my ears. It was much less painful than you would imagine. Just then the Eries, who did not want to lose their miracle man, rushed the village, killed a dozen or so of the Cayugas and took the others prisoner. It was their turn to be tied to a number of trees and listen to the most impassioned among the Erie warriors tell them what they were going to do to them before they killed them. To begin with, their ears were to come off. I had lost mine, now they were to lose theirs. As a compliment to me, you understand. I was pretty weak from the loss of blood, but I got up (I spoke Erie fluently) and told them that they were fools and knaves and deserved to be punished by God for their wanton cruelty, and I took the knife which they were sharpening for the ear-operations and cut the ropes with which the prisoners had been bound and gagged and told them that they were free. A terribly risky thing to do, but it worked and the Eries and the Cayugas made peace.

"Well, they heard about this in Quebec and the Bishop was not pleased. We Jesuits are always suspected of being a little too independent. Some one traveled all the way from Quebec to the lake to remonstrate with me and tell me that I ought not to have acted quite so independently. If the Eries and the Nations meant to destroy each other (a policy which was not regarded with disfavor in the capital) it was their good right to do so and I should not interfere. I should 'refer' everything to headquarters. That was the express will and desire of His Highness, the Governor General.

"I asked the Episcopal emissary whether I ought to have asked the permission of His Grace to have my ears cut off and he answered that I knew perfectly well what he meant and that I had better look for some other field of activity, for that my usefulness among the Eries had come to an end. I took the hint and went to the land of the Cayugas. They were surprised to see me. They suffered from a bad conscience and they told me so and said that they were afraid that I had only come to punish them. But I told them frankly that I had chosen their land as my place of residence because they were terribly savage, had no conception of decency or kindness or charity and that I had come to teach them those virtues.

"I have now been among them for fifteen years. I have baptized some nine thousand men, women and children during that period. I have learned a little medicine (as you may remember to your horror), I have built a sort of hospital and a school where I teach the girls how to take better care of their children, a strange job for a man in my position, and I have enticed a few young priests away from the fleshpots of Quebec and Montreal (it is a new city, but full of worldliness they tell me), and I have founded a small republic of kindliness right here in the heart of the great American wilderness. But I am grateful that the voyage to Canada is so difficult, for if my dear Bishop should ever deign to visit me, I fear that that would be the last of my noble experiment, where Christ resembles an Indian chief and God himself bears a close likeness to the Great Spirit whom the natives have worshiped since the beginning of time."

I saw the "noble experiment" a few weeks later, as soon as I could be transported. It was a cold voyage, but I suffered no harm and I spent three very happy months with Father Ambrosius, for he was a native of Grasse in southern France, where his father was a honey-merchant and he himself had spent his childhood among the bees and had even taken the name of that stern Milanese bishop who was also the patron saint of the Apiarian guild.

I could not yet walk a great deal, but the weather was very bad and I did not miss much. During the day I spent my time composing a French-Dutch-Cayugan dictionary, more to have something to do than from any desire to turn philologist. But when evening came, the two of us would sit in front of the large open fire, which the grateful parishioners always kept well supplied with fuel, and we would talk. And this was a novel and exceedingly pleasant experience to me, because now for the first time in my life I was face to face with a Christian whom I could not only admire but like, a fine man, even a noble man, a cheerful man of infinite good humor, a patient and humble man who went quietly ahead and did as much good as he could without spending any vain regrets upon the harm his neighbors were supposed to be doing to him. And one evening we had it out in a session that lasted till early dawn.

It began with a confession-of-sins on my part. I told him frankly that I had such an intense dislike for the usual professional Christians that it was difficult for me to be even commonly decent to them. Wherever and whenever I had met them I had found them mean and intolerant and suspicious and of a self-righteous arrogance which made it practically impossible for an ordinary human being to associate with them and keep his temper or self-respect.

"But," the Father asked, "are you quite fair? Don't you mix up two things that are entirely different? Remember even in the days of the Emperor Titus, all Jews were not alike. There were the Pharisees and the Sadducees and there were those who left father and mother and glory and riches to follow a certain carpenter from Nazareth. And what have you ever seen of the latter?"

I confessed that I had run across very few of these, and then Father

Ambrosius made the casual remark that was to change my entire point of view. "Life," he said, "is not real. It is based upon fairy tales. It all depends upon the story we prefer."

It was a somewhat cryptic utterance. I said, "Continue. I vaguely think that I know what you are driving at, but I am not sure." And he went on. "You see, most people think of life in terms of hungry people chasing little rabbits and catching them and killing them and eating them up and they make a great ado about our 'daily bread,' as if our daily bread were the most important thing in the world. It is important, of course. We have got to eat if we want to live, but that is only part of existence. Even these poor, benighted savages are not out there in the fields catching rabbits all day long. Sometimes they catch so many that they have food enough for a fortnight. That means thirteen days of leisure. Then, not being upset by the fear of an empty stomach, they can dwell in the realm of the imagination—of that sphere which some people have called 'other worldliness.' Then they compose their fairy stories or they talk about the fairy stories of their ancestors or they embellish the ancestral fairy story with a few details of their own, according to the temper of the times and the change in their form of living. You see, it is really very simple. Their daily bread keeps their bodies alive, but their souls would die without that daily ration of fairy stories."

That seemed a pretty radical speech on the part of a priest and I gave expression to my astonishment by a question. "But surely," I asked him, "you are not going to claim that your religion, your church, all this"—and I waved my hand towards the wall which was covered with crude pictures of saints made by one of the Cayuga chiefs who had a bent for painting—"surely, you don't mean to say that this is merely your particular fairy story?"

"Yes," he answered quite casually. "Of course I would not confess this to my Bishop, and that is one of the reasons why I am just as well satisfied if His Grace remains quietly in his palace in Quebec and lets me stay here. But, yes, this is my fairy tale. It consists of three words, 'Love one another.' Three words spoken on a barren hillside of that brutal land called Judea. The fairy story part—the incredible part, is this, that they were ever uttered at all—that some one in this world—in this world of greed and lust and hatred and cruelty, had the unbelievable courage to utter them.

"That is my fairy story, that some one had the unbelievable courage to utter them.

"But, of course, that isn't enough for most people. It is a little too simple. Too spiritual, perhaps. They don't want to know what Jesus said. They want to know what he wore, how he looked, how he had brushed his hair that morning. That is their fairy story, a tale of outward and inconsequential details. But they are entitled to it if it pleases their fancy and satisfies their curiosity. They are entitled to it and should not be interfered with, no matter how absurd their ideas may appear to us who believe ourselves to be living on a somewhat higher intellectual plane. And what I say of my fellow-Christians I would maintain about all people . . ."

"The heathen included?" I interrupted.

"The heathen included, and even those who call themselves 'agnostics.' For their fairy story tells them that there isn't any fairy story at all and that in itself is the strangest fairy story of all."

I shook my head and said only one word, "Quebec!"

"You are quite right," Father Ambrosius continued. "If His Grace knew about this, shall I say 'slight variation' upon the somewhat more rigid articles of faith which are read every day in his cathedral (these slight variations on his own fairy tale, in the terms in which I see the world), there would be trouble. Or no. His Grace is much too subtle a diplomat to cause trouble. I would be promoted to some higher post in the interior of France, where they would let me lead the singing on Sunday, or I would be called to the capital to instruct the sons and daughters of our nobility in the rudiments of the French language. But never again would I be allowed to utter a single syllable that had to do with a religious subject and I would die a most respectable and peaceful death, whereas now I shall probably try to interfere in the next war with the Hurons and be slowly roasted to death over one of their famous greenwood fires and that will be the end.

"But in the meantime I am having a glorious time for I am successful. My method has proved the right one, the only possible one, at least in this part of the world.

"Can you see what chance I would have if I had come here and had said, 'My dear children of the forest, everything you believe and hold true and sacred is just so much hocus-pocus. I despise it, and to show you the depth of my contempt I shall spit upon your gods, I shall curse them and I shall take a hammer and shall destroy them.

"Not a person would have listened to me. Or if perchance they had taken the trouble to listen, they would have tied me to a tree and would have left me to the mercy of their dogs. They are a pretty savage lot, even to-day. Don't ask me what they were like twenty years ago.

"No! that system never would have worked. I had to go about my business in a very different way, if I wanted to have them listen to me. And so I came here one day accompanied by an old Canadian trapper who knew this region and who had married a Cayuga woman, way back in the early days of Champlain and who had been with him when he started on his famous voyage to China and ended in Lake Huron.

"It was a dangerous trip, let me assure you. My guide spoke the dialect fluently and he could claim relationship with one of the chiefs who lived on the next lake. Otherwise we probably would have been killed right away.

"Champlain was a great leader, a wise man in many ways, but like so many of our race, he must play a part, wherever he was—must pose a little before the crowd—must show everybody what a fine fellow a Frenchman could be. I don't blame him. Those pious people who pride themselves upon the fact that they never 'show off' usually have very little to show. But upon occasion that attitude can be a nuisance and sometimes it becomes a downright danger.

"When the Hurons and the Five Nations tried to slaughter each other, Champlain would have done well to leave them alone. He could then have concluded a treaty with the victors and in that way he would have strengthened our position along the Saint Lawrence. I am not now talking as a minister of the Gospel. I am talking plain, ordinary common sense from the point of view of an explorer or a statesman or a colonial governor—of some one, in short, who wants to found a colony in the heart of a wilderness filled with painted savages. But, no, Champlain must take his little blunderbuss and when the Hurons and the Nations have their little quarrel, he must join the fray and do a little shooting of his own, and having come from the North, he can't help but be on the side of the Hurons and his bullets kill a couple of the braves who are leading the armies of the Nations and thereafter, of course, these good people hated us like poison or like traitors (very much the same in my opinion) and any Frenchman who went to the southern banks of the Saint Lawrence did so at the risk of his own life.

"I was very young in those days and terribly interested in my work. I had not the slightest leaning toward martyrdom. But it never entered into my head that I could be killed. Of course I was not going to be killed! I was so absolutely convinced that no harm would come to me that I refused to take a gun. Finally I let myself be persuaded to take a small hunting rifle but I decided that I would not use it when I got near to a native village. Just to show them how well I meant.

"The old trapper and I crossed Lake Champlain and went west. First through the land of the Oneidas, where we met no one (they had suffered terribly from the smallpox during the last four years) and then we cut through part of the mountains that belonged to the Mohawks and finally we reached the dreaded region of the Cayugas. After about ten days we struck the first settlement. The trapper explained who he was and how his wife had died the year before and how he was now on his way to see her relatives and bring them some trinkets she had left and some money. That sounded plausible enough and they believed it.

"But what was I doing there? Was I a spy sent by the French who had turned against them when they were fighting the Hurons and the Algonquins? I reassured them. I was a Frenchman, but I was merely a 'learned man,' a sort of 'medicine man' who went through the world listening to the stories the different nations could tell me about their gods. Some of these were quite interesting and some of them were not quite so interesting, but I had heard that the Cayugas and Senecas had a God that was more powerful than those of any other race on earth.

"Well, that flattered their pride and while my Canadian trapper was paying a visit to his ex-relatives-in-law, I sat and listened to the Old Men from one village after another while they told me about their Great Spirit and their Evil Spirit and of the mysterious magic powers, the so-called 'secret soul' that lay buried in every man and in every cloud and in every blade of grass and in every grasshopper and even in the arrows which they shot at their enemies.

"When I had listened for almost six months and knew all there was to be learned, I told them how tremendously interested I had been in what they had told me and then I appealed to their sense of fair play (which as a rule is very strongly developed among those fighting races, much more strongly than among the peaceful tribes) and I said, 'Now you have told me your story of how the world was created and who rules it and what the evil spirits try to do to us to make us unhappy, and now you ought to listen to my story,' and they answered that that was right and as it should be, and so I built myself a small altar out in the open, near the shore of the lake underneath a very large tree, as fine a setting for the house of our Lord as one could hope to find on either land or sea.

"Then I began to tell them very slowly and very gradually (and I hope rather tactfully) what my story was and why I thought it better than theirs. And by the grace of God and through the mercy of His saints, I was successful. I was able to show these poor children of darkness the way to the Light. And to-day nine of the frontier villages that belong to this tribe have accepted my story. They have given up the way of the heathen and have confessed themselves Christians. Truly, Heaven has blessed me far beyond my merits."

Here Father Ambrosius stopped talking and he looked at me as if he expected me to give him an answer. But I could say nothing. All my life long I had heard of the faith that moved mountains and here I suddenly stood in the presence of the greatest of all miracles, the miracle of absolute and unquestioning simplicity of heart.

It was a strange experience, and I was still sitting in silence when Father Ambrosius got up and went to his bedroom to get his moccasins and his coat.

"I am sorry that I shall have to leave you for a little while," he said, "but things are not well in the village. The people seem restless. They are in fear of something and I don't know what. I think that I have taught them to look upon life in a more reasonable and intelligent way. But such things take time. Once in a while their old devils whom I chased away some fifteen years ago try to come back and then I have to fight hard to hold my own. This seems to be one of those occasions. What has happened this time is still a mystery to me, but I shall probably know in another two or three weeks. Meanwhile it won't do any harm if I am seen about the village a little more than usual. It gives my children a feeling of confidence. 'Behold,' they say, 'the Father is about watching over us and all is well.' Don't wait for me. Don't sit up for me. It may take me a couple of hours. Go to bed and happy dreams!"

And he left me and I hobbled to my couch and the room was filled with a strange light and when I looked out of the window, behold! the sky was a bright red, and at first I thought that it must be the northern lights, which had been particularly brilliant the last few days. But then I noticed that the glow came from the west and with a shock I realized what had happened. Some one had set fire to a village on the other side of the lake.

Chapter 35

A FAIRY TALE IN THE WILDERNESS AND WHAT BECAME OF IT

Poor Father Ambrosius! The next two weeks were the most miserable of his whole life. Everything he had worked for came tumbling down with a crash and a smoldering ruin was all that remained of his efforts of the last twenty years.

I did not see the end. I only saw the beginning, and that was sad enough. For this was not merely a physical defeat of a man pitched against a group of enemies, it was the moral debacle of a fine and noble and courageous soul, beaten by the innate stupidity of nature-in-the-raw.

The good Father thought that his "fairy tale" had triumphed. He had filled the dreadful universe of these naked savages with the visions of his paradise—his wondrous heaven populated with beautiful angels and long-bearded beneficent saints—a realm of endless golden streets and infinite shining righteousness—the future home of all good little children willing to share his dream. And they had said, "Yea, verily, great Master," and they had come to hear him say mass and they had sent their children to listen to the wondrous chronicles of the Holy Family of Nazareth and their women had stayed after service to weep over the fate of one who had been utterly without blemish and yet had taken upon himself the agonizing task of shouldering this world's sins. And invariably when he had asked them whether they regretted having given up a belief in the gods of their fathers, they had answered him that nothing on earth could make them return to the worship of those false witnesses and he had been happy and he had persuaded himself that they spoke the truth.

But alas and alack! Without a single word of warning the old gods of the forest had suddenly reappeared from the mountain fastnesses wherein they had been hiding these many years. They had come proud and haughty as exiled princes who claim what is theirs by right of birth and their trembling subjects had welcomed them with open arms. Not because they loved them better than their new rulers. By no means. These ancient task-masters of their souls were dreadful tyrants. But they were flesh and blood of their own flesh and blood. They knew them and understood them, even though they hated and despised them. And when they stood once more outside the village-gate, waving the familiar old banners that had been handed down from father to son for thousands and thousands of generations, the humble subjects were as little birds before the gaze of the snake. They wavered. They grew pale. They fell upon their knees. They prostrated themselves in the dust of the road and whispered, "Yes, ye great and glorious Majesties, we thy servants welcome thee with open hearts and open arms," and everything was as it had been since the beginning of time and the work of Father Ambrosius disappeared as the smoke of one's fire on the shores of a stormy sea.

And all that because two little boys had tried to shoot the same wild turkey at the same moment and had had a quarrel as to who had seen him first.

As far as we could make out, this is what had happened. Those so-called Indian countries are not countries in our sense of the word. The Indians live by hunting. Here and there a tribe that is a little more civilized than the others will try its hand at agriculture or to be more precise, the Indian men will allow their women to try their hand at raising corn and grain, for the average Indian male is a noble grand-seigneur, brave as a lion when he is on the war-path, but lazy as the sloth when he is peacefully residing at home. Those tribes therefore need enormous tracts of land to keep themselves provided with the necessary number of deer and rabbits and bears that are needed for their daily support. And these hunting fields are not clearly defined tracts of land for there are no frontiers as we know them in Europe, but the Indian has a great respect for tradition and as a rule he respects the domain that is supposed to belong to his neighbor with scrupulous care. But once in a while these pieces of land overlap each other and then there is always a chance for trouble. And that is what had occurred in this case.

It seems that several centuries before the Eries, who now lived further westward, had occupied this part of the continent. But although they spent the greater part of each year on the shores of one of those big lakes that exist in the West and that many hold to be part of the Arctic Sea or even the Pacific Ocean, they still retained a vague hold upon certain rivers and brooks that ran through the land of the Cayugas and every year a number of Eries would walk all the way from their own country to that of the Cayugas (for these savages have never learned the use of the wheel and must carry everything on their own backs if they want to go anywhere) to spend a few weeks hunting turkeys and other small birds within the grounds that hundreds of years before had belonged to their ancestors.

It was a very unpractical arrangement, but the Cayugas respected the claims of the Eries because they had always done so, which in their language means a number of years all the way from twenty-five to a hundred. For when an Indian has once done something "always" he will continue to do so until the end of eternity.

This particular winter the Eries seemed to have come east a little earlier than usual. Perhaps there was some other reason for their unexpected appearance. There had been vague rumors of trouble between the Eries and those Hurons who lived on the other side of the big lake and it seemed that the Eries had suffered a severe defeat and that they were trying to get away before the coming of spring allowed the Hurons to descend upon them in full force.

But I only heard about this much later when I was safely back in Nieuw Amsterdam and besides, it made very little difference how and why the Eries had come at such an early date. They were there and that was enough or in this case, too much. For one morning an Erie boy of about fourteen had gone forth turkey hunting and a Cayuga boy of the same age had started upon the same errand and by a most unfortunate combination of circumstances, the two had seen the same turkey at the same moment. Each one of them had shot his arrow and both arrows had hit the mark. The turkey was dead and the boys had rushed eagerly forward to get hold of their prey. And then they had seen each other. And of course they had both grabbed at the dead bird and then one had said, "It is mine, I saw it first." And the other one had answered, "No, it is mine. I saw it first."

And then they had dared each other to touch it and then they had fought, but being of equal height and weight, the struggle had lasted quite a long time and then one of them had lost his temper and he had pulled his knife and stabbed the other boy in the back and then he had taken fright and had run away, leaving the corpse out in the open.

But in his excitement he had forgotten his knife, and therefore a small band of Cayugas, also looking for turkeys in that neighborhood and finding the body, had known that it had been an Erie who had committed this murder and a little later, meeting two peaceful Erie women going to a brook to do their washing, they had set upon them and had killed them, for such was the law of the tribe, or rather, such had been the law of the tribe until Father Ambrosius had tried to replace this dreadful code of an eye for an eye by the more merciful doctrine of a forgiveness which had first been promulgated on a hillside in distant Palestine.

But now they had smelled blood and everything they had learned during the last twenty years had been forgotten. They were Cayuga warriors and one of their clan had been killed without provocation. Such an action demanded revenge. And with a fell cry of joy, the ancient gods came rushing forth from their hiding places and joined in the fray. Before another week had passed, at least two dozen people had been killed on both sides. And when Father Ambrosius tried to remonstrate with his beloved children about the folly of such a course, they would listen patiently enough, but they would not let themselves be convinced. "Your God, who is now also our God, is a lover of peace! But the god of our enemies is a lover of war! Just now, he is stronger than your God and we must turn to our old gods to help us, lest we all perish."

They were genuinely sorry that all this had happened, but it had happened and they did not intend to accept defeat without putting up a terrific fight. The God of Father Ambrosius told them to turn the other cheek. They were very sorry but no Cuyaga had ever turned the other cheek unless in the game of love. They were more than sorry, they were humbly apologetic. But for the moment there was only one thing for them to do and they meant to do it, and every night they would leave their villages and go murdering and pillaging among the villages of the Eries and every night the Eries would go murdering and pillaging among the villages of the Cayugas and a vast number of people were killed and an enormous amount of material damage was done and nothing was ever decided, but gradually the Eries, who had got heavy reënforcements from the West, began to be more and more aggressive and the red glow that had lighted up the sky the night before was the first of the Cayuga settlements that had gone up in flames.

The question was, When would we ourselves be attacked? If it had been a few months later, the other four nations would undoubtedly have come to our support, but it had been a very severe winter and the roads were so thickly covered with snow that our messengers would need at least two weeks to reach the camps of the Oneidas and the Onondagas and in the meantime, we knew that we were left entirely to our own devices.

An effort was made to surround our village with a wooden palisade, but the ground was frozen so hard that it was very slow work and only a few yards were done when we heard that the community nearest to ours had been attacked during the previous night and that every man, woman and child had died fighting. Our town was to come next, and the situation was exceedingly serious.

Twice Father Ambrosius had tried to get in touch with the leaders of the Erie band, but they had refused to meet him. They were afraid of this mysterious man whose reputation had traveled all through the land of the Indians and who was thought to be possessed of some magic charm that made him invulnerable. Indeed, so far did this respect for the person of Father Ambrosius go, that the Eries sent one of their chiefs to our camp under a flag of truce to tell the Father that he was at liberty to go back to his own people any time he cared to do so. He was even offered a safe conduct through the land of the Eries if he wished to travel to Quebec by way of the River of Canada.

The good Father answered that he could not possibly return to his own people since at that very moment he was among those whom he considered his own people and he used the opportunity to suggest to the Erie chieftain that he and the Cayugas bury the hatchet or if they could not do that, declare a truce to find out whether the matter could not be settled by the payment of an indemnity. After all, boys would be boys and hot-tempered boys would occasionally do very foolish things, such as killing each other for the sake of a turkey that was not worth the hilt of a single knife. But that was no reason why grown-up men should do war upon each other and should destroy whole townships and should slaughter hundreds of innocent women and children, all of it because "the honor of the tribe had been touched," and he used the opportunity to tell the story of the Great White God, who had come into this world to teach all men that they are each other's brethren. But the Erie Chief merely listened and although he listened most politely, he said nothing, but drew his blanket around him, turned on his heels and departed whence he had come without uttering a single word.

That evening Father Ambrosius turned to me as we were having our supper and casually remarked, I have ordered your Mohawk guides to be here at seven in the morning. You won't be able to walk very far, but I have shown them how to make a stretcher and they will be able to carry you part of the way." And I answered, trying to be just as casual, "That is very kind of you, but of course I shall not go."

"But why not? I have got to stay. I have based my whole life upon the phantastic belief that love will be able to overcome all the evil of this world. Since I have been willing to live by it, I ought also to be willing to die for it. But you, you are a free man and you ought to go."

I agreed. "Yes, I suppose I should go, but we have a proverb at home—one of those homely little sayings that are drummed into our ears when we are still very young, until they become part of our philosophy of life and that proverb bids me stay."

"I would like to hear it."

"It is a very simple one. 'Out together, home together.' I don't suppose that that is a very elegant translation, but it has the virtue of being quite accurate. And when we were boys, it served a purpose. If we went on a trip together, no matter what adventures might befall us, we never thought of turning backward until all our comrades were safe and ready for the return trip. I am here. I stay here. And if we die, we die together. Then I shall at least have some one to show me the way to the Pearly Gate and that will be very pleasant."

Shortly afterwards Father Ambrosius made ready for his customary evening's round and I hobbled off to bed. I was still very weak and the cold weather caused my legs to ache a great deal more than they had done during the milder weeks early in February. Father Ambrosius had noticed that I tossed around a great deal of the night and he had made me a sleeping potion out of a plant which grew all over the hills near our lake and which bore a close resemblance to the Valeriana Officialis of our apothecary shops at home. It had a pungent smell and an acid taste. That evening, I noticed that the acid taste was stronger than usual, but I paid no attention to this as I had caught a cold a few days before and my sense of smell and of taste was not functioning any too well. I took off my coat and hat but kept on the rest of my clothes and went to bed.

When I woke up, I was lying on a stretcher on the ground. It was snowing hard but on one side a roughly made lean-to offered me some protection against the storm that was raging and it had also acted as a barrier against the snow. My two Mohawk guides, bundled up in their blankets, were sitting by my side.

"We thought that we might me able to keep you a little warmer this way," they explained. "As soon as the storm grows less, we shall try and make a fire."

I said, "Never mind the fire. Pick me up and take me back."

But they neither answered, nor did they make the slightest effort to get up. I grew angry and reached for the gun that I had seen lying by my side, but one of the Mohawks whispered, "We unloaded it by special orders." And then I understood everything.

But how did it happen that I had not awakened when they put me on the stretcher? And then I remembered the strange taste of my sedative the night before. In order to save me, Father Ambrosius had taken his precautions carefully and in order to be sure that I left, he had drugged me. For one addicted to fairy tales, the good priest had shown himself a good deal of a realist.

Well, there I was, and what was I to do next? Go back, but how was I to walk all that distance in that raging storm, I who had not walked a mile by myself during the last three or four months? I needed the help of my Mohawks if I were to accomplish anything at all and in order to gain their good will, I had to proceed very carefully and use tact. I first asked them what time it was and they told me that as far as they could make out it was two hours after sunrise.

When had they taken me away from the village?

They thought that it was shortly before midnight. The Father had come to them earlier in the evening and had told them to be ready to start in about three hours. They had packed their belongings and the Father had given them each an old-fashioned arquebus and four loaves of bread. Then they had sat in their tent and had waited until he came back. The Cayugas had not expected an attack that night on account of the threatening blizzard and had mostly stayed indoors. Shortly before midnight, Father Ambrosius had called for them and had conducted them to his cabin where I lay in so deep a sleep that at first they thought I was dead. They had put me on the stretcher and then the good Father had taken them to the outskirts of the village and had told them to make for the hills and not stop until it was daylight. I asked them whether he had given them any message. They said "No, he made the sign of the cross over you before he left and then returned to the camp and never looked back once. Then we picked you up and here we are."

I asked them what they meant to do and they said we would continue our way eastward as soon as the weather should improve a little.

I asked them whether they had heard anything all during the night and they nodded yes and I asked them whether it had been bad, and they said, "Yes, very bad. Everything must have been burned down."

And I asked them whether they would help me return and they answered no, and I called them cowards and pigeon-hearted turn-tails and all the other terrible names for which an Indian under ordinary circumstances will kill even his own father or brother, but they took it calmly and answered, "We are neither cowards nor pigeon-hearted turn-tails. We are only obeying the Father's instructions, because we love him." And as I was too weak to walk by myself, I had to submit and the next morning it stopped snowing and they built me a small sledge and placed me on it and wrapped me in their own warm blankets and we slowly and painfully began our voyage towards the east.

After five days we reached the first village of the Oneidas and when we told our story we were most kindly received by the Chief who gave us his own tent to live in and himself went to stay with his father-in-law and I paid my two Mohawks, who had been most faithful in their duties and gave them a letter to My Lord Stuyvesant in Nieuw Amsterdam, recommending them to him very seriously and suggesting that they be given some token of recognition by the Company, and I remained with the Oneidas until May when the snow had melted and the trails were passable once more.

Then members of all the Oneida tribe gathered in a valley near our camp and we went to a place which is called Owasco in their language and there we waited until the forces of all the Five Nations had come together and we marched against the Eries and when I asked permission to join the expedition, they told me that they would be very pleased if I would come, for they had heard that I was a famous medicine man (the old story of the Mohawk chief whom I had cured more than a year before, something which seemed to have made a profound impression upon the whole neighborhood) and for the first time in my life I found myself obliged to sit on top of a horse, a strange and terrible experience, as the animal moved all four feet at the same time and had the most uncomfortable habit of trying to nibble the buds of the shrubs we passed and of stopping in the middle of the rivers. But I was rapidly regaining my strength and if it had not been for the particular circumstances under which I was taking the trip, I would have enjoyed myself thoroughly.

After six days of trekking (there were about 300 of us and we moved very slowly) we approached the neighborhood of the lake where the quarrel between the Eries and the Cayugas had taken place the previous winter. But we could find no trace of the former. They had apparently been warned by their scouts and had completely disappeared. We afterwards heard what had happened to them after they had fled. A strong band of Senecas had tried to intercept them on their way to the Big Lake and in order to escape from any possible ambuscades they had swung a little towards the south. In this way they had been obliged to pass through the territory of the Susquehannocks, who had surprised them one evening, just when they were pitching camp and who after a short but fierce battle had killed every man, woman and child of them and had left their bodies to rot where they lay.

Such had been the end of an absurd little quarrel that had arisen when two boys had tried to capture the same turkey.

With the enemy gone, there was really nothing for us to do but return whence we had come. But I wanted to see the spot where I knew that my dear friend must have met his death and early one morning, accompanied by about a hundred warriors, I marched to the spot where our village had been located only a short time before. The snow had melted and the country was glorious with the flowers of spring. But the Eries had done their work so well that it took me the greater part of the morning to find the exact location where the massacre had taken place. Of the tents of the Indians nothing remained, but at last we discovered an ash heap and I decided that that had been the house in which I had spent the winter. Strangely enough, we found no skeletons, but the chief who was with me assured me that this was nothing unusual.

"The Eries would have been afraid of the ghosts of those they had slain unless they had first got rid of their corpses. They must either have buried them or they have thrown them in the lake, for as we all know, those who go down in that lake are never again found, as the spirit that dwells at the bottom keeps them there and makes them his slaves."

I had heard of this custom and was familiar with the fear the aborigines felt towards their dead and when the chief asked me whether I was ready to return, I said "Yes," for the scene was full of sad memories for me and there was no use in my staying there any longer.

But ere we broke camp I walked to the big oak tree that stood near the lake and underneath which Father Ambrosius had first explained the beautiful mysteries of his fairy tale to a curious group of old men and women. The tree had been left standing. It was the only one that had not been damaged by the fire. I walked past it to go to the lake when I saw a black object lying amidst the violets and dandelions which covered the hillside. I went nearer and looked at it. It was a skeleton dressed in a long, black cassock. It was lying on its back and the arms were spread wide. The empty sockets were facing the sky. Three arrows with little green feathers at the end were sticking out of his chest. And there Father Ambrosius had written "finis" to his fairy story.

We buried him where he lay and placed some heavy stones upon his grave and I carved a crude cross upon one of these and scratched the initials F. A. on both sides and after a little hesitation I added the letters S. J. Then I knelt down and said a prayer—for the first and last time in my life—and asked God to be very kind to the sweetest man I had ever met and let him dwell in that part of Paradise where the little children lived who still remembered what all the grown-ups had forgotten. Then I went back to the others and an hour later we were on top of the nearest hill and had our final glimpse of the lake.

And ever since I have wondered whether I had been the last white man to cast his eyes upon this lovely landscape which is so far away from the civilized world that even the most ambitious hunters and farmers will never dream of settling down there.

Chapter 36

NEWS FROM HOME

When I returned to Nieuw Amsterdam I discovered that my prolonged absence had caused great consternation. Bernardo, who was apparently still staying with his Mohawk friends, had written to Captain de Vries to tell him of the rumors he had heard about me: that I had reached the ultimate confines of the land belonging to the Five Nations—that I had met with an accident—that I was being taken care of in the house of an Indian chief near one of the smaller lakes a few miles east of the Pacific Ocean—and that I had probably been killed during the famous raid of the Chickasaws against the Onondagas early in the winter of that year.

This strange hodge-podge of information and misinformation had made the excellent captain take a special trip to the capital to try and obtain some further details from the hunters and trappers who gathered together every spring to sell their beaver and bear skins to the traders of the Company. They had indeed heard of some commotion in the region of the small lakes, but some thought it had been a quarrel between the Oneidas and the Algonquins and others knew for certain that it had been merely a little border skirmish between the Cayugas and the Cherokees, who lived almost a thousand miles further toward the south and were then in open warfare with the English who had settled in Virginia, but no one seemed able to tell him just exactly what had happened.

He was delighted therefore when he heard that I had returned and wrote me that he intended to visit Nieuw Amsterdam within a fortnight and hoped to see me. Meanwhile, after the years of comparative freedom, I had grown so accustomed to being my own master that I could no longer stand the restrictions imposed upon me by living in rented quarters. And as I had spent very little of My Lord Andries' money during the last two years (what I had with me when I met with my accident, Father Ambrosius had carefully packed in an old cassock of his and had put it underneath my pillow on the stretcher when he saved me from the massacre) I decided to invest a few hundred guilders in a little house of my own.

I bought a small piece of land from the bouwery which stood in the name of Wolfaert Gerritszoon. I got the land very cheap because it overlooked quite a large swamp, but this swamp which for the greater part of each year was very full of water, gave me the illusion of being near a lake. I found two Indians on Staten Island who said they could build me a wooden house such as were customary among the tribes of the Five

Nations, and they proved to be excellent workmen and in less than a month's time my own house was ready for occupancy.

As soon as it had been finished, I sent word to Bernardo asking him to come and join me but he favored me with a rather cryptic reply. It was a small piece of parchment with a rough drawing of an Indian on it, an Indian who bore a slight outer resemblance to Bernardo himself, and underneath it the cryptic words: "The Ten Lost Tribes have been joined by one more."

I therefore gave up hope of seeing him until I should be able to travel north once more and meanwhile waited for Captain de Vries who had been delayed by some trouble that had recently occurred in the settlement of Rensselaerwijk (the usual story of a greedy farmer selling a plentiful supply of gin to some of the natives who thereupon had got very drunk, had run amuck amongst the villages and had killed three women and two children before they themselves had been shot), but who finally made his appearance early in the month of August during a spell of such hot weather that my beloved swamp ran almost entirely dry and reminded me by its appalling smell of the happy days of my childhood spent among the mud flats of Veere. Not only did he come but he brought me a package that was most welcome to me as it contained nine letters which Jean-Louys had sent me during the previous two years.

"I ought to have sent these to you when I first heard that you had returned," he told me, "but people are so often careless with a small package like this, and so I thought I would wait and bring them myself. I could have sent it to the Fort, but the Governor is in one of his tempers. Some more trouble about that Board of Aldermen of the late but not lamented Willem Kieft, and I would rather not meet him when he is playing the rôles of Nero and Simon Maccabee all in one, stamping around in his little room and complaining that everybody in the whole colony is a traitor and ought to be hung. I know the old man means well, but when he gets in that mood, he is a hopeless bore."

"On the contrary," I answered, "I saw him only yesterday about the final sale of this piece of land. I want to buy that swamp too, otherwise some honest farmer will come here and drain it out of sheer force of habit and I would love to keep my little lake. I found him as soft as butter and as mild as a day in June. You never will guess what he was doing."

"Reading you his last missive to the Board of Eight, calling these worshipful gentlemen a gang of grasping rapscallions, low, lying, thieving scoundrels?"

"By no means! He was writing a poem. A poem about a sunset and a red sky and the happy husbandman slowly wending his way homeward."

"Was it as bad as all that?"

"It was worse. It was, I think, the most sentimental piece of poetry since the day of Tibullus, Tibullus with a wooden leg and a bald head. The whole thing was rather pathetic. For the old man no doubt is trying very hard to do his best and the Directors at home as usual are succeeding in doing their worst. And some fine day all this will come to a sudden end and there will be a terrible disaster and the old man knows it and he can't do anything about it and so he spends his leisure hours writing sweet little elegies about pink sunsets and the virtues of the old Roman matrons. And now please let me have my letters."

The captain gave me a small bundle done up carefully in a leather bag. "Keep the bag," he said, "and read your letters. I hear that our grand duke is laying out a place of his own somewhere around here."

"So he is. The house has been begun. Go and have a look at it and be back at three and we will have dinner."

The captain left me and I spent the next four hours catching up with life on the other side of the ocean. There were nine letters in all. I had thought that they were all from Jean-Louys, but one proved to be from Selim. It was very short and sounded rather sad.

"This big city has grown very lonely," he wrote, "since you and Bernardo have left. Jean-Louys is a charming person, but he is mixing more and more mathematics into his omelettes and I do not like to sit down to a meal when I have first been invited to draw the cubic root from the soup and find the decimal points in the pudding.

"It may be true that God is merely an abstraction and a formula which M. Descartes will solve for us one of these days, but my brain is not strong enough to follow our friend there. And so I sit by myself much of the time.

"Of late I have been greatly diverted by the visits of the Reverend Simon Gallinovius, the son of honest Jan Kippenei, whom you will remember from our trip to the Diemermeer. The old fellow kept the third tavern on the left side of the road outside the Saint Anthonie gate. His promising young offspring desires to make a name for himself and hopes to do so by converting the diplomatic representative of the grand Padisha. Can't you see me going up for baptism in an enormous green turban and that long red robe of office that goes with my high rank? Well, I cannot, but he apparently can. He thinks it would be a fine feather in his dignified biretta.

"His mode of attack is rather unique and causes me a great deal of amusement. He has actually taken the trouble to read the Koran in a Spanish translation. He tells me that he has come to the conclusion that Mohammedanism and Calvinism are the same, as both creeds believe in the pre-ordination of every fact connected with human existence. This undoubtedly is a new point of view and it ought to be interesting to the sort of people who are able to take an interest in that sort of thing.

"But I am bored and the banks of the Bosphorus begin to look more and more attractive to this peace-loving exile. Three more visits from the long-winded Gallinovius and I shall set sail for the land of my fathers.

"What am I doing here anyway? What are any of us doing anywhere, anyway? When a man gets in that mood, you may be prepared for any sort of news.

"I embrace you and the excellent Bernardo. Mark my word, that boy will turn native if you do not look out. He is as much of a wanderer as I am. He is almost as lonely. Allah have mercy upon the likes of us. Farewell!"

Followed by a postscript: "Your good friend Rembrandt has been to see me once or twice. That man has a veritable passion for Turks. He wants me to pose for him. I asked him whether he was running short of models and he said, 'No, but my models are mostly Dutch vagabonds. I can dress them up in silks and satins and put a turban on their heads, but that does not make them Turks. They remain what they were before, Dutch vagabonds who happen to be dressed up in Moslem finery.' Perhaps I shall oblige him one of these days, if only the chicken-egged divine will leave me alone."

The letter was more or less what I might have expected. I turned to the forty or fifty pages covered with Jean-Louys' precise handwriting and I found that they contained a complete history of the last two years, as far as he and I were concerned.

The French often exasperate me. Not infrequently their actions fire me with disgust. They are unreliable and careless to a degree. They have no conception of neatness or order as these virtues are practiced at home. They are quarrelsome and vain. But when I have worked myself up into a complete and perfect detestation of the French nation and all its works, some individual Frenchman will do or say or write something that makes me forget all the manifold annoyances I have suffered at the hands of his race and makes me feel that the world without France would be as dull and uninteresting as a wedding party without music.

These letters of Jean-Louys had a beginning, a middle part (a core would be a better expression) and an end. They told me nothing too much and nothing too little. In their way they were as perfect as the meals he sometimes served us and which left one with a feeling of utter contentment without the unpleasant accompanying sensation of being too replete. I liked these epistles so much that I gave them to the Governor to read and he told me that they had given him more and better information about conditions at home than all the endless reports from his directors. He asked to be allowed to keep them a little longer and eventually forgot to return them when I unexpectedly sailed for home. He sent them after me on the *Drie Croonen*, but the ship went down on the coast of Virginia and was never heard of again. I therefore must rely upon my memory to reconstruct the most important items they contained.

Every letter began with the news that just before writing it Jean-Louys had visited my house on the Houtgracht and had found my son to be in perfect health. The child had completely forgotten me (as was of course to be expected), he was growing up to be a fine boy, had nice manners and went to see Master Rembrandt twice a week to be instructed in the art of drawing. He seemed to have a decided gift for that form of art and Rembrandt was devoting a great deal of his time to helping the boy along.

Then he talked of more serious matters. The long expected had happened at last, peace had been declared between Spain and the Republic and the latter had been fully and most officially recognized as an independent and sovereign nation. The old Prince had not lived to see this final victory of the cause for which he had fought so long and so bravely. He had died a few months before. His end had been very sad, a complication of diseases as a result of the hard life he had led during his endless campaigns. His legs had been so swollen that he could no longer mount on horseback. Then he had had several attacks of lung trouble and finally his brain had given out and during the last two weeks of his earthly existence his nurses had been obliged to take care of him as if he had been a small child.

His son, the one who had married the English woman, had succeeded him as commander-in-chief of the army and might cause considerable trouble. For he was a very ambitious young man who wanted to gain as great a reputation as a strategist as his father and uncle had enjoyed before him. It was generally known that the young Prince had used all his influence to avoid the conclusion of peace until he should at least have added Brussels and Antwerp to the territory of the Republic. But the Burgomasters of Amsterdam were dreadfully afraid of such a step. They feared the rivalry of Antwerp if it should ever be made a Dutch city. They had control of the Scheldt and as long as Antwerp remained a city in the hands of their enemies, they were able to treat her as such and by closing the Scheldt they could ruin their old rival. Amsterdam therefore had declared flatly in favor of an immediate conclusion of peace and as usual, Amsterdam had won.

Their Lordships of the Town Hall and His Highness the Prince now regarded each other as open and avowed enemies and it was feared that hot-headed young Willem was planning a coup against the city that had dealt such a blow to his pride. Thus far nothing had happened, but this friction between the two most powerful bodies within the State had caused a feeling of uneasiness which was doing a great deal of harm.

This came at a very inopportune moment, as business conditions were already very bad. As long as the Republic had been at war with Spain, it had been possible for us to organize a world-wide system of smuggling at the expense of our Spanish opponents. But now that Spain was a friendly nation and no longer a foe to be plundered at will, these smuggling concerns had lost millions of guilders.

Then there were the large number of industries that had been engaged, directly or indirectly, in building ships and making cannon and fabricating gun-powder and looking after the thousand and one needs of an army that was forever in the field and a navy that was rarely in port. Of course the ship yards could now begin to work for the commercial marine and sails and ropes would probably be needed as much as before, but there were many articles for which there was no longer any demand. That would mean a great deal of loss to the original investors and it would mean that thousands of people would be thrown out of employment and this was already becoming very noticeable to any one who ever walked in the direction of the harbor. Where formerly the shipping firms had been obliged to resort to crimps and soul-sellers to get their vessels manned, their offices were now besieged by hordes of hungry men, often accompanied by equally hungry women and children who asked that they be given a chance to take a trip to the Baltic or the Indies.

Then there were the soldiers and the sailors of the navy, all of them out of a job and taking every day more and more to organized brigandage as a means of gaining an honest livelihood. All this of course was greatly affecting the money market and the failure of two or three important houses which had speculated upon a continuation of the war and had filled their store-houses with enormous quantities of supplies which now went for a song, had shaken public confidence so severely that it would be years before the situation could possibly hope to return to normal.

And of course, as Jean-Louys remarked several times, the poor artists will be the first to notice this scarcity of ready money. Rembrandt had told him that he had not had an order for a new portrait for over six months and the others seemed to fare no better. During the first moment of triumph there had been a slight demand for allegorical pictures to celebrate the manifold victories of the Dutch nation. But the two most important orders had gone to Flinck and to van der Helst, two of Rembrandt's pupils. The master himself had been passed. He had tried his hand at an imaginary historical picture representing the pacification of Holland and he had made a number of sketches for it. But no one wanted it and it was still standing in his studio at the time of writing. So were a great many of his other pictures. Nothing he touched seemed to be a success nowadays. He still had an occasional order for a portrait, but he was rapidly being forgotten for a number of younger men who not only charged less but were much more obliging when it came to giving their model his own way.

Indeed, throughout those eight letters there ran an undercurrent of deep and serious worry about the house in the Jodenbreestraat. The terrible nurse was still there, more noisily devoted to little Titus than ever before, but growing more and more unbearable as the years went on. Often indeed it seemed as if she were going out of her mind. Then she would button-hole the unfortunate visitors who came to see her master and would not let them go until she had told them all her woes—how she slaved and worked for little Titus, how she had even made a will in his favor leaving him everying she had in this world, how she, through her own exertions, was keeping the household going because "he," pointing to the door of the master's work-room, was too lazy and too indifferent to attend to anything, but she was not going to stand for it much longer. She could tell a great many things about herself and the famous Rembrandt van Rijn that would astonish the world if it ever became known, a great many things, and had they ever seen the pearls he had given her and the golden ring? And so on and so forth, to the great embarrassment of the unsuspecting visitors who gradually began to avoid the house of the master rather than expose themselves to one of the whining parties of the wild-eyed nurse with her eternal wail that Rembrandt had not done right by her.

No one knew what this situation would lead to, but several friends had at last combined to go directly to Rembrandt and suggest that he have the woman examined by some medical man who was familiar with the subject of lunacy. Rembrandt had listened patiently, as he always did, and had thanked them for their kind interest. He had agreed that the woman ought to go, but he had hinted at several difficulties which made it impossible for him to be as drastic as he wanted to be.

What those mysterious "difficulties" were, Jean-Louys could not tell me. Some people thought that Rembrandt had borrowed money from Geertje which he was unable to pay back at that moment. The inheritance of Saskia had never yet been settled. Any lawsuit involving money would cause the court to examine the financial affairs of both parties and the general opinion was that Rembrandt was not in a position where he could afford to have the magistrates pry a little closely into his business arrangements.

He was working harder than ever and was turning out a very large number of exceedingly beautiful and interesting etchings. But he had retired so completely from the company of his former friends that no one knew exactly how he stood in regard to those funds he was supposed to be administering for the benefit of his small son. No one even could say within five or ten thousand guilders how much there was left for the boy. Everything was all in a terrible muddle and as Rembrandt himself never kept any accounts—invested his money in a most haphazard way—buying an interest in a shipping firm one day and a painting by Raphael the next, it was impossible to make any sort of a guess as to the funds that were at his disposal.

A few goods friends had offered to arrange matters for him—to put some order into this chaos—but he had thanked them most kindly but also most determinedly. He himself would attend to this matter as soon as he had finished a new etching on which he had set great hope. It was a picture of Christ healing the sick and he meant to sell it for a hundred guilders, a record price for etchings. That print would once more bring him into the public eye. Then he would be able to enjoy a little leisure from the pot-boilers he had been obliged to make the last three or four years and he would call on some good and reliable notary to come and help him with his accounts and straighten everything out. Until then, he would just have to put up with the woman as best he could and meanwhile she was full of care for little Titus.

It was the same old story, but with a different refrain. And it made Jean-Louys fear that there was some other reason for his unwillingness or inability to send the nurse packing. Rembrandt had lived a very solitary life since Saskia's death. For all anybody could tell, he might have promised Geertje that he would marry her, or she might be in the family way, or she might pretend to be in the family way and blame the master. It was very difficult to get at the truth with an hysterical woman like that and so there was nothing to do but wait until the situation had taken care of itself.

And as the weeks and months went by, it was more and more likely that some crisis would occur which would rid Rembrandt of his unpleasant companion. Meanwhile his friends hoped and prayed that this would happen before the situation developed into a public scandal. Already there had been a few veiled references from the pulpit about people who had better heal themselves before they made pictures of the Saviour healing others and one reverend gentleman had gone so far as to hint that one of the figures in the supper at Emmaus closely resembled the servant in the house of a certain famous artist who himself was in the habit of giving supper parties, but of a very different nature.

The problem therefore was to get the woman safely out of the house before this whispering campaign got a little too outspoken, but no one could foretell what would happen, as Rembrandt in all things, both good and bad, was known to be almost as obstinate as the gallant warrior who was then reported to be at the head of the government of the New Netherlands and with this charming compliment at the address of My Lord Stuyvesant, the excellent Jean-Louys, who knew that letters were sometimes opened and read by the authorities, closed his account of affairs in the Jodenbreestraat.

He then told me a lot of gossip about European affairs, most of which I already knew; that the English were on the point of executing their King for a series of crimes which seemed to be rather vague, but that, as His Majesty had gained the reputation of being one of the most accomplished liars of his or any other time and had broken his word so repeatedly that no one could trust him for longer than two minutes at a time, he would probably be condemned to death, but whether he was going to be hanged or merely decapitated no one could as yet foretell; that the government probably would fall into the hands of some one called Cromwell, who was certain to proclaim himself king and would cause a great deal of trouble to the Republic, as he was known to be strongly in favor of a very drastic policy of protection for all British interests; that there was a rather amusing quarrel between the French crown and the nobility of that country, and that an Italian by the name of Mazarini, a former henchman of the infamous Cardinal Richelieu, had now got hold of the French government by making himself indispensable to the old king's wife, a Spanish lady with whiskers and not very bright, whom he flattered in the elegant Spanish manner which he had learned during the days of his youth when he was a flunkey in the suite of Prince Colonna and had accompanied that noble gentleman to the University of Alcala to inspect the original manuscript of the Polyglot Bible and place a wreath on the cradle of the great Don Miguel de Cervantes; that this shrewd Sicilian, a master-piece of Jesuit educational skill, who looked like a Portuguese Jew and who stole money from the Public Treasury with the grace of a Neapolitan prostitute going through the pockets of an English lord, would soon break the resistance of the nobles and that it was extremely doubtful whether the French monarchy would go the way of its English counterpart, although many people in the Republic counted on such an outcome; that the "usual" trouble between Amsterdam and Denmark and Sweden about the tolls levied in the Sund was in the "usual" state of being almost settled by either war or a treaty; that for the rest, nothing of any importance had happened except that the most eminent and learned Doctor Descartes had paid a brief visit to his native country upon which occasion the Spanish-Italian-French cardinal had honored him with an annual pension of three thousand francs and the promise of a position at court, which seemed a strange ambition, for the author of the "Discourse of Method" and the "Principles of Philosophy," but then, even very learned people must eat: and so on and so forth, forty-eight pages long.

I was reading these letters for the third time when Captain de Vries returned.

"A strange experience!" I told him. "The Old World suddenly making its presence felt in the New. I wonder what has happened to me? Those things used to interest me. They used to interest me most tremendously. They were part of my life. And now it is just as if some one were making music in a room in another part of the house. I try to listen, but it means nothing to me, except a little, vague noise—not very interesting and rather annoying and upsetting. What has happened to me?"

"It is the fresh air and the horizon. That strange horizon of ours. In Europe, a horizon means the end of something old and familiar. Here it means the beginning of something new and unknown. That horizon will get you as it has got most of us. Unless those old fools in Amsterdam who rule us without ever having seen us force me to go away (as well they may if they continue their present policy of acting as dry-nurses to ten thousand people at the other end of the ocean) I shall never return to the mother country. I would smother and die for lack of fresh air in one of our nice, respectable little cities. Another six months and you will feel the same way."

I confessed that I had already fallen a victim to the pleasant hallucination of space.

"Then send for your boy and set up as a surgeon right here. La Montagne won't mind. He is getting old and hates to go out nights. The others are quacks. Settle down here. Take you a wife and be happy!"

And I might have followed his advice if it had not been for the scrap of paper that reached me exactly two months later and that said nothing but: "I wish you would come home. I need your help and your friendship very badly," and that was signed with a large capital letter R.

Chapter 37

THE TEN LOST TRIBES ARE JOINED BY ONE MORE

A week after the departure of Captain de Vries, who was obliged to return to Vriesendael, I decided that I would pay a visit to Bernardo, for all efforts to make him write me a letter and tell me in some detail what had happened to him had failed. He had sent me three fine beaver-skins, but never a word and so I made up my mind that I would go north once more and discover for myself how he was getting along in his search for Israel's Lost Tribes.

The colony was once more at peace with the Indians—the weather was lovely and I took the greater part of the voyage in a canoe which to my way of thinking is by far the most comfortable instrument of transportation this world has ever seen. It may be true that the Indians were not intelligent enough to invent the wheel and had to wait for us to come and show them how to make a wagon, but they were bright enough to devise the canoe and I am willing to give a thousand rumbling vehicles for a single quietly moving canoe and my only regret is that we have never been clever enough to adopt this craft for home consumption. It would set us free from the tyranny of the canal boat and I can't think of a single other thing that would do us more good than a whole-hearted rebellion against this depressing and exasperating ark of gossip and scandal.

A noble wish, but an absurd one. Ten thousand skippers would arise in all their might, a hundred thousand horses would stamp their feet in righteous anger. Burgomasters and Estates would be bombarded with petitions of outraged citizens and even more outraged labor guilds and the offending canoes would be condemned to be burned by the public executioner.

Meanwhile as long as I live I shall never forget the leisurely trip I took up the great river on my way towards the North. It was a wonderful experience. A slight haze was hanging over the water. We could only see the tops of the mountains that surrounded the flood and these were covered with the greenest of green trees. We could not make much headway against the current and the trip took the better part of five days. Then three days on foot, but my legs had entirely recovered and I could walk all day without feeling the slightest fatigue.

I had not sent word to Bernardo that I was coming. I wanted to surprise him. Instead of which I was the one to receive a surprise. For when I reached the village where I had bade him good-by two years before

I heard that he had left and was living in a large wooden house about ten miles further towards the North.

I found the house and I found Bernardo, so completely changed, so bronzed and so healthy looking, that at first I took him for an Indian brave and he threw both arms around me and kissed me and took me into the house where a very young and very handsome Indian woman was nursing a baby and he said, "Behold the additional Lost Tribe! and now go back to the good Rabbi Menasseh and give him my love and admiration and tell him that I am never, never, never coming back.

"I have not discovered a trace of the other Ten Tribes. They probably had the same experience I did and once they were lost, they liked it so well that they stayed lost.

"But I have found myself. I am happy. This woman is a joy of grace and beauty. This child is the handsomest thing that was ever born. I shall miss you and I shall miss my other friends at home, but in losing all that I have gained more than I ever thought possible.

"For the first time in my life I am not a Jew, but a man. Nobody here knows or cares whence I came. I had to learn a thousand new things before I could keep myself modestly alive. But I have learned them and now I ask for nothing but that I be allowed to stay where I am. And there is really only one thing you can do for me. Go home and tell them I was eaten up by a bear. There are no bears here but they won't know the difference. Tell them that I went down his gullet loving them all and sending them my blessing. But tell them that I am dead and gone. And now come in and I will cook you a steak. But not just an ordinary steak—a steak I shot and killed myself and afterwards I shall give you some of the wine I made myself and afterwards the woman will sing our son to sleep and if you have ever heard anything lovelier, don't tell me, for I would not believe you anyway."

And that is how Bernardo Mendoza Soeyro, who had the blood of the kings of Israel in his veins, who had spent two years in a dungeon of the Portuguese Inquisition, and who for more than ten years had kept books for Isaac Ashalem, the fish dealer of the Lazarus Street in Amsterdam, came to die as an Indian chieftain and now lies buried underneath a small mound of stones and earth in the forests that are the hereditary hunting-grounds of the famous tribe of the Mohegans.

Once or twice after I returned to Nieuw Amsterdam I heard from Bernardo. When he knew that I was obliged to return home, he sent me a leather suit for my boy "with Uncle Bernardo's love," and a tiny silver box for Jean-Louys "just large enough to hold one thought at a time—the thought of a very dear friend who has found complete happiness," but he never wrote me a letter, except an occasional verbal message that all was well with him and that his new daughter was almost as handsome a creature as his son.

But that was all. He felt that the old and the new could not be successfully combined. His new life meant everything to him. He allowed the old one to disappear from his memory completely.

Years afterwards, it was in the fall of '62, I received the visit of a captain of the West India Company who had come to port a few days earlier in command of the good ship the *Drie Burghers*. He told me that on his last visit to Nieuw Amsterdam the Governor had sent for him and had given him a letter. "This was delivered to me," His Lordship had explained, "for a certain Jan van Loon, a surgeon from Amsterdam who was here for some time during the late forties. I don't know whether he is still alive, but you will easily be able to find out when you get back home. Give it to him with my compliments."

It was a piece of birch-bark, the birch-bark the Indians are so clever at using for a large number of purposes. On it with red paint was a picture of a man lying on what seemed to be a couch that stood beside a tree. There was a woman in the background and five funny little figures that looked like children. The writing, done in a very shaky hand, had become almost illegible.

I took it to Rembrandt, who like so many near-sighted people, was very clever at reading small print, and together we puzzled it out.

"My time has nearly come," it said, "but I am willing to go. It has been a good life and I have cheated fate. For I have been happy after all."

It was Bernardo's epitaph.

Not entirely according to the traditions of the Mendoza family.

But they never knew.

So what was the difference?

Chapter 38

I HAVE CERTAIN DOUBTS ABOUT THE SUPERIOR VIRTUES OF THE SO-CALLED "WHITE MEN" AS COMPARED TO THEIR COPPER-COLORED BRETHREN OF THE NEW WORLD

There still was one part of the Nieuw Netherlands which I had not visited during my tour of inspection and it seemed that that was the most important section for the purpose which My Lord Andries and his brother had in mind. The northern and western regions I had examined quite carefully. They would have been of great value to us four or five hundred years ago when our people were obliged to wear furs or freeze in our damp and uncomfortable houses. But now that even the simplest artisan could afford to have a chimney and with those wonderful new stoves they had recently invented in Germany, ordinary woolens were all that were needed and one hardly ever saw a piece of fur worn from one year to another except among the very rich who wanted to show their neighbors how opulent they were.

The beaver-skins were still useful for hats, but it was so easy for our people to make money in other ways than by hunting that I could not for the life of me see how My Lord Andries would ever be able to induce emigrants to go all the way to America to lead the miserable and dangerous existence of trappers.

Of course if those forests I had visited had been a little nearer to the sea, they would have provided us with excellent timber for our ships. But upon the occasion of my last visit to the Fort, the Governor had shown me a letter from Amsterdam in which he was informed that the Emperor and the King of Sweden and the King of Spain and all the other potentates who had been fighting each other for the last thirty years, had at last concluded peace (after three and a half years of preliminary discussions and negotiations) and if this news was true, it meant that the Black Forests were once more accessible to our wood merchants and the cost of transporting beams and masts from Nieuw Amsterdam to the wharves of the Zaan would be prohibitive compared to the ease with which rafts of German fir-trees could be floated down the Rhine.

I had received several letters from My Lord Andries and his brother since my arrival. They had told me that they wanted to modify their plans a little, if such changes were at all feasible. The West India Company was going from bad to worse. The shares were so little in demand that the Amsterdam exchange had ceased to include them in their list of current stocks. Soon it would be possible to buy thousands of acres for a song. Was there any land that could be used to raise spices? They were glad to hear of the timber possibilities, but expected little of such a development as business with Germany had recently been assured (this bore out the news in Governor Stuyvesant's letter). They still had great expectations of their scheme for the wholesale importation of grain. But was there any part of the New Netherlands where they might expect to grow pepper, for which there was an ever-increasing demand, or nutmeg which was greatly gaining in popularity among all classes of society, or even tobacco?

They had heard that there had been serious outbreaks of hostility in the English colony of Virginia where the best tobacco came from. Rumors on the Exchange even mentioned figures and reported that during the last Indian massacre more than 400 white settlers had been killed. Furthermore, Their Lordships had been informed that most of the colonists were royalists and now that the King had been executed, was there any chance of these people starting a rebellion against Parliament and either declaring themselves independent or, from fear of their Spanish neighbors, accepting the protection of the Dutch Company?

Well, all these were questions to which I could not possibly give an adequate reply without doing a great deal of first-hand investigating. It took about two weeks to go from Nieuw Amsterdam to Virginia by sea and no one had ever attempted the voyage on land. Besides, in order to get there, the traveler would have been obliged to pass through the property of a new and upstart company which besides was in popish hands.

This was not of very great importance, for every skipper who had ever been there (and there was quite a brisk trade between the New Netherlands and the different plantations along the Chesapeake Bay) told me that the Calverts who owned the colony outright (and did not have to bother about boards-of-directors or stock-holders, but who were as free and independent as regular monarchs) were very liberal-minded and intelligent people and cared not whether one was Lutheran or a Papist or even a Jew or a Turk as long as one paid liberally and paid in cash. And most of them added that they would much rather spend a whole winter off Kent Island than a single month in the harbor of Plymouth, where the populace, especially since their own party had been victorious in the mother country, acted with great arrogance towards all foreigners. And especially we Hollanders, whose prince was married to a daughter of the king whom they had just killed, were looked upon with great suspicion.

Then there was the eternal quarrel about the boundary lines between the two colonies. The governors who had preceded My Lord Stuyvesant had allowed their English neighbors to make themselves at home in any part of the New Netherlands. But "Stubborn Piet" was of different caliber from the Kiefts and Krols and Twillers. Settlers from Massachusetts were welcome as subjects of the Gentlemen Nineteen, but unless they renounced their former allegiance they were bade to return whence they had come. Fortunately I would never be obliged to travel north again, and I quietly began to make my preparations for an interesting trip through the southern region that was to take me all the way from the Lange Eiland to the James River and the land of the Powhatans.

Several of the Indian tribes through whose countries I would have to pass, were reputed to be of a very fierce and warlike disposition and several people (even the old governor, who seemed to take a genuine interest in my well-being) counseled me to provide myself with an armed guard as soon as I should reach the neighborhood of the Potomac River.

I must confess that I did not know what to do. I was not my own master but was responsible for my well-being to the men who had entrusted me with their money. In the end I invited both Captain de Vries and Doctor La Montagne to my house one day (I had also begun to lay out a garden and was rather proud of my first efforts) and I put the case before them, as they were the only two men in the entire colony who seemed to have taken the trouble to try and understand the point of view of the natives.

They both declared themselves strongly opposed to the idea of taking an armed guard of colony soldiers. "They would only be a hindrance," the wise old doctor told me. "They will get sick. Most of them are not in the best of health when they arrive here and the water-front usually does the rest. They never take any precautions and as a result they catch every fever and every ache that hides within these forests and marshes. Worst of all, they will go chasing after the native women and that invariably leads to murder and bloodshed and revenge; and as the Indian code asks an eye for an eye and a tooth for a tooth, but is not very particular whose eye and whose tooth it is that get sacrificed (as long as they are the eye and the tooth of a white man) you yourself would be in continual danger."

"Besides," the shrewd captain added, "no number of soldiers you could possibly take with you could protect your expedition against the thousands of natives that live in these southern regions if they really meant to do you harm. On the other hand, if they felt inclined to treat you hospitably, they would appreciate your visit all the more if you came alone and unarmed. Such a policy would flatter their pride. It would show them that you were inclined to trust them—that you regarded them as honorable gentlemen. And no matter how lazy and dirty the Indians may be, they all of them possess the rudimentary instincts of a grand seigneur. Appeal to their nobler emotions and they will treat you as one of their equals. Go blundering through their country with a couple of dozen foreign mercenaries, toting arquebuses and halberds, and everywhere you will be received with suspicion, and a single man putting his hands on a squaw or a girl will mean the sign for a massacre."

All of which sounded so eminently sane to me that I decided to act upon the advice of those dear friends and wrote to Governor Stuyvesant that I was deeply grateful for his offer but that in view of the bad feeling that seemed to exist between the Republic and the commonwealth of Oliver Cromwell and the danger of a war that might be extended to the New World, I did not wish to deprive His Excellency of any of his troops and that I had made up my mind to make the trip alone, accompanied only by my two faithful Mohegan guides, who, as soon as they had learned that I expected to start upon a new voyage, had paddled all the way down to Nieuw Amsterdam to offer me their services.

There was only one more subject of worry—that note from Rembrandt. I felt that he needed me badly. He had treated me with abominable rudeness just before I left, but I could bear him no ill-will on account of that unseemly outburst of anger. I remembered my poor brother and what he had suffered. I had no idea whether Rembrandt was in love with Geertje. I did not think so. He had been romantically devoted to Saskia, but he was a man of terrific physical energy, and sat all day before his easel, while he spent the greater part of the night working at his etchings. It is always extremely dangerous for a man of such sedentary habits to be left alone with a woman who is not only of a rather attractive exterior but whose eyes and lips betray great sensuousness.

In short, what I feared and what Jean-Louys seemed to fear (unless I had very much misread his last letters) was this, that the woman had seduced Rembrandt, or to speak a little less harshly, that circumstances had induced the two to forget the strict rules of morality that prevailed in our country. I cared not a whit for those rules, but I knew our clergy, and the cruel gossip of a town like Amsterdam. One definite word of disapprobation on the part of a well-known preacher and the van Rijn family would be ruined, both socially and economically.

It was a terrible thing to leave a man alone at a moment like that, but I considered myself in the service of the Bicker family until I should have accomplished everything they had asked me to do. Besides a contract was a contract. Wherefore I sat me down and wrote to Rembrandt and told him that if all went well, I would be back in Amsterdam early the next fall, that I promised him to take the first boat available as soon as I should have returned from my trip to the South, and if he had any troubles, to talk them over with Jean-Louys, who was the most trustworthy of friends and of good, sound, common sense, though he usually tried to hide his true emotions underneath a cloak of wit and raillery. And I told him that when I sailed into the harbor of Amsterdam, I expected to find him standing near the Montelbaanstoren with little Titus, to whom I sent my best love. I omitted all reference to Geertje and purposely left her name out of my letter. That seemed the better policy to me, though God knows, I may have been wrong.

This letter I gave to My Lord the Governor and the next day I left for the South. During this trip I made the only discoveries which could possibly have been of any practical use to My Lord Andries and I therefore do not think it proper for me to give an account of this expedition in a book that deals with my personal adventures and reflections.

I left Nieuw Amsterdam late in the fall and returned ten months later after a very successful and comfortable voyage, during which I never for a single moment regretted the wise counsel of my two friends who had urged me to dispense with an armed guard and put my faith in my own courage and good fortune rather than the dozen cut-throats whom the kind-hearted governor had most generously placed at my disposal.

Chapter 39

I TALK POLITICS WITH MY LORD STUYVESANT, WHO TAKES A GLOOMY VIEW OF THINGS

As soon as I reached Nieuw Amsterdam, I called on My Lord Stuyvesant, whom I found little changed, though he complained a great deal of pain in the stump of his leg. This leg had been badly smashed by a Portuguese cannon-ball during an attack on one of the West Indian islands several years before. The wounded man had been sent to Leyden in the hope that one of the surgeons connected with the medical school could save it, but gangrene having set in during the trip home they had been obliged to operate as soon as he reached his sister's house. The operation, however, had not been performed with sufficient care and especially during the hot months of the summer the poor man suffered terrible agonies when he hopped around on one of his daily trips of inspection.

As we handled a great many cases like that in our Amsterdam hospital (in a town which was visited every year by so many thousand ships, broken arms and legs were almost as common as beggars and pimps) I had acquired a certain routine in handling this affliction and I was able, by slightly changing the angle at which the stump was fastened to the artificial leg, to alleviate His Excellency's discomfort. As a result of which he treated me with even greater affection than before and offered me a position of great trust. Indeed, he asked me to act as the personal intermediary between himself and the Board of Directors in Amsterdam.

"For," as he remarked one day when we were sitting on a bench outside the Fort and were contemplating the river front, "here we are possessed of what is probably the finest natural harbor in the whole world and what have we done to assure ourselves of the continued occupancy of this spot? Nothing! Absolutely nothing! There is a fort. At least, we call it a fort. Look at it! Cows grazing on the walls and pigs wallowing in the ditch that should be a moat.

"People blame me. But what can I do? I have no money. The Company has no money. I have no men. The Company sends me endless letters protesting that there are no funds to send me more troops.

"The inhabitants, my beloved subjects, poke fun at me and call me the Grand Duke of Muscovy! If I were as bad as all that, ninety percent of this rabble would be hanging from the trees of Staten Island. I would not even care to hang them here on Manhattan. All of them have come to America to grow rich over night. But as soon as they had set foot on land, they discovered that the Company meant them to stay poor, that they could not plant a tree or cut down a bramble-bush without asking permission from some one at home.

"If they only gave me free rein, I could change all that over night. But Their Lordships won't let me do a thing. They even wrote me a letter last week in which they told me how long the sermons ought to be that are preached here every Sunday and Wednesday.

"Meanwhile, now that they have got rid of their king and are ruling the country to suit their own taste, the English are moving to Massachusetts by the boat-load. I suppose they want to prepare for a nice place of refuge to which they can flee if the Stuarts ever come back. Soon there will be a thousand men in New England for every ten here in the New Netherlands. And mark my words! one of these days there will be war between the Republic and the Commonwealth.

"I don't trust that fellow Cromwell! He is too clever to please me. He is an Englishman and knows his own people. The Stuarts were outsiders and never understood their subjects. But Cromwell does. They have had their fill of revolution. Now they will return to their normal selves and a normal Englishman as I know him wants to grow rich at trade. The old lady who ruled them for such a long time gave them a taste of that sort of thing. Cromwell will try to do likewise. Anyway, he has to if he wants to keep in power. That will cause trouble between his country and our own. The Stuarts wasted money on all sorts of things, but they never spent a penny on their fleet.

"That was a good thing for us. We have been driving the English out of all sorts of places in India and in Africa where they had been settled for two or three generations, and I hear that the Company intends to fortify the Cape of Good Hope. Then we shall control the road to Asia, and mark my words! that man Cromwell will fight before he lets us do it. If there is a war, how am I to defend this colony against the people from the North? Yes, I can build a wall across the island and keep them out of Manhattan, but all the rest will be lost in a couple of months."

I could not take quite such a gloomy view of affairs. "But after all, even if Cromwell has all this in mind, he can't just make war on us some fine day without some sort of excuse. And Their Lordships of the Estates General will be careful not to give him a legal pretext."

"Pretext! Who gives a fig for a legal pretext when he wants to make war on a neighbor who has got something he would like to have for himself? Besides, the pretext for which you are looking already exists."

I looked surprised.

"Of course it does. During the last fifty years we have built more ships than any one else. We carry more than half of the world's trade. Time and again I have written home for ships. But I could not have them. They were carrying goods from Boston to London or from Buenos Aires to Cadiz, or from Archangel to Naples, or from the sun to the moon. And why? Because there was more money in that sort of trade than in working for the home markets. Our friend Oliver will tell his Parliament to pass a law that only English ships are allowed to carry merchandise to English ports. If he does, we must either fight or go bankrupt. And if we fight, I can hold out here for a fortnight. After that, I must either blow myself up or surrender the Fort. I don't want to do either. And so I bombard them at home with letters. They are beginning to hate me. They ask me please to be more moderate in my tone. Moderate indeed! when you are offered the chance to do something big in the New World and they give you exactly five stivers to do it with!"

This was a new side to the old Governor I had never suspected and for a moment I felt inclined to accept his offer. There was indeed a chance to "do something big in the New World" and this chance was being scandalously neglected by the short-sighted men whose greed and selfishness made it impossible for them to look beyond their noses and their immediate profit. But then I reflected that my work lay along different lines. I was a surgeon, not a merchant nor a colonial administrator. I had now been away from my regular practice for almost seven years. I had learned a great many things that I wanted to try out in the hospital at home. No, as long as the human race continued to be suffering from a thousand ailments, it was my duty to go back and try to alleviate some of this pain and misery. And having thrashed the matter out with my excellent friend, the local doctor (for whose sagacity I was getting an ever-increasing respect), I went back to the Fort and told His Excellency of my decision and he agreed that that was perhaps the better course.

"This corner of the world is lost to us anyway," he reflected bitterly; "it is merely a question of years, and you can tell the Gentlemen Nineteen so for me when you get back home, and now let me ask my secretary to give me a list of the ships he expects before the coming of winter and I will see that you get a berth on one of them."

This did not prove an easy matter. The week before I returned to Nieuw Amsterdam, three vessels, the *Unie,* the *Sommelsdijk* and the *Assendelft* had sailed for Texel with cargoes of fur. There was a chance that the *Gouden Spiegel,* which had gone to the Chesapeake Bay, would call at Nieuw Amsterdam on her way to Holland, but early in November a very severe storm swept down the coast of Maryland and the *Gouden Spiegel* was never heard of again.

I therefore would be obliged to wait until the coming of spring before I had a chance to bid farewell to the New World forever. This prospect, however, held no terrors for me, as my two Mohegans had asked permission to stay with me until I should actually leave for home, and as one of them had developed into an excellent cook and as I had plentiful fuel to keep my little wooden house warm during the cold months of January and February, I spent a most comfortable winter, one of the most agreeable and peaceful winters of my whole life.

In the morning I used to help Doctor La Montagne with his sick and in the afternoon I worked at my secret report for My Lord Andries or ordered the notes I had taken on the medical methods and practices of those Indian tribes with which I had come in contact. And twice a week I used to take a musket and went hunting among the hills that have given the settlement the name "The Town of the Many Mountains." Every Sunday I kept open house for those who wished to come and then I discovered that Nieuw Amsterdam, notwithstanding the neglect the town suffered at the hands of the home government, contained more interesting and amiable people than I had had any reason to suspect.

And then, to my great surprise, early in December, two ships came in from home much delayed by the same storm that had caused the loss of the *Gouden Spiegel* and that seemed to have swept across the entire Atlantic. Both of them brought a number of letters from home.

One of them was from my boy, the first written words I had ever received from him and which showed me that he was growing up rapidly, for not only did he write an excellent hand (in sad contrast to the illegible pothooks of his father) but he had interspersed his epistle with diverse quotations from Ovid and all of these were correct. He expressed a polite regret at not having seen me for such a long time and suggested that I might see fit to return to him ere long, but all this sounded very formal and I realized with a painful shock that I had neglected the only person in the whole wide world to whom I was bound by something more enduring than the ties of friendship and I felt grateful that my years of wandering and exile were about to come to an end.

As for Jean-Louys, he had outdone himself this time. Not less than nine letters and all of them brimful of information. Seven of them have been lost, but somehow I managed to save two and these I shall copy here in full as they are worth preserving.

In the first place, there was a minute description of the political situation at home, which seemed to fill him with grave fear and anxiety for the immediate future.

"The young Prince [so he wrote] is proving himself more of a nuisance than anybody had dared to anticipate. As long as his father was alive, he behaved most discreetly—was an amiable and industrious young gentleman—a bit haughty perhaps, but then he was the first member of his family who had been allowed to marry the daughter of a real king. The old Prince, his father, had not been an easy man to deal with during the last years of his life. He was dreadfully jealous of his own son and kept him away from all affairs of state and let us be under the impression that his son cared for nothing besides his horses and his dancing and his theater.

"But as soon as the old chieftain's tortured body had been decorously lowered into the ancestral crypt of Delft, there was an end to the theater parties and the French fiddlers were hastily packed off to Paris. All this happened so suddenly that there was quite a flutter on the Exchange when it was reported that the Prince had departed for the front and was trying to get the war with Spain started afresh. We all were under the impression that the fight had come to an end when Tromp had destroyed the second Armada near the Downs. Since then nothing much of any importance had happened. People vaguely remembered that they were still in a state of war, because so many of their neighbors were growing rich out of smuggling or selling war-supplies. But the thing lacked reality. Ninety-nine percent of the people had never seen a live Spaniard except as an honored business acquaintance, come to Amsterdam to do his fall buying or his spring selling. To the younger generation it seems absurd to suppose that their part of the country could ever again be the scene of actual fighting.

"Of course, the official treaty of peace had not yet been signed, but who cared? Such affairs always took a lot of time, what with deciding who ranked whom when the delegates entered a room or whether a Lord Privy Councilor of His Most Catholic Majesty was entitled to as many salutes as a High, Noble and Well-born Member of the Estates of Zeeland or vice versa. But some day these ancient and worthy gentlemen would discover that the charms of Münster were beginning to pall upon them. Nothing much has happened in that town since the sainted Jan of Leyden tried to turn it into the New Jerusalem with the well-known results. That, however, had taken place more than a hundred years before. Their Excellencies whenever they felt bored could go and look at the iron cage in which the Prophet had spent the last days of his life, but that was about the only form of excitement the city offered, and it was not much.

"And so sooner or later these slow-moving excellencies would affix their signatures to a piece of parchment and all would be over.

"As a result, when it was whispered on the Exchange that the Prince meant to use the massing of a few Spanish regiments along the Flemish border as an excuse for preparing another invasion of Belgium, there were several short and rather mysterious meetings in one of the rooms of the Town Hall of Amsterdam and certain gentlemen whom both of us know, had chartered a special night boat for The Hague and the Prince had returned to his stud-farm in the Woods and the army had gone back to its winter quarters and suddenly the long-expected peace with Spain had been signed and it had been celebratd by four days of as drunken an orgy as had ever been seen this side of Parnassus, and that was where matters stood at the time of writing.

"[Then the letter went on.] Amsterdam came out victorious because it has the key to the common treasure-house. The Prince was defeated this time but mark you my words, he has the army with him and as soon as he has half a chance he will turn against Amsterdam and he will have his revenge.

"Meanwhile, business as usual continues. The panic that followed upon the cessation of hostilities and about which I wrote you in my former letters, has come to an end. The ship-yards now work for private owners and the ordnance makers are selling their wares to those who have taken up buccaneering instead of smuggling. As for the ex-soldiers, they have either been hung or have been locked up in so-called Old People's Homes, which is pretty much the same as far as the final effect is concerned.

"But in spite of these items on the credit side, there are many things that fill my heart, or rather my mind, with serious fears for the future. Our relations with England are getting worse every day. It is quite natural that His late Majesty's son should have fled to his sister as soon as he left his kingdom. And as this country has always been extremely cordial to political exiles, the young man had every right to expect that he would be treated with some sort of consideration. But these Stuarts never seem to learn anything. A king in exile has certain duties. There is only one rôle he can play—the rôle of dignified submission with an accent on the dignified. But Charles must have his wine and his women and his eternal round of parties. I saw him in Amsterdam two years ago, quite by chance, of course, for he was supposed to be traveling incognito. He is almost six feet tall and looks so much more like an Italian than an Englishman that he was bound to attract considerable attention. Ordinary Englishmen we can see here every day. But Englishmen disguised as Sicilians are a rarity.

"It was about six o'clock in the afternoon and he was coming home from dinner with one of the Burgomasters. He was slightly the worse for drink but carried himself well enough. Nevertheless, an Oedipus or a King Lear in his cups is not a very dignified spectacle and so his friends hastened him off to the yacht that was to take him back to his sister, and they did this as rapidly and as decorously as circumstances and his wobbly legs would permit.

"That strange Cromwell person, who contrary to our expectations has not put the crown upon his own unkempt locks, is much shrewder than we had thought. He has more power now than any of the potentates whom he has succeeded. And as long as he is allowed to rule his fellow-men according to his own sweet will, he does not seem to care by what name he is known. But he is beginning to find himself in a very difficult position. He is a usurper and the world in which he lives is supposed to be a world of law and order. He can only hope to maintain himself as long as he is victorious and sticks to a foreign policy that makes everybody rich.

"But of course all these many years of civil war have done the greatest harm to the business of the Kingdom and no one has profited as much from this state of affairs as we in our own beloved little Republic. You will notice the influence of environment upon even a highly intelligent mind. Here I am writing 'our own beloved little Republic' whereas of course I am really a devout subject of Giovanni Mazarini, who, by the way, has got himself into all sorts of troubles with Their Lordships of the Estates General, by the truly Italian manner in which he has been trying to grab Belgium as part of the dowry of a rather vague Spanish princess who was to marry an equally vague cousin of the King of France, and who was then supposed to become the sovereign ruler of a new sort of French kingdom that stretched all the way from the Scheldt to the Pyrenees and from the Atlantic to the Rhine.

"However that may be, or to make a long letter still a little longer, there is going to be a war some time within the near future and that war will decide who is to be the master of Europe. At present we here in Amsterdam have the largest amount of money and therefore we rule the universe pretty much as it pleases us. Soon His Lordship, the Protector, will consult his Bible and at the hand of numerous texts will prove that the time has come to smite the Amalekites.

"And of course the Amalekites will prove to be his neighbors who live on the other side of the North Sea.

"That will tell you what is what, in the field of foreign affairs. As for our good town, there is nothing new to report. We enjoyed a few fires, but none of them amounted to very much. Our population is increasing by leaps and bounds and those who have some spare funds at their disposal are buying real estate just outside the city walls in the hope of selling their land at a handsome profit when the next extension takes place.

"There may be something new in the field of literature, but as you know, I never read Dutch unless I absolutely have to. I live a very quiet life and since the departure of Selim, spend most of my time working. I had a rather mysterious visit the other day of a certain Doctor Paniculus, who at first claimed that he was a French physician, who had studied at Montpellier at the same time as you and wanted to get some news of his dear old friend, the famous Dutch doctor. I soon discovered that he was not a doctor of medicine at all but a doctor of theology and a member of the Society of Jesus, visiting the Low Countries on an errand of piety which, however, he refused to divulge. I asked him whether he had ever heard of the edict against the Jesuits which the Estates General had passed in the year 1612 and which never had been repealed. He answered yes, and pulled a copy of that famous edict out of his pocket.

"'Here it is,' he said, 'and I always carry it with me. If ever I am arrested and they find this, they will surely never suspect me of belonging to that poor, persecuted company of holy men.'

"And then he continued the conversation by asking me what news I had of my good friend, Monsieur Descartes. I told him that I had very little news since that morning in September of '49 when I bade him farewell on the shore near Egmont and saw him safely on board his Swedish man-of-war. Had I had any news from him since he had taken up residence with the Queen? I said no, but that I had heard in a roundabout way that he did not feel very happy in Stockholm and suffered a great deal from the cold.

"And then I asked him by what right he had forced himself into my house to bother me with all sorts of personal questions which surely were none of his concern. But he remained as affable as before and totally unruffled he answered me in a very kind tone of voice, 'It is really none of my business, but I thought you would like to have a friend tell you that poor Renatus is dead.' And I jumped up and said, 'Dead?' And he answered, 'Yes, dead! He died in February from an inflammation of the lungs.'

"And then he told me how my poor learned friend had never been quite happy since he had left the territory of the Republic. Of course, it had been very flattering to be asked to become a sort of unofficial adviser to the brilliant young Queen of Sweden, and to play the rôle of Aristotle at the court of the late Gustavus Adolphus. One was getting along in years. Fifty-four was not exactly old age, but it was pleasant to feel that one could make some provisions for the future. On paper the whole plan had seemed most attractive. A philosopher being called for by a battle-ship and being received with royal honors was something that probably had not happened since the days of Philip of Macedonia. But there the comparison ended. For Christina was no Alexander, though she had so great an admiration for this ancient prince that she often expressed her regret at not having been given his name. She had better brains than most of the men around her with the exception of the chancellor Oxenstjerna whom she had inherited from her father, and whom she humiliated in every possible manner. And driven by her pride and in order to show the old diplomat how well she could manage without him, she had begun to surround herself with famous people whom she gathered from all over the world and upon whom she wasted the greater part of the money her careful father had left her at the time he was shot.

"About half a dozen years ago, she had got hold of Grotius, the man about whom you told me once, the absent-minded professor who started on his honeymoon with two trunkfuls of books. But when he had reached Stockholm, he had soon discovered that he was not really wanted there to show his learning. He had been invited as an object of fashionable interest —the man who had written that famous book that was to do away with war. And the damp Stockholm climate had made him sick and he had tried to get back to Europe, had sickened on the way to Paris and had died in some dreadful little German city on the Baltic.

"And that, so it seemed, was exactly what now had happened to poor Descartes. He had been given a high-sounding title, but in reality he found himself in the position of a superior sort of intellectual court-fool. He was asked to draw up the constitution and the by-laws for a Swedish academy of letters which the Queen meant to found and he was told to do his work in the royal library which was both cold and damp, and he had caught an inflammation of both lungs and had died of this complaint early in February. All this the good father told me and I thanked him and asked him whether I could do anything for him in return and he answered, 'I have been told that you are an excellent cook and I wonder whether you would give me some lunch, for I have got to take the three o'clock boat back to Haarlem.'

"'And where do we go from here?' I suggested.

"'Ah, my friend,' he replied, 'that would be telling!'

"But I was curious, and so during the preparation of the meal (the good father had followed me into the kitchen) I said, 'Without committing any further indiscretion, why in Heaven's name did you come to tell me all this? I am glad you did, but if you had not come, I would eventually have heard the news from some one else.'

"To which he answered me with absolute sincerity, 'I came because you interest us. You are not a professing Christian. We know that. We are also aware of the fact that you are a man of great intelligence. Such men can be very useful to us upon occasions. It is well to keep in contact with them and occasionally, if the opportunity offers itself, render them some small service, such as perhaps just now I have been able to render unto you.'

"I answered that I was deeply grateful but again I asked why he had taken so much trouble on my behalf and what did he expect in return, and just as quietly as if we had been discussing the price of butter or eggs, he said, 'Well, you have a soul and a very useful one. We would like to get hold of it before it is too late and show it certain small errors in its method of reasoning but we are in no hurry. And you need not fear that I shall try and hear your confession before I leave. You will probably never see me again. But I hope that you retain a pleasant recollection of my visit. That is all.'

"To which I replied in all sincerity that I would most assuredly remember him during the rest of my days, and then we sat down to dinner and he showed me a new way of mixing a salad-dressing which is a great improvement upon the one I had always used, and we talked of a thousand different subjects and very soon it was time for him to go and he disappeared as quietly as he had come, but just before he left, he said, 'You ought to turn in some time into the shop of that instrument maker on the Singel near the Torensluis. I think that he has got some of those curious Torricellian tubes which I first saw in Florence when I last called on Galileo.'

"I interrupted him with some resentment. 'Then you have something to do with all the misery that overtook that poor man in his old age.' But he refused to be even mildly ruffled. 'Heaven forbid!' he answered. 'We leave that sort of thing to our dear friends, the Dominicans. They have never got over their famous brother Thomas. What he did not know, surely was not worth knowing, and as far as they were concerned, the world stood still when he died. A great man—the venerable Aquinas, but he died 400 years ago and since then a great many things have happened in this world. I did visit the good Galileo Galilei, but merely to assure him that His Holiness sent him his blessing and would never sign the decree by which he was supposed to recant his heresies. Merely a visit of charity, so to speak, for the old man had always been a most faithful son of the Church and he had been deeply mortified by the sentence of the Inquisition.'

"With this remark he quietly departed and I never saw him again."

The letter set me thinking. I had traveled across three thousand miles of wilderness and water to find a companion of the order of Jesus teaching the heathen of the New World the blessedness of the Christian creed by means of fairy stories and crude little pictures. Jean-Louys at home and in the heart of the richest city of the world and a citadel of the Protestant faith, had received the visit of an unassuming little man who seemed to be an authority upon the subject of science and mathematics and whose visit was based upon the very slender expectation that "he might gain his good will."

I knew that the company of Jesus had set out to regain the lost provinces of God for the service of Him whom they regarded as their Heavenly master. But it had never dawned upon me that they would be quite so ubiquitous and so incredibly efficient in their methods. If they could keep this up for another hundred years, things looked very bad indeed for the thousand and one quarreling little sects of the northern part of Europe. From the land of the Cayugas to the banks of the Amstel River was a long distance—a very long distance, as we measured space on this planet of ours. And yet, they were in both spots at the same time—working and pleading and making themselves useful and above all things, being very amiable and very tolerant and almost incredibly reasonable and plausible.

For the sake of the Protestant cause, it would have been a good thing if that bullet of Pampeluna had been aimed a few inches higher.

Chapter 40

I RECEIVE BAD NEWS FROM AMSTERDAM AND DECIDE TO RETURN HOME

As for the other letter, which somehow or other I managed to have kept all this time, it was of a very different nature and talked of matters a little nearer to our own home interests.

"A week ago to-day [Jean-Louys wrote] I decided to call on Rembrandt. But while going down the Oude Schans and by the merest chance, I ran across your old book-seller on the Rokin who also handles some of Rembrandt's etchings. He first of all asked me for news of you and then inquired whether I had heard of the latest troubles of Rembrandt. I said no, and as the old man has apparently retired from business and seemed glad of an opportunity to talk to some one, he gladly accepted my invitation to come home with me and help me eat my dinner, for I decided that my own business could wait. I had not been near the house on the Jodenbreestraat for almost half a year. The last time I had called there the situation had been so awkward that I had vowed to myself that I would never go there again as long as I lived. The nurse Geertje was still on the premises, and more violent and less accountable than ever. But shortly afterwards, so the book-seller told me, there had been an open break between herself and her employer and after that she had behaved so strangely that her relations had been called in and it had been decided to send her to an asylum for a few months' observation. But she managed to get away from them and then began a series of petty persecutions of Rembrandt—which still continue. For example, she went before a judge and swore that her former master had borrowed money from her and had never repaid her, and another time she complained that he had promised to marry her and had not kept his word, and still a third time she stated definitely that she and her old employer had had carnal intercourse and that he had turned her out as soon as he had done his will upon her. And so on and so forth. Until it had become clear to all concerned that she was stark raving mad and thereupon she had been taken away to the town of Gouda, whence she came from originally, and had been committed to the local lunatic asylum in that city.

"Lunatic asylum is perhaps a little too flattering a word. When you remember what our madhouses here in Amsterdam look like, you can imagine what they are in some small provincial hole like Gouda. They seem to consist of a few extra rooms in the local jail and the turnkey feeds the poor devils whenever he happens to think of it. But anyway, the woman was at last out of harm's way and I rejoiced, for now there would be a chance to see something more of Rembrandt than I had done during the last year and a half, and I always liked the man though he has broken every law of nature in regard to those colors which God meant to be 'white' and 'black.'

"But that was only half of the story which the book-seller told me. For it appears that the lady in question is possessed of certain relatives who are not above a bit of blackmail, whenever it comes handy, and can be practiced without too much risk. And the risk in this case was very small, for Rembrandt, who is the world's most muddle-headed financier, has undoubtedly borrowed small sums of money from his son's nurse whenever he was in momentary need of a few guilders to pay the baker or butcher. Very foolish, no doubt, but you know how he is. When he is working, he just does not want to be disturbed and would take cash from the Devil himself. The whole thing, in the language of your esteemed country, is a mess, a 'rommeltje.' (I think that was the first Dutch word I ever learned.) It is a mess, a hopeless muddle. The 'disjecta membra' are all over the Breestraat and I have no idea what the outcome will be. I shall wait a few days and then I shall go forth and do some discreet reconnoitering and I shall let you know.

"After I had seen my guest out (intelligent book-sellers are the salt of the earth and unfortunately as rare as a fine day in March) I decided that it was too late to go to work and too early to go to bed, and having the Breestraat still in my mind, I took my hat and coat and called on Rabbi Menasseh. I found him at home entertaining a number of people and I discovered that this curious old fellow had developed a new hobby. If Bernardo (from whom I have not heard for five or six years. He used to write in the beginning. Is he still alive?)—but if Bernardo actually finds the long lost tribes, and returns home with the good tidings, he will be a very much disappointed man. For Rabbi Menasseh won't even bother to listen to him, instead he will now tell him of a wonderful new scheme he has developed to bring the Jews back to England. He is completely obsessed by the idea. He allows his printing shop to go to ruin and forgets half of the time that he is supposed to teach the Talmud to little Jewish boys, so full is he of this marvelous project.

"As far as I could make out (for as usual everybody was talking at the same moment) he is firmly convinced that the Messiah is about to return and that the Jews, in order not to miss their opportunity this time, ought to settle in every part of the world and make ready to receive the long-expected no matter where he chooses to land on this pretty little planet. That is not exactly the way the good Rabbi expressed himself, but it will give you a fairly accurate idea of what is in his mind. He must have got his 'universal' idea from the East India Company, which has added so much territory to its former possessions that nowadays it is absolutely impossible for a penny's worth of profit to fall upon this earth without being caught by the pocket-book of some Dutch trader.

"After talking for about half an hour, when at last he came up for breath, I quickly asked him how he hoped to accomplish this purpose, as not a single Jew had been allowed in England since the end of the thirteenth century. But he answered that that was a mere detail. It was the English kings who had been responsible for keeping the Jews out of their realm. They had done so out of spite because the Jews were cleverer traders than their own dull-witted Saxon subjects. How they had hated and feared them, one could learn from that contemptible piece of the famous court hack, William Shakespeare. He had never seen a Jew in all his life. When he was born, there had not been a Jew in England for exactly two hundred and seventy-four years but all the same he wrote his monstrous tragedy about Shylock to make the Jews unpopular and to please the Queen. God, however—God the righteous but wrathful—had heavily smitten the wicked rulers of that ungrateful land. The last one of them had been beheaded like a common criminal and now a new day was approaching. A man who truly walked in the footsteps of Jehovah had been called to lead his people out of the wilderness of superstition and intolerance and soon the Jews would be readmitted to all parts of the British Kingdom and to all of the British colonies, because Cromwell the Just not only respected religious principles of the Jews but also recognized the debt of gratitude which Christianity owed the children of Abraham.

"At that moment, a dark-eyed youngster of about sixteen or seventeen years of age spoke up and rather dryly remarked: 'Undoubtedly he does, dear Master. He undoubtedly loves and respects us for the sake of our high-minded religious principles. But has it ever struck you that he may also have a certain admiration for certain commercial abilities which we as a race are supposed to possess?'

"Whereupon the excellent Menasseh flew into a violent rage. 'Baruch,' he thundered, 'are you going to be another Acosta and turn against your own race? Do you dare to come into my house and tell me to my face that this noble Englishman, this second Moses, this prophet and seer who has the power of a dozen kings yet lives simpler than the simplest of his myriad subjects, is merely actuated by a vile lust for gold? I am truly ashamed of you!'

"But that young Baruch, whatever his last name was, remained perfectly calm and quietly answered, 'No, dear Master, I have not the slightest desire to follow the footsteps of poor Uriel and I hold suicide to be a crime against the orderly arrangement of this world. I fully share your admiration for General Cromwell, but I hear that he is a man who takes everything very seriously and that sometime very soon the people are going to offer him the title of their Lord and Protector. Very likely, if he accepts this honor, he will not only try to protect their souls but also their purses. A few thousand Jewish commercial houses, moving from Amsterdam to London, would not come amiss at a moment like the present. It would be another feather in His Lordship's cap.'

"Here I interrupted him. 'I did not think so good a Puritan would ever condescend to wear feathers,' but the youngster merely looked at me for a moment (he had the blackest eyes I ever saw) and then went on. 'I meant his figurative cap, sir. In this house we are always speaking figuratively whenever the Master does not approve of us,' and he explained that that very afternoon he had been called upon to translate a Latin document which one of his father's neighbors had received from London and in which he was offered all sorts of commercial advantages and opportunities if he (his father) agreed to pack up his business and move from Amsterdam to London.

"As this subject of conversation did not particularly appeal to me, I soon afterwards bade them all a good evening and went home. But this true and accurate report of the proceedings in Menasseh's house will show you what way the wind is blowing in this part of the world. The people live under a cloud. They have fought for three generations to gain their liberty. Now they are free and there is a rival across the North Sea who is trying to cut their throats and they are beginning to realize that this was only the beginning and not the end of their difficulties. They will have to sail their newly built craft very carefully if they want to avoid being shipwrecked before they are more than a dozen miles out of port.

"As I said, they are beginning to realize this and then they look anxiously at the poop deck, where the captain and the mate are supposed to dwell in peace and amity that they may give all their thoughts and attention to the difficult business of navigation, and they see those worthies engaged in a disreputable quarrel that may develop into a regular fist fight at almost any moment. The whole thing is very disheartening. The young Prince, if he is not very careful, will end by making a fool of himself. The Amsterdam magistrates, if they continue to insinuate that they and they alone rule the Republic and that both the Prince and the Estates General exist merely for the sake of outward ornament, will find themselves one fine morning in one of the dungeons of Loevenstein with a pleasant-spoken but fierce princely guard on the other side of their doors.

"What will happen to this country unless the people learn to look a little distance beyond the exceedingly narrow limits of their own towns and villages, the good Lord only can foretell. Without quite knowing how they did it, they have acquired such tremendous colonial possessions that they have become the masters of one of the largest empires that has ever existed. But they are trying to rule this empire with the same system of laws that was originally devised for half a hundred hamlets that belonged to some medieval chieftain of the Middle Ages. When told that now they are a big nation and should behave as such, they blush violently and in great embarrassment they answer, 'Oh, sir!' and run as fast as their legs will carry them to the nearest safe spot behind the familiar moat of some ancestral burgh and hastily pass a bill regulating the hours of the civic garbage collectors or stipulating the fee which wet-nurses may charge for their useful and pleasant services. All I can hope for at the present is that you and Bernardo will be safely back here before there is a war. Otherwise you will have to stay in your jungle forever and we need you here.

"As for our mutual friend, about a week ago I desired a fish for dinner (I still obey the dietary laws my father's confessor taught me as a child) and behold! whom should I meet on the fish-market but the good painter from the Jodenbreestraat himself. I thought that he would try to avoid me, for our last meeting had not been exactly a happy one, but he came right up to me and shook me by the hand and said, 'You have heard of course what has happened?' And I answered 'Yes,' and he smiled rather sheepishly and then looked at me and said, 'Phew!' and I replied, 'Yes, indeed, phew!' and then we both roared with laughter and it was the first time I had heard him laugh for several years and so I decided that the obsession of that terrible female had come to an end.

"Then I asked him whether he had joined our Holy Church and was buying shrimps for his Friday dinner, but he said, 'No danger there! They have got hold of old Vondel and ought to be satisfied for the moment. I had a visit the other day from a young Italian nobleman who asked me whether I would be willing to paint him a Madonna in the manner of Raphael. I told him that I had painted any number of Holy Families in the manner of Rembrandt van Rijn. He was a very suave and pleasant young man and said that was exactly what he wanted. There was a patron of the arts in Rome (unfortunately he was not allowed to tell me his name) who had a tremendous respect for my work and who thought I was the greatest painter then alive. Of course my subjects were influenced a little by the surroundings in which I lived, but if I were willing to make just a few changes, such as providing my Virgin and the Holy Child with a halo—just a very small change, as I would undoubtedly see myself—then he from his side would not haggle about the price. I told him that I was deeply touched and flattered but that I painted the way I painted because that happened to be the way I painted and that I could not change my way of painting any more than I could change the shape of my head. He then asked to be allowed to see what I had been doing recently, and I showed him the sketches I had been making for a large picture of the Good Samaritan and some other sketches for a large piece of Christ and Mary of Magdala which I have to finish next year and a half-finished picture of Abraham entertaining the angels, and he expressed himself as delighted with everything and told me that he would write to his employer and would let me know as soon as possible. And so you see, I may be a rich man again, if I will buy enough yellow ocher for half a dozen haloes.'

" 'Which, of course, you won't do!' I said.

" 'Which, of course, I won't do,' he answered, and then he turned to a woman who was standing behind him with a large household basket and quite casually remarked, 'You had better buy another turbot, for if I am not mistaken, our friend here will share our dinner to-night.' And it was said so pleasantly that I forgot all my previous feelings of irritation at his extraordinary conduct and that night I dined with him and I never saw such a change in any human being before. The house was scrupulously clean and it looked quite cheerful, although the carpets were beginning to give evidence of wear and tear and the door and the floors would suffer nothing from a new coat of paint.

"Little Titus, now quite a handsome boy with long blond curls like his mother, was allowed to stand at the table and he had lost that look of a hunted creature which he had had ever since I first knew him. The meal was well cooked and the food was not thrown at us as in the olden days. I asked him where he had found this jewel, and he told me that she was a peasant girl from a small village near the German border, but she had come to Amsterdam to find employment as a general maid, and that a friend had sent him to her because he knew that he was looking for some one after the Dircx woman had been sent to the madhouse.

"'I know nothing about her,' he confessed, 'except that she seems to have no other relatives than a sister who lives in a village called Breevoort, about a week's distance from here, something that suits me exceedingly well, as I have had enough of servants with brothers and sisters just around the corner, ready to perjure themselves at a moment's notice. For the rest, she is an excellent cook, keeps our rooms in order, is as nice to little Titus as if she were his own mother, and has a pleasant shrewdness when it comes to spending money, a quality which is perhaps not out of place in this particular household.'

"'She is also a very handsome woman,' I ventured to remark.

"'Yes,' he answered, 'she will suit me wonderfully well as a model. I was thinking of using her for quite a large picture I mean to make some time—a picture of Bathsheba.'

"I looked at Rembrandt and I looked at the maid who had then turned nurse and was telling little Titus that it was time for him to say good night and go to bed.

"'Remember David!' I warned him.

"'I have thought of that,' he answered, 'but there is really very little danger of such a thing. I am only too happy that I have found a servant like that. The type is scarce nowadays. They all want to work in a shop doing some dull job like curing tobacco or making paper boxes rather than cook for an old widow man.' And he got up to kiss his son good night and went to the door to open it for the servant, who was of a type that was scarce nowadays, and I noticed that he bade her farewell as if she were a very grand lady and then it suddenly struck me: she is a grand lady, even if she cannot read and write.

"And then Rembrandt took me up to the print room and we looked at his etchings and he showed me how he wanted to change the plate of

THREE HEADS OF WOMEN

HENDRICKJE STOFFELS
(about 1652)

the hundred guilder print for the sixteenth or seventeenth time and when I went home shortly after midnight, it was as if nothing had ever happened between us. We were better friends than ever before and when you return, you will witness a miracle—the man is positively showing signs of becoming a normal and civilized human being. He also seems very hard up. But who cares? He is doing better work than ever before, so what is the difference? And fare ye well and come back to us soon. We miss you."

This letter removed the last vestige of doubt that still existed in my mind whether I ought to return or not. After all, this had not been entirely a pleasure trip. I had been sent out to do a very definite piece of work and I had accomplished my task as far as was possible. I had grown very fond of this new country. I had been happy there. But if My Lord Andries and his brother, who had financed the voyage, were in difficulties at the moment or likely to get in difficulties through their quarrel with the Prince, it was up to me to return home and give them that information which might be of the greatest possible value to them at the present moment. I sent word of my plans to Bernardo. The oldest of my two Mohegan servants offered to take the message personally. Two weeks later he returned.

"Your brother only shook his head," he told me.

That was all?

That was all.

I decided not to sell my house. I had become too much attached to that spot to give it up entirely. I went over my accounts and found that I still had more than one thousand guilders left. I gave each of my two servants one hundred guilders in gold and I sent them back to their own country. The ducats would make them rich for the rest of their days and they had well deserved such a reward. I would explain this expenditure to my employers and they would no doubt approve. As for the little house, I had stout doors and window blinds made for it and asked leave to deposit the key at the Fort. My Lord Stuyvesant graciously promised that he would send one of his men every other week to inspect the premises.

I don't believe in lengthy farewells. To say good-by to a dear friend is too much like a minor amputation and it is not good for either the body or the soul. All herbs that I had collected during these many years (with the exception of those I had gathered with Father Ambrosius and which had been destroyed by the Eries when they burned down our Cayuga village) were safely packed in heavy wooden boxes. I had made quite a collection of living plants and these were placed in rough wooden troughs on the poop-deck near the wheel-house where they would suffer as little as possible from the sea.

I then paid an official call on My Lord Stuyvesant and was touched by the emotion he showed in bidding me God speed.

"It will be the last time we see each other," he said, and stamping the floor impatiently with his wooden leg he repeated those words I had heard him use before: "A century hence this land will be of infinitely greater value than Java and all the Moluccas put together. But they won't believe me at home. They won't believe me. They won't believe me until it is too late."

And he actually wept, but whether it was from anger or grief, I could not say though I am inclined to think it was from the former.

One afternoon, late in June, I had my last glimpse of the city of the hills. I had gone on board early in the morning and for several hours we had drifted down the harbor with the tide. On our right was the Staten Eiland, on the left the farms of Breukelen and Nieuw Utrecht. We passed through the narrow funnel that leads from the inner bay to the open sea. In the distance the white beach of the Konijnen Eiland was basking in the sun. Three or four Indian canoes had followed our ship. They were fishermen on their way back to Heemstede. They came very close to the vessel. One of the men in the nearest boat waved his hand at us and called out something. I thought that he was speaking in his own language and I leaned over the railing and cupped my hand to my ear to understand him better. Then I caught his words. They were in Dutch.

"Goede reis!"

The Indian was wishing his white brother a safe crossing.

Then all the sails were hoisted and we turned eastward.

An hour later I had seen my last of the New World.

Chapter 41

I REACH HOLLAND SAFELY BUT FIND THE OLD HOME TOWN SURROUNDED BY THE TROOPS OF THE PRINCE OF ORANGE

Captain Wouters knew his business and the *Zeemeeuw* was a good ship. We had a prosperous voyage and on Saturday, the thirtieth of July, I set foot on shore near Texel.

The next day I found an Urk fisherman willing to take me and my baggage to Hoorn where I arrived on Monday, the first of August. From there I meant to take a carriage to Amsterdam and so I went on shore and went to the inn called the "Roskam," and for the first time in almost two months, I enjoyed the luxury of sleeping in a real bed.

I had asked to be called early the next morning that I might reach Amsterdam before the closing of her gates. But when I woke up, the clock on the Groote Kerk was just striking ten. I called for the landlord and reproached him for his negligence, but he said: "I am sorry, Doctor. You were sleeping so soundly, and it would have been no use calling you anyway."

"But I ordered a carriage at seven," I interrupted him rather sharply.

"The carriage was here, Doctor, but it went away again. The gates are closed. The garrison has been called out. The town will soon be in a state of siege."

"Listen," I said. "I have been away for quite a number of years. But I am not as much of a simpleton as all that. We are at peace with all the world. Surely the Spaniard has not returned to drive us out of house and home."

"No," he answered, "but the Prince may do so at any moment."

And that was the beginning of a very strange adventure, an episode which might have cost me my life, just as I was on the point of seeing my son and my dear friends once more, after an absence of almost seven years.

I went downstairs to the taproom but found it deserted. It had been closed by order of the Magistrates. And so, for lack of anything better to do, I asked where the nearest barber was to be found, for I had not had a decent hair-cut since I left Nieuw Amsterdam, two months before, and looked more like a Cayuga chief than like a respectable member of the Amsterdam Surgeons' Guild.

I found the little shop full of people but none of them seemed to have come on business for I was at once placed in the chair and my honest colleague set to work with such a will that I was in constant fear for my ears. However, I lived through the ordeal without any serious damage being done to my manly beauty and in the meantime I had listened to such a strange chorus of lamentations and curses that I was really no wiser than I had been before and so, after I had paid for the operation, I asked whether I could have a pipe of tobacco and I was shown into the back room which was so full of smoke that it looked like the anteroom of Hades and groping my way to what looked like an empty chair, I sat down and turned to my neighbor and said: "My good friend, I have been away from the country for quite a long time. I returned yesterday to find everybody in great excitement, as if the Republic were in danger of a foreign invasion. Pray tell me what it is all about, for the people who are in the front room do a lot of shouting, but they say remarkably little."

Whereupon this honest citizen informed me that he was in the shipping business and was too busy with his own affairs to take much interest in politics, but if I wanted to know, he could tell me in about two minutes' time, and I answered him that I would gladly give him two hours if only he would enlighten me and then he said:

"Well, it is really all very simple. The Prince of Orange is an ambitious young man who wants to make a name for himself in the only way princes apparently can make a reputation for themselves—by killing a large number of their fellow-men. In other words by conducting a number of successful campaigns. In order to do this, he needs two things, a war and money enough to pay his soldiers. The war part is simple enough. There is always some potentate somewhere in Europe who has a grievance against another potentate and our country, which is now considered the richest nation on earth, is of course a most welcome ally to any monarch who would like to indulge in a little display of gun-powder, if only he could put his hands on a small sum of ready cash.

"But there, my dear sir, is the rub!

"The treasure-chest of these United Provinces stands right in the heart of the city of Amsterdam and, alas, Their Lordships of the Town Hall, who hold the key, are strangely lacking in imagination when it comes to fighting. Each time before they actually engage in a quarrel they sit down before a large table on which there is nothing but a sheet of blank paper. Then they take their goose-quills and start figuring. On the one side they spell out the word 'Debit,' and on the other side the word 'Credit,' all according to that excellent system of book-keeping which the late Master Stevin taught us some thirty years ago. Then underneath the word 'Debit' they write down everything the proposed campaign will probably cost them in guilders and stivers. But underneath the word 'Credit' they write down everything they may safely expect to gain as a result of their ultimate victory, and, mind you! they never start upon such an enterprise until they are mathematically certain that they will gain something. It is a great invention, this new system of book-keeping. If the illustrious uncle of His Royal Highness had ever suspected to what purpose it would be used within so few years after his death, I am sure he never would have made that clever Fleming his quarter-master general.

"Now it is too late. When the Prince let it be known that he expected to conclude a treaty with the King of France and start another war with the King of Spain and conquer the whole of Flanders and make himself Lord of the sovereign city of Antwerp, those of Amsterdam promptly threw the key to their strong-box into the Zuyder Zee and told His Royal Highness how very much mistaken he was if he thought that they would ever lend themselves to such a thing. They had paid out good money for almost eighty years for no other purpose than to break the neck of their hated old rival on the Scheldt and now they were invited to waste further millions to call it back to life for the greater glory of a young man whom they regarded as an intruder and a common nuisance.

"The idea was preposterous. They told His Royal Highness so in very plain terms and when he insisted, they instructed the Estates of their own province (a beautiful arrangement, my dear Sir, for the Estates of Holland, as you probably know, are the same as the Town Council of Amsterdam and the Town Council of Amsterdam is the same as the Estates of Holland)—well, not to bother you with too many details, the town of Amsterdam, speaking ex cathedra, and in its capacity of the greatest money lender of our beloved Republic, told His Royal Highness that he would not get a penny!

"His Royal Highness, considerably annoyed, began to rattle his sword. His Royal Highness has a cousin who is in command of the armies in the north, in Friesland. The cousin also commenced to rattle his sword. Whereupon the Estates hastily dismissed more than two thirds of the army and put the rest on half pay.

"All that is common history. It occurred just before you arrived. But what has happened since Saturday last, I really could not tell you. There had been rumors that the Prince meant to march upon Amsterdam. I do a good deal of business with England and as long as a month ago one of my correspondents in Hull wrote me and asked me what truth there was in the reports that circulated in London that the Prince of Orange meant to attack Amsterdam. I thought nothing of it at the time. The people who rule England nowadays hate the Prince because he is married to one of their Stuarts and of course they would be delighted to start a story like that if they could do him harm by making him a suspicious figure. Then a week ago I got a letter from a friend in Gothenburg who said that the French ambassador in Stockholm had told the consular agent of the free-city of Hamburg that the Prince meant to surprise Amsterdam, hang a dozen members of the town council and make himself king of the Seven United Provinces. I threw that letter into the paper basket. It seemed too utterly foolish. And so, you see, we have had warnings enough and now it has happened."

"Yes," I interrupted him, "it has undoubtedly happened, but just exactly what has happened?"

But that he could not tell me.

"I really don't know," he said, "anything more than you do. I came here to get a little information, just as you did, and I found everybody excited and everybody talking at once and nobody listening to anybody else. Meanwhile, the gates have been closed and the troops have been called out and there you are. But listen! What is that?"

And with his pipe he pointed to the front-room whence there arose a great ado of shuffling feet and of chairs that were hastily being pushed aside as if a large number of people had suddenly taken to flight.

We rushed into the barber-shop and found it empty but there were no signs of violence. The crowd was patiently standing in the middle of the street listening to an old man who had climbed on a stone bench and was reading something from a piece of paper.

"What has happened?" I asked some one who stood just in front of me.

"Shsh," he warned me. "Listen and you will know. He got news from Amsterdam—a letter from his son. They smuggled it through."

Meanwhile the old man on the stone bench continued:

"'It seems at first to have been the plan to take our city by surprise— to hide a company of soldiers in a peat ship and send it into town and then let them come out in the middle of the night and kill the guards and open the gates, as we did in Breda in '37. But this is probably mere talk. Everybody is so excited that the wildest rumors are taken for gospel truth.

"'All we know is that day before yesterday the man who carries the mail from Hamburg to Amsterdam came riding into town as if the devil were on his heels. He asked to be taken at once to see one of the Burgomasters. It was half past seven in the morning and all of the Burgomasters were in The Hague on this business of dismissing the troops, except My Lord Cornelis Bicker. So the mail-carrier was at once taken down to My Lord Cornelis' residence, who received him in his bedroom and heard him tell how that night, in a heavy fog, just as he had passed through the village of Muiden, he had found himself among several companies of soldiers, who seemed to have lost their way and asked him the nearest road to Amsterdam. He had told them, because he was afraid that otherwise they might do him harm, but before they could stop him, he had slipped away in the dark and he had driven his horse at break-neck speed, because he felt sure those soldiers meant no good. Most likely they belonged to a group of mercenaries who had been thrown out of work by the recent peace and who had heard that Amsterdam was the richest city in Europe and who meant to take the town and plunder it.

"'Well, My Lord Cornelis got down to business right away. He gave orders that all the gates be closed and that the militia be called to arms and before ten o'clock ninety new cannon had been mounted on the walls and ships were sailing down the Amstel and the Y to prevent these marauders from attacking us from the side of the water.

"'At eleven o'clock the foreign soldiers actually appeared before one of the gates and asked permission to deliver a letter. Then at last we knew. They were not foreign mercenaries at all. They were native troops commanded by Willem Frederik, a cousin of the Prince, and they demanded that the gates be opened to them "peaceably," that they be allowed to "reëstablish order" and prevent their master from suffering further insults at the hands of the government of Amsterdam.

"'Of course, we from our side refused to accede to this request and as a result we are now being besieged by the army of His Highness. I have just heard that the road to the North is still open and I shall give this letter to the ferry-man to Buiksloot and ask him to send it on to you in Hoorn. We have supplies for at least ten days. In the meantime some solution will have been found. The Prince himself is said to be in Abcoude or in Amstelveen, we don't know exactly where. We are building fortifications outside our gates and since this morning we have begun to cut the dikes on the sea side. Another three days and His Highness will have to move his headquarters to more solid ground.

"'That is all the news. The future is in the hands of God. If this letter gets through, please give a liberal reward to the messenger.'"

There was a postscript.

"'Bread and meat have gone up about a hundred percent since last Friday morning, but the Town Council has just threatened those who mean to make undue profits from the present emergency with fifty lashes and confiscation of their property. That will probably do some good. Farewell.'"

The old man slowly folded his son's letter and climbed down from his perch and the crowd dispersed. Now at last we knew where we were at and I became conscious of only one thing—I had arrived in the nick of time.

The Bicker family which had shown me such great favors in the recent past was in need and I, through the information I had obtained during the last seven years, might be able to help them. I decided to get into Amsterdam at whatever cost. Through sheer luck, at that very moment I bumped into the same gentleman with whom I had had the conversation in the barber-shop.

"I would like to talk to you," I told him, and he answered: "My office is just around the corner. Suppose you follow me there."

Once inside his private room where no one could possibly hear me, I explained who I was and told him enough about my recent exploits to show him how necessary it was for me to get to Amsterdam without any loss of time. The merchant listened patiently. Then he said: "It would mean a great deal to me, too, to get a message into that town to tell my partner to let me know what I ought to buy while the siege is going on. I had thought of sending my son. He has a small boat of his own. But he is only eighteen and apt to be a little reckless. If you will go with him, it will be different. But the trip is a bit risky. No ships are allowed to leave our port until further orders. Will you wait until to-night and take a chance?"

I told him that I would gladly take all the chances in the world if only I could get into the city and I went back to my hotel and told the landlord to lock my room and that I would that evening try and return overland to my ship at Texel to get the rest of my belongings, and he said that that was a very sensible thing to do, for I would not be able to continue my voyage to Amsterdam for at least another two weeks, unless the Prince decided to bombard the city and set it on fire, and shortly after seven that evening I left my inn and went to the house of my merchant friend and two hours later he took me to the water front and pointed a small yacht out to me and said: "Here is a letter to my partner which I hope you will deliver the first moment you have a chance. Now slip quietly on board that little yacht and I will go and talk to the guards at the end of the harbor. The tide is running out and you may be able to slip through without being noticed."

So I climbed down the wet little iron ladder to the deck of the yacht and some one caught my feet and whispered: "Be careful and don't step through the roof. This is rather a flimsy affair," and by and by my eyes accustomed themselves to the dark and I found myself sitting in the cock-pit while a young man with very broad shoulders and very competent hands was loosening the last two ropes and was doing this so carefully that they made hardly any noise when they splashed into the water. A few minutes later we were into the middle of the harbor and half an hour later we were out on the Zuyder Zee. Nothing had happened. No one had tried to stop us. The old merchant apparently had so interested the guards in his conversation that they were looking the other way when we passed them.

The boy, who was both skipper and mate of the little vessel, knew how to sail a boat and early the next morning we found ourselves outside the Gouw Zee between the island of Maarken and Volendam. I had been able to sleep a couple of hours in the small cabin and offered to take my turn at the helm, but the youthful captain was as fresh as the day that was just appearing above the horizon and he would not hear of it.

"I know this water," he said, "and I know the tides and in less than half an hour we will be in the Pampus, where there are all sorts of currents and besides, look way in the distance there. Do you see those black dots? They look like men-of-war. We soon may be in for some trouble. We might as well find out right away. Our conscience is clear and they can't do anything to us anyway." And he set course for the south and two hours later we found ourselves surrounded by seven war vessels which were slowly cruising northward. They flew the flag of the Estates General and we did not know therefore whether they were in the service of the Prince or of the city of Amsterdam. But just as we were debating what to do next, one of the ships, the *Sint Joris*, veered around in our direction and a voice from the poop-deck shouted: "Lower your sails and come alongside!" And these words of warning were followed by two or three shots from muskets which passed directly over our heads and hit the water with a great splash.

Now I am no hero and there are few things I hate quite as thoroughly as being a target for inexperienced and panicky sailors and so I let go as fine a string of vituperations as were ever heard on these placid waters and some one leaned out from one of the after port-holes and shouted: "That must be old Jan van Loon. He always was an artist at that sort of thing!" And behold, there was my good friend, Master Pieter Zuydam with whom I had studied in Leyden years before and who afterwards had become a ship's surgeon, and whom I had not seen for at least a dozen years. But I felt happy that he recognized me, for now at least there was some one who could vouch for me to the commander of this squadron and as a matter of fact, as soon as I had set foot on board the *Sint Joris* I was taken to the captain, who listened most civilly to my story and agreed that I ought to proceed to Amsterdam with all possible haste and present myself to My Lord Andries.

"But don't try to go any further in that pretty little yacht of yours," he warned me. "You will get in trouble every ten minutes as we fear that the Prince may try to force the harbor. I will tell you what I will do. The *Enkhuizer Maagt* has to go back anyway. She has got trouble with her rudder. You go on board her and I will give instructions that you be allowed to pass without further molestation."

I then bade farewell to my excellent young skipper, promised him that I would deliver his father's letter, was rowed on board the *Enkhuizer Maagt* and at one o'clock in the afternoon I found myself in the docks of Amsterdam, behind the Kattenburg redoubt and at half past one, set foot on shore at exactly the same spot from where I had left, almost eight years before.

But I had no chance to meditate upon this strange way in which I was returning home, for every minute now was valuable.

There was quite a crowd of people at the quai and they all seemed eager to hear the latest news from the front. Besides, I still wore the clothes I had bought in Nieuw Amsterdam and I must have looked rather queer. But two sailors, seeing that I was about to be mobbed, jumped out of the boat and made room for me and I walked up the Oude Schans and in half an hour's time I was knocking at the door of my house.

It took some time before I heard footsteps in the hall. Then the little peep-hole in the upper part of the door was opened and a frightened voice asked who was there. I said it was I, the master, returned from his foreign travels, but the voice inside said: "Go away! The master is in America. You are an impostor. Go away, or I will call the guards." And I might have found it impossible to enter my own house, when by rare good luck, my neighbor on the Houtkade, the foreman of the cannon foundry of the Hemonys, happened to leave his house and he recognized me and saw the predicament in which I found myself.

"This is a strange welcome," he said, warmly shaking me by the hand, "but we are all of us a little bit nervous these days. I myself have not been to bed for over three days and nights until this morning, when I snatched a few hours' sleep. Now let me knock and explain to your maid that she can let you in."

A few minutes later the door opened and the honest servant, full of tears and regrets, rushed out to explain how it had happened and to tell me how happy she was to see me once more and ask me to forgive her, but I told her that she had only done what was right and that I was grateful to her for taking such excellent care of my interests, even after those many years, and then I went into the house for the great moment when I should see my son again—the great moment about which I had dreamed for so many years—for which I had prepared so many fine speeches—just what I would say and what my son would answer and how we would both be so overcome by emotion that neither of us would be able to talk.

The boy was in the garden, picking radishes which he put into a little basket. He looked up when he heard my footsteps, and he wiped his muddy hands on his trousers.

Now it was going to happen!

I would open both arms wide and with a voice choked with tears, I would whisper, "My son!" and he, dumbfounded, would give one shriek, "Father!" and then he would throw himself at my breast.

Instead of which the child held one large, red radish up for my inspection and said: "Look, isn't this a big one?" I answered: "Yes, quite a big one." It was not a very brilliant retort, but one had to say something. Then I asked him: "Do you know who I am?" And he wiped his nose with the back of his muddy little hand and said: "No, unless you are the man who has come to fix the chimney."

And I said: "I am your father." And he answered: "Oh?" and went on picking radishes and so I stammered a bit helplessly: "Isn't there something you want to say to me?" And suddenly he smiled brightly and came up to me and put his hand on my arm and asked: "Did you bring me a bear? Nurse told me that if I were a good boy, father would bring me a bear when he came back. Did you bring me one?"

I told him that I had tried to bring him a bear but one fine day the bear, who was very homesick, had jumped overboard and had swum right back to America. And in this way we talked quite happily for about half an hour and then I heard a clock strike and with a shock I remembered that I had work to do that day and I said:

"Father must run now, my darling boy, but he will soon come back and stay with you always. So kiss me and then I must go." Whereupon he gave me a furtive kiss and accompanied me to the front door. But just when I was leaving the house, he called me back and said: "But, father dear, do you really mean to go out in that funny-looking cap?" And he pointed to that garment with a great deal of embarrassment.

"Why, yes, of course," I said. "That is a beaver-skin cap. Everybody wears them in Nieuw Amsterdam."

"Perhaps so," he answered, "but nobody does in Amsterdam." And then he waved his small hand at me and disappeared into the house.

Twenty minutes later I reached the Town Hall. I had anticipated considerable trouble in penetrating to Their Lordships. I had heard my grandfather tell of the siege of Leyden and how all day long eager crowds of excited people had been waiting outside the Town Hall to hear the latest news. I found two guards standing near the door and an officer of the town militia with a large orange scarf (that part of the uniform apparently had not been abandoned, although it would be a long time before any one in the city would exhibit that color as a token of jubilation) asked me what business had brought me there. I told him that I was in a hurry to speak to My Lord Cornelis Bicker, the first Burgomaster.

"Sorry," he said, "but he isn't here to-day. He caught a cold yesterday inspecting the ramparts. He is staying at home all day long. You might find him there if he is well enough to receive you."

All this was not exactly as I had expected it to be, but I consoled myself with the thought that Amsterdam was so big and so strong that the people could afford to regard a calamity like this as a sort of insignificant incident and act accordingly with studied nonchalance.

When I reached the house of My Lord Cornelis there was not even a guard there, but two private coaches waiting near by showed me that something unusual was taking place.

I knocked, and the same maid (a little older of course, but very much the same) opened the door.

"Good morning, Doctor," she said as if I had been away two or three days instead of almost eight years. "Good morning, Doctor, you want to see the master? The doctor purged him this morning. I hardly think that he can see you."

"Suppose you ask him, nevertheless. I come on very important business. He will understand. Tell him I landed an hour ago."

The maid bowed me into the small room on the left of the hall, meant for visitors of the humbler ilk. A few minutes later she returned. "The master is very sorry," she said, "but the purge is just beginning to work and he thinks you had better come back to-morrow morning, rather late."

Then I really did not know what to do. I had rushed back to the city I loved and for whose fate I felt such a keen concern, and I had seen myself rushing in upon the last meeting of the brave little band that had undertaken to defend this citadel of civic independence, and just as they had come to the conclusion that all was lost, I would open the door and say: "My Lord, despair not. I bring you tidings of an even greater land where you can settle down and enjoy the fruits of your industry without the interference of ambitious young potentates and of tyrannical princes."

Instead of which I was asked to come back the next afternoon when the indomitable hero of this glorious last cause should no longer be sitting on the ——!

I took my funny beaver-cap and slowly walked through the hall. The maid opened the door and then a voice from upstairs called out: "Is this Master Jan van Loon?" and the maid said: "Yes, My Lord." And the voice continued: "Ask him to be kind enough to come upstairs for a moment."

And so I mounted the well-known stairs and at the head was welcomed most cordially by My Lord Andries, who patted my shoulder almost affectionately and said: "What marvelous luck that you should have returned at this precise moment. Come in and meet some old friends and then let us tell you what we think you could do for us."

I entered the room and bowed politely to the four gentlemen there present, three of whom I knew by sight and who had been members of the town government when I left in '43.

"I suppose you all remember Master Jan van Loon," My Lord Andries said. "He has just returned from a very interesting voyage to the New Netherlands."

"Yes, My Lord," I interrupted him. "And coming back at a moment like this, when I find my beloved city in such a state of distress, I am happy to say that my mission had not been entirely in vain. I have discovered a territory infinitely larger than that of our Republic, perfectly suited to . . ." But before I could go any further with this speech which I had rehearsed a thousand times, My Lord Andries held up his hand. "That is very interesting, Doctor," he said, "very interesting, what you are telling us there. We would like to hear more, but for the moment we must talk of other matters. For the moment we must try and get rid of that foolish boy who intends to storm our gates. As soon as he is gone, we will have a chance to consider the future. This hour belongs to the present and it is of the present we want to speak to you. Do you know Huygens?"

"My Lord of Zuylichem?"

"Exactly."

"Yes, I have enjoyed his friendship for many years."

"Very well. We want you to render us one more service. For the moment there is only one thing for us to do, persuade or flatter or cajole this young hot-head to go back to The Hague and call off his army. We are not sufficiently prepared to stand a siege. As soon as he is gone, we can make plans for the future and no doubt we shall meet His Highness again some day under somewhat different circumstances. We have good reason to suppose that he will feel satisfied if we promise him that I and my brother Cornelis, the Burgomasters, shall retire from our posts and shall remain excluded from office for the rest of our natural lives. How long that 'rest of our natural lives' will mean, we don't of course know. Probably a couple of years or until we are strong enough to turn the tables on His Royal Highness and can perhaps induce him to return to his ancestral estates in Germany. But all that is neither here nor there. We will attend to those matters when the proper moment comes.

"To-day we are face to face with an emergency and if we can solve that emergency by offering ourselves as scape-goats and sacrificial lambs, so much the better.

"You know My Lord of Zuylichem, but you will have very few other acquaintances among the entourage of His Highness. He has dismissed most of his father's counselors and has taken on a new set of his own.

"You will probably be able to make your way to Amstelveen without attracting any attention. If any soldiers should stop you, you can tell them that you are a surgeon on the way to visit a farmer near the Noorderbrug. Find My Lord of Zuylichem and tell him, discreetly, very discreetly if you please—tell him that my brother Cornelis and I are willing to withdraw from public life if the siege is lifted at once."

"Is that the only message?"

"That is all we want him to know for the moment. My Lord of Zuylichem is a very intelligent man. He will understand and will take the necessary steps. It is now five o'clock but it will be light until eight. You can take my carriage as far as the Overtoom. There you probably can hire a peasant cart and with a bit of luck you will be able to see Huygens still this evening. Good-by and good luck!"

I bade my adieux but as I was leaving the room, My Lord Andries called me back. "Better not wear that Indian headgear," he advised. "It might attract a little too much attention. The rest of your clothes are all right, but here, take my hat!" And so I went forth upon this new adventure in the hat of one of Their Lordships who rule the destiny of the common man until they get into difficulties, when suddenly they bethink themselves of one of their humbler neighbors, call him a good fellow, pat him on the back and make use of him until the crisis has come to an end.

With a loud clatter of horses' hooves we rolled through the streets of Amsterdam which except for an occasional citizen carrying a halberd or a musket looked about as peaceful as under ordinary circumstances, but as soon as I reached the gate, the scene changed. A hastily scribbled note, however, which My Lord Andries had given me, did wonders and the Captain of the Guard told me that it was possible to proceed as far as the Overtoom. "There you will have to ask again," he said. "But an hour ago, the road was still free."

The heavy door of the gate therefore was opened and the bridge was lowered and the coachman carefully drove his horses across the slippery stones on the other side of the moat and then suddenly we found ourselves in the midst of several hundred men with spades and wheelbarrows, busily engaged in building a low bulwark of clay and mud which was to protect the gate from being surprised by a sudden attack on the part of the enemy's cavalry. Where the road broke through this earthen wall, two officers were standing together with a civilian, eagerly studying a map which the civilian held spread out before them.

We had to drive very carefully on account of all the workingmen and at that point we came to a stop because one of the horses slipped and almost fell and in so doing kicked through one of the traces. The coachman came down from his box to fix the matter and meanwhile I looked at the small group that was directing the work. I did not know the officer, but the civilian, who seemed to be in command, looked singularly familiar. At that moment he took his hat off to shade his eyes, and I recognized him. It was Jean-Louys.

He knew me at once and gayly waved his sheet of parchment, said: "Excuse me," to his two companions, and rushed over to the carriage.

"Slowly," I called out. "Slowly! you will slip."

"A thousand slips," he answered, "for the pleasure of seeing you again. And what a rentrée! How marvelously staged! What action—and what actors! And our humble leech enthroned upon the seat of the mighty. And so soon! When did you arrive?"

"About four hours ago."

"And now bound for Amstelveen on business for Their Lordships! What a diplomat was lost when you took to pills instead of to a pen!"

"Thanks for the compliment," I told him, "but how about yourself? The great philosopher, the pupil of the one and only Descartes, wallowing through the mud, building a little wall. . . ."

"Ssh!" he warned me. "Not so loud. Remember Romulus and Remus. This is a most respectable piece of defensive architecture, constructed entirely according to the principles of siege-craft as laid down by His Late Majesty the King of Sweden, Grand Duke of Pomerania and Hereditary Polisher of the Northern Star. You forget I was once one of His Majesty's most trusted officers. But what glorious absurdity! what a buffoonery! This poor clown outside who calls upon Beelzebub to come forth from his hiding place—then is scared to death when he sees that the old devil means business, and who now does not know what to do—whether to shoot or not to shoot. And we from our side also seriously playing at war—hauling guns to the parapets—hiring all the loafers in town for a guilder a day to stand guard and see that no peasant women from Slooterdijk smuggle in a couple of Orange-men beneath their petticoats. Oh, it is a glorious sight! Philosophers building salients and leeches trotting forth upon diplomatic missions!

"Bon voyage—for you will be in a hurry. Come back soon and we shall have dinner and we shall talk, talk, talk!"

Fifteen minutes later I was at the Overtoom. There had been a few hussars there that morning belonging to one of the regiments of the Frisian Prince of Orange, but they had gone away again after each one of them had ordered a couple of schnapps and had paid for them too. This last item, the fact that they had actually paid for their drinks, had filled the hearts of the near-by farmers with such surprise that they were still standing near the lock, talking about it. When I asked for a carriage to take me as far as Amstelveen, one of the older men asked me whether I meant to pay for it too.

"Surely," I answered, "as much as you care to ask."

They all opened their mouths wide and stared at each other.

"This is a new sort of a war, boys," the lock-keeper finally said. "A war in which people are polite and say pardon me before they shoot you and pay for what they get. You had better make the best of it and inspan right away."

I chose the farmer who seemed to live nearest and half an hour later I was on my way to Amstelveen, where I arrived shortly before sunset without any further untoward adventures. Three times I was stopped by mounted patrols who asked me who I was and where I was going, but when I answered them that I was a surgeon on my way to a patient, they promptly apologized for having stopped me and let me go.

Just outside the village I dismissed the driver, gave him his money and a tip and told him that if he cared to wait at his own risk, I might need him again in a couple of hours for the return trip. He said that he had nothing else to do and would go to the nearest tap-room. Any time I wanted him I need only send word to him and he would be there in two shakes.

Tipping is a strange business. Give a man one penny less than he thinks he deserves, and he will be ready to knife you at the first possible opportunity. Give him one half-penny more than he had expected, and he will be your friend for life.

The honest rustic was as good as his word. An hour later I found him at exactly the same spot where I had left him and he had even found me some bread and sausage. "For you must be hungry," he said. And he drove me back at such a rapid pace that I was able to knock at My Lord Andries' door just when the clock of the South Church was striking twelve. In the meantime, I had had many strange adventures and I had learned once more that this planet of ours is not exactly ruled by either the wisest or the noblest of God's creatures.

When I left my carriage, I had no idea in the world where I would find My Lord of Zuylichem. I decided to walk right to the village and ask the first man who looked as if he had some authority and as if he would be able to tell me. But the road was quite deserted as it was supper time, and all the soldiers engaged in this gigantic drama seemed to be in their quarters to eat their evening porridge, like well-behaved children. And the farmers were no doubt waiting on them and watching, lest these unwanted guests depart with the family silver and china.

In front, however, of one of the houses near the center of the village, one that also seemed a sort of village-inn, I saw a young man standing who was apparently engaged in the business of angling, though what he expected to catch there so late at night was somewhat of a puzzle to me. And when I came a little nearer, I noticed that he could not be fishing, for he had stuck his rod deep into the mud of the ditch and then I saw that it was not a fishing rod at all which he held in his hand, but a bamboo cane, and that he was trying to discover the depth of the water.

"Yes, my friend," I said to myself, "the locks near Muiden are open and two or three more days like the present one and a favorable wind and you will be hastening back where you came from, unless you want to get a pair of very wet feet." But I kept this pleasant thought to myself and merely said: "Pardon me, young man, but could you tell me where I could find My Lord of Zuylichem? He is said to be somewhere around here with His Highness."

"Lord of Zuylichem be damned!" the young man answered. "Do you know this part of the country?"

I said yes, that I did.

"Very well," he continued. "Then tell me how long it will be until the water here will be getting higher than the land."

I did not like the insolence of his tone but neither did I want to expose my mission to any danger by answering in too sharp a tone of voice, and so I said: "Well, I could not tell you for sure. The locks near Muiden were blown up yesterday. This afternoon I hear they cut the dikes near the Plague House and to-morrow they will be cutting the Amstel dike near the Omval. Then with a bit of a wind—and I see that the wind is turning towards the east this evening—there ought to be about three feet of water here by Thursday."

"Damn your eyes!" said the young man, waving his cane at me. "And now what do you want? You are probably a spy, sent by the bastards in that town to find out what I am doing." And more threatening: "Who are you, anyway?"

"I don't suppose it is any of your business," I replied, not without some heat, "but since you ask me so pleasantly, I will tell you that I am the barber from Ouderkerk and have been sent for by My Lord of Zuylichem to wait upon him."

"A strange time of the day to have one's whiskers attended to, but wait a moment and we will find out."

And he went to the door of the inn and shouted: "Huygens! Hey, Huygens, come here. A friend to see you."

And indeed, there was My Lord of Zuylichem, not a day older than when I had seen him last and he recognized me at once and came to me and took both my hands in his and shook them most cordially, whereupon the insolent young man whistled a loud phew! and disappeared inside the house.

As soon as I knew that no one could understand us, I whispered: "I want to speak to you alone. I have come on very important business. Have you a room to yourself here?"

"No," he said, "I am sharing a little cabinet next to the sleeping quarters of His Highness—I am sharing it with his valet. The valet is a Frenchman and I don't trust him. Let us walk up and down the road. That is the safest place."

And he took me by the arm and marched me up and down until I had delivered my message and had told him that unless the Prince accepted this sacrifice on the part of the Bicker family and was contented to save his face by some such sort of a compromise, the town would cut all the dikes and would defend itself unto the last.

This threat did not seem to impress My Lord of Zuylichem deeply. "I know our friends inside those walls just as well as those outside," he remarked dryly. "They won't fight an hour longer than is profitable. But those over here" (waving his free hand in the general direction of the village inn) "are not going to fire a single shot unless one of their soldiers happens to get too much to drink and stumbles over his own musket. What you say is right. We must find a way out that allows both sides to save their faces. The Bickers can gracefully retire from office for a couple of years without suffering any great financial or social loss. They are rich and that little Bicker girl will probably marry Jan de Witt before very long and the day may come when I will have to ask her to use her influence with her husband to get me a job as messenger-boy of the Council of State. You go back to Amsterdam to-night, my dear friend, if you can do so without breaking your neck or getting shot by a drunken Hessian. And you tell them that I will do as they asked me."

"But are you sure of all that without first speaking to His Highness?"

"Listen! His Highness wishes to God he had never started this thing. It may cost him his head or at least, his job, though it does not look as if any of the other cities were losing any sleep over Amsterdam's predicament. But he has bitten off much more than he can chew. Leave everything to me. Tell the Bickers to send us an official delegation of the sort of people who can bow themselves nicely out of a room. The Prince likes that and meanwhile I will draw up some sort of an act of agreement. With a bit of luck, all will be over by to-morrow night, except the pumping. I suppose it will cost you a pretty penny to get all this land dry again."

"To tell you the truth, I don't think we have cut enough dikes to do any considerable damage."

"Only as a sort of sample of what could be done?"

"Yes. Just about that. Enough anyway to frighten the youngsters in your army. That blustering ensign who called you just now seemed quite upset by the prospect of getting his feet wet."

"Whom do you mean? The young man with the bamboo cane?"

"Yes. The one who called you."

"He has reason to be worried. That is the Prince."

Chapter 42

THE PRINCE IS FORCED TO GIVE UP HIS NEFARIOUS DESIGNS AND FOR THE FIRST TIME IN MANY YEARS I AM ABLE TO FRY EGGS ON MY OWN KITCHEN TABLE

The rest of that memorable day belongs to history. I found my Overtoom farmer still waiting for me and without any further adventures we reached the city gate where we found everybody wide awake and looking rather sheepish, as if something awkward had just happened.

I did not discover at that moment what it was, but several days later I heard the story from one of the sergeants who had cut his finger trying to charge his musket and who had got blood poisoning in the wound.

Shortly after eleven o'clock that evening the guards had been alarmed by something that sounded like the charge of a regiment of cavalry. They had fired a volley and thereupon the enemy had disappeared but an hour later there had been another charge, answered by another volley, and so on all during the night.

Why this had not started a panic all over town, no one knew unless it were due to the fortunate circumstance that the wind was blowing the other way.

In the morning, as soon as it had become light enough, a patrol had gone out to reconnoiter. They found a couple of horses belonging to a dray-man who lived near the gate peacefully grazing just outside the ramparts. As a rule, those animals were tethered, but upon this occasion they had managed to get themselves free and they had spent a happy night trotting up and down the beautiful rampart which Jean-Louys had been constructing the afternoon before.

As for myself, as soon as I had delivered my message, I felt that I was at liberty to return home. But My Lord Andries and his brother (who had apparently entirely recovered from his recent indisposition and was now full of his usual energy) begged me to stay awhile and partake of some refreshments, as I must be very hungry and tired after such a long day, and I accepted gratefully and they sent to the kitchen for some bread and cold fish and butter and beer—a lot of beer—and then only I discovered how tired and thirsty I was and from sheer exhaustion I fell asleep right there in my chair and they put a rug over me and let me sleep, and when I woke up, it was full daylight and I felt as if I had been pulled through the eye of a needle, but soon I was joined by the two brothers who told me that a delegation from the magistrates was already on its way to Amstelveen and that they hoped that the whole business would be over before nightfall, and thereupon we breakfasted together and at ten o'clock I was at last on my way home, having returned his hat to My Lord Andries and wearing once more that strange peaked affair that had so upset the feelings of propriety of my young son and heir.

It was a warm and lovely day. Word must have gone about that the siege would soon be lifted, for the streets were much fuller than the day before and everywhere I went groups of men and women were standing around, talking about the latest news from the front, and the children improved the occasion by making even more of a nuisance of themselves than usual. About a dozen rotten apples and at least three cauliflowers were heaved at my beaver cap before I had gone more than halfway and so I knew that we were fast returning to normal conditions.

But at home I found everything in the greatest possible commotion. My small son looked the depth of despair and as soon as he saw me, he threw himself into my arms and cried: "Oh, father, I am so sorry! I thought that you had been angry with me for poking fun at your strange hat and I felt you would never, never, never come back to me!"

Whereupon I told him that father had been busy all day and all night long to help the government save the city from the Prince and he stamped his foot and said: "I hate the Prince!" But I told him that the Prince was probably doing what he thought was right, just as we were doing what we thought was right, and that there was very little reason for hatred as no harm had been done. And then I said: "Now come upstairs with me and I will wash and comb my hair and then we will go out together and buy a new hat."

In that way I took my first walk with my son and I felt very proud of myself. It had often struck me that I led much too lonely a life—that I ought to go out in company more—that I ought to marry again and perhaps have more children. But I was afraid. In all my life I had only met one woman whom I really felt that I could love and (what is more important) be patient with, even if I had a dozen headaches and she had asked me the same foolish question three dozen times. She was very handsome and she was very intelligent. She knew what I was going to say half a minute before I said it and I knew what she was going to answer before she had so much as opened her mouth. It had sometimes happened that I had not seen her for two or three months and then I discovered that I knew all the things that had happened to her and she knew all the things that had happened to me. She had liked me from the very first and I had liked her from the very first and she probably would have taken me and then I had lost courage. I had seen my brother go to his death through a woman, a heartless and silly and stupid creature who destroyed him to please her own vanity and I was afraid.

I told myself that this woman would be entirely different. I knew that she would be entirely different. And yet I did not dare go near her.

Then a number of other little incidents had occurred. I began to watch my friends. All of them were married. How many of them were really happy? How many of them were better off now than if they had stayed single? I did not know. I talked it over with Jean-Louys, the only man with whom I could talk about such things. He did not know either. He would not even offer a guess.

"I tried it once," he said. "I had to have a woman or go crazy. God had made me that way, but nobody had taken the trouble to tell me so. Wherefore I drew heavily upon the recollection of all the idiotic medieval sagas I had read as a small boy and came to the conclusion that I was another Abélard or Tristan. But I wasn't. I was a young specimen of the male order of our tribe and I was seventeen or eighteen and I experienced a hunger for the female order of our species that was perfectly normal but quite appalling.

"The moment they noticed my condition, parents and relatives and all the priests in the world came rushing down upon me and filled my head with a lot of nonsense about it. That made it all the more attractive. The girl was willing. I sinned. She sinned. We both sinned, and we had a glorious time. Did the parents and relatives and priests rush to their churches to thank God that two people had snatched a moment of happiness off the granite rock of Fate? They did not. They separated us and perhaps it was just as well. I saw the girl ten years later. She had married a wine merchant and had borne him eleven children. She was fat and dumb and had whiskers and I hated the sight of her.

"It is a difficult subject and you had better ask some one else. I suppose it is a good thing for the average man to marry. He has no resources outside himself. His wife therefore, no matter how stupid she may be, will probably amuse him instead of leaving him. He has some one to sleep with who has got to pretend that she likes him whether she really does or not. He has some one to cook for him and wash for him and look after his children. For that sort of person it is a fine arrangement—an ideal arrangement—but for people with brains—for people like you and me who have work to do in this world, it is nonsense to think of marriage. It dulls the spirits and it leads to endless misery.

"Women are vain. They like to show off. They like to be the center of whatever society they happen to frequent. They hate a man who is just above the average. They detest one who is really clever. When they run across a male being with a first rate set of brains, they are ready to commit murder. Such a fellow is their natural enemy. He robs them of the attention they want to draw unto themselves, no matter whether they are buying fish or dancing a minuet. You might marry your wonderful woman. A week afterwards she would be scratching your eyes out because His Lordship, the third assistant Burgomaster, had returned your salute without paying as much attention to her as to you."

This was sound advice no doubt, but not exactly helpful. It only bewildered me a little more than I had been before and I had left for the New World without ever having settled the question. For all I knew, the woman might be still waiting for me or might have married some one else years before and might have forgotten me completely by now.

These thoughts came running through my mind as I walked to the hat store on the Oude Singel, proudly listening to my son who told me how that old bridge, just off the Verwersgracht, had come down one day underneath the weight of a heavy piece of basalt which they were moving from the stone yards along the Amstel to the Dam to be used in the construction of the new Town Hall, how the horses that pulled the cart had been dragged into the water and had stood there for almost a whole day with their noses just above the surface until a boy had dived into the gracht and had cut them loose. And when we came to the bridge, I saw that it had been recently rebuilt and right in the middle of it there stood a familiar figure holding a pad of paper in one hand and a pencil in the other.

It was Rembrandt, not a day older than when I had last seen him, making a sketch of some boats that were unloading a cargo of peat for one of the big bakeries that work for the city's hospital.

He was so engrossed in his work that he did not notice me and I waited until I was right behind him and then I said: "Why not go to the walls and paint My Lord Banning Cocq, now that he is engaged in defending our city against the attacks of our enemies?"

Whereupon he turned around and threw both arms around my neck and kissed me on both cheeks (to the terrible confusion and shame of my small child, who hastily looked the other way) and then he said: "The poor child! Here his father returns home after years of absence, during which we have all of us missed him so much that more than once we were on the point of joining him and his band of warriors on the other side of the ocean. And here he comes back, wearing a most beautiful beaver cap and with just as little sense as ever."

"Wait a moment," I interrupted him, at the same time pulling my son from underneath the wheels of a dray, loaded heavily with barrels of salted fish. "I agree about the cap but why this slur upon my sanity? I can assure you I never felt better in all my life, nor of a better mind."

"Then why do you prattle about enemies and old Banning Cocq, whom I painted a thousand years ago, fighting somebody."

"Oh," I answered, "I was only joking. Everything seems to be going nicely now and so I suppose we can be funny about it. I was thinking of something that happened on the walls yesterday."

"The walls? What walls?"

"Why, the walls near the Haarlemmerpoort."

"They are all right. I saw them last Sunday. I took Titus for a walk to the lake. Nothing the matter with them then!"

"Of course not. I was not thinking of the walls themselves but of something that happened to the soldiers who were on guard."

"But there aren't any soldiers on guard there nowadays. There have not been for years. A few of them spend the night sleeping in the little room over the gate and that is all."

"Rembrandt," I said, "don't be silly and don't try to be funny. You know perfectly well what I mean. The walls have been manned again ever since the siege began."

"Siege?" he asked. And then I discovered that he had not heard a word about it—that he did not know that almost any time during the last three days the Prince might have bombarded us and might have blown him out of house and studio. It seemed incredible but it was true. I had had to come all the way from America to tell him that there had been an outbreak of civil war.

"But what, in the name of Heaven," I asked him, "have you been doing with yourself these last four days?"

"I have been working," he answered. "I have been doing some portraits of my brother Adriaen and his wife. He has an interesting head. Plain but interesting and I can't stop painting just because some prince of something decides that he is bored and that a little fighting would be a welcome change. Of course, if they had bombarded the city, I might have been killed. Then I would have died putting an extra coat of paint on Adriaen's nose. Like another Archimedes: Noli tangere fratrum meum. It would have been a fine death and they would have remembered me ever so much longer than they will do now. Meanwhile you have spoiled my sketch for me. I hate to tell you how I have missed you. What are you going to do now? Whither are you bound?"

And he took my son by the other hand and he led the way to the hat store and half an hour later, once more provided with a respectable headgear, black of color, and of a most conservative pattern, we returned to the Houtgracht.

But just as I was about to turn the corner, Rembrandt shouted: "Oh, no, my dear friend, that will never do! To-day you belong to me." And he took me and my boy to the house on the Breestraat and he pushed the door wide open as I had seen him do in the old happy days when Saskia was still alive, and he shouted:

"Hendrickje, go out and kill the fatted calf. The prodigal has returned." And a moment later I was looking into as handsome a pair of brown eyes as I had ever seen and a pleasant-looking girl was curtseying to me and was saying: "Oh, I suppose you are the doctor of whom the master has so often spoken. I am very glad, Sir, that you are back. I have known your son for some time. He sometimes visits us and plays with Titus."

And that is how I first met Hendrickje.

I was to see her daily for almost ten years and I was to be on terms with her of the most genuine friendship.

But I never knew a person who was as kind and simple and under=

standing as this peasant girl who could neither read nor write—this peasant girl whom the ministers of our town degraded to a common whore and who was more fit to sit on God's foot-stool than ninety-nine out of every hundred little saints who were allowed in the Divine presence.

For the little saints, as a rule, had only saved themselves. And this big-hearted sinner, who was cast out by the respectable part of the community, lost herself in order to save the man she loved.

Chapter 43

I WRITE MY OFFICIAL REPORT AND WHAT BECAME OF MY RECOMMENDATIONS ABOUT AFFAIRS IN AMERICA

The next six months of my life were very busy and very interesting, and therefore very happy.

Everything came as the Bickers had planned. The Prince, who by this time had realized his mistake, was glad to accept the compromise they suggested. It allowed him to retire more or less gracefully from a position that had become exceedingly difficult.

Nothing had happened according to his plans. The "money-grubbers" of Amsterdam for whom His Highness and his French friends had often expressed their unbounded contempt, had not shown the white feather but had prepared for action with an energy and a display of personal courage that no one had dared to predict. The common people in Amsterdam, the staunch old friends of the House of Orange, who according to the words of their pastors were "ready to rise as soon as the Prince should show himself outside the city gate," had done nothing of the sort. They had rushed to arms, but only to defend their beloved town against the foreign mercenaries who were threatening the safety of those who were supposed to be their masters.

A week before in The Hague, after an excellent dinner, it had all seemed so beautifully simple. The poor, down-trodden members of the working classes would take their muskets and would rush to the Town Hall shouting: "Death to the tyrants!" Perhaps they would even hang a couple of Aldermen and so much the better!

They had taken their muskets and had indeed rushed to the seat of government but only to cheer for their noble saviors and vow fidelity unto death.

Yes, there was no use talking. It had all come very differently from what one had had reason to expect. The polite exchange of some very polite notes (beautifully polished by My Lord of Zuylichem and his friends from the Dam) had settled the whole matter in a most tactful and agreeable manner. Within a week, the regiments of His Highness were back in their usual quarters and My Lord Cornelis and his brother Andries had packed their papers and documents, had surrendered their seals of office and had gracefully withdrawn from public life.

It was observed, however, that the vacancies caused by their withdrawal were not at once filled with other candidates, but remained unoccupied, as a silent but eloquent protest against a policy which had tried to achieve by means of violence what could have been accomplished equally well in a perfectly legitimate manner.

The other members of the government residing outside of Amsterdam who had dared to oppose His Highness' projects and who (as we now discovered) had been lifted from their beds by a company of hussars and had been incarcerated in the castle of Loevenstein without any process of law, were allowed to return to their homes.

For the moment Amsterdam was obliged to accede to the demands of His Highness in regard to the strength of the army, but Their Lordships counterbalanced this decision by increasing the strength of the town militia from twenty companies to fifty-four, and they constructed a series of block-houses around the city which doomed all future surprise attacks to absolute failure.

Thus ended one of the strangest episodes in the history of our country, in which water had flowed more freely than blood, for not a single soldier had lost his life. A great many of them developed serious colds in consequence of the muddy state of the territory in which they had been forced to operate. And that was all.

The holes in the dikes were speedily repaired. The farmers who had suffered damage or who claimed that they had suffered damage, were repaid according to the reasonableness of their lamentations. A number of bad poets on both sides wrote very bad poetry in honor of the success or failure of the famous "attentat." Two or three very ugly pennies were struck to commemorate the courage of the defenders or the attackers, and the siege of Amsterdam belonged to the past.

As the relations with The Hague remained more or less strained, we were not kept very carefully informed about the secret negotiations which His Highness was reported to have continued as soon as he had returned to his Palace in the Woods. I am afraid that those would have brought our country into serious difficulties with all the world. For it now seems quite certain that His Highness not only meant to conclude a treaty of amity (and 60,000 men) with the King of France who was then at war with his Spanish neighbors, but also that he was contemplating an invasion of England to bring the Stuarts back to the throne and make an end to the rule of Cromwell and his Puritan cohorts.

To what extremes of misery these ambitious schemes would have led us it is impossible to state. Early in October the Prince had gone to his estates in the eastern part of the country to do some hunting. On the 27th of October, he complained of feeling ill. The local surgeon could not diagnose the complaint and sent the patient back to The Hague. The trip in a draughty coach must have aggravated his condition. When he reached The Hague it was plain that he was suffering from "variola minor," or small-pox. He was bled twice, but rapidly sank into a coma. On the sixth of November he died. A week later his widow was successfully delivered of a son. The child was called Willem after his father, and for convenience' sake was numbered Willem III.

We all piously but fervently prayed that the boy might take after his great-grandfather. As for the father, we peacefully forgot him and that was perhaps the kindest thing to do.

And as for myself, I never regretted the humble rôle I had been allowed to play during those momentous days. Through the good services of Captain Wouters and the landlord of the Roskam in Hoorn I received all my trunks and my valuable collection of American plants and shrubs in perfect order. Only two or three specimens had died. All the others, wonder above wonder, had survived the hardships of the voyage. I made a present of them to the Botanical Garden in Leyden where they proved of great value to the students of botany.

My papers, too, which I had entrusted to the captain, I received back without losing a single letter, and after copying them and rewriting parts, I was able to offer my report to Their Lordships within less than six months after my arrival. They expressed themselves as being highly grateful and appreciative of my efforts and my devotion to their interests. As I would surely understand myself, the great change in the political situation which had temporarily deprived them of much of their power, made it impossible for them to act immediately upon all my suggestions. But they would carefully consider everything I had told them and would take the necessary steps as soon as possible.

That ended my personal participation in the great American adventure. My Lord Andries died in '52 and his brother followed him to the grave two years later and I lost contact with the Bicker family.

In the year 1652 Nieuw Amsterdam received full civic rights and the government of the town was copied upon the system of government which prevailed in our own country.

Four years later, in '56, the town of Amsterdam paid the West India Company 600,000 guilders for a tract of land along the Delaware River where a new and independent colony was to be founded, to be known as Nieuwer Amstel. All over the land the new board of directors advertised for immigrants willing to go to the New World and devote themselves to the business of raising grain. In my report of the year '51 I had definitely indicated this region as most suitable for the purpose which was in the minds of Their Lordships.

In how far, however, they had acted upon my original recommendations, I am unable to tell. The sons were not like their fathers. I had been sent out to do a certain job. I had done it. I had been well paid for my efforts. That ended the story as far as they were concerned. And as far as I was concerned, too.

Chapter 44

THERE WAS ONE WOMAN I LOVED AND I LOST HER

At first it had seemed best for me to return to my practice.

During my last interview with My Lord Andries he had asked me suddenly what I expected in a way of reward. I told him that I expected nothing. I had been paid generously for my services and was content.

"No," he then replied, "but what I mean is this. Isn't there some office you would like to have? We are no longer as powerful as we once were, but our former colleagues still listen to us attentively when we offer to make a little suggestion."

But I assured His Lordship that this was out of the question. We had always been very simple people. None of my ancestors had ever held public office and we were little gifted for that sort of work. I would only have made myself slightly ridiculous and would have lost the respect of my neighbors if through the influence of powerful friends I should suddenly reappear as some High- and Noble-Born Keeper of the Official Accounts or Inspector of the Local Pawnshops. No, I could not think of it! But His Lordship could render me one great service, the nature of which I then explained.

The shares of the East India Company, which my uncle in Veere had left me, had increased in value and assured me a comfortable competence for the rest of my days. I therefore need not resume my practice. But two trips across the ocean and a long residence in the New World had shown me once more how terribly neglected the surgery was on board those vessels that belonged to the regular navy or to the merchant fleet. And that was in time of peace when nothing much more serious ever occurred than a broken leg or a twisted ankle. What it would be like in case of war, when the wounded lay piled three deep in the hold of the vessel while the surgeons worked by the light of a candle and sawed off arms and legs amidst the groaning of the dying and the stench of the dead, I did not even dare to imagine. I wanted very much to continue my researches in the field of anesthetics. And if Their Lordships would talk to their friend and colleague, Doctor Tulp, and would ask him to bring about some sort of an arrangement which would allow me to continue my studies along that line in the hospitals of the city, I would be deeply grateful.

My Lord Andries was as good as his word. Within less than two weeks after our last interview, Doctor Tulp sent for me. He had been one of the four men who on behalf of the city had taken part in the negotiations with the Prince and who had signed the final agreement which had raised the siege and he was generally recognized as one of the strongest men in our town. He received me most charmingly, asked a great many very intelligent questions about my travels in the New World and declared himself to be in hearty sympathy with my plans for the future. Indeed, he then and there gave me practically carte blanche to do whatever I wanted to do within my particular field of investigation.

Of course, a great many of my colleagues objected strenuously when I knocked once more at the hospital's doors and demanded that they did not operate upon their patients without at least giving me a chance to try and alleviate the sufferings of these poor people by first bringing about a state of semi-consciousness. Some accused me of being a meddler with God's will and others called me a quack and a charlatan who merely wanted to make himself conspicuous. They even went so far as to tell their poor ignorant customers that I had sold my soul to the Devil and meant to cast a spell upon them as soon as they should have lost consciousness, and often my experiments failed because the patients had been thrown into such a state of panic by these lies and they fought so violently to escape from my administrations that in several instances they were threatened with heart-failure and I had to desist and leave the room.

But gradually when it was observed that I charged nothing for my labors and that both the surgeon and his victims benefited greatly from the absence of that hideous pain that often ruined the poor victim for life (even if he survived the knife and the saw), the medical faculty slightly relented and the sick too began to drop their suspicions whenever my name was mentioned, until in the end, hardly an operation was performed without my assistance.

I was often asked to give away the secret of those vapors with which I filled the victim's lungs before he was fastened to the operating table. A secret, of course, it never was, for I freely told all of my colleagues who showed a serious interest. But until I should have perfected my methods a little more thoroughly, so that all elements of danger had been completely removed, I thought it wiser not to put the result of my studies into print.

All the mountebanks and medicasters who make the rounds of our country fairs would at once have set up as "painless surgeons," and with their total lack of training in the true principles of medicine and the chemical sciences, they would undoubtedly have done much more harm than good.

These vapors which I used were a very dangerous thing in the hands of an unskilled amateur. Out of love for my fellow-men I therefore decided not to put my method into book form until I should have made it absolutely fool-proof. I have not reached that point even to-day. But a large number of reliable surgeons have received their education in this field of medicine at my own hands and the story that I meant to keep this form of treatment a secret in order to enrich myself is now no longer believed by any one except those whose ignorance and arrogance it has been ever my pleasure to reveal.

My personal life therefore continued to run its placid course as it had done eight years before. I seriously thought once more of contracting matrimony. I was still afraid of taking the step, but my son needed a mother and I, let me confess it, craved some sort of human relationship which would allow me to put the interests and desires of another person ahead of my own.

Besides, then as now, I hated to be alone. All day long I worked. At night unless I had some one to talk to, I usually returned to my laboratory. I was rapidly degenerating into a perambulating handbook of medicine. It would be pleasant to go back to the Houtgracht after a day in the hospital and be able to think of something besides chloral solutions. But the number of my female acquaintances was very small. And so I bethought myself once more of the one charming person whom I had known several years before. I discovered that she had left Amsterdam and was living in the country with a brother of hers, who was a minister of the Gospel but a man of sense and breeding. I wrote her a long letter and explained my point-of-view as gracefully as I could, though I was conscious all the time that my effusions were not exactly a masterpiece of romantic or erotic literature.

Two weeks later I received an answer. A single sheet of paper on which she had scrawled the sign with which astronomers indicate the planet Venus accompanied by the words: "Will it be ♀ or Cannabis Indica?"

I studied this problem for a long time before I began to understand what she was driving at. Then I understood and I took one of the finest beaver skins I had brought with me from Nieuw Amsterdam and with that red paint with which the Indians ornament their faces and arms and chest when they go forth to war, I drew a single picture on the back of it—♀.

For I was in a very serious mood and it was to be Venus, while my experiments with hemp as a means of bringing about senselessness from pain were to come second.

After another fortnight (just before the day of St. Nicholas) I received a package containing a large heart made of gingerbread. It showed two figures, a ♀ and a ♄ intertwined with gold laurel leaves. I accepted the challenge, even if she identified me most uncomplimentarily with the ancient god known as Saturn.

I left for the country that same afternoon and two months later, after all the endless formalities of both the Church and the civic authorities had been complied with, we were married.

My wife was all and everything I had ever dared to hope for. She was companion and mistress and good friend and wise counselor. She could laugh with tears in her eyes and weep with a smile. She upset all my previous notions about women and made me feel ashamed of many things I had said and thought upon that subject. And she died when our first child was born and her last words were: "It would have been wonderful if only you had had a little more courage many, many years ago." And then she said: "I am in great agony. Perhaps our friend Cannabis will come in handy after all." And I sent to the hospital for my apparatus, but when they brought it she was dead, and so was the child.

And that was the last of my efforts to join the ranks of my neighbors who led what they were pleased to call "respectable and regular lives."

Respectable my life has been and to spare.

God only knows how dull and respectable!

But "regular"—never.

Since that day there have been three things that have kept me going: my son and my friends—my work—and the recollection of one year of perfect happiness. It was not much, I know. It was not very much. But it was so infinitely more than came to most people that I had reason to be contented. Contented and grateful and perhaps a little proud that I had cheated Fate out of twelve whole months of perfect passion and complete companionship.

"But it might have been different if only I had had a little more courage."

It seemed like a fitting epitaph for all my failures.

Chapter 45

OUR NEIGHBOR, MENASSEH BEN ISRAEL, DECIDES TO LEAVE AMSTERDAM FOR LONDON

So much for my own personal adventures during the year following immediately upon my return. But there were other threads I had to pick up and some of those had become pretty badly entwined and it took considerable trouble to straighten them out.

Jean-Louys of course had not changed in the least during the many years I had not seen him. He was the only man I ever knew who had achieved contentment as a result of philosophic reasoning.

There were certain outward circumstances which had made it easy for him to conclude a truce with those influences that are the natural enemies of a pleasant and equitable existence. It is true that he possessed few things which he could call his own. At the same time he had had a tremendous number of experiences. This is a clumsy way of saying what I really mean to say. Jean-Louys was a man without any vain regrets about those many might-have-beens which play such havoc with the lives of most of us. His soul was a well-regulated mansion in which all the doors were neatly closed and were kept closed, no matter what provocation there might be for him to throw a look into the past.

The usual "if-onlys" and "when-thus-and-thuses" had never been allowed to encumber the hallways and corridors of his memory. They simply were not allowed on the premises.

Whatever was dead and gone was dead and gone and stayed that way.

Jean-Louys himself contributed his success as a practical philosopher to his interest in logarithms.

"Logarithms," he used to say, "like all mathematics, are intimately connected with neatness and orderliness If I am neat and systematic in solving my problems, I simply cannot make mistakes. If I neatly proceed from one solution to the next, the final result must be perfect. Apply that same rule to human conduct and in less than no time human society would be perfect."

I doubted whether this was really the solution for the manifold difficulties of existence. Rather did I attribute the Frenchman's success to a different conception of what I might call the technique of living, as practiced in his own country, among the class of people to which he belonged in consequence of his noble birth.

During that long winter I had spent in the cabin of Father Ambrosius in the land of the Cayugas I had learned a great deal about the educational methods of the Jesuits and they of course are the people who

REMBRANDT PAINTING HENDRICKJE

CORNELIS CLAESZ ANSLO

nowadays get hold of the children of the aristocracy as soon as they are old enough to wash themselves and eat without the help of a pusher. The members of the Company of Jesus who devote themselves to that sort of pedagogical work are very clever—brilliantly clever. They realize that man is but an imperfect replica of His divine example. As a result, they don't expect too much—try to make virtues as attractive as possible and show themselves pleasantly surprised and deeply grateful when one of their young charges does his best and attempts to achieve a fair degree of perfection.

If at first he does not quite succeed, they do not scold him but admonish him in almost tender fashion until by a system of trial and error, they make him realize from his own free will that he will be much happier if he follows the counsel of those who are older and wiser than he himself, and that the rules of conduct which he is asked to obey are the result of centuries of trial and experiment and not a haphazard collection of regulations devised by an inconsequential spiritual tyrant who looked for something to do to while away the tedious hours of a sleepless night.

Perhaps such a philosophy of life is in keeping with the warm and agreeable climate of the South. We, in northern lands, forever hiding from rain and cold, follow a different method of thought. Our preceptors, their ears glued to the thunderous "THOU SHALT NOT! THOU SHALT NOT!" that resounded once upon a time from the summit of Mount Sinai, have only one purpose: to make sin as vile and as hateful as possible. At the same time they put their ideals of good behavior so high that not one child in a million can ever hope to come up to those elevated standards. And as a result, there is an everlasting conflict between Good and Evil that is most upsetting to the peace of mind of the young pupil and can only do him harm. He knows that he can't possibly ever hope to reach that degree of perfection which is held up before him as the goal of all his endeavors. At the same time he is in dreadful fear lest he stumble and gain the ill-will of a God who is the most vigilant and exacting of judges and executioners. He is "good" and stays "good" not because he has learned from his own experience and observation that being "good" is the same as being "intelligent" or being "sensible." He remains "good" merely from fear of being discovered in an act that is considered "bad." But all the time he is in secret rebellion against his innermost desires and the thousand and one curiosities that he must repress unless he is willing to risk a descent to the very bottom of Hell.

And when he reaches the so-called years of discretion, and discovers that the sun does not stop shining nor the tides stop running because a certain number of people have failed to obey the Mosaic commandments, he feels that he has been cheated. Then he either tries to make up for lost opportunities (as happened in the case of my poor brother) or he keeps to the narrow path but becomes a man with a grudge against Fate—the most unfortunate and pitiable of all human beings, bar none.

Jean-Louys, as a product of the former school of training and besides, a man of wide learning and possessed of vast worldly experience, had achieved happiness because he had put his intellectual and spiritual house in perfect order as a result of which it was impossible either to surprise or disappoint him.

But among my Dutch friends, I found a great deal of work to do. Most of them were at sixes and sevens, both with themselves and with their surroundings and no amount of pleading or reasoning seemed to make the slightest impression upon their firm conviction that this was a miserable vale of tears and that man was doomed to pass through the valley of life with a maximum of sorrow and a minimum of joy.

And to my great surprise I discovered that the excellent Rabbi Menasseh ben Israel was by no means that paragon of resignation and submission which I had been led to suppose from the letters of Jean-Louys. I mentioned this to the Frenchman and he agreed that the good Rabbi seemed far from happy when we called on him.

"But things may have changed somewhat in the meantime," he suggested, and this I found to be true after a very short period of investigation. All was not well with the Jewish community in Amsterdam and Menasseh took this internal strife very much to heart. At first I thought that the refusal of Bernardo to return home with me might have been responsible for the state of irritation in which I found him whenever I called, but soon I discovered that I was mistaken.

"The poor boy!" he said. "Why, I am glad he has found some happiness at last. Few people ever went through such sufferings as he did. I suppose, since we over here paid for his trip, he ought to have sent us a little more detailed account. All I have had so far consists of a single letter, saying: 'No, they are not here,' and signed: 'Your loving pupil, Bernard, not of Clairvaux but of Mohegania.' And that was not very much and rather less than I had expected. It was not exactly the sort of literary document I would have liked to show to those of my constituents who had financed the expedition. I just lied about it when they asked me and told them that the dear boy had found the field of investigation so much larger than any of us could possibly have foreseen that it would take him several more years before he could come to any definite conclusions and in the meantime they must exercise patience. Now if you will join me in this little fib and will bear me out if they should happen to ask you, no great harm will be done."

"Yes," I answered, "but after a while they will begin to wonder. We can stave them off one or two years, three perhaps, but then they will insist upon adequate answer."

"And I shall not be there to give it to them."

I looked at him in surprise. "Surely," I said, "you don't mean to die before then! You must be younger than I am and I mean to live another fifty years."

And then he told me of his worries and of his plans to leave the Republic and settle in London. It was the old, old story of prosperity proving more dangerous and disastrous than the adversity that had gone before. When the Jews first fled to Amsterdam they were poor and miserable and humbly grateful that they had been allowed to escape with their bare lives. They had built themselves a small synagogue and being given every opportunity to develop their natural-born gifts for commerce and barter, they had done exceedingly well and soon had been counted among the richest inhabitants of the city. Then they had built themselves a larger synagogue and at once they had been beset by endless unforeseen difficulties.

One group wanted their children to be taught the Torah rather than the Talmud. Others preferred the Talmud to the Torah. They all had taken sides and before any one knew what had happened, there had been two synagogues instead of one, which fought each other with the fury and bitterness of brothers engaged in a family feud. No sooner had the quarrel been brought to a successful ending (mostly by the good efforts of Menasseh himself, who having lived among the Catholics of Portugal and the Protestants of La Rochelle, felt very little love for useless strife) than the unfortunate incident with Acosta had taken place. The terrible, almost inhuman, humiliations to which this poor suffering creature had been obliged to submit himself before he was readmitted into the fold of the faithful had done a great deal of harm to the good name of the Jews, who had found a refuge in our country. His examination had not attracted very much attention. In so far as it had become known, it had been regarded as a purely local affair of the Jewish colony and a feeble attempt on the part of the Rabbis to bring the matter to the attention of Their Lordships the Magistrates by accusing their victim of having attacked the doctrine of the immortality of the soul, was quickly squashed and the Rabbis had been told to mind their own business.

But when Acosta, in the utter loneliness of his heart, had asked to be reaccepted as a member of the fold, and as an act of penance had been obliged to stretch himself full length across the threshold of the Temple, that every one of the True Believers might step over his prostrate body and spit on him, word had come from the Town Hall that those of the Synagogue should remember when a good thing ceased to be a good thing and should not indulge in practices that were contrary to all the established customs of the country in which they enjoyed such signal hospitality.

A week or so after this occurrence poor Acosta, who had been brought up as a Portuguese nobleman and who could not stand the idea of the ignominious dishonor he had suffered at the hands (or rather at the feet) of the rabble from the Amsterdam ghetto, quietly and unostentatiously put a bullet through his heart. This had caused a tremendous scandal all through town. A few of the dominies undoubtedly approved of such severity of doctrine and one or two of them had even tried to comment discreetly upon the fate that awaited all those who undertook to oppose the will of the Lord Sabaoth and his trusted servants. Their Lordships, however, had feared the bad impression the incident might cause abroad and they had sent for those responsible for the administration of the Synagogue, who had been responsible for the tragedy, and had told them in very plain terms: "One more such occurrence and all of you are put on board ship and are returned whence you came!"

Those stern words of warning had not missed their purpose. For more than ten years the Jews had rigorously kept their private religious differences out of the courts and carefully abstained from doing anything that might once again bring them in the center of the public interest. But now fresh difficulties threatened to make an end to this era of good understanding.

It was all on account of this young Baruch de Spinoza about whom Jean-Louys had already written me once or twice in his last letters and whom I had met years before at Menasseh's house. A bright boy. A very bright boy. The son of immigrant parents but a little too inquisitive and much too independent. He was not yet twenty but he had already mastered Latin, outside his studies in the Law, and he was full of ideas which he had got from Plato and Aristotle. Furthermore he had concluded an intimate friendship with a number of Dutch scientists who were known to hold very liberal views upon all problems connected with religion. And furthermore a little over a year ago he seemed to have met some one who had introduced him to the works of Descartes. All this could lead to no good end and honest Menasseh was greatly perplexed by the problem of how to keep this youngster from jumping over the traces.

"He has some money of his own," he concluded his recital of woe, "and does not depend upon our good will for his living. He has concluded some very powerful friendships with people who are well regarded by Their Lordships. If we are ever obliged to excommunicate him, there will be another scandal compared to which that of Acosta was mere child's play. For Acosta had been alone so much of his life that he had grown a little queer—yes, I might even say that he was no longer possessed of his reason when he committed suicide. But this young Baruch is a very likable youngster, and as bright as a fresh daisy. I have done my best to keep the peace and so far I have been successful. But the day will come when I will no longer be able to prevent my colleagues from jumping at his throat. And then—what turmoil there will be! And how all our neighbors will shout: Look at those dirty Jews! They can never live in peace with any one. As soon as they are no longer persecuted by some one else they must start squabbling among themselves and do all sorts of cruel things to their own people out of sheer wickedness of heart."

That there was a good deal of truth in all this, I could not possibly deny, and I heartily agreed with Menasseh that he might just as well find himself another and happier home before the crisis actually occurred.

"I would like to go somewhere," he said, "where we aren't quite so prosperous. As long as we are poor we are the finest people on earth, but as soon as we grow rich, we are terrible!" And he told me of his plans to move to London.

"That General Cromwell," he said, "is not in the least the man most people imagine him to be. He is head and shoulders above the average run of his followers. I think that he even would have spared the King if His Majesty had not proved himself such a scoundrel. I have written to him, to Cromwell I mean, and I know that he has regarded my letters with considerable favor. There have not been any Jews in England for more than three centuries. It is time we returned there to prepare the way for the coming of the Messiah. I can take my printing-press with me and I can just as well publish my books there as here. And it will be much easier to preach good sermons in a community where there are not quite so many opulent parishioners who say to themselves: 'How now? I gave ten ducats to the poor last year and this man comes and preaches a sermon upon the dangers of greed!'"

That much about the troubles of Menasseh ben Israel, who was one of the most intelligent and broad-minded Jews who ever dwelled in our city. Eventually he was to make good his threat and was to move from Amsterdam to London. But ere he could put this plan into practice, a great deal of water was to pass underneath the big Amstel bridge. Water mixed with blood and troubled by the agony of men who had died in battle.

When I was a small boy and learned my catechism, I was taught that God had created man after His own image just 4,000 years ago. That is a long stretch of time—4,000 years. But the human race seems to be very slow to learn its lessons. For every time two nations, like two dogs, want the same thing, the same bone or the same slice of territory, they know no better way of settling their difficulties than by turning themselves into the semblance of wolves and by fighting each other until they are both of them so completely exhausted that neither of them is able to enjoy his ill-gotten plunder.

Our first war with England broke out in the year 1652. The cause was mutual jealousy. We were jealous of England's success in Asia and America, and England was jealous of the rapidly increasing riches which we derived from the spice trade in the Indies and from being able to engage in the carrying trade more profitably than any of our neighbors.

In order to deprive us of the revenue derived from that particular form of commerce, Cromwell in the year 1651 did exactly what Jean-Louys had predicted that he would do. He made Parliament pass a law which practically excluded our ships from all English harbors. For our vessels could only be loaded with goods manufactured at home when they set sail for a British port and we manufactured very little that was wanted in England.

Of course, these real, underlying causes were never mentioned when the British representative in The Hague addressed himself to the Estates General with his ever-increasing lists of complaints.

Almost twenty years before seven Englishmen, accused of living where they had no right to live, had been most brutally executed by soldiers of the East India Company in the island of Amboyna.

That was perfectly true. Our only possible excuse for this crime was that it had happened during the unsettled days of helter-skelter grabbing of islands and empires when there had been neither law nor decency to regulate the behavior of the contending parties.

I think that Their Lordships of the Estates General were perfectly willing to pay an indemnity to the descendants of those poor victims, but Parliament asked for 300,000 pounds sterling, or 3,600,000 guilders in our own money and that seemed a little too much.

Then there was another grievance. Our Admiral Tromp had destroyed the second Spanish Armada in the roads of the Downs without first asking England's permission. That had happened a dozen years before and as it had been to the direct advantage of the British people to see Spain deprived of the last vestiges of her naval power, nobody at home quite understood why this should be held up against us as an act that ought to be answered by a declaration of war.

Then there was the murder of an English diplomatic agent at The Hague, who had been killed by an irresponsible group of drunken Royalists who had found a temporary refuge in that city.

And finally (and here we were on more solid ground) there were the very cordial relations which had existed between the Prince of Orange, now defunct, and his late father-in-law, the pretender to the throne of England.

All during the year '51 and the first half of '52 there was friction between the two countries. But of what actually happened I knew very little. It was the period of my second marriage. During those months there was so much to interest me at home that I rarely visited one of those taverns where one could hear the latest news. I saw a good deal of my friends, but they unfortunately regarded politics as a pastime unworthy of the attention of intelligent human beings. And so, for once, I was deeply ignorant of the state of the country and I sincerely hoped that I would continue to dwell in that condition of blessed ignorance for the rest of my days.

But when I returned from my wife's funeral, I found the walls of our city plastered with announcements of the Admiralty, offering all those who enlisted a bonus of sixty florins and a promise of a pension for their relatives in case they got killed in the service of their country. For a moment, in the bitterness of my heart, I thought of enlisting. Then I turned on my heel and went home. I found my son playing peacefully in the kitchen.

"My boy," I said, "something terrible has happened. The country is at war."

He clapped his hands and ran away to tell his nurse. I heard him in the hall.

"Oh, goody! goody!" he said. "We are going to fight and I am going to be a soldier and I am going to kill all the dirty enemies!"

And then I decided that I still had a purpose in life.

Chapter 46

WE ONCE MORE FIGHT THE ENGLISH

The war lasted two years and it affected our lives in a great many ways. The quarrel between the Prince and Their Lordships of Amsterdam had done very little good to the development of adequate means of defense for the country as a whole, and as a result we suffered one defeat after another. Within less than ten months, we had lost more than 1,600 of our merchant vessels. Tromp, the greatest naval strategist of our time, had been killed in action and a naval engagement that lasted three days and three nights had ended in a draw. Considering our lack of preparation, we had to count ourselves fortunate that the English were prevented from landing on our coast, but our trade was temporarily at least completely ruined. In Amsterdam, vast fortunes were lost through the depreciation of all commercial paper. More than 2,000 houses stood empty and were for sale without any one wishing to buy them and the Magistrates felt so thoroughly disheartened that they decided not to build their new Town Hall according to the original plans of Master van Campen but to do with one story less, merely in order to save a few thousand guilders.

But in England too the struggle was making itself felt in a very unpleasant and painful fashion, and General Cromwell, who at last thought his position sufficiently strong to make himself Lord Protector of the former Kingdom and who expected a certain amount of opposition to this project (as was only natural), was all in favor of concluding a hasty peace.

As soon as he had received solemn assurances that the Republic not only would cease to support the Stuarts but would also exclude the young son of the late Prince Willem from all participation in the future government of the United Seven Netherlands, he declared himself satisfied. The Navigation Act of course was maintained, but our sailors soon discovered so many ways in which they could circumnavigate this particular bit of law that no one worried very seriously about it and that most people were even willing to overlook the very humiliating additional articles of peace which bade all Dutch ships lower their flags whenever they met an English rival as a sign of outward deference and respect.

As always under such circumstances, everything was arranged for us by Their Lordships of the Estates General who were now once more the undisputed rulers of the country. They told us just as much or just as little as they thought was good for us. The fact, for example, that at the conclusion of peace they meant to exclude the House of Orange from all public office they kept a profound secret until it was much too late for the mass of the people to do anything about it beyond giving vent to a certain degree of anger by shoving in a few windows and booing those who were suspected of having taken a more direct part in the negotiations which had led to this fateful decision.

And in regard to the conduct of the war, too, we were kept in complete darkness and had to content ourselves with poor little scraps of news that would not have satisfied a cat.

In consequence whereof most of the common people soon lost all interest in the struggle except in so far as they were directly hit in their purse by those taxes that are the inevitable concomitant of such a struggle. And I, disheartened by my short-lived happiness and perhaps more tired from my eight years' voyage in foreign parts than I knew, withdrew almost completely from public gatherings and came to depend more and more upon the companionship of my friends.

But the house in the Jodenbreestraat, which for the first time in its history was beginning to look like a real home, saw more of me than ever before. I was welcomed there both by Rembrandt himself and by the handsome Hendrickje with the utmost cordiality. They showed the same sentiments toward Jean-Louys and the four of us spent a very happy time while the Lord Protector over on the other side of the North Sea and Their Lordships, our own Protectors, fought each other to the death to decide who should get the greater part of certain spoils that belonged to neither of them.

Chapter 47

I MEET MY COLLEAGUE, DR. EPHRAIM BUENO, WHO HAD TAKEN CARE OF REMBRANDT'S FAMILY WHILE I WAS IN AMERICA

A dozen or so years before, ere I had started upon my American adventure, Jean-Louys, Bernardo, Selim and I used to meet each other nearly every Sunday morning to spend the day in some tavern at not too far a distance from town.

Now Selim had departed to partake of the quiet pleasures offered by the hospitable shores of the Bosphorus—Bernardo had become a Mohegan chieftain and Jean-Louys and I remained alone, and since even the best of friends will tire of each other if they have to listen to each other's everlasting monologues, it was quite natural that instead of going on long Sabbatical walks, we should drift into the habit of spending at least part of the day with our painter friend of the Breestraat.

Only extreme youth can be hilarious and full of good spirits early in the morning. We, however, were fast approaching an age when one likes to be alone for at least part of every twenty-four hours, and we used to improve the time when other people went to church, puttering around the house, until a little after eleven, Jean-Louys would drop in on me and then the faithful Jantje would invariably remark:

"I suppose His Highness will stay for dinner." (He was the only baron she had ever met and she meant to make the most of her opportunity.) And Jean-Louys would slap his hands in surprise and would say, "Ah, my beautiful Antoinette, but that would cause too much trouble." To which she would reply, "No trouble whatsoever. I have already counted on your being here." And they both would laugh right heartily, and we men would retire to my working room where we talked of this and that until Jantje came to tell us that "the food was on the table." I had tried to teach her for many years to say, "Monsieur le Baron est servi," but at the last moment she always lost courage and the much less elegant but rather more direct announcement was the only compromise she would accept, although even this form of invitation to partake of her culinary efforts appeared to her as a direct manifestation of that French effeminacy which according to her innermost conviction would some day destroy the whole fabric of our noble northern civilization.

After dinner, during which we had been joined by my son who had a seat and a knife and a spoon of his own (I never approved of the prevailing habit of keeping children standing at the table and letting them eat only with their fingers), we went back to the workroom to smoke a pipe of tobacco, and as soon as the chimes of the South Church had announced the third hour of the afternoon, we took our hats and capes and walked around the corner to the house on the Jodenbreestraat which by this time had acquired a look of pleasant familiarity and no longer made the impression that it had been finished only day before yesterday. And inside too there had been many changes. The ground floor still looked like the store-room of a dealer in antiques—statues and bits of old armament and a most heterogeneous collection of pictures gathered from all the four corners of the European continent. On the top of a large oaken cupboard, two large globes and a foreign-looking helmet which a few weeks previously had adorned the head of Rembrandt's brother Adriaen.

The staircase which led to the second story was half hidden by a bit of tapestry that had once been the pride of a small Flemish castle in the neighborhood of Antwerp which had gone up in flames during the siege of 1585. On the table in the center of the hall, a large marble wine-cooler and a couple of daggers of Italian provenance. Over the door that led to the Side Room, was a Venetian mirror in an ebony frame. I only mention the things one remembered seeing when one entered. The others would fill a small catalogue, and as all of them were sold at auction long before the death of their owner, it would indicate a serious lack of piety were I to try to enumerate them.

But the old disorder had somehow undergone a change. During the last days of Saskia's life and immediately after her death, one felt that there was something wrong in this house. Tables and chairs and pictures and globes were all thickly covered with dust. Milk pitchers were standing in doorways where they did not belong. An occasional pail of forgotten garbage would strike an unpleasant note next to the green velvet covering of an ornamental Spanish chair.

Now everything was neat and clean and spick and span. People were living in this house, not just camping out like the mutilated soldiers and their wild women in the wooden shacks just outside the Haarlem gate.

But it was in the big living room in the back of the building, in the so-called hall, that the "vita nuova" the "new life" upon which Rembrandt seemed to have embarked, made itself most thoroughly felt. It still served as sitting-room, dining-room and reception-room to the whole of the family, and Rembrandt continued to sleep in the large bed built in the wall in which Saskia had died. Some day I suppose people will learn not to sleep in beds in which patients with pulmonary trouble have died. From my own experience I would say that it is a very bad thing to do. But I have never been able to convince any one else. Even Rembrandt, who by nature was a man of good sound common sense, would not hear of it when I told him that he must never let little Titus come near anything his mother had worn. He laughed at the idea and said that we doctors were always trying to scare the poor laity merely to show the world how learned we were, and he pointed to Titus and asked me whether I had ever seen a boy that looked as strong and healthy as he did.

I was thinking of that when I first met Titus again after almost eight years of absence. He must have been ten years old, running on eleven. A handsome and pleasant-looking youngster endowed with his mother's fine profile with that same agreeable smile that Saskia must have had in the days Rembrandt drew the little picture of her in a large straw hat —the only drawing we found among his belongings when we cleaned out his room on the Roozengracht. But the child did not give one the impression of being very robust. His cheeks were a little too thin for his age and his large, wondering eyes shone with that strange brilliancy one so often finds in those whom the gods love so well that they deem them worthy of an early death.

My first impulse was to talk to Rembrandt about my suspicions— suggest that the boy be kept outdoors a great deal of the time and not be allowed to spend the greater part of his days in the etching-room where the acid vapors caused even a healthy man to gasp for breath. But I felt a certain hesitancy about taking such a step on account of Doctor Bueno, who had taken care of Rembrandt's household after I left for America.

Bueno was a Jew. His full name was Ephraim Bueno after his father from whom he had learned his profession. He was a pleasant and modest little man and from all I had ever heard about him an excellent physician. But of course his position in the community had always been a little difficult.

In the first place, it had not been until just before the war with Cromwell (I think it was in the year 1652 but it may have been a few months later) that the Portuguese immigrants of Jewish extraction had been given full civil rights. Up to that time, from a strictly legal point of view, they had been merely tolerated. And this had made it impossible for them to join one of the guilds. Even when they opened a shop or started a business of their own, they had been technically guilty of a breach of law. Quite frequently the Guilds had sent delegations to the Town Hall to ask the Magistrates to interfere and forbid these unwelcome competitors from exercising their trade at all. But Their Lordships had too great a respect for the commercial abilities of these profitable immigrants to take any such steps. They did of course not dare to treat the representatives of these ancient and honorable corporations as curtly as they sometimes treated the clerical powers who came to them for redress from some threatened heresy. The town militia was entirely composed of members of the different guilds and only the officers belonged to the class of the rich merchants. The Magistrates therefore were very polite and sometimes almost obsequious in the way in which they listened to such complaints as came to them from the united bakers or butchers or carpenters or cartwrights or soap manufacturers. But no sooner had these worthy guild members left the premises, highly flattered by their reception and quite convinced that very soon something was going to be done about it, than the petitions and requests wandered into the aldermanic stove and the matter was referred to the Kalends of the Greeks.

For our town, first and last and all the time was a business establishment. Since the average Portuguese Jew had proved himself an excellent and most industrious citizen, he was considered a good business asset and all attempts to oust him or turn him into a pariah failed as systematically and as efficiently as the efforts on the part of the established Church to turn Amsterdam into a new Zion on the basis of Doctor Calvin's shorter catechism.

But until the Jews finally were accorded full civic rights, their position was always a trifle difficult. Their surgeons, no matter what degrees and titles they could offer as a token of their competence and ability, really had had no right to practice until the year 1651 and if one of the Burgomasters had ever been foolish enough to enforce the strict letter of the law, he could have ordered all Jewish doctors to be driven out of the town by the hangman on the ground that they were mountebanks and quacksalvers and had no right within the jurisdiction of the city.

I therefore was very careful in the way in which I treated Ephraim Bueno. I had a great respect for his learning and did not want to hurt his feelings. Sometimes if I happened to be within hailing distance and some slight accident took place (once, one of the pupils burned himself heating a copper plate and once Titus had an attack of coughing which frightened Rembrandt almost out of his wits), I would be called in and then I did whatever was necessary (in the case of Titus it was only necessary to tell him not to eat so many green nuts), but as soon as the emergency was over I invariably sent a hasty note to Doctor Bueno asking him to proceed to the Breestraat as soon as would be convenient. It was Bueno himself who put a stop to my somewhat exaggerated civility.

"My dear colleague," he said one day, as we were returning from the hospital together, "we Jews are sometimes said to be very thin-skinned, and perhaps we are a little too suspicious about the intentions of our neighbors. But my people have lived here now for half a century. We shall probably live here as long as this town lasts. Suppose we cease insulting each other by being so frightfully polite and become friends." And he added as an afterthought, "I am a Jew and that, as many of my neighbors never tire of reminding me, is pretty bad. But we both of us are leeches, and that is infinitely worse."

And in this he was quite right. For as soon as I had returned to Amsterdam I had been struck once more by the anomaly of our position. In the New Netherlands there had been so few physicians that the people, depending upon our good will, had usually treated us with great respect. But the Republic was overrun by every form of charlatan and the public seemed either unable or unwilling to differentiate between serious practitioners who had studied at half a dozen universities and had spent seven or eight years walking the hospitals, and those jugglers and bone-setters and ointment vendors who frequented the country fairs.

In the eyes of the "better classes of society" we still belonged to the guild of the "tonsorial artists" or "whisker-pluckers" of my childhood, and no amount of labor on our part seemed to be able to overcome that prejudice.

Indeed, I remember how shortly after Rembrandt's death, I was requested one day to come to The Hague and pay a professional visit to My Lord Jan de Witt, who at that moment was the recognized leader of the Republic, and how His Lordship bade me stay for luncheon and introduced me to one of his youthful cousins (cousins of his wife, to be exact) whose name was Bicker and who curiously enough was an ensign in a regiment of the Scottish guards. I, trying to be pleasant to the young man, said something flattering about his relatives, whereupon the young man, affecting a strange English accent, said, "Oh, yes! I think I remember my uncle telling me that you used to shave him whenever he could not leave the council-chamber on account of the press of business."

This remark was not a success, for My Lord Jan slowly contemplated his cousin with two eyes that were as cordial as icicles and casually remarked, "I am sorry that your regimental duties will not allow you to sit down with us at table," and took my arm to show me the way to the dining-room without paying any further attention to the bewildered young man who was left to the mercies of the maid who in that simple household still fulfilled the rôle of a butler.

No, our own social position had never been a very happy one. People needed us and at the same time they were ashamed of associating with us because in their heart they were ashamed of the illnesses which we were supposed to cure and which as a rule they had brought on through some carelessness of their own.

It was pretty bad. But as Bueno said to me one day, it might have been infinitely worse. We might have been artists!

Chapter 48

CONCERNING THE POSITION OF ARTISTS IN A COMMERCIAL COUNTRY

Ephraim Bueno had meant his remark as a jest but there had been considerable truth in what he had said. The position of the artists in those early days of our independence was a very curious one indeed. I had heard from my colleagues who had studied in Italy how the different princes and kings and grand dukes who ruled that country considered themselves deeply honored if a painter or a sculptor or a poet of renown deigned to honor their courts with a visit. From my grandmother I had learned how in Flanders in the days of her youth a whole city would go forth to meet the man who was to provide their church with a new picture or statue of the Madonna. I had not quite believed her when she told me that famous artists were often requested to accompany the king or even the emperor on his peregrinations through his realm. But during my own lifetime (it must have been in the early thirties, for I had just moved to Amsterdam) we were much surprised to hear that Rubens, the Antwerp painter, had just been sent to London to act as ambassador of the King of Spain at the court of Charles Stuart, and I remember that I heard many people say that they thought such a step a very dangerous precedent, for painters ought to remain painters and diplomats ought to be gentlemen, and I am sorry to say that this was the general attitude of pretty nearly all classes of society.

There may be those who can explain this curious attitude toward the arts, but I cannot. Doctor Bueno's bitter remark that a first-rate salesman was of some practical use in a commercial community, but that a sculptor was not, was probably more or less true but if it were wholly true, then how about Venice and Genoa and such towns as Florence or Bruges? All of those cities had been mere political counting-houses, like our own Republic. They had been ruled by bankers and cloth manufacturers and salt-merchants, plain, practical business men who loved a soldo just as dearly as our own little potentates loved their golden doubloons. I have seen pictures of these worthies and they looked for all the world like the older brothers and cousins of our Burgomasters. I have read a few stories about them and they were every inch as mean and as generous and as shrewd and as corrupt as Their Lordships of the Town Hall. But they apparently felt flattered whenever a painter or a musician was willing to come to one of their parties or dropped in for dinner, whereas our artists are forced to stand with their hat in their hand and listen very obediently when one of our great whale-oil magnates or some half literate buccaneer who has recently returned home rich with the plunder of a dozen spice islands demeans himself sufficiently to address a few words to one of those "paint-spillers."

I am not exaggerating. I was present not so long ago when an unbearably patronizing young man (he bore my own name, but was no relation) asked old Ruisdael why his son, instead of taking up painting, had not joined his cousin in the frame-making business.

There is a man by the name of Hobbema living in an attic on the Roozengracht not far away from the house where Rembrandt died. I am told that he is the best landscape painter we have ever had, but the other day, in the boat to Haarlem, I overheard two young business men cursing him roundly as an impostor because one of them had bought a landscape from him for two hundred guilders and had been told by his father that he could have had the thing for one quarter the price if he had only jewed the poor devil down a little harder.

Not to mention poor Hals of Haarlem, who died only a few years ago, who was undoubtedly as great a man as Rembrandt, who was forced into bankruptcy by his baker (can one man eat quite so much bread?), whose belongings at the time of his death, amounting to three mattresses, one cupboard and a table, were sold at public auction for the benefit of the poor-house in which he had found refuge.

No, I have never quite understood why it should be that way in our country and so very different everywhere else. But if I sometimes wondered and worried, my anxiety was certainly not shared by the victims of this deplorable public negligence.

After I returned from America I spent a great deal of my time in the company of painterfolk but almost without exception they accepted their fate as something that was too self-evident to be a subject for public discussion or commiseration. Whenever they were together, they talked shop. They talked of different methods of grinding paint or of a new combination of acids with which to treat their copper plates or a better method of laying on a coat of varnish, only upon some very rare occasions did they curse their poverty and declare Rembrandt to be an outrageously lucky fellow to be able to live in a house of two stories and to have been allowed to marry the daughter of a burgomaster.

But taking them by and large and as a group, they were a singularly contented body of men. A few of them of course got despondent and gave up in sheer despair and drank themselves into oblivion and an early grave by spending twenty-four hours of each day in the gin-shops with which our town was so richly blessed. But the vast majority lived like masons or plumbers—like unsuccessful masons and plumbers, I ought to say, and not to be compared in any way with the genuine masons and plumbers who were employed on Jacob van Campen's new town hall on the Dam.

Without exception they were very hard workers. The world accused them of keeping irregular hours, of being seen about the streets at all hours of the day and night. There was some truth in this. They did indeed lead very irregular lives. As a rule they were too poor to be able to pay much rent and as they needed at least one large room for a studio, they were apt to go to the outskirts of the city and look for an old barn which they then converted into a more or less suitable workshop. For our painters, unlike those in Italy, don't seem to be able to work out of doors. They will sometimes make a hasty sketch of a landscape or a tree or a few boats out in the open, but then they run home as fast as they can and spend the next three weeks finishing the picture for which the sketch serves them merely as a reminder but not as an inspiration.

But since they spend the greater part of the day right there in the studio which also serves them as dining-room and sitting-room and bedroom and kitchen and nursery (for they rarely can afford more than one room) the whole place is almost always in a state of extreme disorder.

Then their rich neighbors, who live in a house with five or six different apartments, see the poor painterman sitting at his easel between a pile of yesterday's dishes and day-before-yesterday's cutlery—see the baby's laundry hanging from a rope stretched along the ceiling—observe his wife busily engaged making the weekly supply of pea-soup over a little charcoal fire in the corner, shake their heads and say, "Oh, my, oh, my; what a careless fellow. No wonder he is always hard up." But they entirely overlook the fact that poverty is more apt to provoke slovenliness than vice versa.

People, however, will cling to their preconceived notions as tenaciously as they will cling to the tables and chests and drawers which they have inherited from their parents. And I have long since given up trying to convince them of the error of this view. For even after I had brought them to the point where they were forced to agree with me and told me, "Well, perhaps there is something in what you say," they would find other reasons why the artist should not be regarded as a respectable member of society. And one of these was the so-called clannishness of all those who made their living by their brush or their wits.

"Why don't they ever associate with us?" I have heard respectable merchants ask. "Why do they spend endless hours in each other's studios? Why do they marry each other's daughters?"

To which I would make answer as follows:

"Why do you who are in the export business or grain trade always marry each other's daughters? Why do you who sell whalebones or distill gin know all other whalebone dealers and gin-distillers and rarely see any one outside your own profession?"

But then of course I was shouted down by a tumult of protests. "Oh, but that is different! We have got to know each other to get along in business, we marry our competitors' daughters because we know fairly accurately how much the father will be able to give her. We are practical men of business and at the same time we like to sit down with people with whom we can talk about our own work."

"Very well," I would then continue my line of reasoning, "why shouldn't painters also like to meet men and women with whom they can talk their sort of shop?"

It was no use. I butted my head against a granite wall of prejudice and accomplished nothing. The artist was an amiable loafer, not able or willing to do an honest day's work and therefore deserving all he got in the way of poverty and neglect. One could of couse be an artist and at the same time a respectable member of society. But such a combination was an exception almost as rare as that of Doctor Tulp, who was a gentleman and a member of the town government, although he had started life as a physician, or Gerard ter Borch, who painted portraits in Deventer and was said to have served one term as Burgomaster of that city.

Yes, ours was a strange country.

But there was one consolation. With the exception of two or three rather weak brethren, I never knew a member of the Guild of Saint Luke who cared a tinker's dam for the opinions of any one who did not belong to his own profession. Not because he thought himself superior to his surroundings but because he was by far too busy to bother about such unimportant little details as the respect of his community. Life was short and at the very best one had only ten hours a day during which one could paint. That was the answer to the second riddle of the artist's far-famed "queerness." The fellow was never idle and what was infinitely more important, he was interested in his work.

I wish that his neighbors could have said as much.

Chapter 49

TWO OF MY OLD FRIENDS ARE GONE AND IN MY LONELINESS I BEGIN TO SEE A LITTLE MORE OF REMBRANDT

But to return to Amsterdam, life at first was rather dull and we missed our old friends. Selim had become a man of vast importance in the land of his birth (returning sea-captains told wonderful stories about the luxury displayed at his palace and of the two hundred women, which were said to be guarded by no less than three hundred eunuchs) and Bernardo had disappeared in the American wilderness without leaving a trace. Jean-Louys and I tried to continue our Sunday walks but we soon discovered that peripatetic duologues were very apt to degenerate into sedentary monologues, accompanied by too much beer.

For a while we did our best to make Rembrandt join us, but I never knew a man who had such a thorough-going aversion to exercise of every sort. I used to scold him and Doctor Bueno used to back me with great cordiality whenever I told him that no human being could lead the sort of life he did without digging his own grave with his easel and his chair. I delivered endless lectures on elementary physiology, quoting a great deal of wisdom which I had borrowed from Jean-Louys, who in turn had culled his information from the writings of Monsieur Descartes. I used to explain how the human body was a sort of machine and just as windmills could not do their work without wind or water-mills without water, so the human body needed fresh air and exercise to keep in good condition.

I drew graphic pictures on the back of some of his sketches, showing him that the lungs were in reality nothing but a pair of bellows that had to be kept going all the time by moderate exercise, for otherwise (the metaphor was slightly mixed) the organ would give forth no sound whatsoever. From organs I would jump back to sailing vessels that were useless and deteriorated without wind, which is merely fresh air in motion. But I might as well have talked to the skeletons that were hanging from the municipal gallows near the harbor for all the impression I made.

Rembrandt never lost his temper and I admired his patience until I discovered one evening that he did not even listen. He just went on painting and let me talk. Only the week before he had complained to me that his heart caused him trouble—that he would wake up in the middle of the night with his heart beating like fury, and a severe pain in both shoulder-blades I told him to ask Doctor Bueno to examine his heart and then I said: "When do you notice this trouble most?" He could not quite remember but he thought that it came when he had spent the whole day at his etching-press. "You see," he remarked casually, "those boys of mine mean well, they do their best, but if I want a really good copy, I have got to do it myself. I have not had many orders for portraits of late—you know how it is when there is a war. Everybody is scared. Everybody saves all the money he can. And portraits, after all, are a luxury. But people will buy etchings. They are good investments and I had orders for several hundred. So in the evening when those children had gone to bed, I used to strike off a few copies myself."

"At what time did you begin?"

"About seven."

"And when did you stop?"

"Oh, sometimes quite early. Other evenings I worked until four or five."

"Without stopping?"

"Yes. Sometimes I stopped for a quarter of an hour or so and had a glass of beer. One gets thirsty. It is hard work."

Seven until four or five—that meant nine hours of standing on his feet in a small room that was suffocatingly hot, pulling the wheel of a press that was almost too heavy for a cart-horse.

"Man alive!" I answered him. "No human being can stand that sort of exertion. How long have you been doing this?"

"Oh, not so very long. Since January last year when orders came in for those plates."

January of last year—that meant fifteen whole months of a sort of labor that would have killed a hod-carrier in less than six.

"But of course," I said, "when you do that sort of thing, you don't paint?"

"Yes, I paint the greater part of the day in my studio, as long as there is any light. Then I take the candles and go to the press-room."

"How many candles?"

"One as a rule. Sometimes when my eyes begin to bother me, I light a second one."

"When your eyes begin to bother you? Do they bother you much?"

"Not very much. We all of us have good eyes. We got them from our father. Bad lungs from our mother and good eyes from our father. No, there is nothing the matter with my eyes, I still can do a dry-point without using any glasses. But after five or six hours, I find myself weeping big tears as if I were walking in the wind and after ten hours, I get funny pains."

"What sort of pains?"

"As if some one were sticking a pin into my eye-balls. Not the pain on the side of my head of which I just spoke to you. That only comes when my heart does its funny tricks. But irritating little pin-pricks and sometimes I have to stop for a few minutes until they disappear again."

Truly, the man was hopeless.

"Has it ever dawned upon you," I asked him, "that if you go on working that way you may end by losing your eyesight completely? A fine painter you would be with your eyes gone!" And I made ready to leave. At once he changed his tone. "Don't be angry with me, Doctor," he begged me, "you are probably right and I am undoubtedly wrong, but what will you? I can't stop. I have to go on."

"Why?" I interrupted him.

Rembrandt wiped both his hands on his blue painter's smock, a habit which made some of his enemies of the popular Italian school say that he carried his best works on his belly—took a bottle of acid from a low chair that stood in a corner of the room—reached down—picked up the bottle—took out the cork—looked at it and smelled it, and said, "That is the sixth cork in two weeks. That stuff is too strong. I told them they had made it too strong. I must get a glass stopper." And then added, "I will be good for this once and obey orders. My whole head aches and I might as well call it a day. You ask me why I work like a madman? Very well. I will tell you. Because I am really a little crazy."

"Professionally speaking," I interrupted him, "I never noticed it."

"Of course not. I am not crazy in the sense the Dircx woman was crazy. You need not lock me up. But I know that I am not an ordinary, well-balanced and respectable member of society and I know that no matter how hard I try, I never shall be. That is what is the matter with my work. So far I have kept out of the poor-house. But only because I happen to have inherited all that money from Saskia. The inheritance is a little slow in collecting, but anyway it gives me credit, which is almost as good as having money. You can buy whatever you want and people ask no questions. Are glad to sell to you.

"But if I did not have that money, I don't know what would have happened to me long ago. My work does not sell.

"In the beginning, the first ten years after I came here from Leyden, I was a sort of curiosity. I was the fashion. In those days many people were still alive who remembered the Rebellion. Of course you and I, theoretically speaking, lived through it too. But what did we ever see of it? Nothing! We paid our taxes and once in a while some former soldier with his arms or his legs gone would ask us for something to eat in the street and if he were very much of a bother, we called the guards and had him arrested.

"The people—I mean all the people like that grandfather of yours of whom you have so often told me, or my own father, or my own grandmother—men and women who had escaped with their lives but whose brothers and sisters and sons had been hanged and burned and broken on the wheel—that generation seems to have understood more or less what I was trying to do. They had all of them started from very simple beginnings. So had I.

"There was a time when I used to pretend that I was a great nobleman. That was just after I married. I liked to dress up. Saskia was a lovely girl. I liked to dress her up. I liked to imagine that we were really fine folks. She was, but I am the son of a miller and my brother is a shoe-maker and all the satins and silks in the whole world and all the feathers and frills will never make me anything else.

"That is why that older generation liked my work. That is why the younger generation is afraid of me. I think they realize that I am a fairly good artisan. I can paint, if I say so myself, and they know it. But I can't paint the way they want me to paint and they know that too.

"Of course you will say that I ought to be practical and ought to try and paint the way they want me to paint. Well, I will tell you a secret. I have tried and I have tried very hard, but I can't do it. I just can't do it! And that is why I am just a little crazy.

"An ordinary person who sells raisins or herring or cheese or who makes pictures for a living carefully studies his market, which after all is his bread and butter. When the taste of his customers changes, he speedily changes the nature of the goods he is trying to sell them. If they want their herring dried instead of pickled, he buys a couple of acres of land and hangs his fish up in the sun until it is as hard as a rock. If they want their cheeses painted red instead of yellow, he paints them red instead of yellow. If the fashion of the moment prescribes Italian landscapes with Italian skies and Italian beggars eating—what is the name of that stuff? macaroni?—he will paint them Italian landscapes with Italian skies and Italian beggars dropping handfuls of noodles into their gaping mouths.

"Personally I don't blame those people, as I have heard it said sometimes, when I am accused of being too proud or too haughty to paint differently from the way I paint. It isn't that I am too proud or too haughty. I just can't do differently—that is all. And so I stick to my own line and I suppose I shall stick to it until I go to the poor-house or the cemetery and you may put a stone on my grave, saying: 'Here lies a fool' and you will never have been so right in all your life as on the day you ordered that inscription."

Chapter 50

REMBRANDT BECOMES TALKATIVE AND FAVORS ME WITH A FEW OF HIS VIEWS UPON ART

This was one of the longest speeches I ever heard Rembrandt make. And contrary to his habit, he used it to mention a few of his theories on art.

Notwithstanding the war, which continued with uneven success, there was a good deal of money abroad at that time. Thousands of people were losing all they had; but a few hundred, who had been shrewd enough to speculate in grain and wood and gun-powder and all the other supplies of which the fleet was in such great need, made vast sums of money. Not knowing what to do with their newly found riches, they were buying luxuries right and left.

One day pictures would be all the rage. The next day it would be china. The little Japanese cups that had sold for three florins apiece had gone up to three thousand. The china craze switched over to pearls, and when all the wives of all the profiteers had been provided with ear-rings as large as carrots, pearls became vulgar almost over night and the Nurem berg watch-makers reaped a fortune with queer and extraordinary time-pieces that showed not only the minutes but also the seconds and that played a little tune when the hour was struck, just like the bells of the new town hall.

As they had heard that there lived a painter in the Jewish quarter whose house was a museum of everything that one could possibly hope to collect, a good many of them found their way to the Breestraat.

In the beginning, Rembrandt felt rather flattered, and thought that this meant a renewed interest in his own work. But very soon he discovered that those noisy visitors with their even more noisy wives did not care in the least for his own art—very often were ignorant of his name—called him Ronnebrandt or Remscheidt—patronized him in most outrageous fashion—gave Titus sweet-meats and patted his head and said he was a nice little Jewish boy and then asked the master how much he would take for an enameled Turkish sword or a piece of ivory carving from the Indies. Then he would grow angry at such an indignity (for he well knew the value of his own work) and instead of making these miserable war profiteers pay an outrageous sum for some article which he himself had bought in a moment of weakness and for which his visitors were willing to pay ten times the original price, he would show them the door in a most abrupt fashion (he still could speak the vernacular of the Weddesteeg in Leyden with great fluency) and then these amazing guests would depart and would spread it among all their friends that this man Rompot, that so-called artist, who gave himself such airs, was an ill-natured ruffian and that one ought to give him a wide berth and have nothing to do with him.

Until the rumor had gone all over town that the painter of the Jodenbreestraat, you remember, the one who had done that queer picture of Banning Cocq, was a sullen and crabbed barbarian—a morose and splenetic fellow—whose swinish ill-temper had turned him into an involuntary recluse, shunned by all his neighbors for his violence and irascibility.

This was of course entirely beside the truth. Rembrandt was by nature an easy-going and friendly person, perfectly willing to meet his neighbors with a smile and only asking to be let alone. But that was just it! Our newly rich did not like people of an independent character. They had touched their caps to their betters for so long that now they rejoiced to be in a position where (through their purse and their financial influence) they could oblige others to raise their hats to them. And any one who stood squarely on his own feet, went his own way, asked for no favors and (infinitely worse) accepted none, was something so utterly baffling to their sort of mentality that they could explain his attitude in only one way, by accusing him of a haughtiness of spirit that was as foreign to his nature as malice, envy or the very suspicion that such things existed in this world.

Here I am conscious of a doubt. If this diary of mine should ever fall into the hands of one of my descendants (if my son is to survive) and should be read by them two or three hundred years hence, wouldn't they instinctively feel that I have exaggerated my friend's character? Wouldn't they say, "This mysterious grandfather of ours seems to have had a sober enough eye when he contemplated the rest of his contemporaries, but when it came to Rembrandt (of whom we have heard very different stories) he feels compelled to indulge in the most noble-sounding terms, as if his friend were a paragon of all the virtues. Yet, when we contemplate his life, as it is revealed to us by the records of the Bankruptcy Court and the Public Guardians of the Amsterdam orphans, we meet with an irresponsible fellow who bears very little resemblance to the glorious picture revealed by our great-great-great-grandfather."

And when I say that I never met a man so little given to petty jealousy or so indifferent to malice, I do not mean to imply that Rembrandt was a saint who after a lifetime of seclusion and meditation had finally attained such a degree of spiritual perfection that he had become immune against the temptation (forever present in all of us) to regard every man as his possible rival and therefore as his potential enemy.

Nothing could have been less true than that. Rembrandt was of this earth earthy. He was fashioned out of the common clay of our land and our land, lest we forget, lies fifteen feet below sea-level. But he had one enormous advantage over the majority of his neighbors. Like most other artists he had a purpose in life and he was too busy with his own problems to enjoy that leisure which is the breeding ground of gossip and spite.

This devotion to a single ideal sometime manifested itself in very unpleasant ways. I never knew him to read a book. He owned quite a library—the hall was full of them, but every one of them had to do with the arts, wood-cuts by Lucas of Leyden, copper-plates after etchings by Raphael, the world's best pictures done in copper-plate reproductions, wood-cuts of Lucas Cranach, copper print reproductions of Guido Reni of Bologna and dozens more of the same sort. All of the best painters of the last two centuries were represented—Rubens and Titian and Jordaens and Michelangelo and Miereveld, Carracci, van Dijk and dozens of others, not to forget Albrecht Dürer's famous handbook on perspective.

But when it came to the so-called "belles lettres," to literature as such, almost any ordinary household in Amsterdam, however humble, could have boasted of a better selection than this luxurious museum of the Breestraat.

I have spent all my life among books. When I am called in for a consultation in a house where I have never been before, I try if possible to cast a glance at the book-closet. One minute's examination of the different titles will tell me more about my future patient, his habits and tastes and even the probable nature of his ailment than hours devoted to a mere physical examination. But if I had tried this method with Rembrandt, my diagnosis would have been completely wrong.

For I don't think that I ever found more than five or six ordinary books in his house during all the many years I knew him intimately. One of these was a tragedy in blank verse, called "Medea," wished on him by the author, Jan Six, the linen merchant (afterwards one of the Burgomasters) by whom Rembrandt was befriended for a while and from whom, to his own great detriment, he borrowed a small sum of money. The others were devotional books, Josephus' "History of the Jews," Bibles and collections of sermons. And all of them, including some interesting products of the calligrapher's art by his friend Coppenol, had been presents, for with the single exception of a German treatise on military strategy which for some reason had caught his fancy, I don't think that Rembrandt during the whole of his life ever spent a single penny on books. I don't believe he even felt the need of them. If he had done so, he would have bought them by the cartload, for he had no sense of the value of money and bought whatever he wanted with the same sublime unconcern as that which is manifested by a very small child which pulls its mother's most beautiful glass vase off the table and lets it fall on the floor and break into a thousand pieces, and will feel itself completely justified by the smiling excuse, "I wanted it."

Whatever he "wanted," Rembrandt got and our more or less veiled hints that life just simply wasn't that way, that one had to trim one's sails according to the wind and other bits of proverbial wisdom did not make the slightest impression upon him and never evoked any further comment than an admiring, "But isn't it beautiful?" it being almost anything from a painting by Giorgione to an ebony chest for little Titus's diapers.

Being fearsome of the ultimate results of this indiscriminate buying, I sometimes hinted at books as a substitute for the infinitely more expensive objects of art with which he filled his room. At one moment he got greatly interested in a certain Adriaen Brouwer, a pupil of the incomparable Frans Hals of Haarlem. This young man, of phenomenal ability, had died in the poor-ward of an Antwerp hospital at the early age of thirty-two. His works therefore were rather rare and in the dozen or so years after his death (he died in the early forties) they had greatly increased in price.

One evening I found the whole of the front room filled with Brouwers, a most heterogeneous collection, a woman and a child and a pastry cook and a couple of gamblers and a cook busy with a very greasy dish, all of them done with the most beautiful economy of line and color.

"Aren't they wonderful?" Rembrandt asked me, who had kissed Titus good night and was coming down the stairs with a candle in his hand.

I said yes, that they were very interesting but that they must have cost him a small fortune and I pointed to one which probably represented my household expenses for more than half a year. Then I congratulated him on his success and said that I was glad he had done so well recently.

"Done well recently?" he asked and lifted his candle so that I should better be able to see the picture of a small studio (also done by Brouwer) which up to that moment I had not noticed. "Done well recently? Good God! I have not sold a thing for over two years."

"Then your Indian venture must have turned out prosperously." (For though he had tried to keep it a secret from me, I knew that he had been speculating in the shares of a rather doubtful Indian Company.)

He was a little surprised. "Oh, you mean those three ships. You heard of those?" (Who had not heard of them?) "No, they were not exactly what one would call a success. There was some trouble with the crew of one of them and the others suffered so badly from scurvy, they only got as far as the Cape. No, the money I put into that affair is lost, I am afraid."

"But I suppose they wanted cash for these Brouwers?"

"They did. I borrowed it. Aren't they marvelous?"

And then he took me in the side room, lit a fire, got me a bottle of ale and spent at least two hours explaining his conception of the uses of money and the duties of artists toward themselves, and he defended his point of view so plausibly and so reasonably that I went home convinced that he was right and that I was a hopelessly prejudiced miser who would never be able to look beyond the rock-ribbed system of "never spend more than you can afford." Which (if we were to believe our elders) was the foundation stone of the Republic's prosperity and greatness.

"You have been telling me to be careful," he began. "Everybody I ever knew has been telling me to be careful. You are a man of tact (that is why I like you) and rather than tell me outright not to buy pictures and helmets and all those things in this room and in the others" (he made a gesture that meant to include the whole house) "you have encouraged me to buy books—and read. 'If he is kept busy reading,' you probably said to yourself, 'he won't spend so much time among the Jews, inspecting their antiques.' But what good has the reading of other people's books ever done to an artist?

"You remind me of those people who have been coming to me ever since I was fourteen years old and had smeared some paint (very badly I am afraid) on a couple of pieces of canvas. 'My dear boy,' they used to say, 'this is all very nice and very pretty but it will never lead to anything. You can't learn your trade here. We in the North are all of us barbarians when it comes to the arts. Italy, the South, that is the country for you.'

"And then they would recite long lists of names of boys from Amsterdam and Haarlem and Leyden and Dordrecht, from every village and hamlet in the Republic who had gone to Rome and Florence and Venice to learn 'painting.'

"I used to make them very angry with my attitude. 'Painting,' I used to say, 'is nothing but seeing. You see something that impresses you and then you paint it, or if you have a gift for something else, then you draw it or hack it out of a piece of marble, as the Greeks used to do, or you make a tune out of it and play it on the organ as old Sweelinck used to do when we were children and he got so excited one day about a thunderstorm he had just heard that he turned the 116th prelude into an imitation thunderstorm and seven people in the congregation fainted in their pews and had to be carried out.

"And then I would add that it did not depend so much upon what you saw as how you saw it and that a good artist could get more inspiration out of a dead bullock hanging from a ladder in some mean village butcher-shop, than a bad one out of half a dozen beautiful churches in the village where Raphael himself was born.

"All this sounded like terrible heresies to the good people among whom I grew up. They took me aside and whispered into my ear that if I knew what was good for me I would not be quite so plain-spoken and express such open contempt for those marvelous Italian artists whom all the world held to be the greatest craftsmen after the sculptors of ancient Greece. In those days I was a great deal more impatient than I am to-day and I would lose my temper and would waste my time on foolish arguments—trying to prove that I had never said that the Italian painters were not among the greatest that had ever lived—that all I meant was that the

Italians living in Italy should get their emotion (the word inspiration is good enough for theologians and for amateur artists) from Italian subjects, but that we people living in Holland should get our emotions from the subjects with which we were familiar in our own country and not from something a thousand miles away.

"But no, I was all wrong and even such a broad-minded man as My Lord Constantin, who has been a kind and steadfast friend to me all my life, could not see it that way and broadly scolded me because I refused to take the opportunities that were offered me to go to Italy. When I told him that his beloved Italians cared so little for their own great men that they were willing to let all of their best pictures be sold abroad, so that one could get a better idea of the work of Raphael and Giorgione and Titian right here in Amsterdam than in Florence and Rome (except of course the things they have painted on the walls of churches and monasteries that can't be pried loose) he did not quite know what to say and replied that anyway the trip would be good for me, that I was too young to spend my entire time working in a stuffy studio, that it was bad for my health never to take any exercise and sit or stand everlastingly in front of an easel, that I would die young if I overdid it as much as I was doing . . ." ("In which he was quite right," I interrupted him, but got no answer) . . . "and ended up by telling me of the wonderful landscapes he had seen on his way to Venice and that landscapes were only possible in a region where the sun was a brilliant ball of golden fire and not a greasy speck made by the nose of an inquisitive child on a pane of window-glass as it is in our own muddy country.

"But I would not be convinced and answered him that a rainstorm, if seen and felt by some one with the ability to see and feel rainstorms as intensely as some of the Italians were able to see and feel the sunsets over their native lagoons, would make just as good a subject for a picture as his dearly beloved Forum by moonlight and a dozen years later (it was in '43 if I remember rightly) I sent him a copy of my etching of those three trees with the rainstorms in the distance, and I wrote him:

"'My Lord, do you remember a talk we had when I was twenty-five years old and was just on the point of moving to Amsterdam? And will you graciously accept this poor etching as a token of my extreme gratitude and tell me whether I was right when I said that rainstorms could be made just as interesting as sunsets?'

"And he answered me with his usual courtesy that he was beginning to understand that after all, perhaps I had been right and in '50 when he was here a few days incognito, after the Prince had attacked the town, I showed him that picture of a windmill that was afterwards sold to some one in England and I asked him once more: 'My Lord, isn't that mill as good in its own way as the little house that Giorgione painted in the background of his Concert?' (a picture which is in Paris but of which I have seen some very fine copies) and he looked at it for quite a while as if he were thinking of something that had happened long, long ago and as if he were speaking to himself, he said:

" 'Of course, that pretty young woman would hardly be playing the flute the way she does at the foot of your mill,' and I answered, 'Your Lordship is right, but neither would the Graces of Botticelli bombard each other with snowballs.' And then he said yes, that I might be right after all, but like poor Jan Asselijn, whom we buried last year, I might have done both, and I asked His Lordship point-blank: 'Do you think his work was so much better than mine?' and he answered: 'No, of course not, and besides, he was really a Frenchman, so the comparison was not quite fair. I happened to be looking at the etching you made of him, that is probably why I happened to mention him.'

"And then, abruptly changing the subject, he said: 'I want to ask you something. It has always puzzled me and I have always wanted to ask it, but I never had the opportunity, but what are you really trying to do?'

"And I told him as best I could (just as I told you a moment ago), how when I was very young I had thought that painting was merely a matter of seeing, of feeling, of sensing some particular object or idea and translating what you saw and felt into lines or bits of color.

"And then one day I was working in my father's mill and something happened to me. I don't mean that I was painting in my father's mill. In those early days I was not encouraged very much to become an artist. My people were simple folk and very pious. They had the usual prejudice against the arts and especially against the artists. When one mentioned the word painter, they thought of Babylon and Sodom at once, and when I first told them that I wanted to be a great painter, like Lucas van Leyden, who was the first man whose works I had ever seen, they shook their heads and said 'No,' they wanted me to be a good Christian and get ahead in the world.

"I seemed to have a fairly good brain—I was much cleverer than my brothers. One of them could succeed father in the mill and the others would be taught a trade that they might spend their days as God-fearing members in good standing of some honorable guild of artisans. But as for me I was to go to the university and get a degree so that my parents could say, 'Our son, the Doctor of Laws,' and have something to console themselves for the hard labor which had been their share all during the time they were bringing us up.

"That plan never came to anything. I actually went to the university but I was a dreadful failure as a student. I never went to a single lecture. I wrote my name in a big book and got a piece of paper informing me most solemnly that Rembrandus Hermanius Leydensis or some such thing was now, at the age of fourteen, if you please, a duly enrolled stud-litt—whatever that meant—in the glorious university of Leyden, and entitled to all the rights and privileges connected with this distinguished rank.

"But it was no use, I never went near a professor or a book (I cared as little about books then as I do now) and instead I went to Jaap Swanenburch, who was a famous man in our town—he was one of those who had learned their trade in Italy—he had done the job so thoroughly, he even came home with an Italian wife who used to throw plates and knives at him every time we had a pretty model, to the great joy and delectation of his pupils—and when Swanenburch came to the Weddesteeg one day and told my parents that I had it in me to become a most successful and fashionable portrait painter, but would they please pay my tuition, they forgave me for having played hookey from my scholarly duties and as Swanenburch's charges were less than the tuition fee of the university, they decided that they might as well let me stay where I was and work out my own salvation according to the best of my own abilities.

"But before that time, I could only draw when no one was looking my way and every afternoon after school time, my brother Cornelis and I used to go to the mill on the wall and help father with his work.

"Have you ever been in a mill? You have. Ever been in a mill on a bright, sun-shiny sort of a day? Well, then you have missed something. For the wings do curious things to the interior on a day like that. The windows of a mill are usually very small, but when the sun is shining brightly, especially in the spring when the air has just been cleaned by three weeks of wind or rain, the whole inside of the mill is flooded with a curious and very brilliant sort of light—a strange light that is like nothing else I have ever seen—though I must add that I have not traveled very far and that I may be all wrong when I say that it is only to be found here on this floating pan-cake of ours, where the sun and the fog are apt to do all sorts of queer things to the light, both inside our houses and out of them.

"Well, it was just such a day in April—I remember the date, for the experience made a great impression upon me. It was the fourteenth of April and Cornelis and I had been told to go and count a number of sacks that lay on the first floor and carry them up to the second floor where the grinding was done and stack them up neatly in a corner. We counted our sacks and carried them to the second floor and my father inspected them and found that one or two needed repairing and told us to get a needle and thread and attend to the job then and there. I got a needle and thread and sat down in a corner to repair the sacks, while Cornelis was sent away on an errand. It did not take me long to finish that task, but I was afraid that if I told my father that I was through, he would give me something else to do and so I said nothing, but sat very quietly in my little corner and pretended to be very busy. There was a brisk eastern wind blowing outside and the wings went past the window, g'chuck—g'chuck—g'chuck, just a sort of guttural sound like the snapping of a musket and then the sudden swish of those enormous wooden arms, cleaving the air. And every time one of those wings passed by one of the windows, the light was cut off for perhaps a hundredth part of a second—just a flash—too short to measure by the clock—but visible, just the same—very visible indeed, for every time it happened, the room became pitch-dark.

"Now you may remember that when we were young, the country was suffering from a plague of rats—perhaps as a result of the siege and the large number of people who had died—but anyway, our houses and our cellars were all of them full of rats. And there were people who did nothing all their lives long except catch rats—professional rat-catchers. They were usually old soldiers and very dirty and very picturesque and I have drawn them quite a lot, for they were interesting-looking scoundrels.

"That morning one of them had been at work in our mill. There were so many rats in that mill, we sometimes were afraid they would carry the old building back to Noordwijk where it came from. The rat-catcher who liked to work in the dark would not be back before evening and one enormous wire cage full of rats was hanging by a strong chain from a rafter of the mill. Those rats—great big fellows—would have eaten through any kind of rope but though all of them seemed to be sitting on their hindsides, gnawing at the steel chain that held their cage, they hadn't a chance in the world. But through the scurrying and pattering of all these excited little bodies, with their bright beady eyes and their long, disgusting tails, the cage was slowly beginning to swing from left to right and it was making a curious shadow upon the wall. And all the time, the wings of the mill kept swishing past the window and every time they swished past, the room would be pitch dark and then for just one, two, three seconds, it would be filled once more with brilliant sunlight.

"But I had seen that sort of thing hundreds of times before and it had never struck me as anything very remarkable. And then suddenly—it really came to me just like the revelation that came to Saul—I noticed that that cage was not merely hanging in the light or in the air, as I had always taken for granted, but that it was an object surrounded by a whole lot of different sorts of air—all of which were of a different texture. In the beginning it was not at all clear to me and I can't expect to tell you what I mean in two words, but you know of course that there are a number of colors, like yellow and blue and red and combinations of colors and we painters are supposed to know all about those colors and their combinations and that is how we paint our pictures. We tell stories in daubs of color, just as others tell stories in lines or with the help of words or notes. At least, that is what I had always taken for granted and I had done my best to learn how to use those colors.

"But that morning in the mill, there weren't any colors, at least, none of the colors with which I had been familiar from my earliest childhood, when some one gave me my first box of paints. The light in front of that rat cage was different from the light behind it, which was different again from the light on the left of it and all these different sorts of light did not remain the same, but changed every moment. Of course, when I say 'light' I mean air and when I say air, I mean light. What I really mean is the space which fills all our rooms and all our houses and the whole world —the stuff we breathe, and through which the birds fly. And then the idea suddenly struck me (and that was the moment when I turned from Saul to Paul) does all this space—this air—really have a color in our sense of the word and is it possible to translate that color into terms of paint?

"Let me show you" (here he picked up a pewter mug that was standing on the table)—"let me show you. You see that mug. It is about three feet away from you. And now" (moving it towards himself) "it is only two feet away. Suppose I want to paint this. I can get the illusion of distance by applying the rules of perspective which Master Dürer of Nuremberg laid down in that little book of his. That would be enough when I use a pencil or pen and ink. But when I use color, I ought to be able to create that impression of distance in some other way—in the way nature does it, or rather, in the way I suspect that nature does it. For I have now spent the greater part of every day during the last forty years—Sundays included, to the horror of my good parents—trying to solve the problem and I know just as little about it to-day as I did when I first began.

"Your French friend, the Baron, told me the other day that those famous mathematicians of whom he sometimes talks work quite differently from the way we would expect. When a mason builds a house, he first digs the basement and then builds the first floor and next the second floor and so on until he gets to the roof. But mathematicians, so it seems, first make the roof and fit in the rest afterwards. 'They have suspicions,' the Frenchman remarked. They 'suspect' that two times two is four and accept their 'suspicion' as an established fact and then work backwards and by working backwards, they finally 'prove' that two times two is indeed four. I may have got this a bit mixed, but I think that is the way he reasoned it out. They first 'suspect' and 'surmise' and then they 'prove.' Of course, those are not the sort of ideas with which to entertain my own relatives nor those of Saskia either. They would either giggle sheepishly or run to their dominie and suggest that I be locked up in the asylum. And I am not quite certain that I am making myself clear even to you.

"But from that moment on, from the moment I saw those excited rats in their wire cage, hanging from the rafter of my father's mill, until to-day I have been convinced that every object in the world is surrounded by a substance (call it light or air or space or whatever you like) which somehow or other it must be possible to express in the terms of light and shade and half a dozen primary colors.

"Sometimes I even think that at least in a few of my pictures I have solved that problem pretty well. But I confess that I have been working backwards, painting the picture first and trying to discover afterwards why I had done what I had done. People, always looking for the outlandish and the unusual, whisper that I have a secret. Secret fiddlesticks! I am a mathematician who works in vegetable matter and who started out with a formula and who is now trying to prove that it works and is correct."

It sounded very plausible but I warned him that I had once heard of a mathematician who had hit upon a new formula that appeared to be perfect and who had died just before he had succeeded in proving his point.

"Yes," he answered, "that is the risk I run. I too may die before I have been able to find out exactly how this problem should be solved. But I am content. A few times when painting people, I have caught certain effects that seem to bear out my theory. What I would like to know, however, before I die is this—how did I happen to get those effects? Why are people able to say, when they look at one of my pictures, 'That man is actually sitting on a chair in a room, not leaning up against a mere back-ground of chair and room.' Or, 'That angel is really floating through space, not falling or resting on a cloud, but floating!'

"I probably would have been more of a success in my work if I had not been told by my father to repair sacks in his mill on that particular morning. Now I waste half of my time or more on a problem that no one has ever solved before me—that no one, as far as I can find out, has even thought of. Rubens is a great man, but he does not even suspect that there is such a thing as I have been trying to put into paint for the last thirty years. Hals comes much nearer to it. That man Brouwer (you scolded me because I bought so many of his pictures) has done marvels in that field. They tell me there is a man in Spain, working for the King (his name is Velásquez, or Velázquez, I don't quite know) who seems to be working on that basis. I have never seen any of his paintings and it is always difficult to imagine what a picture looks like merely from hearing some one else describe it.

"Of course, the public has no notion of what I am trying to do. Perhaps four hundred years from now, if any of my pictures are left, they will say to each other: This fellow van Rijn at least was on the right way and was going in the right direction. But my neighbors—they see that one picture is very good, and how in the next one I tried a new method to prove that two times two actually makes four and have failed pretty completely, and they sneer, 'This man is a mere amateur. He does not take his art seriously. He does not paint things the way we ourselves see them.'

"Heaven forbid that I should ever see things the way they do! They may (and very likely they will) let me starve, but they can't rob me of the conviction that I am right and that they are wrong. Any one can learn to paint the things that are there. But to paint the things that one merely suspects to be there while one can't possibly prove that they are there—that, my good Doctor, that is the sort of task that makes life interesting. And that is the sort of thing that makes other people be afraid of me. And now let us go to the Back Room."

"For a game of chess?" I asked.

"No, no more chess. Life is too short. At least for me. Too short for books and for chess—too short for anything except one single problem and one that I shall never solve. But if you will come with me, I will show you something. You remember the etching I made of Doctor Faustus, one or two years ago? Well, it wasn't right. I have worked a lot of dry-point into it since then and now at last I think that I know what is necessary to make it right. I will let you see it and then you will understand how it is possible (even in black and white) to make different sorts of light that flow into each other like wine that is poured into a glass of water. Speaking of which, Hendrickje shall make us a kettle of bischop, but please don't scold me any more if I continue to buy pictures instead of books. In the first place, it won't do you any good. I shall buy them anyway. And in the second place, I need them. There is always a chance that they will teach me something new. I am almost fifty. More than two thirds of my days are gone and there is still so much to do. So terribly much."

We went to the Back Room. Rembrandt lit two candles and got the plate of Doctor Faustus. Titus was fast asleep in one of the two beds built in the wall. Hendrickje went to get the wine and the spices that were necessary for our drink. The kettle was standing on the floor in front of the fire. She leaned over to pick it up just as I looked her way. And suddenly my professional eye registered an unmistakable professional fact. She was pregnant and in her seventh or eight month.

That too was a problem in space but one which Rembrandt seemed to have overlooked.

Chapter 51

I BEGIN TO UNDERSTAND THAT ALL IS NOT WELL IN THE BIG HOUSE ON THE JODENBREESTRAAT

It is very strange, but there are certain things which one man just can't possibly tell to another. He may, under certain circumstances, draw his friend's polite attention to the fact that he is a scoundrel or a thief, but he can never, and under no pretext whatsoever and however discreetly, inform him that his cuffs are badly in need of the laundry—that his collar needs starching nor that his coat after all these many years and many meals of spinach and soft-boiled eggs, would fill the heart of a dozen Josephs with envy and desire. Nor can he go up to even the most intimate of his friends and say, "Pardon me, but isn't that housekeeper of yours on the point of giving birth to twins?"

But for once Fate intervened in a very welcome and discreet fashion. Hendrickje suffered an accident, and as Rembrandt's regular doctor was out of town for the day (he had left by boat that morning to go to Ouderkerk for a funeral) they sent for me who lived just around the corner. When I arrived, I found Rembrandt painting in the large back room while Hendrickje was lying panting and gasping for breath in the same bed in which, almost a dozen years before, Saskia had died. I thought of course that her apparent lack of air had to do with her physical condition, but Rembrandt at once told me what had happened and then I understood the cause of her ailment to be much simpler.

She had gone upstairs to clean the studio as usual that morning. The evening before, two of the pupils had been biting a plate in a new mixture that was supposed to be more effective than the usual "eau forte." It consisted of nitric acid and blue vitriol and a few other ingredients but nitric acid was the chief substance used in this particular compound. Those bright boys had become so deeply engrossed in their task that they had forgotten to close the bottle containing the acid. The faithful Hendrickje had paid no attention to the strange odors in the room—had carefully swept and cleaned and brushed—had breathed the poisoned air—had felt how her chest was gradually beginning to ache and how her eyes were beginning to smart—and how she was weeping bitter tears—and in great panic she finally had left the room, telling Rembrandt she was going to faint and would he please send at once for the surgeon.

It was not a very difficult case. I asked to be shown the room in which she had worked, for I thought that she might have tried to burn some old rags which sometimes make a very dangerous smoke. As soon as we entered the studio, Rembrandt noticed what had happened, pushed open both windows, looked for the jar containing the acid, closed it and then called for the two pupils whose ears he boxed with such an experienced hand that these young men probably remembered until the end of their days that a bottle of nitric acid was no child's toy and should be treated as circumspectly as a loaded and cocked gun.

We then took Hendrickje out of the badly ventilated back room and put her down on a couch in the garden and immediately she began to feel better. A few minutes later she fell asleep and as my morning had been spoiled more or less anyway, I decided to stay a while and reassure Rembrandt who was in a great state of perturbation.

"I have lost one wife in this house through what was more or less my own carelessness," he said as soon as we had returned to the studio where the mild hurricane that was blowing in through the open windows had not only driven away the acid fumes but had also upset a picture of Hendrickje on which Rembrandt was working. It showed Hendrickje wearing the big pearl ear-rings of Saskia which he had bought about fifteen years before and which had figured so prominently in the famous libel suit which he had been forced to bring against some of his wife's relatives who had accused him and his wife of being spendthrifts and ne'er-do-wells. That libel suit had come to nothing. The court had found Rembrandt to be technically right, but as he was only a painter and Saskia only the wife of a painter and both of them therefore "private persons" of no particular account, the amount of damage which they claimed had been reduced from 128 to eight golden florins and so in the end the case had cost Rembrandt infinitely more than he had got out of it. He still apparently retained the pearl ear-rings for in the picture, Hendrickje was wearing them and when Rembrandt had dusted it off with a piece of soft cloth, I noticed that it was a very fine piece of work. Perhaps he had made Hendrickje a little more of a "lady" than she actually was, but all the kindness and goodness of her beautiful eyes were there. I liked it and I told him so and he sat down in front of his easel and mixed some white with ocher to touch up the ear-rings (slightly damaged by the fall), and said, "I am glad if you think that all those things are there. I have worked on this very hard. She has been very good to Titus and to me. I would like to do something for her."

This was more or less my opportunity.

"I was obliged to examine her when I came in," I said, "for to tell you the truth, my first impression was that she was pregnant. And I discovered that she was. That isn't what you mean when you say that you wanted to do something for her?"

I knew that I had committed a terrible blunder. I had done one of those incredible, unbelievable things of which one is guilty once or twice in his life and which one never is able to forget—which come back to one at the most unexpected moments—during sleepless nights and cause cold shivers to run down one's spine. And no sooner had I spoken these words than I regretted them with a thousand regrets, but it was too late.

Rembrandt, however, picked up the knife that was lying on his palette, put some raw umber on it, with which he lightly touched the background, stepped back, the better to look at what he had done, and then remarked in a most casual tone of voice: "No, that is not what I meant. I was thinking of this picture, for it is one of the best things I have ever done and people will look at it and will admire it—and her—long after we shall be dead. And as for the other little item you just mentioned, that I am sorry to say was an error on our part. We are both of us glad it happened, now that it has happened, but it was a mistake. It happened once before, but you weren't in town at that time and the child died. Pity, for it was a girl and it would have been nice to have a girl. Perhaps we shall have better luck this time."

He made this announcement as if he were telling me of some new picture he was planning to paint and I really don't believe that it meant very much more to him than that. The picture was merely an incident in life, an interesting episode in which one pitted one's intelligence against the unwilling forces of nature. The child was an incident in life in which nature pitted its unreasoning forces against the intelligence of man. Sometimes man won. As a rule nature won. It made no difference. Everything that "was," was to Rembrandt a manifestation of the existing order of things. Some people tried to solve the problem by worrying. Others tried to solve it by working. Rembrandt worked—pictures, etchings—children. Everything was as it should be—no questions asked—no answers either expected or given—world without end. Amen.

"But," said I, who after all had been brought up in the atmosphere of profound middle-class righteousness (and can a person ever rid the garden of his memory from the weeds of inviolable respectability?) "but surely, now that Saskia is gone and you are a free man, you can marry Hendrickje and I think" (what hideous spirit of mental bumptiousness possessed me that morning?) "that you ought to."

Rembrandt smeared some more ocher on his palette knife.

"I ought to, all right," he answered, falling into the vernacular of his childhood days. "Sure, and I know it. I ought to, even more than all right, but I can't."

"Why not? You are a free man."

"I am. I am absolutely free. I could marry anybody I pleased, provided she would have me, as soon as the banns had been read. I know all that. We have talked about it. But it can't be done."

"Why not?"

"The will."

"You mean Saskia's will?"

"Yes. Poor Saskia meant well. She loved me. She left me a will and all her earthly possessions."

"But that will is perfectly good."

"Of course it is. But the possessions are not. They looked very imposing on parchment. But they did not exist. Or if they did, my dear Frisian relatives got away with them. I don't know and to tell you the truth, I no longer care. It does not matter. I have too much to do. I think I have found a new way to handle a lighted candle in a picture I may be asked to do for the new Town Hall. I will show you the sketch. I think I now know how it ought to be done. The theme is Potiphar's wife. I tried something like that twenty years ago—a nude—but I didn't like it. I like to paint my figures clothed. The nude was a good thing for those old Greeks who made their statues that way—they were accustomed to see nude bodies. We are not. We never see more than three or four of them in all our lives and we can't paint what we do not see every day—what we do not know by heart. Yes, I want to do that again. Potiphar's wife, or something like that. And then I bought an old piece of armor—paid 300 guilders for it—rather expensive, but a fine piece of work. I am going to use that for all sorts of things for I have never done brass the way it really looks when the sun shines on it, and I want to try my hand at some more landscapes and I have got at least two dozen etchings to do. You see, work enough for ten years! If I live that long. If I wanted to get all those other problems straightened out, I never would be able to do anything else."

"Are they as bad as all that?" I interrupted him.

"Much worse. The only way I can go on is by forgetting that they exist. One of these days the public will come back to me. They will understand what I am trying to do. I am a fast worker. In less than a year I will be able to paint myself out of this financial hole. Then I can pay my creditors and marry Hendrickje. I am fond of her. Terribly fond. She is a nice girl. A good girl. She gives me everything I want. I would be a scoundrel not to marry her, but she will have to wait until then. And she does not mind. She says it makes very little difference to her and meanwhile it keeps this household out of trouble."

"But meanwhile will you be able to keep her out of the town gossip? Surely the neighbors will notice her condition and will talk?"

Rembrandt dropped his palette knife and looked at me with anger blazing in his eyes. "What of it?" he asked brusquely. "What of it? They talk anyway. They always have talked. They always will talk. That is what they are in this world for. To talk. They can't do anything else. They can—how does the Bible say it?—they can hew wood and draw water and talk scandal about their betters. The neighbors, indeed! Damn the neighbors! I am not thinking of them. Neither is Hendrickje. Let them go on carrying bricks and slopping around with pails of water. That is all they are good for. But this house is worth saving. Hendrickje likes it. Titus loves it. I have been happy in it. Some mighty fine pieces of work have been done right here in this house. We ought to save the house. That is what we are working for now."

I did not see the connection and told him so.

"Do you remember the will, Saskia's will?" he asked me.

I told him that I did so only in a very vague way, not having the sort of mind that easily retains official language.

"Well," Rembrandt said, "Saskia was not only very fond of me, bless her, but she also had great confidence in me—absolute confidence—and she wanted to show how she felt in her will. Her relatives had said rather nasty things about me—that I was a spendthrift and a wastrel—that I did not know the value of money—that money slipped through my fingers like water and that I would rather spend 500 guilders on some picture that interested me than use the money to pay my grocer. Perhaps they were right. I was never very good at figures and when I think what I am giving the world—what I have already given it—such little details don't matter.

"Anyway, Saskia left everything to me—absolutely and outright—no guardians to watch her son's interests—no notaries to poke their inquisitive noses into our affairs—no Chamber of Orphans to come and ask embarrassing questions. I was to handle everything but on certain conditions. I was to give Titus a first rate education and establish him in some profession of his own as soon as he should become of age. In case, however, I died or married again, her fortune was to pass directly to Titus. Do you get the meaning of that? In case I married again, Titus was to have everything. If I married Hendrickje, then according to the terms of the will, I would have to go before the courts and fill out endless papers and swear a dozen oaths and turn everything over to Titus. And how am I to turn over 'everything' when there isn't anything—when there never was anything except promises and still more promises and law-suits and family feuds, but no cash. Even when I wanted to buy this house, I had to borrow. We ought to have been able to pay for it in full. But always something was happening in Friesland and every cent we ever got out of those people we had to take out with a block and tackle.

"Meanwhile the whole world has taken for granted that I am a rich man. It was, 'Rembrandt, buy this!' or 'Rembrandt, I got a little Italian picture. The moment you see it you will buy it.' Or, 'Rembrandt, my kids have not had a square meal for a fortnight and my wife is expecting her seventh. You are a rich man. Let me have ten guilders.' And I am a weak man where it comes to money. We never had any when we were children. It was fun to be considered a Croesus. Anyway, what did it matter? Some day that inheritance would be paid out in full and I would have almost 50,000 guilders to pay all my creditors.

"Meanwhile I painted, but since the Banning Cocq picture, the public does not seem to like my work any more. What could I do? Move away?

Give up this house? The moment I whisper a word about wanting to sell, I shall have all my creditors on my back. I have got to keep up appearances if I want to keep up my credit. And the moment my credit is gone, we shall all be in the poor-house. Titus—Hendrickje—I. The kind friends who encouraged me to borrow when they thought everything was fine will fall upon me like a pack of wolves. It would be the end. And so" (with a final dab at the foreground of Hendrickje), "don't ask me, 'Why don't you marry the girl?' for I can't and she knows it and she is very wonderful about it. It won't be easy for her, but she says that she understands and so I think that for the moment we had better let matters stand where they are."

I agreed with him in the main but I am one of those persons who likes things done in an orderly fashion. I cannot work unless I am neatly dressed, well shaved, my hair well brushed. The room in which I work has to be neat. My desk has to be neat. Otherwise my brain won't work. And being a man of such precise, almost meticulous, habits, I like to have my business affairs in order. I know that I have no talent for financial problems and I therefore leave them to some one else who knows more about them than I do. But I don't think that I could live if I were not sure that at any moment I could open a drawer and undo a bit of red string and convince myself, within two or three hundred guilders, just exactly what I had and what I owed others and what others owed me. I know it is rather foolish to lay so much stress upon such things, homo est quod est and that is the way I am made. And so, though I did my best not to sound too much like a schoolmaster, I could not help saying: "But, Rembrandt, my friend, you must know approximately where you stand!" But he smeared his hands on his smock in a most unconcerned fashion, smiled pleasantly at me and answered:

"I have not the faintest idea and that is the truth."

Then I tried to reason with him. I explained to him that he never would be able to get out of debt without first knowing approximately how much debt he had—that fighting unknown debts was like trying to fight an invisible enemy in a dark cellar—that system and order was the only way in which one could ever hope to slay the monster of bankruptcy. But he was unable to consider the matter seriously and tried to distract my attention by conducting me into the press-room where three pupils were busy with a large etching of the Crucifixion, and presently he discovered a flaw in the shading of the figure of the bearded Pharisee in the foreground and called for one of the boys to sharpen him the steel needle he had bought that afternoon, for he would not bother to bite the plate again but would make his correction by dry-point and finally he forgot all about me and I watched him working by the light of a single candle (a terrible strain on his eyes and disastrous to anybody who has to make a living by one of the arts) and I stayed in the room for about an hour and then, realizing that I might sit there until four in the morning without being noticed, I went downstairs, found Hendrickje fast asleep and little the worse for her accident, and went home where I found a letter from My Lord Constantin written from his country place in which there was little mention of pictures but a great deal about politics.

"These are strange days," so the old gentleman wrote, "for those of us who like to contemplate the historical landscape from a more or less philosophical angle. History, as I have been told since childhood, does not repeat itself. But as certain human emotions are eternal and invariable, certain political conditions, arising directly from those human emotions, bear a very close resemblance to each other.

"Take this bugaboo of self-government, of democracy, or whatever you wish to call it. The average man feels feebly and vaguely that he ought to stand on his own legs—manage his own affairs—and he clamors for a Republic—for a Res Publicae—in which every free man shall have the right to express his own feelings in regard to the management of the state. As long as the country to which he belongs, or the city or the village of which he is an inhabitant continues to dwell in peace, he is perfectly at his ease and struts about in his gay colors, a sword at his side and pats himself on the back and says, 'I am a pretty fine fellow, master of my own destiny, etc., etc.' But the moment he sniffs the first suspicious odors of danger—the moment he is brought face to face with a crisis—all his courage and all his high spirits leave him and he runs to the marketplace and cries: 'A leader! Give me a leader! Give me some one who is stronger than I am myself. Give me a man whom I can follow when he leads. I am only a weak little creature—all these fine phrases were merely self-deception. Take me by the hand and tell me what to do.'

"As soon as we had got our liberty we felt that we had no longer any need for a man on horseback—a handsome young general on a prancing steed. And we got rid of the House of Orange. Henceforth our people were to rule themselves. The rabble of course were not consulted. They never had been and most likely they never will be. Our Burgomasters and Magistrates and our Aldermen and our merchants were to rule the Republic.

"Meanwhile, on the other side of the North Sea our English neighbors were doing the same thing. Being by nature more violent or more logical than we are, they cut their ruler's head off and declared themselves a Republic—just as we are—and Parliament, as representing the wish of the people, was to rule. This condition of affairs lasted exactly three years in both countries. Then they drifted into a war with each other, as they were bound to do, seeing that they both wanted the same thing at the same moment, and behold! England is still nominally a Republic, but it is ruled by a successful general who calls himself only a Lord Protector, but who is more powerful than the old Kings ever thought of being. For one thing, he has presented himself with a standing army of 30,000 men and every time a Stuart dared to ask for a corporal's guard of his own to keep order in the garden of St. James' Palace, there was an outcry of tyrant and murderer. Now an obscure country-squire from a county no one had ever heard of enjoys more power than any sovereign, duly anointed and booted and spurred by Holy Church, ever dreamed of exercising. And all the little people flock to his standard and shout: 'Long live our Chief!' and if he told them to throw themselves from the cliffs of Dover, they probably would do so because they have no confidence in their own weakness but full faith in his strength.

"And at the same moment we on this side of the North Sea are beginning to repent of our courage of a few years ago. We are scared. We don't know how this war with England will come out. Just when we had decided that we would rule ourselves and that it was folly for free men to submit to the descendants of a little German robber-baron, we seem to lose courage and the old, old story is about to repeat itself.

"Two years ago we got rid of King Log and to-day amidst the enthusiastic plaudits of the multitude, we are trying to bring in King Stork. Yesterday your old friend, Jan de Witt, was made Pensionary of Holland. The title itself means nothing. The office in the hands of that man means everything. It makes him Dictator of the entire Republic. He can raise an army if he wants to and he can build himself such a fleet as the world has never seen before. He can spend all the money he wants. He is his own Minister of Foreign Affairs and his own Minister of Justice. He has a complete spy system at his disposal, to keep tab on his neighbors. By formal resolution of the Estates (passed only a couple of days ago) every private citizen is being urged to watch over his neighbor and to report him to the police the moment he suspects him of disloyal sentiments—disloyal sentiments to My Lord Jan, of course.

"What the House of Orange never dared to do, this son of wine merchants (or were the de Witts in the wood business?) from a third-rate little provincial town does and everybody says, 'How perfectly wonderful! how fine! how noble!' Because we are at war with a very dangerous enemy—because we are afraid of our own shadows—because we know that we can't ever hope to win without accepting the leadership of some one whom we feel to be abler and stronger than we are ourselves.

"And behold! at once the country takes new courage. Stocks go up which ever since the battle of Dover have been going down. The rate of interest on the public debt has gone down from five percent to four percent. We cannot quite undo the harm of the first year. Tromp is dead. Van Galen is dead. We have lost more than sixteen hundred merchantmen, but Jan de Witt has taken hold of things and we are sure that everything will come out all right and that we will yet win the war.

"I refrain from drawing any conclusions.

"But I have read my Plato.

"I think that I have read everything that was ever printed upon the curious subject of a Res Publicae and upon the even more extraordinary subject of government by the average citizens rather than by the few exceptional men. It makes rather inspiring reading when one has nothing else to do—when the day's chores are over and the motherland at peace with everybody. But as soon as there is need of action, that sort of literature becomes just so much trash—useless books of learning without the slightest practical value.

"It is all very puzzling, but as for myself, I have always served a prince and I shall be content to do so until the day of my death.

"Farewell.

"If you could see my late strawberries (my own invention, my own specialty, raised by the care of my own hand) you would rejoice. And I would rejoice too, for it would mean that you were here and I must confess that I miss your agreeable company."

I laid the letter aside and went to bed.

The next morning I got up early.

During the night I had evolved a little plan that seemed to promise good results.

It was impossible to let Rembrandt go on the way he was going.

It was time for some one to do something and I meant to be that some one.

I took my hat and coat and instead of turning to the left as I did every morning on my way to the hospital, I turned to the right and made for the quarters which Jean-Louys had occupied these last five and twenty years.

For although for once I meant to be a man of action, it would do no harm to proceed cautiously.

I knocked at the door and entered and behold! Jean-Louys was lying on the floor before a large flat bowl of water on which there floated a tiny ship made out of paper. By his side knelt a sort of red-bearded giant who was working a pair of bellows with which he was engaged in creating a mild hurricane in the vicinity of the paper vessel.

"Come in and join me," Jean-Louys shouted, without, however, moving an inch from his uncomfortable position. "Come in and join me. I am playing Jupiter and this is my Aeolus. I am at work on a new problem. I have discovered something new, infinitely more interesting than logarithms. And it will make us all rich. Come in and join me. Have you breakfasted? No? Then you will stay with me. This cut-throat here was for five years chief onion-soup-maker-in-extraordinary to the Dey of Algiers. Ten minutes more and you will know why the old Dey drowned three of his favorite wives rather than give up such a cook!"

Chapter 52

JEAN-LOUYS GETS A NEW SERVANT, AND I HEAR FOR THE LAST TIME FROM BERNARDO

As soon as the onion soup had been placed upon the table (this is the only disguise in which I can bear that useful bulb) the red-bearded giant left the small dining-room and Jean-Louys, who had been as eager as a small child to tell me all about his new playthings, poured the tale into my ears.

"First of all I must tell you about that man. He can't understand what I say for his hearing has been greatly impaired and his speech too, as you may have noticed. He is a Frenchman. He comes from my own part of the country. That is probably why we understood each other from the first moment, though he was dead drunk when I picked him out of a gutter and brought him here.

"This is the way it happened. I had gone out to get some fresh bread. I was finishing some work and had not been out for days. It was a nice evening and I decided to take a walk. Down near the water front they were very busy. The next day about thirty ships were to leave for Batavia. It was the usual scene—drunken sailors and drunken women and a band or two and the usual crimps and soul-snatchers eagerly watching lest their prey wander off into the byways of the Nieuwe Waals Island and be stolen by their rivals before they could get them safely on board and pocket the reward. You know the system. They don't get paid until their cargo of human cattle has been delivered.

"It was a disgusting sight, but I suppose that sort of thing is unavoidable if we are to have nutmeg in our wine, and what would scrambled eggs be without a little pepper?

"I got away from the Island as soon as I could and returned home. On the corner of the Oude Schans a man was lying in the middle of the street. He seemed dead. But I could see no wounds and he was still breathing. Drunk or drugged, I thought, and then I heard him mumble a few words. They were in the dialect of my own part of the world!

"A dialect is a passport to the heart of every other man or woman who speaks it. I tried to lift him, but he was very heavy and in a stupor. I hailed two suspicious-looking characters who were lurking around, probably with the intention of robbing this poor devil, and offered them five stivers each if they would deliver the drunk at my house. They pocketed the money and deposited their burden on the floor of my room. I gave them each an extra shilling. They were very grateful. One of them before leaving told me:

"That boy will be all right before morning. That is the work of Squinting Mike, the Irish crimp. He is the greediest of them all. He puts drops in their beer. He once killed two Swedes that way and almost got hanged for it. The Swedish agent pushed the case hard, for it was not the first time his people had been packed off to the Indies that way. But there was some dirty work. Mike was allowed to get away and fled to Hamburg. He came back last fall. Now he is up to his old tricks. That boy will be all right in the morning. Perhaps he will have a headache. Thank you for those two shillings, mister. You don't happen to have a drink for two poor devils that are down on their luck?"

"I gave them each a bottle of beer (I don't like the stuff myself anyway), and they left me alone with my new-found friend. I covered him up with an old coat and in the morning, when I woke up, he was busy dusting the room. I got his story.

"My master Descartes laid down the rule: 'I think. Therefore I exist as a human being.'

"I would like to go a little further and offer an amendment to that fundamental law of life. As soon as all people shall have learned to think, they will be able to exist as human beings.

"Until that moment (I doubt whether it will ever come) we shall continue to live like wild animals. That red-bearded giant is only twenty-seven years old. Listen to this. He is the son of a sheep-farmer near Dax, a drunken father, nineteen brothers and sisters and a third step-mother. The other wives had all died in childbirth. At the age of seven he was sent out with a flock of his own. One day, during a thunderstorm, three of them were killed by lightning. The father was so angry with the boy that he hanged him by his arms from one of the rafters of the sheep-pen. The village priest heard of it, hurried to the farm and cut the boy loose, and took him home.

"As soon as he had recovered (in two or three weeks' time) the father came to the parsonage and demanded his son. The priest refused to surrender him. The father went to the bishop at Dax with a present of five sheep. He got a legal document which forced the priest to surrender the boy to his 'legal parent,' as if parenthood had anything to do with the right to maltreat one's offspring.

"The next day the boy ran away, walked all the way to Bordeaux and hid himself on board a vessel bound for Canada. He was discovered, given a severe beating and put on shore in La Rochelle where the ship had gone for supplies, and for a cargo of rum to sell to the natives of the St. Lawrence River. He was eight years old by this time. It takes a lot of starvation to kill an infant at that age. But one day he fainted in the street and was carried inside the nearest house. It belonged to a Huguenot minister, a certain Guiton, a cousin of the famous mayor who conducted the defense of the city during the siege. The Huguenot kept him and used him in the kitchen. That is where he learned to cook so well. He must have been a remarkable man, that minister, for he let the boy stay a Catholic.

"During the siege the minister's house was hit by a shell of Richelieu's artillery. The whole family was killed with the exception of the minister himself, who was tending the dying on the walls and this boy who was cleaning bottles in the cellar at the moment of the disaster. When the town was taken, the minister was obliged to sign a paper that he would never preach again. He refused to sign and went on preaching. He was condemned to fifteen years at the galleys. The boy was allowed to go, as he had remained a Catholic. He found out what he had to do to be condemned to the galleys. Then he stole a loaf of bread from a military bakery and was given five years on the galleys. It was almost a year before he could discover the whereabouts of his former master. In the meantime his ability as a cook had been discovered. He was offered a job as ship's cook. He refused, but some officers took an interest in him (the story of his deliberate effort to be sent to the bagnio had somehow leaked out in the meantime) and he was given a seat at the same oar with his former master.

"After two years—two years spent chained to a wooden seat or chained to a bench in the land barracks—their vessel, while returning from a trip to Corsica was overhauled by a Tunisian pirate. There had been a great deal of sickness among the French galley-slaves, due to the bad food they were given. The captain of this particular vessel was a young man from Touraine who had tried to have an affair with one of the nieces of the Cardinal. But the women of the Mazarin blood did few things for the mere sake of the doing. She hinted that he might be more successful if he approached her occasionally with the trifling gift of a couple of pearls or a diamond bracelet.

"The young man was as poor as a church mouse but he had influence. He was made captain of a royal galley. In his greed, he even let his own officers starve. So you need not ask what happened to the men. The poor devils were no match for the corsairs. In less than an hour the Tunisian had overtaken them.

"You probably know the bounties which My Most Christian Majesty bestows upon those of his faithful subjects who are generously allowed to work in his galleys. He gives them two sets of chains, one for their legs and one for their arms—a pair of breeches—a straw hat and a little wooden pear which is suspended from their neck by a thin iron chain. When the ship goes into action, the creatures are ordered to put that pear into their mouth. It allows them to breath but it stifles their cries when they are wounded or dying, so that the soldiers won't be disheartened by the agony of this poor, dumb cattle when it is on the way to meet its creator. This wooden pear saved my friend's life. The Tunisians fired a volley which hit the Frenchman from in front. The old

Huguenot minister got a bullet in his brain, and was killed outright. Our friend in the other room was hit just a little lower. The bullet struck him in the mouth, but the wooden pear stopped it. All his teeth were knocked out and splinters got stuck in his vocal cords. Otherwise he was all right. In less than a month he was pronounced cured, but he never could talk again above a whisper.

"During the next three years he sat chained to a bench of a Tunisian galley. Otherwise nothing was changed in his life. Then by accident his culinary abilities were discovered. He was promoted to the kitchens of the Dey. They gave him a fine uniform and three wives and paid him for his services.

"One day a Dutch trader loaded with rum, dropped into the harbor of Tunis. The Dey, who was a faithful follower of the Prophet and at the same time a heavy toper, entertained the captain with great honor and the poor cook thinking that this man must therefore be a personage of distinction—an admiral or vice-admiral, at the very least—hastily smuggled himself on board the vessel that night when the Dey and all his guests were deeply under the influence of the Dutchman's floating cargo.

"The next day he discovered his mistake. The ship belonged to the West India Company and was in the slave trade. At first they talked about throwing the Frenchman overboard. Then they noticed his gigantic strength (any one who survives four years at an oar in one of His Most Catholic Majesty's galleys has the constitution of an ox) and they taught him the trade of a sailor. They used to ply between Cormantyne on the Gold Coast and Virginia, with an occasional side trip to Nieuw Amsterdam for repairs. A year ago they met an English man-of-war off the Cape Verde Islands. They did not know that war had been declared between England and Holland until the Britisher fired a salvo that made them lose half of their foremast. Then they decided that something was wrong and fled. They were faster than the Englishman but they had a heavy cargo on board—more than eight hundred black men and women. The Frenchman and two Dutchmen were ordered to throw the cargo overboard. They refused at first, but the captain threatened to shoot them down unless they obeyed his orders. They threw all of those eight hundred odd human beings overboard. The ship was followed by sharks until they reached the Canary Islands. There they lost their Englishman. But there was no use going to America without a cargo and so the captain decided to return home by way of Scotland. They ran out of water and had to land in Ireland. Ten men were sent on shore. They fell into an ambush, laid by a band of natives, who rushed upon them shouting, 'Armada! armada!' probably thinking that they were Spaniards belonging to the great armada of almost a century ago. The Frenchman and one German boy, who were the last to land, could reach the boat and escaped. All the others were taken prisoner and clubbed to death. Half of the crew and the captain died from lack of water. The survivors brought the ship home.

"This poor devil, when he came for his pay, was told that he was a stowaway and owed the Company money. When he insisted, they threatened him with arrest. He did odd jobs around the harbor for a few months. Then some one asked him whether he did not want to enlist on board an Indiaman. The pay was good and he would get fifty guilders in advance. That seemed riches to him. He accepted. His new acquaintance suggested that they go somewhere and have a drink in honor of the event. He agreed. They went to an obscure basement, but he does not remember where. Indeed he remembers nothing until he woke up in my room.

"I did not quite know what to do with him. I got a room for him with my amiable vegetable woman. Then I asked him what he could do. He said he could cook and sail a boat. I let him cook. He was a wonder.

"One evening, just for the fun, I did what I had never done. I hired a small sailboat and told him to take me on a trip on the Y. That was the second great emotion of my life. The first one happened when I stumbled upon that little volume by John Napier and discovered logarithms. The second one came to me when for the first time since I was born I experienced the feeling of a fresh young breeze filling the sails of that little cat-boat. It was like flying into space—at least what I think flying into space must be like—if we can ever hope to do it. Then and there I fell in love with sailing. I did not tell you. It seemed so silly, at my age, to be as enthusiastic as a boy with his first pair of skates. But I bought a boat of my own last week. A small yacht. It used to belong to a family in Zaandam who lost their money early in the war. It has a large cabin and room for two passengers. Poor François, that is the name of my new man, sleeps in the front part of the ship. There is a small stove on board. The ideal home for a philosopher. As soon as my new book is done, I shall retire from the world and live entirely on board my own yacht. I like the sound of that. How does it strike you?"

I told him that it struck me as a brilliant idea. As a boy whenever I stayed with my uncle in Veere, I had done a great deal of sailing and I loved to be on the water. But I feared that Jean-Louys, accustomed to spend his days in scientific studies, might find life on board a little dull and I told him so. Would he be able to live for days at a time without his mathematics and his logarithms?

"But that is just the beauty of it!" he shouted with enthusiasm. "As soon as I had been on the Y a couple of times and knew more or less how a boat like that was handled, I went to my book-seller and asked him to give me a volume on the theory of getting a vessel in motion by means of the wind. I know what happens when I use an oar. I did not know what happened when I hoisted sail. I can guess more or less at what occurs, but I want to see a problem expressed in terms of mathematics, before I believe that it is true. There were a lot of books on how to build boats, but no one ever seemed to have asked himself exactly what takes place when a ship sails before the wind or tacks. So I thought I would try and find out. The Magdeburg mayor, with his notions of a vacuum, had given me an idea. I am trying it out in the wash-basin in the other room. But that won't interest you. You come and sail with me some time and I shall never even whisper a word about my formulae. If you, from your side, will promise not to talk about Cannabis Indica. And at night we shall drop anchor in some quiet spot and shall drink malmsey and talk of olden times and of our walks with Selim and good Bernardo. Those were good days! I wonder what has become of them?"

Since I am once on the subject, I might as well mention now under what circumstances I last heard from Bernardo. It was in '65, a year after Nieuw Amsterdam had been taken away from us by the English, who attacked the city without any declaration of war, and two years after the death of King Louis.

In this letter, addressed to Jean-Louys and to me (it made the trip in less than four months, which was a record, considering the fact that at that time we were at war with England and the ocean and the North Sea were both infested with priveteers) Bernardo no longer used his own name but signed himself by means of an incomprehensible Indian hieroglyphic, the picture of a man lifting both hands toward High Heaven, and whenever he spoke of his neighbors, he called them "My people." For he had completely identified himself with the copper-colored aborigines among whom he had settled down almost twenty-five years before. But his letter showed that, mentally at least, he had not changed and that although he had preferred to cast his lot in with natives, he himself had not in any way "gone native" as we used to say of those Europeans who having been sent to the Indies to administer the Javanese and the Malayans on behalf of the white races had cut themselves loose from their own civilization and through indolence and from lack of sufficient force of character had degenerated into a species of nondescript human beings as thoroughly despised by their former compatriots as by those whom they tried to flatter by an all too sincere imitation.

He sent us both his most affectionate regards and "to all the old friends who were so good to me and who now seem so far away. As for me, there is little to say. I am happy. Happier than I ever thought I could be. My children are fine boys. They hunt and fish. They know nothing of those dreadful things which I have spent the greater part of my life trying to forget. Their mother is very kind. I never regretted for a moment that I married her and joined her tribe. We are breaking camp. The Massachusetts people have become our neighbors. We are moving further westward. The Dutch were hard task-masters, but they did not despise us. When they were not actually engaged in killing Indians, they did not refuse to associate with them on terms of equality. And so we have pulled up stakes and to-morrow we move westward until we shall find new hunting grounds. I am sad at heart, for I am leaving the only spot in the world where I have found contentment of the soul. But my sons are eager to go and so all will be well. The land of which I have heard the old people talk lies several weeks away from here near the big lake where the Eries used to dwell. They have suffered greatly during the last ten years from sickness and many of their hunting grounds lie deserted. But it is far away from Nieuw Amsterdam and I may not be able to communicate with you for a long time to come. And if this be my last greeting to you on this earth, let it tell you once more with what deep gratitude and love I think back to the days when you took me into your heart and gave me your friendship."

Then followed the strange little manikin, lifting both hands wide stretched up to High Heaven, and that was the last time I ever heard of Bernardo.

When My Lord Stuyvesant came home for the last time, a year after the surrender of Nieuw Amsterdam, to give an account of himself during the last years of his administration and to explain why he had not taken sufficient measures to defend the city against the forces of Colonel Nicolls (a charge which he answered by referring the honorable directors of the Company to their own letter-files in which they could read how for a period of nineteen years he had never ceased to draw their respectful attention to the utter state of neglect of the colony entrusted to his care) I had the privilege of visiting him at the little village near Leyden where he was staying with his wife's relatives.

He received me most cordially. He told me that during the four months preceding the actual attack upon the city he had not received a single letter from home, hinting in any way at friction between the Netherlands and the King of Great Britain. He had heard in a vague and roundabout way that His Majesty had bestowed the greater part of the American coast upon his brother, the Duke of York, but as Charles II was notoriously generous with other people's possessions, he had paid no particular attention to this news. It was probably part of the day's royal gossip. And as His Majesty was said to contemplate a more active policy against the Puritans of the Northern settlements who had given refuge to the judges who had condemned His Majesty's father to death—who had made themselves guilty of all sorts of cruelties against those who differed from them in matters of religion—who had driven perfectly harmless men and women who refused to share their views into the wilderness to be tortured to death by the natives—and who had passed special laws condemning other Englishmen who were followers of George Fox to have their ears cut off, their noses slit and their tongues pierced by hot irons, whenever they should be found within the jurisdiction of the Massachusetts company, it had been perfectly natural for My Lord

Stuyvesant to draw the conclusion that this military expedition was directed against the rebellious inhabitants of the New England colony rather than against the peaceful citizens of the New Netherlands who had done nothing to incur His Majesty's wrath.

I was glad to hear shortly afterwards that my old friend had been able to convert his former employers to this point of view and that no further steps were contemplated against him. As for myself, the news he brought me was not very encouraging. Regarding my little piece of property near Nieuw Amsterdam (now called New York after the brother of His Majesty) that probably was safe enough as the English commander had shown the greatest possible generosity in dealing with his new subjects. But when I asked him what he knew of the migration of the northern Indians from their ancient homesteads towards the great lakes of the West, he shrugged his shoulders and answered, "Nothing! Absolutely nothing!"

He had heard in a very indefinite and roundabout way that some such migration had been contemplated and that the advance guard had actually left for the West late in the fall of '64. But it had been an exceptionally early and severe winter. Rumors had come to Nieuw Amsterdam that the first group to undertake the distant and dangerous journey had been caught in a blizzard and that all of them had frozen to death. Whether Bernardo had joined this group or had waited until spring, it was of course impossible for him to tell.

During the next half dozen years I asked every captain bound for the mouth of the Hudson to make inquiries and inquire among the natives who loafed around the trading-posts what they knew. But all to no avail. Bernardo's letter of the year '65 was the last token of life I ever received from his hand. The wilderness had swallowed him up. He had always craved oblivion. He had got his wish. May his end have been as happy and peaceful as those years he spent away from a civilization he had every reason to abhor and detest.

As for Selim, he had a habit of reminding us of his continued existence and prosperity by messages and presents that bobbed up in Amsterdam at most unexpected moments. His greatest coup took place in the year '60. I remember the date because it occurred just at the time the whole country was in a violent state of excitement about those three judges of the late King Charles, who had found a refuge in the town of Delft when the House of Stuart was returned to the throne of England and who had expected that the ancient right of asylum (of which our country had long been so proud) would protect them against the vengeance of their new sovereign.

As soon, however, as His Majesty had sailed from Scheveningen for the mouth of the Thames, he had begun to bombard the Estates with requests for the surrender of these "murderers." The country had been sharply divided upon the subject. Most people still smarted under the remembrance of what their own fathers and mothers had suffered at the hands of a cruel potentate and those declared that it was against the very spirit of the founders of the Republic to comply with such a demand. But others, short-sighted as merchants so often are, argued: "No, it would be foolish to refuse to comply with His Majesty's wishes. We need his good will for we need his country's trade. The Lord Protector and his followers who ruled England during the last ten years were our worst enemies and did their best to destroy our prosperity. Why should we be over-sensitive about a few of the disciples of this man Cromwell, who hated us and made war on us whenever he could, if by surrendering them we can gain the good will of those who are now in power and with whom we have never had any quarrel? We can easily placate our own consciences by persuading ourselves that this is a purely internal political question which does not regard us at all—which the English must solve as they themselves see fit."

While this discussion was going on, leading to violent discussions in all the ale-houses and in the cabins of every canal-boat (I am sorry to say that in the end the "practical minded" gained the victory and that the three unfortunate Britishers were surrendered to His Majesty who had them butchered in the approved royal fashion) there appeared at my door one day a personage who introduced himself as a certain Captain Jan Krol, a cousin of the former governor of the Nieuw Netherlands (though not inordinately proud of the fact)—who stated that he had that week returned with his ship from Stamboul and that he brought me a little present from an old friend of mine.

This little present, carefully carried into the house by two stalwart sailors who had waited outside with a wheel-barrow, consisted of a queerly shaped bale or sack, made of a pale yellowish matting and spreading a strange but exceedingly pleasant odor vaguely reminding me of the water-front of Nieuw Amsterdam.

When my son with a pair of scissors cut it open, as if it were a fatted pig, it disgorged thousands of little brown beans, no larger than a full-sized pea, and they rattled all over the stone floor of the kitchen and looked most appetizing, though none of us knew what they were, though we suspected them of being a new kind of vegetable or something that was to be boiled in the soup. When half of the bag was emptied, we came upon a letter of Selim's, hidden in a beautifully wrought small golden box.

"Allah is great, O my friends, for once more Allah is Allah and I am the humblest and most faithful of his servants.

"I hope your health is well. I also hope you will enjoy this small present as much as I enjoyed your charming companionship during the days I dwelled within your hospitable but dampish gates.

"At that time, now so far behind us all, you may remember, we were occasionally treated to a cup of that 'chaw' which ships returning from Kathay had obtained from the Portuguese at Macao. It may have been a popular beverage among the yellow denizens of the great empire of the East, but if I recollect rightly, we did not like this lukewarm soup any too well and merely partook of it only out of politeness. But now, my friends, the gates of Paradise have been opened—the Houris have descended upon earth—the marvelous Black Water from the Realm of Sheba's glorious Queen is about to pour down your unbelieving and unworthy gullets.

"Nevertheless, drink this supreme Abyssinian draft—this divine cure of all human ailments, O my beloved friends, and think in kindness of him who now dwelleth in the fear of Allah, the One and Only God, who rewardeth those who truly love Him beyond the merits of mortal man and surely beyond the merits of the black-souled sinner you once knew as your affectionate companion,

SELIM,
"Now His Majesty's bearer of the most
sacred horse-tail and groom-in-extraordinary to the Padishal mule."

The letter itself was not remarkable, but the accompanying gift caused a commotion which few of us who took part in concocting that unfortunate potion will ever forget, no matter how long we live.

For no one in those early days knew what those little beans really were or how they should be prepared and served.

I took some of the beans with me and asked Francen, the apothecary, who consulted his entire pharmaceutical library, but could find nothing that would give us a hint. We therefore decided that though it might cure "all human ailments" it was not primarily a medicine.

Then Jean-Louys, who notwithstanding his oft repeated assertion that he was only interested in mathematics, read (on the sly, of course) about every book that appeared upon every conceivable subject, remembered that several years before in a certain learned treatise of one Jacobus Golius ("I happened to pick up his book because the old fellow is also a teacher of mathematics," Jean-Louys excused himself afterwards) which pretended to be a history of the reign of the great Emperor Tamerlane, he had once come across a passage that might throw some light upon our problem. According to the famous Leyden professor (who himself had spent a number of years among the Moslems as secretary of the Dutch Legation in Morocco) the Mohammedans sometimes held a form of divine service which for sheer length surpassed anything ever heard of in our own part of the world, though several of our ministers prided themselves on never giving their audiences less than three whole hours of divine service. But whereas in our churches, no one minded an occasional snore, the God of the Moslems greatly resented such a lack of interest on the part of his adherents.

And then, sometime during the twelfth or thirteenth centuries of our era, certain merchants returning from Abyssinia reported that they had discovered a wonderful new drug that would keep one awake for days at a time. It grew on a small shrub and its exhilarating qualities had first been noticed when flocks of sheep ate from this shrub and did not go to sleep for a whole week.

The pious Mohammedans thereafter fortified themselves with this concoction whenever they meant to attend any of the high festivals of their creed. The old-fashioned and orthodox Moslems had of course denounced this innovation as a trick played upon the faithful by Satan, just as the true believers in our own time are fighting the organs in our church which they declare to be an invention of the Devil and a survival from Sodom and Gomorrah. But in the end, so Golius reported, the berry-eaters, or berry drinkers (for they preferred the extract to the dry bean in its natural state), had won out and soon afterwards all over Arabia people were in the habit of partaking of "coffee" (so the shrub was called after that part of Abyssinia where it came from and which was known as the province of Kaffa), and notwithstanding a long series of edicts passed by the Mohammedan Church against this "wicked and impious custom, worthy of a thousand deaths," and notwithstanding some very drastic efforts on the part of the Sultan to suppress the bean altogether, every true Moslem partook of a hearty dish of coffee at least once a day.

So much for old Golius. From his writing it seemed to us that a few hours' soaking and boiling was all the little beans needed to make them palatable.

But no sooner had we come to this conclusion than behold old Coppenol, the writing-master and one of the world's most irrepressible bores, whose only excuse for living consisted in the encouragement he had given Rembrandt when the latter was still in some doubt about his ability as a painter (and whom Rembrandt had repaid by a lifetime of forebearing friendship), this learned old pedant must come forward with a new theory.

According to him the little brown beans of our friend Selim were in reality nothing but that mysterious "nepenthe" of which Homer speaks in that part of the work known as the Odyssey. According to the famous Rhodian poet, "nepenthe" was an herb which hailed from Egypt and those who partook of it were immediately granted complete forgetfulness of all their ills and woes. Coppenol was so delighted with this brilliant discovery (I wish Rembrandt had not wasted quite so much time painting and etching the pompous fool) that he finally persuaded Jean-Louys to give him a chance to prove his point and to invite all his friends to a regular feast of oblivion.

This was to be held at the Breestraat as the hall in the back of Rembrandt's house was the largest room then at our disposal. Accordingly, one fine Sunday evening, about twenty of us gathered together for supper and Coppenol, as originator of the new "mystery" (an Eleusinian mystery in the Jewish quarter of Amsterdam in the fifties of the seventeenth century!) was delegated to prepare the lethal potion. He had not the slightest idea how to set about this task, being one of those unfortunate persons who have twenty thumbs on each hand whenever it comes to anything less complicated than writing the whole of the Lord's Prayer on the back of a stiver or turning his own name into the motive for an animated barn-yard scene. He had, however, developed a mystic theory that since the word "nepenthe" consisted of two parts, the beans should be mixed with a quantity of water that equaled their own weight—half coffee and half water, in the terms of the pharmacopoeia.

While he was busy with his brew, we partook of the usual Sunday evening supper, a dark peasant bread, the recipe for which (and it was a most excellent recipe) Hendrickje had brought with her from her own village, and some herring. After that, those of us who cared to do so were given the opportunity to drink a pipe of tobacco in the studio, where Rembrandt had just begun a new portrait of Hendrickje, looking out of a window and wearing the pearls that had brought so much unhappiness to Saskia and himself, and finally (it must have been about ten o'clock) Coppenol sent up his grandson to tell us that the divine symposium was ready.

We each got a large earthen jar filled with a thick, brownish soup. We each of us drank the horrible stuff to the last dregs. Then we waited. Then Abraham Francen left the room as if compelled to keep a sudden appointment. Next two of the pupils, invited to this party for the occasion, darted out of the door. Next I saw Hendrickje turn a deadly pale and heard her excuse herself from our company. Within twenty minutes, the whole of the gathering found itself reassembled in the back yard. For the "divine nepenthe" had not given us oblivion. It had only made us dreadfully ill.

Francen, an experienced apothecary, then bethought himself of hot milk as a possible antidote and the whole neighborhood was searched (it was the Sabbath day and all the shops were closed) for fresh milk. The proprietor of a Jewish creamery on the corner of the Vlooburgstraat nobly rushed to our rescue. He even went so far as to heat the milk for us, since none of us had strength enough left to handle that heavy kettle, and soon afterwards (having meanwhile turned Rembrandt's neat little garden into something not quite so neat) the illustrious band of artists and apothecaries and writers and chirurgeons (not to forget the excellent Hendrickje, who had her hands full with small Titus, who boylike had licked the pot with his fingers and who had coffee all over his hands and face and his brightly starched Sunday collar) regained their former health and composure, swearing due vengeance on unfortunate Selim who had undoubtedly made his offering in the kindest of spirits, but who might have gone just a little further and might have sent us one of his fifteen pastry cooks to let us know how the stuff should be prepared.

News of this unfortunate occurrence soon spread through the town. Sermons were preached on the iniquity of feasting on the Sabbath day. Others, less uncharitable, who pretended that they had drunk coffee before in Smyrna and Constantinople and Famagusta, offered us plentiful advice. According to some of them, we should have ground the beans first and then should have drunk them mixed with hot water and cloves. Others suggested hot milk and cinnamon and still others both water and milk and sugar and mace, and one even vowed that no true Moslem would partake of the beverage without a small pinch of ambergris.

Several years afterwards, when the newspaper brought us news of the attempts made by our old enemy, King Charles, to suppress the Cornhill coffee-houses as breeding places of discontent and the hatching-ground of anti-royalist plots, we also learned something more definite about the true way to prepare the little poisonous beans. But for those of us who had partaken of that feast at Rembrandt's house, the advice came too late. We stuck to beer or bischop and although Selim continued to send us strange-looking bales and barrels containing even stranger-looking products of his native land (as an expression of his undiminished affection for his old friends), we never quite trusted their contents sufficiently to engage in another nepenthean feast.

We used to thank the noble Turk in high-flowing language and we distributed his gifts among the beggars who especially during the years following immediately upon the great English war, infested our streets as badly as they had done in '48 after the end of the rebellion, but we ourselves declared an embargo against all things Mohammedan and strictly lived up to this rule.

All of which has carried me far afield from the subject that was in my mind when I began to write this evening, but as I have said before, writing is very much like living, and human existence refuses to be bound by the orderly rules of the tables of multiplication but wanders all over the planet. I started out in this chapter to explain how I had called on Jean-Louys to ask him to give me some advice about Rembrandt's hopeless financial situation. Instead of which I first indulged in a short essay upon the charity of His Most Christian Majesty and then, for good measure, I added a few observations upon the nature of certain supposed blessings that came to us from the Orient.

Well, all these separate little items played their modest part in producing that sum total of experiences and sensations which the world knows as Master Jan van Loon and as such (since I am mainly writing about myself) they are not only necessary but also unavoidable.

But now I return to the end of my interview with Jean-Louys. At one time in his career he had been obliged to handle large sums of money. He had even tried to discover the theoretical mathematical formula that must underlie the highly practical system of double-entry book-keeping which Simon Stevin had introduced into the Republic. He was an ideal person therefore to act as one's financial counselor. But when I had explained my predicament to him, I found him quite uninterested and deliberately aloof.

"What does it matter?" he asked me, with true and tantalizing philosophical calm.

"Everything," I answered, slightly upset by his indifference.

"But why? The man paints better than ever before. In a hundred years, no one will know or care whether he died in the poor-house or in the second-best guest-room of his illustrious friend, My Lord Six."

"I know that. But meanwhile he has to support a son and a wife, or at least a woman who will soon be the mother of one of his children. They need three meals a day and he himself would die if he ever had to give up that museum he calls his home."

"It might be good for his work."

"Also it might kill him—not to speak of Hendrickje and little Titus."

Jean-Louys confessed that he had never thought of it in that light. Then he asked me what I meant to do.

"I don't know," I answered. "If I did, I would not be sitting here bothering you with my questions. Every time I mention it to Rembrandt himself, he gets fidgety, takes me to his studio to show me a new picture he has just started, explains a new idea for some large allegorical figure for the new Town Hall (as if they'd give him a chance to work there!) and hastily tells Hendrickje to bring me something to eat or to drink, as if I were a small child that had to be placated, and changes the subject."

"Yes," Jean-Louys said, "it probably makes him feel uncomfortable. As we all know, he is a man of but one single obsession. He wants to paint. All the rest to him is detail and therefore a negligible quantity. You will never find out anything from him directly."

"And yet I have got to know a few things if we are to avert a disaster."

"You never will. It is not in your line. How about your friend Lodewijk?"

"But he has never handled any of Rembrandt's business affairs. He happens to be my banker and not Rembrandt's, if Rembrandt allows himself such a sensible luxury, which I doubt."

"Of course he is not Rembrandt's banker, but he makes a living handling other people's money. It is his business to know the financial condition of everybody in town. I happen to be a mathematician and therefore I am familiar with what all the other mathematicians in Holland and France and England are writing or saying or doing. You are a surgeon and you are careful to follow the work of your competitors here in Amsterdam and in Lisbon and in Bologna and in every other part of the world. People who play the dangerous game of your friend Lodewijk must be even more careful than we. You go and see him to-morrow and you will be surprised to find out how much he can tell you. And if he puts his mind to it, he can give you a complete balance-sheet before the end of next week. I don't think that that balance-sheet will make you any the happier. But if you must have it (and seeing that you belong to this pig-headed race, you probably must, once you have set your mind on it) he will undoubtedly get it for you, neatly written out on a piece of paper and showing a deficit of fifty or sixty thousand guilders. If I were you, I would leave the matter alone and come sailing with me to-morrow. I think I have got hold of a new idea about rigging the sails so as to cause more of a vacuum. To-morrow at ten you had better come. You may be present at the birth of a new era in navigation."

But all the ships in the world could not have dragged me away from my original purpose. And at the very moment Jean-Louys and his faithful man-servant were crossing the banks of the Pampus, I was knocking at a well-known door on the Singel.

The night before, little Titus had come to my house to ask whether Mother could perhaps have half a dozen eggs for there was nothing to eat in the house and Father had not yet had his dinner.

Surely it was high time that something be done!

Chapter 53

I VISIT MY BANKER AND LEARN SOMETHING ABOUT THE DEPLORABLE STATE OF REMBRANDT'S FINANCES

When I entered his office, I found Lodewijk busy cutting himself a new pen.

"What a day!" he shouted as soon as he saw me. "What a day! Was there ever such a climate in all the world? My sixth pen this morning. They melt in your hand—like fresh butter."

Then when he had fashioned the nib according to his desire: "Well, what can I do for you to-day? Want to know how your shares are doing? They are bearing up well under the bad news from the front. But you must not expect too much these days. We ought to be glad if we get through without losing more than ten or fifteen points. What is it you want?"

I told him.

He listened patiently, but did not seem surprised.

"I know all about that," he answered. "We all do. That man owes everybody money and is in debt way over his ears. It is a bad case. He will end in the bankruptcy courts."

"That is what I feared," I told him. "That is why I am here to-day. Exactly how bad is it?"

"Ah, there now! I can't give you a balance-sheet with all the details. When I said that I knew all the case, I meant that I knew enough never to give the man a single penny, if he came here to ask me for a loan. Further than that, my interest did not go. But if you want to have details, come back in a week's time and you shall have them all."

And then he dropped the subject and talked to me about certain of my own affairs which I shall mention in some later chapter, and he took me out to a small eating house in the Wolvenstraat where a greasy, bearded and squint-eyed Armenian kept what he called on his sign-board outside a truly kosher Jewish restaurant and he fed me a mixture of strange Turkish dishes which made me think of Selim's little brown beans which had made us all sick, and then I left him and went to the hospital, though I am sure none of my patients felt as miserable as I did that afternoon. And a week later I called again at the Singel and received a short report, writ by Lodewijk himself, and containing a number of facts which made me suspect that my worst fears were about to come true and that the position of Rembrandt indeed was hopeless.

"Don't expect too much," Lodewijk warned me. "This is not a stockholder's report. As a rule we disciples of Mercury know a great deal about our neighbors' private affairs. Or if we don't know, we can at least find out. But this is hopeless. Hopeless, I tell you! The man himself does not know how badly off he is. He is one of those chain-borrowers—the most disastrous form of all possible financial transactions. He will borrow one thousand guilders from one friend for the period of a year and at 5 percent interest. And at the same time he will borrow 1,500 from another friend for eight months and at 7 percent. Five months later he will borrow 900 guilders for thirteen months at 6¾ percent from another party. With half of that he will repay Friend No. 1, from whom he will immediately thereupon borrow another 2000 florins for one year at 5½ percent and which he will use to repay Friend No. 2 one third of what he owes him and Friend No. 3 two sevenths of his debt, plus accumulated interest. As he seems to keep no accounts of any sort and carries all those complicated manipulations in the back of his head (which is already very full of other things which have nothing at all to do with finance) you will understand the hopeless muddle in which his affairs are after almost twenty years of chaos.

"To make matters still a little more complicated, he occasionally borrows money on pictures that have not yet been painted or on others that have already been promised to a third party. For good measure he has hypothecated his house a couple of times and as to what he has done with his wife's inheritance, of which he was the trustee for his little son, nothing less than the day of the Last Judgment will ever solve that puzzle.

"But here you are, my friend. Here is the report as I pieced it together from two dozen different sources. Sit down in that corner and read it while I cut myself a fresh pen. It is raining again. It always rains in this damned country. Now sit down and read."

I did as he told me. I sat down and read and as I have kept that report I can copy it in full.

"CONFIDENTIAL

"For your own exclusive information. The subject of this investigation is the son of very simple folk, but his parents were not without means and possessed among other things one wind-mill, two small houses and a parcel of real estate in one of the poorer quarters of the town of Leyden. There were six children. Several of those seem to have died young. Those who are still alive have never done very well and are now actually in reduced circumstances. It is said that their brother (the subject of this investigation) supports them and keeps them out of the poor-house.

"As for the subject of this investigation, who hereafter will be designated as N.N., he was the brightest of the family and destined by his parents to follow a legal career. As such he was inscribed in the University of Leyden in the year 1620 at the age of fourteen. It does not appear that he ever actually followed any courses of lectures, having in the meantime made up his mind to become a painter. In 1630 his father died. The oldest son, having suffered an accident to his hand which made it impossible for him to work, remained behind, as a charge on the other brothers and sisters, but they each received a small amount in cash. N.N. took his share and left Leyden and moved to Amsterdam and took a studio on the Bloemgracht, afterwards moving to the Anthonie Breestraat, also known as the Jodenbreestraat, where he lived for upward of six years.

"At first he was a great success in his own field of work. He had developed a new style of painting which for a dozen years was very fashionable. He had customers among the richest and noblest families of our city and was even commissioned to work for the Prince, though in that case it appears that he had considerable trouble in getting his money. Meanwhile he had become engaged to a girl from Leeuwarden, the daughter of a former burgomaster and well-known political leader, called Rombertus van Uylenburgh. The girl was an orphan and said to be wealthy. After the death of her parents she had first lived with two of her sisters in her native province and had then moved to Amsterdam and first came to live with a female cousin, the wife of Dominie Jan Corneliszoon Sylvius, who had been called to this town in 1610 and was considered a very powerful and eloquent preacher.

"N.N. met the girl through another cousin of hers, one Hendrick van Uylenburgh, who at that time was a dealer in antiques and who also acted as 'entrepreneur' for fashionable painters—that is to say, he acted as go-between for rich people and poor artists and then charged the artist twenty or thirty percent for his services if a sale were made and a picture was ordered. N.N. married the girl in June of the year 1634 and went to live with her in his house on the Breestraat which even at that time he had already begun to convert into a museum, spending the greater part of his considerable earnings on old paintings, bits of statuary and fine silks and brocades.

"After his wedding he added pearls and diamonds and other bits of jewelry to his collection. He is still said to have those. As for his annual revenue during that period, we can find no details but during the first ten years of his residence in Amsterdam he seems to have received an average of about 500 guilders for his portraits. In addition to his own pictures he had the right to sell the work of his pupils which must have netted him between 2,000 and 2,500 guilders a year. As we were unable to find out how much profit he derived from his etchings during this period, it is impossible to state the sum total of his annual income during this period, though it probably exceeded the sum of ten thousand guilders.

"But already in the year 1638 he seems to have been in financial difficulties. That was the year in which he bought himself the house in the Breestraat which he occupies at the present moment. The house belonged to one P. Beltens. It was the second one from the bridge. N.N. is still living in it to-day. The original price was 13,000 guilders. One fourth was to be paid a year after taking possession and the rest at regular intervals within six years. Why he bought a house so entirely above his own position in life is not clear except that at that period he is said to have tried very hard to come up to the social standards of his wife's family, an attempt which also made itself evident in his art, for every time he painted either himself or his wife, he evidently tried to make the world believe that he was a member of the Medici family of Florence, rather than the son of a humble miller in the little town of Leyden. And even at that moment, when he was willing to spend any amount of money upon such old pictures or pieces of silver as had struck his fancy, he was unable to pay the installments on his house. Of those 40,000 guilders which according to local rumor his wife had inherited from her parents, he never seems to have received a penny, for he had to wait until his mother died in 1640 when he received as his share in her inheritance a sum of 2,490 florins, before he was able to offer the former owner any money at all.

"Eventually, with an unexpected inheritance from an aunt of his wife (who was also her god-mother), and with a part of his own savings, he was able to pay off one half of the 13,000 guilders he owed the heirs of aforementioned P. Beltens. Thereafter he seems to have forgotten about the house for he did not even attempt to keep up with the accumulated interest which has been growing larger and larger every year, until to-day it represents the sum of 8,470.06 guilders, which is entirely beyond his present financial means. For in the meantime he appears to have contracted debts on all sides. As all of them have been made with private persons, it is impossible for us to discover the actual amount for which he is involved. Besides the eight thousand odd guilders for the house there is an I.O.U. for 4,180 guilders made out to the order of Cornelis Witsen, the well-known city councilor. Another I.O.U. for a similar amount (4,200 guilders, to be exact) is in the possession of Isaac van Hertsbeeck or Hartsbeeck, a local merchant. These curious amounts N.N. appears to have borrowed to placate the former owner of his house in the Breestraat, who for the last eight years has been obliged to pay the taxes on this piece of property and who has at last threatened to sue him unless he sees some money coming his way.

"Meanwhile, although the house does not really belong to him unless he shall have paid the full contract price, plus the accumulated interest and plus the accumulated back taxes, he is said to be contemplating making both the house and the adjoining yard over to his son Titus as half his share in his mother's inheritance of 40,000 guilders. This, however, is merely a bit of gossip. For in order to do such a thing, he would be obliged to make a public declaration of his affairs to the Board of

Orphans and as he himself never seems to have received a penny from that Uylenburgh estate (which appears to have existed only on paper), it is not very likely that he will take such a step. For the Board of Orphans is well known for its very strict methods of accounting and a father who is suspected of having made away with part of his son's inheritance, even if he could prove that it was a fictitious inheritance, would run the risk of doing several months at hard labor in the city jail. I therefore return to those debts and transactions which can be more or less identified. From his friend Jan Six, the linen-weaver of the well-known family, he borrowed a thousand guilders which My Lord Jan, however, seems to consider such a risky investment that he has recently offered the I.O.U. for sale and according to rumor on the Exchange, he is willing to accept anything at all. Then he seems to have borrowed or to be in the midst of negotiating a loan of about 3,000 guilders with a surgeon by the name of Daniel Franssen and finally there are countless small items to different persons all over town. These consist either of unpaid grocery bills and baker bills and doctor bills and for money he owes to frame-makers and dealers in brushes and paints and oils and manufacturers of copper plates and printer's ink or of small amounts from fifty guilders upward of tiny sums borrowed under one pretext or another from those unfortunate tradespeople.

"In the meantime N.N. has lost favor with the public. He ruined his reputation with a picture of the company of Captain Banning Cocq which he painted in the year his wife died, in 1642. The members of that company were so outraged with the arrangement of the figures (but upon which he himself had insisted) that several refused to pay him and he is said to have received only 1,600 guilders instead of the 5,250 for which he had contracted.

"If said N.N. owes you any money, I would, as your banker, advise you to get hold of it as soon as possible. You had better take a few of his valuable antiquities if he is willing to give you those in settlement of his debt, but don't count on ever getting a stiver in cash. N.N. is hopelessly involved. His reputation of having married a rich wife will perhaps carry him a little longer. But sooner or later the day must come when his credit has reached its end and then there will be quite a scandal for N.N. has nothing and he owes everybody. The conclusion of our investigation is as follows:

"Assets: Heavily mortgaged house full of objects of art on which, however, it will be very difficult to realize at the present moment owing to the unfavorable economic conditions which are the result of the present war with England; very little good will and no cash or securities whatsoever.

"Liabilities: The total amount is unknown but they must be well over 30,000 guilders.

"Credit standing of the person under discussion—o."

I slowly folded the paper and made ready to put it in my pocket. "I suppose I can keep this?" I asked Lodewijk.

"You can keep it, my friend. But please don't let it fall into the wrong hands. It is bad enough as it is. I am very deeply afraid that poor painter's goose is about cooked."

Then he dropped the pen with which he had been busy figuring all that time and rubbed his hand across his bald head.

"Too bad," he said, as if he were speaking to himself. "Too bad. Poor devil! I suppose he sees certain things we don't happen to see and so he fails to notice certain other things quite as important and which we ordinary human beings must have before our eyes all the time."

I stared at him hard.

"Lodewijk," I remarked, "did I hear you mumble 'quite as important'?"

"No," he answered. "I was wrong there. I suppose they are less important. As a matter of fact, I know that they are less important, but what will you? We all must keep alive. And there is but one way to keep alive—hunt with the pack and stick to the well-known tracks."

"But suppose you are so constituted that you simply must leave the beaten track and look for a path of your own or die?"

Once again Lodewijk rubbed his hand across his head.

"Then," he slowly replied, "you are just out of luck." But more than that he would not say.

THE JEWISH SYNAGOGUE

THE BANKRUPTCY NOTICE

Chapter 54

I ONCE MORE TAKE UP MY SEARCH FOR SOME DRUG THAT SHOULD KILL THE PAIN OF THOSE ABOUT TO UNDERGO A SURGICAL OPERATION

Here of course the question arises, why didn't I help Rembrandt at that critical moment in his life? I was supposed to be his most intimate friend and I was wealthy. Why didn't I tell Lodewijk, my banker, to take care of that ghastly "list of creditors" and give Rembrandt a chance to begin all over again and this time with a slate that could be kept reasonably clean?

Well, the answer is very simple. If I had still been able to put my hands on part of that money my uncle had left me, Rembrandt never would have gone to the poor-house. But my money was gone. Temporarily, at least. And when the crash came, I was absolutely helpless. All I could do was to gain enough by my practice to keep my own family alive and slyly give an occasional couple of guilders to Hendrickje for her household expenses. But the bulk of my fortune was no longer at my disposal and this is the way that had happened.

All my life I had hated pain.

Pain to me seemed absolutely unnecessary in a world that was meant to be a happy place of abode for intelligent men and women. The few times I myself had suffered pain, I had felt like an object of pity and contempt. Yea, worse than that. For some queer reason I never could disassociate the word "pain" from the word "dirty." Most of my neighbors of course did not know what I was talking about when I told them that a person in pain made a dirty impression on me. They were good Christians and had been brought up to believe that pain was a necessary concomitant of all human existence.

Had not Jehovah in the first book of the Old Testament condemned Eve to bear children in pain?

I knew he had. My grandfather had read that chapter to me for the first time when I was six years old and had added that any God who had seen fit to condemn women to such incredible agony merely because he was out of sorts that day and angry and was searching for an object to wreak his vengeance upon—that such a God might be good enough for the savages to whom our missionaries in the Indies preached, but that he was no fit company for decent people.

Perhaps it was the memory of that morning, perhaps it was the recollection of a particularly brutal little operation I was obliged to undergo at the age of nine (an infected finger that was opened up by a dumb surgeon with a very dull pair of scissors), but whatever the reason, all my life long I had had one obsession—pain! And all my energy (when I was not directly working for my daily living) I had concentrated upon one single object, how to diminish the amount of unnecessary pain there was in this world.

What I mean by "unnecessary pain" I hardly need describe or define. We are so hopelessly ignorant of the inner construction and the secret mechanism of our bodies that there are a number of afflictions against which we are without any means of defense. Any surgeon or doctor will at once recognize what sort of diseases I have in mind. As the source of these unfortunate morbid conditions is invariably located in one of the organs that lie beyond, or rather below, our reach, it will probably always be impossible to relieve patients who suffer from such maladies. They will have to die. We can try and make their end as merciful as possible, but that is about all we can do.

But there are many other disorders which I would like to call "extraneous ones." That is to say, they are by their very nature "foreign" to the normal human body—they are mere mechanical accidents like broken arms or legs or skulls—or they are the result of a wrong method of living and manifest themselves in the form of gravel or stones and cause endless misery to people who are otherwise quite well and hearty—or they are the result of old age, like decaying teeth or cataract of the eye—they are in short only incidentally part of our natural share of pain and happiness and it always struck me that if we could relieve human beings of that particular form of gratuitous horror, we would add a great deal to the sum total of comfort and happiness in this world. And why, since we have got to stay on this planet for forty or fifty years and it is, in all likelihood, the only planet we shall ever visit, shouldn't we try to make our stay as pleasant as possible? My chosen purpose in life therefore was to find a way to make people temporarily senseless while undergoing an operation.

I have already written something about my experiments with different sorts of alcohol (feeding my patients gin or rum until they were so drunk that they were senseless) and with the mysterious mandrake root. But none of these had been satisfactory. The poor inebriates became hopelessly sober as soon as the knife touched them and as for the mandrake, I never succeeded in arranging the dose in such a way that it brought about thorough insensibility. As a rule my patients became very sick after the use of the extract which the apothecaries recommended as the most satisfactory and the spasms caused by their nauseous condition not infrequently ruined the work of the surgeon and caused the patients to die from internal bleeding.

But now I must mention a curious meeting I had in Nieuw Amsterdam about the fourth year after my arrival in America.

One day a ship flying the Swedish flag and called the *Westergotland*, dropped anchor in the outer bay. Just then we were a little suspicious of

Swedes in our part of the world. Letters had recently arrived from Holland addressed to His Excellency the Governor telling him that according to certain very definite rumors on the Amsterdam exchange, the Swedes meant to establish a West India Trading Company of their own and intended to establish themselves on territory which (theoretically, at least) belonged to us. Wherefore, His Excellency was urged to exercise great watchfulness and keep an eye out for all suspicious-looking vessels that were seen in the neighborhood of the Hudson or the South River, which the English have now rebaptized the Delaware.

The *Westergotland*, however, seemed a harmless enough sort of a craft, bound from Virginia to Gothenburg with a load of tobacco. Off Cape May she had met with a storm which had blown her mizzenmast overboard and she had come to Nieuw Amsterdam for repairs. As only ships flying the English flag were supposed to carry British goods, she dare not put into one of the harbors to the north or south of us for fear of confiscation. That, at least, was the story of the captain who openly boasted of the fact that he had got an entire three hundred barrels filled with contraband tobacco and nobody any the wiser. And as we had no reason to love the people of that particular colony, it was decided to offer Captain Frederiksen (that was his name) all the facilities at our disposal so that he could continue his voyage with the least possible delay.

Nevertheless, a new mast in those early days, when the town had less than 4,000 inhabitants, was quite a big affair and the *Westergotland* remained in Nieuw Amsterdam for almost a whole month. Her crew of course was allowed to go on shore as often and as freely as they pleased and it was then that I made the acquaintance of a very curious personage.

Most of the sailors on board the *Westergotland* were either Swedes or Norwegians, the officers were all of them Swedish, but the doctor was a Portuguese. Now in those days it was a little out of the way for a merchant vessel of scarce 300 tons to carry a surgeon. When the sailors on such small craft happened to fall ill, they either got better or they died, but whatever the outcome of their disease, they were allowed to make their choice without the assistance of one of those ship's leeches who were a disgrace to the profession, being as a rule almost as incompetent as they were drunken and as drunken as they were incompetent.

This old Portuguese (he must have been sixty if he was a day) made a notable exception. He was a fine-looking man, his manners were most gracious and he seemed to be well versed in his craft. How a man like that had come so far down in the social and professional scale as to be a ship's doctor on board a Swedish smuggler was something that puzzled me until I came to know him a little better, and then I found out that he was not only a medical man, but that for about twenty years of his life he had been a pilot in the service of the Portuguese government.

Then, of course, the whole thing became very simple. The *Westergotland* was not a Swedish privateer but was in the service of the King of

Sweden and was engaged in spying out the central part of the northern American coast, preparatory to establishing a Swedish colony at some point between Florida and the possessions of the Gorges family, just south of the Saint Lawrence.

I felt absolutely convinced that this was the case and mentioned it to His Excellency. But as we had no other proof except this bit of circumstantial evidence, it was quite impossible to take any further measures against a vessel that flew the ensign of a sovereign with whom our country was in a state of peace and eventually the *Westergotland* departed amidst an exchange of the most cordial civilities between her skipper and our grouchy old governor, and three weeks later she foundered with the loss of everybody, just off Sable Island, as we heard from a French fisherman who disabled by the same gale had drifted into the sound between the main land and the Lange Eiland and who was now waiting for permission to re-victual his vessel before he went back to his codfish on the Grand Banks.

But to return to my Portuguese. He had a long and very imposing name. He spelled it out for me one day on the fly leaf of my Vesalius and it read: Dom Sebastiao do Conto Quevedo de Oliveira Mortaria. Upon that same occasion he also told me the story of his life, but that was of no great importance to me, except in so far as it helped me to solve the question that had been puzzling me ever since he had set foot on shore in Nieuw Amsterdam, "how did it happen that a man of such evident accomplishments had been obliged to leave his own country and take service with a foreign potentate who lived at the other end of the map?"

It could not be drink, for he never touched a drop. It could not have been women. In the first place, he was too old now, and in the second place, he had an almost morbid aversion for women. Then one night he told me himself. It had been "hasheesh."

What hasheesh was, I did not at that time know. The name sounded Oriental to me and in this I had guessed right. Hasheesh was the Indian name for hemp. Not the sort of hemp we raise at home and which we use in our rope yards, but the resin from the Asiatic hemp, Cannabis Indica, which is prepared in a special way and which is then used by the natives of India as a drug to make them forget the miseries of their existence and make them dream they have arrived in Heaven.

When he had been in Goa for about five years, my unfortunate Portuguese friend had caught a sudden chill which had given him a severe case of rheumatism, and which had caused him such dreadful sufferings that he had been ready to commit suicide. Then a native physician had introduced him to the use of hasheesh and he had become an addict to that dangerous drug which gave him temporary relief from his pain but which had made him a total failure as a responsible member of society.

Eventually the rheumatic affliction had left him, but he had never again been able to live without his daily portion of hasheesh. He knew that the stuff was killing him, but he could not help himself. And in the course of our conversation (he was a brilliant talker and would keep me up night after night with his stories of the early days along the coast of Malabar) he told me all about the various drugs that could be made of hemp—about charas, ganja and bhang, which were all three of them different trade names for products of the hemp industry—and he described to me in detail just exactly what his sensations were whenever he was under the influence of his hasheesh.

Finally he persuaded me to try the stuff one night. He suggested that I smoke the dried leaves, rather than take it internally. He gave me a pipeful. After five or six puffs everything went dark around me and I knew nothing until I came back to life about an hour later. I was then lying on the floor, having fallen off my chair when I went into a coma. It was only then that I discovered that I had hurt myself rather badly against the sharp edge of the table. I had quite a gash in the side of my scalp but had noticed no pain until that moment.

As for my distinguished Portuguese colleague, he was sitting in his chair fast asleep and he remained there until the next morning.

I did not remember that I had had any dreams, either pleasant or disagreeable. I just had "not been" for the half hour I was under the influence of the drug. I could notice no bad after-effects except a violent headache, but as that might very well have been caused by the blow on my head when I hit the table, I could not say that it had been caused by the hasheesh.

At that time I was so busy with other drugs that I had not thought about my experiment any further. Presently the Portuguese had taken his departure and I had gone into the interior on another trip of exploration and Cannabis played no further rôle in my life until returning home on board a slow-sailing merchantman and being obliged to assist them, one of the sailors was cut for the stone (a hideous performance, with the victim fastened to a rough wooden plank and screaming his head off like a pig that was being butchered) I suddenly bethought myself of Dom Sebastiao do Conto Etcetera and his pipe and the idea struck me: "Why not try Cannabis when I get back to my hospital?"

Then of course the siege of Amsterdam had intervened, but finally, about six months after my return, I had begun my experiments in all seriousness. I had gathered hemp from all parts of the world, canappa from Italy and konopi from Russia and cañamo from Spain—even Iceland had contributed a quantity of hampr. Among the ships' captains who sailed for foreign ports, I became known as a poor deluded though harmless fool who had a hemp obsession, probably as they suggested because his grandfather or grandmother had been obliged to look through a hempen window, which was their facetious way of suggesting that these ancestors of mine had been hanged. But they were very obliging, nevertheless, and after a couple of years there was nothing connected with the use of hemp as a narcotic with which I was not thoroughly familiar.

I found several of my colleagues among the surgeons willing to co-operate with me, but the majority of them turned against me as one man. They denounced me as a meddler and innovator and quack and absolutely refused to listen to me or attend one of my operations during which the patient had been put into a state of coma by means of the fumes of Cannabis sativa.

In the end they even objected to my using the operating room of the hospital for my "childish experiments," "getting it all messed up with the smell of that filthy Indian manure," as one of the learned leeches expressed himself, and when I paid no attention to their objections they went to the Town Hall (everybody who had a grievance always rushed to the magistrates) and petitioned Their Lordships that they forbid me to perform any further operations with the help of that "pagan and nauseating drug."

Their Lordships, afraid as usual of what would happen if the clergy caught hold of the word "pagan" as a text for more sermons upon the laxity of the town government in regard to the enforcement of "true Christian morals," asked me to come and see them, spoke to me very affably, praised my zeal and my unselfish devotion and politely requested me to drop all further experiments for, "after all," as one of the Burgomasters said, "if the public is foolish enough to want to feel the pain when it is being operated upon, why not give it what it wants?" An argument at once so simple and so cunning that I could do naught but answer: "Indubitably, My Lord," and promised for the sake of convenience that no more fumes of burned hempleaves would pollute the delicate walls of the city hospital.

But I did not mean to give up. And after a few weeks' meditation I hit upon a plan which would safeguard me against interference on the part of my fellow-physicians and at the same time would allow me to continue those scientific investigations without which my life would have been as dull as soup without salt. This time I first went to my banker to ask him for his opinion and advice, for in all such matters he was possessed of a dry sort of common sense (kindness of heart tempered by a bitter knowledge of the world) which I had learned to esteem very highly during the many years he had been my financial adviser. He had of course heard about my experiences at the hospital. He considered it his business to keep informed about everything that happened in our city and I will say that he was the most reliable perambulating newspaper I have ever met anywhere.

"Yes, my boy," he tried to console me, as soon as I had explained the nature of my errand, "you are getting along in years now—you must be well in the fifties—but in some matters you are as inexperienced as a child of seven. Now what did you expect? You wanted to play the benefactor of the human race and then you found that the human race did not appreciate your kind intentions and now you are sorry for yourself."

"Of course not," I interrupted him. "I am not quite as young and as foolish as all that. Only I hate to see waste of any sort. Pain is waste—waste of perfectly good energy that could be used to a better purpose. Waste of time—waste of money—waste of human happiness. I am not sentimental about it. I am entirely practical."

"Good. But you know what becomes of those entirely practical people who want to benefit humanity? They have usually been killed for their troubles. They have been thrown down wells—hammered on a cross—hung from the highest gallows in the land. And when they escaped the fury of those miserable mortals whom they tried to help, they fell into the hands of the Gods who do not want us to be either too wise or too happy lest we get on to their game and discover that they aren't all we were made to believe when we went to the Rabbi to be told about the glories of Heaven. But all this is talk and talk like this belongs to that waste you hate so much. What doth our young Prometheus mean to do now?"

"I mean to go on. Some day people will come to their senses and appreciate what I am doing."

"Your pretty colleagues kicked you out of their hospital."

"So they did. But that makes no difference. I am a surgeon in good standing. I could perfectly well treat my patients at home. If the house is not large enough, I could hire a couple of other houses. I could build myself a new hospital."

"Fine! And who is supposed to pay for all this?"

"I!"

"Out of your annual income, when you don't send a bill to even half your patients?"

"No, out of my capital. Quite easily, with enough extra money to keep the place going for a couple of years."

At first Lodewijk did not answer.

Then he picked up his latest goose-quill and rubbed the feathery end pensively across his chin. And then he said:

"Blessed be the fools, for they shall see the shadow of God. When do you want that money?"

I told him and that morning we settled everything. He was to convert twenty-five of my shares of the East India Company into cash and was to look for a suitable location for my hospital.

When I left, he put his arms around me and suddenly kissed me on both cheeks.

"It is nice," he said, "to have a few harmless idiots like yourself wandering about on this planet of ours. How dull life would be otherwise. How terribly dull! So dull, one would be almost tempted to turn respectable."

Chapter 55

I FOUND A NEW SORT OF HOSPITAL

I found a house on the Groene Burgwal that entirely suited my needs. It had been recently built for a distiller who had made so much money during the war that he could no longer afford to live in such an unfashionable part of the town and had moved to a small palace on the Heerengracht, where he was ignored by all his dignified neighbors but highly esteemed by the trades people who openly boasted that the rich gin-maker was a better investment than a dozen Burgomasters' families, where the sugar was kept under lock and key and the salt necessary for the soup was weighed on a pair of scales, lest the cook be spoiled and be encouraged to become wasteful.

To my great surprise the distiller was a very intelligent citizen. Except for a certain vanity that seems to be the inevitable in those who have risen in the world through their own exertions, he was a simple-minded, yea, almost humble-minded person, but a very shrewd observer of both man and his ways.

"Since these fools insist upon forgetting their woes by drinking evaporated grain, why shouldn't they drink my gin, which I guarantee is as pure or purer than that of any of my rivals? I know it is not a very inspiring trade I am engaged in. But my gin is as good, as gin goes, as any gin now on the market, and so as long as the blunderheads will drink, I will continue to make the stuff, provided I do not have to taste any of it myself."

This strange philosopher, whose name was Anthony van Andijk ("Just call me Teunis, will you? That Andijk business I added to please my wife. She is a good woman but her father was a beadle in Medemblik and she will never get over it.")—this cheerful Teunis had come up from what we were pleased to call the "dregs of society." His father was a common longshoreman who worked for the Greenland Company and as a boy he had shipped on board an Enkhuizen whaler which had been captured by a Duinkerk privateer (practically within sight of the Texel dunes) and had been taken to Bordeaux because the captain hoped to get a better price for her there than in his home port.

After years of misery as cabin boy on different foreign ships, young Teunis had finally returned to his home town. At one stage in his career he had decided that he would try and walk from Bordeaux to Amsterdam. But in the city of Cognac he had been arrested as a vagrant and in order to escape being sent to the galleys he had hastily taken service with a brandy-maker who had taught him several secrets of the distiller's art which had been of great value to him when he finally was able to set up in business for himself.

The first time I met him he asked me point-blank what I wanted his house for, since it seemed that I already had one perfectly good house of my own and I could not live in two houses at the same time. I told him. I explained my plans in a rather perfunctory and I am afraid slightly patronizing fashion. But he paid no attention to my superior mode of talking and when I had finished, he warmly shook me by the hand and said: "Doctor, that is the first time I have ever heard of a rich man who was trying to do something for poor people without wanting to get something out of the deal himself. I am for you, Doctor. And what is more, I am with you."

And indeed in all our business transactions he was most generous and when it came to refashioning the premises, he used to be on the job every day from six in the morning until seven at night and he bossed the carpenters and the masons so eloquently and so successfully, that in less than three months the house was ready for occupancy. It consisted of a study for myself and a room where I could examine patients at my leisure—an operating room, and a room where I could conduct my own experiments.

On the second floor the building contained about twenty small rooms for patients and on the third floor were the living quarters for the fifteen women whom I hoped to train as nurses for the special sort of work I had undertaken to do. As soon as plans had been formulated for my hospital, I had tried to persuade a few of the deaconesses from the city hospital to come with me, but most of those had religious scruples since I was trying to make people escape the pain which the Almighty had meant them to suffer on account of their wickedness of heart and as punishment for their sins.

Two of the deaconesses, however, were willing to follow me and no one could have asked for more devoted and intelligent service than was given by those women, both in assisting me with my work and in training a dozen young and very ignorant but serious-minded and well-meaning girls who were Moravians and whose parents had fled to the Republic after the battle of the White Hill in which their people had been so decisively beaten and which had been a great blow to the cause of Protestantism in central Europe.

As for the work that was done in my place, I leave it to the unprejudiced members of our guild to say whether it was worth while or not. One thing is certain—our rate of mortality was much lower than that of the regular hospitals. Perhaps this was due to the fact that I kept every patient in a separate little cubby-hole of his own, as I had noticed that the larger the number of patients confined to one single room, the smaller their chance of escaping with their lives. What caused this mysterious connection between over-crowding and dying, I did not know then nor do I know it to-day. Maybe the vapors exuded by sick bodies exercise a harmful influence upon others. Maybe it is the general mood of depression which is noticeable as soon as a number of people are able to tell each other about their symptoms. But we lost only forty percent of all our serious cases and that was quite a record, the figures of the general hospital running well into eighty percent and during some parts of the year (especially during the fall and the winter) going higher than ninety percent.

I had let it be known that my hospital was open to all surgeons who wanted to use my operating room and who cared to avail themselves of my method of rendering people senseless. At first none of them dared to come near what they pleasantly called "The Hempyard," the name usually given to the meadow on the other side of the Y where criminals were hanged. But when it appeared that this hempyard was much less deadly than the official city clinics, they slowly began to patronize No. 17, Groene Burgwal, and everything was going along so nicely that I felt great hope for the future and when Lodewijk (who hated sickness in every form) at last decided to visit our Lazaretto (where he made fast friends with the faithful gin-distiller, who by this time had taken over the entire financial management of the place) I asked him whether he remembered our conversation the day I had decided to risk my entire capital on this one enterprise and what he had to say now?

He answered, "Nothing. I have nothing to say. Everything seems to be going very nicely. But remember Solon, my boy. Remember Solon— 'nemo beatus ante mortem'—you aren't out of the woods yet."

"Perhaps I am not, but just now, I don't seem to espy any lions or tigers."

"Of course not, but that does not mean that they are not there. They may be asleep or probably they are looking at you from behind the shrubs and you have been too busy to see them. Remember Solon, my young friend! The poor-of-spirit are always with us and there is no limit to the amount of harm they can do."

Alas! He was right. As I was to experience within a very short time and to the great detriment, not only of myself, but of all those who had put their confidence in me and had believed in the unselfishness and integrity of my intentions.

Chapter 56

THE MINISTERS TAKE A HAND IN REMBRANDT'S AFFAIRS

It was a far cry from a broken-down old Portuguese doctor on the banks of the Hudson River and a little peasant girl from nowhere in particular who happened to be in the family way, to a public riot in the streets of Amsterdam and the loss of that sum of money with which I would have been able to save Rembrandt from his disgrace. But the world has seen stranger coincidences than that and the episode attracted the attention of many who otherwise would never have heard of me or the work I was doing.

Hendrickje was pregnant. I had noticed it that time she hurt herself and Rembrandt sent for me. Soon afterwards, others had noticed it too and then the trouble had begun. Not among Rembrandt's friends. They understood the situation and knew why he could not marry the girl. Even the exceedingly respectable family of My Lord Jan Six (is there anything in this world more careful of its dignity than one of our linen-weaving or beer-brewing dynasties trying to break into the slightly superior class of the hereditary magistrates?) did not appear to be censorious of a conduct which must have shocked them quite as much as the bankruptcy of one of their nearest relatives.

I never quite understood the friendship that had sprung up between Rembrandt and the rich linen merchant. But then, I never even met the young man. Rembrandt had repeatedly suggested that I accompany him when he called upon Jan Six and had accused me of being super-sensitive and of being a snob, and had assured me time and again that I would find naught but the simplest of manners within the Six household. To which I invariably repeated that I had no doubt about the perfect graciousness that reigned within this charming home on the Kloveniersburgwal, and that I had no doubt but his friends would receive me with the utmost cordiality. Unfortunately their ways were not my ways and my ways were not their ways and what the habits and customs and prejudices of many generations had put asunder, we had better not try and put together.

And in the end it was shown that I had been right. For when the great financial crisis came in Rembrandt's life Jan Six sold the note which Rembrandt had given him to a professional pawnbroker and all that Rembrandt saved out of those years of intimacy and friendship was a presentation copy of a very mediocre Greek play in very mediocre verse. Whereas the Six family was left in the possession of a number of paintings and etchings which will keep its name alive long after the last of their descendants shall have returned to dust.

Verily, as we say in our language, it is bad policy to eat cherries with the mighty. They get the cherries and you get the stones—if you are very lucky.

Upon this unfortunate occasion, however, both My Lord Jan and his relatives showed themselves rather more broad-minded than I had had reason to expect. Of course they had never met Hendrickje and had made no move which showed that they recognized her existence. But at least they continued to be on cordial terms with her husband (for as such she now invariably referred to Rembrandt) and that was more than could be said of most people.

They were shocked.

They disapproved.

If this sort of thing were tolerated once, where would the world end?

And since most people are in the habit of considering their own prejudices as part of the divinely inspired laws which underlie the structure of a well-ordered universe, it was quite unavoidable that the scandal on the Jodenbreestraat should become the most popular subject for family discussions and tea-party gossip. For although it was still considered good form among the higher classes of society to have a few bastards (all the children of the late Prince Maurice, although born out of wedlock, had been baptized by the court preacher of the House of Orange and had received high honors and dignities in the service of the Republic) the prospective arrival of an illegitimate infant in the household of a painter was still considered an event of such enormity that it could not be allowed to pass unnoticed by the reverend clergy who were supposed to be watching day and night over the morals of our New Zion on the Zuyder Zee.

And fortunately on this occasion at least the dominies had luck with them, as I shall now have to relate.

"Misfortunes never come alone," says an old Zeeland proverb, and during the days that followed I was often reminded of this bit of ancestral wisdom. And whereas under ordinary circumstances the birth of the little van Rijn child might have caused only a temporary storm in our domestic tea-cup, a most unfortunate combination of regrettable little incidents caused it to assume the shape of a national scandal.

It all started in a little village in Friesland. I have forgotten the name of the place. It was one of those terrible villages where the people looked like cows and the cows looked like people and where nothing ever happened until from sheer boredom and exasperation the inhabitants were willing to believe any bit of news that would bring them a little excitement.

In this miserable village, where half of the people had been dead for years but had never become aware of the fact because no one had taken the trouble to tell them so—in this far-off hamlet it had been necessary to repair one of the walls and these alterations had in turn caused the temporary removal of several graves. As the last occupant of these tombs had died more than thirty years before, it was not expected that the architects would find anything beyond a few skulls and skeletons. But imagine the surprise of the grave-diggers when they suddenly came upon a corpse that was as good as the day it had been interred!

"A miracle," the people shouted who saw it. "This man was a saint. He was too holy to be returned to dust."

"On the contrary," a young and eager candidate of theology, who was preparing here for his final examinations, whispered. "On the contrary! This man was a sinner of such magnitude that even the worms refused to eat him."

As it was of course much pleasanter to believe evil than good of a departed neighbor, the populace heartily shouted amen, and immediately they began to delve into the past of this poor fellow to discover what crimes he might have committed to deserve such a fate.

This proved to be rather difficult, as the man had been dead for at least thirty-five years. During his days on this earth he had been a very humble shoemaker who had distinguished himself by nothing except his somewhat exaggerated respect for the wise precepts of his Lord and Master, Jesus Christ. He had been charitable to a fault and had not contented himself with surrendering one tenth of all his possessions to the poor, but had often gone hungry himself that others, who were even more miserable than he himself, might be fed.

An old farmer in a neighboring village remembered him well and spoke of him in the highest terms. The deacon of the church he had attended (now well in the eighties) stated emphatically that so good and pious a man had rarely trod the unworthy soil of this planet.

Indeed, at first it seemed as if those who had proclaimed him a saint had been right, but the theological candidate refused to be convinced. "All this," he argued, "only proves that the man was also a very clever prevaricator and was able to hide the traces of his wickedness in such a way that he finally died without ever having been found out." And of course the quest into the fellow's past continued as merrily as before.

Now it happened that the widow of the mysterious corpse was still alive. She was a woman of about seventy and no one knew anything against her that was not highly favorable. She had only one child, a daughter who was married (and very respectably) to a master carpenter in Haarlem. Surely all these family details were commonplace enough to discourage even the most hardened scandal-mongers. But the young cleric kept on snuffling. The old woman was in her dotage and spent most of her days sitting in her little home—tending half a dozen cats and telling those who were willing to listen (and they were very few) what a fine man her husband had been. She was also very superstitious and terribly afraid to die. By playing upon her fear of the Hereafter, and by colorful description of the horrors of Hell, the unscrupulous parson finally got the whole story out of her and no Castilian explorer crossing the parched wastes of the great Mexican desert could have experienced greater happiness at the sight of his first lump of gold than this man of mercy when the trembling old crone at last revealed unto him the well-tended secret of her husband's one and only transgression.

She had never been married to him. They had never been united in holy wedlock. They had lived in sin, but it had all been done with the best of intentions and then she had related the story which soon afterwards was to become known to everybody in the Republic, for it was a sad tale and our ballad singers made the most of it.

It had really been her fault and she was willing to take all the blame upon herself. She had been a wayward girl and had got into trouble with a man who had deserted her. Her father, when he suspected her condition, had thrown her out of the house. She was wandering from village to village (she herself hailed from the neighboring province of Groningen) until she had reached that little town in Friesland. It was very late when she arrived and she was half starved and she had knocked at his door because he was still working and looked friendly as he sat there hammering at his bench. He had taken her in and had fed her. The next day she had been very sick. He had kept her there and had sent for an old woman who lived next door to nurse her. She had been sick for almost two whole months. When she got better, her condition had become noticeable. She then had told her benefactor the truth. He said that he wanted to marry her. But he could not do so as he was already married. Only his wife had lost her reason shortly after the birth of a child that had died in infancy. She had developed a case of religious mania and finally had escaped with the help of one of the many priests who still infested the country, notwithstanding the severe edicts promulgated against them. This man had taken her to Trier, where she had joined the Catholic church and had entered a nunnery. All efforts on the husband's part to bring her back had been unsuccessful. The Archbishop of Trier had openly boasted of his victory over Antichrist and even the Estates General, to whom the matter finally had been referred, had been powerless.

That had happened twenty years before and all that time the husband had heard nothing of his wife. Attempts to find out whether she were still alive had brought no answer. The prioress of the cloister where she was supposed to dwell had answered that those entrusted to her care were dead as far as the world was concerned, the moment they set foot across the sacred threshold and all further communications addressed to her had been returned unopened. The shoemaker had left his native village where all this had happened and had moved to that forgotten little town in northern Friesland, so as to avoid meeting his former friends. In his new home no one ever suspected that he had ever been married. In his compassion for the poor girl whom God had conducted to his doorstep, he had then decided upon a desperate plan. He had spread the news that he meant to marry her but that she wished to have the ceremony performed among her own people in Groningen. They had actually gone to the town of Groningen for a fortnight and had then come back as husband and wife. The child had been born shortly afterwards and the village elders had smirked pleasantly about their old shoemaker who apparently had not been such a saint as they had always held him to be. But as no couples among our peasants ever marry until they absolutely have to, the matter had soon been forgotten.

No one could have been more devoted to a child of his own than this humble shoemaker to that of another man and as for herself, why, the woman had never had an unhappy day in all her life until the day her "husband" had died from old age and hard work, when she had buried him with all decency and had settled down to spend the rest of her remaining years honoring his memory and tending her cats.

The story struck me as rather marvelous when I first heard it. But in the hands of that miserable zealot up there in the Frisian hamlet, it became a monstrous tale of seduction and deception which filled the hearts of all good Christians with the utmost delight and satisfaction. God's hand became plainly visible in that pathetic, shriveled corpse which had been so unceremoniously brought back to life and literally thousands of sermons were devoted to the gruesome sufferings of that soul which had been refused admittance to both Heaven and Hell, as too vile for even the lowest dungeons of Satan's abode.

Hysterical outbursts of this sort have one advantage, they never last long. But just when the details of the case were beginning to be known in Amsterdam and when every self-respecting disciple of John Calvin was ransacking his Old Testament for suitable texts with which to bolster up the case of God vs. the Shoemaker, the fact that the painter Rembrandt van Rijn was living openly with his house-keeper was brought to the attention of a certain dominie by the name of Zebediah Hazewindus, and what then happened was something of which the people of our country may well be ashamed till the end of their days.

It is unnecessary for me to go into the details of the affair. They are only two well known.

On the twenty-fifth of June of the year '54 the members of the Amsterdam council of churches, gathered together in a plenary session, decided that "since a certain Hendrickje, also known as Hendrickje Jaghers, had now for a considerable space of time been living in open concubinage with a painter called Rembrandt van Rijn at the latter's house in the Breestraat, she therefore was to be ordered to appear before the consistory within eight days of the issuance of this summons and explain to the consistory what excuse she could offer for so scandalous a conduct."

This message was delivered at Rembrandt's house one evening about six o'clock when he and Hendrickje were just enjoying a little respite from the efforts of the day's work on the stoop of their house. It was brought to them by the sexton of the West Church, who also acted as beadle. The sexton was well known to the neighbors. The message was not known, but they could guess at its nature. And soon all through the street and then through the next street and through the next street, the news had spread: "The painter and his woman will have to appear before the dominies. Serves them right! We always told you so. Nothing good can come from that sort of goings-on."

And although no one dared to "say" anything, a great many people "looked" things and that was hardly desirable for a woman in Hendrickje's position. But in one small detail these good neighbors were mistaken. The neatly folded piece of paper bearing the seal of Amsterdam's church council did not mention the name of Rembrandt. When I called later in the evening and was shown the document and asked why he had not been summoned, together with Hendrickje, he could at first not give me any reason. Then it dawned upon him. "I am not a member of the church," he said. "That is probably why they left me out. Years ago, I forget just when, I withdrew or resigned or whatever one does when one bids farewell to the church. I let the ministers know that I would not attend divine service any longer and would refuse to pay my church-taxes in the future and would they please take my name off their register, and they answered me that I could not do this unless I could offer proof that I had joined some other denomination. I hardly knew what to do and so I talked it over with old Anslo, whom I had known for years. I asked him whether there would be any objections if I joined his own church, that I was not a very regular church-goer and perhaps not even a very good Christian. He said no, that the Mennonites did not believe in bothering people about their beliefs, that they would be glad to have me join them whenever I cared to come but would not worry me or bother me if for one reason or another I decided to stay away.

"So I joined the Mennonites and I have never been sorry. Anslo was a nice man. I liked to hear him preach. He never told me how wicked I was, but did his best to show me how good I might be if only I tried just a little harder. Yes, he was a good man. I am glad now I went to him. I would be doubly glad if it were not for Hendrickje."

The girl who had been studying the paper in her hand now looked up at us. "Yes," she said, rather dryly, "I have no doubt of that. But meanwhile, what shall I do?"

Without a word Rembrandt took the summons out of her hand and tore it up into a thousand bits.

"Do nothing," he answered. "Do nothing and forget about it. The dominies can of course make themselves very disagreeable to us, but that is about all. But they can't send a company of town guards to come and fetch you to make a public confession. You are safe—perfectly safe—and so that is that."

And he threw the little bits of paper into the air so that two little Jewish boys who were playing on the sidewalk shouted: "Oi, oi! lookit! lookit! it is snowing!" and then started fighting for the "snow" until nothing remained of the clerical document but a mess of dirty scraps which lay spread all over the Breestraat.

But although Rembrandt was entirely right when he proclaimed so bravely that the dominies could not send a company of town guards to drag Hendrickje to their solemn conclave, it was soon proved that those worthies were not entirely defenseless. They had other means at their disposal to make their displeasure felt and they were not slow to avail themselves of these convenient instruments of spiritual torture.

A great Parisian lady might of course have snapped her fingers at such a manifestation of clerical meddlesomeness but Hendrickje was not a great Parisian lady, but a simple little Dutch peasant girl from a simple little Dutch peasant village with all of the peasant's traditional regard for those standards of respectability which she had learned as a child. To be publicly cited to appear before the consistory of the big town of Amsterdam, accused of the dreadful sins of "lechery and adultery" (strange what delight pious people take in dirty words. If there are nine decent ways of expressing a certain thought and one indecent one, they will invariably choose the latter) was as terrible an experience to her as if she had been condemned to undress right in the middle of the municipal market-place. And I noticed the effects of this ordeal when a week later she was presented with a second summons which did not even reach her hands, as Rembrandt jerked it from the fingers of the beadle and threw it in the gutter without even bothering to open the seal.

Upon such occasions, the spirit of his old grandfather, who had been a notable fighter in the early days of the rebellion, would suddenly break through that decorous exterior which he had retained from the days of his marriage with Saskia.

"Get away from here, you damn black crow!" he shouted at the poor fellow, who had delivered the message, and who was beating a hasty retreat. "Get away and stay away and don't bother my wife any more. If your masters have aught to tell me, let them come themselves and I shall throw them in the Anthonie Sluis. You dastardly, meddling old fool! Mind your own damn business and let me paint my pictures."

All of which was no doubt quite natural and more or less to be expected (there is nothing quite so wholesome to the physical well-being of the human race as an occasional outburst of first-class cursing), but a little beside the point. After all, the consistory had not told Rembrandt that he must not paint pictures. It had told his housekeeper that she must not live with him in sin. And it continued to do so until poor Hendrickje, in her great distress and misery, saw no other course than to obey their solemn command and present herself that she might confess her guilt and ask for their solemn forgiveness.

Exactly when she made her appearance before the consistory, I never found out, for she kept the fact hidden from Rembrandt. One afternoon she quietly slipped out of the house and when she returned, it was all over. She went right up to her room and to bed. In the middle of the night, Rembrandt sent Titus to ask me whether I would please come at once. Hendrickje seemed to have a fever. Her mind was wandering. She talked of hell-fire and of Satan, who was chasing her with a torch made out of a burning sheaf of grain. Then she wept as if her heart would break, calling for her mother and saying that she would be a good girl and that she had only done it because the man had been so good to her. "He is good to me and you and father were bad to me," she kept on crying.

I gave her some hot milk to drink and put a cold poultice on her forehead, and after a short while she calmed down. In the morning she was happy and cheerful, as if nothing had happened.

The following Sunday when I called after dinner, as I was in the habit of doing, I asked her (really without thinking very much of what I was saying), "And well, Hendrickje, what was the sermon about this morning?"

But she looked crestfallen and answered, rather indifferently, "I don't know. I did not go."

Three days later, I discovered the reason why. As punishment for her sinful way of living, she had been forbidden to partake of the Lord's holy communion.

That may have been good church discipline. But it was not the best thing in the world for a woman who was eight months pregnant, as we were to find out soon afterwards.

Chapter 57

HENDRICKJE HAS A CHILD AND THE CLERGY OF AMSTERDAM EXPRESS THEIR OPINION UPON MY RESEARCHES IN THE DOMAIN OF PAINLESS SURGERY

In September of the year '54 the blow fell.

During the first week of that month I had suddenly lost two of my patients. They had died while I was administering the usual dose of hemp and the thing had been a great surprise to me as the operations for which they had been brought to the hospital were not of a serious sort and under ordinary circumstances their chance of recovery would have been very good. But they passed out after a few whiffs of the Cannabis fumes and all efforts made to bring them back to life were in vain. Both of them were middle-aged women and like most women in our country who have been forced to bear children ever since they were nineteen or twenty, they were not in good physical condition.

News of this disaster became soon known all over town and those who had always disapproved of my methods were delighted. They had always known that something like that would happen some day. If I were allowed to go on I would eventually kill the whole population of Amsterdam. The authorities ought to interfere and close that so-called hospital. As for me, I ought to be forced to resign from the Surgeons' Guild. I had defied the will of God and now see what had come of it!

Within less than twenty-four hours I received an official document bearing the signature of one of the Burgomasters. I was told not to administer any more hemp until the matter should have been officially investigated. Three physicians of good repute were delegated to perform an autopsy upon my unfortunate patients and report to Their Lordships. One of these three doctors was a good friend of mine. The other two belonged to the old school of medicine and regarded me secretly as an impostor and mountebank.

The bodies were taken to the dissecting room. Afterwards the doctors reported unanimously that death had probably been due to natural causes as both women seemed to have suffered from inflammation of the valves of the heart and under those circumstances any sudden shock to the system might be fatal. As they would have died with almost equal certainty if the operation had been performed without an anesthetic, the administration of a pain-relieving agency could not, under those circumstances, be held responsible for the unfortunate outcome of the case. This was very pleasant news for me but unfortunately Their Lordships did not deem it necessary to communicate the findings of their committee to the public, and all over town the murmurs continued about the surgeon who was in the habit of poisoning his patients in order to get hold of their bodies and then study them by cutting them up into little pieces which afterwards he fed to the rats.

That was trouble No. 1.

Trouble No. 2 happened immediately afterwards.

Now that I had come to know Hendrickje a little more intimately, she was no longer as shy with me as she had been in the beginning, and so she told me of her worries in connection with her coming confinement. She had had a baby before. It had been born a year after she had come to live with Rembrandt, but the baby had died immediately afterwards and she had had a most dreadful time and had almost died from pain. Even now, whenever she thought of it, she shuddered with the memory of so great an agony. She fully expected that this time the child would have to be taken by force and if that were the case, would I perform the operation? I examined her and realized that she might be right in her fears. She had an unusually narrow pelvis and the child was already very large. I promised her that I would do as she asked me and suggested that she come to my own place, where I had plenty of room and could work much better than in the stuffy, built-in beds of the ordinary household. At first she hesitated. Simple people seem to think that there is something sacrilegious about children that are born outside their own homes. But Rembrandt was greatly in favor of this arrangement, and during the first half of the first week of October Hendrickje came to the hospital.

Five days later she had her first pains. Her labor lasted three whole days. In the end she suffered so terribly she asked that she be killed and even tried to climb out of her bed to throw herself out of the window. On the morning of the fourth day, when it looked as if I would have to perform the Caesarian cut (I was afraid the child would otherwise die), she told me that she could stand it no longer and asked me to give her some quick-working poison. Instead of that, I administered my hemp extract. She was so exhausted that it worked almost too well, for she was still unconscious long after the midwife had washed and cleaned the newborn infant (a girl it was, and in the end no operation had proved necessary) and wanted to bring it to her for its first meal. She recovered very rapidly and a fortnight later she was back in the old house on the Breestraat, looking very handsome and very happy and quite like her old cheerful self.

The child was baptized in the Old Church on one of the last days of October. The minister must have received a hint from the Town Hall that further censorious remarks on their part were considered out of place, for little Cornelia was duly registered as the daughter of Rembrandt van Rijn and Hendrickje Stoffels and no embarrassing questions were asked.

But for me it was only the beginning of my trouble.

Hendrickje had been deeply grateful. So grateful, indeed, that she told the dry-nurse who took care of her how good I had been to her and how I had saved her from any further pain when she thought that she could no longer stand the ordeal. The dry-nurse, a very competent and well-meaning woman, but like all the members of her guild, an uncurable chatterbox, had told the neighbors.

"And you know, Doctor Jan gave her something at the last moment and then she never felt any pain at all. Isn't that wonderful? Though of course, it is not quite what we read in the Scriptures."

And then the fat was in the fire.

A week later, the Reverend Zebediah preached his famous sermon on "Childbearing without God's curse." And two weeks later the whole town knew about the scandalous and blasphemous proceedings that went on in the hospital of "this libertine and Arminian who pretended to be wiser than God." Once the rumor had started it was utterly impossible to stop it.

Within a month, Hazewindus felt himself strong enough to lead a delegation of outraged citizens to the town council to ask for my immediate arrest and to suggest that my "place of business" be closed for all time. He went to see Their Lordships, followed by thousands of his parishioners.

I would rather not write about what followed, for in a way it was a very sincere tribute to the confidence which Their Lordships placed in me personally. They promised the young parson that they would hang him from the highest gallows at the disposal of the city of Amsterdam if he ever bothered them again in this matter, and had the bailiff kick him bodily out of the council-chamber.

I hoped that that would be the last of my difficulties and that now I would be left in peace to continue my experiments. But two days later, during the middle of the night, a mob of several hundred men and women, proceeding very quietly and very orderly, as if they obeyed a single will, suddenly broke into the hospital, carried the eighteen patients they found there out into the street (fortunately it was not a very cold night) and then set fire to the premises, disappearing in as quiet and orderly a fashion as they had arrived.

When I came upon the scene of the conflagration, the house was already doomed. It burned until the next afternoon. Of my invested capital which was to be used for the good of humanity, nothing remained but four charred walls and a pile of smoldering beams and red-hot bricks.

That was the end of my dream.

I petitioned the Magistrates and insisted upon an indemnity. My property had been destroyed as the result of a riot which they had failed to repress.

They told me that I was entirely right and that they would take the necessary steps to satisfy me. After deliberating this item on their calendar for seven whole years, they finally voted me about one third of the sum for which I had asked. After another four years, they paid me half of what they had promised me. When I hinted at the unfairness of such an arrangement and suggested that I should at least receive five or six percent accumulated interest on my money, I was informed that Their Lordships had been exceptionally generous in dealing with me and that I should be contented with whatever I got, on pain of not getting anything at all.

And that is the reason why I could not move a finger to help my poor friend during those dreadful years of his bankruptcy.

Once more the shrewd Lodewijk had been right. I had tried to benefit mankind—whether wisely or not it is not for me to say. According to the best of my ability, I had tried to be of some service to those who were less fortunate than I. And they had risen in their wrath and had destroyed me because I had dared to deprive them of what was dearer to them than life itself—their own misery.

The Reverend Zebediah Hazenwindus preached a triumphant sermon.

And I went back to general practice to make a living.

Chapter 58

I NOTICE THAT BY LOSING MY CREDIT I HAVE ALSO LOST THE RESPECT OF A GOOD MANY OF MY FELLOW-TOWNSMEN

The first few weeks after the disaster, I was too busy to pay serious attention to anything that did not have to do with the removal of burned bricks and charred wooden beams. For the city, which had neglected to protect my property while it was still intact, took a deep interest in it, now that it had become a ruin, and I was bombarded with letters from the Town Hall. "Would I please remove the eastern wall which was in danger of collapsing and would I kindly see to it that the timbers of the former roof were removed from among the débris, as they were said to be smoldering, and might start a new conflagration."

And one day, when a sudden storm blew a few bricks from the one chimney that still remained intact (they did not fall into the street and caused absolutely no harm), I was fined two hundred guilders for "criminal negligence."

For although the attack on me, or rather on my humanitarian intentions, had failed with Their Lordships, the Burgomasters, those Aldermen who were supposed to superintend the building activities within the limits of our town, were a great deal less independent than Their Lordships who occupied the Mayor's bench and they had to pay considerable attention to the wishes (both implied and outspoken) of the rabble that had declared itself my eternal enemy.

Here I ought to mention a curious coincidence. The same morning when my house was invaded by two sheriffs with a warrant for the immediate payment of my fine (also a most extraordinary procedure, as the usual time was six weeks), part of the rear scaffolding of the new Town Hall collapsed, killing three masons outright and seriously wounding a dozen. But in that case there was no investigation, there were no fines and no punishments, as (according to a semi-official statement issued shortly after the accident) there was serious proof that the foreman who was in charge of that part of the work was "well-known for his blasphemous conduct and his lack of respect for the shepherds of God's own flock," and that under the circumstances the wrath of a righteous Jehovah could not possibly have been averted. And because that foreman had been an infidel no compensation was ever paid to the widows and the children of the workmen who had lost their lives.

In the end I fared a little better than these poor masons and hodcarriers. But for the moment I was in very difficult straits. I had gradually fallen into the unfortunate habit of not charging anything for my services beyond a nominal sum, which in most instances was never paid. Suddenly I found myself obliged to turn a "calling" into a "profession," and I discovered that those same patients who had been only too delighted to accept my services for nothing, while I was fairly well-off, deeply resented my charging them a small fee when through circumstances entirely beyond my own control I was once more obliged to work for a living.

Indeed, a good many of them seemed to feel that I was an impostor and not a few accused me openly of having merely feigned riches so as to be able to charge them more afterwards. In this matter, the very poor behaved with infinitely more delicacy of feeling than those who could well afford to pay a moderate fee for medical assistance. It was an interesting time for me. During the last twenty years I had lived in an artificial economic vacuum, where the severe laws of human survival, which dominated the entire social fabric of our commonwealth, had been almost completely suspended by the presence of an invisible substance which I had come to know quite intimately under the name of "credit."

To this day I have been unable to understand the true nature of this mysterious invisible substance, which is intangible yet opens all doors which has neither volume nor body, yet is able to remove a thousand difficulties that face ordinary citizens which can not be detected by either eyes or ears or the sense of smell, and is nevertheless possessed of such concrete qualities that ninety men out of every hundred recognize it at a vast distance and allow themselves to be influenced by its presence as if it were some wonderful talisman come to us from the Holy Land of Ophir.

When did I first become conscious of its existence? It is hard to tell, for I had been brought up in a very simple fashion in a small community and every one I knew lived on a modest margin of comfort and every one paid his way as he went along. But shortly after the death of my grandfather's brother, I began to notice that some subtle change had taken place in the relations between myself and those of my neighbors with whom I came into daily and regular business contact. My needs had always been modest and whenever I needed something I was in the habit of going to the nearest or most convenient store, asking for the article in question and paying cash for my purchases. Like most people who lead sedentary lives, I am a creature of habit and when I once happened to patronize a store, I was apt to go there for the rest of my days, unless the proprietor died or sold me a fish that had been dead a little longer than was strictly necessary.

As a result I was on the most cordial personal terms with most of the tradespeople who looked after my needs. They consulted me when their wives suffered from vapors (women often do after bearing a dozen children in as many years) and sent for me when their infants had tried to swallow a gherkin that was three times too large for their gullet and that needed merely an experienced finger, to be pushed into the insatiable abdominal cavity they erroneously called their "stomachs."

But one day these good old friends had become quite obsequious in their attitude toward me. I was no longer "the Master" or "Master Jan" or "Hey, there," but "Doctor van Loon," and they bowed a little lower than before and insisted upon escorting me to the door or sending some small urchin with me, to carry a package that I could quite easily have dropped into one of the smaller pockets of my coat. And they would refuse to let me pay spot cash. "Oh, no, Doctor, surely we could not expect that of you!" or "That will be quite all right, Doctor. We will take the liberty to remind you of this small indebtedness at the end of the year." And when I insisted upon settling my debts then and there as I had always done, they would loudly lament that I no longer thought them worthy of my confidence and that I was on the point of deserting them for a rival. Until from sheer inborn laziness and my great natural dislike for every sort and variety of business detail, I gradually gave in and said, "Very well. Send me a bill whenever you want, but don't trust me too much. I am no Burgomaster!" Whereupon they invariably smirked and bowed very low and answered with an attempt at joviality, "Hee hee! that is a good one. Not trust *you!* Why, we know all about *you,* my dear Doctor. You can have this whole store and on credit too. Just say the word and it is yours." All of which puzzled me until I mentioned it to Lodewijk during one of my monthly visits, and he gazed at me for a while from behind a fresh goose-quill and then looked up at the ceiling and then pushed back his chair and muttered:

"What a lot this poor man still has to learn! What a terrible lot! He has rubbed shoulders with the great God of the Golden Pouch. He is a man set apart. The Token is upon his brow and he knoweth it not."

But when I asked him for an explanation of these cryptic words, he refused to tell me anything more and merely added: "Enjoy the day while it lasts. The breath of good fortune is like the dew of early morn. It turns drops of water into pearls and makes a shining scimitar of every humble blade of grass. Then—a short whiff of sunshine and a short whiff of fresh air. And behold, the glory is gone! A cow comes along. The grass is eaten. The farmer on his way to work says, 'Damn these wet pastures. My feet are all soaked.' Enjoy the day, my son, while it lasts, and farewell."

Well, I neither enjoyed the day, as the excellent Lodewijk bade me do, nor did I dislike the experience with any particular feeling of resentment, but I continued to be puzzled, for not only did I observe a change among those who were my more immediate neighbors and therefore might have heard something about my good fortune, but in the most remote parts of the busy town where I had never been before and where no one could possibly know me, yea, in cities and villages far removed from Amsterdam, it was the same story. As soon as people heard my name, they became eager to please me and be of service and everywhere I heard: "Never mind the bill, Doctor. Pay us whenever it is quite agreeable to you. We can wait, there is no hurry. Just suit your own convenience."

And often when I tried to press the money upon them, they showed signs of annoyance, asked me whether they had done or said anything to incur my displeasure, and in order not to hurt their feelings, I had to submit to their wishes. For I was a person set apart. I enjoyed unlimited credit.

Then came the fire which temporarily at least swept away all my possessions and behold! with lightning-like quickness, everything was changed.

Those same tradespeople with whom I had dealt uninterruptedly for the last twenty years were still polite, very polite indeed, but they no longer bowed quite so low, nor smiled quite so broadly when I entered. Nor did they hasten quite so eagerly to the door when I left and although my bundles might be heavier than formerly (as I now often am forced to buy my household necessities in the bulk for greater cheapness) they were always so terribly sorry but "the errand boy had just stepped out for a moment and so, if you don't mind carrying this little package yourself, etc., etc."

Well, I did not particularly mind, being of a sound constitution and able to support heavier burdens than a dozen pounds of dried beans or a couple of Westphalian hams, but again I was puzzled. For during the previous years, I had become quite accustomed to my privileged position in life and as a rule I walked out of a shop without even trying to settle for my purchases, knowing that at the end of the month or year the owner would call on me to receive not only his bill but in addition a small gift of wine or brandy as a slight token of my good will and esteem.

Therefore it came as somewhat of a shock when I was suddenly reminded of the more direct sides of minor business transactions by such remarks as: "We hope you don't mind if we ask you to pay us now, but you see, the war and the unsettled conditions nowadays, and to-morrow we must meet a draft against us for three hundred guilders." Or again: "Of course, we don't want to push you, but our silent partner told us yesterday that he absolutely forbade us to extend any credit to any one, no matter whether it was the King of France himself."

The only exception were the book-sellers of the Rokin and Damrak. While I was in the New World I had a great many opportunities to speak the English language and gradually I had learned that tongue sufficiently well to read it not only with pleasure but also with considerable profit. One day Menasseh, who was in constant correspondence with his friends and sympathizers in London, showed me a book that had been sent to him recently. It was called "Hamlet," and was the work of that same William Shakespeare whom I have mentioned before and who had died about the time I was born. I had never read this play and took it home with me. I found it rather uninteresting as it was the story of a weak and vacillating character, a young prince who would have amounted to a good deal more either as an assassin or a respectable husband if he had served a couple of years before the mast with old Martin Tromp. But in it I found one character I liked, a courtier called Polonius or Palanias (I forget which), who suddenly, when his son is on the point of leaving him for a long voyage, rises to a degree of common sense which one would hardly expect in an author as vague and romantic as this William Shakespeare.

Speaking out of my own experience, I know that it would have benefited me infinitely more if as a child I had been forced to listen to the gentlemanly and practical wisdom of this experienced court-official rather than to the grandiloquent laws of Moses which told me how to avoid a number of terrible crimes (the very existence of which until then had been unknown to me), but which left me completely in the dark when it came to those highly important items which had to do with our common, everyday existence and which we unfortunate boys and girls were supposed to solve for ourselves without any guidance whatsoever. But I had discovered one omission in this Polonian decalogue which filled me with surprise. Polonius forgot to mention something that is of the very greatest importance. He never told his son to make friends with his book-seller. That is one of the few hard and fast rules which my own son learned as soon as he was old enough to spell c-a-t, cat, and c-o-w, cow.

For the book-seller is a man who carries a magic key in his pocket, and if you are able to gain his good will he can and will unlock such wondrous treasure-chests for you that you never need experience another dull moment as long as you live.

The book-seller of course is in business to make a living and he will charge you for his services, as is not only his good right but also his duty. But listen, O my son, and treat thy book-seller as thy best friend and he will repay thee beyond the miser's fondest dreams of unearned increment.

I shall not be able to name all of those with whom I came in contact during my long quest of printed matter. There were Louis and Daniel Elzevir in that pleasant little shop on the Damrak, Jan Blaeu, who is still alive and a close personal friend, although he has come up in the world and we now must call him Doctor Blaeu. There was Johan van der Bergh, from whose shop-window I could watch the progress of the new Town Hall, and half a dozen others who were my most trusted companions in the days when I was suspected of being quite wealthy and who almost forced their wares upon me when an adverse fortune had suddenly turned my riches into a smoking and blackened deficit. They knew that I could not exist without a fairly heavy diet of parchment and paper.

They asked no questions, raised no suspicious eyebrows. They said, "Here are our shelves. Help yourself and let the future take care of itself."

And finally there was one other man, outside of my own personal friends (who were veritable pillars of loyalty and faithful affection), a man whom most people considered the most aloof, the coolest, the least responsive of ordinary mortals and who during this unfortunate crisis in my personal affairs showed himself to be possessed of such deep understanding that he made me his grateful slave for the rest of my life. That was My Lord Jan de Witt, who at that time ruled the Republic as if he were its undisputed master and sovereign instead of being merely a paid official of the Estates General.

Shortly after the disaster, I received a note dated from the well-known house on the Kneuterdijk in The Hague, asking me to call at my own convenience the next time I was in the city as My Lord Jan wanted to consult me as he was not feeling quite well.

This, however, I found to be only a pretext—a slight indisposition as the result of a too sedentary life. I told him so and suggested a suitable course of exercise and a diet, a bit of advice which any practitioner in The Hague could have given him at much less cost and trouble. I even went so far as to tell him that for such little ailments, he might call with perfect safety upon a couple of local physicians whose names he suggested. Whereupon His Lordship answered:

"I had thought as much myself, but there are some other matters I want to discuss with you. Suppose you stop for dinner. We shall be all alone and I can't promise you much. I shall do better after next February when I am married. But if you will take pot luck, I hope you will stay."

He conducted me into the dining-room (which I noticed had been done over entirely in the new French style) and we had our dinner which consisted of a vegetable soup, some cold ham and brown beans and Delft beer. His Lordship excused himself for the simplicity of the fare.

"I hear," he remarked, "that my cousins in Amsterdam are beginning to follow the English fashion of serving meat every day. But I think that I will remain faithful to our simple provincial habit of one roast a week. It is better for one's blood."

Nor did he offer me a pipe of tobacco after dinner, saying that he reserved the weed for the evening, and even then in great moderation, as he derived greater contentment from a few chapters of Quintilian than from half a dozen pipes. "And at much smaller expense," he added as an afterthought, "and now that I am on the point of founding a family of my own, I ought to think of such things."

After the dinner had been finished and we had wiped our hands on the wet towel which the man in black livery offered us (My Lord Jan apologized for the presence of this male creature in his household, but explained that since the Bickers were accustomed to men-servants, he had decided to introduce this innovation into his own home, so that his wife would find herself among familiar surroundings), my host asked me whether I were in a hurry and when I answered no, that I expected to return to Amsterdam by the night boat, he invited me to come upstairs to his study a moment and let him talk to me as there were some problems he wanted to discuss with me.

"Of course," he began, "all this is entirely confidential. I am your patient—you noticed how I took no mustard with my ham—and everything I am telling you is in the nature of a confession, made by a sick man to his medical adviser. Sit down in that easy chair and listen and then tell me what you think about my idea."

I sat down and His Lordship began with a short review of the war as it had now been fought for the greater part of two years. "It will soon come to an end," he said. "We are neither of us getting anywhere. I am afraid that we are a little too well balanced. A few months more and the war will be over. We will both of course try and get some advantages out of the negotiations of peace, but mark my words, it will be a stalemate. Then we will prepare for the next war. I am sorry but I don't see how it can be helped. In every village as you may have observed there is always one dog who lords it over the others. As long as we human beings still have so much in common with dogs and as long as we will fight for every bone, we shall probably continue to build warships and quarrel for islands in India and rivers in America. It seems absurd that it should be that way. And for good measure, add the ambitions of those private families toward the south and the east of us, who used to be highway robbers a few centuries ago, whom I now have got to address as Royal Majesties or run the risk of getting my letters back unopened.

"I am not yet fifty years old and the other day my brother and I figured out one evening that we had lived through nine major wars and fifty-one minor conflicts since we were born. I had a visit the other day from a Rabbi in Amsterdam, I don't know whether you know him, a certain Menasseh ben Israel, an interesting old fellow who told me that he had made a wonderful discovery. He had been able to decipher a mysterious passage in the Pentateuch and now he knew for certain that the moment of the coming of the Messiah was merely a question of weeks or months. I told him that as far as I remembered, the Messiah had paid us a visit some sixteen hundred years ago, but he answered that that had not been the right one. He was very polite about it and kept on repeating that he did not want to hurt my feelings, but that so-called Messiah of which we Christians made such a great ado, had been merely one of the minor prophets and not a very good one at that. But the true Messiah was about to appear among us and it would be well if we, who ruled the destinies of the nations of this world, made suitable preparations to receive him.

"I asked him what he wanted us to do and he replied that he wanted us to establish a reign of peace and righteousness. He really was a most engaging person and absolutely sincere. He told me that he intended to go to London as soon as peace should have been declared to see the Lord Protector on the same errand. In the meantime he expected to convince me of the truth of his views, for no other country on the Continent was as powerful as the Republic of the United Seven Netherlands and no man in the Republic was as powerful as I and when I asked him how we should bring about this reign of peace and righteousness, he looked at me with some surprise and said, 'Why, My Lord, by making all nations love each other like brethren and by turning the whole of this earth into one vast commonwealth like the Republic of the United Seven Netherlands which is one country, yet composed of seven independent and sovereign states.' If he had to rule them, as I do, he would know just how much of 'one country' they are!

"But he did not know and I did not disillusion him. If he actually intends to visit England soon and pay his compliments to our friend the Protector, it is better that he arrive in the British capital fully convinced that we are a strong and united country. And as for the rest of his ideas—did you ever see the plan one of the kings of France, I think it was the fourth Henry, worked out for a league of all the nations of Europe? A most intelligent and intriguing project. But hopeless, quite hopeless! He wants to scramble us all into a vast omelette. But what is the use of trying to make a decent omelette if two or three of the eggs are rotten? And when he has worked it all out and enumerated what we should be allowed to do and not be allowed to do, he forgets one simple little item, he does not tell us who will be the policemen who will make us do what we should do. He leaves that part to Providence and declares the meeting closed.

"A most admirable ideal but almost as vague and futile as that of our friend the Rabbi.

"Meanwhile our enemy across the water and I, though we are not officially on speaking terms, have been discussing a plan of our own that may prove more practicable. Of course you understand that I am still talking as your patient and that all this is strictly between us. I have the uncomfortable feeling that somewhere in my office there is a leak and one of these days I will catch the traitor and have him hanged. But I know that I can trust you and all this will make it more clear to you what I am trying to do when I make you the offer I am about to make.

"The Lord Protector and I are practical men. We know what the common people do not seem to understand, that if our countries go on fighting each other for another fifty years, we will both of us be ruined. We know that all that talk of Parliaments of Nations and Estates General composed of delegates from the Emperor of China and the great Khan of India and the seven hundred and eighty-three little German princes, not to forget the Grand Duke of Muscovy and the Grand Padisha of Stamboul and the black potentates of the Gold Coast won't ever be anything more than they are now—pleasant dreams of well-meaning rabbis and other visionaries. The world respects only one thing, and that is force and such a body would never be able to command the slightest respect.

"The people in Scandanavia have tried it out and they have failed. The Holy Roman emperors seven hundred years ago tried something of the sort and they failed. Charlemagne succeeded. But he had an army, he was able to say 'do' and everybody did, for he was possessed of a powerful army, and when he said 'don't' even our own wild ancestors obeyed him, because they were afraid of him.

"Our Lord Cromwell seems to have read his ancient history with profit. He suggests that we make peace and then conclude a treaty. We are the two most powerful nations in the modern world. Together we could rule the whole planet as we would see fit and I assure you, if ever we decide to go in for a partnership, we will know how to make the others obey us. We would simply divide the world between us.

"We here in Holland would keep the Indies, paying England a certain sum for the expenses they have incurred, developing their property there during the last seventy years. The English on the other hand would be given free rein in America, with the exception of Brazil, without which our West Indian Company would go bankrupt, for that settlement of ours in the north, that bit of land around the fort of Nieuw Amsterdam, will never amount to anything. The English are welcome to it any time they care to take it. And small loss.

"Of course, Spain and France would object, but they are Catholics and our own people and the great majority of the English would regard a war upon them as a holy pilgrimage and would give us all the money we need. For that money we would equip and maintain a fleet. The English would contribute sixty ships of the line and we would contribute forty. That makes one hundred modern war vessels and together these would amply suffice to blow every galley of the Bourbons and Habsburgs out of existence.

"As I said, both our people and the English would consider this a holy war and if we allowed the clergy to organize all this territory and keep it free from Catholic competition, there would be such a rush of missionaries that there would be hardly a dominie left at home and that would make the business of ruling these premises a great deal easier. Of course, Their Lordships of Amsterdam will fight this project tooth and nail. They would be heartily in favor of the scheme if England were left out of it and perhaps they are foolish enough to think that they are strong enough to go it alone. I may be able to persuade them to come over to my views, and I may not.

"In the meantime, I have certain other worries. The world at large seems to believe that we derive our great wealth from Indian trade. We don't. We get our daily bread and butter out of the North Sea and the Baltic. Herring and grain have made us what we are. And herring and grain will probably continue to make us rich for a long time to come. The North Sea is at our disposal whenever we are not at war with England, and even then that source of revenue does not completely run dry. But the Baltic worries me. Without grain, we are lost. We are the grain dealers and grain carriers of the whole world. Without us, the bakers in Madrid and Naples and Lisbon might just as well close their shops. Even the Pope would go hungry if one of our ships did not drop in occasionally at Civita Vecchia, where by the way we have a bright young man to represent us as our consular agent. But of course this monopoly is full of danger for ourselves. We don't raise a blade of all that grain. We get it from Danzig and we carry it home through the Sound. Have you any idea of the lay of the land?"

I assured His Lordship that I did, for all this sounded remarkably much like certain lectures on politics and economics to which I had listened almost a dozen years before in the study of My Lord Andries Bicker, and his brother, the Burgomaster. But I said nothing about all this to the man who so soon was to marry their daughter and niece and merely remarked in a casual tone of voice that I had always had a liking for geography and was quite familiar with the map of those northern countries.

"Well, then," My Lord Jan continued, "you know yourself how full of danger that road to Danzig is, as long as all those Baltic countries continue to fight among themselves. There are the Poles who rule that whole part of Russia and Lithuania where the grass-fields are. I use the word 'ruling' advisedly for if I am to believe our agent in Warsaw, they are the most unruly mob that were ever entrusted with any sort of power. They call themselves a republic but have a king whom they elect and who has less power in his own country than my cat has in the kitchen. Every person of noble blood has a finger in the governmental pie and ninety-nine out of every hundred citizens seem to be of noble blood. The rest are Jews who attend to the civil administration and the bookkeeping of that crazy concern. But every one from the King down to the lowest stable-boy will take a bribe and the situation therefore is not very serious. We simply pay our way and buy grain or officials as suits our needs.

"Then there is Sweden. In that country we have to do with a monarch who in more than one way resembles our own Prince William—the one who just died. He too was trained to be a great general. And then the Thirty Years' War came to an end, just when he was about old enough to ride a horse. Now of course he is looking for a nice little war of his own, for once a young prince like that has tasted the joys of leading a charge on horseback (I must confess that sort of thing is rather out of my own line, I prefer a chair or a ship) he will never be happy till he has trotted across at least a dozen battlefields.

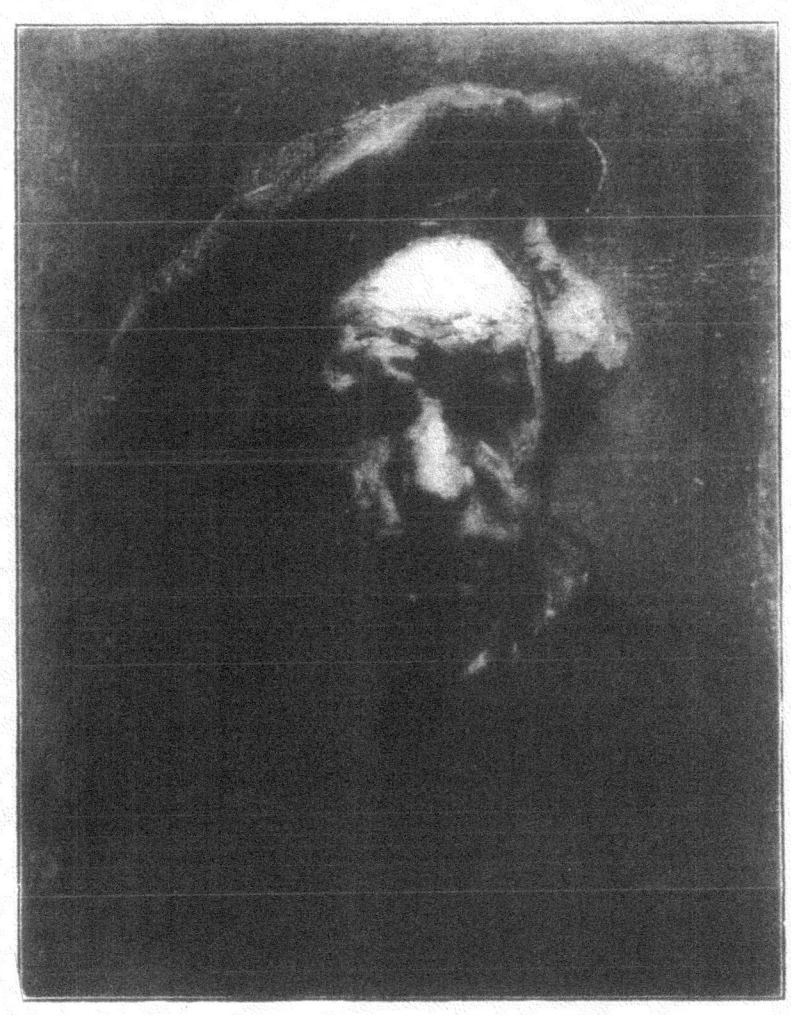

SELF-PORTRAIT
(about 1659)

OLD MAN SEATED IN AN ARMCHAIR

"But he will need money for his little adventures, and he will be looking for a bargain. There is only one bargain in the whole Baltic. That is the crazy Republic of Poland.

"I received a letter from Stockholm last week telling me that young Charles is assembling 50,000 men to march on Warsaw and Cracow. I suppose he can take both cities without any great difficulty, for I know of no people that make such magnificent fighters as the Swedes. Then all the neighbors will get frightened. Then Denmark will be forced to join the Poles and that is where we come in, for that means that the Sound will be blockaded and that we have no grain. We have got to be prepared for that moment and it won't be my fault if we aren't. I have been studying the problem of our navy very carefully and have conferred with all of our admiralties. We ought to have one admiralty board instead of half a dozen, but the time isn't yet ripe for such a step. Meanwhile I have suggested three innovations and I think that they will be accepted.

"The first one has to do with the ships themselves. No good waiting until we are at war and then chartering a couple of hundred merchantmen and converting them into fighting craft. The owners ask exorbitant rates—the sailors are not accustomed to military discipline and half of the captains are pirates. I say nothing about their ability or their courage. They are marvelous seamen, and in nine cases out of ten they will blow their ships up rather than surrender them. But they have always fought on their own. It is difficult for them to obey orders. When a battle has started, they get so excited they forget everything except the one particular enemy they have engaged and hope to capture. The admiral can hoist a dozen signals but they see nothing but that one fellow they are trying to get. As a result of which, we have lost at least two engagements during the present war in which we ought to have been victorious. And of course a converted merchantman can never be as good a fighting machine as a vessel built for the purpose of modern naval strategy.

"So that is item No. 1 and as all the admiralties have agreed with me that I am right, there won't be many difficulties on that point.

"Then I come to item No. 2. Sailors are sailors and soldiers are soldiers. There is no use asking a mackerel to climb a mountain or a dromedary to swim across the Channel. Therefore I am going to introduce regular sea-soldiers on all of our ships, troops of specially trained men who will be called 'marines.' They will have their own officers and they will be used for all operations on land which have never been much to the taste of the regular sailors.

"And now I come to the third item, a very important one which so far has been most scandalously neglected. I mean the medical care of both sailors and marine soldiers. I want to reorganize that whole department. Will you take care of this for me?"

The question left me dumbfounded.

"But, My Lord Jan," I answered, "you know what has just happened to me?"

"I do," he said.

"And you understand the opposition there would be to such an appointment if you were kind enough to suggest it to Their Lordships of the Admiralties?"

"I have taken that in consideration."

"You know that all over the country the clergy would denounce you for having made an alliance with a man who has sold his soul to the devil?"

My Lord Jan was a very quiet man—a soft-spoken man of terrific power but a power held absolutely under control. It was the first time I saw him angry and his anger (as in most people of his temperament) did not show itself in a sudden rush of blood to his cheeks. It manifested itself only in a slight twitching of his lower lip. Upon this occasion his lower lip twitched so hard that I almost heard his teeth chatter.

"As long as I have any influence in the government of this Republic of ours," he answered, slowly thumping the table with the knuckles of his left hand, "those clerical gentlemen will be taught to keep their place. I remember a very old aunt of my grandfather. She lived to be a hundred and three years old and she was born before Luther hammered his articles of faith to the doors of the Wittenberg church. She was a witty woman and until the last day of her life (she died sitting upright in her chair, knitting a petticoat for her great-great-grand-nephew) she was in full command of all her faculties. She was, of course, a Protestant, but at heart she had retained a great deal of affection for the old faith.

"'They tell you children it was the bishops and the cardinals that caused it all,' she used to say. 'The bishops and the cardinals who were a little too greedy and selfish. Well, don't you believe it. Of course they were greedy and selfish, for they were men, and all men are greedy and selfish, and it is only we women who ever do anything for anybody else; otherwise would I have spent all my days cutting diapers and knitting stockings for a breed of children that deserved to have gone stark naked? No, it was not the greed of those on top. It was the greed and selfishness of those at the very bottom. It was that horde of begging friars that caused all the trouble. Dirty, ill kempt, slovenly, ignorant, arrogant yokels—peasants in a cowl, who thought the world owed them a living—lazy rustics who had spent their childhood behind the pigs and cows and were tired of working quite so hard. These voracious holy men who had the manner of the hogs they tended in their younger years' (like so many good women of that ancient day, the old lady affected the picturesque vocabulary of her own scullery-maids) 'forced their way into our houses, ate our food, drank our wine, slept in our beds, kissed our servants and any refusal to extend to these pious trenchermen the most complete and cordial hospitality meant the chance of being denounced to the henchmen of the Inquisition as a suspicious character and a friend of that demon Luther. It was this unwashed rabble that made our people rise up in rebellion. The bishops were no angels. They stole. But they stole in the grand manner. They used their plunder to build churches and endow hospitals and buy lovely pictures and the common people did not mind. They felt that they were getting their money's worth in a glorious and free public show. But when those pilfering peasant boys tried their hand at the business of ruling their powerful neighbors, then the trouble started.'

"I often think of that queer old character (she had not left her house since the death of her husband some fifty-two years before—she never took a breath of fresh air and as I just told you, she lived to be more than a hundred) when I am called upon to deal with the affairs of the Synod and am asked to interfere in some church quarrel. I am not a free-thinker, as I am told you are. The Church means a great deal to me. My life is a difficult one and I could not live without the consolations that come to me from certain parts of the Gospels. But I have absolutely no patience with the attempts made by so many of our dominies to hoist themselves into the seats of the mighty. It is their business to look after other people's souls, just as it is our unquestioned duty to watch over their physical well-being, see to it that they get enough to eat and are able to practice their trade in peace.

"God has appointed us to this high task because we are the ablest of our nation. If he wanted us to be ruled by shoemakers or hod-carriers or doctors of theology, he would have given them the power which he has now laid down in the hands of the merchants who have made this country what it is to-day. I have on my table here at least three dozen 'official complaints' sent to me by different church councils. Every one of these, although signed by half a dozen vestry-men, is really the work of some bright peasant-lad who thinks that he can tell us, the members of the Estates General of this sovereign Republic, what we ought to do because he has been able to escape from his father's farm and has studied theology at one of those universities which we have provided for his benefit and convenience at a great expense to the state.

"Just now they are upset by the popularity of the doctrines of a certain Descartes, a Frenchman who lived for a long time in our country. They want his works suppressed. They want me to forbid all gatherings where the ideas of that Frenchman are discussed. They want me to dismiss all professors who have ever read a single page of his works. I won't tolerate it! I won't tolerate it for a moment! This is a country in which every man ought to be allowed to think as he pleases, within certain definite limits laid down by the law. We have to be strict with the Catholics. But they are an exception. They would mistake our mildness for weakness and would abuse our hospitality. It will be centuries before we forget the murder of Prince William, and the murder of so many of our own grandparents. We can't have the Anabaptists run naked and wild through our streets, proclaiming the coming of the Kingdom of Heaven. But they were exceptions. As long as the different sects observe a certain discretion, our magistrates won't interfere with them. The same goes for the philosophers. Let them come and philosophize as much as they will, all we ask is that they do not interfere with the peaceful running of the government.

"And the same holds true for the reverend gentlemen who preach their sermons from the pulpits of our own churches. We have had the Inquisition here once and no one wants to see it again. I have heard what that man in Amsterdam has done. My influence in that city is not very strong. It will be a little stronger as soon as I shall have married into the Bicker family. I shall do all I can to see that you get justice and get reimbursed for the loss you have suffered. The man who caused that outbreak will not only be obliged to leave town, if I can do anything about it, he will be exiled from the territory of the Republic. In the meantime, as a public vindication of yourself and as an expression of my belief in your own integrity and the usefulness of your aims, I offer you this post of chief-surgeon of the fleet. The admiralties, I am sure, will follow my suggestion and there will be no difficulty about your appointment. Will you accept?"

The offer came so unexpectedly that I did not know what to say. The Pentionary was not known as a person given to sudden impulses. As people used to say of him, he never ventured across the ice of a single night's freezing. It was his policy to wait until the frost had lasted at least a couple of weeks and the ice was as solid and reliable as a road built of Belgian blocks. That he should offer me so high a dignity at a moment when from every pulpit I was denounced as a menace to the country of my birth, showed that he was firmly intent upon seeing this matter through to the bitter or happy end.

But I did not know what to answer and I asked His Lordship for a week's respite to talk over my problem with some of my friends. He assented. There was no hurry. Nothing could be done anyway until the end of the war. And so I bade him farewell and took the night boat back to Amsterdam.

That night boat was an innovation. It was pulled by relays of three horses and reduced the distance between Amsterdam and The Hague to a little less than eight hours.

I did my best to sleep.

But I was kept awake for the greater part of the night by three citizens who were discussing the recent goings-on in Amsterdam.

They differed upon many points, but agreed upon one point—that I, the man responsible for this outbreak of public wrath, should have been hung as an example to all other enemies of Zion.

Chapter 59

I LOSE A FAITHFUL BANKER AND AN EVEN MORE FAITHFUL FRIEND

The next four weeks I spent almost entirely on board ship. Not on board one of those war-vessels with which I had been asked to associate my future fate, but on board the little sailing-craft of Jean-Louys, who indeed had turned the most enthusiastic and indefatigable of amateur sailors. His French mate and cook and body-servant proved indeed a jewel of the first magnitude. He could handle a boat in any weather and in any sort of a sea. He could present us with a four-course meal, half an hour after we had arrived in some village of the Zuyder Zee from which the last inhabitant seemed to have moved long ago. And he seemed to belong to that curious and restricted tribe of human beings that can live entirely without sleep, for no matter what time of day or night one appeared on deck, there he was busy with some task of his own and as cheerful and obliging as he was silent.

During the first five days, we enjoyed the companionship of Rembrandt. He had not wanted to come but we thought it would be good for him to enjoy a little change after the harrowing experience of his wife (we invariably referred to Hendrickje as his wife and he seemed to like that). And we told him that he could bring all the sketchbooks he wanted and could sit on deck all day long and draw as much as he wanted.

Jean-Louys had even persuaded him to take along a dozen copper plates for the purpose of doing dry-points of sea-gulls and distant bits of shore-line.

But almost from the first he complained that his plates would show spots—that his needles would rust, and that the sea air would ruin his pens, so that he could not work at all. And after two days he began to grow restless.

"This is nothing for me," he complained. "This sort of existence is too soft and too easy. Another week of having this man blacken my shoes for me and giving me things to eat which I can't recognize when they are on my tongue, and I will jump overboard and swim home."

We argued with him that the lovely little cities along the Zuyder Zee would provide him with an almost unlimited number of subjects for landscapes and seascapes and what not. But he remained obstinate and refused to listen to us.

"I appreciate your hospitality," he told Jean-Louys. "But the life does not suit me. Besides, I can't work in this light. No more than I can work on land, I mean on really dry land, where there are forests and open sandy spaces covered with heather. I tried it once. I was going to walk to Arnhem and from there to Breevoort where Hendrickje comes from. One of her brothers was still living there and there was the usual difficulty about an inheritance. I was to settle that difficulty. Imagine me settling other people's inheritance troubles!

"But anyway, I went and I hated it. The light was too dry. Just as here the light is too wet. For my work—for the things I am trying to do—I need the sort of light that is neither too wet nor too dry. I don't know how to describe it. I would like to call it a sort of suspended light, but that expression is very vague and can hardly tell you what I mean. And I don't quite know myself, except that I am unhappy when I have got to work in any other sort of atmosphere. We have got that particular light in Amsterdam. I suppose because the town is nothing but a stone pancake afloat on a sea of mud. Everything in my workshop is bathed in that light. It does something to the shadows, too. Here the shadows are too hazy. On land far away from the sea they were too abrupt, too severe and too sudden, and that is no fun for me—any ordinary painter can paint that sort of shadows. But the shadows at home have a lucid quality, a little velvety as if they had been mixed with oil. They look as different from ordinary shadows as the wet clay of the Diemer Polder looks from the sandy soil I saw between Utrecht and Arnhem. I suppose I am talking nonsense, but as soon as we get to Monnikendam I hope you will set me ashore and let me peacefully walk home."

Jean-Louys did more than that. He returned to the Y and landed Rembrandt almost within stone's throw of his own house. We presented him with a pail full of fresh shrimps.

His home-coming, as we afterwards learned, was not very happy. Two sheriffs were waiting for him with an order for his arrest unless a bill which he owed his frame-maker for almost five years were immediately settled. Hendrickje had gone out and had pawned one of Saskia's famous pearl ear-rings and the sheriffs had been satisfied and had gone their way. But all this we did not learn until we returned to Amsterdam several weeks later, and in the meantime we had gone as far north as Medemblik and as far east as Blokzijl and we had talked of everything under the sun, but mostly of this one problem: should I accept My Lord de Witt's offer or not?

Of course in my heart of hearts I knew that I should not, but then again it seemed such a wonderful opportunity that I felt that it was my duty to say yes, and then again it struck me as almost wicked to let such an opportunity go by, and then again I told myself that I was not the sort of man for an executive position like that and that all the official bother to which I would be exposed would soon kill me, and then again I tried to persuade myself that with the backing of the powerful pensionary, I would be able to overcome all bureaucratic difficulties and in the end, I flipped a six-stiver piece and it said "no," and when I told

Jean-Louys, who was sitting on deck (I had consulted the oracle in the cabin, feeling slightly ashamed of myself for my superstition), he burst out laughing and said, "That is the way it always is. Do you remember the story in Boccaccio of the traveler who wanted to go swimming in the Nile and asked one of the natives whether that part of the Nile was ever visited by sharks from the North Sea and the native said, 'No, there are no sharks here.' And so he went swimming and when he had enjoyed his bath and come out of the water, he asked the little Selim-boy how he had known that there were not any sharks there and the boy answered, 'Where there are such a lot of crocodiles there are no sharks.'

"And that is the way it goes in life. Always and everywhere where there are sharks there are crocodiles, and where there are no crocodiles there are sharks, and here you are, a most skeptical bone-setter who takes no stock in all the old women's stories of his childhood, a man who openly defies Jehovah and the first chapter of Genesis, and when you want to know whether to start out upon a new venture, you flip a coin! The most avowed agnostic I ever knew used to consult a pack of piquet-cards every time he went on a voyage. When I was in the army in Germany, I used to be friends with a noble, swash-buckling Swede (Heaven only knows how he got there. Perhaps he had swash-buckled a little too freely among his own people) and that Swede, who was the bravest man I ever knew, was so blasphemous that he could make a dozen imperial dragoons blush at one and the same moment, and he respected neither Heaven nor Hell and he vowed that all religion was merely a sort of dangerous drug with which wily priests tried to stupefy dull people, but he would never take part in a charge (and he was a superb horseman) unless he had first stroked the pelt of a black cat and in the end (and that will show you how useful he was) his commanding officer was obliged to have the regiment carry a couple of black cats with it wherever it went to keep old Torenson happy and contented.

"It is no use trying to teach people to depend solely upon their reason. They have got to have something to bolster up their coruage—it does not matter whether it be sharks or crocodiles, but they have got to have something.

"For the rest, of course you are entirely right. You and I are not the sort of people that would ever fit into an organization. We are lonely wanderers. We are the pussy-cats that explore the region beyond the furthest known back-yard. If you said yes to My Lord Jan, you would discover that there are just about nine thousand other pill-rollers and leeches in this Republic of yours who were firmly convinced that they had a better right to the office than you. And you would start out with nine thousand irreconcilable enemies and you would never be able to accomplish anything at all. On the other hand, if you refuse the Pensionary's gracious offer and let it be known that you have refused it, every single one of those nine thousand Aesculapian disciples will vow that you are a great man and deserving the highest praise for your discretion and modesty.

"Go to The Hague and tell His Lordship that you are deeply sensitive of the honor he has done you by asking you to become his surgeon-general, but that you feel that you ought not leave your patients here to the extent of accepting his very kind offer. If, however, he comes to employ you in an advisory capacity, you will be delighted to comply with his wishes.

"That is the thing, my dear friend. Always try and keep near the throne, but at the same time hide yourself behind some convenient draperies to avoid the gaze of the crowd. That is to say, if you really care to accomplish something useful. If you merely want to cut a fine figure—wear beautiful feathers on your hat—the regal dais will better suit your purpose. But I am afraid that God never meant you to be a courtier. If he had, he would not have let you be born in this country."

I knew how much the ultimate success of my plans meant to Jean-Louys. Like many very sensitive people, he had to hide his emotions behind a display of skeptical fireworks which might deceive those who only knew him slightly, but not his friends. And beneath all this levity there lay a kernel of good, sound common sense. As soon as he had returned to Amsterdam, I wrote to the Pensionary telling him that I did not think it quite fair to leave the people to whom I had devoted myself for so many years but that I would be delighted to come to The Hague whenever he wanted me and act as his adviser in all matters pertaining to the medical care of the fleet. His Lordship most kindly agreed to this arrangement, but he told me that in that case and unless I were duly enrolled, he would experience great difficulty in persuading Their Lordships of the Admiralties to pay me a regular salary, and as it would probably take considerable time before my accounts with the city of Amsterdam were straightened out, I might find it difficult to make both ends meet. But I could answer him that he need have no worries on that score. For when I returned to Amsterdam, I found a short note from Lodewijk, my banker in the older and more prosperous days.

"I encouraged you in your folly," he wrote. "You never were a spendthrift and I feel that I am partly to blame for that absurd venture that ended exactly as I had predicted. In due course of time, Their Lordships of the Town Hall will undoubtedly reimburse you. But the wheels of the official deities grind slower than any other piece of machinery known to man. To atone for the sin of having told you to go ahead, instead of throwing you out of my office that memorable morning, I shall send you an order for two hundred florins on the first of every month until you get your money or at least part of it back. This will keep you out of the poor-house. How to keep people like you out of the madhouse is a problem that puzzles me infinitely more."

I took his two hundred florins. It would have broken his heart if I had refused them. They arrived on the first of every month. They arrived on the first of every month for more than ten years, when I was at last able to begin and pay some of that money back. The day before I received the first installment of the compensation which the town at last had decided to make to me, Lodewijk died. In his will he had made a stipulation that my debt to him should be canceled. When I finally received the bulk of my money and began to build my second hospital, I asked leave to call it after this most faithful friend. But his widow refused.

"Lodewijk," she told me, "had considered himself fully repaid by your friendship and his wife and children feel the same way."

Chapter 60

OUR JEWISH NEIGHBORS, WHO HAVE COME TO US TO ESCAPE FROM THE INTOLERANCE OF THEIR SPANISH MASTERS, SHOW THAT RELIGIOUS BIGOTRY IS NOT RESTRICTED TO ONE SECT OR RELIGION

The war came to an end. And as the ships returned home, I met a great many of the captains (for I now spent about half of my spare time at the admiralties) and I heard stories of such surpassing heroism that I was obliged to revise most of my previous notions about the human race or at least that particular part of it to which I myself happened to belong.

Quite often when I was visiting Jean-Louys in his tower near the water front, I had been an unwilling witness of the departure of our brave tars. Disorderly crowds of drunken, disheveled men and drunken, disheveled women, with here and there a howling, bedraggled child, pacified by an occasional raisin drenched in gin.

This mob would slowly come down the quay, pushed forward by large numbers of town guards and looking and behaving exactly like a moaning herd of sheep that were being taken to the slaughter-house.

Now and then a drum and fife corps would try to start a patriotic air or even a hymn, but after a few bars of some well-known tune, shrill, ribald voices would interrupt the musicians with one of those blasphemous ditties that seem to have sprung straight from hell and at once the whole of the crowd would join in—improvising words as they went along and indulging in a wild orgy of dancing and bucking and skipping, accompanied by gestures of such utter vulgarity that even the town guards would blush and they would repeat this performance until after hours of jostling and shrieking, the embarking stations had been reached where the rum-soaked cattle were unceremoniously pushed into a large number of flat-bottomed barges and at once turned to the big vessels that lay at anchor just off the Rijzenhoofd Bulwark.

That was the last we saw of them until we heard our first vague reports of battles and encounters and victories and an occasional defeat.

But one day, years later, a number of high plenipotentiaries assembled around a green table in a large hall in the center of Westminster, affixed their names and seals to a yellow piece of parchment, and shortly afterwards the tired ships would painfully limp back into port—without sails, without masts, without a scrap of that paint that had made them look so spick and span when they had gone forth to war. Then anxious women would come once more around the ancient bulwark and numb-faced children would cling to the rotting wharves and every time a boatload of sailors approached the shore, they would all of them rush forward and scan the faces, many of which were still black from gunpowder or covered with bandages that clearly showed the untrained hands of the bungling nautical doctors.

Then there would be anxious questions: "Is that you, Piet?" or "Have you heard anything of Klaas, who was on the *Zilvere Ster?*" or "Jan! oh, Jan! are you there?" And sometimes the answer would be, "Yes, I am here, as fit as a fiddle," but more often there would be a gruff, "Go home, woman, your Klaas is dead," or "They are bringing your Piet home on a stretcher. His legs are gone." And then there would be cursing or weeping (according to the nature of the woman who was told that she could now spend the rest of her days scrubbing other people's floors and hallways) and silent groups would mutely separate themselves from the main body of spectators and would move desolately toward that part of the town where lived those "gallant gentlemen" whose name only a fortnight before had been on everybody's tongue and who early the next morning must begin the endless round of those workshops and offices where the "No sailors need apply" signs told them how deeply a grateful country had really appreciated their self-sacrificing valor.

For that was the queerest part of it all—those drunken, disorderly and disheveled ruffians who had to be conducted to the arsenals between lines of heavily armed town guards, for fear that they would set fire to the city if they were left to themselves—those selfsame rowdies, once they were on board and realized that they were fighting for their own women and kids and that hovel they considered home—would perform deeds of such unheard-of courage and of such incredible loyalty, that each one of them, if personal heroism is really a safe-conduct to Heaven (as was held to be true by the ancient Greeks) had more than fully established his claims to at least ten square yards of the celestial domain.

They were not very communicative, these "common sailors," and even their sluggish brains revolted at the recollection of many of the sights they had seen—at the sickly sweet smell of blood that would be forever in their nostrils. But gradually little bits of narrative prose, far superior to any poetry ever composed by one of our peaceful, home-staying bards, would find their way into the ale-house gossip of our everyday lives and Homer himself in his most inspired moment could not have devised such deeds of valor and devotion. There were men who had continued to fight when only five or six of the entire ship's crew had been left alive and who, when nothing could save their floating charnel-house from sinking, had boldly jumped on board the enemy craft and with their bare fists almost had captured their former aggressor.

One sailor in the midst of an encounter had managed to swing himself on board the vessel that flew the admiral's flag, had reached the top of the mast and had removed the English colors, thereby causing a most useful panic among the other British men-of-war, who thought that their leader had been killed. Trying to jump back into the rigging of his own vessel, he had missed his footing and had dashed his brains out on the deck, forty feet below, but with the enemy's flag still tightly held between his dead teeth.

The son of Admiral Tromp, commanding a vessel in the harbor of Livorno where the reigning grand duke had forbidden him to take action against his English rivals, who were at that time in the same harbor, had waked up in the middle of the night to find his craft in the hands of the English, who had broken the truce. Rather than surrender, he had jumped overboard and after swimming for more than three hours, he had finally been picked up by a Dutch sloop. With that sloop he had rowed back to his own ship and had recaptured it.

Captain Jan van Galen, during the battle that had followed, had had one of his legs blown away by a cannon-ball. But rather than go to the sick-ward and have his wounds attended to, he had told his officers to carry him to the top of the poop-deck from where he could better watch the battle while he slowly bled to death.

On one occasion a small squadron which was convoying one hundred and fifty merchantmen, fought a much larger English force during the greater part of three days and three nights and then only gave up the fight because they were completely out of gun-powder. Nevertheless, they not only had saved all of the merchant-men but they succeeded in escaping themselves with the loss of only two of their ships.

Truly the men who could perform such acts of valor deserved a better treatment than they usually received and I was very grateful that with the unwavering support of the Pensionary I was able to do something for them.

Up to that time the operating room of those few vessels that had any operating room at all (on most of them the surgeons worked right among the guns) was located way down deep in the hold of the vessel and below the water-line. As a result these places were pitchdark and absolutely devoid of fresh air. The surgeons were obliged to amputate arms and legs (the usual wounds) by the light of a candle and as they were not allowed to make a fire and heat their irons on account of the proximity of the powder-room, they had no adequate means of closing the arteries except by using large quantities of lint, a method which failed in ninety out of every hundred cases.

Besides, the transport down the narrow stairs of such desperately wounded men was a form of torture which one would not have meted out to one's own worst enemies. In order to change this and provide better facilities for the medical staff on board our men-of-war, I suggested that the admiralties offer a prize of 500 florins for the best plan that should remove the sick-ward from the bottom of the ship to one of the upper decks, without interfering too seriously with the manipulation of the heavy guns which filled the two top decks. As the sum was a very large one, practically all the nautical engineers of the entire Republic took part in the contest, and for several months my office resembled the draughting room of a ship-yard.

I remember one strange meeting I had during that period. One night the maid told me that a foreign-looking gentleman wanted to see me. "He carries a small ship's model under his arm," she added. "He is probably one of those funny people," and she pointed to the diagrams and specifications that were spread all over the walls and the floors.

The visitor proved to be what the maid had predicted. He had come to show me an invention of his own. Unfortunately it had nothing to do with the problem in which I was interested. It was a new device to raise the angle of gun-fire without the clumsy arrangement then in use. I told the mysterious stranger that he had come to the wrong place with his little model, that he ought to take it to the admiralty which undoubtedly would be greatly interested. He answered that he had already been to three of our admiralties but that none of them had shown the slightest desire to examine his invention any closer and that he was now thinking of selling it to the English or the French.

I replied that that did not seem a very patriotic thing to do and he readily agreed. "But," he added, "what am I to do? I am a poor schoolmaster and have a daughter who is a cripple and I need the money and I thought that you perhaps could help me, as I have heard of you from one of my pupils," and then I discovered that he was the famous Dr. Franciscus van den Ende, of whom I had heard a good deal, but whom so far I had never met.

This van den Ende was a curious citizen who lived in a sphere of mystery. He had come to Amsterdam during the early forties and had opened a book-store which had not done any too well and which a few years afterwards he had been forced to close for lack of cash and customers. He had then started a Latin school of his own and had revealed himself as one of the most competent teachers we had ever had in our city. He had a veritable genius for making irregular verbs palatable and in his hands, even the most refractory hexameters would behave with the docility of so many tame kittens. Within a very short time all the little boys of our best families were learning the fact that "all Gaul was divided into three parts" at the school of Monsieur van den Ende. For the doctor was a native of Antwerp and preferred that appellation to the more soberminded Dutch "Meester."

He knew of course that his neighbors were slightly curious about his antecedents. But before any inquiries could be made in his native town, he had told us all about himself and about the reasons that had caused him to move northward.

He had, so it then appeared, started life as a Jesuit, but had lost his faith and had been forced to flee for his life. The story of course appealed to us and it had given him an excellent standing with the Magistrates who prided themselves (and rightly) upon the fact that Amsterdam was the most tolerant and liberal community of the entire world. But now I discovered that van den Ende was something more than a good classical scholar. He also appeared to have devoted several years to medical studies and showed by a few casual remarks (in answer to a few equally casual questions on my part) that he understood his subject thoroughly. And so I told him to forget all about his ship's model which did not interest me anyway, as I was interested in saving people's lives and not in destroying them and took him down to the dining-room and invited him to partake of some refreshments for I have found that it always pays to be pleasant to a colleague, even if you never expect to see him again.

Thereupon we talked of many things—of the superior way of teaching as practiced by the Jesuit fathers, who shape the material in which they give instruction so as to suit the individual pupil, rather than making the pupil fit the material he is supposed to study (as we do in our country) and of several other subjects that were of interest to both of us, and then quite unexpectedly the Belgian said: "But of course I already know all about you and your views." And when I asked him how that was possible, as this was the first time I had had the pleasure of meeting him, he answered: "No, but I have a pupil who has a great admiration for you, a Portuguese Jew by the name of Benito d'Espinoza," and then I recalled that this was the man of whom young Baruch Spinoza had been talking to me and of whom he had said that as a school-master he was worth at least five dozen ordinary rabbis and Talmudic pedagogues.

I repeated this observation to van den Ende (where is the man of ability who does not like an occasional bit of flattery?) and he was much amused by it.

"A marvelous brain, that Portuguese has," he told me, "but they are going to have a lot of trouble with him," and the conversation once having taken this particular form, we quite naturally drifted into the discussion of a topic that was beginning to assume rather alarming proportions—the problem of the Jews who in ever-increasing numbers were flocking to our town. For just about a week before Doctor van den Ende called on me with his little ship, one of those absurd things had occurred that although utterly insignificant in and by itself might easily have led to bloodshed if the town militia that week had not been commanded by an officer who was not only a strict disciplinarian but who was also possessed of a sense of humor and a delicately trained taste for the grotesque.

The Jews in our town were not obliged to live in ghettos as they had always done in Spain and in Poland and in Germany. They were free to settle down wherever they pleased but out of force of habit they invariably flocked to the same neighborhood. But of course the Portuguese immigrants stuck closely to the Sephardic Synagogue and the Polish and German Jews remained within stone throw of the Ashkenazic temple.

They were both in my own part of the town and I often walked around the island of Vlooienburg or Fleaburg (as it was soon called by the people) and I was quite familiar with the habits and customs of these strangers who even now, after having been with us for almost a whole century, continued to address each other in the Portuguese and Yiddish tongues and who spoke our own language (which is supposed to be theirs) as if it were a foreign tongue not worthy of their attention. And so of course I knew all about the famous Doctor Alonzo ben Immanuele, commonly known as the Tongenkijker or Tongue-looker.

His real name was not Alonzo nor was he an Italian as he pretended to be, nor was he a direct descendant of the famous Jewish friend of Dante, as he claimed to be upon every possible occasion. He was the son of a Frankfort mohel and had studied to be a mohel himself until he fell in love with a Christian girl and in consequence thereof was disowned by his family. When he tried to communicate with the object of his affection, the parents of the girl had called the police who amidst the plaudits of the Frankfort mob had thrown him into the river Main (it was the month of January if you please) and when he had scrambled onto an icefloe they had shot at him with their guns.

They had missed him but he had left Germany for all time. Eventually he had taken service with a French surgeon who had gone to Bologna to study anatomy with Malpighi. Being an exceedingly clever boy he had picked up considerable medical information in the course of the two years he had spent at that famous Italian university, blacking his master's boots during the day-time and spending the midnight hours reading his textbooks on materia medica. And when the Frenchman returned to Paris, il Signore Dottore Alonzo ben Immanuele continued his peregrinations northward until he reached the city built upon the humble bones of a million defunct herring, where he felt himself so completely at home that he decided to stay there the rest of his days. But as the town seemed already well provided with doctors and apothecaries, Moritz Schmultz (for that was his real name as I had the chance to find out) came to the conclusion that he must do something that would make him widely conspicuous if he did not want to die in the poorhouse.

Among his scanty baggage he carried a discarded doctorial robe of his former master. To this he added the sort of peaked cap the rabbis had been obliged to wear in former times and in this garb he now began to wander through the streets of Fleaburg announcing in a fine flow of Italian-Yiddish and German-Hebrew that he had discovered a new method of treating the sick. All they had to do to get cured was to show him their tongues from behind the window panes of their rooms. He would then make his diagnosis and send them the proper medicines. The consultation was free but a slight charge was made for the medicine to pay for the bottles and the corks and the labels, etc., etc.

The usual story and with the usual result. The man was soon rolling in money. Every morning at eight he would make his appearance on the famous island and would slowly proceed from the Amstel to the Uilenburgwal and back again.

He was accompanied by a coal black negro whom he passed off as an Arab and a direct descendant of Ishmael, the unfortunate son of Hagar, a fable which would have given grave offense to the Christian part of the population if they had ever heard it, but as soon as the Professor had crossed the bridge of the St. Anthonie locks and had entered the domain of the Goys, the honest blackamoor was re-baptized Sebaldus and became a Nubian slave who had been set free by Admiral de Ruyter during one of his campaigns against the Tunisian pirates and who had come to Amsterdam to receive instruction in the true faith according to the Heidelberg catechism.

It is hard to believe that this genial impostor had made such a deep impression upon the inhabitants of the Jewish quarter, that as soon as Sebaldus, alias Hagarson, had rung the big brass bell which he carried in his left hand (in his right hand he held the satchel which contained the doctor's nostrums) the windows of scores of houses would be opened and everywhere anxious mothers would appear with small children whom they would lift halfway out of the windows (upon one occasion a small boy was actually dropped into the street, but as he landed on a pile of rubbish, no great harm was done) and all those unfortunate infants would be obliged to stick out their tongues at the famous doctor who would contemplate that organ for a few minutes with a profound frown upon his face and would then whisper a few words in an ununderstandable vernacular (it was supposed to be Arabic) to his black-faced familiar who would thereupon rush into the house and leave a bottle of "Elixir Vitae Salamonialis" with the afflicted family in exchange for one guilder if it was for a boy and ten stivers if the patient happened to be a girl.

I once had an opportunity to examine two of such bottles, a male and a female one. As far as I could make out, they contained nothing more harmful than a mixture of water and Tamarindus Indica and were worth exactly two cents wholesale. But when I told the man who had bought them for seventy times that amount (a dreadfully poor butcher who never made more than three guilders a week) he waxed very angry and hinted that I was trying to kill my colleague's trade because I was envious of his success.

For there could be no doubt about it. The Tongenkijker was an enormous success. Not only professionally, but also socially. From far and near people were flocking to Amsterdam either to consult him or merely to see and enjoy the free show which he put up right in the heart of a highly dignified and respectable Christian city. Why the Magistrates never interfered with him, I don't know. But they either considered it beneath their dignity to take any notice of him or they believed (as many, other governments had done before) that a bit of ridicule would be good for the souls of these obstinate heathen who so tenaciously clung to their self-imposed ghetto and therefore (unless it was a case of murder or rape) they usually left the Jewish quarter severely alone and told the police to do likewise.

But the Portuguese Jews, much better educated and infinitely more polished than their Polish and German neighbors, regarded this absurd comedy with profound abhorrence and did all they could to bring about the arrest of this saltimbanque and if possible his expulsion from the territory of the city of Amsterdam.

The Town Hall, however, remained deaf to all their petitions and supplications and in the end they took matters into their own hands and staged a regular riot during which the unfortunate Inspector of Tongues was almost drowned in the Amstel (he seemed to have a fatal tendency to get himself ducked) and in which several people would undoubtedly have been killed if it had not been for the tact of the officer of the guard, who had succeeded in restoring order without firing a single shot.

The affair, however, caused a good deal of discussion and no less alarm. For what was this world coming to when foreigners who had come to us in sack-cloth and ashes to find a refuge from foreign persecution could so far forget their duties towards their hosts as to stage a pitched battle right in the heart of the city of their habitation? And for no better cause than that they failed to approve or disapprove of a silly old man who ought to have been left to the mercies of the police?

The more enlightened among the Jews (regardless of the party to which they belonged by birth) tried to pacify Their Lordships of the Town Hall by promising that they would do all they could to prevent a repetition of such an unseemly outbreak. But the rabbis, especially those of the Ashkenazic fold, would not listen to any compromise and exhorted their followers to further violence. In the end it became necessary to have the entire Jewish quarter patrolled by armed guards, for more than six weeks, and the militia who were called upon to perform this extra duty felt very bitter about it and even talked of burning down the whole of the Fleaburg Island.

The plague, which had been very severe in Leyden the year before and which was beginning to make itself felt in Amsterdam with increasing severity, may have helped to quiet the mob. Dr. Alonzo ben Immanuele received a gentle hint to go and practice his beneficent arts elsewhere and peace and order were gradually restored but many people began to ask themselves what the end would be.

"Only a short while ago," so they reasoned, "those people came to us on their knees, begging us to give them shelter and protect them against their enemies, all of which we did. More than that, we allowed them to worship as they pleased, though their faith is anathema to most of our own citizens. Then they asked to be given permission to have butchery stores of their own and to have a Sunday of their own and they insisted upon wearing a garb that was quite different from the clothes which we ourselves wore at the time and they continued to speak the Spanish or Portuguese or Polish or German tongues of the countries that were such cruel task-masters to them, so that there is hardly one among every hundred of these foreigners who can write an ordinary business note in Dutch. And now, after having shown in every possible way that they wish to keep themselves apart from the nation which has offered them a home, they are beginning to take the law into their own hands and they try to settle their private quarrels as if they owned the city and as if there were no magistrates whom God has placed over us that they might rule us all with diligence and wisdom, and that will never do!

"No, it will never do, and if they continue to behave in this fashion, they had better return to Lisbon and to Madrid and to Warsaw for while we don't particularly want them to say thank you to us for our kindness, neither do we care to have our community ruled by these upstarts who came here after we had purged the land of those enemies that were theirs as well as ours and who now want to reap the benefits which they did not help us sow and on top of that, try to tell us how we ought to run our own government."

There was a great deal of unreasonableness in this accusation for the vast majority, both of the Portuguese and German Jews, were almost fanatically grateful to those whom they invariably addressed as Their Saviors and they were not only loyal to the country at large but most generously inclined toward the particular city in which they happened to have settled down. Their rabbis, however, were an unruly lot and they bore a close resemblance to the clergymen of our own official church. As a rule they belonged to the lower classes of society and seeing little opportunity in following a business career, they chose the clerical profession because it promised to give them an outlet for their ambitions. But as no upstart can ever hope to rule without first discovering a "grievance" around which he can rally his followers, the rabbis, exactly like our own beloved dominies, were forever detecting dangerous issues which they thereupon attacked with the utmost violence and a complete disregard for the truth.

These were sad days for Menasseh, who spent almost every evening at the home of Rembrandt, presumably to talk of the illustrations for his forth-coming book, but in reality because he did not care to stay in his study, where at any moment he might be disturbed by the visit of one of his fellow rabbis. Poor Menasseh! His first great dream of finding the descendants of the Lost Tribes among the inhabitants of the New World had come to nothing. Next, in order to forget his miseries he had thrown himself upon the study of the Old Testament and he had done that with such fury that soon he had begun to hear mysterious voices and then one day he appeared among us boldly announcing that he had stumbled upon a hitherto unrevealed bit of prophecy that would set clear everything that had been dark thus far.

Being profoundly bored by that sort of hocus-pocus, I never quite understood what he was actually trying to prove. But it had something to do with Nebuchadnezzar or rather with Nebuchadnezzar's dream, which was supposed to be a prophecy of the coming of the Messiah, not the false Messiah whom we worshiped but the real Messiah who had not yet put in an appearance, et cetera, et cetera.

Next he got that Babylonian dream associated with the stone with which David slew Goliath and the stone which served Jacob for a pillow when he had his famous dream and it was all very muddled, but Menasseh himself was so full of his new idea that he persuaded Rembrandt (much against his will, I am afraid) to make a number of illustrations for the book which was to explain these mysteries to an unsuspecting and indifferent world.

The book was written in Spanish and not in Dutch and that may have been one of the reasons why Rembrandt never quite realized what he was doing and made such a bad job of the pictures. As he himself was beset by a thousand troubles during all this period, his friends hesitated to tell him just how bad these illustrations were. But the publisher of the Nebuchadnezzarian dream, being a business man and looking upon the venture from the angle of profit and loss, was inspired by no such delicate sentiments and simply threw the Rembrandt pictures out and had some ordinary hack do another set of plates which proved much more satisfactory from a popular point of view.

But when this happened, Menasseh himself was no longer among us. His Messianic premonition had left him no rest. He had missed meeting the Lost Tribes but he meant to be present when the great prophecies went unto fulfillment. His position in Amsterdam was no longer a very pleasant one. Doctor van den Ende had been right when he told me that young Espinoza would some day, very soon, be the cause of considerable difficulties among the Jews of our town and Menasseh was forced to agree with him. He was very dejected about it.

"Those Rabbis," he complained, "seem to have forgotten all we ever learned during our many years of suffering and persecution in foreign lands. Here we can enjoy a new and happy home of our own and they are all of them on the look-out for trouble. First it was d'Acosta, but he was not very bright and a little bit crazy. But this Espinoza boy has more brains than all of us put together. Instead of letting him go his own way, they are going to try and turn him into an errand-boy of the synagogue, a nice little fellow with a little brown coat on who goes around to all the people on Friday night to see that they clean their cupboards neatly and that they don't eat a chicken that has not had its head cut off in the right way. It is terrible!

"This Baruch, he is proud. He won't submit. He will fight back and the Christians will say, 'See those Jews, they are always the same. Quarreling again among themselves, as they did even in the days of Nebuchadnezzar.' And speaking of Nebuchadnezzar—did I ever tell you of his dream . . . ?"

And the poor man would be off again to tell you about his great discovery.

Poor honest soul! He left us soon afterwards and went to England where the Jews were once more being admitted for the first time I believe in four or five centuries. In London he fought valiantly and successfully for the good rights of his own people to be granted the right to live in the New Commonwealth. In the beginning he used to write to us—short letters in fluent Spanish and not such fluent Dutch. Then he complained that he was too busy to correspond, for the Lord Protector had granted him a pension and he was now able to devote all his time to the task of preparing the way for the coming of the Messiah, whose appearance might be expected at almost any moment. Then for a long time we had no news from him. But in the summer of the year 1657 I happened to be in Veere for a few days to see about the repair of the houses I had inherited from my grand-uncle and which were badly in need of new floors and stairs. One day, quite early in the morning, the Baptist minister from Middelburg was announced. He begged that he be excused for disturbing me at such an unseemly hour but in the hospital at Middelburg there was a sick man—he seemed to be a Jewish divine—who had asked after me and as it was known that I was in Veere at that moment, he had thought it his duty to warn me I thanked him most cordially and together we walked back to Middelburg where we arrived at noon.

The sick man was Menasseh. He was suffering from a pulmonary ailment and was already unconscious when I reached his bed-side. I heard that he had arrived in Flushing two days before with the body of his son Samuel, who had died in England and whom he wanted to bury in Amsterdam. He had been sick when he reached Flushing and had fainted in the coach that carried him to the ferry to the next island. The coachman had therefore driven him to the God's House and the matron had warned one of the ministers that she had a patient who seemed on the point of dying. But when it appeared that the man was a Jew, and a Rabbi at that, there had been little enthusiasm on the part of the official clerics to attend him in his final hours.

The Baptist preacher having been informed of the good woman's predicament had then offered his services and having heard how the patient in his feverish wanderings had repeatedly mentioned my name, he had taken the trouble to come all the way to Veere and warn me.

Together we watched over the patient and when evening came, he had a moment of consciousness. He recognized me. He smiled and whispered: "I love all my good friends in Amsterdam. Tell them so. And tell them to be prepared. The hour is at hand. The Messiah will come. Surely he will come!"

And thus Menasseh had died at peace with all the world and two days later we had buried him, together with his son Samuel, and this had been the end of a good and righteous man and a true friend whom we could badly spare at the very moment when the little group of people who fought for a more intelligent and charitable world was so dreadfully in need of his patience and his humor and the satisfaction one derived from his oft-repeated meditation:

"Ja, am Ende, wenn wir nur wirklich wüssten—if only we knew—if only we knew!"

Chapter 61

MY SON BEGINS THE EDUCATION OF HIS FATHER

Meanwhile little Titus, Rembrandt's son, had grown up to be a boy of almost fifteen and my own offspring was also approaching that age when a father looks at his perambulating resemblance and asks himself: "What in the name of high Heaven am I going to do with that boy?"

Titus, I am sorry to say, was causing Rembrandt more worry than my own boy was causing me. In the first place, he was not at all robust. He had inherited his father's face but his mother's delicacy of nature—her beautiful hands—her slender bones but also her weak lungs, and general lack of resistance. Really, it was too bad. If only it had been the other way around! If he had inherited his father's frame, who had the physique of a cart-horse, but the face of a good, honest, hard-working blacksmith or carpenter, which lacked all the charm and vivaciousness that had belonged to his aristocratic wife.

Jean-Louys and I had often speculated whether on the whole it was better for one to have started out with good blood or with a good education and how much education could do for one who had been born under humble circumstances and whether one who was born of good blood could ever quite belie his origin. And we had both come to the conclusion that there were so many exceptions to whatever rules we felt tempted to establish that we had better drop the subject as beyond our power of solution.

In the course of these discussions, Jean-Louys had hit upon a very clever new definition of "education," as different from mere "ability," by laying down the rule that "ability" allowed one to get along without "education," whereas "education" allowed one to get along without "ability." But when I suddenly asked him, "Yes, but what has that got to do with the subject of which we were talking?" he had answered, "Nothing at all, but it is past two o'clock of the night and then one is no longer supposed to talk sense," and so we had gone to bed and the matter never had been decided, which was a pity, for in the case of little Titus I felt that I was face to face with a problem which I for one would have great difficulty in unraveling. The poor lad seemed to have inherited from both parents exactly those qualities which were bound to be of absolutely no help to him in making his way. His handsome looks were of very little use to him, because he was a boy, and the talent for painting which he undoubtedly possessed, was so slight and insignificant as to be almost negligible.

He gave one the impression of an amiable and rather tender boy with excellent manners (the work of Hendrickje, though where she had learned them herself I never was able to fathom) and the best of intentions but without any force or stamina. I asked his father what he intended to do with him afterwards and Rembrandt, in that vague way in which he dismissed all subjects that had not some direct bearing upon his work, answered:

"Oh, I suppose he will become an artist."

And when I continued: "But how will he live?" he said:

"Oh, well, I suppose he will live somehow or other."

And he peacefully continued with the portrait of Jan Lutma, the goldsmith, on which he had been working for quite a long time, and which needed a general overhauling.

But how was that poor innocent and rather incompetent child ever to survive in a world that had been turned completely upside down by the war?

His father had had a difficult time making both ends meet, but he at least had worked in a normal world. The peace of Westminster, however, had destroyed all the old values. Even a great many of those rich merchants who ruled our towns and our country for so long and who seemed so firmly entrenched that nothing could possibly happen to them, even they had suffered reverses from which they were never able to recover and were forced to go back to a much simpler way of living than that to which they had been accustomed for three or four generations. And among those just a trifle below them on the social ladder there was hardly a person who in one way or another had not felt the influence of that great upheaval. Either their ships had been destroyed by the English or they had speculated in wood or gunpowder when they should have concentrated all their forces upon cornering the market in hemp and meanwhile other younger or more ambitious and perhaps a little less conservative and undoubtedly much less scrupulous firms had grabbed all the right profits at the right moment and had made millions. They were now buying up the town houses and country houses of those who had guessed wrong, and they were buying themselves noble carriages and an occasional coat-of-arms to put upon the doors of those vehicles. But their taste in furniture and art and music was as bad as the manners they displayed both in public and in private and the pictures they bought came almost exclusively from Antwerp and Paris where regular picture-factories were now working for "le goût Hollandais."

How mild little Titus, with his mild little portraits (they were a very weak and therefore bad reflection of those of his father) would ever be able to sell one of his works to the barbarians of the new era of prosperity was something I could not quite see. But the boy was still very young and might decide to do something different when he reached the age of discretion.

As for my own son, he never caused me any trouble. He seemed to have inherited absolutely nothing from anybody, neither from his mother nor me, nor for that matter from his grandfather or grandmother. Instead, he jumped right back to his great-grandfather, my own beloved grandfather, and I rejoiced in this biological miracle. For nothing could have been more to my taste than to see all those qualities of independence and enthusiasm and efficiency return in that flesh and blood that was so very much my own.

The youngster had absolutely no interest in the work that had occupied me ever since the days of my childhood. He was very nice to sick people and in a mild and non-committal way he felt rather sorry for them too. But he did not like them. He was too sound himself to have much sympathy for those who were suffering from some ailment. Nor did his grandsire's characteristics manifest themselves in a tendency toward things military. He told me once that he would not mind fighting but that it seemed a silly thing to do. It was too destructive—too aimless to suit practical taste. He wanted to make things. And he wanted to make them not only with his brains but also with his hands, for he had fingers that were as strong as steel nippers and he liked to use them. And from childhood on (so I was told, for during the first ten years of his life I had been in America) he had been busy with windmills and toy-carriages and miniature dredges. But when I returned from Nieuw Amsterdam he was no longer pottering around with tiny little mills made out of packing cases and pieces of sail which he had begged or stolen at the water front (a proceeding which seems to have shocked his faithful nurse more than anything else he ever did during a somewhat obstinate and turbulent career) but he had graduated from such futile pastimes and was beginning to revaluate his practical engineering experiments into terms of certain abstract mathematical formulae—formulae which meant nothing at all to me but which he explained to me as representing wind-velocities and the friction of wood upon wood and of stone upon stone and other intricate details of that mechanical world that will forever remain closed to me.

Where exactly he had learned all this I was never able to find out. I had first sent him to a school which was famous for the excellence of its Latin and Greek teaching. But there he was a complete failure. He went to sleep over his syntax and his copybooks contained diagrams of new hoisting devices instead of those terrible Greek verbs, the knowledge of which was considered an indispensable part of a gentleman's education. But whenever I tried to make this clear to him, he merely looked pained and bored and upon one memorable occasion informed me that I was talking through my hat (he used an even less complimentary expression which I must refuse to repeat here)—that he had no desire to be a gentleman if I meant by this that he would be allowed to spend five years at some university drinking gin and running after the servant girls of the town and generally misbehaving himself in those ways that were then considered highly fashionable among the young men of leisure who deigned to patronize those institutions of erudition and that anyway, he could learn more from ten minutes' talk with the owner of the "Cow" (a well known mill just outside the Saint Anthonie gate, where he was in the habit of spending a great many of those hours he should have been at his desk at school) than from four entire years aimlessly pawing the dreary pages of a Greek grammar.

I then spoke of the beauties of ancient poetry and he quietly looked at me and said: "But, father, have you ever heard the regular swish-swish of a mill that is running full speed? Could anything be more wonderful or more beautiful than that?"

I then began to discover for myself what must have been clear even to Adam, who certainly was no shining beacon of intelligence. (What a pity that our earliest ancestor should have been such a terrible bungler! Just suppose that he had been a bright fellow like Jacob or Joseph! Ten to one he would have beaten Jehovah at his own silly apple game, but it is too late now to waste vain regrets upon such a hopeless case of stupidity.) I was beginning to understand that we can't teach our children anything at all. We can expose them to education in the hope that they will catch some of it. But just how much or how little they catch of it depends upon certain mysterious elements in their make-up, the exact nature of which will probably remain hidden to us for all time.

But I know this much, that if a boy has a definite "tendency" toward certain subjects of learning, he will "catch" those subjects, in spite of every obstacle. But if on the other hand he has no such "tendency" he remains what we physicians call "immune" and we can expose him as much as we like, but he will never succeed in making that subject an integral part of his mental equipment.

I was not always as sane upon the subject as I am now after my son has been trying to educate me in this direction for almost twenty odd years. But on the whole I am happy to say I suspected the existence of this pedagogic axiom long before I had been able to prove it and as a result the boy has never given me any trouble and I have given him as little trouble as was possible, considering that I was his father and therefore more or less his natural-born enemy.

Poor Rembrandt! I was sorry for him when on Sundays, as sometimes happened, we took our boys out for a walk. Little Titus was usually bored, would want to go back home and color his pictures or look at a book. After half an hour he would complain that he was tired. After an hour he would sit down and weep for he really was not strong and got exhausted very easily.

Meanwhile my own young barbarian would occupy himself with some mechanical contrivance he had put together during the previous week—would try it out on the waters of the Amstel where the winds blew ever fresh, would talk of the day when mills would not only pump water and grind flour and saw wood but would also peel rice and make oil and perform Heaven only knows what other miracles.

Then Titus would look at him and would say, "I hate mills. They are ugly. They make such a noise."

And the answer would be: "Pooh! Ugly! They are useful. Useful things are never ugly."

As for Rembrandt, he would listen to this childish conversation, but it never seemed to penetrate to him what they were saying.

"They are young," he used to comment, once in a while. "They will grow out of it, both of them."

But there I had my doubts.

Does any one ever really "grow out" of something that was put into him even before the day of his birth?

Chapter 62

WE BUILD A NEW TOWN HALL AND REMBRANDT ALMOST PAINTS A PICTURE FOR IT

During the fall of the year '55 it became more and more clear that the situation in the northern part of Europe must soon lead to a crisis. Our Baltic granaries were in danger and without those supplies, half of our people would have starved to death.

I don't think that there were a hundred burghers in the entire Republic who cared a straw for the Poles, either as a nation or as individuals, while our relations with the Swedes had always been most cordial and furthermore the Poles were Catholics of a most pronounced and bigoted sort and the Swedes belonged to our own church, although they took to Lutheranism, rather than to Calvinism. Nevertheless, when it was seen to be a question of guilders and stivers, all personal considerations were curtly set aside and as soon as Danzig had been taken by the forces of King Charles, a squadron of our ships was sent to that town—it was recaptured and was given back to the Polish king.

The situation was not entirely clear. Even after this event we were still supposed to be at peace with the Swedes and My Lord de Witt strongly urged a union between the two great Scandanavian powers, Sweden and Denmark, with the Republic of the United Netherlands as the "honest broker" keeping the peace between the two rivals and preventing them from flying at each other's throats.

But this plan failed as ignominiously as his project for that English-Dutch treaty which he had explained to me upon the occasion of our memorable interview. In both instances it was the town of Amsterdam that rudely upset his calculations. The great pensionary was a "party man." He firmly believed in government by the "best people" and the "best people" of course were his own relations and their friends, the rich merchants of our big cities. But he was a man of such brilliant parts that, almost against his own will, he was sometimes obliged to look beyond the immediate interests of his party. Whereas Their Lordships, who ruled us from the big new building on the Dam, believed the world to end at the city boundaries and invariably put their own profits ahead of those of the country as a whole. They were wise and sagacious magistrates and I hasten to add that as a rule their policies coincided with those that were considered most favorable for the Republic as a whole. Nevertheless, it was a very unfortunate system of government, for it allowed a single community to override the clearly expressed will of all of its neighbors.

But it had been that way ever since the beginning of our independence and I suppose it will continue to be that way until the end, for I don't know of any man or party powerful enough to change it unless one of the princes of the House of Orange succeeds in making himself our king, something which seems hardly likely at the present moment when the only surviving member of that family (with the exception of a few negligible cousins in the northern part of the country) is a young boy who suffers dreadfully from headaches and who does not seem predestined to live very long.

In this particular instance it fortunately was proved that Amsterdam had chosen the wiser course. Since the death of my old friends, the Bickers, the affairs of the town were managed by a member of the van Beuningen family. The first half century of our independence offered wonderful opportunities to young men. Jan de Witt was only twenty-eight when he was appointed to the highest office in the state. And Conrad van Beuningen, at the age of thirty-three, had more power than many of the dictators of ancient Greece about whom we read in our history books. He belonged to a family that was greatly interested not only in the Baltic grain trade but also in the spice trade of the Indies and he was supremely endowed both by nature and by years of serious study for the rôle he was to play during the next twenty years. He was good looking and he could speak well in public—an accomplishment which I am sorry to say has been sadly neglected in our community, since we are rather apt to frown upon every form of rhetorical elegance except that extraordinary variety which is practiced in the pulpit.

But His Lordship was not given much to sermonizing. As a matter of fact, he was a person of very liberal ideas and it was said (though no one could offer any definite evidence) that he preferred the wisdom of Seneca and Marc Aurelius to that of Calvin and Knox. But as he was enormously rich, such accusations were never uttered beyond a whisper and it is only in recent years, when it seems that he is afflicted with the family curse of insanity, that people are beginning to speak out a little more openly about his heretical tendencies.

But in the year 1656 of which I am writing at the present moment, no one in his senses would have even dared to hint at such a possibility. And His Lordship could devote all his time and all of his tremendous energy toward a realization of those plans which should turn the Baltic into another Zuyder Zee, into a lake that should be dominated by Dutch interests. His friend, the Pensionary in The Hague, agreed with the views of Amsterdam in a general way but was inclined to proceed a little more cautiously. He had had more to do with navies than van Beuningen and knew how precarious a thing even a well-equipped fleet remains even under the most favorable circumstances and how little one can depend upon it in time of need. A sudden storm or an unexpected fog and victory may suddenly be turned into defeat. Besides, ships cannot be constructed over night. It takes fourteen months to build one of those gigantic modern men-of-war which measure six or seven hundred tons, but one unfortunate hit in the powder-magazine will send them to the bottom of the ocean in less than a minute's time.

Therefore while the Pensionary was just as anxious as the Burgomasters of Amsterdam to bridle the ambitions of the Swedish monarch and keep the old Baltic granaries open for the Dutch trade, he felt less inclined to risk the whole of the navy upon this one venture.

"How about England?" he asked his friend in Amsterdam. "Suppose that the Lord Protector avails himself of the opportunity which is offered by the absence of our ships in the north to stage a landing on the Dutch coast. What will happen then?"

Those of Amsterdam answered him that since the Republic was at peace with England and even had concluded a treaty of amity with that country, we need have no fears from that angle.

"What are official documents between nations?" the Pensionary replied. "Since when has a piece of paper prevented a people from attacking another when it seemed to their own interests to do so?"

And he cited a large number of instances in which empires and kingdoms and republics had treated the most sacred treaties as mere scraps of paper because it was to their advantage to do so. But Amsterdam refused to give in and since our town paid most of the taxes of the province of Holland and since Holland alone paid almost half of all the taxes of the entire Republic, Amsterdam had its own way and for five entire years our navy was kept busy in the north.

During this campaign some of the measures which I had been permitted to suggest were tried in practice and on the whole I am grateful to say my fellow practitioners on board approved of them and gave me their hearty coöperation. I myself was present at the encounter in the Sound when the Swedes under Wrangel were defeated, although it cost us the life of one of our ablest commanders, the famous Witte de With, who was a wild-man-of-the-sea, who could swear almost as well as he could fight, and who had hacked his way through so many naval engagements that he seemed to be possessed of a charmed life. On this occasion the tide carried his vessel on a bank, but he turned it quickly into a castle and defended himself until almost all his men were dead and he himself lay dying, causing so much admiration by his conduct, even among his enemies, that the next day they sent us his corpse with full military honors.

I arrived just too late to be with de Ruyter when he bombarded Nyborg and entered Copenhagen. I was allowed, however, to visit that town during the winter our admiral spent there and found it of very pleasing aspect, reminding me in many ways of our own city of Amsterdam, though it struck me that the people were a great deal gayer than our own and much less inclined to rowdyism.

I found it hard to account for this difference in outward behavior of the two nations. I have heard it claimed that the bad weather of our low land, the eternal fog and rain in which we are obliged to dwell from the day we are placed in a damp cradle until the hour we are lowered into a water-soaked grave, is at the bottom of our depressed mood and depressing ways. But surely nothing could be viler than the climate of the Danish capital which like my own town of Veere resembles a pancake afloat on a sea of mud. So it can't be that.

Others have told me that: "It is the difference in religion. These people are Lutherans, whereas we are Calvinists."

I am willing to grant that I would rather have gone fishing with the Wittenberg reformer than with his Genevan colleague, but what I saw here of the Lutheran ministers did not exactly give me an impression of levity of spirit. Indeed, I found them to be very much like our own dominies—perhaps a trifle more human but not very much, and just as eager to force their own views upon the rest of the world as the best or worst of our Amsterdam clerics. The most likely solution was given me by a young man who was one of the aides of Admiral van Wassenaar.

The latter, a very rich man and lord of the village of Obdam, an hereditary member of the Estates of Holland and the owner of a vast country place near The Hague, had begun life as the colonel of a regiment of cavalry. But during the recent English war, he suddenly had been ordered to take command of the fleet and he had stepped on board his first vessel as ignorant of naval strategy as a baby is of playing the harpsichord.

He owed his sudden rise in the world to the fact that he was a staunch supporter of the party that opposed the House of Orange, whereas de Ruyter and Tromp and Evertsen and all the others were suspected of leanings toward the little Prince. However that may be, the admiral-on-horseback had proved himself a very able man and a person of tact who had gained the respect and affection of his subordinates by his pleasant manner and his willingness to listen to their advice.

At the time I was summoned to his flag-ship he was suffering badly from podagra. A draughty ship's cabin was no ideal place of residence for a man thus afflicted, but he bore his pains with great fortitude and spent most of his time playing backgammon with his aide, who had developed a technique of losing that was truly admirable. This young man, the son of a Frisian nobleman and a French mother, but who vowed that he would never again set foot in that part of the world where a square foot of air weighed ten million Flemish pounds, was an amateur student of politics of no mean ability and he had developed a social theory which greatly amused me, although I soon realized that in most of what he said, the wish was father to the thought.

"The trouble with our country," he used to say while we paced up and down the deck, waiting for the Admiral, who was a handsome man but rather vain and very particular about his outward appearance, to finish his toilet, "the trouble with our land is the lack of standards which is due to the lack of a court. In some ways that is our strength, but in many other ways, it is one of our great weaknesses. It is true we can't just suddenly be lifted out of our beds and taken to a dungeon in some prison, as happened to the husband of one of my mother's cousins. It took the greater part of a year to discover where he was kept and next it took the combined efforts of the Estates of Holland and Friesland and five personal letters of the Grand Pensionary to get him out again. He had, so it appeared, laughed a little too loudly when one of the Mazarin girls was murdering the King's French a little more atrociously than usual. The Cardinal had observed that smile and His Majesty had obliged his faithful servant with a little slip of parchment, beginning, 'de par le Roi.'

"Good! I grant you that sort of thing is quite impossible here, and we will put that on the debit side. We have no sovereigns by the grace of God. As a result, we have fewer priests and not quite so many scaffolds. Whatever violence is committed is the work of the riffraff that has been preached into a frenzy of destructive holiness by the gentlemen of the cloth, but it is not the result of a sleepless night or indigestion on the part of one of the Lord's anointed.

"But now take the credit side. We are a circle without a center. As a result, politically speaking, we wobble, and socially speaking we are nowhere at all. We are supposed to be 'a country.' The poor innocents in Paris or London are still under the misapprehension that we are 'a country.' The day they discover that we are nothing of the sort, but merely an aggregation of squabbling, squealing, fighting, quarreling little provinces and cities and hamlets, each one with the pretention of being the equal of the grand duchy of Muscovy, they will fall upon us and divide us among themselves, as Philip of Macedonia fell upon the so-called independent democracies of ancient Greece and took away their liberty.

"Being a race of merry pirates, the inhabitants of our seacoast, who are devils when it comes to discipline, but perfect angels when there is any fighting to be done, may be able to hold out a little longer than if we were some inland state like that curious kingdom of Poland where I spent six whole months or one hundred and eighty-five days this spring and where every truckman and stevedore is a count or duke in his own right and has the power to veto any law he does not like.

"But I was telling you what is wrong with our social system. Well, we have no rallying-point—we are without any standards whatsoever. Standards of conduct and standards of beauty and standards of customs or manners may not be necessary for such a genius as that painter friend of yours of whom you have told me so much, and who lives with his cook and has children by her and quietly goes on painting, but most of us are no geniuses, and without standards we are lost, like ships at sea without a compass.

"As a very young man I went to London and I was there again as a sort of secretary during the negotiations at Westminster. The difference between the London of the Stuarts and the London of the Roundheads was incredible. I was very young when His late Majesty was still possessed of his head, and when one is very young, everything looks fine. But the people still had manners—they still had a code which told them what to do under all occasions and it made the whole social machinery run smoothly and evenly and quite pleasantly for all concerned.

"But two years ago—Heavens above! what a difference! One heard the social machine creak and groan. Each one of the men and women one met in the streets seemed to have worked out some little system of behavior of his or her own, and as not two of these systems were alike, the result meant continual friction—a chaos of conflicting interests which made me feel as if I were being entertained by my uncle of Witmarsum, who is famous for his dog-kennels and whose chief pastime in life is to invite his friends and relatives to be present when the brutes are being fed.

"We had a few audiences with the Lord Protector and I have never met a more charming or a more urbane man in all my days. But then, he was a landed nobleman of the old school and had been brought up under the monarchy.

"But take France or Italy, for I believe you told me that you had been there once. In each one of those countries there is a court with a king and that court is the bureau of standards for everything that has to do with a civilized existence. His Majesty decides that he must no longer dive into his goulash with his fingers, but use a fork, and the whole country, or at least that part of it that wants to be considered civilized (and the rest does not matter), hastens to go to the silversmith's shop and order a couple of forks for every member of their respective families.

"Or His Majesty wants to build himself a new palace. He knows nothing about bricks and mortar himself and therefore he sends for the best architects in the land and says: 'Messieurs, go to it.' I don't mean to say that you and I will invariably agree that they are the best architects according to our own tastes, but never mind, they are bound to be among the best, otherwise they would not have got the job.

"Or His Majesty becomes enamored of a beautiful damozel and wants to honor her by such a feast as this world has never seen. He sends for the best fiddlers and the best dancing masters and says: 'Gentlemen, it is up to you to show us what you can do and please don't disappoint us, for our royal displeasure would be fatal to your reputation.' Do they work their poor brains overtime to please His Majesty? I assure you they do. And their music and their plays set a standard for all others.

"Or again His Majesty wants to enliven the dull walls of his castle. He asks who are considered the best painters within his realm and tells them to get out their palettes and their brushes and give him what is the best. I repeat, this 'best' may not be the 'best' according to your taste or according to my individual taste, because we happen to be people of profound discrimination, but at least it is a sort of norm for those hordes of patient subjects who have no more idea of taste than my dog Nero has of how to catch storks.

"And the result is a pleasant average of behavior and of comedies and tragedies and paintings and sculpture and of cookery and dancing and love-making.

"In our Republic we have a few people who are far above that average, for we are a nation that is by no means devoid of ability and talent—I might even say genius. But our 'average' is bad. We really have no average. We have whatever it pleases every man and every woman (and sometimes every child) in every street of every town and village to give us. It is good enough for them. It suits their needs. We don't like it? Very well, we know what we can do about it! And so while we have worked ourselves up to the rank of a God-fearing, prosperous and highly respectable nation, we have in everything that does not pertain to our fear of God, our prosperity or our incredible respectability, remained what we were four hundred years ago when my ancestors killed your ancestors with pitchforks and bludgeons. We have remained a rowdy mob of self-embarrassed and clumsy yokels who either giggle or moan and as a rule giggle when they ought to be moaning and moan when they ought to be laughing. . . ."

But at that moment the Admiral had finished his toilet and sent for me and I never quite heard the end of this diverting speech. But I think that I know what young Aitzema had meant. Denmark was a country dominated by a single big town and that town, ever since it had been founded, six hundred years before, had been a royal residence and school of manners which was attended by pupils from all over the land. Whereas we at home had been left to our own devices—every man for himself and the Devil take the hindmost! Which the Devil had not failed to do, as I discovered the moment I returned to Amsterdam.

For the last eight years we had been building a new Town Hall. As soon as the Peace of Westphalia had been signed and our independence had been recognized, Jacob van Campen had been ordered to draw up plans for a new civic center. The old Town Hall was considered a little too shabby for a city of quite such magnificence as ours. Besides, the building had grown much too small and no one felt very sorry when it burned down during that memorable Saturday night in July of '52 when a cousin of Rembrandt's friend, Burgomaster Six, saved the books of the city bank and gained the everlasting devotion of the grateful depositors.

For eight long years one part of the Dam, right behind the ruins of the old Town Hall, had been hidden from our view by a high wooden fence. Meanwhile we had heard stories of the wonderful things that were going on behind that fence, which by then had become an excellent advertisement for the thoroughness of our public school system, as the usual dirty words were written as low as a foot from the ground, showing that even the youngest of our children were able to write and spell correctly.

Every citizen knew exactly how many Norwegian pines had been sunk into the ground to give this building the necessary stability. (I was the only exception, having no brain for figures, but the number ran somewhere between twelve and fourteen thousand, which made a forest of respectable dimensions.) And every citizen knew the width of the basement and the height of the towers had been carefully recounted, together with the number of rooms (including, as I remember, three different and separate jails) and the number of chimneys and the water reservoirs on the top floor which were to protect the building against fire.

But what had interested us most of all had been the plans for the interior decorating of all these many stately mansions that were to be occupied by Their Lordships the Burgomasters and by the high court of justice and by the aldermen and sheriffs and by the tax-gatherers and by all the many other dignitaries that made up what we were pleased to call our "magistrates." There would be need of a great many pictures and who was better fitted for such a task than Rembrandt? He had shown them that he could handle the most complicated subjects in a superb way and that size and shape of the canvas meant nothing to him provided he were really interested in the subject. Accordingly ever since I returned from America I had made it a point to speak to every one who possibly might have some influence with the authorities to say a good word for the man who was the ideal candidate for this very important task. And many of those whom I approached had answered, "Yes, that is a good idea. A very good idea. He is the fellow who painted that large picture that now hangs in the Doelen?" And without exception they had promised that they would do their best to give my friend at least a few of the orders that were to be placed among the local painters.

But when I happened to meet them again, they were always full of excuses. "Yes, they had mentioned his name to His Lordship, the first Burgomaster, the last time they saw him." Or again, "The big reception room which is a hundred by a hundred and twenty feet is just the sort of room that man Rembrandt ought to do, but the roof was not quite ready yet and therefore it was impossible to judge of the light effects and until the roof should have been finished, it would be impossible to make a decision."

Meanwhile I learned that Bol and Flinck and Jan Lievens and several others were busy in their studios on portraits and allegorical works that were to find a place in the new edifice, while Jan Bronchorst was about to submit elaborate plans for the ceilings of the new court room.

The public at large did not take a great deal of interest in this whole matter. As long as Their Lordships had thought fit to place their orders with such and such painters, well, why talk about it? Their Lordships undoubtedly knew what they wanted and Their Lordships undoubtedly knew best.

When it became known that practically all the necessary bits of sculpture had been commissioned to a certain Aert Quellin, who was a native of Antwerp, a voice was heard here and there asking whether we had no artists of our own who could do that sort of work just as well as a foreigner, but since it was conceded by every one who laid claim to a genteel taste that the Belgian painters were far superior to our own— much less coarse in their subjects and infinitely more refined in their treatment of the nude (and as furthermore Quellin happened to be one of the ablest sculptors of our time), these murmurings were never taken very seriously, and on the whole the populace approved most heartily of the choice of their rulers.

I knew both Flinck and Bol from the days they had been Rembrandt's pupils and I went to see them. They were quite loyal to their former teacher and wished that they could be of assistance to him. But both of them agreed that it would be suicidal for them if they should try to agitate on his behalf in any way that might be constructed as a personal interference with the plans of Their Lordships.

"Even now," Bol told me frankly, "we may at any moment be replaced by some Fleming who paints more in the Rubens manner than we do. Rubens is the great man here. He and Jordaens are our heroes. Rembrandt? Why, he is either too dark or too muddy or too something to please our public. Both Flinck and I and practically all the men that studied with our old master have been obliged to change our technique, become a little more Flemish, a little more Rubenesque—if you understand me—to keep our customers. If we had not done that, we would now be starving to death. If you don't believe me, go to any of the art-dealers and ask them whether they will take a chance on Rembrandt. Yes, here and there a man who sells to the Italian trade. Perhaps because there is so much sunshine in Italy that they can stand something a little dull better than we. But the others? They won't touch him. They won't come near him. And if we went to Their Lordships and suggested the name of Rembrandt, they would show us the door, and ask us to mind our own business, which consists in being just as Flemish as we can be."

I knew that they were right, but refused to give up. The next time I was in The Hague, I mentioned the subject to My Lord de Witt.

"I don't know much about such matters," he confessed, "and the Lord have mercy on my soul if it ever should become known that I had dared to make a suggestion concerning anything that had to do with the purely domestic affairs of that very independent city. If it should be rumored that I was in favor of yellow curtains, Their Lordships would at once order every curtain in the whole place to be dyed a bright green. No, I dare not interfere in any way, but I will give you a letter to my uncle. He is a man of sense and a man of taste and not without influence in his own country."

This was expressing it very mildly, for every one knew that nothing could be accomplished in Amsterdam without the silent approbation of the famous Lord of Polsbroek.

This title was one which he had acquired in later life by buying himself the seigneurial rights to the village of Polsbroek. Why he did this, I do not know, for as simple Cornelis de Graef he was known far and wide as the uncrowned king of Amsterdam and as one of the strongest men in the Republic. He was not really an uncle of My Lord Jan but of his wife, the former Wendela Bicker. That, however, made little difference. If the two men had not been related at all, they would have appreciated each other just as genuinely. For they both were far above the average in intelligence and integrity and as neither of them coveted outward glory, or dignity (having enough of the latter not to be obliged to worry about the former) there was no danger of their ever getting into conflict about mere matters of policy.

Whether My Lord of Polsbroek was as staunch a party man as his famous nephew or had secret leanings towards the House of Orange, no one was ever able to discover. He never quite gave himself away, being perhaps too much of a philosopher to make a good politician. It was his business to see that Amsterdam remained the most prosperous city of the old continent and for that reason he wished to remain on cordial terms with the government of the Republic as represented by the Estates General who met in The Hague. His nephew by marriage happened to be the most influential person in the Estates General. It really was a most perfect arrangement. The uncle acted as general adviser to the nephew, while the nephew kept the uncle informed about everything that happened in his corner of the woods. From such partnership great things are born and as long as both men lived, the country enjoyed such affluence and such uninterrupted good fortune that the period of their coöperation will probably go down into history as the Golden Age of our Republic.

But in the matter of art, I found His Lordship was about as helpless as his nephew had pretended to be.

I found him in his house on the Heerengracht to which the family had moved when they ceased to be cloth-dealers and were promoted to the rank of merchant-princes. But nothing could have been more delightful or cordial than his reception. Like all men of big affairs, he seemed to have plenty of time for everything and bade me be seated and at once spoke most sympathetically about the loss I had suffered.

"An outrage," he said, "a perfect outrage and absolutely inexcusable.

But what will you? The rabble needs a victim once in a while. I am sorry that this time the popular lightning (which is about as reasonable as that of the great god Zeus) has struck one for whom I feel such sincere personal regard. And you shall have full redress. You shall receive full compensation for everything you lost. Unfortunately such things proceed rather slowly. That is one of the most regrettable sides of our form of government. If we lived under a monarchy, such a wrong could be settled in one quarter of the time it takes to do such a thing here. One royal signature and the difficulty would be out of the way. Also if the royal signature for some reason were not granted, you would never see a cent of your money, and your children and grandchildren could die in the almshouse and His Majesty would not care. Here, under our system of government, you are at least reasonably certain that part of the funds will be in your hands before you die and that your son will get the rest. I wonder why governments always work so slowly? But an official exchequer is like those ingenious bow-nets with which in the days of my youth, I used to catch eels. Everything can go in, but nothing can ever go out. However, in what way can I hope to be of service to you to-day?"

I told him. He threw his hands up in a gesture of despair.

"Ask me something else," he said. "Ask me something easy like declaring war upon the Emperor or making the East India Company publish a true account of their last year's budget. Ask me to have you appointed ambassador-in-extraordinary to the court of the Great Khan. Ask me to have the Amstel diverted into the North Sea instead of the Zuyder Zee. But don't ask me to risk my position and my prestige in a matter of this sort."

I looked at him and was dumbfounded. Here was My Lord of Polsbroek, without whose permission (as the people used to say) it could not even rain in Amsterdam, confessing to me, a poor leech, that he could not order a few pictures for his new Town Hall from the greatest painter alive and for what reason—for what reason on earth? I asked him. I asked him humbly and politely, but nevertheless I asked him. What considerations of a political nature could oblige him to give me such a disappointing answer?

"What considerations of a political nature?" he burst forth. "Politics be damned. I will appoint any man to any place I please as long as it is a matter of politics, but that is just it! This is not a matter of politics. This is a matter of religion—of theology—of the one thing I have vowed I would keep clear of, all the rest of my live-long days."

"But surely," I answered, "Your Lordship need not ask Rembrandt to paint an allegorical picture that could possibly shock the pious. He is most excellent at portraits. You must need a great many portraits for the new Town Hall. Allegorical pictures never were his strong point anyway."

"My dear Doctor," he said, and looked at me the way I had noticed other people look before, when I had asked a particularly foolish question, "don't you see how it is? You may think that we are almighty at the Town Hall, that we can do as we please. We can to a certain extent but we have to proceed very carefully. After all, there are window-panes in our houses and it costs a lot to replace them. The clergy still has a hold upon the masses that we philosophers are a little too apt to overlook. And numbers count, especially in a city like this that has no court and therefore no life-guards. Some of our colleagues know this and make use of it to excellent purpose. I have one in mind, a certain Valckenier. His father made a lot of money in the East India Company. He is one of the most unpleasant people I have ever met and he has a temper that is as nasty as the bite of a sturgeon. But he is intelligent and he has a terrific amount of ambition. He wants to succeed van Beuningen if that poor man should ever be shipwrecked on one of his endless voyages. He has not a friend among the members of the city council. But he needs a party —some one to back him up. We watched him turn pious almost overnight. He has not one single quality of a true Christian and is a hateful and spiteful man. But every Sunday—three times every Sunday—you can see him in his pew in the new church.

"The 'small people' worship him as one of their own. What would he say, or rather, what would he not say, if I suggested to give a commission for an official portrait to a man who lives in open sin with his maidservant? He would drop a hint and the dominies would pound their pulpits and would start their usual fulminations against the new Sodom and would preach sermons about the whore of Babylon and it might end in bloodshed.

"And now I don't even consider the possibility of his finding out that you, of all people, suggested this to me. You—a mere surgeon who tried to cheat Jehovah out of his allotted measure of pain—you, an iconoclast who tried to set woman free from one of her most disastrous burdens. Why, we would have to turn the whole city into an armed camp if I so much as suggested the name of this man van Rijn for a single piece of work.

"Ask me some other favor and it is granted before you even express the wish. But let me die in peace. Our day will soon be over. I have spent much of my time reading books of history. For every five years that the world has been ruled by Reason, the human race has insisted upon five hundred during which it should obey the dictates of its own passions and prejudices and follies and foibles. You see, I am quite eloquent upon the subject. Mankind has but one enemy, its own stupidity, but it loves that enemy as truly and as devotedly as many a poor simpleton who is married to a shrew loves and obeys the creature who has turned his existence into a living hell.

"I would like to oblige you. I will give orders that the new Town Hall be burned down if that pleases you. But as for giving an order to your friend van Rijn, no, that I won't do because I can't do it."

I saw his point and thanked him for his courtesy and took my leave.

The new Town Hall was inaugurated with many ceremonies. There was a service in the Old Church and a service in the New Church and a procession of all the dignitaries connected in any way with the government of the city and there were public performances on the Dam and there was music and a great deal of patriotism and a great deal of drunkenness, as is apt to occur on such occasions. I spent the day quietly at home and in the evening went to Rembrandt's house and helped him polish some plates, for he was in the midst of one of his attacks of etching when he was apt to work twenty hours a day.

But ere I finish this chapter, I must run ahead a few years and tell of something that happened much later.

In the month of February of the year 1660 Govaert Flinck, who was still working on the decoration of the big gallery in the Town Hall died. He had been sick for quite a long time and it was known that he would not be able to finish the work he had begun. Just then my old friend and colleague, Doctor Tulp, was treasurer of the town of Amsterdam. He had achieved much greater honors in the world than I and was then one of the most respected burghers of our town. But we had always remained on a pleasant and cordial footing and besides I knew that he had a great admiration for Rembrandt, who had painted his picture some twenty odd years before when they were both still comparatively young men and at the beginning of their respective careers.

Since that time, Tulp never again met Rembrandt, and the last time he had had his portrait painted he had had it done by a foreign artist. Nevertheless I decided to say a good word for Rembrandt and as the Town Hall was no longer a novelty and no one paid much attention to it except those who went there on business and native Amsterdamers who had to entertain guests from abroad and whom they dragged right from the boat to the Dam to behold the "eighth wonder of the world" and tell them that in the globe carried by the Hercules who guarded the entrance gates, there was room for at least three people enjoying a meal at a middle-sized table—as in short the Town Hall and its decorations were no longer in the public and in the clerical eyes, the excellent Tulp complied with my wishes and Rembrandt was told to continue the work which his own pupil had not been able to finish.

It was to be an historical picture representing the great Batavian hero, Claudius Civilis, who for a short period of years had set our country free from the rule of the Romans. All this of course had happened a long time ago and no one knew exactly where or under what circumstances, but every well-behaved child could reel off the date: "100 B.C. the Romans arrived in our country and 50 B.C. Claudius Civilis sets our country free from the Roman yoke."

Rembrandt showed less enthusiasm than I had expected. This order was what he called "mustard that comes after the meal," and true enough, it was not very flattering for him to be called in only as a sort of stop gap. But once he had started, his enthusiasm grew by leaps and bounds. He decided that since this was a conspiracy, the scene must have been laid at night and in the dark, when the Romans were supposed to have gone to bed. He chose an enormous canvas, almost sixty feet square, the largest canvas he had ever handled, and he made the Batavian rebel the center of a festive meal, during which he explains to his friends and followers what his plans are for the coming uprising.

The problem of having the entire scene bathed in the light of a few small oil lamps fascinated him. He spent months on it and produced something so weird and mysterious that it made me feel queer to look at it. The figure of the one-eyed Claudius dominated the scene. The sword in his hand glistened ominously. I expected great things of this work of art and eagerly awaited the day when it should be hung in its place.

Rembrandt was to get only 1,000 florins for the whole picture (no more than Flinck would have received), but I was sure it would cause so much talk that he would be completely rehabilitated in the eyes of his neighbors and what was even more important from a purely practical point of view, in the eyes of the art-dealers.

But the magistrates rejected it. They rejected it flatly and unceremoniously. Some said that Claudius Civilis looked too much like Hannibal. As the Carthaginian hero had also lost one eye in battle, they had some excuse for this complaint, but it really had very little to do with the value of the picture as a work of art.

Others said it was too dark. Still others complained that the light was all wrong, that no one ever had seen a lamp that threw such shadows. It was never hung in the big gallery. It was at once removed to the garret to be stored away until some future date when Their Lordships should decide what else they could do with this monstrous canvas that was by far too large for any ordinary room and much too beautiful for ordinary people. To this day I do not know what became of it. I have heard that it was cut into four pieces and sold to a junk dealer.

Just about a year ago I happened to have a patient who had been secretary to My Lord van Beuningen during his last voyage to Sweden. He told me that in Stockholm he had seen a picture that looked very much like a sketch that was hanging on my wall. The sketch in question was a small pen and ink study for the Claudius Civilis which years before I had fished out of Rembrandt's fireplace (fortunately it was summer), into which he had thrown it in a moment of despair. I asked the young man whether he was certain and he said yes. I asked him how large the picture was and he answered, "About half of the wall of your room."

Then I begged him to describe it to me a little more in detail and I recognized the central part of the Claudius Civilis picture.

But it may have been merely a copy. Or the young man was mistaken. For although I wrote to Stockholm and for years afterwards interviewed every one who returned from the Swedish capital, I never could discover another trace of this lost masterpiece.

The open space in the gallery left behind by the death of Flinck was filled in by some local talent whose name I have forgotten.

And Rembrandt was obliged to split his fee with this young man, as it did not seem fair to Their Lordships that a man should be paid for work he had not really done.

Chapter 63

REMBRANDT RECEIVES A CALLER. HE PROVES TO BE AN OFFICIAL FROM THE BANKRUPTCY COURT

It is curious how one loses track of time when one is at sea. Besides, my trips of inspection to our squadrons in the Baltic took place at such irregular periods that I have no very clear recollection of any of them. They have become one vast blur upon my memory—a blur composed of uncomfortable berths in uncomfortable cabins—of miserable hours of wetness and depression in some small boat that was being rowed to the flag-ship—of miserable hours of wetness and depression a short while later in the same little boat that was now being rowed back to shore—of quarrels with superannuated but obstinate ship's surgeons—of pleasant dinners with captains who had but one wish in life—to invite the Lords of all the Admiralties on board their ships and then make them stay on deck to take part in some major engagement, of long, placid sails along the flat coasts of northern Germany and Denmark and of sick and wounded people who hated to die and whom one could not possibly hope to save for lack of even the most primitive and elementary sanitary precautions.

Here and there in this blur there is a short breathing space caused by a week or perhaps a fortnight on shore. It was during one of these periods of respite that after a hard day's work preparing a report for the Pensionary that I decided to take a walk and a walk with me always led right around the corner to Rembrandt's house.

The house looked no different from other times, but as soon as I had entered, I knew that something was wrong. Two strange hats were lying on the table in the entrance and I heard the noise of unfamiliar voices coming from upstairs. I went into the living room where I found Hendrickje busy putting little Cornelia to bed. She asked me to go into the little garden by the side of the house and wait for her. Shortly afterwards she joined me.

"We have had a terrible day," was the first thing she said. "I am very tired. If you don't mind, I will sit down with you for a moment." For though we all liked her sincerely and treated her in every way as if she were really Rembrandt's wife, she could not get over a certain shyness when she was in the company of those who belonged to what she still considered a higher class of society.

"What has happened?" I asked her.

"Oh, just the usual thing. People with bills. Grocers and bakers and the butcher. Then more people with bills. Paint dealers, money lenders. I don't know them all by name but it was pretty awful."

Just then Rembrandt himself appeared in the doorway.

"I got rid of those two," he said. "I wonder how many more there will be to-day?"

"Perhaps none," Hendrickje suggested.

"No, when they once begin to come, they go on the whole day. Can I have something to drink? Is there any gin left in the house? I shall have to work all night to make up for these interruptions."

Hendrickje got the gin. Rembrandt took two glasses.

"Such days are terrible," Rembrandt said. "I have just started two new pictures and those fools come and talk to me about money! Well, I have not got any. That is simple enough, isn't it?"

There was a knock on the door.

"Don't open," Rembrandt told Hendrickje, who had got up. "Don't let them in. They will go away soon enough."

"But then they will be back early to-morrow morning."

"In the meantime I shall have been able to do a whole night's work."

"What are you doing now?" I asked him.

"Mostly oil. I am doing one etching, a portrait of Jan Lutma, the goldsmith. His family ordered it. But for the rest, just pictures. Biblical subjects. There are not many portraits ordered these days. And those who order won't pay. Last year I did one for a Spaniard, a portrait of his daughter. He paid me seventy-five guilders in advance and then he said that he did not think the likeness was any good and wanted his money back. He is still after me with his lawyers. No, the war has killed the portrait business and besides, I am too old now to sit before my easel and be told what to do and how they want little Wimmie to hold a dead parrot and how little Susie must absolutely wear that dress of brown and pink. If there are any dead parrots to be put in the picture, I will put them where I like them myself. And so I paint Biblical pictures. When I do that my models can't talk back. If I want to put Joseph here and Potiphar there, they don't say, 'Ah, sir, but we would rather face the other way around.' They stay where I put them and when Jacob blesses the little children no one is going to tell me what color the counterpane of his bed should have. Meanwhile these people out there seem to have given up hope. At least, they have stopped knocking," and he poured himself another gin.

"A lovely day," I said, to say something.

But this merely angered him. "A lovely day? Good God! A lovely day indeed! Yes, the sun was shining, I believe, but if you had had my sort of a day—"

"What has happened?"

"Oh, the old story."

"People who want money?"

"That is no longer a story. That is a legend. But it is about Titus."

"But the boy is perfectly well, isn't he?"

"Better than ever. But it is about his inheritance."

And then I understood what he was driving at. It was the question which I had found mentioned in the report Lodewijk had given me.

What I had dreaded for such a long time seemed at last to have happened. The uncles and aunts of young Titus had asked for an accounting and Rembrandt apparently had done nothing about it, had put their letters aside and had not even taken the trouble to answer them. Thereupon they had insisted upon a public inspection of his books (as if the poor man had ever heard of such a thing as book-keeping!) to see whether at least part of their nephew's non-existing fortune was still intact and present.

And now they had threatened him with court proceedings and had hinted that they would ask the Chamber of Orphans to attach the house in the Breestraat and sell its contents at public auction that Titus might receive his legal share of his mother's inheritance.

I wish that I had been in town when that had happened, for most likely he would have come to me and I would at least have been able to send him to a reliable advocate who could have advised him. But Rembrandt, confused and panic-stricken, had asked the first person who happened to come to his studio to give him the name of a lawyer—"any lawyer will do"—and that person happened to be an art dealer of rather doubtful reputation who had called on him in the hope of selling him a spurious Michelangelo and he had answered, "Yes, so and so is an excellent man. Ranks as high as the best of them."

And he had sent Rembrandt to a shyster. This fellow probably knew that the situation was hopeless but in order to keep his hands on at least part of his patient's tangible assets, he suggested that Rembrandt have his house on the Breestraat transferred officially to Titus, as "part of the boy's maternal inheritance."

The meaning of this move should have been clear to any one not quite as inexperienced in such matters as Rembrandt. It was an attempt to placate the Uylenburgh relatives by swindling the other creditors. How this lawyer ever was able to persuade Rembrandt to accede to such a desperate plan I do not know, except that he probably did not pay the least attention to anything that was being said beyond a vague and pained "yes" or "no" and "Will this take long, or can I go back to work now?"

But of course in order to make this transfer "official" (and nothing less would be accepted by Titus' uncles and aunts), the deed of transfer had to be attested before the Chamber of Orphans, an institute that was known for its severity and its scrupulous honesty.

They, so it seemed, had asked no questions, well knowing that not a soul in the world would dare to appear before them and ask them blandly to register a house as "orphan's good" when said house was no longer in the possession of the donor but had belonged since years to a syndicate of creditors. But for the nonce, these worthy gentlemen were mistaken. Rembrandt, totally ignorant of business methods, had not even bothered to tell them that the house was heavily mortgaged. The transfer had been made and the next morning of course all the other creditors knew what had happened. To say that then the fat was in the fire was to express it mildly. The two hats I had seen in the hall belonged to two of the main creditors. They had insisted upon being received. They had called Rembrandt a swindler, and I could hardly blame them for being very angry. They had asked that the deed giving Titus his father's house as part of his mother's inheritance be revoked within twenty-four hours and they had threatened that unless he give them his written promise to this effect and give it to them then and there, they would serve papers in bankruptcy on him before the end of the day.

Rembrandt had listened to them vaguely and had then requested to be excused for a moment. He had wanted to ask Hendrickje what he should do. But the door of the studio had been open and it was still light. Just when he passed that open door he had noticed something he had for a long time wanted to change in the colored turban of Potiphar. He had picked up a brush to make this small correction. Then he had forgotten all about his visitors and he had continued to work until the loud slamming of the front door suddenly reminded him of the reason for which he had come upstairs.

At first he had felt rather ashamed of his rudeness, but in the evening when I saw him his annoyance had made place for merriment.

"Served them right," he said. "Served them right for disturbing me on a day like this. And now they will probably leave me alone."

But at that moment there was another knock at the front door, a knock that sounded official and refused to be denied.

"I will open," Hendrickje said.

"You had better," I added.

"Oh, very well," was all that Rembrandt remarked.

A moment later, Hendrickje returned. She was followed by a little man wearing a long brown cloak and looking for all the world like an undertaker's assistant.

"Have I the honor to address Mr. Rembrandt van Rijn?" the little man asked.

"Never mind the honor," Rembrandt answered roughly. "What do you want?"

"Nothing, except to give you this."

Rembrandt automatically picked up the large yellow envelope which the undertaker's assistant gave him.

"What is this?" he asked.

"An order in bankruptcy," the brown beadle answered.

"Oh," said Rembrandt. "So soon? Well, I suppose you can't help it."

"I most surely can't, sir!" the little man said. "It just happens to be my business."

"Then perhaps you will have a drink?"

"I would not mind at all."

Hendrickje got another glass. Rembrandt poured it full of gin, but took none himself.

"Your health," said the little man, as he poured the glass down his throat with one gulp and wiped his mouth with the back of his hand. Then he bowed low and wished us all a good evening. A moment later we heard him slam the door and all was quiet until the chimes of the South Church began to play the hour.

"What time is it?" Rembrandt asked. "It stays light so late these days."

"Ten o'clock," I answered, counting the strokes.

"Then I had better go back to my studio. I suppose I am in for a hard time. Well, I am young still. I painted myself into these difficulties. Now I will have to paint myself out of them again."

But he never did.

From that day on until the hour of his death, he remained an "undischarged bankrupt."

Chapter 64

THE HOUSE ON THE JODENBREESTRAAT STANDS STILL AND EMPTY

The next day half a dozen of us, all good friends of Rembrandt, gathered at his house to see what we could do. We knew that all efforts to save this sinking ship would be useless. The question before us was how we could transfer the passengers of the doomed vessel to another one with as little delay as possible and without causing any more annoyance to any one than was absolutely unavoidable.

They could not remain in the house for they were not allowed to touch a thing and the officials of the Bankruptcy Court could now come in at any moment to make an inventory of all the furniture and the paintings. After that they would not even be allowed to sleep in their own beds. I offered Hendrickje and little Cornelia the hospitality of my own house. They could have my room and Titus could share the room of my son. The others agreed that this would be a good plan, as Cornelia was only two years old and still needed a lot of care being by no means a very strong child.

That left Rembrandt on our hands. We had to find quarters for him, for if he were left to his own devices, God only knew what he would do. He must have seen this disaster coming upon him slowly for at least ten years. But he never apparently had realized how serious conditions were until that little undertaker-man in the brown cloak handed him the big yellow envelope. Ever since he had walked aimlessly through the house—picking up one piece of his collection after another—holding it in both hands and looking at it for a long time as if he were saying good-by to it. We had to take care of him as if he were a small boy, whereas Titus, to whom no one among us had ever paid very much attention, now suddenly stepped forward as if he were a full-grown man, sent for the baker, the grocer, and the vegetable-man, explained the situation to them with as few words as possible, and made arrangements through which his father obtained at least a few days' further credit.

Then some one, I think it was Francen (the art dealer, not his brother the surgeon) said: "There is quite a good place in the Kalverstraat, called the 'Keyserskroon.' It belongs to a fellow by the name of Schuurman and it is not too expensive. It is a large place. I think it used to be an orphan asylum. If all this has to be sold" (and he waved his hands around him), "the auction could be held right there, and meanwhile Rembrandt could live there."

I interrupted him. "Wouldn't it hurt him terribly to be present when all this is sold?"

But Francen was less sentimentally inclined than I.

"Undoubtedly it would," he answered, "but just now it is not so much a question of how to save his feelings as how to save his family. If he is present or if it is known that he is about, the dealers won't dare to offer as little as if they knew that he weren't there. Don't you other gentlemen agree?"

The others agreed, and I too could see the reasonableness of Francen's point. And in order to prove that I was sincere in this, I offered to tell Rembrandt what plans we had made for him and his family.

I found him in his studio cleaning his palettes. "I don't suppose these belong to me any more," he said. "I don't suppose that, strictly speaking, I am even allowed to touch them. But I can hardly let them go to ruin. They have been very faithful servants so far."

I assured him that no one, not even the most strict-minded notary, could object to his keeping his tools in order, and then I told him what we had decided for him and his family. He listened, carefully scraping the paint off his large round palette, and merely nodded his head.

"When ought we to leave?" he asked.

"Oh, there is no immediate hurry. Sometime within a week or ten days."

"Then why not to-day? You know, it is rather hard on me to stay here any longer, now that all this is about to be taken away from me."

"Very well," I replied. "I will ask Hendrickje."

I found her in Cornelia's room packing. She was perfectly quiet and self-possessed.

"It really does not mean so much to me," she explained. "I have always been poor and to tell you the truth, all this luxury was just a little too much for me. But it will be terribly hard on him. His heart is in these things. I hope it won't kill him."

I told her that I did not think it would. He came of a strong race and could stand a blow better than most people. Then I went back to the meeting and reported what we had decided. The others thereupon went home, but Jeremias de Dekker, the poet, and I remained behind to see whether we could be of any further assistance. I sent Titus to the shop of a carpenter who lived on the Oude Schans, to ask him for the loan of one of his assistants and a cart and had the fellow take Hendrickje's belongings and Titus' small trunk and Cornelia's cradle to my home just around the corner. I told de Dekker to go with them to see them safely to their new place of residence. Then I went upstairs and helped Rembrandt put a few clothes and shoes and shirts and sheets and blankets in a small leather portmanteau.

When this had been done, he returned to the studio.

"I don't suppose I can take any of these things," he said.

I told him that I was afraid that could not be done.

He picked up a large surgeon's needle, which I had used for small operations until it had got too blunt, when I had given it to Rembrandt who was forever complaining that he could not get a piece of steel that was really fit for a good job at dry-point work. He held it out for me to see and asked: "You gave this to me, didn't you?"

"No," I replied. "I merely loaned it to you."

"Then it still belongs to you?"

"It most certainly does!"

"And you will let me borrow it a little longer?"

"With great pleasure."

For a few moments I saw him rummaging among the left-overs of old tubes and old brushes on a small table in the corner until he produced an old cork.

"I will just cheat the creditors out of the cork," he said, putting it on top of the steel needle, so as not to hurt the point, "and out of the copper plate. They won't notice the difference, and if they do, well, then, they can put me in jail for it. But I have got to have something to make me pull through the next few weeks." And he slipped the needle and the copper plate into his pocket.

I picked up his satchel and carried it down stairs. There was a knock at the door. I opened. Two men in black capes were standing on the stoop. I asked them their business.

"We are from the Bankruptcy Court and have come to make an inventory," they answered.

"Isn't that rather soon?" I asked them.

"Yes," they replied, "but some of the creditors are afraid that if we are not quick, part of these belongings might disappear."

To my intense horror, I noticed that Rembrandt was standing right behind me. It was impossible that he should not have heard that last remark. I saw him take the small copper plate out of his pocket and hold it out to the oldest of the two men.

"You were right," he said, "I was on the point of stealing this. You had better take it."

But the official shook his head.

"I know how you feel," he answered, with more consideration than I had expected. "I know exactly how you feel, sir. You are not the first man I have ever met under these unfortunate circumstances, and most likely you won't be the last. But cheer up and don't take it too much to heart. You are a famous man. A few years from now you will come back here riding in your own coach and four."

And he saluted the master most politely while he took a piece of paper and pencil out of his pocket and with a short, "I am sure you will pardon me," began to jot down:

"The entrance hall—one picture by—who is it?—one picture by Adriaen Brouwer representing—"

But I had quietly taken Rembrandt's arm and had pushed him toward the door.

For a moment we stood silently on the stoop, and then turned towards the left, carrying the heavy satchel between us.

Rembrandt never entered his house again.

Two years later it was sold to a shoemaker who turned it into two small apartments. One of these he kept for himself and the other he rented to a butcher. For all I know, they are living there yet. But I am not certain, for I have not set foot in the Anthonie Breestraat for more than ten years. A street or a house in which one has been happy becomes something very sacred. And when that happiness has departed, there remains nothing but a melancholy memory. And one should not spend too much time among the dead. The living need us so much more.

Chapter 65

OUR FUGITIVES FROM THE SPANISH INQUISITION SHOW THAT THEY WERE INTELLIGENT AND EAGER PUPILS AND YOUNG BARUCH D'ESPINOZA IS FORCED TO LEAVE AMSTERDAM

The month of August of the year 1656 was one of endless blue skies and a brilliant white-hot sun. All day long, the green-pastured polders lay basking in her bounteous favors while the long twilight of the evening invited the soul to contemplate the mysteries of existence in a spirit of such philosophical resignation that one felt almost inclined to accept life at its face value and declare in favor of happiness as against worry and doubt.

I have forgotten the exact date but it was sometime during the last week of that month of August that my son and I were sitting on the stoop of our house on the Houtgracht and were talking of nothing in particular when we suddenly received a visit from Baruch d'Espinoza. Young Spinoza (for that extra "e" had proved a little difficult for our Dutch tongues and Spinoza seemed quite sufficient for all practical needs) —young Spinoza had never been at my house before. I had often met him at Menasseh's, where he used to drop in at all hours of the night to smoke a pipe of tobacco (of which pastime he was inordinately fond)—to listen to the conversation, and perhaps, if any suitable opponent were present, to play a few games of chess.

Since the days of Saskia's death when I had tried to teach the game to Rembrandt (who, however, had no brain for anything mathematical) I had not touched either pawn or knight. But especially after the disastrous collapse of my hospital plans, I had begun to find a certain relaxation in games of that sort and Spinoza and I had spent many nights over the austere board of ivory that was one of the show-pieces of Menasseh's simple household. I had come to like that young Jew with the melancholic eyes, offset by a merry and somewhat mocking twinkle, but I was a great deal older than he and his Dutch was not very good and I knew neither Spanish nor Portuguese while Spinoza was ignorant of English. Hebrew, Chaldean and Syrian were not exactly convenient vehicles for the interchange of ideas and we therefore had to fall back upon Dutch with a little French and Latin to help us over the rough places. But we had never been very intimate and I was therefore somewhat surprised to see him appear at that hour of the day and a little puzzled by his earnest mien, for as I just said, it was one of those rare evenings when everything is peace and harmony.

However, I was sincerely glad to see him and bade him be seated while my son would get him a pipe of tobacco from my study. But he said no, he had come to consult me, he wanted to see me professionally, and could I spare him a moment?

Of course I could and so we entered the house and I showed him the way to my work-room. As soon as we had entered, Spinoza took off his cloak and his coat and opened up his shirt.

"I wish you would have a look at me, Doctor," he said. "I tried to get a book out of a trunk in the attic and in the dark I ran up against something and hurt myself, I am afraid."

"A strange attic, my young friend," I answered him, "for it is now eight o'clock and it won't be dark before ten."

He hesitated a moment and then replied, "My mistake. Please pardon me, I meant the cellar." And at this clumsy fib we looked at each other and both burst out laughing. At that moment the difference in years, that had stood between us like a granite barrier, melted away like anger before a kind word and from that moment on we were the best and most cordial of friends.

"I am a very poor liar," Spinoza apologized. "We were brought up very strictly and lying was considered the worst offense next to working on the Sabbath day. As a result, I cut a very poor figure in polite society since half our conventional conversation consists of little white lies. But please don't talk about what has happened to me. It is true that I ran into something, but it was a knife. I want to know how much harm the fellow has done. He has cut my cloak rather badly and the knife may have been poisoned."

I opened his shirt a little wider but found only a slight abrasion of the skin but no blood. All the same and in order to be entirely on the safe side, I cauterized the wound and then bandaged it. When I had helped him back into his coat he picked up his cloak.

"A good job for a tailor," I said, pointing to the rent in the right shoulder.

"No," he answered, "I think that I will keep this coat as a souvenir of my own people. It will probably be the last thing they will ever give me."

And at that remark the reaction set in and he turned pale and trembled a bit. "I never realized," he apologized, "that they felt so bitter about it." And he took the small glass of French brandy which I hastily handed him (a special bottle which I kept in my work-room for just such emergencies), swallowed it at one gulp, choked a little, and said, "I will be all right now," but I begged him to stay, and we returned to the stoop (my son had gone back to his plans for a mustard-grinding mill upon which he had been working furiously ever since the beginning of summer) and we sat and smoked and talked of what a strange world it was in which people would try and murder their neighbor for no more serious reason than that they held different opinions upon subjects which forever must remain a matter of taste and a question of personal preference.

At the same time I felt greatly incensed that such a thing could have happened right in the heart of our beloved town of Amsterdam. Our city was comparatively free from murder and violence. Of course, with a large floating population of sailors and with immigrants and political refugees from every part of the world there was a certain amount of shooting and stabbing. But Their Lordships of the Criminal Court had eyes that saw everything and arms that reached far and fingers that never let go of anything that had come within their grasp. They were no spoil-sports. Neither did they believe in bringing about the Kingdom of Heaven by a set of paper laws. A certain amount of drinking and feasting was bound to go on in a port where sailors who had spent seven or eight months at sea would arrive with their pockets bulging with ducats and their souls starving for a little excitement. But no matter how these unfortunate wretches intended to amuse themselves or how drunk they meant to get before they once more fell into the hands of the ever-watchful crimps, there must be no outward disturbance of peace and order and those who upon rare occasions forgot themselves so far as to hit their opponents with a stone jar or slash them across the face with their clasp knives, could count themselves fortunate if they escaped with their lives and were merely condemned to spend four or five months rasping Brazilian wood in one of the local prisons.

As for premeditated murders, I don't believe they happened oftener than once every three or four years. And here I was sitting face to face with a harmless young Talmud scholar who had just shown me a scar on his chest as evidence that he had been the victim of an attempt at assassination.

It was very puzzling and even after Spinoza had told me the cause, I felt deeply angered, for if once we decided to overlook such an occurrence, no one could foretell what the end might be. I therefore refused to give him my word that I would not mention the episode to any one. As a surgeon I was under oath to make a report of every case of violence that came under my observation, but I compromised in so far that I promised not to bring the matter to the attention of the chief of police, who was reputed to have the delicacy of touch of a sledge-hammer, but that I would carry it directly to one of the Burgomasters and let him decide what steps should be taken to prevent a repetition of such an outrage.

In order to take no further risks, I kept Spinoza at my house that night, where he slept on a cot in my work-room, and early the next morning I presented myself at the house of Cornelis de Graeff and asked an immediate audience. I found His Lordship still in his dressing-gown and slippers having his breakfast.

"A man of my age should take it a little more easily," he apologized. "I have given up eating anything at all at this early hour of the day and only take a cup of a new beverage my doctor has recommended in very high terms. It is made out of little beans which grow in Mexico and is called chocolate. Will you try some?"

I tried a cup which I found pleasant and palatable, though a little too rich to my taste and hardly the sort of thing on which to start the day if one tried to reduce one's weight. But I had come to discuss more serious matters than the diet of a middle-aged gentleman with a tendency toward a fatty degeneration of the heart. I had come to speak of something that went to the very root of our national existence. Did we in our Republic grant unto every one living peacefully within our gates and minding his own business the right to believe whatever he pleased, or did we not?

"In theory," His Lordship said, pouring out another cup of the steaming stuff, of which he seemed very fond, "in theory we don't and in practice we do. Or rather let me put it this way. Among all the nations of the earth, we seem to be the only one that gives dissenters at least what our English neighbors call a 'sporting chance.' We do not exactly invite them to build their churches within the heart of our cities, but if the Papists want to keep a little chapel of their own within stone throw of this house (as you and I and every man, woman and child in the whole city know they do), well, that is their business and provided they don't begin to hold a procession down the Singel and provided they don't try and blow the Town Hall up with gunpowder (as they tried to do in London), they will never be disturbed, as long as we have the present form of government.

"And the same goes for all the other sects. Baptists and Lutherans can't be appointed to office, that is all. For the rest, they are as free as a bird in the air. Even the Jews don't have to live in a ghetto. If nevertheless they stick together, they do so because they like each other's company, not because we make them. And now I suppose you will want to tell me about the case of young Spinoza. I know all about it. I had a report on it last night from the high sheriff. They even know who did it, but he had an accomplice who rowed him across the Amstel and he escaped. He will never dare come back. You can count on that. If he does, we shall hang him from the roof of the Town Hall with his mouth full of lard. I am a peaceful man but we must have law and order."

I thanked His Lordship for his consoling news. And then (though I was obliged to partake of a second cup of chocolate to prolong the interview) I asked him whether he knew anything of the cause of this most unfortunate incident and whether he meant to take measures to prevent a recurrence of such an outrage.

"The usual course," His Lordship answered. "When I had the pleasure of seeing you here last, I told you that I am not without influence within this community, but that I keep aloof from everything that smacks of theology. Then you wanted me to do something for your friend Rembrandt and I said, 'No. He is in the bad graces of the dominies. I shall leave him severely alone.' Now you ask me what I intend to do with young d'Espinoza. Nothing! I shall do just exactly nothing. He left his own church and his own people, for which I for one most assuredly do not blame him. He told the Rabbis quite plainly that they were blind, trying to lead the blind, a sentiment in which I happen to concur most cordially. He refused their offer to bribe him with an annuity if he would forswear his heresies, for which I admire him unreservedly. And when they excommunicated him—and by the way, I have a copy of that sentence of excommunication and I shall drop these worthies a hint to soften it considerably if they ever have another candidate for those uncomfortable honors—when they expelled him from their church, the young man behaved with the utmost dignity—did not try to defend himself—did not bring the matter to the attention of the Magistrates, but quietly withdrew from the public gaze and continued his studies without a word of comment or complaint."

"But surely," I argued, "if Your Lordship is animated with those lofty feelings of admiration of our unfortunate friend, he will take steps to protect him."

His Lordship picked up a small sheaf of papers.

"If it were a mere matter of dispute within the Jewish church itself, I surely would, but will you look at this."

I took the hefty document. It was a report written by a number of Protestant ministers whom the magistrate had consulted regarding the theological aspects of the case of which they must have been aware for quite a long time. The ministers, however, in their petition expressed themselves as in complete sympathy with the Rabbis. They declared that any one who doubted the physical existence of angels and who questioned the immortality of the human soul (as Spinoza had done), no matter to what faith he might otherwise claim to belong, should not be accorded further hospitality in a Christian city like Amsterdam.

They expressed the view that all this agitation was a direct result of the leniency with which the Magistrates had treated the nefarious disciples of that pernicious ex-Jesuit, known as René Descartes, and they suggested that Their Lordships back up the Rabbis in their demand that the culprit be brought to justice. I read the ten or twelve pages and silently handed them back to His Lordship.

"The same old story," I said.

"The same old story," he answered. "Always and everywhere, the same old story, the same little men with the same little minds, trying the same despicable tricks and as a rule, with the same degree of success."

"But surely you won't do what they ask you to?"

"Partly yes and partly no. A single Jew is not worth a riot. I am afraid in this matter I will have to act somewhat like the late Pontius Pilate.

But we can't afford the risk of a bloody uprising because of one honest man. I will see to it that nothing happens to your friend while he remains in town. Even now he is being guarded, though he may never know it. I have asked him to visit me here this afternoon. I will explain the situation to him. They tell me that he is reasonable as well as very intelligent. I shall request him to leave town for a short while. Merely in order to oblige us.

"There is a nice country place in Ouderkerk which belongs to Dirk Tulp, a son of your colleague, my esteemed colleague. He is married to one of those Burghs who are related to every one in town. Very respectable people and very intelligent and liberal. Dirk Tulp happened to visit me last week and I mentioned the difficulty to him. He told me that if the matter ever came to a head we could tell our young Jewish friend to come and visit him at Tulpenburg for a couple of months. The house is full of books on philosophy and mathematics. The air is healthy and the landscape, though a bit flat, is full of color and charm. Dirk has an excellent cook and is quite a connoisseur of tobacco. Could you imagine a more delightful spot in which to recuperate from the excitement of an excommunication and an attempt at assassination?

"You will tell me that I ought to stand up for my principles—that I ought to fight this battle unto the last ditch. If it were merely a question of principle, I would rather drown the whole city than give in, as I was all for doing six years ago. But no theological dispute on earth seems to me worth the bones of a single Amsterdam citizen. Our amiable friend will enjoy every possible protection as long as he is within our gates. No one shall touch a hair on his head or a penny of his patrimony. And in addition he will have several months' holiday with delightful friends."

"Yes," I interrupted, "that is all very well and no doubt Spinoza will agree that Your Lordship has acted in a most generous manner, but suppose he ever wants to come back?"

"Then he will take the first boat for Amsterdam and sail for home as quietly as if nothing had happened."

"And the Rabbis and the Dominies and all the rest of them?"

His Lordship turned the can with chocolate upside down and drained the last drop into his cup. "Two months from now," he said, "they will have found something else to get excited about. When wolves lose the scent of one victim, they turn on their heels and trot off in a different direction to look for some other wretch they can devour."

And with those words he bade me a good morning and went upstairs to prepare for the affairs of the day.

When I came home I told Spinoza what had passed between us and I found him quite well pleased.

"I am no martyr," he told me. "I never had the slightest inclination that way. I suppose I am too healthy for such a rôle. I want to laugh a great deal and work enough to support myself the rest of my days so that I can spend my evenings studying philosophy. That is a very simple program and Tulpenburg will serve my purpose quite as well or even better than most other places."

Early the next morning four soldiers of the guard and a corporal called for him and I accompanied him part of the way and when we came near the gate he invited us all in for a glass of beer, at which the honest soldiers, being staunch Calvinists and rather ashamed of the company they were obliged to keep in the execution of their official duty, looked decidedly uncomfortable. But in the end, they accepted and we spent an hour waiting for the boat, drinking rather bad beer and listening to a brilliant dissertation upon angling. For it appeared that this dangerous heretic was also a most accomplished fisherman and once this was known, the ice was broken and the soldiers lost all reserve and shyness and when the boat pulled out they waved their hats at him and gave him three hearty cheers.

And such was the departure into exile of that shy-looking youngster of whom I was to see so much during the rest of my days, who wanted to work, to be merry, and to philosophize.

A strange creed, but by no means a bad one.

Chapter 66

REMBRANDT SHOWS SIGNS OF BEGINNING OLD AGE

The greater part of the year '57 I spent with the fleet in different parts of the North Sea and the Baltic. My son proved himself a somewhat erratic but conscientious and trustful correspondent. His letters were not exactly samples of orthography and his style resembled that of an architect writing out specifications for a bricklayer, but as a rule he managed to tell me that which he thought would interest me and thus I was kept fairly well informed of what was happening to my own family and to that of our friend.

Hendrickje was still living at the Houtgracht. In the beginning I had been afraid that there might be trouble between herself and my own faithful Jantje. For servants as a rule do not take very kindly to those of their own class who are supposed to have done rather better in the world than they have themselves and are very touchy about any "uppishness" on the part of the latter. But in the first place, Hendrickje was the simplest of all people and the disaster that had overtaken her had made most people willing to forget that she was Mrs. van Rijn only by act of common courtesy and not in virtue of a stamped and sealed document handed to her by the register of the matrimonial records.

Besides, Jantje was a good soul and deeply devoted to the small bundle of clothes and smiles called Cornelia and the two women lived peacefully together beneath the same roof without ever causing the slightest amount of friction or jealousy. As for the two boys, they were so absolutely different that it was easy for them to remain on friendly terms. Titus stuck to his paint-box. And my own son stuck to his mills and his calculations and they met at meals and sometimes they took a walk together to the Diemermeer or to Ouderkerk (where Spinoza was still living with his friends, the Tulps, and where the boys were always certain of a free meal) but for the rest they left each other severely alone and caused very little trouble to their elders.

Rembrandt's position was a little more difficult. He had a good enough room in the Keyserskroon but he was lonely and he complained that he could not work. I offered to fix up my workroom for him as an atelier, but he complained that the light was wrong and that he could not use it and then he had once more met the little shyster lawyer who had been his adviser in the matter of the transfer of his house to Titus (that very questionable affair that had almost got him into jail), who apparently had told him with a great ado of words that he need not have been in such a hurry—that he had a perfect legal right to stay in his house until the day before the sale was actually going to take place and being nervous and dispirited, he had believed the fellow and had gone to see de Dekker and Francen to ask them why they had told him to do a thing he had never wanted to do, and he had been quite disagreeable about it.

To which they had answered him quite truthfully that they had only taken him away so soon because they were afraid that further residence in the house would expose him to a great deal of unnecessary suffering and that furthermore, the sale of his goods might begin at almost any moment and then he would have been obliged to leave under even more harrowing circumstances.

But he refused to believe them—vaguely talked of a plot (what sort of a plot he did not explain) and locked himself in his room for days at a time—drinking a great deal more than was good for him and alternately spending entire days in his bed or working at his etchings with such uninterrupted violence that he was beginning to experience trouble with his eye-sight. The latter piece of information did not in the least surprise me for there is no greater strain on the eyes than scratching tiny lines onto a shining plate of copper by the flickering light of a candle.

Fortunately the next letter brought better news.

Rembrandt had left his hotel and would not return there until immediately before the sale of his furniture and his art treasures. He had at last accepted my offer to come and live in my study and was painting again. As soon as he had once more felt a brush in his hand, most of his worries had dropped away from him like the water that drops from the back of a duck. He no longer drank gin to forget his worries. He was extremely sober, as he had always been in the past but he continued to complain that he was not feeling quite well and he was worried about the sale of his belongings. At least once a week he would send Titus or my son to the office of the Bankruptcy Court to ask when the sale would begin and invariably he got the answer: "Not yet. A few weeks more. The times are bad. We must wait until the war is a little further behind us and then we shall get better prices."

And he had to wait all this time in miserable uncertainty, for the only way in which he could hope to escape his bondage was by means of that sale. If it brought enough, he would be able to pay his creditors and would be discharged by the court. If it did not produce enough, he would continue to be a bankrupt and every portrait he painted and every etching he made would belong to his creditors.

Finally, in the fall of '57, the commissioner appointed Thomas Jacobszoon Haringh to start the sale as soon as convenient. Rembrandt once more moved to the Keyserskroon and waited. But the first bids showed that the public had not yet recovered from the ravages of the recent conflict and after a week, Haringh went to the commissioners and suggested that the bulk of the articles be reserved until next year when there would be a chance of them selling at double and triple the amount they brought now.

The commissioners acceded to this request and the paintings and drawings and etchings which Rembrandt had collected with such great care and discrimination and at such tremendous outlay of money, went back to the store house.

Meanwhile the creditors continued to hold unofficial meetings and devised innumerable little tricks that should put them on the preferred list. But of all this I know nothing except the few odds and ends of gossip that I picked up talking to my friends. As far as Rembrandt was concerned, that part of his life was over—was dead and buried—was forgotten as if it had never been. He knew what his collection was worth and felt certain that with the efficient handling of Haringh, who was a personal friend of his, it would produce much more than he owed. If the creditors therefore would stop bothering him, so that he could do his work in peace and make a few extra guilders for Hendrickje and the children, all the rest would come out all right, but they must wait—they must wait and not bother him, bother him morning, noon and night.

He finally grew so exasperated at the continued interruptions he was forced to suffer from the side of his tormentors, that he asked Jantje not to open the door unless she had first made certain that the person who called was a personal friend and did not belong to the dunning guild. And in that way, the spring of '58 went by and affairs in the North were hastening to their final conclusion and as for the moment I had done all I could possibly hope to do, I returned to Amsterdam and found my house occupied by a happy little family, Rembrandt painting and Hendrickje busy with Cornelia and doing as many of the chores as she was able to do (for she remained ailing most of the time) and my son working on a project for a sailing-carriage that should be quite unlike that of Stevin in that it also would be able to navigate against the wind, and Titus coloring pretty little pictures which unfortunately did not show a great deal of originality.

We let the boys sleep in the attic (a change which delighted them) and I took their room and the next day after dinner I had a long talk with Rembrandt and listened to his complaints. For that interminable year of enforced idleness and waiting had done him little good and when he first opened his heart to me, it seemed as if he were suffering from every disease ever known to Galen or Hippocrates. His head ached. A million little ants were crawling up and down his arms. His fingers tingled as if they had been frozen. When he sat still for ten minutes, his feet would fall asleep. He had pains in his back and in his chest and was sure he was going to die of the same disease that had taken Saskia to her grave. But what worried him most of all was the strange notion that there was something the matter with his bones, that they were, as he himself called it, "melting away" and that some day soon he would not have any bones at all—that he would collapse in the street and would be carried home dead.

Where and how and from whom he got the idea that such a disease existed, I do not know unless he had heard it from some itinerant quack on the market-place who might have tried to frighten his audience with the old stories about the "pulverized man" to sell them his "Elixir Ossificationis."

I soon realized that nothing was the matter with the poor patient except a too sedentary life—too much loneliness—the bad habit of eating indifferent food at irregular hours—and as a result, a tendency to meditate a little too consistently and too profoundly upon his own pains and woes. But I knew from practical experience that it would do me no good to tell him, "Cheer up, my friend, all this is imagination pure and simple. A few days of fresh air and sunshine and you will be well again." I hoped to be able to cure him but I could not begin to do this until the sale of his possessions should have become an accomplished fact and he had been definitely discharged from all further obligations and in the second place until he had had some great new success—until some token of recognition on the part of the public at large had made him feel that after all he counted for something in the hearts of his neighbors and had not been forgotten by them as completely as he now thought.

In the meantime I could only mark time and pray that his profound melancholic moods would not drive him to suicide. I watched him very carefully. I accompanied him whenever he went out for a walk or sent my son to go with him. In the beginning I also suggested that he join Jean-Louys when the latter went forth again upon one of his famous sailing expeditions but I soon had to give this up as Rembrandt detested life on board ship as much as he had always done and complained that he would rather sit in jail (but only on dry land) with the worst bore in the world than listen to the wittiest conversation of the most brilliant Frenchman alive, if he were obliged to go to sea to hear it.

Jean-Louys, on the other hand, declared that he had never quite understood why he had been born until that former galley-slave had initiated him into the secrets of navigation. And as for me I divided my Sundays between walks to Watergraafsmeer and along the Amstel, and trips on the Zuyder Zee and meanwhile I waited and Rembrandt waited and Hendrickje waited and we all waited until finally in the fall of the year '58, exactly two years after he had first been declared a bankrupt, the last chest and the last picture and the last etching press and the last half dozen chairs were auctioned off and were removed from the Keyserskroon by their new owners.

The famous collection of etchings of Dutch and French and Italian and German etchers, which he had been collecting with such great discrimination for at least twenty years (for he had bought the first ones when he was a mere boy) were offered to the public on the 24th of September of that same year. Then the book-keepers of the Bankruptcy Court got busy and a few weeks later we were able to compare figures.

According to Rembrandt himself (but he was a most unreliable guide in all matters pertaining to finance) he had spent between 30,000 and 35,000 guilders to buy all these treasures. According to the estimate of the officials of the Court (who as a rule are very conservative in such matters) the sale ought to have produced approximately 13,000 guilders, which would have been enough to satisfy at least the most clamorous of the creditors and give Rembrandt a chance to begin again without any further obligations. And according to the balance sheet that was produced after everything had been sacrificed, Rembrandt had realized a trifle less than 5,000 guilders or about one seventh of his original investment.

The house had fared a little better. Liven Symonse, the shoemaker who bought it, paid 11,000 guilders for it. And of these 11,000 guilders Titus' relatives (after a terrific legal battle) salvaged 7,000 guilders for their young nephew who now had a regular guardian (a certain Jan Verwout, a very decent fellow, by profession and inclination a clerk) but who throughout all this remained pathetically loyal to the man who according to his mother's relatives was a mere spend-thrift and good-for-nothing paint-slinger, but according to himself, the best and kindest father that any boy had ever had.

Chapter 67

HENDRICKJE GOES INTO BUSINESS

The situation, instead of having been improved by this painful sacrifice, had become considerably worse. The creditors were still hanging around outside my door and with the persistence of wolves they besieged my house day and night to see whether Rembrandt had perhaps painted another picture which they could then attach and claim as their own. I knew two of the members of the Bankruptcy Court and went to see them and I found that they understood and even sympathized with our position but it was absolutely impossible for them to suggest a way out.

Our nation, when it turned its back upon the ancient faith, had abolished the old saints, but their place had been taken by a new celestial spirit, and the name thereof was "Respect for Property." Little children no longer prayed to the holy men and women of a by-gone age who had taught them "Thou shalt love" but reverently bowed their knee before the image of an austere and relentless God who spake, "Thou shalt possess."

Whether this change had been a change for the better or a change for the worse, I cannot here decide. I will merely say that it had taken place and that those who failed to take account of the existence of this deity were most severely punished.

Rembrandt, driven by his inner urge to create—a man mad with painting—who could see things that no human being before him had ever suspected, had alas been blind when he passed the temple of the new deity to which the faithful hastened at every hour of the day and at many hours of the night.

He had been punished.

He had been cast out. And he would never (of that, alas! I felt convinced with absolute certainty) be able to rehabilitate himself in the eyes of the respectable part of society.

The problem that had faced those of us who loved him in spite of his many failings (and perhaps a little on account of them) was this—how could we make the rest of his days tolerably happy? And then, when none of us seemed to know quite what to do, it was the faithful Hendrickje who showed us the way out of our dilemma.

She was not at all well. Adversity had struck her a terrible blow and she was failing fast. Rembrandt thought that he was a very sick man and on the point of dying and he was forever telling Hendrickje what she ought to do for Titus and for little Cornelia when he should be gone, but I knew that he would survive her for a long time, while she, who never complained, had at the very most three or four more years to live.

I think that she realized this herself but she was a woman of incredible courage. There was not a task in the house she considered too much for her. She took care of little Cornelia. She cooked for Rembrandt and Titus, refusing to let my own Jantje do this for her. She repaired their clothes and knitted their stockings for them and she kept tract of every cent that came into the house, though how she managed to hide these few poor pennies from the ever-present eyes of the hungry creditors is more than I can understand.

And then one evening she came forward with a plan. She asked whether she could speak to me alone for a moment and of course I said yes and as it was a pleasant night in June (we used to have two or three pleasant days every June, but the rest of the month it would usually pour) I took her out into the garden and there she told me what she wanted to do.

"That poor man," she said, "ought never to be trusted with another stiver. He is blind when it comes to money. His mind is on other things. He would give away his last shirt or exchange his only pair of breeches for a picture he saw if he should happen to want it at that particular moment. I never really was happy in that big house. It was too grand and too rich for me. I did not belong there. I was always afraid that I would break something and in the end, there was hardly room for one to sit down. Besides, I never knew what he would bring home next. It makes me feel uncomfortable to think how we are abusing your hospitality, but for the rest I have never been as happy as I am right now. Only, I know, that as soon as Rembrandt gets discharged by the Court, he will go right back to buying things. Not because he wants them—it is so hard to explain this. The things themselves mean nothing to him—it is not that. But they seem to fill a gap somewhere—they are bits of upholstery for his mind—and when it comes to his work, he is in some ways the strangest man I ever knew and some ways, the weakest.

"And so perhaps it is just as well that for a short while at least he should stay where he is at present. Only he must go back to his painting and etching or he will die. And what I have been thinking about is this: suppose that Titus and I started a little art store of our own and then hired Rembrandt to work for us—paid him just as a carpenter pays the assistants he hires or a bricklayer. One of my own brothers is a mason and hires two men to help him and one of those once had trouble with his wife who tried to attach his wages and then the judge said she could not do it and that is how I happened to think of it.

"Of course, Titus is still very young and I don't know anything about pictures, but you could help me or Francen or de Jonghe or some of his other friends, but I wish you would think of it and perhaps ask a lawyer and see whether we could not do something of that sort, and then we could once more have a place of our own, for we have put you to all this inconvenience quite long enough."

I took both her hands and assured her that she could stay until the end of her days and at the same time I was deeply touched not only by the kindness of her heart and her loyalty but also, I might as well confess it, by the clear common sense of her suggestion.

The next day being Sunday, I asked Rembrandt to take a walk with me to the Overtoom where I had not been since that memorable day in the spring of '50 when I had seen the Prince of Orange there, trying to find out with his bamboo cane whether the water was rising.

We took some bread and cheese with us, for I knew that Rembrandt felt embarrassed every time I was obliged to make some small extra expense on his account and he would not have liked it if we had gone to an inn.

We sat by the side of the canal and watched little white clouds that looked like sheep placidly grazing in an enormous blue pasture and I delivered myself of a short speech I had carefully prepared that morning. For I knew that Rembrandt had an almost physical aversion to any concrete discussion of his painful financial situation, but the thing simply had to be done if we were ever going to get him back on his feet. And upon this occasion too, as soon as he noticed what direction the conversation threatened to take, he took a small sketchbook out of his pocket and fished around for a piece of crayon. But I said, "Never mind, those sketches can wait until some other time. Suppose you listen for a moment now to what I have to say. I am not going to preach to you. I just want to see whether we can't find some way out which will allow you to go back to work."

At once he became suspicious.

"You mean to say that I have abused your hospitality long enough?" he asked, stiffening up.

"Rembrandt," I said, "you are a full-grown man with a son who will need a razor ere long. Now don't behave like a child. These years have been damnably hard on you and I don't blame you if your nerves are a bit frayed. As far as I am concerned, you can stay until you die, and you know it."

"Of course," he answered, "I am sorry, but I feel as if I were locked up. My head is full of ideas. They seem to come faster than ever. I need space. I need a room of my own in which I can putter around. You know that sometimes I find it difficult not to shriek when I have done a bit of work on a plate and want to try and find out what it looks like— just one proof would be sufficient—but all I can do is mess it up with a bit of black and then wait until two or three days later when some friend is perhaps kind enough to let me use his press for a few minutes. And I can't turn your house into a workshop. The smell of paint and the smell of acid would be all over the place. Your patients would stay away. They would think you were busy cooking some evil poison. I don't know how I can ever thank you for all you have done for us—"

"You can thank me," I interrupted him, "by listening for about ten minutes and keeping your mind on what I am going to say."

"Very well," he said, "I will be good." And he closed the sketchbook and put it back again into his pocket.

"Well, then," I said, "we know where you stand financially."

"I would hardly call that standing!"

"Never mind such details. And I am not going to talk economy to you. It would not do any good. If you were the sort of person who could keep his accounts straight, you probably would be a book-keeper at the West India House to-day instead of being—"

"Yes. Instead of being what?" he interrupted me.

"Instead of having painted a few pictures that the world will recognize—"

"That the world will recognize three hundred years after I am dead."

"Perhaps, and perhaps sooner. What your friends want to do is to get you back to a place of your own where you can work."

"But what would be the use of my working? As soon as I had finished a picture, Hertsbeeck or de Coster or Ornia or one of those noble patriots would appear with an order from the Court and would carry it away under his arm. The Court would credit me for a few guilders (they never pay me the full price) and twenty years from now I would still be in debt."

"That is just what we want to prevent, or rather Hendrickje, for she it was who thought of the idea. We will help you. But let us start from the beginning. I don't want to criticize you, but I don't think you were very happy in the choice of your lawyer."

"He seemed a nice fellow."

"Perhaps so, but that does not quite make him a good lawyer. How did you get him?"

"Oh, a man who stopped and looked at a picture I was drawing of the South Church and with whom I happened to get into conversation (he was born in Hazerswoude and had known one of my father's aunts—she was quite an old woman when she died)—he told me about him and gave me his address."

"An excellent recommendation! And when did this happen?"

"When I had that trouble with Geertje's brother."

Here was something that was news to me. I asked him what that trouble had been and when it had taken place.

"Well," Rembrandt said, "you remember that nurse I had when Saskia died?"

"I am afraid that I shall never be able to forget her."

"Yes, she was pretty bad. But I felt sorry for her. Then afterwards I had to send her to Gouda, to an asylum. And I promised to pay for her keep. Anything to be rid of her! I was very busy at that time. She had a brother Pieter and he took her down to Gouda. I gave him quite a sum of money. In those days my credit was good and I could raise as much as I wanted to. Well, two years ago, just before all this happened, I thought that I would try and get some of it back. The fellow refused to pay me. Perhaps I had no right to ask for it. I went to see that lawyer. He found out that the brother was in Amsterdam. He was a ship's carpenter and on the point of sailing to India. He was afraid that he would try and get away and we had him put in a debtor's prison. It was foolish of me. But I was in a terrible state just then. And I had come to hate that woman until I was glad to be nasty to her brother. Nasty is the word. I am not very proud of what I did. Then Francen got me a decent lawyer—Arnout Vingboom—you know him. He got the case straightened out.

"Then it is 'out' now—straight or crooked but 'out'?"

"Absolutely out."

"And there are no other troubles, no further lawsuits? No cases in court?"

"None. Except those in the Chamber of Horrors."

"Very well," I answered, and then I explained what Hendrickje had suggested. "It seems an excellent idea to me," I finished. "What do you think of it?"

He sat silent for a while and picked up a few pebbles that were lying in the grass and threw them into the water.

"Funny," he said at last. "And that is the woman whom they did not think fit to partake of Holy Communion."

"That is something else again," I suggested.

"Yes," Rembrandt said. "That is something else again. Of course I accept. Let us go home and tell her. And to-morrow I can begin working again."

Chapter 68

HENDRICKJE AND TITUS FORM A PARTNERSHIP BUT ARE NOT VERY SUCCESSFUL

But he did not begin to work that next morning nor the next, nor for several weeks afterwards. For that evening Francen came in and he had still another plan that seemed almost as good as Hendrickje's.

"I thought of this," he told us, "the moment I left you yesterday. But let us place ourselves in the position of Rembrandt's creditors. What do they want? They want their money. How they get it is all the same to them provided they get it and get it fairly soon. Of course Rembrandt can go back to painting portraits. That is really his business, but portraits are slow work and now that everybody is either bankrupt through this damned war that has just come to an end, or afraid to spend a stiver, through fear of the next one, the portrait business will hardly be profitable. I know that I myself have not sold a picture for almost two years. But I have sold a whole lot of etchings during that same period. Etchings are the thing for the present. Twenty years ago, it was tulips. To-day it is etchings. Not because most of the people who buy them like them particularly. They never even look at them. But they have heard of others who bought an etching for a few pennies and sold it the next day for hundreds of guilders and they hope that they will be equally lucky. There always has been a demand for Rembrandt's etchings. Even when people no longer liked his paintings (I don't mean to hurt his feelings, but he will know what is in my mind)—even when he painted pictures they could not quite follow—they could not quite understand—they paid good prices for his etchings. Now what I would like to know is this: what has become of the plates?"

"I don't know," Rembrandt answered. "They were sold. Mostly to local art-dealers."

"You could find out to which ones?"

"I think we could," Hendrickje said. "Titus kept a list of them."

"Well," Francen continued, "they won't be of much value to them. They can have others make prints off them, but that is never quite the same as when the artist does them himself. We ought to be able to get those plates back. We may have to pay something for them, but in the past these fellows have made a lot of money out of you, for whenever you wanted one of their antiques, they would ask you anything that came into their heads and you would pay it. Perhaps we can make an arrangement by which we promise to pay them a small royalty for every print. But we ought to get them. A few days ago I heard just by chance where

520

we can get a good press for very little money. It belonged to some one who has given up etching and has taken a job as a servant."

"Not Piet de Hoogh?" Rembrandt asked.

"No, some one nobody ever heard of. He had bought himself a press when etchings became fashionable. Hoped to make a lot of money easily. Found it would take him at least ten years to learn to turn out something that could be sold to the public and was glad to be offered fifty guilders a year as butler with a family on the Heerengracht. Anyway, it means that we can lay our hands on a first-rate press for about sixty guilders. I will buy it and donate it as my contribution to the new venture. To-morrow Rembrandt can go and look for a place to live that will have some sort of a room that can be fixed up as a studio. Hendrickje meanwhile can buy beds and sheets and a few pots and pans and Titus and I will make the rounds of the art-shops and see what we can do about the old plates."

"And I?" I asked. "What shall I do?"

"For the moment," Franceen said, "you shall take it easy. You have done quite enough as it is. Unless you want to ask Vingboom when he can give us a little of his time, and then I will take those three innocent babes to see him and have a regular contract drawn up. This is beginning to sound like one of those plays of Joost Vondel in which Virtue appears at the end of each act to offer us her bright consolation. And now, if the doctor will send out for a mug of beer, we will drink to the health of the new firm, 'van Rijn, van Rijn and Stoffels.'"

I thought the occasion was worthy of something better than mere beer and went into the cellar myself to get one of my few remaining bottles of papish wine. And going down the narrow stair-case I bumped my head, as I had done these last twenty years, and I swore and stopped to rub the sore spot, and standing there in the dark and thinking of what I had just seen and heard, it struck me that the situation would have been more fit for the pen of gruesome Aeschylus than that of our own amiable Vondel.

The greatest painter of his time being kept out of the poor-house by the combined efforts of a sick girl who had nothing in this world beyond her beauty and her kind heart and a boy of sixteen or seventeen, who loved his father and who would probably die as soon as Nature, in the pursuit of her own mysterious purposes, had driven him into the arms of a woman.

Then I got the bottle I had promised to bring up and we spent a happy hour, talking of the future.

It was the first time I had seen either Hendrickje or Rembrandt smile for more than two years.

Chapter 69

THE VAN RIJN FAMILY FINDS A NEW HOUSE

The first thing for us to do was to get the permission of Titus' guardian, for his affairs were by now so hopelessly interwoven with those of his father that the latter could not take a step without being taken to task both by the members of the Court of Bankruptcy and those of the Chamber of Orphans.

Verwout had soon discovered that he was too busy to devote the necessary time to the case and he had been succeeded by a certain Louis Crayers, whom I had never met before but who sent me a brief but courteous note saying that he would be glad to see me and my friends the next Friday at eleven in the morning. Abraham Francen and I, however, had agreed that nothing is ever accomplished in this world by committees and we decided to do everything by ourselves. Then when the arrangements should have been completed, we could tell the others what had been done and ask them to give the new household such help as they thought fit.

At the appointed hour we were ushered into Crayers' office. We found him very busy so that he could not spare us a great deal of his time, but he was an easy man with whom to transact business, for he went right to the point and treated the whole affair as if it were merely a problem in mathematics, which indeed it was.

"Gentlemen," he said, "I hope that you will understand my position. I have given my word—and an oath before that court means an oath, let me assure you!—that I would protect this boy's interests to the best of my ability. Besides, I like the young man. I am sorry he is not a little stronger physically, but his mother was very delicate, so they tell me, and he seems to take after her more than after his father. All the same, I have rarely seen such a pleasant and affectionate relationship as exists between van Rijn Sr. and his son. As for the father, I never knew him very well but in my spare time I sometimes buy a few etchings. No, I am not just keeping up with the fashion. I was collecting etchings when most of the people who are buying them nowadays were making ten stivers a day digging ditches out there in the new part of the town. I am too busy a man to give much of my time to the arts, but I recognize the genius of the older van Rijn. A little too muddy for my taste in some of his pictures, but when he is at his best, I don't know any one who is better. But when it comes to business, may God have mercy upon me for the language I used when I first studied the documents in this case!

"I don't want to sound harsh, but in this instance it would have been infinitely better for the boy—of course, I am speaking strictly from a business point of view for I know how devoted he is to his father—but looking at the matter in a less romantic way, it would have been infinitely more advantageous for him if his father had died instead of his mother. But that is neither here nor there. The mother is gone and we have to deal with the husband.

"You want to know what I think about your plans. Well, I am heartily in favor of them, provided the rights of my pupil are absolutely protected. That last point I can't insist upon strongly enough, for I don't think that old van Rijn will ever mend his ways, financially speaking—he is too old and even if he were twenty years younger, he would be just as bad. I just wish you had seen the mess I had to straighten out! It was absolute chaos.

"When the appraisers of the Bankruptcy Court went through that house, they collected three pailfuls of bills—old bills—new bills—paid bills—unpaid bills—protested bills. The house looked neat enough, so they told me, but in all the cupboards, behind the pictures and the mirrors, they found bills.

"But not only bills. What was infinitely worse, they discovered almost as many notes and drafts and checks, all made out to Rembrandt and which he had never taken the trouble to present and turn into cash. They even found a dozen envelopes and a few small bags containing money which he had put somewhere and then had forgotten all about—just plain carelessness. Of course I tried to collect some of this paper, but in many instances, the people were dead, had been dead for years or had moved away and could not be traced. The amount we lost that way must have run into several thousand guilders.

"Under ordinary circumstances, I would call this 'negligence' and with any other man I would have thought of bringing the matter to the attention of the Court. But van Rijn is not an ordinary man. He lives in an imaginary world of his own and has no sense for the realities of life. For example, I asked him whether he still had any relatives from whom he might expect to inherit something. He said yes, there was a grandson of his aunt, a certain Piet van Medemblick, from whom he would probably get several thousand guilders when he died, for so at least he had been told by one of his brothers the last time he saw him.

"I looked into the matter and found that he had spoken the truth. He was to inherit some money from this distant—well, let us call it cousin. But I also discovered that this mysterious cousin, his father's sister's son's son, as he was called in the official documents, had taken service on board a ship that had sailed for the Indies at some unknown date early in this century and that the ship on which he traveled was reported to have sunk off the coast of Portugal three weeks after it had left Texel; that during the last 45 years, not a word had been heard from this Piet van Medemblick, but that according to the law as interpreted by the municipal courts of Leyden, the man could not be officially declared 'dead' until at least half a century after he had first disappeared; that therefore the heirs would get nothing until the year 1665 and that even then, with all the accumulated interest, van Rijn's share would probably not exceed 800 guilders. A rather vague prospect, as you will see for yourself and yet he was firmly counting on 'the inheritance of my aunt's grandson' as if it were something tangible—a chest of pearls—sent to him by the Emperor of China.

"I shall support you, Gentlemen, in all you do for your friend (whom I bear nothing but good will out of respect for his great ability) and at the same time I shall use every means at my disposal to protect the interests of young Titus. Therefore whatever you do, I shall insist upon a contract, but for the rest, you will find that I am entirely on your side."

We thanked Crayers for his patience and courtesy and asked whether he had any suggestions to make about the contract.

"No," he answered, "it had better be a regular partnership contract. I have a friend, Notary Listingh, who does that sort of work for me and who is a very reliable man. Of course if you have some one you would rather suggest—"

But we assured him that we had no preference and agreed that the first thing to do now was to find a place where our friends could live—some sort of place that could be used as a shop and where Rembrandt could work. As soon as that should have been done, we would return to Crayers and ask him to make out the necessary papers. Then we made our adieux and began house-hunting.

But this proved to be no easy task. During the war, very little building had been done and as a result people were paying enormous prices for very inferior accommodations. They were living in old barns and in converted stables and in deserted cellars and attics and on the outskirts of the cities. A good many families were obliged to content themselves with such shelter as under normal conditions would not have been thought fit for pigs. At last we found something, but entirely through luck, the sort of luck that was (as is so often the case) somebody else's misfortune.

One day a young man came to me who told me that I had been recommended to him by a friend. He had got some dirt into a little open wound on his right hand and it had caused an infection and would I please oblige and open it for him, without hurting him too much and his name was Lingelbach—Joannes Lingelbach, and his father was a German from Frankfort-on-the-Main and he himself was a painter and he had worked in Italy and hoped to go to Paris where he heard there was a much better chance for painters than in Holland, and ouch! that hurt—but not as much as he had expected—and so on from the moment he came into the house until the time he left with his hand neatly bandaged and his arm in a sling.

Three days later he came back to let me change the bandage and by this time I had house-hunting on the brain and before he left me I asked Lingelbach whether he knew of any houses for rent anywhere and he answered, "Why, yes, of course I do. My father is the owner of the Labyrinth on the Roozengracht—at the end of the Roozengracht. You may know him? Old David Lingelbach? He used to manage the Orange Tree on the Looiersgracht twenty years ago, the first man to build a labyrinth in Amsterdam. Well, he had to break away several houses to make room for his present place but right opposite us there are three houses left, and one of them is free, at least half of it. I happened to see it yesterday."

"Is the rent very high?" I asked.

"I am going to have supper with the old man to-night," he answered, "and I will drop in and ask and let you know to-morrow."

The next day he brought me the information I wanted.

"It is only the left half of the house that is for rent," he said. "It has one large room and I had almost taken it myself—it has a fine big window on the north and would have made a wonderful studio. The other four rooms are much smaller and there is a kitchen and the rent is 150 guilders a year, but you may be able to get it for a little less. The landlord is called van Leest. He lives on the premises. I talked to him. He seemed a very decent sort of person—not the usual type. You had better go and see him for there are mighty few houses to be had in this town nowadays."

I took Rembrandt out to the Roozengracht late in the afternoon of that same day. Hendrickje said that she did not feel up to the walk and she remained at home, but on the corner of the St. Anthonie Lock we met Titus and my son, who were coming home together and they went with us.

We saw the house and we saw van Leest and we signed a lease then and there at a rental of 125 guilders a year.

A week later the van Rijn family moved into their new quarters.

All of the old friends had contributed something to their household. Francen gave them four beds, Dusart contributed the sheets and pillows, van den Eeckhout and Roghman looked after the kitchen utensils, Suythof took care of the tables and chairs and I presented him with the large brass chandelier that used to hang in my own room which he had used as his studio for almost two years, and to which he had become very much attached. We rented a cart and filled it with the pictures he was working on and as many of his copper plates as we had been able to get hold of and then we put Hendrickje on top of it, together with Cornelia (who by this time had grown big enough to be immensely pleased and greatly amused by this unexpected trip across town), and we drove them to their new home.

When we arrived, we found everything in terrible disorder, beds, tables, wash-basins and chairs all standing pell-mell in the front room, and sheets and pillows and pots and pans filling the sleeping quarters in a most picturesque and disharmonious fashion. We had expected to meet Rembrandt on the door-step, ready to welcome us, but we could not find him anywhere.

Then Hendrickje, inspecting her new domain, opened the door to the large room in the back of the house. Rembrandt was sitting in the center, right on the floor, in the most uncomfortable position imaginable, painting away for dear life at a large canvas that stood leaning against a barrel containing the family china.

"Oh," he said, without looking up. "Are you there? I hope you will pardon me, but the light was so good—I thought I had better begin."

"Yes, dear," said Hendrickje, "that is quite all right." And she came back to us and quietly started unpacking the small satchel containing Cornelia's clothes and toys.

Chapter 70

I PAY A VISIT TO A STRANGE COLONY OF PEOPLE WHO ACTUALLY THINK FOR THEMSELVES

I thought that I had better leave the van Rijns to their own fate for a while to give them a chance to become a little more accustomed to their new surroundings and meanwhile I gave myself a week's holiday and went on a trip which I had planned to take for quite a long time. I often was obliged to go to The Hague to see the Pensionary on business (he continued to give me his confidence in a most gratifying way) but I had not been in Leyden for years and now I meant to go there on an errand that was not wholly pleasant.

Also partly owing to the kind interest of My Lord Jan de Witt, the town council had once more paid some attention to my claim for the indemnity they had promised me at the time my little hospital was wrecked by the mob. But Burgomaster de Graeff was growing old and his influence was waning while that of his enemy and rival, the highly objectionable Valckenier, was waxing stronger every day. And Valckenier, who had come to power through his associations with the Church, was my sworn enemy and had repeatedly declared—both in private and in public—that as far as he was concerned, I would never receive a penny, for "so he reasoned" the fire that had destroyed my property was not "the work of men's hands but a direct manifestation of Jehovah's all highest displeasure."

When driven into a corner by the arguments of My Lord of Polsbroek, who reasoned that if this riot had been an expression of God's will, the magistrates of Amsterdam, who wanted to hang the ringleaders of this attack upon private property, would have been guilty of sacrilege (a line of reasoning bound to cause great discomfort to a greedy and selfish creature like My Lord Valckenier, who whenever there was the slightest disturbance in town caused both his houses to be guarded by the militia), this pugnacious official had thereupon completely changed his line of attack and had suggested that the question be decided merely upon its scientific basis and that the medical faculty of the University of Leyden be asked to submit a report upon "the desirability or otherwise of performing painless operations according to the method suggested by a certain well-known Amsterdam surgeon."

The motion had been put over for two weeks, in the hope that Valckenier would change his mind. Instead of which he called upon his followers to rally around him and they did this, partly by a series of sermons delivered in the principal churches of Amsterdam and extolling the sublime profits to be derived from physical pain and partly by staging three or four popular manifestations on the Dam right in front of the new Town Hall.

Why I suffered no personal violence during that period I do not know, but I rarely left my own street during those days, being hard at work upon plans for a new hospital as soon as I should have received my money from Their Lordships and I am proud and happy to say that my neighbors, without a single exception, were most loyal to me and upon one occasion at least came near to drowning two young hoodlums who had smeared my door full of red paint.

But "excitement" was the one thing no member of the government wished to see at that particular moment. There was a feeling of unrest all over the country. On the other side of the North Sea things were not going any too well from our point of view. The Lord Protector, Oliver Cromwell, had died in the year '58 of an intermittent fever, which his enemies declared to be the punishment of Heaven but which according to his friends had been brought about by the death of his daughter, to whom he was passionately devoted. His son Richard had succeeded him but he was not the man his father had been and after a few months, a revolution had broken out which had once more brought the House of Stuart to the throne of England. But on his way back to the country from which he had been absent for almost a dozen years, the new King paid a visit of state to our country, where he had been received with even more splendor than the old Queen Dowager of France, when she had deigned to honor our city with her presence in '38.

Those, however, who had come in personal contact with His Majesty felt serious forebodings for the future. And those who had been present when His Majesty was slightly under the influence of intoxicant beverages (the wet climate had probably forced him to drink a little more than he was accustomed to) all those dignitaries reported that he had spoken of his Dutch hosts in very unflattering terms as "those bastards who had been friendly to the murderers of his father" and "mean-eyed greengrocers who ought not to be tolerated in a world of gentlemen." And other sentiments a little less elegantly expressed but just as eloquent and ominous as the two examples I have just given.

And although His Majesty upon the occasion of his leave-taking at Scheveningen (His Majesty was entirely sober that morning and a little repentant for having seduced the daughter of the majordomo of the palace of the late Prince Maurice, which had been most graciously placed at his disposal when His Majesty reached The Hague) had delivered himself of a most gracious speech extolling the virtues of the noble land that was the home of his charming nephew (who, however, was not present upon this occasion, as My Lord de Witt had expressed a fear that the excitement of bidding farewell to his beloved uncle might have a bad influence upon the health of the young man, who was considered to be quite delicate) no one believed him when he proposed a toast to the "prosperity and happiness" of the country that would ever be the subject of his most sincere devotion and gratitude.

For as soon as the last sail had disappeared from sight, it became known in The Hague that His Majesty during his last interview with a financial deputation from among the members of the Estates General, had called them a lot of Shylocks (an expression which had greatly puzzled these worthies as none of them seemed to have ever heard of the works of William Shakespeare) and had broadly hinted at the revenge he would take upon their accursed land for having treated him quite so niggardly in the matter of his royal loans.

Every one in the Republic therefore felt that sooner or later we would be at war once more with England and under those circumstances, an outbreak of religious fanaticism was just about the last thing that was wanted. The more liberal-minded among the Magistrates therefore allowed themselves to be intimidated and the medical faculty of Leyden had been duly requested to favor Their Lordships of Amsterdam with an opinion upon the subject which I have just mentioned—should a surgeon actually try to alleviate the pain of those about to submit to an operation or was such a method opposed to the best traditions of surgical practice?

Now if this question had been asked fifty years before, I would not have been disturbed by the possibility of a negative answer. For the University of Leyden had been the creation of our great Prince William and his friend Coornhart, the Haarlem engineer and former secretary-of-state, both of whom were men of wide experience and a tolerant point of view.

But of the old academic freedom of spirit for which they had fought so bravely, very little remained in the year 1660 except the memory, and even that memory was held up to public scorn by the second-rate successors of the original founders.

Under those circumstances, I was greatly perturbed when I heard that my views upon the subject of anesthesia were to be submitted to a group of men who were sure to condemn them without ever taking the trouble of a thorough investigation, and I decided that I had better go to Leyden myself and try to save whatever I could save by a personal demonstration of my method and a general explanation of the motive that had inspired me to start such a line of investigation.

I went and I was politely enough received by my colleagues of the medical school, but when I was asked to appear in a full session of all the faculties (and the theological men were powerful enough to insist upon such a procedure) I at once noticed a spirit of deep hostility which boded little good for the future. And after I had listened to them for hours—to an endless series of quotations from the Bible, all of them expressing profound disapproval of any attempt to interfere with human pain and to an equally formidable list of passages from Hippocrates and Galen explaining that pain was a necessary and unavoidable concomitant of illness, I felt that my case was lost then and there and that I might just as well return to Amsterdam by the evening boat.

Nevertheless, I made one more effort and addressing myself to the Rector Magnificus, who was in charge of the University's policies for that year and who happened to be a surgeon like myself, I asked that I be not condemned on the ground of a few passages in books that had been written twenty centuries before, but that I be judged upon my actual performance. I told him that I had brought my apparatus with me and would be happy to give a demonstration of the excellent results that could be obtained by my method at any time, anywhere they decided. I would invite the members of the theological faculty to be present too, that they might judge for themselves whether the sight of a patient sleeping peacefully on his couch was not preferable to that of a poor wretch who would not only curse those who inflicted this pain upon him but who would also blaspheme the God who had ever allowed him to be born.

Finally the matter was put to a vote and a vast majority of those present pronounced themselves as opposed to "any further discussion of the matter" and in favor of "a written report that should be submitted to Their Lordships of Amsterdam in due course of time and after serious deliberation on the part of those who are entrusted with the care of the true principles of the Christian religion."

That was the end, and the meeting was adjourned and I was allowed to return to my room at the inn and await the departure of the first boat for Haarlem, which left at six the next morning.

And then there was a knock at the door and a stoop-shouldered man, dressed in a long black coat and his hat well down upon his eyes, entered and put both arms around me and saluted me most respectfully and most cordially, and of all the people in the world, I recognized young Spinoza, whom I had not seen for almost four years and from whom I had had practically no news ever since I bade him adieu on board the ship that carried him to his exile with his friends of Tulpenburg.

So, knowing his weakness, I ordered two pipes of tobacco and I also asked that a fire be made (my visitor had a cold and was coughing quite badly, a dry, racking cough which somehow frightened me) and then we sat down and talked and Spinoza told me all that had happened to him ever since he had been asked to leave the territory of our city.

That sentence of exile, as My Lord de Graeff had suggested to me before it was put into execution, had never been meant seriously. After spending three or four months with his friends at their home in the country, Spinoza had quietly returned to Amsterdam to find that nobody seemed to remember his case. He had been able to attend to all his personal affairs without in any way being molested by the authorities and had then returned to the country and (not wishing to be a burden to his friends) had taken a room in a farmhouse near Ouderkerk and had spent his time studying optics (a branch of science that had interested him ever since, as a boy, his parents had apprenticed him for a while to a glass polisher to learn the trade of grinding lenses for spectacles) and writing a treatise upon the colors of the rainbow while spending his leisure time reading the ancient philosophers.

But Ouderkerk had been a little too near to Amsterdam. There were a number of young men in the city with a tendency for spiritual hero-worship who had already proclaimed him their leader and that was just about the last thing he wanted to be.

"I have seen enough of Rabbis and Prophets," he said, "to last me for the rest of my days and I have no ambition to become one myself. An abstract idea, incorporated into a concrete system of thought, soon loses its value. It dies and becomes fossilized and while fossils may be interesting to antiquaries who study the condition of this earth thousands of years ago, they are of small use to those who live in the present. And why study philosophy if you do not mean to practice it while you are still on earth?

"And so, in order to escape becoming another Joshua or John the Baptist (not to mention poor Jesus," he added, "who spent all his life trying to escape a fate that his followers finally forced upon him) I went to Rijnsburg."

How had he happened to choose Rijnsburg?

"Well," he answered, "at the Tulps' I had met a great many Collegiants and I liked them. You know who they are?"

I did. Yes, in a rather vague way. Rembrandt's brother who had stayed with him a couple of years before had talked about them one evening and he had been quite scandalized. They were heathen, he had told us—pagans—they had no right to call themselves Christians—they had no ministers and listened to no sermons. He had wanted them all killed off, as the Anabaptists had been killed off a hundred years before. When the quarrelsome old man had gone to bed, Rembrandt had told me something more about them.

It seemed that a certain Mennonite preacher of whom he had made a portrait some twenty years before had been related to this sect and had told him a great deal about those strange people who were different from the rest of our Christian neighbors, in that they really tried to live like Christ himself. The sentence had struck into my mind and afterwards whenever the conversation drifted to the Rijnsburg community, I had always been careful to listen.

In the early part of the century, right after the Synod of Dordrecht, when those despicable quarrels took place that led to the execution of My Lord of Barneveldt and that put all power into the hands of a small group of Calvinists, certain dominies of Rijnsburg suspected of liberalism had been among those who were forced to abdicate on account of their principles. But Rijnsburg, a village about an hour from Leyden, had once upon a time been the seat of a famous abbey. When the Reformation abolished all such Popish institutions, the property as a whole had been taken over by the Estates of Holland, who ruled it independently as if it had been a piece of conquered territory, and this fact had made the sleepy little town a harbor of refuge for all those who elsewhere were being persecuted on account of their religious beliefs. And when the Synod forced the Estates to dismiss the Rijnsburg clerics who had dared to encourage the liberal movement in their city, two brothers by the name of van der Kodde, well-to-do and intelligent farmers, had begun to hold services of their own and no one had been able to prevent them because they were responsible to no magistrate and the Estates, having dismissed the local clergymen, felt that they had done enough for the time being and refused to take any further steps to oblige the Synod.

Every Sunday therefore in an old barn the friends of the Koddes had come together to listen to the reading of the Holy Scriptures (mostly of that part that I hold to be of any true value, the New Testament) and to join in a common prayer. After that they used to sit in absolute silence until one of those present felt that the Holy Ghost urged him to say something, when he got up and spoke what was on his mind and sat down again as soon as the inspiration ceased.

Such séances had been denounced by the dominies of Leyden as absolutely sacrilegious and they had preached a regular crusade against these dangerous heretics who lived without benefit of clergy, gave liberally to the poor and who in every possible way tried to follow the example of the earliest Christians in being kind and charitable and cheerful and in treating all men as their brothers.

But the authorities had been firm in defending the good right of those people to their own opinion and no one in Rijnsburg had suffered harm on account of his ideas. Gradually in other cities there had been similar small groups of people who thought and acted likewise and once or twice I had even heard of Collegiants meeting in Amsterdam.

In many ways therefore Rijnsburg was an ideal community for a man like Spinoza and I told him that I thought he had been very wise to go there and he agreed and then he said:

"I heard that you were here last night from my landlord, Doctor Hooman. He had been told that the people here were being urged to give you a good sound beating. So I thought I would come and try and see what I could do to help you (not much, I am afraid, but I am still deeply grateful to you for what you once did for me) and to ask you to come with me to Rijnsburg to-morrow. The Hoomans have a room for you. It is a very quiet place, but we can walk and talk about things. I have at last begun to write. That French baron, that friend of yours, was right. I only met him once and then he told me that the only practical way to reach a definite answer to any problem was the method known as the mathematical one. I am trying it out in my first book that discusses the methods I mean to employ in the others."

"And after that?" I asked.

"After that I mean to turn the whole of the universe into my private laboratory and investigate everything."

"A fine ambition," I answered. "You must be very happy. For only happy people set out to do the impossible."

But as it was very late, I made an end to the conversation, sent for the landlord, told him to prepare another room and the next morning, after a hearty breakfast and another pipe of tobacco, we set out for Rijnsburg and soon had the towers of Leyden far behind us.

I stayed an entire fortnight instead of a week and met every one in the small town. It was a strange experience. I had been obliged to spend almost sixty years in a country which loved to call itself a Christian nation, before I was to come face to face with the real spirit of Christ and then I found it in an old, converted barn.

Chapter 71

I GET REMBRANDT AN ORDER FOR A FINAL PICTURE

When I returned to Amsterdam, I heard that Hendrickje had been quite sick, that Titus was working hard, trying to convert the little front room into an art store, and that Rembrandt himself was busy with the sketches for that allegorical picture in the Town Hall which was to find no favor in the eyes of Their Lordships and that was to find a final resting place in the rubbish corner of the aldermanic attic.

But of course at that moment we could not know all this and the mere fact that he was busy once more made him so happy that even Hendrickje was caught in an occasional smile and Titus had started to dream once more of becoming a famous painter instead of spending his days as a peddler of pictures and bric-à-brac.

They were delighted to see me, wanted to know all about young Spinoza and whom I had met in Rijnsburg and what the Leyden professors had said (they had said nothing, so far), and they kept me for dinner and told me that the house was a great success but of course, the creditors still continued coming around, trying to find something that might possibly be considered to belong to Rembrandt himself ("The clothes on my back are all I have left," he interrupted us), but the Roozengracht was far removed from the center of the town and only those who really cared for them would take the trouble to walk that long distance, and by the way, my friend, the Frenchman, had come to visit them several times but he had looked very ill and had come in a coach, accompanied by his sailor, who had to support him when he climbed the stoop, but he had made them promise that they would not write to me and tell me that he was sick, and Francen had been in and he had just returned from Haarlem where he had seen Hals, old Frans Hals, I surely knew whom they meant, and Hals had laughed right merrily when Francen had told him that he was a good friend of Rembrandt's.

"Give him my regards," Frans had said, "and tell him that now I can call him brother. And also tell him that he was a lucky devil. For when he went bankrupt, some of the grandest people in town were proud to be among his creditors while I was sold out at the behest of a baker, a common, ordinary, everyday baker, whom I had tried to please by painting a picture of him while blowing his horn to tell the people that the fresh bread was ready. And when I went broke, all the sheriffs could find in my house were three mattresses, a table and a chest of drawers, and he, so I hear, had a house as full of things as the palace of the late King Solomon."

And Francen had brought other news. Hals was painting again, painting again although he had not done a stroke of work for almost twenty years (he could not sell anything anyway, so what was the use?) and he wanted Rembrandt to come and see him, for he had made a wonderful discovery but he was eighty years old and would not be able to make use of it himself. "But tell Rembrandt," he had said, "that being poor is the best thing that can possibly happen to any painter. For if you are poor, you can't afford to buy all those expensive colors you use when you are young when your father pays the bills; and then you have got to get results with only two or three pots of paint and it is then that you learn to suggest tints rather than put them down in the original red and yellow and green and blue—just suggest things—indicate them—and if you can do that and can do it really well, people will sometimes see what you mean just as well as they used to do before—when you could still afford to paint in all the colors of the rainbow." And so on and so forth, for the old man was getting to be a little vague and repeated and contradicted himself continually, but then, he had been in the poor-house for so long, no wonder he was no longer as bright as in the olden days.

And oh, yes, they had almost forgotten to tell me, but Crayers had sent word that the case of Titus against that man van Hertsbeeck, who had got part of the bankruptcy money that really belonged to Titus ("Good God!" I said to myself. "Still another case? Is there no end to these lawsuits?") would probably come up for a decision before the end of the year and that he was sure van Hertsbeeck would have to pay Titus several thousand guilders and that would be wonderful, for they still had to manage very skimpily ... and so the evening went by and when at last I went home (it was ten o'clock and I was almost thrown into the canal by some playful roisterers who had been evicted from old Lingelbach's labyrinth as it was long past closing time)—when finally I went home, I was happier than I had been for a long time. For just ere I left, Hendrickje, her cheeks flushed by fever and her eyes wide with excitement had drawn me aside into a corner of the room and had whispered: "He works all day long, and everything is all right."

Indeed, for the moment at least, the Fates that had so doggedly followed this poor man's footsteps seemed to have wandered off in search of some fresh victim, for not only did the creditors gradually begin to leave him alone, but I was at last able to get him a commission that was exactly the sort of thing he liked to do best.

Except for my son, I had only one relative in the town of Amsterdam. How we happened to be cousins, I did not know. My grandmother had explained it to me any number of times, but I was not greatly interested in the man and invariably I failed to listen just at the moment when she said, "And so you see, his mother's sister's grandfather was the uncle of your father's uncle's nephew," or something of the sort. But we observed a certain outward cordiality towards each other, which rarely exceeded the bounds of mere politeness, and we made it a point to call upon each other every New Year's morning when we would say, "Good day, Cousin, and I hope you have a very happy and prosperous New Year." But that was all for we had nothing in common except the accidental tie of blood and a dead great-great-grandfather.

This particular van Loon was a few years younger than myself and a cloth manufacturer in a small way. But as he was not married and had more spare time than most of his colleagues, he had been several times elected into the board of managers of the cloth-workers guild and this year again he was one of the Syndics, as he happened to tell me when I met him by accident on the corner of the Rokin where he had his store (he was also in the retail business) and where he lived with an old servant and three very fat and very lazy cats.

I congratulated him on his new dignity and asked him, more as a matter of having something to say than through curiosity, whether he and his colleagues had made any plans yet to have their picture made. He said no, they hadn't thought about it yet. And then, through a sudden impulse, I found myself putting both my hands on his shoulders and I heard myself blurting out: "I have got just the man for you. He is a splendid painter and he won't charge you much a terrible sum either. When will you pose for him?"

But the dried-up draper looked hastily around to see whether any one could possibly have observed my unseemly behavior (he was most correct and respectable in all his personal dealings) and then asked me curtly, "Who may that be, Cousin?" and I answered, "A man by the name of Rembrandt, Cousin," and he again, "I have never in my life heard of him, Cousin," and I, "That does not matter, Cousin. I will take you around to see him and then you can judge for yourself, Cousin. Good night now, Cousin, and I will call for you to-morrow at ten in the morning."

God only knows how I was able to persuade this dry-as-dust wool-carder and his equally uninspired confrères that Rembrandt was the man for them, but it is a fact that I finally persuaded them to sign a contract for a picture and at a very fair price.

I was curious to see how Rembrandt would go to work about this picture. It was a long time since he had painted anything of the sort and in the meantime, as he himself put it to me more than once, he had been pulled through the mangle so repeatedly that nothing remained of his former self except his skin and his bones and his honest homely face. Twenty years before it had been all the same to him what size canvas he needed—what sort of color he used, nor had he given a fig for the opinion of those who in the end would be asked to pay for the picture.

This time he had to take the smallness of his studio into consideration, he must be careful not to waste any of the bright lakes and the expensive others which Titus had bought for him on credit and as he needed money and needed it badly, he must be very considerate of the feelings of his customers and give every one of them an equal chance.

I am not the best possible judge of paintings, but it struck me that Rembrandt had never come quite so near his ideal as this time. I was reminded of the somewhat incoherent message which Francen had brought back from Haarlem and which Hendrickje had related to me on the evening I returned from Leyden, that strange artistic last will and testament which exhorted the younger man to try and "suggest color" and "to hint at things rather than expose them in concrete form and color."

Everything in this picture was a matter of suggestion and yet one actually felt the presence of those honest, commonplace drapers as if one had been present at one of their meetings—one sensed that they were secretly very proud of the high office which their fellow members had bestowed upon them and at the same moment one knew that in their heart of hearts they were convinced that this much envied dignity had come to them entirely in recognition of their outstanding probity and the unimpeachable integrity of their business morals.

It was the strongest picture I had ever seen, and of one thing I am sure, no one had ever achieved such a brilliant effect with the help of such incredibly sober means.

I was delighted, and the day after the picture had been finished, I hastened to the house on the Rokin where the sign of the Pelican hung out to tell all people that this was the Drapery Shop of Gerard van Loon and Sons (the old man was all that remained of those "sons") and I found the honorable syndic eating his midday meal consisting of a bowl of lentil soup and he looked at me with considerable surprise, for he was not accustomed to familiarities of this sort, and I said:

"Good morning, Cousin, have you seen your picture?"

And he answered, "Yes, Cousin, and none of us are particularly impressed by it, but we will pay the man all the same."

And I turned on my heel and he called after me, "Don't you want to stay, Cousin, and share my meal with me?"

And I answered, "No, thank you, Cousin, some other time I shall be delighted."

And I went home to talk with my son about a new sort of saw-mill which he wanted to construct—a saw-mill that should be able to take care of three trees at the same time. He had gone to see one of our neighbors, the only wood-dealer left on the Houtgracht, and the man had been delighted with the plan and had told him to go ahead and construct a working model and very likely (if it could be arranged with the carpenters' guild) he would let him build one for him in Zaandijk.

The boy (he was taller than I but my affection for him was so great that I could never think of him except in terms of a child—a sentiment which sometimes caused considerable difficulty between us)—the boy, who in his own way loved me very deeply, noticed at once that something was wrong.

"What has happened, father?" he asked. "Uncle Rembrandt in trouble again?"

"No," I protested, but he knew that I lied.

"Too bad." He spoke quietly to himself. "Too bad. Uncle Rembrandt is a fine fellow and I like him tremendously, but he just has no sense. Who wants to go on painting pictures when the world needs mills?"

I suppose there was an answer to that question, but (for that moment, at least) I must confess I could not think of it.

Chapter 72

A CHAPTER MOSTLY PERSONAL AND NOT DEVOID OF ENCOURAGEMENT

The Leyden faculty did what I had expected it to do and sent a lengthy report to Their Lordships the Burgomasters stating that in the opinion of the High and Noble Born Faculty of the Illustrious University of Leyden, I was not entitled to an indemnity from a purely medical point of view. They could not of course express themselves upon the political aspects of the case—a riot was a riot and rebellion against their divinely appointed masters was ever a crime on the part of mere subjects. They must, however, leave that aspect of the unfortunate incident to the judgment of the worldly authorities. But they, as the sworn guardians of the spiritual and scientific truth, could only regret that a supposedly respectable member of their guild should have so far forgotten the lessons of his early training as to try and set himself up as the equal of God.

A copy of this report was forwarded to me and I in turn sent it to The Hague for the consideration of the Pensionary. After this public reprimand, he might find it inconvenient to retain my services as unofficial adviser to the committee that was trying to reorganize the medical service of the navy. By return boat I got my letter of resignation back. At the bottom of it, written in the illegible hieroglyphics of this illustrious statesman, was written one word, "Perge," and underneath it a scrawl which I finally deciphered as J. de W.

I should not be ungrateful and try and create the impression that all my life long I had been a victim of circumstances and had received absolutely no signs of recognition. On the contrary, a small pamphlet I had written upon the subject of my peculiar method of performing major operations had been translated into Latin and had apparently been read all over Europe, for I was continually in the receipt of letters from London and Paris and Vienna and even from Rome and Madrid, telling me how different surgeons in those distant cities had followed my instructions and had achieved the most satisfactory results. And three scientific academies appointed me a corresponding member of their institutions and they informed me of my election by means of beautifully calligraphed parchment bulls.

But I would cheerfully have sacrificed all these expressions of public approbation for that one word of my dear friend, who in the midst of ruling the affairs of a nation, yet found time to say "continue" to an humble doctor who a week afterwards was denounced in a meeting of his own guild as "a disgrace to his profession and a menace to society."

Chapter 73

POOR HENDRICKJE GOES TO HER FINAL REST

I now come to the years between 1661 and 1668, when a great many things happened, but few, I am sorry to say, that contributed in any way to the happiness of either myself or my friends.

In the first place, there was the sickness of Hendrickje. She had never quite been well since about a year after Cornelia's birth, when she had caught a cold and, refusing to stay in bed long enough, had developed pulmonary trouble which soon made me fear that she too was a candidate for an attack of phthisis. It seemed unbelievable and too cruel for words. Saskia had died of this dreadful disease and now Hendrickje was going the same way.

Rembrandt, who was singularly blind to symptoms of this sort, noticed nothing. He sometimes commented upon his wife's lack of appetite and her general listlessness, mildly complained when she refused to accompany him upon one of his walks through the deserted fields that surrounded his home on all sides, but as a rule he closed the sentence with a cursory, "Oh, well, she will be all right again soon enough. When spring comes, we will take her home for a change of air. That will put her back on her feet."

But when spring came she was much worse, and when summer came she was not any better, and one day in the fall she asked me to send for the same notary that had helped her and Titus draw up the agreement about their little art store, but to be careful that he did not call when Rembrandt was at home, for that she did not want him to know how badly she felt. She could still walk about a bit and she hoped to deceive him about her condition until the very last.

I knew that on the seventh of August Rembrandt was going to take Titus to see his friend Joris de Caullery, who was living in The Hague at that time—who had been ailing for several months, but who had now sufficiently recovered to pay a short visit to Amsterdam to attend to some private business affairs. On the seventh of that month, accordingly, I walked with Notary Listingh to the house on the Roozengracht and Hendrickje made her last will.

She had little enough to leave, poor dear, but all she possessed, she bequeathed to her daughter Cornelia, or in case of her death, to her stepson Titus. Furthermore, she stipulated that Rembrandt should be the only guardian of her child and insisted upon including a paragraph which stated that if Titus should inherit her property, the revenue of her investments (such as they were) should be paid out to Rembrandt, who was to enjoy them until the day of his death. As she could not write, she merely made a cross at the end of the document. I was asked to sign too, but just then Christiaen Dusart happened to drop in with a small picture he had finished the week before and which he wanted to show to Rembrandt. The notary thought it better that Dusart should be one of the witnesses than I, because Rembrandt or Titus might otherwise think that I had been in some way responsible for the strange stipulations of this extraordinary testament which might well be shown to further generations as a lesson in loyalty and unselfish devotion. One of the occupants of the other half of the house in which the van Rijns lived was the second witness, and got a guilder for his trouble.

When everything had been done according to the law, Hendrickje was so exhausted that she had to go and lie down.

For a few weeks it seemed that she was growing a little stronger, but in October she happened to see from her window how a drunken vagabond tried to stab a woman who had resented his unproper advances with his clasp-knife. The excitement proved to be very bad for her. She went to bed and never got up again.

She lived almost a year longer. She never complained, and until the end she kept as busy as she could. Her love for Rembrandt and for her two children (Titus regarded her entirely as his own mother and she apparently knew no difference between her own child and that of Saskia's) never waned but on the contrary grew stronger as she felt herself more and more slipping away from this world. And she was so strong in her determination that no one should suffer on her account that until the last moment, neither Rembrandt nor Titus appreciated the seriousness of her condition.

One morning Rembrandt found her unconscious on the floor. Apparently she had tried to get up to open a window to get some fresh air. She had often had attacks of choking and then fresh air had been the only tning that would bring her any relief. Titus was sent off as fast as his legs could carry him to fetch me. When I reached the house on the Roozengracht, Hendrickje was dead.

That afternoon we discussed the forthcoming funeral. Rembrandt wanted to bury her in the Old Church together with Saskia. But since the death of his first wife, he had moved to the other part of the city and the law provided that all dead people must be buried "in the church nearest to their most recent place of abode." In case the surviving members of a family wished to make other plans, they were obliged to pay the undertaker an extra sum for "every church the procession should pass on their way to the holy edifice they had selected for the interment."

Such a procedure was out of the question; it was too costly.

Early the next morning (it was the 27th of October, 1662) Rembrandt sold the grave containing the remains of Saskia to a certain Pieter van

Geenen, who paid him cash. With that money he was able the next day to buy a grave in the South Church. And there Hendrickje was buried.

God must have been delighted to welcome her to his Heaven. But she must have been terribly lonely without her man and her children for truly, beyond those, she had had no existence.

Chapter 74

JEAN-LOUYS SAILS FORTH INTO SPACE

And now I must recount another incident of that same year of grace, '62, which filled my heart with great and sincere sorrow.

When I had returned home from Leyden that evening and called on the van Rijns, they had told me that Jean-Louys had been at their home that afternoon, in a carriage, bringing them a present of a barrel of excellent wine from Bordeaux, but looking so haggard and so pale that they were afraid he must be suffering from some dangerous disease.

With his usual affability, however, he had laughed away their fears and declared that he had never felt so well before in all his life. And indeed, when I hastened to his house he seemed not only in very good spirits but his color was good and his eyes were clear and he was full of all sorts of plans which he began to explain to me before I had even sat down.

"Look at this," he said to me, showing me a drawing that I held to be the outline of the skeleton of a centipede but that proved to be a design for a new sort of ship he intended to build. "I am going to sell the old one," he told me. "A nice little boat, but too cramped for comfort and all wrong from a scientific point of view. It pulls itself backward when it should push itself forward. That is too complicated for your sort of brain, and so just take my word for it. There was only one solution. Submit the matter to mathematics. I did. I got an answer that surpassed my highest expectations. Half a year ago they began to build this boat after my own specifications. It will be ready next month. And this summer you shall have such sailing as you never even dreamed of."

I tried to bring the conversation back to more general subjects, but it was no use. Jean-Louys had temporarily gone insane and boats were his delusion. Imagine my horror when I came home and found that my son had been actually working on that new mathematical caravel for the last six months without my knowing anything about it. He left the house every morning several hours before I got up, for I was getting old and beginning to feel the need of a little extra rest, and by attending to all my correspondence and literary work in bed between six and eight in the morning, I found that I could accomplish much more during the actual working hours of the day.

"Yes," he told me, "Uncle Jean showed me those plans I don't know how long ago. It is going to be a wonder, that boat! It is costing him a tidy sum, too, but he seems to have sent to France for a tun of gold and he does not care what he spends as long as it is for his navy, as he calls it.

I have learned an awful lot about the ship-building trade. I even may give up mills and go in for ship-building myself."

In June of '62 the *Descartes* was ready. The name at first attracted no attention. Of course every skipper in port was enormously interested in this strange contraption which had such a stern as no one had ever seen before, at least in our part of the world. All day long they would stand on the wharf (the vessel lay off the Kattenburg) and discuss the possible pros and cons of such a construction. Then a few ventured to row out and inspect the *Descartes* at close range. They were cordially invited on board—taken into the cabin—plied liberally with that marvelous French brandy that came from the land of Cognac, and that was still a curiosity in our land, and were treated with that bonhomie which one sailor should show to another.

Soon a mob of curious people was besieging the ship and the harbor authorities, suspecting that this might be part of a deep-laid smuggling plot, sent a lieutenant and three soldiers to make a personal investigation. But all the papers were found to be in perfect order and nothing would have come of the matter except that the name *Descartes*, which was mentioned in the official report, caught the eye of My Lord Valckenier, who was now one of the Burgomasters and who read every official document from the beginning to the end and who declared himself deeply hurt that a foreigner who had enjoyed the hospitality of our country for such a long time, should be so insensible to the prejudices of the majority of his neighbors as to call a craft that was to sail from a Dutch port after a pagan philosopher who was generally known to be one of the worst enemies of the Christian faith.

This was perhaps no matter of which Their Lordships could take public cognizance but Valckenier suggested that the Baron de la Tremouille be requested to change the name of his ship. The other Burgomasters agreed. They did not anticipate the prospect of four weeks of anti-Cartesian sermons with any great pleasure. Besides, this was hardly a matter of principle but merely one of convenience.

Jean-Louys was asked to re-baptize his vessel. He asked for a week's time in which to make up his mind, as he was wavering between *Buttercup*, *Moses and Aaron* and *Young Love*. He was granted a respite of five days.

By the end of the fourth, he was gone and so was my son. I did not worry, for I knew that he was well able to take care of himself and that he would turn up again ere long. Four days later he walked into the house, tired and unshaven but cheerful. He explained his muddy boots by telling me that he had walked back all the way from Hoorn.

"It was a wonderful trip," he said. "That ship is a marvel. I wish that Uncle Louys had taken me all the way. But he wanted to try and make Dokkum by the outside passage and he was afraid it would take me too long to reach home. He expects to be back again in about six weeks. Here is a letter for you. If you will pardon me, I will go and shave and wash."

The boy went upstairs and I took the letter. There was nothing extraordinary about that letter but before I had opened it, I suddenly knew: "This is the last message I shall receive from Jean-Louys on this side of the grave." I have had such instinctive premonitions four or five times in my life and I have never known them to fail. I still have that letter, and here it is:

"Carissime [it began, and then continued in French],

"Your boy will bring you this letter. He is a fine fellow. Let him build his mills and be happy.

"And now a word by way of explanation why I left you for good without saying 'good-by.' I don't like this business of bidding farewell to good friends in the conventional way. It is a little too much like a major operation without the benefit of your beloved Cannabis.

"I am not going to Dokkum, God forbid! I told your son that I was going there because it seemed the easiest way of explaining to him why I thought he had better return home. If I had let him know my real destination, he might have insisted upon keeping me company. A voyage from Texel to Bordeaux would have been a trifle too long for a young man of his age who still has to make his career. And the *Descartes* (I did not change the name after all) is bound for the mouth of the Garonne, for I am going home.

"A strange idea, I grant you, that I, of all people, should be wanting to go home. I seemed to be a man without a country—without a family—without any place I could call my own. I liked to pose as a piece of animated logic—of perambulating reason. But now that I realize that I have only a short time more to live, some strange and hitherto unsuspected instinct bids me go forth that I may die among my own people.

"For my days are numbered. The heart has about finished its task. It is getting tired and has sent me repeated warnings that soon it will cease its labors altogether. Well, I am contented. It has been a faithful servant and deserves a rest.

"But let me talk of other and more cheerful matters. We have been friends—we have been good friends—we have been brothers in the best sense of the word.

"It would be an insult if I were to say thank you for a gift that you tendered me so willingly and so gladly.

"Whenever I have been obliged to listen to people who talked about the uselessness and emptiness of all earthly existence, I have felt inclined to tell those unfortunate pilgrims that they had failed in their quest for the only positive good that life has to offer to those created after God's holy image. The excuse for all the pain and suffering that are our share while we dwell on this planet is implied in one single word and that word reads 'companionship,' the companionship that is based upon perfect mutual understanding.

"You and I and Bernardo and even poor Selim have had our share of that divine blessing. Let us give thanks and pass on to the next subject.

"I shall be in my grave within a year. In less than twelve months' time, I shall have received an answer to the Great Riddle—if an answer there be. Otherwise I shall just sleep and what more sublime reward for three score years of valiant fighting than the peace and quiet of eternal oblivion?

"And now one more short meditation before I bid you my final adieux.

"Has life been worth while? Would I do it again if I were given the choice?

"Let me answer those questions in reverse order.

"If I were given the choice once more I would answer 'No. A thousand times, no!' At least not if I had to promise that for a second time I would commit all the same follies of which I have been guilty the last sixty years. If I were told that I would have to see as many things that were ugly and wasteful and senseless as I have been obliged to witness since I reached the age of discrimination, if I were asked to associate with as many fools as it has been my sad privilege to encounter during my peregrinations across half a dozen different countries I would say 'No.' But I hasten to add that this second question (which people are asking themselves all the time) is really a very silly one. No one was ever consulted about his own birth. One moment he was happily unaware of everything. The next one he found himself struggling amidst hundreds of millions of crawling little creatures, all of whom obeyed but a single impulse, the urge that bade them to survive.

"Only a coward would shirk such an imperative duty. A man of parts accepts the inevitable, and I too have accepted and while I breathe, I shall say 'Yes' to whatever fate has still in store for me.

"But has it been worth while? Has it? I don't know for sure but on the whole I feel inclined to say 'Yes, it has been worth while.' Not on account of those so-called 'realities' which I have learned to despise but on account of the unrealities which are the only solid structure upon which a wise man will attempt to build the edifice of his individual contentment.

"When I was very young my careful father tried to drum it into my head that the acquisition of tangible possessions was the beginning and the end of all human happiness. And all through life (and not the least in that country of yours which has given me its hospitality for so many years) I have heard that endlessly reiterated commandment: 'Thou shalt try to accumulate as many worldly goods as possible that thou mayest call them thine own.'

"Remembering that Christ had admonished his followers 'not to live by bread alone,' the spiritual leaders of those nations that pretend to follow his example ceaselessly urge their flocks to mix their porridge and their potatoes with a mysterious substance which they call 'religion' and which I am sorry to say has never been very much to my taste. For I understood the words of that bewildered young Jewish peasant in a somewhat different sense. He wished to elevate his greedy and grasping fellow-tribesmen from the ranks of the animals of the field and he realized that the only thing that sets man apart from his brethren of the bush and the fields and the sky and the waters of the ocean is his ability to create himself an imaginary realm of the spirit into which he can escape whenever the unbearable actualities of breeding and killing (the twofold basis of all animated existence) are on the point of slaying his high courage or (what seems to me even worse) threaten to turn him into a cynic.

"For that, I think, is the greatest piece of wisdom to be found within the endless and ofttime dreary pages of the Holy Book and to the best of my ability I have tried to make good use of it, ever since I have been allowed to shape my own life as I saw fit without the unendurable interference of parents and teachers and other people who meant well by me.

"Have I chosen the right path or the wrong one?

"I do not know, but I am willing to leave the final decision to those Deities whom I will meet face to face within a very short space of time.

"I will confess that the selection was difficult and that it took me years to find the right one. Like all young men, grown up amidst the traditions of a feudal society, I was taught that true romance was only to be found within the arms of woman. I tried to make that dream come true but was unable to do it. For woman, as soon as she was captured, avenged herself for her defeat by destroying her captor or by turning him into her slave.

"I loved my freedom above all and withdrew from all further competition within a field where the victor was also the vanquished.

"Then I went forth to war, because the clash of arms (so I had been taught to believe) made one forget all else. Dull marches in the company of dull drudges—sweat and blood and boredom and as a reward, the conviction that we had accomplished something that had better been left undone.

"Then I tried to find oblivion within the garden of the Muses, but the Muses were jealous mistresses who like their fair sisters of the Earth asked for everything and gave as little as possible in return.

"I finally closed the gate of that spurious Paradise behind me for all time and began to wander.

"Oh, to be free and drift from town to town and from country to country without a care and a responsibility! But at night, all alone in some inhospitable room with no other companionship than a pair of muddy boots and half a dish of stale food—no, that sort of life offered me only a temporary means of escape but no definite solution.

"And then, by chance and through mere unaccountable accident, I stumbled upon that little book of young Napier. And suddenly within the thirty or forty pages of that tiny volume I found my fairy-story, my own particular fairy-story. And the goddess whose magic wand then and there turned a commonplace old tower on a commonplace old canal in a dull Dutch city into an enchanted castle where a man of my character could live happily for ever afterwards, was called Mathematics, and the ancients worshiped her as the mother of all science.

"Ever since that moment I have dwelled contentedly within her delectable domain—tilling her fields and watching over her flocks in return for the highest reward which man is able to receive on this earth—complete oblivion of himself by means of the work of his choice.

"Now the time has come to depart and a well-behaved guest leaves the house where he has been happy, quietly and with the least possible amount of embarrassment to his fellow-lodgers.

"My incomparable François tells me that there is little danger connected with this voyage and that I shall be home by the end of next month. I have complete confidence in his ability to handle this craft safely. But if he should prove to be my Charon and the Bay of Biscay should assume the dark shape of the River Styx, waste no useless tears upon the memory of one who contemplating the few fleeting hours that separate him from Death, can honestly state, 'Yea, verily, it has been a good life.'

"And now I, the most selfish of creatures, shall tell my faithful servant to open me a bottle of the wine that comes from the land of Cassenac and I shall fill his glass and I shall fill mine and together we shall drink a toast to the man who honored me beyond all others by calling himself my friend."

The letter was not signed but it ended with a postscript.

"Present my humble duties to that poor old bear Rembrandt. All his life long he has dwelled in a land of make-believe of such infinite beauty and integrity that the world has passed it by with a shrug of the shoulders and a sneer of malice and envy. Now he is old and sick and growing stout and soon he will be an object of pity to the little boys on the street and when the end comes, the commissioners of the poor will take him to an unknown grave in an obscure corner of one of your chilly churches. But was any one ever richer than this poor wreck? He lost everything when he surrendered to the dreams that were within him and by so doing he gained all."

Four weeks later a convoy of merchantmen returning from Batavia reported that just outside the British channel they had met a queer-looking little vessel that flew the French flag but that had hailed them in broken Dutch and had declared that it came from Amsterdam and was bound for the south of France.

But I never was able to find out whether Jean-Louys had finally reached the land of his birth or had sailed for another shore from which no one has yet returned to tell the tale.

Chapter 75

A FORGOTTEN MAN IN A LONELY HOUSE GOES ON PAINTING PICTURES

Strange though it may seem at first, Hendrickje's death did not seem to have made a very deep impression upon Rembrandt. This, however, was not due to any callousness of heart on his part, as I heard some people say—people by the way who had never met him and only knew from hearsay. But there seems to be a saturation point for mental suffering as well as for physical pain, and during the last ten years Rembrandt had been dealt such terrible and incessant blows by fate that there was nothing now that seemed able to make any impression upon him whatsoever.

After the very indifferent reception of the Syndics he knew that as far as his artistic career was concerned, there was to be no "comeback" for him. He was, in the common parlance of that day, "out of the running" and a "back number."

I tried to console him once by telling him of something I had found in one of the old Greek writers, how the Athenians were running a race in the Stadium and how the public, seeing a man a few feet behind the very last of all the others, began to chide him for his slowness until they discovered that the unfortunate victim of their displeasure was so far ahead of all the others that he merely seemed to be running in the rear, while as a matter of fact, he had already won the prize. But this neither amused nor interested him. He merely grunted a casual "yes" and went back to his easel.

For he worked very hard those days—entirely too hard to please me when I looked at him with a professional eye. He rarely left the house either during the day or during the night. He was glad to see his few remaining friends and was polite to them and occasionally he even tried to be cordial. But all the time his mind was elsewhere and when addressed, it took him some time before he realized that he had been spoken to and that one expected an answer. Then he would smile a feeble smile and would stammer "Yes" or "I hardly think so," and would at once sink back into those meditations with which he endeavored to drug his soul.

The English (who whatever their faults, are possessed of a much richer literature than we ourselves) have a proverb which says that kites rise against and not with the wind. That may be true but if the wind turns into a hurricane and blows too strong, the string that holds the kite is apt to break and the unfortunate kite comes tumbling down and is smashed to pieces on the ground.

Rembrandt came of a strong breed of men. His father and grandfather and great-grandfather (not to speak of his maternal ancestors) had fought their way through the great rebellion and had lived to tell the tale. They had been the sort of people that would never bend, but even the hardest iron will break if it is exposed to too severe a blow. Sometimes when I saw Rembrandt late at night, his short squat figure (much too stout around the hips on account of his lack of exercise) scratching away at some copper plate by the light of a single candle (the whole family sat and worked or read by the light of one single candle— they could not afford more), I wondered how long it would be before the crash came.

I tried to convince him that he must take at least one short walk every day but he said, "No, I am too busy."

I tried to persuade him that he ought to go out oftener and visit his friends—that it would be good for his painting and his etching if he refreshed his mind once in a while by an evening of laughter and jest, but he merely shook his head and replied: "No, it can't be done. I am too busy."

Then I made it a point of walking across the town whenever the sun was shining and the weather was fine and knocking at the door and saying, "Titus, go tell your father that I am here to take him for a stroll." And in less than a minute Titus would be back with the message: "Father is sorry but he is too busy right now. He wants to know whether you won't come in and sit in the studio while he finishes something he is doing."

And I would find him busy with his sketches for still another picture of Haman's downfall and disgrace, a subject which seemed to occupy his mind a great deal in those days and of which I have seen him start and finish at least three full-sized pictures.

He rarely spoke of his work in those days but everything he did was in a minor key. Gone were the days of the laughing cavalier and of Saskias and Hendrickjes, dressed up like the ladies-in-waiting of those merry foreign queens.

In his bare little house there was nothing left that could serve as a fitting background for such scenes of gayety. And as he had never read much, and considered the pursuit of mere literature as a rather scandalous waste of time, his choice of subjects was necessarily limited and he had to fall back upon the memories of his childhood days and those were of course restricted to the Biblical incidents of which his mother had told him when he was a small boy.

But the Christ he painted was not the handsome young prophet of his Italian rivals, preaching the good tidings among the sun-baked bowlders of some Palestine hill. No, it was invariably the man of sorrows—Christ being scourged—Christ bidding farewell to his followers—Christ standing in deep thought before the walls of the Temple! And the other problems that filled his mind until he had to rid himself of this obsession by recounting them in the form of pictures—all of those had to do with that feeling of doom—that sense of futility, and that defiant air of hopeless rebellion which had descended upon him the moment he had walked for the last time out of his house in the Anthonie Breestraat.

Often I have sat in his studio and have watched him for hours while he was busy with his painting. And every time again I have been reminded of a picture he had painted years before when he was still quite young, of Samson threatening his father-in-law who had cheated him. The strong man who for reasons which he has not been able to fathom (of which, as a matter of fact, he is totally unconscious) has been struck what he considers an unfair blow, and who defies Fate—who thumbs his nose at Providence—shakes his fist at the Deity himself, and with boy-like bravado shouts: "All right! I will show you! I will show you!"

For he was showing them. He was showing them with a vengeance.

In that shabby room in a mean house on the Roozengracht, such miracles of color were now being performed that the world for ages to come will sit before them in stupefied silence and will say: "Beyond that point, no man could go without lifting himself to the rank of the gods."

Provided that any of these pictures would survive long enough to allow mankind to catch up with their maker. And that to me seemed highly doubtful. For nothing Rembrandt finished during those days was ever sold. And where they are at present, only a year after his death, I could not possibly tell. A praying pilgrim he painted during that time I saw only a few months ago in a pawn-shop in Leyden and it was hanging between a cheap fiddle and an old pair of sailor's trousers. What has happened to the others, I do not know, but I have my fears. An intelligent art-dealer with an eye to his grandsons' fortune would have hired himself a store-house and would have filled it with the pictures Rembrandt finished during the period he lived on the Roozengracht, and which he was unable to sell for half a guilder or even less.

But why expect such foresight among the vultures of the world of art?

Chapter 76

REMBRANDT HAS ONE MORE PUPIL

By the end of '64 it became clear that Rembrandt would not be able to afford the rent of the Roozengracht house any longer and that he would have to look for cheaper quarters. Titus found a place just around the corner and the whole family once more pulled up stakes and went to live on the Lauriergracht. There they had only three rooms and in every one of them the light was bad. It was then that Titus thought of the possibilities of having his father do some book illustrations which would probably be more lucrative than painting pictures.

He went to a publisher but the publisher had probably heard of the failure of the drawings which Rembrandt had submitted for Menasseh's book on Nebuchadnezzar and would not listen to the plan.

"If only your father knew something about steel-engraving, then I would have a job for him." And Titus in his eagerness to get his father an order (any order at all), had answered, "But my father is one of the best steel-engravers there are in town. Just give him a chance!"

The publisher had agreed. Would Mr. van Rijn please engrave a picture of Jan Antonides van der Linden after a portrait that Abraham van den Tempel had painted of him half a dozen years before? Rembrandt said that he would. But he was an etcher and not an engraver and the experiment ended as disastrously as that of the Nebuchadnezzar book he had done ten years before. And Rembrandt was once more at the mercy of his creditors.

Although I was no longer rich in those days, I would have been delighted to help him but he would not hear of it. "You have trouble enough of your own," he invariably answered when I talked of taking over some of the burdens of his household, "and I am still strong enough to take care of my children myself."

He was immensely pleased when one day a young man who said that his name was Aert de Gelder asked to be allowed to become his pupil. De Gelder, who then must have been about twenty years of age, hailed from the town of Dordrecht and was a pupil of that Samuel van Hoogstraten who shortly after the English war had moved to England where it was said that he had done very well and had become quite a rich man. As van Hoogstraten too had for a short while worked in Rembrandt's studio, the old man felt touchingly grateful and de Gelder proved to be not only an apt student but a kind and loyal friend, which Rembrandt had not been able to say of all of his pupils.

But unfortunately I was not able to see much of Rembrandt during this period. For we were on the brink of another war with England and I was obliged to spend the greater part of my time in The Hague, so as to be at the beck and call of My Lord the Pensionary, who was about to venture forth upon the most dangerous but, as it proved to be, the most glorious adventure of his entire career.

Chapter 77

FOR THE FIRST TIME IN MY LIFE I MEET A REAL STATESMAN

The Peace of Westminster of the year '54 had theoretically at least made an end to the hostilities between ourselves and England. But in practice there never had been a cessation of that warfare which is bound to spring up when two countries, almost equally matched, are contending for the monopoly of the world's trade.

To make matters worse, King Charles considered the fact that his young nephew, the Prince of Orange, had been definitely and for all time excluded from the government of the United Netherlands as a personal insult directed in the first place against himself and his illustrious house and he eagerly looked for a pretext to make war upon us.

He had the loyal backing of the vast majority of his subjects, who for some curious reason appeared to be under the impression that the Lord Almighty had given them the sea, as He had given them the River Thames, merely another piece of private property to be used and administered as they themselves saw fit.

Against this point of view a great many European nations had protested, but all to no avail. Their ships, like ours, were forced to salute English vessels wherever they encountered them—they had to submit to search upon the slightest suspicion of carrying contraband (and the definition of contraband was a very vague one which might imply anything from gun-powder to dried figs), and through the so-called "Act of Navigation" of the late Lord Protector, any foreign vessel suspected of being engaged in the trade between an English port and an English colony could be confiscated, without offering the owner a chance of appeal before a duly constituted court of law.

Our two countries were of course supposed to be "united" by a number of treaties of mutual esteem and good will but I have never taken much stock in such written documents as a possible bulwark of peace. When two nations are really convinced that their future safety depends upon fighting, even the most sacred treaties in the world become merely a pile of useless parchment that may just as well be sold to the junkman for all its intrinsic value, and such a point, I am afraid, had been reached when the world began to date its letters Anno Domini 1665.

At that moment both England and Holland wanted the monopoly of the trade in the Indies and in America (Spain and Portugal had so far dropped behind in the race that we did not even consider them as possible rivals) and as neither of them felt that they could change their policies without risking the prosperity of their respective merchants, there was but one possible solution—fight it out and see who was the best man.

All during the previous twelve months the news from London had been exceedingly alarming. No one less than the brother of King Charles himself had been put in command of the British forces and it was said that Parliament was ready to vote two and a half million pounds sterling for new ships and that all the English navy yards were working overtime and were building very large and powerful ships that were undoubtedly meant to be used against the Dutch.

Early in February of the year '64, a secret agent of the Pensionary in Paris had been able to get hold of a letter written apparently by no one less than the Clerk of the Navy Board (a certain Pepys or Peeps, a former official of the Treasury so I was told, who had been a past master at making the public revenues flow into his own pocket) and addressed to the British consular official in Livorno where several of our merchantmen who had left Smyrna too late to venture across the Straits of Gibraltar, were spending the winter.

It contained some general information for the benefit of an unnamed British commander who was to be expected in the Mediterranean as soon as the winter storms should have slightly abated and then there was a page filled with pothooks and dots and dashes which no one could make out. As My Lord Jan had recently had some very unfortunate experiences with one of his own confidential clerks (who had sold very important political documents to the enemy) he did not dare to entrust this missive to one of his subordinates but showed it to me and asked me what I could make of it. I had once told him of my efforts to decipher a page of manuscript of the famous Leonardo da Vinci which an Amsterdam antiquary had sold to me, telling me that it contained some observations of that learned and many-sided man upon the subject of anesthetics, and how I had been obliged to give up in despair.

The intercepted letter of the British naval official was, however, of a very different nature and I realized at once that it was merely a short tachygraphic account of something to which the consular agent in Livorno undoubtedly held the key. I went to all the book-sellers in Amsterdam and finally got hold of a little book on the art of stenography, devised by a certain Thomas Shelton and published originally in 1641.

At that time there had been quite a craze in our country for "short writing," and the Sheltonian system which claimed to be equally handy for English, Latin, German and Dutch, had been studied by a great many people. But it had been discontinued soon afterwards as being a little too complicated for quick reporting and it was just by chance that I still came across a copy in that second-hand shop. I bought the volume for a few pennies and that night I was able to decipher the interesting part of the letter of this Mr. Pepys and in that way we learned that before the end of the year, England expected to have a fleet of 160 ships of the line, with 5,000 guns and manned by 25,000 sailors; that this armada was expected to make an end to all further "depredations and arrogance of those insulting and injurious neighbors who live on the other side of our sea) ("those neighbors" were we and "our sea" probably meant the North Sea), and that His Majesty would probably start the war by an attack upon "those outlying colonies in Africa and Asia, but especially in America which our enemies have been either too lazy or too confident to fortify."

This statement coincided entirely with something which Sir George Downing, the British ambassador, was said to have said a short while before during a meeting he had with a few members of the Estates General. This man Downing was a very dangerous person, for whom none of us felt any respect. He had come to our country originally in the year '57 to prepare the way for Oliver Cromwell's plan for a Protestant League of all European nations.

But when this idea came to nothing through the usual jealousies of the different countries, Downing remained in Holland and as soon as the Lord Protector had died, he had hastened to make his peace with the new sovereign (not a very difficult thing to do as King Charles spent several weeks at The Hague). In order to show his zeal he then had set to work to bring about the extradition of the three of the judges of His Majesty's brother, who were still in the Low Countries (and who were promptly put to death in a most barbarous fashion), a piece of perfidy which made every decent man in the Republic avoid him as if he had been afflicted with the plague.

But this odious villain (who incidentally spoke and wrote our language perfectly) was just the sort of man Charles wished to keep as his representative at The Hague and it was during an interview he had with a committee from among the members of the Estates General that he had pointed to a map of the northern part of the American continent and had uttered the ominous words: "I am sorry, My Lords, but I completely fail to find those New Netherlands of which you have been telling me so much," thereby indicating that as far as the House of Stuart was concerned, no one had any claim to any part of North America except the English.

A few days later when I handed a copy of my translation of the secret English letter to the Pensionary, I took the liberty to draw his attention to this cryptic utterance of the British traitor, and he said, "How now, Doctor, are you getting scared about your house in Nieuw Amsterdam?" And I answered, "Your Lordship well knows that another loss more or less would make very little difference to me just now, but I would hate to see us lose a possession that promises to be so immensely rich in the future."

Whereupon he reassured me and said, "A month ago I already sent for two of the directors of the West India Company and told them of the danger to their colony. They have been duly warned. But those people are hopeless. They are never able to look beyond the question: Will it cost us anything, and sending troops and guns to the mouth of the Hudson would undoubtedly cost a great deal of money. My only hope is that that one-legged fellow—what is his name?—yes, that that man Stuyvesant, who is not without spirit, will hold out long enough until I can send our own navy across the Atlantic. He is said to be as obstinate as a mule and he may be able to save the situation. If God is with us. Otherwise we are lost."

But God apparently was not with us, for in August, long before there had been any declaration of war, a British squadron suddenly appeared in the Lower Bay and as My Lord Stuyvesant had neither men nor money, nor cannon nor gun-powder, he was soon obliged to surrender.

This had been the last straw, and we, from our side, were now beginning to prepare for war in a most serious fashion. During those days My Lord Jan seemed to be everywhere at the same time and able to do everything just a little better than any one else, regardless of their special training for the office to which they had been appointed.

Together with his brother Cornelis he developed a new sort of craft, much heavier than any vessels we had ever equipped before. These ships carried as many as 80 or 90 guns and the cannon were no longer of iron as in the olden days but of bronze and copper which not only carried much further than the iron ones but could be worked much more accurately and also (which was very important) much more quickly. Their Lordships also paid serious attention to the food of the sailors. They increased the pay of the enlisted men and of the sea-soldiers and (for the first time since we had had any navy) saw to it that only thoroughly trained doctors were engaged for the coming campaign. And My Lord Cornelis was appointed to accompany the fleet as "civil commander" to see that everything be done according to the wishes of his brother.

But in spite of all those precautions we suffered one of the worst defeats of which our history bears the record. I don't know what was the underlying cause of this disaster, but I have a suspicion that party-politics had a great deal to do with it.

The Pensionary had been able to make over the ships, but he was no wizard and could not change the minds of the sailors. Most of those had been reared in the traditions of the House of Orange and despised the rich merchants who now ruled our land as upstarts and usurpers. They loathed being commanded by "civilians," and in this term of contempt they included My Lord of Wassenaar, who had been elevated from the rank of a colonel of cavalry to that of an admiral because of his loyalty to the de Witts. I do not mean to imply that they were right. Wassenaar was a brave and able man, but it was perhaps just as well that his ship was blown up during the unfortunate encounter off Lowestoft. The effect at home of this defeat was terrible. The Exchange went to pieces in a terrible panic. The shares of the East India Company reached the unprecedented low rate of 440 percent. All our harbors were full of ships that could not reach their destinations because command of the sea was now completely in the hands of the English. How the Pensionary changed all this and gradually brought order into the chaos of seven different squadrons with seven different commanders, each one of whom wanted to conduct the war according to his own notions of naval strategy, can be read in any book of history that deals with this period.

But this miracle of organizing the apparently unorganizable was duly performed and when late in the year '65 de Ruyter returned after having conquered the English colonies on the west coast of Africa (as a return compliment for their unexpected visit to the shores of the Hudson), the picture of the war changed completely.

In June of '66 well within sight of the English coast, our ships met those of the enemy and fought that memorable battle that lasted four days and four nights and if a sudden fog had not come up during the afternoon of the fourth day, the entire British fleet would have been annihilated.

But a few months later, just off Dunkirk, we were once more defeated, for Admiral Tromp, who was an ardent supporter of the House of Orange, refused to come to the assistance of de Ruyter, who was his commander-in-chief and a friend of the Pensionary. As a result of his disobedience Tromp was promptly dismissed from the service. He thereupon tried to start a rebellion among the sailors who were devoted to him, and it was necessary to forbid him from ever showing his face on board another ship before order was restored.

Something drastic had to be done to give the country renewed confidence in its navy. While the whole nation was still divided into two hostile camps—those who took the side of Tromp and those who declared in favor of de Ruyter—I unexpectedly received a note from the Pensionary asking me to call on him at his home (not at his office) the next Friday night, the eighteenth of January of '67, a little after nine in the evening.

At the appointed hour I knocked at the door of His Lordship's house on the Kneuterdijk and was at once ushered into a room where I found My Lord Jan himself, together with his brother Cornelis, Admiral de Ruyter, Colonel van Ghent of the marines (who had succeeded Admiral Tromp as second in command of our fleet), and some one whom I did not know by sight but who proved to be a certain Colonel Dolman, who (if I caught the name correctly) was in command of a regiment of infantry in Brabant.

The Pensionary presented me to those high dignitaries and then told me why he had asked me to come and see him.

"These gentlemen already know about my plans," he explained. "I expect absolute secrecy from you in this matter. Ever since the treason of Buat, we have run the risk of an uprising among those who support the Prince. It was possible to cut off the head of a single traitor, but I have no army and I am powerless against the mob. As soon as we shall have forced England to accept our terms, the sea will be open, prosperity will come back and we can then begin the reorganization of our party, which will be absolutely necessary if this country is to remain a republic."

Thereupon he explained the details of the coming campaign to me and ended by asking me if I were willing to join the expedition.

"I want you to be chief-surgeon on the ship on which my brother will sail as the civilian commissioner. You will have an excellent chance to try out some of your new ideas and see how they work below deck."

I gratefully accepted the honor that was tendered me so generously and spent the next five months helping His Lordship with his preparations for a fleet of eighty ships that were to gather at the mouth of the Meuse early in June and were to sail from there for an unknown destination.

Early on the morning of the 14th of June of the year '67 we hoisted anchor. Except for the commander-in-chief and his immediate assistants, no one knew whither we were bound. As Admiral van Ghent had just returned from an attack on Edinburgh, we supposed that we were heading for Scotland to try and start a revolution there, as it was well known that the Scotch were not in sympathy with the war which King Charles had forced upon their fellow-dissenters in the Low Countries and might start a rebellion of their own at any moment.

But when I appeared on deck after supper on the evening of the seventeenth, I saw before me a low flat coast which I recognized as that of southern England. And true enough, that night we dropped anchor off the mouth of the Thames and the next morning, all the different captains were called to the flag-ship for a council of war (at which I of course was not present) and on the 19th of June of the year 1667, immediately after sunrise, we sailed past the fortifications of Sheerness, landed several thousand troops under command of that Colonel Dolman whom I had met at His Lordship's house on that mysterious evening early in January, and prepared for a general attack. Sheerness was taken the next day and destroyed together with all stores and all the ships that were lying in the harbor, and on top of the ruins we raised the flag of the Estates General.

On the 22d of June we were through with our labors and proceeded up the Medway, which is an estuary of the Thames. There we found to our great dismay that the enemy had sunk a number of their ships across the only navigable channel and furthermore had stretched an enormous iron chain from one shore to the other, defending this barricade by means of a dozen batteries of large caliber.

But one of our captains by the name of van Brakel hoisted all sails and notwithstanding the fire from shore, smashed through that chain and opened the road for the rest of the fleet. Once more we landed a number of troops, destroyed the vessels that were supposed to defend the river at this point, took the *Royal Charles* that flew the flag of the British admiral and the *Unity*, sank six large English war vessels and continued our way until we reached the town of Chatham.

There were those among us who thought that the Pensionary meant to start an uprising among the former adherents of Oliver Cromwell, who had fallen upon sad days since the return of the Stuarts. Others (especially among the sailors) hoped that we were bound to plunder that town London, though I, as a medical man, could see little use in capturing a city that was suffering so greatly from a very serious form of plague which undoubtedly would kill more of our people in one hour than we had lost during an entire week of fighting.

Soon, however, it became clear that the Pensionary had other plans for our expedition.

Negotiations for peace had been started a short time before and he intended to use our presence on British soil as a warning of what would happen if the plenipotentiaries of His Majesty did not accept our terms. We remained where we were, blockaded the Thames, bombarded Harwich, destroyed a number of ships near Gravesend and in a general way made our presence so definitely and thoroughly felt that in less than six weeks news was received of the conclusion of peace.

We gained a number of colonies in South America, but lost the New Netherlands. For this I was sorry, but I found that few people shared my feelings.

"That part of the world is absolutely useless anyway," they used to reason. "What did we ever get out of it? A few beaver skins, but even the beavers were beginning to die out. And what else? Trouble and more trouble and nothing but trouble and endless expense. Now we have Surinam, where we can raise sugar. An excellent bargain."

And they were loud in their praises of the political sagacity of the Great Pensionary who had given them the flourishing town of Paramaribo in return for the poverty-stricken village of Nieuw Amsterdam which now was called New York in honor of His Majesty's brother and which the English hoped to develop into a second Boston, by making it the capital of a separate province that stretched all the way from New England to Virginia.

Ambitious plans, to be sure, and as I had spent the happiest years of my life there, I hoped that they would come true. But I never ceased to regret that our short-sighted worship of immediate gain had made it impossible for us to administer that part of the world for our own benefit. It is true, we were no angels. But neither were we Puritans.

Chapter 78

AND STILL REMBRANDT CONTINUES TO PAINT

I returned to Amsterdam in the latter half of August. His Lordship the Pensionary had sent me a very flattering letter in which he expressed his gratitude for my services and commented upon the fact that during the entire expedition we had only lost fifty men. But this was not so much due to my skill as a surgeon and to the organization of the medical corps (for which, to a certain degree, I had indeed been responsible), as to the fact that the English in their panic (their country had not been invaded for almost six centuries) had rendered only a very limited resistance.

I was mustered out at Texel and from there hired a boat to Enkhuizen, from whence I made the rest of the voyage on foot, finding it agreeable to take a little exercise after so many months of close confinement on board a war vessel. I hired a man to row me across the Y and walked home through the twilight, happy to be once more among my own people and filled with a deep sense of pride when I contemplated the magnificent stone houses and palaces that had been going up during the last four years and that had been built in spite of a very costly war.

My son was not at home. The excellent Jantje, who had kept everything spick and span during my absence, explained that he had probably gone courting. For the first time I realized with brutal clarity how old I had grown. It seemed a few days ago that I had looked at this ungainly bundle of pink flesh, saying to myself, "Good God! will that ever grow up into a human being?" And now, but for the grace of God, I might at almost any moment stand revealed as a grandfather. But before I had been able to develop these frightening meditations to their fullest possibilities, Jantje handed me a letter, adorned with a big seal, which I recognized as the arms of Amsterdam and which, so she told me, had been delivered only that morning.

I opened it.

Their Lordships the Burgomasters informed me that in view of the "outrageous rebelliousness" which had caused the destruction of my property, they had voted to grant me the first part of my indemnity. Thirty thousand guilders in cash awaited my pleasure at the Town Treasury any time I cared to call with two witnesses who would be able to identify me.

I was dreadfully tired from my long and unaccustomed walk, but without bothering to get my hat I rushed out of the door and ran as fast as my old heart would permit me to the house on the Lauriergracht.

Rembrandt had retired to his workshop. Titus was in the front room with Cornelia, ordering a number of etchings which they were hanging on strips that had been stretched across the windows, that they might dry during the night. They were delighted to see me and at once took me to the studio where Rembrandt lay awake on a narrow cot.

"Look who is here," Titus shouted. But all Rembrandt answered was, "Please take away that candle. The light hurts my eyes." Then he recognized me and tried to get up. I bade him not exert himself and took possession of the only chair I could find. Titus and Cornelia sat down on the side of the cot. As soon as I had become a little more accustomed to the darkness of the low-ceilinged room, I examined my old friend a little closer. His eyes looked bloodshot and he seemed to have trouble breathing. He was in a bad shape.

"Rembrandt," I said, "I have come with good news for you and for the children. I have got back part of my money. Now, what can I do for you?"

I realized that this had not been a very tactful way to approach the subject, but in my enthusiasm, I had blurted out the first thing that came to my mind. But there was no immediate reply. Finally, a very tired voice said, "Nothing. It is too late." And then I realized how terribly he had altered during the three months I had not seen him. And I began again and this time a little more carefully, to explain that soon I would be amply provided with funds and that I wanted Rembrandt to share in my good fortune. But nothing seemed any longer able to make an impression upon him. We sat there, the four of us, during the greater part of the night and finally Rembrandt was able to formulate a wish.

"If it would not be asking too much of you," he told me, "I would like very much to go back to the house on the Roozengracht. It had such excellent light and this place is so dark that I am afraid I shall go blind if I have to work another six months in this dark cellar."

Then he excused himself. "If you don't mind, I would like to try and go to sleep now. I lie awake the greater part of every night and tomorrow I must be up early. I want to start work on my Prodigal Son. Titus thinks he has found some one who wants to buy it."

He reached out his hand which was covered with paint and a little shaky. "Please don't think I am not grateful," he said. "I am deeply grateful. But I am very tired and I have not seen any one for so long that I am not much good at conversation nowadays." And he pulled his blankets over his head and turned his face towards the wall.

I remained talking to Titus and Cornelia for a few minutes before I went home.

"No," Titus said, "you must not think that things are as bad as he imagines them to be. I have got my money at last, I mean that share in my father's house. Crayers had to go to the Supreme Court to get it but the judges found for us, and a few months ago van Hertsbeeck was told to pay me on pain of being sentenced to jail if he should keep me waiting. You know, it was half of the money that was paid for father's house when the Courts sold it to pay his debts. It is quite a sum—almost 5,000 guilders."

"Congratulations," and I shook the young man warmly by the hand. "And what do you mean to do with it?"

He looked at me a little sheepishly. "I think I will use it to get married," he answered.

"And who is the lucky girl?" I asked.

"Magdalena van Loo. She lives on the Singel with her mother. I will bring her around to see you to-morrow."

I turned to Cornelia, who was green with sleep. "And you, my darling," I said, "you too will soon say good-by to us to get married, won't you?"

She shook her head with that wisdom that seems to be part of those children who have spent their earliest years without the society of their own contemporaries and solemnly answered, "No, Uncle Jan. I am never going to leave you. I am always going to stay right here with father."

And the poor girl meant it.

Chapter 79

TITUS MARRIES

I am reaching the end of my story.

Why dwell upon the misery of those last years?

Yes, financially Rembrandt was a great deal better off than before. Titus had got hold of his five thousand guilders which he administered carefully, almost penuriously, for he knew from sad personal experience what poverty meant and he now had a wife of his own to support.

As for the wife, the less said the better. She was of equal age with Titus—they both had celebrated their twenty-seventh birthdays just before they were married. And she too had inherited a few thousand guilders from her father and would get a few thousand more when her mother died.

But she was a person without any charm or any color. She felt convinced that she could have done a great deal better if she had only tried a little harder. She tolerated her father-in-law (who painted a magnificent likeness of her and Titus which she did not like as it made her look a little too old), and she was patronizingly pleasant to her half-sister-in-law whom she called a bastard behind her back.

Was Titus in love with her?

I never was able to discover.

He seemed fond of her in a quiet sort of way, but I felt that he would have married almost any one who had taken the trouble to set her cap at him. Like most men who are predestined to die young of pulmonary trouble, he had strong sexual desires. But being a very dutiful son and sincerely devoted to his father, he had suppressed all such longings as long as he was responsible for the welfare of his family.

Now that he was at last able to afford a wife of his own, the inevitable happened and what that inevitable was, most people will know even if they have not been trained for the medical profession.

During the whole of that year I was very busy with the plans for my new infirmary. I had no intention of giving up my search for a more effective method of bringing about a state of artificial unconsciousness when people had to submit to an operation. But the regular hospitals remained closed to me as before and I had to have a place of my own if I wanted to make any progress.

One evening, early in September of the year '68, Rebecca Willems, an old servant who took care of Rembrandt's household now that his son was married, came to me quite late with a note signed by Cornelia. She asked me to come at once to Titus' house on the Apple Market, as her brother had been suddenly taken ill and seemed in a bad way.

When I arrived, he was unconscious from loss of blood. He had suffered an internal hemorrhage and I knew that he was doomed. He rallied a little towards morning, but died during the afternoon.

Rembrandt was present. He sat in a corner of the room. Cornelia and Rebecca took him back to the Roozengracht. He was sick for two weeks afterwards and could not attend the funeral of his son.

When Cornelia, trying to cheer him up, told him that Magdalena expected a baby, he shook his head.

"Merely some one else for me to lose," was his only comment.

He had reached the end of his strength and courage, and he knew it.

Chapter 80

I READ A FINAL CHAPTER IN GENESIS

But somehow or other, after a few months, he seemed to rally. At least, he tried to paint again. But when he had sat in front of his easel for forty or fifty minutes or so, he used to complain of pains in his back. He tried to do some etching while lying in bed, but his eyes had grown so weak that they no longer could stand the strain of that sort of work.

In the end he merely puttered around in his studio for a couple of hours every morning and then went back to his cot. He rarely undressed but slept in his old paint-covered smock, like a soldier who is desperate but who wants to die in harness.

In the month of March of the next year, his first grandchild was born. It was a girl and it was called Titia after her father. We thought that it would do him good if he attended the baptism, and he finally allowed himself to be persuaded. But he could hardly stand on his feet during the short ceremony and his hands shook so severely when he tried to write his name that Frans van Bijlert, the other witness, had to help him.

I used to drop in every other day to tell him the latest news and cheer him up by little bits of local gossip which often seem to divert the sick. He was politely grateful, but answered little in return.

Once or twice he asked after Saskia, as if she had still been alive and occasionally he mentioned Hendrickje.

"She was a good girl," he used to say. "She was very good to me and to the boy. If it had not been for her, I don't know what we would have done."

I sometimes asked him whether he wanted me to read to him, but he said no, he had so much to think about.

And then one evening in October of the year '69, when I was sitting by his bedside (he had not been able to get up for about a fortnight), he surprised me by asking that I get him the family Bible. It was in Cornelia's room and when I called to her, she brought it and put it on the table.

"I wish you would read me that story about Jacob," he said. "Do you know where to find it—the story of Jacob wrestling with the Lord?"

I did not know where to find it. Cornelia remembered that it was somewhere in Genesis. I turned the leaves until I found the name Jacob and then searched up and down the pages until I came to the passage which he seemed to have in mind.

"Yes," he nodded, "that is it. Where Jacob wrestles with the Lord. Now read that to me. Just that and nothing else."

And I read:

"'And Jacob was left alone; and there wrestled a man with him until the breaking of the day.

"'And when he saw that he prevailed not against him, he touched the hollow of his thigh; and the hollow of Jacob's thigh was out of joint, as he wrestled with him.

"'And he said, Let me go, for the day breaketh. And he said, I will not let thee go, except thou bless me.

"'And he said unto him, What is thy name? And he said, Jacob.

"'And he said, Thy name shall be called no more Jacob, but Israel; for as a *Prince* hast thou power with God and with men, and hast prevailed.'"

But when I had got that far, the sick man stirred and I stopped reading and looked at him and I saw him slowly lift his right hand and hold it close to his eyes and look at it as if it were something curious he had never observed before. And then his lips moved and very softly I heard him whisper:

"And Jacob was left alone. And there wrestled a man with him until the breaking of the day . . . there wrestled a man with him until the breaking of the day . . . but he did not give in and fought back—ah, yes, he fought back—for such is the will of the Lord—that we shall fight back . . . that we shall wrestle with him until the breaking of the day."

And then, with a sudden effort, he tried to raise himself from his pillow, but could not do it and he stared at me in a helpless sort of way as if asking for an answer that he knew would never come.

"And he said, thy name shall be called no more Jacob but Rembrandt," and while his gnarled old fingers, still covered with the stains of ink and paint, fell back upon his breast, "for as a Prince hast thou had power with God and with men and hast prevailed—and hast prevailed unto the last . . . alone . . . but hast prevailed unto the last."

But when Cornelia a moment later looked at me with questioning eyes and said, "Thank Heaven! for now he is asleep," I went up to her and took her by the arm and answered, "Thank Heaven, indeed, for now he is dead."

EPILOGUE
by a DISTANT DESCENDANT

If Doctor Jan had not been killed during the battle of Kijkduin and had lived a few years longer, he would have seen the name of Rembrandt van Rijn completely disappear from the face of the earth.

Within less than a fortnight after Rembrandt's death, the body of Magdalena van Loo, the widow of Titus, was gently lowered into a grave in the West Church, not far away from that of his own.

As for Cornelia, on the third of May of the year 1670 she married one Cornelis Suythof, a young painter who could not make a living at his art and who that same year sailed to Java on the good ship *Tulpenburg* and went to work for the East India Company.

Then on Saint Nicholas day of the year 1673, Cornelia gave birth to a son who was duly baptized and received the name of Rembrandt Suythof and who apparently died shortly afterwards. Five years later, another son was born to the couple, Hendric Suythof. What became of the parents, we do not know.

A few years more and they disappeared from view as completely as if they had never existed.

Titia, the daughter of Titus and Magdalena van Loo, lived a little longer, but only a very little. When she was seventeen years old, she married the youngest son of her guardian, a certain Frans van Bijlert, who was in the same business as his better known colleague, Kilian van Rensselaer, although his shop was in a less fashionable part of the town, on the Kloveniers Burgwal. They had a raft of children, whose funeral notices are duly recorded in the mortuary books of the West Church which soon became a sort of general receptacle for those who had a drop of Rembrandt blood in their veins.

But ere she herself died, in the year 1725, Titia could still have read the following estimate of her grandfather's work in a book that was considered the standard of good taste for all those who had genteel aspirations during the first quarter of the eighteenth century:

"In his effort to attain a mellow manner, Rembrandt van Rijn has merely succeeded in achieving an effect of rottenness. The vulgar and prosaic aspects of a subject were the only ones he was capable of noting and with his so-called red and yellow tones, he set the fatal example of shadows so hot that they seem actually aglow and of colors that appear to lie like liquid mud on the canvas."

The man responsible for this piece of poetic prose was a painter by the name of Gerard de Lairesse, born in the town of Liége in Belgium in the year of mercy 1641. He had studied the rudiments of his trade in his father's studio, and then learning "where the big money was" (that expression, alas, is as old as the Pyramids or older), he had moved to Amsterdam where he had covered endless miles of patient canvas with allegorical representations of whatever subjects were suggested by his patrons.

For a moment there had been danger of his fall from grace for as he modestly confessed in his "History of Painting" he himself had been tempted to try Rembrandt van Rijn's style of painting but soon he had recognized his mistake and had abjured "these errors and had abandoned a manner that was entirely based upon a delusion."

There it stands for every one to read: "Rottenness of effect . . . the fatal example of shadows that were so hot as to appear to be aglow . . . vulgar and prosaic aspects of every subject . . . colors that appeared to lie like liquid mud on the canvas . . . a manner founded on a delusion."

A funeral in an unknown grave—a half open coffin from which the bones had been removed and thrown on the rubbish-pile . . . an undischarged bankrupt until this very day . . . as it was in the beginning . . . is now and probably ever will be . . . world without end. Amen.

In Den Houtuin,
Veere,
May 27, 1930.

HENDRIK WILLEM VAN LOON.

. . . to give them beauty for ashes, the oil of joy for mourning, the garments of praise for the spirit of heaviness.

CPSIA information can be obtained
at www.ICGtesting.com
Printed in the USA
BVHW041031070719
552787BV00018B/476/P